Additional Praise for *The Age of Deleveraging*

"Gary Shilling provides a compelling and comprehensive assessment of the looming deflationary backdrop. This is a highly valuable resource to help the investor navigate through the post-bubble economic volatility of our times."

—David A. Rosenberg, Chief Economist and Strategist Gluskin Sheff + Associates

"Particularly given what's unfolding in world markets, this is a must read. It's well written, engaging, enlightening, relevant, and very up to date with today's economic landscape. It concludes with 12 specific sell ideas and 10 specific buy ideas. Buy it."

—Ed Hyman, Chairman of ISI Group, Inc. (broker dealer) and ISI Inc. (funds management)

"Gary Shilling is a master at recognizing the reversal of long term trends while everyone else is still looking in the opposite direction. Even more important, he shows his readers how to protect themselves and profit from his insights. It's vintage Gary!"

—Terry Savage, nationally syndicated *Chicago Sun-Times* financial columnist and author of *The Savage Truth on Money*

"Gary Shilling told you so—and now, in this primer on the forces of economic and financial gravitation, he's telling you again. Pay heed!"

—James Grant, *Grant's Interest Rate Observer*

"Gary Shilling is a rare bird: a certified economist who nonetheless is thoroughly imbued with common sense—and has stellar records in two of the world's more parlous occupations, forecasting and investing, to prove it. His latest book, *The Age of Deleveraging*, is a gift, pure and simple, to the legions of investors who want to know what's hit them as this "post-Lehman world" flirts with deflation and—more urgently—what to do now. Read it and profit."

—Kate Welling, Editor/Publisher, Welling@Weeden

"Gary Shilling's book provides insight into leverage, excessive speculation and the underlying deflation in our economy. He is unique among his colleagues for the persistence in which he has maintained these views."

—Richard S. LeFrak, Chairman and
CEO of the LeFrak Organization

The Age of Deleveraging

Investment Strategies for a Decade of Slow Growth and Deflation

A. Gary Shilling, PhD

WILEY

John Wiley & Sons, Inc.

Published by John Wiley & Sons, Inc., Hoboken, New Jersey.
Published simultaneously in Canada.

For general information on our other products and services or for technical support, please contact our Customer Care Department within the United States at (800) 762-2974, outside the United States at (317) 572-3993 or fax (317) 572-4002.

Wiley also publishes its books in a variety of electronic formats. Some content that appears in print may not be available in electronic books. For more information about Wiley products, visit our web site at www.wiley.com.

Library of Congress Cataloging-in-Publication Data:

Shilling, A. Gary.
   The age of deleveraging : investment strategies for a decade of slow growth and deflation/A. Gary Shilling.
      p. cm.
   Includes index.
   ISBN 978-0-470-59636-4
   1. Investments—United States. 2.   Investment analysis—United States.
3.   Deflation (Finance)—United States. 4.   Economic forecasting—United States.
5.   United States—Economic conditions—2009- I.   Title.
   HG4910.S458 2010
   332.6—dc22

                                                                2010021341

Printed in the United States of America

10 9 8 7 6 5

Contents

Foreword

viii

Acknowledgments

xii

Introduction

xiv

Delveraging, especially of the global financial and U.S. consumer sectors, will dominate the worldwide economy for years. It's centered on five traumas so far. Three more possibilities loom.

Chapter 1   **Spotting Bubbles**   1

Economic and financial bubbles are time-honored and part of immutable human nature. I love to be among the few to spot them and predict their demise. They follow a well-defined pattern as they expand and burst.

Chapter 2   **Making Great Calls**   29

They involve important events that the consensus doesn't foresee and unfold for the stated reasons. Here are five I've made: the 1969–1970 recession, the early 1970s inventory bubble and 1973–1975 recession, disinflation starting in the early 1980s, the demise of Japan's 1980s bubble, and the dot-com blow-off in 2000.

Chapter 3 **The Housing Bubble (Great Call 6)** 53
Why I saw it coming in the early 2000s, how I forecast its demise and the way I personally profited.

Chapter 4 **The Financial Bubble (Great Call 7)** 95
The great disconnect between the financial and real worlds started three decades ago and accelerated in the 2000s. Soaring financial leverage, especially in the global financial and U.S. consumer sectors, made collapse inevitable.

Chapter 5 **The Results of Denial** 123
The 2007–2009 recession and financial crisis started in early 2007 with the subprime mortgage collapse, spread to Wall Street at mid-year, then moved to U.S. consumer retrenchment and global recession in late 2008. Investors thought every crisis was the last, and governments had no foresight or master plans.

Chapter 6 **Slow Growth Ahead** 159
Global slow growth in the next decade will result from U.S. consumer retrenchment, financial deleveraging, increased government regulation and involvement in major economies, low commodity prices and the shift by advanced lands to fiscal restraint.

Chapter 7 **No Help from Anywhere** 225
Four more reasons for slow global growth: Rising protectionism, continuing U.S. housing weakness, deflation and weak state and local government spending.

Chapter 8 **Chronic Worldwide Deflation** 273
Deflation comes in seven varieties, but is fundamentally driven by supply exceeding demand. Productivity-saturated new tech and globalization will drive the good deflation of excess supply while slow economic growth introduces the bad deflation of deficient demand. As the two combine, I look for chronic price declines of 2 to 3 percent annually.

Chapter 9   Monetary and Fiscal Excesses   311
The inflation-wary Fed will probably withdraw excess reserves if inflation looms. Federal deficits over $1 trillion will persist as weak economic growth forces government job creation and helps push those dependent on government to two-thirds of the population. Still, government stimuli will continue to only replace private sector weakness at best.

Chapter 10   The Outlook for Stocks   339
Corporate earnings grow with GDP in the long run. With slow growth and deflation in prospect as well as falling P/Es, stock appreciation will be muted and below dividend yields. History favors market timing over buy and hold, even more so in this environment.

Chapter 11   Twelve Investments to Sell or Avoid   363
Big-ticket consumer purchases, consumer lenders, conventional home builders, collectibles, banks, junk securities, flailing companies, low tech equipment producers, commercial real estate, commodities, Chinese and other developing country stock and bonds, and Japanese securities.

Chapter 12   Ten Investments to Buy   425
Treasury bonds, dividend-payers, consumer staples, small luxuries, the dollar, asset managers and advisers, factory-built houses and rental apartments, health care companies, productivity-enhancers and North American energy.

About the Author   493
Index   499

Foreword

When one thinks of the term "Renaissance Man" in conjunction with the world of investing, trading, and economics there are really very few names that come swiftly to mind. Wall Street is simply not known for its sense of art, or history, of philosophy, of literature, or of music. There are some from the past that come to mind of course, as great philanthropists to the arts, but they were philanthropists simply to buy a place in history rather than as a respecter of history and the arts. I have been fortunate, however, to have met a true Renaissance Man, and you are fortunate enough to be about to read one of his books. When I think of a Renaissance Man on Wall Street, I think instantly of my dear friend, Dr. A. Gary Shilling. Gary is a gentleman who can, with the best of them, launch into a discussion of Shakespeare's tragedies, and can instantly recognize the composer of a piece of classical music—and perhaps even name the conductor and the orchestra playing the piece in question. He understands the lessons of history through the ages and can discuss with alacrity and clarity the importance of the adjusted monetary base as reported by the Federal Reserve Bank of St. Louis or, just as readily, the implications of a revision to monthly durable goods orders. Gary is a true Renaissance Man, and he's taught me much.

I first became aware of Gary's economic forecasting abilities back in the early 1970s, when I was one of the young economists at Cotton, Inc. in Raleigh, North Carolina. My duties were to forecast cotton supply and demand statistics as well as generate a view on the economy that we could send to the cotton producers of America, who were our clients. Looking about for economic wisdom, I came upon Gary's work. He was White, Weld's Chief Economist, as I recall. He was the only economist on The Street at the time who was forecasting a severe recession. Everyone else was forecasting protracted economic growth. Gary was right. The recession of the early 1970s was the worst recession to that point in the post-World War II period. He earned my respect.

Gary was bearish again regarding the U.S. economy in the early 1980s when his peers on The Street remained steadfastly bullish. Applying simple logic and historical precedents to the situation, Gary's view was again proven right. Others, sadly, were proven wrong.

I followed Gary from afar for nearly a decade. Having chosen in the early 1980s to set up my own firm that would focus on writing a daily commentary on the global capital markets, I chose to "screw my courage to the sticking point," and called his office to request a meeting. To my great surprise and true delight, he said he'd be happy to meet with me. I remember to this day our meeting in a wonderful old building in lower Manhattan, where he graciously spent an hour or two talking about the markets, the economy, and his interest in Shakespeare, music, and history. From that point on, I've been an even greater fan of the man and his work.

Thereafter I read, with delight and great expectations, his books on topics such as inflation and economics as well as his monthly newsletter to clients around the world . . . never to be disappointed. In all his work, Gary's wisdom is more than merely evident; his writings are cogent, rational, and, far more often than not, they are utterly "spot on." Too, they are often witty.

Gary taught me the importance of technology shifts in matters few others could explain. For example, few today think about the Erie Canal, but in its time it was a huge shift for the better in the United States, opening up the western states to trade with the eastern seaboard in a manner previously unimagined. Gary's insights into why the wheat trade suddenly became an important part of the history of Buffalo, New York, which became perhaps the leading milling city in the then young United States, taught me why it was, through extension, important that Silicon Valley grew as it did in the 1970s, 1980s, and 1990s. He also taught me the importance of "good deflation" and "bad deflation." And of the benefits of rising production and falling prices of goods and services during the growth of agriculture in the nineteenth century, and how that could be extrapolated to technology today.

Gary taught me the importance of being an iconoclast in the world of economics, for it is he who sees with a different eye that survives the ebbs and flows of the investment world. He taught me the necessity of being away from The Street, where he and I could see with some sense of clarity what others might be seeing too closely and thus unclearly. He taught me the importance of keeping a long-term perspective, and the importance of having interests outside of Wall Street. So Gary has his bees . . . he's a well known beekeeper and gardener . . . he has his Shakespeare . . . he was once the Chairman of New Jersey Shakespeare Festival, a regional theater company . . . he has his music, and he putters around the house. And most importantly, he has his family. He's what, in the Midwest, we call "a good man." This is high praise.

Over the years we've talked on the phone countless times, discussing the markets and viewing them with perspective. We've invested together, and we've sent clients to one another. We've had dinner; we've laughed; and all the while, I've learned far more from him than he's ever learned from me. In this new book, *The Age of Deleveraging*, Gary shares his newest ideas on the global economy, and I cannot recommend it strongly enough to anyone with even a tangential interest in how markets and economies work. I guarantee . . . and one is always warned never to guarantee anything in the markets . . . that you will come away from this book understanding how the United States and the global economy functions. You will be a better investor having read this book, and you will become enamored of this great gentleman.

To finish, let's not forget that despite his "Renaissance" visage, Gary has his feet in the modern world. After all, in years past he's entertained Keith Richards of the Rolling Stones and his family at his beach house on Fire Island. The tale of how this happened is another story for another time, but suffice it to say that when the world of the Rolling Stones and the world of Shakespeare can meet in the world of A. Gary Shilling, magic happens.

So, I wish you well in reading this excellent book and learning, as I have, what Gary offers. We are all the better ... materially ... for this.

Dennis Gartman
The Gartman Letter, L.C.
July 2010

Acknowledgments

This book is the result of literally decades of research and analysis, so many, many people have been involved over the years. Still, the actual writing of it took place from January through mid-April of 2010. The first months of the year are my "free time" for projects like this. From mid-April through October, my honeybees need lots of attention. So do my yard and gardens at our residence in Short Hills, New Jersey, and our beach house in Point O'Woods on Fire Island off the south coast of Long Island, New York. Then comes November and all the activities leading up to Thanksgiving and Christmas. So it's January 2 before I can catch my breath.

Assembling a book of this length and depth in three and a half months put a lot of strain on our organization, coming on top of an already hectic schedule. I'm delighted, however, that everyone worked long and hard, and with good cheer.

I'm especially indebted to our extremely able editor, Fred Rossi. In addition to the usual superb job he does in editing our monthly newsletter, *Insight*, and managing our growing distribution list, he typed and edited this book. I must confess that I broke into a museum and stole an ancient writing instrument called a pencil with which I wrote every word. But since I'm not completely antediluvian, it's a mechanical pencil. In any event, Fred did a magnificent job, as usual, in translating my chicken scratches on white lined pads into English—and did so in his usual calm, cheerful manner.

Colin Hatton, the senior man on our research team, also deserves my special thanks for much of the data, charts, and analysis in this book. Despite being only two years out of college, Colin has an excellent grasp of economic and financial data and a wonderful memory for the huge number of charts from which we selected the relatively few contained in this book. He also made a number of very helpful suggestions for the analyses that supported my arguments and forecasts. And Colin did it all with an unusual calmness and willingness to work long hours.

I also appreciate the work of Nestor Pura, a new research associate who nevertheless contributed to the analysis and charts. And I thank Jack Redmond, who took time from his investment advisory duties to unearth important financial data.

My most able assistant, Beth Grant, played an extremely critical role in keeping us all calm and focused on getting this book written on time and without the inefficiencies of personal blowups. How many times did Beth, in her extremely pleasant way, say, "Gary, how's the book coming?" I got the message loud and clear! Beth is the glue that keeps our firm together.

Finally, I thank my wife of almost 48 years, Peggy, for understanding the pressure I was under and for accepting the many evenings and weekends when I was not spending time with her, but bringing chapters of this book home from our offices and writing in the solitude of my den or on the dining room table. Even our female yellow Labrador retriever, Honey, seemed to understand the situation. Rather than bug me to go out and throw a tennis ball for her to retrieve, she lay down on the floor while I wrote, providing silent support and companionship.

Introduction

I n 2007–2008, almost all investment categories suffered huge losses as the global financial crisis and worldwide recession unfolded. Stocks in almost every market worldwide; corporate, municipal, and junk bonds; commodities; residential and commercial real estate; foreign currencies; emerging market stocks and bonds; private equity; and most hedge funds bit the dust. Indeed, in 2008, the only winners were the traditional safe havens—Treasurys, the dollar, and gold.

But in response to massive government bailouts of financial institutions here and abroad and huge worldwide fiscal stimuli, those many depressed investments revived vigorously, starting in early 2009. So most investors believe that 2008 was simply a bad dream from which they've now awoken. We're returning to the world they knew and loved, with free-spending consumers supporting rapid economic growth, fueled by ample credit and backstopped by governments. After all, they reason, the recent experience proves not only that major financial institutions are too big to be allowed by governments to fail, but that the same is true for underwater homeowners. Monetary and fiscal largesse is so extensive, they believe, that economic overheating and serious inflation are the next major problems.

But the optimists don't seem to realize that the good life and rapid growth that started in the early 1980s was fueled by massive financial leveraging and excessive debt, first in the global financial sector, starting in the 1970s, and later among U.S. consumers. That leverage propelled the dot-com stock bubble in the late 1990s and then the housing bubble. But now those two sectors are being forced to delever and, in the process, are transferring their debts to governments and central banks.

This deleveraging will probably take a decade or more—and that's the good news. The ground to cover is so great that if it were traversed in a year or two, major economies would experience depressions worse than in the 1930s. This deleveraging and other forces will result in slow economic growth and probably deflation for many years. And as Japan has shown, these are difficult conditions to offset with monetary and fiscal policies.

The insidious reality is that this deleveraging doesn't occur in a straight line, but in a series of seemingly isolated events. After each, the feeling is that it's over, all may be well, but then follows the next crisis. When the subprime residential mortgage market collapsed in 2007, most thought it was a small, isolated sector. But then it spread to Wall Street with the implosion of two big Bear Stearns subprime-laden hedge funds in June of that year. Most hoped the Fed actions that summer had ended the crisis, but as the financial woes spread, Merrill Lynch suffered a shotgun wedding, major banks like Citigroup and Bank of America were on government life support, and Lehman went bankrupt in September 2008.

Then the third phase struck as U.S. consumers stopped buying in the fall of 2008 and the fourth, the global recession, coincided. The optimists hoped the $787 billion fiscal stimulus package in the United States and similar fiscal bailouts abroad would take care of all those problems, but were surprised by the eurozone crisis in late 2009 and early 2010. Nevertheless, that's just the fifth step in global deleveraging. The combination of the Teutonic north and the Club Med south under the common euro currency only worked with strong global growth driven by the debt explosion, but now that's over.

As I discuss in this book, further traumas on this deleveraging side of the long cycle lie ahead. They may include a crisis in U.S. commercial real estate that could exceed the one in housing, a collapse of what

I believe is a Chinese house of cards, and a slow-motion train wreck in Japan.

I hope this book convinces you that the deleveraging process has years to go and that economic and financial markets have not returned to business as usual, at least not to the world of rapid growth supported by oversized and growing debt. If you agree with me, you'll appreciate the investment strategies that I see as appropriate for a decade of slow growth and deflation. In Chapter 11, I cover 12 investment sectors to sell or avoid, and in Chapter 12, I discuss 10 you should consider buying.

During the past fascinating decade, I played three roles. First, I was an eyewitness to history, watching speculation survive the Internet bubble collapse in the early 2000s due to massive monetary and fiscal stimuli, and then the spread to commodities, foreign currencies, emerging market stocks and bonds, hedge funds and private equity, and especially housing. I saw the housing and financial bubbles expand and then explode. I watched the fears of financial meltdown spur gigantic monetary and fiscal bailouts. I experienced the witch hunts that followed, the inevitable result of widespread losses and high unemployment.

Second, I've been a participant in this drama, not only chronicling it in our monthly *Insight* newsletter, but also continually warning of the impending collapses in the housing and financial bubbles. And I was involved through a very profitable year in 2008 for the portfolios we manage when all 13 of our investment strategies worked—most gratifying, in contrast to those who never acknowledged that those bubbles existed, much less could burst.

Third, I've participated as a forecaster in successfully foreseeing the expansion and then collapse of the housing and financial bubbles. More recently, my forecasts have focused on the continuing deleveraging that the bursting of those two bubbles commenced, and the resulting investment strategies for the next decade.

This book describes all three of these roles. I hope you find it enlightening, provocative, instructive, and at times amusing. It would probably have been more convincing had you read it in early 2009 in the depths of the recession and financial crisis, but it may be more useful today.

A. Gary Shilling
May 2010

Introduction to
Paperback Edition

Since I finished writing this book in May 2010, events to an amazing degree have confirmed its analysis and forecasts. Consequently, most of my investment recommendations back then have done very well and still make sense.

Greek Bailouts

The €110 billion bailout of Greece in the spring of 2010 was supposed to give that country time to get its economic house in order, drastically slash government spending and deficits, and return to the public markets for sovereign debt financing. Nevertheless, I wrote that "the likelihood that Greece will shape up and fly right is slim," and it has been. The probable decline in real Greek gross domestic product (GDP) of 5 percent this year, the inability to sell substantial government assets, and the resulting budget deficit that's more likely to hit 9 percent of GDP than the government's target of 7.6 percent in 2011 forced the second Greek bailout plan in July 2011.

That plan, however, is in jeopardy because Germany, Finland, and other solvent northern eurozone lands are reluctant to keep bailing out the weak countries in order to keep the eurozone intact. Greece, Ireland, and Portugal, the countries aided so far, account for only 6 percent of eurozone GDP. Nevertheless, the sovereign debt crisis has infected Spain (10 percent of eurozone GDP) and Italy (16 percent), requiring European Central Bank (ECB) support for their bonds, and contagion threatens France (21 percent).

The latest government leader discussions center on fiscal policy integration in the eurozone to match the monetary union under one currency, the euro, and one central bank, the ECB. But, as I wrote in Chapter 12, the critical differences and mutual distrust between, say, Greece and Germany make this highly unlikely. Also, the proposed euro bonds to replace individual eurozone sovereign issues are problematic since the profligate Club Med southern countries would place an ever-growing debt burden on the Teutonic North's credit rating. With the financial mess in Europe and declining consumer and business confidence, a eurozone-wide recession is increasingly likely.

Chinese Hard Landing

The hard landing I forecast for China, with annual economic growth dropping from double digits back to recessionary 5 percent to 6 percent levels, has also become more probable since May 2010. The Chinese government is determined to curb the property bubble and inflation that resulted from the massive 2009 stimulus program—equivalent to 12 percent of GDP—enacted in response to the global recession that disrupted China's export-driven economy. By August 2011, consumer prices had risen 6.2 percent from a year earlier, and food prices, crucial to the many living at subsistence levels, were up 13.4 percent.

China's crude economic policy tools point to a hard landing. So does the reality that the U.S. Federal Reserve, with all its sophisticated techniques, effected only one soft landing in 12 tries in the post–World War II era, with the other 11 resulting in recessions.

I also forecast in this book that a hard landing in China will knock the foundation out from under the global commodity bubble since commodity bulls believed that China, aided by other developing countries, will soak up the world's industrial and agricultural commodity supplies indefinitely. In fact, the prices of copper, a key industrial commodity, and sugar in the agricultural arena commenced their massive declines in February 2011.

I also wrote in this book that the decoupling theory, which maintains that China can grow independently of U.S. consumer demand for its exports, was disproven by the 2007–2009 global recession, and that the theory's revival in 2010 would be equally debunked. China and most developing lands still depend directly and indirectly on U.S.-bound exports for growth.

Japanese Train Wreck

Chapter 12 describes Japan as a slow-motion train wreck since its ability to finance the huge government debt internally and still have capital left over to export will succumb to ongoing U.S. consumer retrenchment and, therefore, weakening demand for Japanese exports. Then it will need to import capital and pay global interest rates, ending the government's ability to finance its net debt-to-GDP ratio of 117 percent at 1 percent for 10-year bonds.

I didn't forecast the March 2011 earthquake and tsunami in Japan, of course, but they probably speeded up the train wreck. Exports were curtailed by supply chain disruptions, some of which may linger. Meanwhile, the national disaster-linked surge in imports will be longer lasting in the form of building materials for reconstruction and more energy imports to replace shut-down reactors.

Slow Growth So Far

The basic argument in this book is that the global economy is in the Age of Deleveraging. I point to nine forces that are likely to limit U.S. economic growth to a slow 2 percent annually for many years to come. As I finished writing it, however, many believed that massive monetary and fiscal stimuli had rekindled the economy and returned it to earlier salad days. The 2008 collapse in the economy, stocks, commodities, and foreign currencies was just a bad dream from which we'd awaken, they were assured.

Stocks in the United States and elsewhere were on a tear that commenced in March 2009 and lasted until July 2011 before nose-diving. Rallies in other investments that were killed in 2008 were also robust. In mid-2010, the U.S. new home ownership tax credits convinced many investors that house prices were bottoming, so they eagerly bought foreclosed property for quick flips at higher prices. In August, Fed Chairman Bernanke signaled another round of quantitative easing, which sent stocks and commodities skyward, even before the formal announcement in November.

Nevertheless, the economy has not returned to robust growth. Real GDP grew at a mere 0.4 percent annual rate in the first quarter of 2011 and an anemic 1.3 percent rate in the second quarter. Growth at those slow rates or lower is in prospect in coming quarters, with a recession likely in 2011 as sentiment of U.S. consumers and small businesses falls, as real household incomes decline and high unemployment persists, as business frets over the uncertainty of government regulation and future sales, as housing remains mired and prices retreat due to excess inventories and weak demand, and as state and local governments cut costs and jobs as they confront ongoing deficits and underfunded public employee pensions. Abroad, the European financial crisis is poised to spread globally and recession threatens, while the economic growth engine in Asia sputters.

No Magic Bullets

Equally important to the investment climate is the realization that earlier massive monetary and fiscal stimuli, while probably having some positive effects on the U.S. economy, did not return it to robust health and that policy makers have no magic bullets left to fire. The net effect of quantitative easing phase 2 (QE2) was to add $600 billion to excess bank reserves at the Fed, which now total $1.5 trillion, while banks are too scared to lend and creditworthy businesses and consumers don't want to borrow. That quantitative easing did temporarily propel stocks and commodities, but didn't aid lower-tier homeowners through lower mortgage rates, and actually harmed financially stressed Americans the Fed hoped to help due to higher grocery and gasoline costs.

Fiscal stimuli in 2009–2010 in the form of personal tax cuts, unemployment benefits, aid to state and local governments, and so on are expiring in a still-weak economy after pushing federal budget deficits to $1.3 trillion annually. Despite the gigantic size of the fiscal stimuli, they have offset less than half the private-sector deleveraging. Since early 2006, U.S. government borrowing has risen from 3 percent of GDP to 8 percent, a 5-percentage-point jump. But in the same time, private-sector borrowing dropped from 16 percent of GDP to zero, a 16-percentage-point decline. Nevertheless, this deep government red ink spawned a backlash that forced Congress and the administration to enact huge deficit cuts—$2.4 trillion over the next decade—in the midst of a faltering economy.

Nine Growth Retarders

To date, then, economic performance is confirming my forecast of slow growth that will persist for about a decade due to the nine causes I cover in this book (see Table 6.4 on page 182).

1. Consumers are shifting from the 25-year borrowing-and-spending binge that drove their saving rate from 12 percent to near zero to a saving spree, with the saving rate now back to 4.5 percent, and are also paying down debt. As I predicted, the high volatility of equities in the past decade has made individual investors no longer trust their equity portfolios to substitute for saving from current income. Few participated in the 2009–2011 near-doubling in stock prices as they dumped stock mutual funds in favor of bonds.

   Declining house prices since I completed this book have further depleted home equity and the ability of homeowners to use it to fund spending. The postwar babies are increasingly aware of their underfunded retirement funds and need to spend less, save more, and work longer in order to enjoy comfortable retirements. And persistent high unemployment encourages those with jobs to save for contingencies.

2. Financial deleveraging is proceeding and reversing the trend that financed much of the global growth in recent years. U.S. banks have been forced out of profitable but risky activities like off-balance-sheet vehicles, derivatives, and proprietary trading by losses, bank management fear, and government regulation. They're back to core spread lending, which is being squeezed by the flattening yield curve as banks also contend with losses on troubled mortgages they originated and sold earlier to investors. Also, the Fed's "Operation Twist," which involves selling shorter-term Treasurys while buying long-term issues further flattens the yield curve. European banks face severe losses on questionable sovereign bonds as well as dollar funding problems as U.S. money market and other fearful lenders retreat. This curtails their lending to U.S. and other dollar-based customers.

3. Increased government regulation and involvement in major economies is not only stifling innovation and reducing efficiency but also creating so much uncertainty that businesses refrain from hiring and investing. The detailed regulations to implement the 2010 Dodd-Frank U.S. financial regulation law are largely yet to be established and, therefore, uncertain. Also creating unanswered questions are the legal status and implications of the 2010 health care law that expands insurance coverage to 32 million Americans. Political gridlock in Washington also slows economic growth due to uncertainty over future laws and the implementation of past and future regulations.

4. Declining commodity prices are just beginning to curb spending in commodity-producing countries. Some Middle East oil producers are cutting government spending in response to the fall in crude oil prices. Commodity-exporting emerging economies such as Brazil earlier were plagued by huge capital inflows and surging currencies because of their high interest rates compared with near-zero developed lands. More recently, the swoon in commodity prices and stocks universally is reversing the process. Their currencies are retreating as foreign investors head for the exits and local-currency bonds are dumped.

5. Developed countries are moving toward fiscal restraint. As mentioned earlier, in mid-2011 Washington enacted a plan to reduce

the 10-year federal budget deficit by $2.4 trillion. The eurozone financial crisis is forcing Greece and other troubled countries to slash their deficits—actions that are deepening their ongoing recession. In 2010 the United Kingdom embarked on an experiment to drop government spending and employment not only to reduce future deficits but also in the hope that lower government involvement in the economy will energize the private sector to more than make up for the cuts. So far, the net effect has been a weaker economy. That forced the Bank of England to increase its quantitative easing massively.

6. Protectionism has grown in the past year and a half and threatens global growth. China continues to battle the United States and Europe over favoritism for Chinese firms in selling to government enterprises. Brazil has initiated a "Buy Brazil" policy to favor local producers that are being pummeled by the strong real.

7. The U.S. housing market keeps slipping under the weight of 2.0 to 2.5 million in excess inventories over and above normal working levels. Those surplus units will take five or six years to absorb in a climate of heavy foreclosures, stringent mortgage lending terms, high unemployment, and the realization that, for the first time since the 1930s, house prices can and do fall, eliminating the bedrock of home-buying zeal. Excess inventories, the mortal enemy of prices, are pushing house prices down toward the 20 percent further fall that I predict.

   Since I finished writing this book in May 2010, investors, forecasters, and Washington politicians are joining me in realizing that until the housing market is cleared, the resumption of meaningful U.S. economic growth is highly unlikely. Even then, the likely flattening of house prices and memories of past declines and horrendous losses are likely to keep residential construction from returning to its earlier substantial role in promoting economic growth. Home ownership is no longer desirable for many.

8. Goods and services deflation is not yet established and thereby curtailing spending as buyers anticipate lower prices. But as commodity prices drop, the early 2011 fears of inflation have faded and I foresee the media chatter shifting to deflation before long. Worldwide excess supply, globalization, competition from many developing

countries that depend on exports to the United States for growth, and falling U.S. real incomes and wages seem destined to initiate widespread chronic deflation of 2 percent to 3 percent per year.

Already, five of the seven types of deflation I explore in this book are in place. Financial assets led by stocks, tangible assets (notably residential real estate), industrial and agricultural commodities, real U.S. incomes, and almost all foreign currencies against the dollar are deflating.

9. State and local governments have contracted considerably since I finished this book in May 2010. From the early 1970s until recently, state and local government spending accounted for a steady 12 percent of GDP, only second in size to consumer spending at 70 percent. Since April 2010, state and local payrolls have fallen by 420,000 employees, or 2.1 percent, with many more cuts in prospect. And these job losses have a bigger-than-average negative impact on consumer spending since state and local employees are paid 44 percent more on average than private-sector workers. As noted earlier, municipal budgets remain stressed due to weak tax collections and the expiration of federal aid. Pension fund underfunding is being enhanced by the realization that projected investment returns are too high and the assumed current value of future benefits is too low.

Markdowns

The recent and prospective slow economic growth and the still-huge size of excess debts continue to persuade me that we are in The Age of Deleveraging. The financial sector globally and U.S. households, the two sectors that built up massive leverage in the past three or four decades by huge outside financing, have worked down only 10 percent or so of those excesses on their way back to previous norms. The deleveraging that remains will take many years to complete. And the decline will likely be punctuated by further traumas such as another 20 percent decline in U.S. house prices, a hard landing in China, major disruptions and restructuring in the eurozone, and frequent and severe recessions.

Even the most Pollyanna of optimists are realizing, since I finished this book 17 months ago, that the good life and rapid growth of the 1980s,

1990s, and early 2000s—funded by massive financial leverage—won't return any time soon. It's become clear to all that deleveraging involves not only increased saving and debt repayment but also the price markdown of many assets, including houses, many forms of commercial real estate, mortgages, stocks here and abroad, commodities, some foreign currencies versus the dollar, and junk securities.

Investment Strategies

Given the high degree to which events have confirmed the predictions I made in this book, completed in May 2010, it's no wonder that most of the investment strategies I advocated have worked well since then and continue to appear attractive.

This book discussed 12 investment areas to sell or avoid, starting with *big-ticket consumer purchases.* These are postponable, largely discretionary items, such as autos, appliances, airline travel, cruise lines, destination resorts, casinos, ski resorts, and so on. When times are tough, these expenditures suffer, as witnessed by the heavy hotel vacancies and low casino activity in Las Vegas and Indian casinos. As consumers cut out the frills, gambling casinos have suffered. In 2010, U.S. commercial casinos employed 34,564 people, 30,000 fewer than in 2006 before the Great Recession started. At the other end of the spectrum, Procter & Gamble, which has always emphasized premium household products at premium prices, in September 2011 appealed to frugal shoppers and those forced down from middle- to lower-class status by launching a new dish soap, Gain, at a low price—the first such strategy change in 38 years. "Forever frugal" consumers has become the watchword of producers and retailers of consumer products.

Meanwhile, Wal-Mart has revived its layaway plan due to consumer requests. Consumers who want to avoid using credit cards can have merchandise set aside, make periodic payments, and then pick up the items, usually Christmas gifts, after the last payment is made in December—debt free.

From the beginning of 2011 through September, a representative group of these stocks fell 38 percent compared to the 8 percent drop in the Standard & Poor's (S&P) 500, demonstrating their weakness relative to the total equity market.

I also disfavor *credit card and other consumer lenders.* Since the fourth quarter of 2008, U.S. consumers have reduced their credit card debt by 21 percent as they delever, and this trend is likely to continue. So far in 2011, some of these companies' stocks have actually risen, however.

Conventional homebuilders and related companies, I predicted, would be in the doghouse for years as house prices fall, foreclosures mount, and distressed houses are dumped on the market at prices that undercut newly constructed homes. That's clearly been true so far, with one homebuilder exchange-traded fund (ETF) down 23 percent from the end of 2010 through September 2011 versus the S&P 500's 8 percent drop.

With goods and services deflation yet to be established, the related weakness in *antiques, art, and other tangibles* lies ahead. But *banks and similar financial institutions,* another on my sell or avoid list, are obviously under pressure. As noted earlier, their profitable but noncore activities are being eliminated, bank loans and leases have been declining, lending interest spreads are being compressed, and banks are under pressure to make good on troubled loans they sold earlier to investors, including Fannie Mae and Freddie Mac. This is reflected in bank ETFs, with one falling 26 percent and another down by 25 percent compared with the 8 percent S&P 500 decline in the first nine months of 2011.

The zeal for yield in the low-interest-rate environment of the past several years pushed the prices of *junk bonds* up and the yields down close to record lows. Money was so available for low-rated issues that it took real skill to default, and default rates dropped to less than 1 percent, levels not seen since 2007, just before the Great Recession pushed them up to 13 percent.

Starting in early 2011, however, the spread between junk bond yields and 20-year Treasurys has jumped from 3.6 percentage points to 6.5 percentage points in September. In part, this reflects the decline in Treasury yields, but also higher junk bond yields, as investors anticipate tough economic times and leaping defaults for low-rated securities. I continue to believe these securities should be sold or avoided.

My forecast to avoid *flailing companies* with below-average revenue growth, high fixed labor and other costs, and big debts is also unfolding in the current stock bear market and should continue to be valid in the slow growth, deflationary, and globally competitive world I foresee. Ditto for *old-tech capital equipment producers* in an atmosphere of worldwide excess capacity and the resulting low demand for more of it.

Commercial real estate is also the victim of excess capacity, especially office buildings and retail space as high unemployment and weak consumer spending reign and Internet shopping continues to explode at the expense of bricks-and-mortar stores. There are exceptions, however, that we continue to favor. Rental apartments will continue to benefit from the single-family housing bust, as discussed later. Medical office buildings should be in high demand as a result of the growing use of medical services and the shift of medical providers from small practices to hospital employment. And self-storage facilities will continue to thrive as people downsize from McMansions to smaller single-family houses and apartments and store their excess treasures. In 2011 through July, commercial real estate prices overall fell 1 percent.

Commodity prices were still rising in May 2010 when I finished this book, but peaked in early 2011, as noted earlier. From the peak in February, copper prices were down 32 percent as of the end of September, measuring anticipated declines in global manufacturing since copper is used in almost every factory-produced good. The Thomson Reuters/Jefferies CRB (TRJ/CRB) index of all commodities declined 20 percent from its late April top. I expect these declines to continue, especially if the hard landing in China I'm forecasting materializes and removes the foundation from the bullish commodity structure, as noted earlier.

Developing country stocks and bonds remain unattractive, in my view. As noted earlier, kingpin China seems destined for a hard landing as officials there combat the undesired effects of their massive 2009 stimulus program—the property bubble and high consumer inflation. In addition, almost all developing economies are driven by exports, most of which have been purchased directly or indirectly by U.S. consumers.

Now, however, American households are retrenching to the detriment of emerging country exports. When I finished this book in May 2010, both emerging country bond and stock prices were leaping. Recently, those bond prices have fallen as domestic and foreign invetsors retreat. As with U.S. junk bonds, investors are beginning to worry about slower growth and recessions in Asia and Latin America, and rising risks or even defaults on emerging country bonds.

Emerging market *stocks* were also zooming in 2010, but investors more recently have begun to worry about slower growth, including a hard landing in China. Since early May 2011, those equities on average are down 27 percent, but still expensive, in my view. They would need to fall 48 percent from here to return to the low level of late October 2008.

Since I finished this book in May 2010, the earthquake and tsunami speeded up what I had described as a slow-motion train wreck in Japan, as discussed earlier. Despite Japan's rebuilding efforts, its basic flaws remain, including its heavy dependence on exports for economic growth and to allow internal financing of its huge government debts. Consequently, with the global economic slowdown under way, the Nikkei 225 dropped 14.9 percent in the first nine months of 2011.

Buy Strategies

The buy recommendations listed in this book are headed by my 30-year favorite and proven winner, *Treasury bonds.* In 2011 through September, they have performed magnificently, with 30-year Treasury bonds rising 28.5 percent in price with 2.9 percent in yield, for a total return of 32.8 percent, compared with the 8 percent total return loss on the S&P 500. One well-known bond manager sold off all his Treasurys early in 2011 and then sold more short. He said back then that owners of government bonds were like frogs slowly being boiled alive and oblivious to the risks of owning Treasurys. As they say, the rest is history. I have a toy frog on my desk, and I've been known to croak occasionally—and the water temperature has been just fine.

The 30-year Treasury prices may continue to rise and the yield fall from 2.9 percent at the end of September back to the 2.5 percent reached in late 2008 in the aftermath of the near meltdown on Wall Street and demise of Lehman Brothers. That would push up the price of 30-year coupon Treasurys by 8 percent, and 13 percent for 30-year zero-coupon bonds. As noted earlier, deflation fears may soon dominate as global economic growth slows and worldwide recession looms large, all to the benefit of Treasury bonds.

In the United States, financial and economic uncertainty as well as the unattractive alternatives of falling stock and bond prices and pitifully low returns from money market funds should continue to make Treasury bonds attractive. Foreigners are also likely to keep favoring Treasurys as a safe haven from slipping Asian economies and unresolved if not unresolvable financial woes in the eurozone.

High-quality income-producing securities such as highly rated corporate and municipal bonds as well as companies that pay meaningful, secure, and rising dividends in such industries as utilities, health care, and consumer products also remain attractive in the long run. Nevertheless, many of these stocks suffered in the mid-2011 bear market, but less so than stocks in general as dividends cushioned their decline. One broad-based ETF fell 0.5 percent in total return—price change plus dividends—in 2011 through September compared to the 8 percent drop in the S&P 500, also on a total return basis.

I recommended *food and other consumer staples* as long-run investments in a slowly growing economy in which consumers are cutting out the nonessentials and concentrating on the necessities of life. Other investors agree and have favored these defensive stocks in the troubled stock market of mid-2011. Through September, an ETF for consumer staples rose 3.2 percent compared to the S&P 500 loss of 8 percent.

It's probably too early to tell whether my *small luxuries* theme will be a long-term winner. The idea is that consumers, even with depressed incomes, want the best status symbols they can afford, be it moderately priced cufflinks from well-known jewelers, premium beers and liquors, or even tablet computers that are very conspicuous since they're far too big to hide in owners' pockets.

The *U.S. dollar* was definitely out of favor back in May 2010, but our investment advocacy of the greenback has proved valid more recently. It isn't that the United States is doing everything right, but that the buck remains the only major global currency, is the safe haven in a sea of worldwide trouble, and is the route to Treasurys after which foreigners lust. I've been especially bullish on the dollar against the euro in view of the nonstop sovereign debt crises in the eurozone.

From early May through September, the buck rose 11 percent against the euro. It has also climbed 13 percent against the Australian dollar since late July. I'm negative on the Aussie because of a likely break in the Australian housing bubble as well as that country's close link to China. They've been digging up the Island Continent and shipping out the iron ore, copper, coal, and so on to feed China's commodity bubble that, as noted earlier, I expect to burst with its hard landing. Emerging currencies such as the Brazilian real and the Mexican peso have reversed their earlier rallies and reached 2011 lows versus the dollar in mid-September 2011.

Investment advisers and financial planners will benefit in years to come from helping the vastly undersaved postwar babies prepare financially for retirement in an era of low investment returns. In 2011 through September, however, a group of five of these firms that specialized in this field had stock losses of 30 percent, probably reflecting the falling stock market and investors' hunger for the safety of cash rather than stocks.

In the hardcover version of this book, I advocated *factory-built houses and rental apartments,* but have since eliminated factory-built homes in view of the industry's near demise. The rationale is that with heavy foreclosures, high unemployment, and the realization for the first time since the 1930s that house prices can and do fall on a nationwide basis, Americans are separating their abodes from their investments. Earlier, the two were combined in single-family, owner-occupied houses. Increasingly, young families are likely to stay in rental apartments until their kids are really old enough to need single-family homes, and empty-nesters who hate lawn maintenance will sell their suburban money pits, move to rental apartments, and invest elsewhere.

Aging postwar babies will also enhance the demand for rental apartments, and in the past two years, vacancy rates have been falling while asking rents climbed. An index of apartment real estate investment trusts (REITs) that my firm has assembled rose 1 percent in the first nine months of 2011, anticipating future growth as well as reflecting the dividend-like required payout of 90 percent of REIT profits.

The broad *health care* field is another of my long-run investment favorites, and in the January to September 2011 period it worked well, with a major ETF rising 2 percent. The aging postwar babies, increased usage of increasingly expensive medical technologies, the new health care law that is scheduled to add 32 million Americans to insurance rolls, and the migration of physicians from private practice to hospital employment all promise to keep this sector growing rapidly, despite government and private pressures to contain costs.

Perennial business zeal for cost control will benefit *productivity enhancers,* be they high tech, low tech, no tech, or outsourcing. These should be important supplements to the slashing of labor costs in recent years by American businesses. Nevertheless, the high-tech sector, which, of course, is broader than productivity enhancement and includes consumer gadgets, suffered a 5 percent fall in a broad ETF in the January to September 2011 period.

North American energy still appears a long-run winner as Americans increasingly want to reduce exposure to unstable foreign sources such as Venezuela, Russia, the Middle East, and Africa. I continue to favor conventional energy, not renewables, which rely on huge government subsidies. The recent bankruptcies of two U.S. solar panel makers, as well as the possible expiration of ethanol import duties and subsidies at the end of 2011, illustrate my concerns.

Shale gas development has made that clean-burning fuel plentiful and cheap, and investments are under way to increase its usage by converting it to diesel fuel. The stocks of natural gas producers leaped early in the year but fell in August and September along with commodity prices in general. Producers of fuel from Canadian oil sands, another major source of North American energy, were also about flat in the first nine months of 2011.

The Age of Deleveraging Continues

On balance, then, events since I completed this book in May 2010 have confirmed its forecasts and enhanced my conviction—and I hope yours, too, as you read it—that we are in the Age of Deleveraging. The process has only started in earnest and will take many years to complete. As a result, the investment strategies discussed here—those advocating buying and those recommending selling—should be valid for a decade of deleveraging and the resulting slow growth and deflation.

Chapter 1

Spotting Bubbles

With the bursting of the U.S. housing and global financial bubbles in 2007–2008, it was inescapably clear that they were indeed bubbles. Earlier, few had agreed with me that the explosive growth and gigantic financial leverage in these two areas destined them for collapse.

Of course, if the majority doubted the sustainability of a rapidly expanding economic sector, a bubble in it would never develop. Indeed, at its peak of expansion, a bubble appears the most credible and most likely to continue to enlarge since the greatest number have invested in it and fervently hope for its continuation.

But they are then enveloped by the "willful suspension of disbelief," which constitutes not the poetic faith to which Samuel Taylor Coleridge applied the term, but the essence of investor irrationality at bubble tops. And at that point, there are no more gullible investors left to keep expanding the bubble. My good friend and retired senior investment adviser at Merrill Lynch, Bob Farrell, the dean of Wall Street technical analysts, taught me decades ago that a speculative market peak is formed when everyone who can be sucked in has been sucked in. So there are no more potential buyers left, but lots of potential sellers.

I make a practice of spotting economic and financial bubbles and then predicting their demise. This isn't easy because there always is some fundamental logic behind them. Bubbles aren't pure fluff, but initially well-founded activities that just get carried to irrational extremes. And, of course, every bubble is different, with a fresh and plausible explanation for its endless expansion. Also, there are so many intelligent and otherwise calm people who are telling the world that the prices of tulip bulbs or houses will soar forever. And how do you think I felt as a professional investor in the late 1990s when I saw the dot-com boom as a huge bubble waiting to burst? (See Figure 1.1.) My attempts to sell those stocks short as they continued to climb were frustrating, to say the least. My angst was even more intense at cocktail parties when amateur investors would revel over the new issues they'd bought and seen leap 5 or 10 times in price the first day of trading.

To see bubbles for what they are and predict their demise with unpleasant consequences, you also have to be willing to see negative sides of the economy. That goes against the grain of most Americans, who are eternal optimists; even more so, investors and especially spokesmen for big banks, brokers, and mutual funds, as well as the media who are

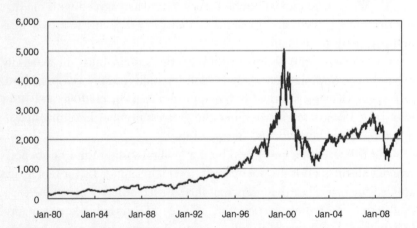

Figure 1.1 NASDAQ Composite Index, 1980–2008
Data source: Yahoo! Finance.

paid to be upbeat. Back in 2006–2007, when I forecast that the *subprime slime*, as I dubbed it, would spread to the rest of housing, then to financial markets, and ultimately precipitate the worst recession since the 1930s, I was regularly chastised by the bulls during TV appearances. Some were downright insulting, deprecating, and thoroughly unprofessional.

Bubbles Last Longer than Expected

It's also true that bubbles tend to expand more and last longer than I and other skeptics expect. That's because they have entered the realm of irrationality that knows no bounds, while I'm trying to examine them with rational analysis. Furthermore, I have a bias toward forecasting a sooner rather than a later collapse of a bubble.

Suppose that in January 2006, I told you, as I wrote in my monthly *Insight* newsletter back then, that "evidence of the housing bubble's demise is mounting" and that a 20 percent decline in prices nationwide "is not a wild forecast, and may be optimistic." And I went on to say, as I wrote at the time, that "a severe housing bust will be detrimental to the earnings and stock prices of homebuilders, building materials producers, mortgage and subprime lenders, and related entities like Fannie Mae and Freddie Mac."

Your reaction might well have been, "Wow! That's scary! When do you think the bubble will break?" I might have replied, "It may be about to break, but it could last another several years, considering the loose lending practices, low interest rates, securitization of mortgages, and expectations of ever-rising house prices that are feeding it." Or I might have said, "I think we're right at the peak now." In fact, house prices did peak in the first quarter of 2006 (see Figure 1.2), but I had no way of knowing that at the time, and forecasting accuracy isn't my point here. Rather, it's the fact that putting an immediacy to my forecast is much more likely to get your attention and spur you to act on it than if I place the catastrophe in the distant and indeterminate future.

Great Calls

Despite these handicaps, I'm zealous to spot bubbles because they provide excellent opportunities for great calls, which I define as having three

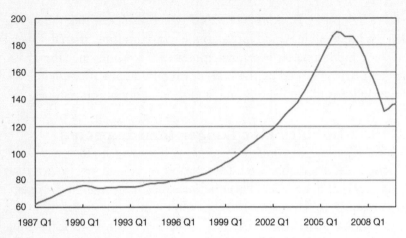

Figure 1.2   Case-Shiller National Home Price Index, 1987–2008 (1Q 2000=100)
Data source: Standard and Poor's.

components. First, a great call has to be important. An accurate forecast of next month's payroll employment doesn't make the cut because later revisions are likely to change the number considerably, and several more months of data would be necessary to confirm any change in trend. By contrast, my forecast in early 1973 that a massive inventory-building was taking place and would collapse into the (then) deepest recession since the 1930s obviously was an important forecast.

Second, a great call needs to be nonconsensus, as my forecast in 1973 certainly was. Almost every other forecaster thought that global shortages of almost everything were driving the economy and would last indefinitely, as opposed to an unsustainable inventory-building spree. Of course, being in the minority does subject you to the slings and arrows of the numerous doubters that constitute the consensus. But then a great call wouldn't be great unless it bucked the majority in a major way. By definition, it's a forecast that few believe until it has become a reality.

Third, a great call must unfold for the reasons stipulated ahead of time by the caller, not through dumb luck or being right for the wrong reasons. In 2007, some thought that residential subprime adjustable rate mortgages (ARMs) would collapse when those rates reset to higher levels than mortgagors could afford, not because declining house prices would wipe out the slender equity of those marginal homeowners, as I correctly

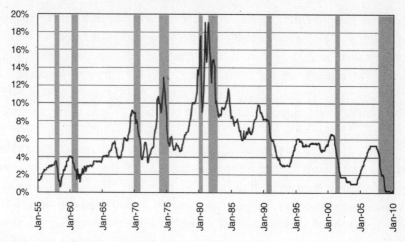

Figure 1.3 Effective Federal Funds Rate, 1955–2010
Data source: Federal Reserve Board.

forecast. The ARM rate resets had little effect because of the dramatic drop in short-term interest rates instituted by the Federal Reserve Bank (see Figure 1.3) before those resets took place.

Lucky Seven

I've made seven great calls in my economic forecasting career, which started in 1963 when I joined Standard Oil of New Jersey (now Exxon Mobil) as an economist, fresh from Stanford's PhD program. I'll discuss them shortly, and you'll see that most of them were forecasts of bubbles' demises. But first, I'll note that those seven great calls work out to one every 6.7 years on average. Opportunities to make these significant forecasts don't occur very often, and when they do, you have to recognize them and make the correct forecast at the proper time.

Still, I think it's fair to say that my record in making great calls is far, far better than most forecasters since the vast majority seldom stray far from the consensus. There's safety in the herd, and if the boss is thinking about firing an economist or strategist for missing a great call, well, the replacement he's considering probably also missed it. Furthermore, most forecasters would rather go wrong in the good company of their peers than risk being a laughingstock for a far-out forecast that didn't pan out. In contrast, I'm uncomfortable in the herd and stimulated when my forecast is in a tiny minority. Maybe that's why I'm no longer with big firms, but instead run my own shop. Of course, my approach can be embarrassing, especially to my wife at times. We'll go to a cocktail party and someone will remark, "Oh, what a beautiful yellow moon tonight!" I've been known to reply, "Are you sure it isn't green?"

Also, the consensus has ingenious ways to deal with missed great calls. In July 2007, only five months from the start of the Great Recession, 60 economists (not including me) polled by the *Wall Street Journal* on average forecast at least 2.5 percent annualized growth in real (inflation-adjusted) gross domestic product for each of the four quarters of 2008. The results were quite the opposite: declines of 0.7 percent in the first quarter, 2.7 percent in the third quarter and 6.4 percent in the fourth, with the only increase being 1.5 percent in the second quarter.

Not to Worry!

But not to worry! The recession wasn't officially called until November 28, 2008, almost a year after it had started in December 2007, when the Business Cycle Dating Committee of the National Bureau of Economic Research, a private outfit, announced its decision. This body is the official arbiter of recessions, and everyone accepts its judgment. That includes every presidential administration and every Congress, since no politician wants to be in the business of declaring recessions. In any event, in late November 2008, the consensus could argue that the downturn must be close to completed since the 10 previous post–World War II recessions averaged 10.4 months in length and the longest, the 1973–1975 downturn, spanned 16 months. Subsequently, many, in effect, declared that the Great Recession that they never forecast and never acknowledged up until then was almost over! I found such statements less than reassuring, but surprisingly few of those forecasters joined the mushrooming ranks of the unemployed.

It's also true that the negativity involved in great calls—realism, as I prefer to call it—can be hazardous to employment continuity. I learned that firsthand when I joined Merrill Lynch in 1967 as the firm's first chief economist and established its economic department. In 1969, I forecast a recession to begin late that year and run into 1970. The forecast proved accurate, but it wasn't being bullish on America, in the Merrill Lynch parlance. That put me at odds with Donald T. Regan, who obviously won because he was running the firm. So I took my entire staff and left, ending up at another Wall Street firm, White, Weld, with no idea that Merrill Lynch would buy White, Weld in 1978. So the story on Wall Street, which was absolutely correct, was that Gary Shilling was the only person fired twice by Don Regan. I promptly established my own firm and at least eliminated the risk of being axed by him a third time.

Fundamental Principles

My zeal to detect bubbles and forecast their demise also fits right in with two very fundamental principles that have always guided my forecasting. First, I believe that human nature changes very slowly, if at all, over time. So people will react to similar circumstances in similar ways. This means that history is relevant. Of course, history doesn't repeat itself, but as Mark Twain noted, it does rhyme. This means that forecasting remains an art, not a science. Still, if you can find circumstances in the past that resemble closely those at present, their resolution back then may be a useful guide to future events.

This was clearly true for me in forecasting the 1973–1975 recession. Over a decade earlier, in the early 1960s, while I was pursuing my PhD at Stanford, I spent a summer working at the San Francisco Federal Reserve Bank. The research department was a rather sleepy place at the time, but that gave me lots of time to browse through the library. Most of the books had uniformly dull titles that contained the words *Economics* or *Finance*, but an unusual one caught my eye: *Hand-to-Mouth Buying and the Inventory Situation*, by George A. Gade, published in 1929.

Hand-to-Mouth Buying

The book title came from the reaction to the traumatic events in American goods production and distribution in 1919–1921. After World War I ended in 1918, there were widespread fears that the cancellation of government contracts for military equipment and unemployment among returning soldiers would precipitate a depression. But by early 1919, the opposite unfolded as exports to Europe leaped, credit expanded, and domestic demand surged in reaction to wartime privations. Robust demand soon more than soaked up excess capacity, and prices leaped, since wartime price and wage controls had been removed.

Exuberant retail demand worked back to raw material producers, and fears of shortages mushroomed. That encouraged the ordering of many more goods than were needed, both to ensure adequate supplies to meet surging demand and to profit from leaping prices. Inventory levels jumped, but their building created excess demand and artificial shortages that only pushed prices higher and encouraged more inventory building.

The transportation system became overburdened, creating delivery delays, more fears of shortages, and more excess orders for later and later delivery. Manufacturers were forced to allocate their production among customers, and demand exceeded their capacity. This encouraged double- and triple-ordering to ensure adequate supplies in the future. Inflationary expectations were rampant as buying in anticipation of price increases further strained supply and further stimulated prices. That confirmed expectations and promoted even more buying in a self-feeding cycle.

Leaping Prices

Prices, according to Gade, leaped 24 percent from the first quarter of 1919 to their peak in the second quarter of 1920. Retailers encouraged customers to buy more than they needed in anticipation of further price increases. But prices got so high that consumer purchasing power was slashed. Parades were held on Fifth Avenue in New York City by people who pledged to buy only the necessities of life until prices came down.

In April 1920, the bubble broke and prices started to fall, ultimately by 42 percent from their peak to their second quarter 1921 level. Falling prices revealed the false basis of demand, and order cancellations spiraled, even for goods in transit and in the production process. Retailers were stuck with goods they had bought at much higher prices. And consumers, many of whom had overbought in the inflationary expectations days, curtailed spending and switched to deflationary expectations as they held off buying in anticipation of still-lower prices. That forced retailers to slash prices to unload unwanted inventories, fulfilling consumer expectations and causing them to wait even longer to buy.

The end result: Massive inventory-building gave way to massive production cuts to liquidate those inventories, causing the 1920–1921 recession with the steepest decline in economic activity of any recession on record. Real GDP fell 13 percent from 1919 to 1921, compared to 3.8 percent peak-to-trough in the recent recession. It also resulted, after the excess stocks were cleared out at massive losses, in hand-to-mouth inventory-buying, the purchase of only those inventories needed to meet immediate customer demand. Hence the title of Gade's book.

Early 1970s Rerun

In the early 1970s, inflation was raging, the result of excess demand that commenced in the mid-1960s due to heavy government spending on the Vietnam War and Great Society programs. Shortages were spreading in commodities and manufactured goods that many expected to last indefinitely, so commodity prices skyrocketed (see Figure 1.4). At that

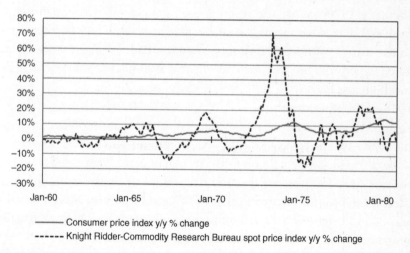

Consumer price index y/y % change

Knight Ridder-Commodity Research Bureau spot price index y/y % change

Figure 1.4 Consumer and Commodity Prices, 1960–1978 (Year over Year percent Change)
Data source: Haver Analytics.

time, I was trying to figure out why steel production was so strong. Our statistical models that related historical steel production to the output of major steel-using industries such as autos, appliances, and machinery indicated that much more steel was being produced than consumed in the early 1970s. Yet the big difference between production and usage was not reported as leaping inventories among producers and steel consumers.

At that time, however, steel service centers—independent warehouses that bought steel from producers, did some fabrication, and then sold to smaller users—did not report their inventories. Maybe these inventories were jumping. We also were hearing stories in and out of the steel arena that fears of shortages had led to double- and triple-ordering of goods and that customers were deliberately understating their inventories in order to convince suppliers with whom they had good relations that they deserved higher spots on their allocation schedules.

Hidden inventories and the strength of business activity in the early 1970s due to inventory-building kept inventory/sales ratios subdued. So the spiking in those ratios, which signals big trouble for retailers, wholesalers, and manufacturers, didn't occur until almost the beginning of the recession. I also remembered *Hand-to-Mouth Buying* and noticed the parallels between the 1919–1920 inventory leap and what was going on in the early 1970s. What was in progress, I concluded, was not shortages forever, but massive and unsustainable inventory-building. Furthermore, in the early 1970s, stock investors' attention had narrowed to the Nifty Fifty, which told me that the end of the economic expansion was nigh, as I'll discuss later.

Inventories, Not Shortages

So in a May 1973 report, I stated that "rapid inventory-building" will "lead to an inventory correction in 1974" and a recession (which actually started in November 1973). This forecast was made well before virtually any other recognized forecaster saw trouble ahead. In a December 1973 poll of forecasters by *BusinessWeek*, I was the only one predicting a 1974 decline in economic activity. In its December 30, 1974 edition, the *Wall Street Journal* said,

Forecasting economic developments can be hazardous any time. A survey of 32 prominent economists taken a year ago turned up only one—A. Gary Shilling of White, Weld & Co.—who correctly predicted that economic activity would decline in 1974. Many forecast substantial growth. It was not an enviable performance and today's uncertainties, at the least, match those prevailing a year ago.

Importantly, our forecast was made five months before the Arab oil embargo in October 1973. In imposing it, the Saudis probably didn't realize its psychological effects, coming on top of shortage fears that had already invaded most commodities (as shown in Figure 1.4) and other goods-producing sectors. For me, however, it reinforced my conviction that a recession was about to commence and led me to predict that it would be the most severe since the 1930s.

Well, as they say, the rest is history. After a shallow decline in economic activity in late 1973, the economy actually revived a bit in the second quarter of 1974. But then all those double- and triple-ordered inventories were delivered. Production was slashed in the fourth quarter of 1974 and first quarter of 1975 to get rid of them, and the 1973–1975 recession was indeed the deepest since the 1930s.

I remember vividly a conversation shortly thereafter with a friend of my dad's, Bob van Hook, the CEO of Henkel-Clauss, a cutlery producer in my hometown of Fremont, Ohio. "Gary," he said, "I knew back in 1973 what you were saying about excess inventory-building. Your dad was showing me your newsletters. But our supplier of cutlery steel would come in and say, 'Our order books are almost full for the next five years. But you're a longtime customer and personal friend, so I can squeeze in your order if you place it now.' So I succumbed, and will be working down that excess steel inventory for years."

Nonconsensus Forecasts

So, as in the case of the big inventory buildup and collapse in the 1970s, history is relevant—my first forecasting principle. It can be very useful in detecting bubbles and forecasting their demise as people react to similar circumstances in similar ways. If you think human nature has changed over the centuries, just ponder this speech from Shakespeare's *Troilus and*

Cressida, one of my favorites. It takes place in the Trojan War, and Achilles is sulking in his tent where Ulysses tells him to get back into action before he's forgotten. This was written 400 years ago—and is just as relevant today when looking at human relationships in and out of business.

> Time hath, my lord, a wallet at his back,
> Wherein he puts alms for oblivion,
> A great-siz'd monster of ingratitudes:
> Those scraps are good deeds past; which are devour'd
> As fast as they are made, forgot as soon
> As done. . . .
> For time is like a fashionable host,
> That slightly shakes his parting guest by the hand,
> And with his arms outstretch'd, as he would fly,
> Grasps in the comer: welcome ever smiles,
> And farewell goes out sighing. . . .
> The present eye praises the present object. . . .

My second fundamental forecasting principle is also relevant to dealing with bubbles: To add value to clients, the key elements of our forecasts must be nonconsensus. As noted earlier, a bubble wouldn't exist if the majority didn't believe it was fundamentally sound and sustainable, so a forecast that recognizes it as the flight of fancy it is and predicts its bursting is nonconsensus.

Consensus forecasts are readily available, and at little cost, from polls of forecasts reported in the media. More important, they tend to be built into business plans and security prices—*discounted* by markets, in the Wall Street parlance. So only a nonconsensus forecast—if it's correct—can add value. This doesn't mean that I simply take contrary stands for the sake of notoriety. I am, and expect to be, judged by my forecasting record. When my forecast in a specific area agrees with the consensus, I pass over it lightly. But when I foresee an important development that's nonconsensus and, in my view, has a high probability of happening, I jump on it with all fours.

Also, please note the difference between my approach and that of the contrarian. The latter always takes the side opposite the consensus. I'm happy to oppose the herd, but only if I think the reverse forecast has a good probability of being correct.

Since most forecasters and investors are perennially optimistic, a non-consensus forecast is usually negative. This doesn't make me popular, especially when I'm correct in my forecast. Begrudging recognition of my accurate prognostication is about the best I can expect. But that goes with the territory. It's like the old saying: If you want loyalty, get a dog. And we have a beautiful, loyal, and friendly female Labrador retriever that my wife named Honey since I'm a serious beekeeper with 80 hives, in addition to my day job.

So you've got to be satisfied with your inner feeling of success and the compliments of the few fellow travelers. But that feeling in itself provides plenty of satisfaction since, to me, the highest intellectual achievement in this trade is to go against the crowd and be right for the correct reasons. It reminds me of Silius Italicus's (A.D. ca. 25–99) statement, "Virtue herself is her own finest reward."

The November 1974 edition of *Institutional Investor* magazine said:

> "Early this year," admits A. Gary Shilling, chief economist at White, Weld, who predicts a painful worldwide recession for 1975, "it was very difficult to convince anyone of our forecasts and, naturally, I worried all the time about whether I was right. Because, in this business, if you're positive and wrong, you're usually in pretty good company, but if you are negative and wrong, nobody is going to forgive you."

A nonconsensus negative forecast, especially the bursting of a major bubble, means that a lot of the participants will lose a lot of money, and that many hopes and dreams will turn to nightmares. Sure, many savvy speculators recognize bubbles as such, but figure they'll get out before they break. Consider those who bought condos in Miami in 2006, before they even came out of the ground, and then made scads of money as they bought increasing numbers and flipped them repeatedly—until flipping ended with the price collapse and they lost everything. Those who buy at the bottom and sell at the tippy top of a bubble are few.

Sitting Out Bubbles

Others, who see bubbles for what they are and sit them out, can avoid losing money when they break. But making money from bursting bubbles usually involves being short stocks, commodities, real estate, subprime mortgages, and so on, one way or the other. And selling short, in the minds of most investors, is unpatriotic and destructive to motherhood and apple pie.

Short sellers, nevertheless, are important to market stability. They keep markets from jumping in unsustainable ways. If short selling of one form or another had been more welcomed and better studied by regulators during the housing and financial bubbles, they might have been deflated much earlier with considerably smaller losses and disruption. Short sellers of individual stocks sometimes ferret out fraud and unrealistic corporate earnings projected by company managements and bullish analysts. Short sellers provide the other side of hedges for those who own bonds, stocks, commodities, currencies, and many other investments. Still, short sellers, especially of stocks, are seldom sought out by the predominantly bullish financial media, and retreat to quiet restaurant corners, hushed phone conversations, and confidential e-mails to discuss stocks that are ripe for collapse. As of November 1, 2009, only 7 percent of Wall Street analysts' rating were "sells" and 48 percent were "buys," with the rest being "holds."

According to the *Wall Street Journal*, Brian Kennedy, a 36-year-old analysts at Jefferies & Co., in early 2009 issued a "sell" rating on CardioNet, accurately forecasting a big cut in what Medicare paid for the firm's remote heart-monitoring system. Some of his senior colleagues criticized him for "rocking the boat." He was muzzled by Jefferies. Bullish analysts at firms that had underwritten CardioNet's stock blasted him, including Citigroup, which issued a report, "Not Worthy of the BEAT-down" (CardioNet's ticker symbol was BEAT), which questioned the legitimacy of Kennedy's report while maintaining its own "buy" rating on the stock. CardioNet's CEO, Randy Thurman, at a health care conference said Kennedy hadn't done "proper due diligence." In a complaint to the SEC, Thurman said the Jefferies report may have been part of an effort to help short sellers.

But then the company was forced to announce that Medicare was cutting its payments for the monitoring system by 33 percent, exactly the amount Kennedy had predicted. The stock fell a cumulative 75 percent after Kennedy's report was issued, and Thurman later said CardioNet "will not be able to sustain operations as a stand-alone company."

Kennedy was dead right, but apparently the criticism got to him. He quit his job soon after the Medicare payment cut announcement and planned to work for an independent research firm with no investment banking business.

Note that in the dot-com bubble, Wall Street analysts pushed new issues underwritten by their firms that they privately said were garbage. When this was revealed, major firms were forced to pay $1.5 billion for independent research to be distributed to their brokerage clients, and their analysts and investment bankers were supposed to be entirely separated. Interestingly, in 2008, Massachusetts regulators accused Merrill Lynch of using "supposedly independent" research analysts to aid in selling collapsing auction-rate securities to unsuspecting clients. The firm replied that regulations covered contacts between equity researchers and investment bankers, but not communications between bond analysts and salesmen. One investment banking firm demanded and got a favorable rewriting of a Merrill Lynch analyst's negative report on those toxic securities.

Short selling is not only frowned upon but can be expensive. An unleveraged short position can make at most 100 percent of the price if the shorted security drops to zero. But the loss is unlimited if the price rises and the investor fails to cover his short positions. That, of course, opens the door to options and other instruments that gain if the underlying investments fall, but it also limits losses. I'll cover later my highly successful investment with hedge fund manager John Paulson, who used these techniques very successfully.

After the 1929 Crash and Great Depression, many felt short selling was a major cause. They believed that short sales had triggered the cumulative downward spiral, and many still worry about this possibility. Of course, they never complain about upward buying panics that can squeeze short positions and cause irrational stock leaps. In any event, in reaction to the 1930s, shorting stocks was prohibited except on an uptick—that is, the price of the most recent sale of a stock had to be higher than the immediately preceding sale.

Over time, however, the use of futures contracts, options, and other techniques largely emasculated the uptick rule so it was eliminated in 2007. Back then, the SEC studied the 70-year-old limitations on short sales and concluded that they were ineffective and an "economically irrelevant" constraint. But the uptick rule was briefly reinstated in late 2008 on many financial and other stocks that were crumbling. Then in early 2010, the Democratic majority of SEC commissioners approved renewed curbs on short selling.

Positive Nonconsensus Forecasts

As noted earlier, the consensus is almost always optimistic, but not always. So there occasionally is the opportunity for a positive nonconsensus forecast. This was true of my great call in the early 1980s on the unwinding of inflation, which I explore in detail in Chapter 2. The rising inflation of the late 1960s and 1970s was devastating to stocks and bonds. Rising inflation pushed up interest rates (see Figure 1.5), which drove down bond prices. In fact, in the mid- and again in the late 1970s, inflation spikes pushed real Treasury bond yields into negative territory. That compounded the losses from falling bond prices.

Rising interest rates knocked down stock price/earnings (P/E) ratios, which normally move in inverse fashion. And inflation very effectively transferred corporate profitability to government, which taxed

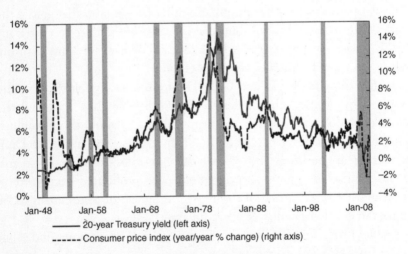

Figure 1.5 20-Year Treasury Yield and Consumer Prices, 1948–2008
Data sources: Federal Reserve and Bureau of Labor Statistics.

the underdepreciation and inventory profits it created. Also, at that time, most companies felt duty-bound to keep their employees' pay abreast of inflation while they viewed their earnings in nominal, not decimated real terms. But stockholders knew the difference from November 1968 to July 1982, when the S&P 500 Index rose 4 percent, but in real terms plummeted 64 percent.

With this miserable performance and the consensus forecast in the early 1980s that high inflation would persist if not increase, most forecasters and investors were very negative on both stocks and bonds. So my forecast back then that inflation would unwind, resulting in strength for both stocks and bonds, was not only nonconsensus but distinctly positive. I reasoned that falling inflation rates would push interest rates down (as shown in Figure 1.5) and Treasury bond prices up. In 1981, when 30-year Treasuries yielded 14.7 percent, I said, "We're entering the bond rally of a lifetime" that eventually would drive those yields to 3 percent. For stocks, I noted that falling interest rates would move P/E ratios up and fading inflation would diminish the transfer of corporate profitability to employees and government. Stocks would benefit immensely from both of these developments, I forecast. And they did (see Figure 1.6).

Figure 1.6 S&P 500 Index, 1980–2010
Data source: Yahoo! Finance.

Bubbles Aren't New

Economic and financial bubbles are the result of nearly immutable human nature, so they've existed throughout history. In any speculative bubble, there always is an underlying grain of truth, as noted earlier. When tulips were introduced to Northern Europe from Asia in the sixteenth century, they were immensely popular. Think about all of those magnificent Dutch still-life paintings that featured parrot and other beautiful tulips. The tulip bulb mania took this reality to illogical extremes. Charles Mackay, in his well-known 1841 book, *Extraordinary Popular Delusions and the Madness of Crowds*, has a wonderful chapter on the 1636 tulipomania, as it was called.

Tulipomania

Mackay notes that in 1636, as the demand for tulips grew, confidence was also growing as seemingly everyone was profiting.

> A golden bait hung temptingly out before the people, and one after the other, they rushed to the tulip-marts, like flies around a honey-pot. Every one imagined that the passion for tulips would last forever. . . .

Everyone from the very wealthy to the lowly chimneysweeps contracted tulipomania, Mackay writes:

> People of all grades converted their property into cash, and invested it in flowers. Houses and lands were offered for sale at ruinously low prices, or assigned in payment of bargains made at the tulip-mart. Foreigners became smitten with the same frenzy, and money poured into Holland from all directions.

Eventually, the folly was seen for what it was and

> Rich people no longer bought the flowers to keep them in their gardens, but to sell them again at cent per cent profit. It was seen that somebody must lose fearfully in the end. As this conviction spread, prices fell, and never rose again. Confidence was destroyed, and a universal panic seized upon the dealers. Many who, for a brief season, had

emerged from the humbler walks of life, were cast back into their original obscurity. Substantial merchants were reduced almost to beggary, and many a representative of a noble line saw the fortunes of his house ruined beyond redemption.

The South Sea Bubble

Mackay also discourses at length on the South Sea bubble of the early 1700s in England. The South Sea Company was formed in 1711, and in return for taking on government debt was granted a monopoly on trade with Latin America. As in any bubble, there was a kernel of economic reality. In this case, it was the idea of trading English-manufactured goods for Latin American gold and silver.

But Spain controlled Latin America, and King Philip V had no intention of granting the English trading access. This reality, however, didn't deter the company directors or the public who bought the shares with gay abandon. Neither did the news that the 1719–1720 Mississippi scheme in France was shaky. That was instigated by Scottish businessman John Law and was among the first to introduce paper money, in that case to restore the French government's finances after the extravagant reign of Louis XIV ended with the king's death in 1715. As Louis predicted, the deluge followed, and Law's scheme only papered over France's financial plight temporarily.

The South Sea Company stock leaped almost 1,000 percent from January 1720 to August of that year, and along the way the company issued more stock with delayed payment to provide leverage for enthusiastic speculators. It then collapsed and the usual skullduggery was revealed later, including members of the government having ensured passage of laws favorable to the South Sea Company.

Other Bubbles Spawned

A fascinating aspect of the South Sea bubble, which has been repeated many times since, was the wide variety of other speculative public companies it spawned in its short life as the speculative fever spread. They were popularly known as bubbles and many lasted only a week or two, but that didn't deter shareholder zeal. One was for a wheel of perpetual motion; another, according to Mackay, "for encouraging the breed of horses in England and improving of glebe and church lands and rebuilding parsonage and vicarage houses." Globe Permits, square pieces of playing cards with a picture of the Globe Tavern near Exchange Alley where shares were traded, were sold with the inscription, "Sail-Cloth Permits." These gave their buyers no more than permission to subscribe to a new sailcloth factory which, of course, never materialized.

The top of the tree was the promoter in London who advertised "A company for carrying on an undertaking of great advantage, but nobody to know what it is." Sounds like today's special purpose acquisition companies (SPACs), known as blank check companies, which are empty shells that promise to use the proceeds of initial public offerings to buy other companies. This 1720 genius required subscribers to put down only 2 percent of the value of their stock. His prospectus promised the project's details in a month when the remaining 98 percent was due. He opened his office at 9:00 A.M. the next morning to crowds of subscribers and took in a fortune by 3:00 P.M. when he closed up. The guy was shrewd enough not to press his luck, and promptly set off for the Continent that evening, never to be heard from again.

Even before the South Sea bubble broke, the government became worried enough that on July 12, 1720, it dissolved all the bubble companies and dismissed petitions to form new ones. Among the prohibited were those "for assessing of seamen's wages," "for improving the art of making soup," "for improving gardens," "for importing walnut trees from Virginia," and "for extracting silver from lead."

Tulipomania and the South Sea bubble had limited substance behind them; some other bubbles had more, but expanded too soon and burst before their promises were achieved. Railroads revolutionized transportation and commerce in the United Kingdom in the early 1800s, generating a bubble that burst in the 1840s. The exercise was repeated in the United States after the Civil War. Between 1866 and 1892, 120,000 miles of track were laid. But excess debt popped the bubble and helped precipitate the panic of 1873. By 1900, almost every U.S. railroad had been reorganized. Similarly, with the electrification of homes in the 1920s came radio. This exciting new technology sired a bubble that burst well before radio achieved its full potential and was followed by television.

Nifty Fifty

Much more recently, in the early 1970s, the Nifty Fifty list of stocks was the focus of investors' attention. These represented rapidly growing companies, some based on solid long-term growth prospects, while others were simply fads. But overconfidence became so extreme that they were labeled the "one decision" stocks. They had such promise that investors only had to make one decision—to buy them—since they never would need to be sold. Nevertheless, disappointments began to multiply, and the favored few shrank.

In its November 1974 edition, the *Institutional Investor* magazine quoted me as saying, "It seemed to me that, for a long time, there was something wrong with the world, and that the stock market was telling us this. Its emphasis was not on the basic structure of the economy, but on motor homes, hamburger chains, amusement parks, and gimmick cameras." I was referring, of course, to Winnebago, McDonald's, Disney, and Polaroid. These represented the fluff of the economy, not its guts. If investors shunned the basic economy, they were anticipating big trouble, I reasoned. The *Institutional Investor* further quoted me as believing that conditions were "totally outside the whole postwar experience" and that we might be on the brink of "some downward, worldwide supercycle of the sort not seen since 1920–1921." The premonitions of investors and me were right. The 1973–1975 recession followed, the deepest since the 1930s because of the 1920–1921-style massive inventory liquidation, as discussed earlier. What was left of the Nifty Fifty collapsed. Panicked investors did make that second decision—and as they dumped Polaroid, they simply knocked a zero off the stock's price, from $140 to $14 per share.

As noted earlier, bubbles feed on the widespread conviction that they will last indefinitely because the world has entered a new solar system. Consider the New Economy concept that was used to justify triple-digit P/Es for dot-com start-ups in the late 1990s. Walter Bagehot, the famed editor of the London *Economist* in the nineteenth century, said that in expanding bubbles, merchants and bankers "fancy the prosperity they see will last always, that it is only the beginning of great prosperity."

The early twentieth century bull market in stocks was seen in the 1920s by the financial editor of the *New York Times*, Alexander Dana

Noyes, as "speculation which based its ideas and conduct on the assumption that we were living in a New Era; that old rules and principles and precedents of finance were obsolete; that things could be done safely today which had been dangerous and impossible in the past." Forgotten in the hot air of a rapidly expanding bubble are the immortal words of the late and great investor, Sir John Templeton: "The four most dangerous words in investing are, 'this time it's different.'"

Well-known value investor Jeremy Grantham has identified 28 bubbles in global security markets since 1920. American speculations in the post–World War II years include the banking stock binge in 1961, the PC stock bubble in 1982–1983, and the zeal for biotech companies in 1991–1992. Didier Sornette, director of the Swiss Federal Institute of Technology and a student of financial bubbles, says that only about two-thirds of bubbles end in crashes, but, of course, those are the ones that get the attention as their lovers lose bundles. And unless human nature suddenly changes, there'll be many more bubbles in the future. The World Bank is worried that too much investment money is "raising concerns about asset price bubbles" in Asian stock markets. Meanwhile, in the *Wall Street Journal*, the International Monetary Fund (IMF) cited "a risk" that leaping asset prices in Hong Kong are being propelled by a surge of funds "divorced from fundamental forces of supply and demand."

The Anatomy of Bubbles

Bubbles often develop in periods of financial and economic tranquility after memories of the last bubble's collapse or other major disruption have faded. Hyman Minsky's *financial instability hypothesis* holds, quite plausibly, that eras of stability spawn big risk taking. The stock blow-off in the late 1920s came at the end of a decade of rapid growth, with industrial production almost doubling between 1921 and 1929 while major price indexes fell on balance.

The dot-com bubble of the late 1990s capped off nearly two decades of declining inflation rates and rapid productivity growth fueled by a consumer borrowing-and-spending binge and soaring stocks. The great moderation of the early 2000s in inflation, financial markets, and the business cycle convinced senior Fed officials and others that skillful monetary policy and new risk-reducing financial instruments made higher debt levels acceptable. Then came the resulting housing and financial collapses.

Furthermore, bubbles tend to unfold in similar steps, especially those involving a new technology such as tulip breeding in Northern Europe in the sixteenth century, the development of the Internet in the 1990s, and securitization and other financial innovations that fueled the housing and financial bubbles more recently.

Overenthusiasm

The first step is investor overenthusiasm. To be sure, bubbles have some real bases, but avid investors hyperventilate and their zeal leaps. This, of course, also attracts scads of new entrants into the business, eager to cash in on the opportunities to raise money cheaply, develop personal and company wealth quickly, and participate in a mushrooming venture. That was equally true in the glass industry in the late 1800s, in autos in the early 1900s, and in computers and Internet companies more recently. At the same time, at that early stage of the nascent bubble, growth—current and anticipated—is so robust and new investment money so plentiful that costs are of little concern.

Then comes the competition. Initial public offerings and other new money become so prolific that even wildly enthusiastic investors become satiated. Over 50 percent of all high-tech initial public offerings in the years 1992–1998 finished 1998 trading below their offering prices. And competition among producers starts to erode selling prices.

At the same time, the participants and investors in the expanding bubble begin to question whether it will indeed be the best thing since sliced bread. In 1882, investors in London rushed into the shares of companies involved in electric lighting, a promising new technology, after the invention of the light bulb. Nevertheless, the boom turned to bust as much of the money went into fraudulent inventions, worthless patent fees, and promotion expenses while regulators delayed electrification in favor of municipal gas-lighting companies.

Bold Reassurances

As bubbles near the bursting point, assurances of their continuity are often heard from those with vested interests. They include, of course, promoters but also businesspeople, government officials, and even academics who want to keep the good times rolling. Yale economist Irving Fisher in September 1929, one month before the Crash, declared that stocks had reached a "permanently high plateau" because Prohibition had increased worker productivity and new "scientific" management techniques were being employed by businesses.

In September 2006, as defaults were beginning to leap, Merrill Lynch bought subprime lender First Franklin for $1.3 billion, spurred by CEO Stan O'Neal's zeal for the mortgage market. Reportedly, he used the Merrill Lynch helicopter on golf outings, but didn't have time to learn about the firm's huge warehouse holdings of collateralized debt obligations (CDOs). In any event, in late October 2007, O'Neal said that "we got it wrong by being overexposed to subprime" and that "both our assessment of the potential risks and mitigation strategies were inadequate." He resigned a few days later, but not to worry. He was replaced in December 2007 by John Thain, the ex-Goldman Sachs Group president who came to Merrill Lynch from the New York Stock Exchange, where he had paved the move to electronic trading.

In 2008, Merrill Lynch was headed for the exit and reportedly forced by the government into a shotgun merger with Bank of America in January 2009. But that didn't stop Thain from making a long series of optimistic statements that became comical since each one was made from even deeper in Merrill Lynch's financial hole. Maybe they're understandable since it's reported that during the interviews for the Merrill Lynch CEO job, Thain didn't ask for details on the positions that were generating billions of dollars of losses. Here's a list compiled by *Reuters*:

Thain's Takes

One of my first priorities at Merrill Lynch was to strengthen the firm's balance sheet, and today we have made great progress towards that by bolstering our capital position through these investments and our announced sale of Merrill Lynch Capital.

—Thain in a statement when Merrill announced a $6.2 billion capital raising, December 24, 2007

...These transactions make certain that Merrill is well-capitalized.

—Thain in a statement after selling $6.6 billion of preferred shares to a group that included Japanese and Kuwaiti investors, January 15, 2008

We're very confident that we have the capital base now that we need to go forward in 2008.

—Thain as quoted by the *New York Times*, January 18, 2008

...Today I can say that we will not need additional funds. These problems are behind us. We will not return to the market.

—Thain in an interview with France's *Le Figaro*, March 8, 2008

We have more capital than we need, so we can say to the market that we don't need more injections. We can confirm that we have tackled the problem.

—Thain in an interview with Spain's *El Pais*, March 16, 2008

In 2007, we lost $8.6 billion after tax, but we raised $12.8 billion in new capital. We raised significantly more capital than we lost. And we did that on purpose so that we could say to the marketplace that we raised more than enough capital. We replaced all the capital we lost. We have plenty of capital going forward, and we don't need to come back into the equity market. The goal is to maintain our current ratings. No more capital raising; I'm sure we have enough capital.

—Thain in an interview with Japan's *Nihon Keizai Shimbun*, April 4, 2008

We deliberately raised more capital than we lost last year...we believe that will allow us to not have to go back to the equity market in the foreseeable future.

—Thain to reporters in Tokyo, as reported by *Reuters*, April 8, 2008

John Thain has been very clear that we have sufficient capital and don't have a need to raise additional common equity for the foreseeable future. When we raised this capital in January, we had a lot of demand so we went beyond what we needed.

> **—Merrill President Greg Fleming in an interview**
> **with the *Times* of London, May 12, 2008**

Today on a pro forma basis we have about $44 billion of equity capital, which actually isn't very much below the all-time high that Merrill ever had. And our philosophy about this is that we are well-capitalized. We're comfortable with our capital position. We, like everyone else, are deleveraging our balance sheet.

> **—Thain on a conference call hosted by Deutsche Bank,**
> **June 11, 2008**

Right now we believe that we are in a very comfortable spot in terms of our capital.

> **—Thain on a conference call after posting Merrill's**
> **second-quarter results, July 17, 2008**

Ex-CEO Thain

Not surprisingly, the ever-optimistic-in-times-of-trouble Mr. Thain got the ax after the Bank of America takeover and the revelation, among others, that he had redecorated his Merrill Lynch CEO office to the tune of $750,000. Nevertheless, the irrepressible Thain surfaced in February 2010 as the new CEO of small and mid-size company lender CIT Group, which had just emerged from bankruptcy after overexpanding into subprime mortgages and student loans.

As overly enthusiastic expectations for a bubble are disappointed, financing dries up. But bubbles grow so rapidly and require so much capital in the process that a closing of the money spigot creates big trouble. Inevitably, bankruptcies and consolidation follow and the companies and investors with deep pockets and steadfast sources of finance are the ones that ultimately survive.

In the late 1800s, the American steel industry, a new tech of the day, had grown too rapidly and was being killed by price-cutting and competition. Furthermore, Andrew Carnegie's Federal Steel was so efficient that no one else could successfully compete. So J. P. Morgan, the moneyman, bought out Carnegie and combined his operations with other less-successful firms to form U.S. Steel. The company then became a huge financial success. Cutthroat competition was curtailed as demand for steel continued to mushroom.

Similarly, big consolidation occurred among the dot-coms after their bubble broke in 2000–2002 and investor disappointment curbed capital sources. Today, in the aftermath of the financial crisis and massive government bailouts, banks continue to disappear and deposits become increasingly concentrated.

Detecting economic and financial bubbles and predicting their bursts and aftermaths constituted many of my great calls. In Chapters 2, 3, and 4, I explore the seven I've been lucky enough to make so far.

Chapter 2

Making Great Calls

As spelled out in Chapter 1, I define a *great call* in the realm of forecasting as containing three elements. First, it must involve an important economic or financial development. Second, it must be nonconsensus. And third, it must evolve for the reasons stated, not just due to dumb luck. I've had the good fortune of making seven *great calls* in my 47 years of forecasting. This chapter briefly discusses the first five. The last two, the great calls on the housing and financial bubbles, are covered in Chapters 3 and 4.

Great Call 1: The 1969–1970 Recession

In 1969, I'd only been at Merrill Lynch for two years as the firm's first chief economist, as noted earlier. Nevertheless, I was increasingly concerned about rising inflation rates, the result of heavy government spending on the Vietnam War and Great Society programs—the guns and butter policy. Furthermore, the Fed had begun to raise its federal funds rate in 1967 in response. So in April 1969, I first forecast a mild recession for 1970, similar to the 1960–1961 downturn when real GDP fell 1.6 percent from peak to trough.

By December of that year, however, I sensed that economic conditions were deteriorating further and forecast the 60 to 70 percent likelihood of a major recession on the order of the 1953–1954 decline when real GDP dropped 2.6 percent, or the 1957–1958 setback when it fell 3.7 percent. In my report to Merrill Lynch clients that month, I argued that a major recession was really bullish since it would knock out "inflationary psychology," then rising with inflation, which was then running 6 percent annually. A mild recession, on which I placed a 30 to 40 percent probability, would leave inflationary expectations intact. In that case, price acceleration might degenerate into runaway inflation, credit demand would probably outrun any reasonable increase in supply, economic distortions would multiply, and the inevitable correction in those excesses could be the most severe in the post–World War II era.

As it turned out, a recession did occur from December 1969 to November 1970, but it was not deep, with real GDP falling 0.6 percent from peak to trough. Still, I regard this as a great call because there had been no recessions since the 1960–1961 downturn almost a decade earlier. Furthermore, the vast majority of forecasters saw no recession in the offing. Stocks were rising after statements by incoming Federal Reserve Board Chairman Arthur Burns and Council of Economic Advisors Chairman Paul McCracken that the Nixon administration wouldn't let the current fiscal and monetary restraints push the economy into a recession.

Inflation Helps Stocks?

In addition, few others at the time worried about the detrimental effects of inflation on stock prices. I recall that back then, Merrill Lynch had wall posters showing graphs of stock prices and the consumer price index (CPI)—both rising in the post–World War II era. The implication was that stocks were a great offset to inflation and, indeed, rising consumer prices might spur equity prices.

I also remember the shock I felt earlier when I learned otherwise—and well before the near runaway inflation of the 1970s wreaked havoc on stock prices, as discussed in Chapter 1. At Merrill Lynch, we developed a statistical model to explain stock prices. We included the usual suspects as explanatory variables—the money supply, business sales, excess capacity, the trend in stocks, and inflation. I even got my friend Bob Farrell to develop a variable that quantified whether the stock market was in a speculative mode or not in each month of the historical sample period. When the sign in the inflation coefficient in the equation came out of the computer as negative, indicating that inflation is bad for stocks, I thought it was a mistake.

I learned otherwise as inflation rolled on and stocks suffered, especially in real terms. And contrary to my hopes, the 1969–1970 recession wasn't deep enough to curb inflationary expectations and their economic distortions, so the inventory bulge of the early 1970s followed, culminating in the severe 1973–1975 recession, as discussed earlier.

Big Waves

I knew my forecast of a major recession would make waves even though it might calm the growing inflation monster. But my report made big waves because of its unauthorized early release by Alfred L. Malabre Jr., a *Wall Street Journal* staff reporter. I foolishly succumbed to his request for an early copy of my report under the strict understanding that he would not use it in print before it was sent to Merrill Lynch clients at the very end of December. But on December, 1969, Malabre broke the whole story on the Dow Jones broad tape with the opener, "The chief economist for the world's largest securities firm said business appears headed into a 'major recession.'"

For all you young folks, the broad tape was printed on $6\frac{1}{4}$–inch wide rolls of paper and spewed out of clattering teletype machines almost nonstop. Malabre later told me that he violated our agreement because the day after Christmas was a no-news day and the people running the broad tape pressured him for copy. I think he simply wanted to grab a byline.

He also said he called Merrill Lynch's head, Don Regan, and apologized for the early release to clear me of collaboration. I think the broad tape story only infuriated Regan, coming on top of my recession forecast report, even though it had been cleared by the director of research. Ironically, I had earlier condensed my report to fulfill a request made to Regan from the *San Jose Mercury* for a year-end article to appear under his name. I asked him if he wanted to read it before it was sent to the newspaper. "Was it okayed by Jim Corbett (the director of research)?" Regan asked me. "Yes," I replied. "Then send it," he ordered.

Fan Mail

Still, the fan mail the firm received about my forecast was uncomplimentary, to put it euphemistically. One letter, which is still framed and mounted on my office wall, was written by H. Mandelcorn of Fullerton, California, and addressed to "Mirrill Lynch" with the greeting, "My dear Mr. Lynch." Apparently, Lynch's first name was Mirrill, and Charlie Merrill really didn't found the firm—it was "Mr. Lynch."

> On Friday, December 26th, A. Gary Shilling stated in a staff letter he believes the probability of a full scale recession in 1970.
>
> Who wants to know about his predictions for 1970 in the news channels?
>
> Is Mr. Shilling trying to help the short sellers? It should be investigated.
>
> I have friends in Los Angeles and New York who deal with your company. I shall contact my friends to see what they want to do about it.

Apparently, Mr. Mandelcorn wasn't a Merrill Lynch customer himself.

> Why doesn't he also predict some good news for 1970? Things are not all bad. Mr. Shilling's news can only encourage a depression.

In any event, Regan slashed my year-end bonus several weeks later and subsequently forced me out of the firm, as I mentioned in Chapter 1.

Great Call 2: The Early 1970s Inventory Bubble and 1973–1975 Recession

You've already read in Chapter 1 about the early 1970s when almost all forecasters and businesspeople thought the world was in a state of never-ending shortages. I, however, correctly saw these shortages as artificial, driven by a self-feeding inventory-building binge as inflationary expectations ruled. And that appraisal of the situation led me to correctly forecast not only the 1973–1975 recession, but also that it would be the deepest since the 1930s. I also called for a major decline in stock prices and the demise of the Nifty Fifty "one decision" equities. The bloodbath started in November 1973 and pushed the S&P 500 down 48 percent to its trough in October 1974. At that point, the S&P 500 was selling at a price/earnings (P/E) ratio of only 7 as investors anticipated the severe recession we'd been forecasting.

What made this great call so great was that it was so nonconsensus, so at variance with almost everyone else's conviction. Sure, the recession that commenced in November 1973 was an on-and-off affair until late 1974, so my forecast of massive inventory liquidation was being severely challenged during its early phases despite the nosedive in stocks. But when those excess inventories were being dumped in the fourth quarter of 1974 and first quarter of 1975, respectively, and real GDP fell 1.6 percent and 4.8 percent at annual rates, there was no question in anyone's mind about what was happening.

Great Call 3: Disinflation

In the late 1970s, the economy was very troubled. Leaping inflation (as seen in Figure 1.5 in Chapter 1) coexisted with high unemployment (see Figure 2.1) under the label *stagflation*. Frustrations over the failed Vietnam War and the Watergate scandal were monumental. I sensed back then that voters were not only beginning to blame Washington for the mess, but they were also feeling betrayed by the earlier overextension of the role and abilities of government.

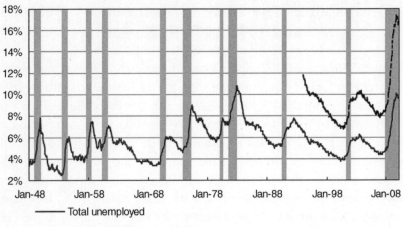

Figure 2.1 U.S. Unemployment Rate, 1948–2008
Data source: Bureau of Labor Statistics.

Government Expansion

Federal government involvement in the economy had been growing since it was initiated in a major way by the New Deal reaction to the Great Depression. It's debatable whether those programs were responsible for economic revival. Indeed, it can be argued that government involvement created uncertainty and fear among businesspeople and markets and thereby impeded recovery. It's also likely that rearmament and World War II were instrumental in ending the Great Depression.

But the economy did revive and World War II was a successful one, so Americans associated increasing government involvement in the economy with economic growth. Both the economy and government's role in it were rising together, but note that you can't prove causality with statistics. I guarantee—absolutely, positively—that every time there's an eclipse of the sun, if you go outside and beat a drum, it will go away.

Washington policy makers also increasingly believed they could successfully manage the economy, to the point that in the mid-1960s, they way overreached their abilities. At that time, administration economists believed they were so skillful at implementing monetary and fiscal policy that they could prevent not only a major recession but minor dips as well—the "fine-tuning" policy. At the same time, the Johnson administration believed that with just a modest increase in government spending—the Great Society programs—the nation's social ills could be cured. And then there was the conviction in Washington that the economy was strong enough to fight a land war in Asia and simultaneously embark on massive domestic spending without creating inflation and other major problems—the guns and butter strategy.

Overreaching

Needless to say, this government overreaching proved disastrous. Recessions proved far less than extinct. Social problems persisted despite huge government outlays, and even grew. And massive federal outlays for military and domestic programs spawned aggregate demand far in excess of supply, with the inevitable result: inflation.

Voters revolted, as witnessed first by Proposition 13 in California in 1978, which severely limited property taxes to 3 percent of assessed valuation. The movement strengthened with the election of President Reagan in 1980 and a substantial shift to the right in Congress. Reflecting voter disdain for national politicians, every presidential candidate since then has run as a Washington outsider, even Al Gore, who lived most of his life there. Furthermore, virtually every meaningful legislated change since then has not been initiated in Washington, but bubbled up instead from the state and local levels. Workfare, which requires welfare recipients to work or enter job training, is a good example, and term limits for politicians is another. Before the federal Consumer Financial Protection Bureau was established in mid-2010, a number of states had restricted payday lenders, auto loans, and costly tax refund loans. While Congress continues to avoid the immigration hot potato, Arizona, Oklahoma, and some cities have put strict limits on illegal aliens.

With this shift in voter sentiment, I realized in the late 1970s that inflation would wane and disinflation would reign in the years ahead—overall prices would still be rising, but at slower and slower rates as they dropped from double-digit growth rates to 3 percent or less (Figure 1.5). I saw excess aggregate demand created by huge government spending as the root cause of inflation, and reasoned that voters were blowing the whistle on government involvement in the economy and spending. And I reached that conclusion more than a decade before the end of the Cold War in the early 1990s and all its huge costs.

We also made our forecast of disinflation well before the Fed under its then-chairman Paul Volcker hiked interest rates massively in the early 1980s (as was seen in Figure 1.3 in Chapter 1). Now, I'm aware that some credit the Fed with precipitating disinflation, and even more believe Milton Friedman's statement that inflation is always and everywhere a monetary phenomenon. That may be true in a direct sense, but my concern is with the prime mover behind inflation.

The Prime Mover

Those who believe the Fed is the basic instigator must think that it was run by a bunch of idiots in the year 1941–1945 to allow the money supply to leap at 26 percent annual rates in 1943 and spawn CPI inflation at 14 percent in 1947 after wartime wage and price controls were removed. In reality, monetary policy then was merely the handmaiden of fiscal policy. To maintain patriotism during World War II, the government didn't want to raise taxes enough to pay for the leap in military spending, which reached almost 40 percent of GDP. So it relied on the Fed and war bond sales to finance the resulting huge federal deficit, which hit 30 percent of GDP in 1943.

This great call on disinflation was no doubt the most profound I've ever made, with far-reaching implications for stocks and bonds, as discussed earlier. But it took years to develop in all its ramifications and was not accepted by many even as it unfolded, so great was the conviction that inflation was a permanent fixture on the economic scene. Some argued that inflation would never retreat without a return to the gold standard since, in a democracy, the majority will always resort to the inflationary money-printing press.

I wrote my first book, co-authored by Kiril Sokoloff, in 1982 and it was published by McGraw-Hill in the spring of 1983. The title was *Is Inflation Ending? Are You Ready?* and in it we argued that inflation was indeed ending, largely because of voters turning against its creator, the federal government. In answer to the second question, we wrote that no, you're not ready. Your investment portfolio is probably loaded with tangible assets that thrive as hedges against the earlier inflation, but you likely don't have enough stocks and bonds, which will benefit from disinflation, as I discussed in Chapter 1.

The book was a bust. Few believed we could possibly be correct in our forecast. High inflation was here to stay. McGraw-Hill actually gave us the remaining unsold copies several years later just to get rid of them. In fact, however, the CPI inflation rate, measured year over year, peaked in March 1980 at a 14.6 percent, three years before our book was published.

But there is a silver lining for that book. In 1986, as our forecasts became manifest to all, the business editors of the *Boston Globe* and *Seattle Post-Intelligencer*, independently, remembered *Is Inflation Ending? Are You Ready?* and reviewed the book ex post. By then, the book was long out of print, so those two reviews were about as handy as a pocket in your underwear in terms of book sales. But they sure felt good!

Great Call 4: The 1980s Japanese Bubble

Japan's revival from World War II was spectacular and in the mid-1980s, its economy was developing bubble dimensions. High and rising levels of consumer saving were driven by a mercantile system that would have made the eighteenth century French green with envy. That saving in turn fueled stock and real estate booms as well as huge additions to industrial capacity. Studio apartments in Tokyo sold for $1 million. The family of a friend of mine from Nomura Securities, the huge Japanese brokerage house, was heavily invested in what were called *pencil* buildings, commercial structures so narrow they looked like pencils, but still sold at high prices due to exuberant demand.

Stocks soared and in the late 1980s, P/Es of 100 were commonplace. The value of all Japanese equity markets exceeded the total of U.S. stocks even though the Japanese economy was only half as large as that of the United States. In the late 1980s, the market value of one stock, Nippon Telegraph & Telephone, exceeded the value of the entire German stock market.

Japan's high household saving rate, mercantile system, and strong yen in the 1980s were also felt by the rest of the world. It targeted industries like autos for global domination and moved swiftly to augment exports with production facilities abroad. Japanese purchases of U.S. icons like Rockefeller Center and Pebble Beach scared many Americans to the point that some Midwestern states moved to limit foreign ownership of farmland.

By the late 1980s, I was convinced that the Japanese economy was in an unsustainable bubble. I knew the end was near when worried matrons at suburban cocktail parties would approach me and ask, in worried tones, "Is my husband's firm going to be run out of business by a Japanese company, or will he end up working for one of them?" When nearly everyone is convinced some juggernaut will roll on forever, it's probably about ready to roll over into the ditch.

Japanese Depression Forecast

So in 1988, I stated that Japan's economy was in the latter stages of a bubble and forecast an imminent end. In fact, I titled a chapter in *After the Crash*, published that year, "A Depression Is More Likely in Japan Than in the U.S." and began that chapter, "Ask most people which industrial economy today is the strongest and they will answer, Japan. Yet if any are to experience serious financial problems and a depression in coming years, Japan is the most likely."

This was a great call because few others expected the Japanese bubble to burst and because its demise had such profound and lasting implications for the world's second largest economy. The bubble lasted about another year. On May 31, 1989, the Bank of Japan started to raise interest rates. That central bank was led by Masushi Mieno, the man who thought stocks were speculative by nature and said he'd never own a share, and was determined to let the air out of the bubble economy.

He certainly achieved his goal! Those rate increases broke the stock and real estate bubbles soon thereafter. The Nikkei stock index hit its high of 38,916 on the last trading day of 1989, fell 81.9 percent to its low of 7,055 on March 10, 2009, and has barely recovered since then (see Figure 2.2). Real estate prices fell 90 percent or more in major Japanese cities (see Figure 2.3). The Japanese economy has remained weak, drifting in and out of decline in this two-decade-long deflationary depression.

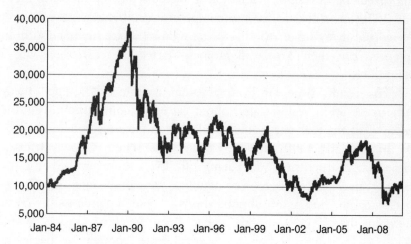

Figure 2.2 Nikkei 225 Index, 1984–2008
Data source: Yahoo! Finance.

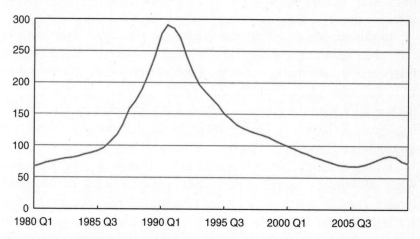

Figure 2.3 Japanese Urban Land Prices, 1980–2008 (1Q 2000 = 100)
Data source: Japan Real Estate Research Institute.

Great Call 5: The Dot-Com Blow-Off

In the late 1990s, the U.S. economy and stock market were really humming—the culmination of a long process that started in the early 1980s. Back then, inflation began to recede. This left American businesses, which had grown lax on cost control and productivity improvement during the inflation-distorted years of the late 1960s and 1970s, as naked to foreign competition as the proverbial jaybird. Autos and many other manufacturing industries faced extinction from imports. But then American business started to restructure with a vengeance.

The results were far from apparent in the 1980s when many Americans were really scared about Japanese competition. But the collapse of the real estate- and stock-driven Japanese economic bubble in the early 1990s alleviated those fears. Then it slowly became clear that restructuring was paying off. Even more noticed was the rise of new technologies—computers, semiconductors, the Internet, biotech, and telecommunications. These technologies weren't new in the 1990s—computers had been invented during World War II—but they had finally grown large enough to begin to drive the economy and unleash their tremendous productivity potential, both in the production of new-tech gear and among its users.

In this atmosphere, corporate earnings leaped in a self-reinforcing cycle. Restructuring and the rise of new tech reduced inflation, which had been very effectively transferring profits to the government and to labor in earlier years. Furthermore, the end of the Cold War and the decline in defense spending as well as other deflationary forces were beginning to blossom. The result was a mushrooming in corporate earnings (see Figure 2.4).

Rising earnings momentum began to convince investors that even faster growth was assured. This, combined with falling inflation and interest rates (as was seen in Figure 1.5), pushed price/earnings ratios through the roof. Also at work was the reality that stocks had been in a long bull market since 1982, with even the 1987 crash only a brief setback (as was seen in Figure 1.6 in Chapter 1).

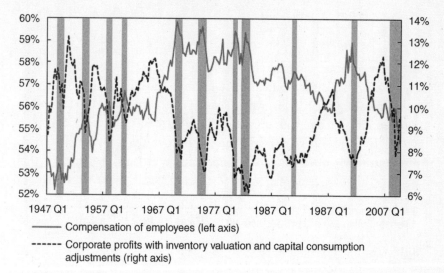

Figure 2.4 Corporate Profits and Employee Compensation, 1947–2007 (Percent of GDP)

Data source: Bureau of Economic Analysis.

Speculation Reigns

As stock market advances of 20 percent or greater were repeated year after year, investors began to count on them continuing indefinitely (Figure 1.6). So they relied more and more on stock appreciation in lieu of saving from current income to fund their kids' education, early retirement, and a few round-the-world trips in between. Consequently, the household saving rate plummeted (see Figure 2.5).

Another measure of the conviction that future rapid stock appreciation was a given was the consignment of dividends to the dumpster and the favoring of companies that paid none. Keep the money and invest it for more profits growth, was the directive from shareholders. Corporate managements cooperated and dividend yields fell to a mere 1 percent, far below the 3 percent level that previously was considered speculatively low (see Figure 2.6).

In the late 1990s, speculation had clearly gripped the nation since the stock market was directing the economy, not the reverse.

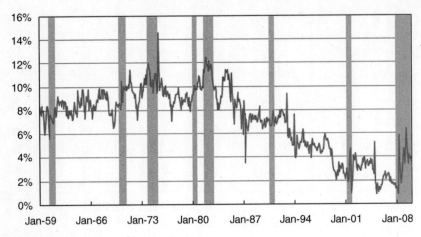

Figure 2.5 U.S. Personal Saving Rate, 1959–2009
Data source: Bureau of Economic Analysis.

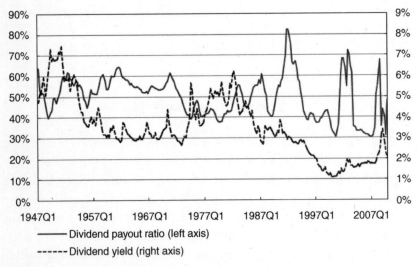

Figure 2.6 S&P 500 Dividend Yield and Payout Ratio
Data source: Standard and Poor's.

Normally, economic conditions—profits, interest rates, inflation, and so forth—determine stock prices. But in the late 1990s, surging stocks created appreciation that drove consumer spending and the economy. Speculation focused on new tech, and the NASDAQ Composite Index became its measure (seen in Figure 1.1 in Chapter 1).

Nothing Lasts Forever

The late 1990s stock appreciation and the economic boom it drove would have collapsed of its own weight eventually, but the Federal Reserve started to tighten credit in June 1999 (as was seen in Figure 1.3) and eventually inverted the yield curve, with the usual bear market and recessionary results.

Speculation was so great in the late 1990s, however, that initially little heed was paid to the Fed's rate-raising campaign. Fed Chairman Alan Greenspan made his famous "irrational exuberance" speech in December 1996, just as the dot-com bubble was beginning to expand, but the Fed did nothing as a follow-up. It didn't even raise margin requirements to send a warning shot across Wall Street's bow.

Indeed, NASDAQ surged in late 1999 and early 2000 to its March peak (shown in Figure 1.1). Internet stocks, the most speculative of the speculative, were still going public at hundreds of times sales with no earnings in sight, and then selling the first day at five times or more the offering price. Some didn't even have revenues, only a business plan, and at least one of these companies wouldn't disclose its plan because its management considered it so revolutionary. Cheerleading Wall Street analysts redefined stock valuations to measure prices in relation to sales, not earnings, to make the numbers look reasonable, as I'll expand on later.

How Wild It Was

The excesses of the late 1990s were legendary. Garage mechanics stopped rebuilding carburetors and put in stock quote machines so they could day-trade tech stocks full-time. Investors planned to accumulate enough stock profits to retire in their forties or even thirties. Teenagers managed mutual funds. Cash was trash. Bonds were only for wimps, and bond mutual funds were of little interest.

As we noted in our February 1999 *Insight* report, when Internet stocks were still skyrocketing and still a year away from their peak,

> Internet stocks are based on a real phenomenon but have reached the
> tulip bulb level of excesses. Most of these companies have no earnings

and little prospect of making money for years, but this hasn't stopped buyers from pushing EarthWeb's stock up 379 percent in three days when it was offered to the public on November 1998, or rushing into theglobe.com, up 606 percent in its first day of public trading. That put a market capitalization on the firm that was 347 times its $1.74 million in revenues. Compare that with five times the revenues for the average stock in the Russell 2000 index of small companies, and note that theglobe.com lost $5.8 million in the first half of 1998. MarketWatch.com wasn't far behind, with a 474 percent gain on its opening day. That put a $1.15 billion value on a company that lost $8 million in the first three quarters of 1998.

Those involved in developing and purchasing new tech thought they were the masters of the universe in the late 1990s, living in the New Economy. The belief that new tech was noncyclical persisted until the 2001 recession, which proved that new-tech companies couldn't exist simply by taking in each other's laundry but needed to sell ultimately to the Old Economy and to consumers. New techies believed that growth potential was so great that any start-up was assured success.

Twenty Follies

As would be expected, the stock market boom and soaring economy of the late 1990s spawned plenty of conspicuous consumption as egos and the yearning to be recognized rose with the leap in paper profits. Around-the-world trips by dot-commers with their kids who were too young to read became the measure of success. Huge charitable pledges and gifts of Internet stocks proved that they had instantly become big philanthropists. After the bubble broke, I assembled a list of 20 follies that the long bull market in stocks had taught investors, all of which had been feverishly believed during the final Internet bubble phase.

1. Stocks will leap indefinitely because corporate earnings will grow faster than the economy and P/E ratios will rise forever in the New Economy world.
2. With a continuous bull market, investors should buy and hold. Don't try to time the market since being out of stocks is the loser's game.

3. With a perennial bull market, dips are opportunities to buy, not warnings to get out of stocks.

4. Stock market data before August 1982, when the long bull market commenced, is irrelevant in the New Economy age.

5. Investment allocation is a precise science, so to maximize risk-adjusted returns, invest X percent in small-capitalization value stocks, Y percent in big-cap growth stocks, and so on.

6. Cash is trash because of lost investment opportunities.

7. Beating benchmarks is fund managers' only goal, with no concern over absolute returns.

8. Index investing always beats active stock management.

9. Sector index funds are wonderful ways to cash in on new tech.

10. Any individual investor can beat the pros.

11. Day-trading is the easy route to riches.

12. Investment fees are always too small to be relevant when compared to investment gains.

13. Pro-forma results are superior to GAAP numbers because they reveal true profits.

14. Stock buybacks are very beneficial to stock prices.

15. Stock options are wonderful since they align management interests with shareholders.

16. Dividends are to be avoided since they dissipate cash that corporations can better invest themselves, and are tax-inefficient.

17. Treasury bonds are for wimps who are too timid and too stupid to grasp the wonderful world of stocks.

18. Defined-benefit pension plan profits are a great and steady source of pretax corporate earnings.

19. Investing Social Security contributions in stocks will cure the postwar retirement problem.

20. In the age of the New Economy, this time it's different.

Our Forecast

My 1998 book, *Deflation: Why It's Coming, Whether It's Good or Bad, and How It Will Affect Your Investments, Business and Personal Affairs*, warned that stocks then were "overpriced in so many ways. Price/earnings ratios are in nosebleed altitudes, price-to-book values are at extremes." I also forecast that, contrary to popular conviction, the coming bear market would not appear in the form of a sudden, sharp decline that would provide a great buying opportunity—like the 1987 crash—but rather "will probably be a Chinese water torture, with sell-offs met with buying that spawns weak rallies, followed by more sell-offs, and so on—a long and frustrating saw-toothed pattern along a declining trend." And that's the way it unfolded (as was demonstrated in Figure 1.1), so this forecast of a collapse of the dot-com bubble, made two years before it started, was my fifth great call.

We continued to warn of this coming development in *Insight* throughout 1998, 1999, and 2000. Near the height of Internet stock mania, in our February 1999 *Insight*, we pointed out that "most of these companies have no earnings and little prospect of making money for years. . . ." We said that the "cycle of overenthusiasm and overexpansion, followed by disappointment and consolidation before the basis of long-lasting financial success is laid"—the pattern we foresaw for Internet stocks—was "the classic pattern for new technologies over the past 150 years."

Although the bull continued to romp on Wall Street throughout 1999, we warned our readers, at the beginning of the Fed's rate-raising campaign in June 1999, that further rate hikes were in store and reminded readers that once the Fed begins raising interest rates, "they will probably keep raising rates until something happens, and that something may well be a major bear market in U.S. stocks." We added that "the lofty level of stocks suggests that it may not take much in the way of rate increases to slaughter the bull."

In our *Insight* report, "Buy the Rumor, Sell the News?" for March 2000, right as NASDAQ was peaking, we explored previous new-tech spurts in the 1800s, in the 1920s, and in the 1960s–1970s and found that initial investor enthusiasm for canals and riverboats, then railroads, later for autos and radio, and more recently the Nifty Fifty tech stocks of the early 1970s, was always disappointing. New tech inevitably kills itself with overinvestment, excess capacity, excruciating competition, and commoditization of its products, and is superseded by even newer tech, we noted. Consumers win big from new tech, but investors have to be lucky to pick the few eventual winners. In previous tech bubbles like railroads in the late 1800s and autos in the 1920s, many companies were started, but few survived. We went on to forecast the same fate for the day's new tech, especially Internet stocks, and wrote, "We question whether the tremendous investment success in new-tech stocks in recent years will continue, even after a major bear market brings them back to earth."

Big Declines

In our January 2000 *Insight*, with the 17-year bull market still going strong, the Fed still hiking rates, and the Dow, NASDAQ, and S&P 500 all yet to hit their all-time highs, I said I was "convinced that a major bear market is in prospect with a 40 to 50 percent decline in the S&P 500 Index" due to continued extraordinarily high stock prices that "appear ridiculous and are crying for correction." In November 2000, once the sell-offs began, I said that "in contrast to the equity bulls, we see this stock weakness as the opening round of a major bear market that will slash 70 to 80 percent from the peak NASDAQ level, 40 to 50 percent from the S&P 500's top, and 30 to 40 percent from the Dow Jones Industrials." In fact, the 2000–2002 bear market slashed NASDAQ 78 percent, the S&P 500 by 49 percent, and the Dow by 38 percent, all amazingly close to my forecast.

In contrast, in March 2000 at the market peak, a Duke University survey of chief financial officers found that 82 percent of these knowledgeable insiders believed their stocks were underpriced, 15 percent felt they were fairly priced, and only 3 percent thought their equities were too expensive.

In both my 1999 book, *Deflation: How to Survive and Thrive in the Coming Wave of Deflation*, and in our November 1999 *Insight*, I warned investors, still blinded to reality by continuing stock appreciation, that a big market drop would mean prices would then have to appreciate much more in percentage terms if investors were to recoup their losses. A 20 percent decline in stock value—the common definition of a bear market—would require a 25 percent subsequent jump to get even again. A 50 percent decline would require a 100 percent increase to get back to even. Therefore, exiting the bull market before its top would benefit investors even if they missed the final jumps, and they would be much better off emotionally for not having suffered big losses, as I discuss in more detail in Chapter 10.

The Bubble Bursts

The bursting of the Internet bubble I forecast earlier was spectacular (see Figure 2.7). Despite the fact that many of those companies had no profits—or any expectation of any profits for years to come—investors earlier continued to buy as the speculative bubble expanded, sending all traditional measures of a company's value completely out of whack. In fact, I warned in the January 2000 *Insight* of the new—and faulty—method of estimating a stock's value, not by measuring earnings but by forecasting potential sales. I said then that I had "no lack of faith in the creative talents of corporate officials and their Wall Street fans to figure out new ways to make even more ridiculously high stock prices seem reasonable" and went on to warn that "these thoroughly convincing valuation measures may well look stupid if the stock prices they are designed to support crumble in the next bear market." As I predicted, by the second half of 2000, earnings again became of paramount importance as Internet stock prices returned to earth and the NASDAQ collapsed. And the highly paid Wall Street analysts who routinely said that

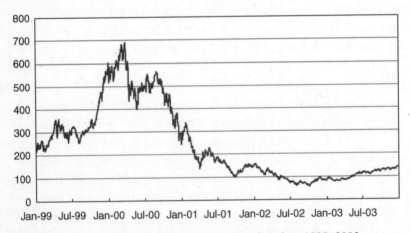

Figure 2.7 Amex Interactive Week Internet Stock Index, 1999–2003
Data source: Yahoo! Finance.

earnings don't matter were being tarred and feathered with monotonous regularity by the press and angry investors.

Furthermore, in our October 1999 *Insight*, long before the popular press picked up on the idea, we warned about, on the one hand, analysts who were rewarded by Wall Street for touting the stocks of companies that had investment banking relations with the analysts' firms while, on the other hand, negative analysts were often punished, excluded from meetings with company managements, or fired for their less-than-rosy outlooks. "Despite their claims of independence, loudly supported by their employers, many analysts today—and almost all of the well-paid ones—really work for corporate finance, bringing in deals, helping to sell them, and currying favor among investment banking and merger and acquisition clients." Later, this practice became well publicized and the SEC barred several analysts from the industry for life for recommending stocks of companies that were their firms' investment banking clients that they really believed were terrible investments, as I mentioned in Chapter 1.

The biggest first-trading-day gain for an initial public offering was the 698 percent leap for VA Linux Systems on December 9, 1999. The huge profits generated by this and other IPOs spawned illegal practices such as underwriters awarding hot IPOs to tech industry executives in return for investment banking business—*spinning*, as it was called. Another such practice was demanding that traders who received hot IPOs, in effect, repay 50 percent and then 65 percent of the resulting first-day profits in commissions they paid the underwriter on other trades.

I also noted that the SEC was aware of this phenomenon and had expressed concern over the guidance on earnings that many public companies were giving to select analysts, "often those who perennially support the companies' stocks." A year later, the SEC issued Regulation FD (for Full Disclosure), which requires public companies to make market-moving data public to all, simultaneously—not just to friendly analysts and big investors first before releasing it to everyone else.

Ad Down

In our April 2000 *Insight*, right at the dot-com bubble's peak, we were intrigued by the gobs of money being spent on advertising by Internet and other new-tech companies, and looked at ad space in detail in a batch of leading newspapers. The results were staggering: Internet ads composed almost one-third of total ad space in a week's worth of the *New York Times* and close to two-thirds of total ad space in five consecutive issues of the *Wall Street Journal*. Clearly, these ads were an important source of revenue, but we foresaw bad news for publishers when the Internet stock speculation collapsed. Back then we wrote, "The flow of money from venture capitalists and IPOs will dry up faster than rain on the Sahara, and the Internets will find it nearly impossible to raise new money." When business atrophies, we noted, "ad spending—especially on corporate image-building—is among the first to go."

A year later, after the bursting of the Internet bubble and the steep decline in the NASDAQ, we took another look at newspaper advertising and saw firsthand the result of the Internet collapse. Internet ads in the *Times* fell to less than 20 percent of total ad space, while those ads accounted for only 42 percent of total ad space in the *Journal*. Quite a comedown, especially for those newspapers' publishers and their stocks.

In our November 17, 2000, *U.S. Quarterly Economic Outlook*, before many were daring to utter the word *recession*, I tied many factors together to present my case for a full-blown recession. I noted the Fed's rate hikes of the previous 18 months; the inverted yield curve; the continuing vulnerability of stocks, which I still viewed as overpriced despite their declines to that point, making consumer real wealth and spending highly vulnerable; the negative effect of continuing high energy prices, and especially the California energy crisis, on consumers' purchasing power; the similarity between the U.S. economy in late 2000 and its structure at earlier business cycle peaks, including increased consumer caution, mounting inventories, and slumping manufacturing; and the prolonged resolution of the presidential election and the near 50-50 split in Congress that would weaken or delay any meaningful fiscal stimulus to revive the economy. The economy peaked shortly thereafter, in March 2001.

Beware the Pollyannas

Many observers believed the worst was over for stocks and the economy at the end of January 2001 after stocks rallied strongly and the

Fed cut interest rates twice. Investors began to tout a soft landing for the economy, with first-half weakness followed by a stronger second half. I didn't buy into this line of thinking and noted that "there are rallies in bear markets, but they end up being brief and temporary, upward blips on the way down." Sure enough, the gains from January's rally were soon consumed by sharp drops as the bear market continued.

I also doubted the advice in 1999 and 2000 of the sky *isn't* falling crowd, which told investors to diversify their portfolios—globally—in order to protect themselves and to take advantage of economic recoveries just picking up steam in Asia and Europe. In my two *Deflation* books as well as my May 31, 1999, *Forbes* column, I said that while global diversification is supposed to greatly reduce the volatility of a stock or bond portfolio, "it doesn't—at least not when you most want it to." I noted that in times of financial calm, markets tend to move independently. A portfolio split 50-50 between U.S. and Japanese stocks during the 1990s, I pointed out, "would have gone nowhere, as Japanese losses offset U.S. gains. The Japanese stocks would have calmed the portfolio, but at a terrible cost." In periods of high volatility, in contrast, U.S. and foreign stocks tend to march in lockstep, and "when Americans are losing money, they often sell first what they understand least: foreign holdings. So stock correlation is low when you want it to be high, and high when you want it to be low." The results speak for themselves: While the U.S. stock market experienced double-digit declines in the 2000–2002 bear market, stock markets in the United Kingdom, Canada, Germany, France, Spain, and Japan also fared poorly (see Figure 2.8).

One reason for global stock weakness is global economic softness. In our September 2000 *Insight*, I noted that earlier universal central bank tightening would soften economies worldwide. Furthermore, I observed, more foreign countries' growth is dependent on exports, which are directly or indirectly bought by U.S. consumers. So a U.S. recession with consumer retrenchment would spawn a global recession, the first since the early 1970s.

My run of good forecasting luck continued in foreseeing the shape of the recovery after the 2001 recession. In early 2002, after real GDP

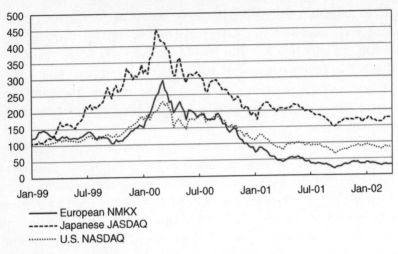

Figure 2.8 Tech–Heavy Stock Indexes (Jan. 1999 = 100)
Data source: Yahoo! Finance.

was reported to have risen in the fourth quarter of 2001, the optimists forecast a strong recovery. In our April 2002 *Insight*, I disagreed and said, "We foresee a sluggish recovery." It turned out to be so slow that even in late 2004, many Americans thought the recession was still running, even though it officially ended in November 2001, and voted against George W. Bush for a second term.

Chapter 3

The Housing Bubble (Great Call 6)

F oreseeing the housing bubble, its demise, and the massive implications was my sixth great call. I was lucky enough to see the
bubble developing in 2002 when we wrote of housing in our July
Insight, "Now it has taken on self-feeding bubble dimensions that will
sooner or later collapse." In the mid-2000s, on one of my regular CNBC
appearances, the producers so identified me with my housing collapse
forecast that they preceded my interview with the film clip of Dorothy's
house falling from the sky in *The Wizard of Oz*. They thought it was a
joke on me, but I was so convinced of my forecast that I saw it as my
leitmotif and insisted that they show the spinning, earthbound house
before every one of my subsequent appearances.

No Puke

The housing boom commenced in the mid-1990s (as was seen in Figure 1.2 in Chapter 1) and got tremendous support when speculation survived the 2000–2002 stock market collapse (as seen in Figure 1.6). Investors never threw in the towel, as is normal at market bottoms. They never reached the puke point at which they regurgitate their last equity and swear never to ingest another one. Speculation never died. It was sustained by the massive monetary and fiscal stimuli, especially after 9/11, which kept the 2001 recession short and mild. The brief federal government surplus in the late 1990s (see Figure 3.1) was the result of the stock bubble and the robust economy it spawned. Tax revenues from realized capital gains, exercised stock options, and leaping incomes were responsible, so the surplus faded with the onset of the bear market. Then followed the recession, massive tax rebates and cuts, and spending jumps for homeland security and the Afghanistan and Iraq wars. The resulting federal deficit measured the huge amount of money pumped into the economy.

Meanwhile, the Fed pushed the federal funds rate it controls down, ultimately to 1 percent (as we saw in Figure 1.3), and mortgage rates

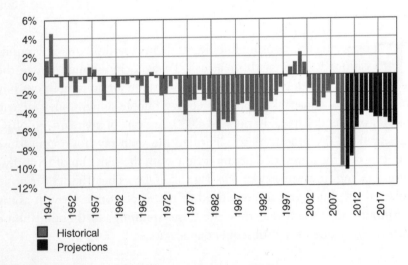

Figure 3.1 Federal Budget Balance—Percent of GDP
Data source: Congressional Budget Office.

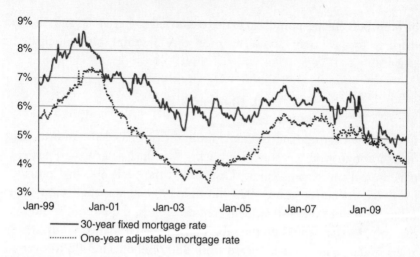

Figure 3.2 Fixed and Adjustable Mortgages Rates
Data source: Freddie Mac.

followed (see Figure 3.2). So housing starts, which normally fall 50 percent in a recession, only paused in the 2001 slump before rising (see Figure 3.3). At the same time, low mortgage rates encouraged cash-out mortgage refinancing and home equity loans that fueled consumer spending. And when the Fed did get around to raising its target rate, starting in June 2004, it did so in an orderly 17 steps

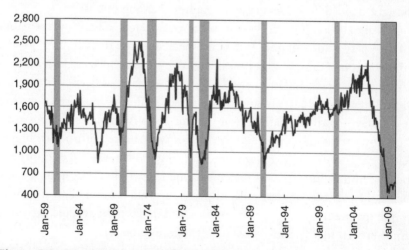

Figure 3.3 Housing Starts (Thousands of Units)
Data source: U.S. Census Bureau.

of 0.25 percentage points each that removed uncertainty and allowed markets to not only adjust to monetary restraint but anticipate it as well.

I Deserve It

Despite the bear market, the rampant bull that preceded it and the lack of a thorough washout convinced many that they deserved 20 percent-plus annual investment gains. That's what the S&P 500 had returned for five consecutive years, 1995 through 1999. It was their God-given right. So if stocks no longer delivered the goods, there must be alternative vehicles that would do the job. Many turned to hedge funds, whose assets under management leaped from $500 billion in 2002 to over $2 trillion in 2007. Numerous pension and endowment funds began to consider hedge funds as an asset class that should always contain a portion of their assets. In the same speculative vein, they viewed commodities as another asset class that would provide big returns. Other new so-called asset classes included foreign currencies and emerging market stocks and bonds. The carry trade also became popular among institutional investors. With low short-term interest rates in this country (as was seen in Figure 1.3) and even lower in Japan, hedge funds, banks, brokers, private money pools—you name it—borrowed massively and bought fixed-income securities in higher-yielding countries.

Not to be left out, individuals voraciously pursued their own versions of the carry trade—highly leveraged speculation in their houses. House prices normally rise and fall with overall consumer prices. In fact, correcting for overall inflation and the increasing size of houses over time, the median price of single-family houses had not increased for over a century—until the bubble (see Figure 3.4). As living standards rose, homeowners could afford bigger abodes with more bathrooms, bigger kitchens, and so on. Then with the housing bubble, the urge to buy the biggest houses they could finance became irresistible. That, plus soaring prices of existing houses, pushed prices up much faster than inflation. Similarly, median house prices rose more rapidly than average incomes, another sign that housing was in an expanding bubble.

Just like hedge funds, homeowners played the spread between their borrowing costs, say 6 percent on a mortgage, and appreciation of their

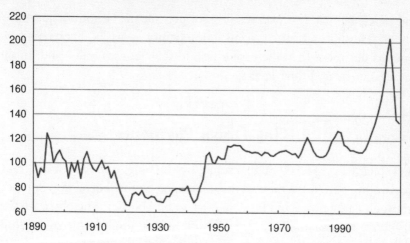

Figure 3.4 Real Quality-Adjusted Home Price Index, 1890–Present (1890=100)
Data source: Robert Shiller.

assets, perhaps 10 percent or more per year in the house's value. And that 400 basis point spread was leveraged 20-to-1 if the down payment for a new homeowner was 5 percent. Furthermore, existing homeowners increased their leverage. During the housing bubble, the percentage of their abodes that people own after subtracting all mortgage debt sank (see Figure 3.5). For anyone with a mortgage, it fell from almost

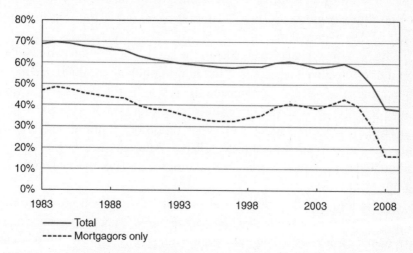

Figure 3.5 Homeowners' Equity as a Percent of Household Real Estate
Data sources: Federal Reserve, A. Gary Shilling & Co.

50 percent in the early 1980s to 16.4 percent in the fourth quarter of 2009. Through refinancing and home equity loans, homeowners have sucked out more than the earlier leap in their houses' value and, in the process, increased their leverage.

Tiny Down Payments

Leverage was especially high among low-income, minority, immigrant, and young families as they were encouraged by the federal government, through Fannie Mae and Freddie Mac, to buy houses. The objective was to create stable families and neighborhoods through home ownership. All well and good, but many programs allowed them to put down 3 percent or less and borrow the rest.

Those first-time buyers were very important to the housing bubble since they were 40 percent of all homebuyers, according to a National Association of Realtors survey at the time. Furthermore, the influence of first-time buyers extends far beyond the modest houses they usually purchase all the way to the top of the housing scaffold. When Ralph Kramden buys a starter home from Al Bundy, Al in turn can purchase Mike Brady's split-level. Then Mike can move his bunch into the McMansion of Reginald van Gleason III. In the bubble years, home ownership expanded universally, among races and all ages, even those over 65 (see Figure 3.6).

Besides the speculative climate in the late 1990s through early 2000s, a number of other fuels inflated the housing bubble. In 2000, Treasury bond investors correctly anticipated the easing by the Fed at the beginning of 2001, so long-term rates, including those on 30-year fixed-rate mortgages, fell (see Figure 3.2). That supported housing and helped prevent the normal recessionary collapse. After the Fed began easing, adjustable rates, which are tied to the short-term rates the Fed controls, dropped.

In addition, lenders fell all over each other to make housing affordable. Long gone are the days when they required 20 or 25 percent down payments on houses. Many mortgage lenders only stipulated 5 percent or less. The average for a first-time homebuyer was only 3 percent in 1999 compared with 10 percent a decade earlier. Some get down to zero

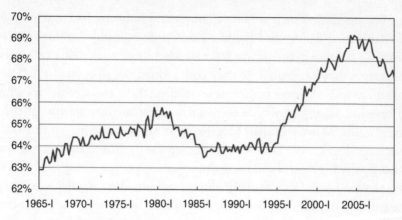

Figure 3.6 Homeownership Rate
Data source: U.S. Census Bureau.

by taking out an 80 percent first mortgage and a second mortgage to cover the remaining 20 percent. Others even pushed the amount lent to 125 percent of the house's value by loading a personal loan on top of the mortgages.

If a homebuyer put down 5 percent back in the boom days and the price of his house rose 10 percent per year, he made a cool 200 percent on his investment, neglecting mortgage interest, taxes, utilities, and maintenance—and he still got a place to live. But it works both ways, so a 5 percent decline in his house's price wipes him out.

Interest-Only Mortgages

Of course, low down payments mean higher monthly payments, but they were held down through interest-only mortgages with no principal repayments for as long as 15 years. Adjustable-rate mortgages (ARMs), with lower starting rates than fixed-rate mortgages (see Figure 3.2), also reduced servicing costs and became increasingly popular. Many ARMs had rates that were fixed for as little as six months and then adjusted up on a regular basis. But implicitly, both lenders and borrowers assumed that the value of the houses would increase so the mortgages could be refinanced before the monthly payments become onerous, perhaps with some cash-out that financed spending, to boot.

Private lenders such as New Century and IndyMac had much looser standards than Fannie and Freddie since, unlike Jimmy Stewart's Bailey Building & Loan in the movie *It's a Wonderful Life*, they didn't retain the mortgages they originated, so they could forget the risks involved. They sold them to Wall Street firms that securitized them and sold the tranches to investors, many of whom were unaware of the low quality of their investments. Many so-called liars' loans or no-documentation (no-doc) mortgage loans were originated with upwardly misstated income and assets by the borrowers and no documentation of true amounts. Lenders also reduced—in fact, virtually eliminated—lending standards to keep the game going after the pool of creditworthy borrowers was exhausted.

Brokers and lenders often hired only accommodative appraisers who gave unrealistically high appraisals to facilitate house sales and subprime mortgages. Many borrowers committed soft fraud in which they bought houses with no intention of ever making even one monthly payment but figuring they'd live rent-free until the sheriff evicted them, perhaps as much as a year later. In fact, more than half the subprime delinquencies and foreclosures in 2007 were not caused by ARM resets but by sloppy underwriting, soft fraud, and falling house prices that nailed speculators who had planned on quick flips.

Too Good to Believe

Securitization not only encouraged loose lending practices, but also greatly magnified the impact of subprime mortgages, which still accounted for only 8 percent of total outstanding residential mortgages at the end of the bubble in the mid-2000s. The explosion of subprime mortgages from 6 percent of acquisitions in 2003 to 20 percent in 2005 resulted from the confluence of powerful inducements. First and foremost was the leap in house prices (shown earlier in Figure 1.2), which convinced borrowers and lenders alike that the risks had disappeared because home appreciation would bail them both out of even the worst situation. Relatively low interest rates (see Figure 3.2) also spurred subprime mortgages.

Securitization was a huge inducement for lenders. The guts of the process are shown in Figure 3.7. Subprime mortgages, of course, aren't

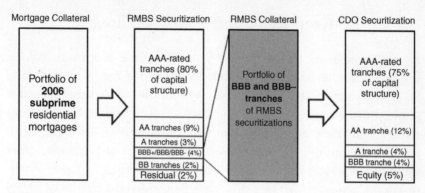

Figure 3.7 A Sow's Ear Becomes a Silk Purse: How Subprime Residential Mortgages Become AAA-Rated Securities

individually rated by rating agencies, but if they were, they'd no doubt be well below the minimum investment grade of triple-B-minus. Still, when they were packaged into residential mortgage-backed securities (RMBSs), 80 percent were often rated triple-A. Why? The rating agencies worked hand in glove with the issuers to structure the securitizations to maximize the amount in the highest-rated tranche, triple-A. That tranche was considered supersafe since it received the first of the monthly mortgage payments; then the double-A tranche was paid, and on down the line. Also, the rating agencies' models to determine the risk of defaults were based on periods in which house prices only rose—declines hadn't really occurred since the 1930s. So few problems were anticipated.

Then (returning to Figure 3.7), and here is where it gets wild, a number of the triple-B tranches of these RMBSs were combined to serve as collateral for a collateralized debt obligation (CDO). And since the combination of a number of triple-B tranches was assumed to reduce risk through diversification and because, again, the rating agencies' models showed almost no likelihood of significant defaults, 75 percent of that CDO was often rated triple-A. Although not shown in Figure 3.7, the magical transformation of garbage subprime loans into triple-A securities was sometimes magnified further as triple-B CDO tranches were combined into a synthetic CDO, or a CDO^2 with, again, a majority rated triple-A. Wow! This truly was the magical transformation of a sow's ear into a silk purse.

Keep the Good Times Rolling

Everyone involved in this process—the subprime mortgage brokers, the mortgage lenders, and the Wall Street securitizers—was well paid in commissions and fees and had every incentive to keep the game going. Furthermore, subprime borrowers were happy as house appreciation built their equity up from tiny or even zero down payments into enough money to finance even bigger houses or to finance other spending. And the ultimate investors were clamoring for those securities in the age-old belief that they were being served a free lunch. They trusted the ratings, so a triple-A tranche based on subprime mortgages that yielded considerably more than an ExxonMobil obligation was such a deal!

Lax regulation also fueled the housing bubble. No serious attempts were made to bring private and, ultimately, bankrupt private mortgage lenders such as IndyMac and New Century under regulatory control. Aggressive lenders such as Countrywide appear to have bought off meaningful oversight with attractive mortgages for many in Washington, and some earlier attempts in Washington to tighten regulation and otherwise curtail the buildup of leverage were frustrated.

In 2005, all the Republicans on the Senate Banking Committee, then chaired by Republican Richard Shelby, voted to prohibit Fannie, Freddie, and other government-sponsored enterprises from holding portfolios and instead make them stick to the less profitable but safer business of guaranteeing packages of mortgages sold to investors. The bill also gave their regulator authority to set capital requirements that then were so low that their assets exceed 50 times their regulatory capital. All committee Democrats opposed the bill and Democrats kept it from coming to a Senate vote.

Attempts to tighten mortgage lending requirements, even before their virtual disappearance, were consistently and effectively axed by housing industry lobbyists. The National Association of Realtors has one of the strongest lobbies in Washington. Fannie and Freddie themselves were major lobbyists on their own behalf and spent $170 million on lobbying in the past decade. Rep. Barney Frank, now chair of the House Financial Services Committee, said in 2003, "Fannie Mae and

Freddie Mac have played a very useful role in helping to make housing more affordable." Even Treasury Secretary Henry Paulson was unaware of the housing bubble, and in 2006 convinced President Bush to set aside his plans to curb Fannie and Freddie and to accept a deal with Rep. Frank that allowed them to keep expanding.

All that support easily drowned out the cries of those in Congress and the Fed who correctly believed that any failure of Fannie and Freddie would easily exceed the $150 billion taxpayer cost of the savings and loan (S&L) bailout of the late 1980s.

For 1996, the Department of Housing and Urban Development gave Fannie and Freddie a target of 42 percent of their mortgage financing for borrowers with income below the median in their regions. The target was hiked to 50 percent in 2000 and 52 percent in 2005. And, to avoid committing government-related money but still encourage housing for lower-income households, the Community Reinvestment Act, first passed in 1977 and beefed up in 1995, mushroomed the bank loans for lower-income families. Of course, everybody, including Fannie and Freddie and the banks, was happy as long as rising house prices kept defaults low and their loans profitable. And securitization allowed the banks to unload risky mortgages with triple-A ratings on others.

Another government subsidy for housing was the Taxpayer Relief Act of 1997, which hiked the demand for more expensive houses by increasing the capital gains exclusion from $125,000 to $500,000 and making it easier to exclude capital gains on rental property. Ironically, government efforts to make housing affordable were probably at best self-defeating. They created artificial demand, which bid up prices, fueling the housing bubble and leading to still more subsidies to offset higher prices.

A very important spur to the housing bubble was the conviction that house prices never decline, and any problems with buying in a bad neighborhood, at the wrong time of year, with too big a mortgage, or having too little income would ultimately be remedied by rising prices. And house prices hadn't fallen since the 1930s, at least nationwide (Figures 1.2 and 3.4), although they dropped in the oil patch in the late 1980s after petroleum prices collapsed, and in Southern California in the early 1990s after the end of the Cold War depressed the aerospace industry.

Bubble Burster

In our July 2002 report, we stated, "Like any speculation, the housing bubble will bust. The only questions are, when and how." We dismissed popular arguments by the optimists that housing was safe as long as interest rates remained low and employment stayed high. They apparently didn't realize that high employment, especially in housing boom states like California, Arizona, Nevada, and Florida, was due to exuberant residential construction that accounted for most of the job growth. In any event, the irrational bubble was too advanced to wait for those rational forces. We noted that "past housing bubbles, such as in Texas in the 1970s oil boom and California in the 1980s, generated huge overbuilding that aided and abetted their collapse. If the bubble persists, overbuilding will develop as surely as the night follows the day," we stated in 2002.

We went on to say that "the housing bubble can also simply collapse of its own weight when prices and expectations outrun even the wildest of dreams." We concluded that "our candidate" as the housing bubble pricker "is financial problems for new and recent buyers, especially those with low incomes and few assets." Our July 2002 *Insight* also said it would take time for a bursting housing bubble to be fully realized and accepted:

> One reason that it takes time for residential prices to react is because the market prices of peoples' houses are not available daily. There is no price quote flashing by on the TV screen or in the newspaper to force homeowners to realize that their homes have declined in value. So, they can put their heads in the sand, arguing that any price weakness, even if they are trying to sell their houses, is short-lived. The neighborhood is temporarily out of favor, one will argue. Or, I have a lousy real estate broker but I'll get a good one. Or, it's the wrong season of the year, but spring and stronger prices are coming. In the inflationary postwar era, with the trend in rising real estate prices, this strategy worked. When homeowners pulled their heads out of the sand, prices had recovered.

Housing starts peaked in January 2006 (Figure 3.3) and prices in the first quarter of that year (Figure 1.2), but few realized there was a major problem until subprime mortgages collapsed in early 2007 and the subprime slime, as we dubbed it, spread to Wall Street in midyear. Until then, most thought that subprime mortgages were inconsequential, totally separate from the rest of housing and, indeed, the economy. Subprime borrowers were people whom, luckily, they'd never have to meet.

Hammering Away

Nevertheless, I kept hammering away on the subprime-led housing collapse and its spreading effects. In my October 14, 2002, *Forbes* magazine column, "Home Sick," I wrote, "The housing boom is soon to go bust. And the way it will come to an end will affect everyone, even affluent homeowners." I noted that "most people don't see housing as overblown, just benefiting from strong demand. They don't see weakness because huge overbuilding is absent." I went on to cite classic signs of a bubble: investors believing there was no place else to go; leaping home ownership for those under 25; a self-feeding price spiral with increasing leverage; low interest rates; and loose lending standards.

My *Forbes* column went on to predict that "the implosion will start among first-time homebuyers with few other assets. They support the housing market through the move-up chain. People like me living in tony Short Hills, New Jersey, really do need to think about home sales in gritty Newark." I went on:

> As housing demand dries up, prices will fall. Those with big leverage will see their equity wiped out, forcing them to sell, pushing prices still lower. Lenders will withdraw and will no longer be as loose with lending as they are today. A question is whether Fannie's and Freddie's losses will force a bailout.

Between mid-2002 and mid-2007, we pounded out over 17 *Insight* reports and numerous articles for other publications on the impending housing collapse. In our December 2002 report, we wrote:

> We continue to see great vulnerability in housing, starting at the bottom end. Lower-income mortgage borrowers, many of whom are

subprime, have exploded in recent years and account for up to half of new mortgages. Around 3.5 percent of homeowners pay over half their pretax income on mortgage debt service. Lower-income families have few financial assets to fall back on and tiny if not negative net worth.

In our January 2004 *Insight*, we wrote:

The recent run-up in house prices makes them extremely vulnerable. Interestingly, the recent leap in house prices and, hence, their vulnerability is found throughout the industrialized world. Since the mid-1990s, prices in Australia, the United Kingdom, Ireland, the Netherlands, Spain, and Sweden have jumped by 50 percent or more in real terms compared to 30 percent in the United States. All have risen much faster than rents, indicating that they're selling for a lot more than their intrinsic worth.

Return to Earth

When house prices return to earth—and price declines of 20 percent in the United States and 30 percent elsewhere are warranted—the effects on the global economy will be serious. An International Monetary Fund study found that in advanced lands, the negative effects of house price declines are twice as great per percent decline in price as stock market crashes. This is because more people own their homes than own equities, they borrow more heavily on houses than stocks, and that greater leverage is more likely to drag down mortgage financiers than is the case with stock margin lenders. Falling house prices will make life very difficult for consumers overloaded with debt. As prices fall, many will see their home equity wiped out.

The 1990s stock bubble and economic boom removed risk concerns from consumer lenders' considerations. So, after saturating creditworthy borrowers, they aggressively pursued subprime borrowers. Of course, those folks, many of whom were in the subprime category because they didn't understand that loans are supposed to be repaid, were only too glad to take the money. In our view, subprime loans are probably the greatest financial problem facing the nation in the years ahead.

In our April 2004 *Insight*, we added:

We see trouble for housing from overly generous lending terms. To keep the bubble expanding, Washington is moving down payments for low-income buyers from 3 percent to zero. Private lenders are pushing interest-only loans and loans that exceed house values. The bubble is insidiously self-feeding as more liberal financing terms spur higher prices that require even more liberal terms to keep first-time homebuyers viable. Look for the bubble's ultimate collapse to slash house prices and destroy much homeowner wealth.

In our June 2004 edition, we said:

Housing is the most vulnerable segment of the economy. House prices have soared way beyond their normal close link to CPI increases. At the same time, Americans have leveraged their houses to the stratosphere.

We noted in our June 2005 report:

Earlier, many observers did not believe that a speculative bubble in housing and its nationwide collapse were possible for two reasons. It costs so much money to move, including real estate commissions, moving costs, redecorations, closing costs, and so on, that speculation would be discouraged. In addition, it's hard to speculate in your abode because if you sell it, where will you live?

But not to worry. Human ingenuity has addressed and largely eliminated those two constraints. Internet brokers, aided by the Antitrust Division of the Justice Department, are whittling away at the cartel-rigged 5 to 6 percent real estate broker commissions, which are ridiculously lucrative at today's high sales prices for houses. And online mortgage brokers have slashed closing and related costs while speeding up financing approvals.

Meanwhile, purchase of multiple houses or condos as investments is leaping. Last year, a quarter of house sales were investments, and 13 percent as vacation homes. Those percentages must be much bigger now. The proliferation of vacation homes and non-owner-occupied houses has caused the normal relationship between housing activity and household formation to deviate in disturbing ways. It makes it easy for speculators to sell one of their houses without vacating their domicile.

That June 2005 *Insight* also said:

The most troubling aspect of the housing bubble is the leverage involved. Household real estate increased by $5.5 trillion in the last five years, about 50 percent appreciation. But people have been sucking out much of that appreciation with mortgage refinancing and, more recently, home equity loans. So, the remaining equity of homeowners remains near record lows.

Leveraging Up

A recent survey found that 2.2 million households in 2004 used home equity to buy additional real estate, up from 1 million in 1994. Many plan to rent their non-occupied houses while they wait for appreciation. But the rush out of rental apartments into single-family houses, aided by these new landlords, has depressed rents and pushed up vacancy rates, creating negative carrying costs for many. So, the individual version of the carry trade—borrow cheap short-term money and invest it in rapidly appreciating houses—is becoming less attractive.

Furthermore, in our June 2005 report, we discussed the effects of the impending housing price collapse on the rest of the economy.

A big crack in housing prices would damage the largest asset of most households and wipe out the home equity of many. And after the earlier stock collapse, it would constitute a one-two punch. The resulting drying up of housing activity would be important to the economy since this sector has accounted for 43 percent of the rise in private sector payrolls since late 2001, by one estimate.

Furthermore, after a housing collapse, a major consumer saving spree would follow as Americans realized that neither stocks nor real estate would provide for their kids' education, contingencies, and retirement. Slower U.S. economic growth would result, with even slower growth abroad since most foreign countries depend directly or indirectly on U.S. consumers to buy their excess goods and services.

Signs of a Peak

Our July 2005 *Insight* was written as the housing peak in early 2006 loomed, and our report that month was titled, "The Housing Bubble May Break Soon." It stated,

> Signs of a peak in housing are significant and growing. The *Time* magazine June 13, 2005, cover story, "Home $weet Home," is a superb indicator that the housing play is about over. By the time the editors of *Time* realize that a fad or the popularity of an individual is important enough to warrant a cover story, the end is nigh. And the picture on the June 13 cover says it all. A man is fondly clutching a cartoon house with more love in his eyes than he probably ever showed for his wife or girlfriend.
>
> Furthermore, as with any bubble, shortly before its demise it is so attractive that nonprofessionals rush in. Recently, Deere is involved in creating a "John Deere Signature Community" in Durham, N.C., where the only links to its products will be garages full of its lawn tractors and other yard maintenance equipment. Orvis is teaming up with Cushman & Wakefield, both brand new to the residential arena, to sell ranch and recreational properties.
>
> The residential real estate business, of course, retains its perennial optimism. Folks there talk about solid demand that will continue for years due to the aging population and resulting demand for abodes and vacation homes. Then there are foreign investors buying houses that look cheap compared to those in London or Tokyo, and housing demand from immigrants. As David Lereah, chief economist of the National Association of Realtors, puts it, "It's the demographics, stupid."
>
> He and his fellow bulls also point to supply shortages, and especially in places like New York City and San Francisco where limited land and tight zoning regulations curtail building. "We simply don't have enough houses on the market to meet demand," Lereah said recently and pointed to low inventories at current sales rates. And to top it off, he said in his February 2005 book, *Are You Missing the Real Estate Boom?*, subtitled *Why Home Values and Other Real Estate Investments Will Climb Through the End of the Decade—and How to Profit From Them*, that "most households are underinvested in real estate. While there can always be a local price bubble, with today's economy, homeowners are in no danger of experiencing a widespread fallout of home prices."

In August 2005, Lereah said, "All of the doom-and-gloom fore-casts of a housing debacle are not only irresponsible, but are downright wrong." Well, flat unequivocal statements can also prove to be wrong—and embarrassing. In late 2005, he said the housing market is "likely to pick up a bit" and is experiencing a "soft landing." In October 2006, he stated, "The worst is behind us, as far as a market correction—this is likely the trough for sales." Even as the housing collapse was gaining steam in January 2007, he stuck to his conviction and said, "It appears we have established a bottom." Not surprisingly, Lereah made *Time* magazine's February 12, 2009, Rogues Gallery of those most responsible for the housing collapse and financial crisis.

Lereah Was Not Alone

Lereah was far from alone in denying even the existence of a housing bubble, much less its demise. Here's a sampling of expert comments. Jim Jubak, senior markets editor for the MSN Money web site, said in June 2005, "For all the teeth gnashing and pundit-moralizing, we really don't have a housing bubble that's anywhere near bursting." Neil Barsky of Alson Capital Partners wrote in the *Wall Street Journal* the following month, "The reality is this: There is no housing bubble in this economy." Jan Hatzius, chief U.S. economist with Goldman Sachs, said in October 2006, "The point of maximum deterioration in housing activity has probably passed."

David Seiders, chief economist for the National Association of Home Builders, said in December 2006, "The downswing in sales hit bottom recently, . . . and we are now expecting sales to show some improvement by the first quarter of 2007." And in February 2007, the Mortgage Bankers Association of America said the housing market "will regain its footing by mid- to late 2007."

In November 2006, when house prices were only down about 5 percent from their peak, I had a debate over the housing outlook with Jim Paulsen, chief economist of Wells Capital Management. It was hosted by my good friend Kate Welling and published in the November 17, 2006, edition of her newsletter, *Welling@Weeden*. I made my usual case for the collapse in housing, with a 25 percent decline in prices—far larger than the 5 to 10 percent decline forecast by other housing bears—with very negative effects on consumer spending and a severe recession. In contrast, Jim was in the soft-landing camp, and saw no serious problem for housing unless interest rates leaped. He said,

> I personally think that the vast majority of homeowners out there are still so darn far ahead that it's just not funny. It's wonderful to have this mid-cycle correction in housing, because it's much better to do part of it now and part of it later, after we do raise rates again, than it would be to have mortgage rates or 10-year Treasurys go up to 6.5 to 7 percent now and to have that prick the bubble. In a sense, we've pricked it without killing it off with an increase in long-term rates—which might be what we do in another year or two. So we may look back at this period and say, "Maybe it was good we let some gas out of that thing." In the meantime, housing may continue to liquidate all the way through from here to there, just at a very slow pace, until we really jack up rates again and destroy job creation.

The Fed had stopped raising rates the previous June 29, over four months before our November interview, and would begin cutting them on September 18, 2007 (as we saw in Figure 1.3). Yet, contrary to Jim's forecast, housing still collapsed.

Inventory Problem

In that July 2005 report, almost two years before excess house inventories murdered prices, we went on to say:

> Extreme speculation and excessive investment may finally sink the housing ship. During speculations, the participants see nothing but shortages and insufficient inventories.
>
> Housing today is no exception. Publicly owned home builders assure stockholders that they build only to firm orders, with virtually no inventories. Note, however, that home builder Toll Brothers' CEO recently bragged about the firm's high level of nonbinding deposits—essentially reservations for new houses that prospective buyers can cancel and reclaim their money.

Speculators assure themselves and all who will listen that they are long-term real estate investors, but many of those houses are rented at less than profitable returns, and only make economic sense if prices continue to rise rapidly. An NAR economist said that "house price appreciation over the last three years has been nearly 20 percent nationwide in each of the years, and that implies there is a housing shortage." Well, sure, a shortage relative to insatiable and self-feeding speculative demand.

But in past bubbles, even the starry-eyed speculators finally realized that huge excesses had been built, and shortages became surpluses overnight as they dumped their holdings on the market, depressing prices in a self-feeding cycle. In addition, when buyers disappear, the supply chain can never be shut off fast enough to avoid huge inventories. And remember that inventory problems are never fully understood by buyers and sellers until they're huge.

What's different about housing? And even if major builders have avoided excess inventories, how about all those small builders with their pickups who each build only a few houses a year but constitute the bulk of that fragmented industry? Has human nature so changed that they're resisting the urge to build extra houses amidst the multiyear surge in prices? Inventories of new homes for sale have yet to move up to alarming rates, or existing homes either. But what will happen when housing buying dries up while supply increases continue to roll and inventories come out of the woodwork? Many of the houses bought in recent years as investments and now rented at unprofitable rates will be dumped on the market. Look for mounting inventories to precipitate a downward price spiral.

Answers for the Optimists

In the mid-2000s, the optimists were always looking for reasons why there would not be a substantial fall in U.S. house prices, so we were continually challenged to reply to their rationales, one by one. We answered the argument that housing excesses were only bicoastal in our July 2005 report:

The housing bubble is not local, but national—not surprising since it's driven by economy-wide forces: investor zeal for high returns but skepticism over stocks, ample cheap mortgage money, and lax lending standards. Indeed, these forces and the housing boom are global. Earlier

U.S. housing booms/busts were driven by local business cycles such as the rise and fall of the oil patch along with oil prices in the 1970s and 1980s. Since houses are much more widely owned than stocks, the bubble's likely demise will shake the economy more than the early 2000s bear market. It could change the good deflation of excess supply we foresee to the bad deflation of deficient demand. The most likely bubble-pricking pin is massive speculation itself, and as prospective buyers stand aside, mounting inventories will precipitate a downward price spiral.

Our June 2006 report reinforced our forecasts by saying,

The speculative housing bubble is beginning to crash from its own excesses, similar to stocks in the early 2000s. The bubble's break will cause widespread pain—and be much worse economically than the 2000–2002 bear market and will guarantee a serious recession that will spread globally.

That report added,

Many speculative markets such as commodities and emerging market equities saw substantial declines recently. We see that as not just a midcourse correction in continuing rallies but the beginning of big declines that anticipate global economic weakness. Weakening U.S. house prices will probably sink consumer spending and the American and world economies before long. Our rough count of the increased value in the last five years of stocks in major countries, emerging market debt and equities, commodities, merger premiums, real estate, and derivatives totals $20 trillion, or 153 percent of U.S. GDP. The demise of speculation could wipe out a big fraction, especially due to deteriorating investment quality and the high correlations among speculative markets in recent years.

Why Buy a House?

In "House Party Horrors," our September 2006 report, we wrote:

The nationwide housing bubble, the first in the post–World War II era, has been propelled by low mortgage rates, loose lending practices, aversion to stocks after the 2000–2002 bloodbath, and conviction that house prices always rise robustly.

Without ever-rising prices, we went on:

who in their right mind would buy an asset that

... is not subject to standardized quantifications and therefore uniform valuation

... has not in recent years returned enough in rent to cover taxes, maintenance, interest and other costs, in most cases

... suffers with aging

... is highly illiquid

... is highly leveraged financially

... and is financed with mortgage loans [that] depend heavily on lender sentiment.

We also said that house prices were

about 25 percent above the norms and made them vulnerable to declines at least that big [that] will do severe economic damage. The average American owns much more house than stocks. Thinly capitalized speculators, subprime borrowers, the low ends of subprime debt, and many lenders, mortgage bankers, and home builders will be wiped out as falling prices and sales and leaping inventories feed on each other. But the major damage will come from the retrenchment of the many consumers who have relied on their house appreciation to bridge the gap between their meager income gains and robust spending growth.

Our November 2006 report, "What Will Collapse Housing Prices?" continued to drill into this theme as we wrote:

The housing bubble is deflating as sales slide and prices begin to drop. For the first time since the 1920s, the bubble is nationwide and we continue to forecast a 25 percent fall in median single-family house prices. The big price plummet may start soon as many speculators give up on appreciation dreams and throw their properties on the market, triggering a downward spiral.

Arrive Too Late

Cheaper energy will not offset losses in house appreciation nor will nonresidential construction growth. The Fed is unlikely to slash interest rates soon enough and big enough to save the day. Washington will be politically forced to bail out hapless homeowners, but as with the S&L crisis, will probably arrive too late to prevent major damage.

Furthermore, our January 2007 *Insight* stated that

> ... housing bulls believe that since prices haven't fallen as sales have plummeted and inventories leaped, they won't. But the bulls are missing the reality. It takes time for house price weakness to sink in because the market prices of people's houses are not available daily.

We also wrote that the housing bubble "appears big enough and the speculative overhang so large that sellers won't be able to wait out the weakness, and a major price drop is likely. Trouble in subprime mortgage land may well spread to many other areas whose inherent riskiness is suddenly unmasked," such as commercial real estate, real estate mutual funds, junk bonds, and private equity.

By early 2007, our forecasts were gaining enough credibility that a number of clients were asking us what we looked at in assessing the outlook. So in our February 2007 report, "What We Watch," we said:

> At present, we're focused on inventories in many areas as the end of the economic expansion approaches. Also housing, especially subprime mortgages, the key to the U.S. and global outlook. If housing collapses, so will many other financial speculations. So we follow stock speculation, buybacks, private equity, aggressive life-cycle funds, China, risky new asset classes, commodities, junk bonds and leveraged loans, executive pay practices, and evidence that speculative peaks are near because everyone who can be sucked in has been.

We also wrote that investors and hedge funds who bought collateralized debt obligations "will be shocked! shocked! over their losses."

Factory-Built Housing

In 1995, I joined the board of Palm Harbor Homes at the invitation of its CEO, Lee Posey, an old friend and economic consulting client. The company, which had just gone public, produces factory-built homes that used to have the trailer park image. Then several things happened. In 1974, the National Manufactured Home Construction and Safety Standards Act was passed in Washington. Administered by the Department of Housing and Urban Development, it standardized and greatly improved the quality of manufactured housing to the point that today, many units match or exceed the quality of site-built housing. Furthermore, since they are built in factories where weather is not a factor, assembly-line production reigns, and high productivity is the rule, manufactured homes per square foot cost about half as much as site-built housing, excluding land expense, for fill-in houses in established communities. That's not true in large developments where builders essentially set up factories on-site.

Furthermore, zoning law changes in many parts of the country now accommodate manufactured homes. And the trend has been toward multiwidth units that are manufactured in widths to accommodate shipping on highways by truck, but then fastened together on-site. When completed, they are almost indistinguishable from site-built houses. Some producers, like Palm Harbor Homes, concentrate to a high degree on multiwidths and furnish them with amenities like fireplaces and brand-name appliances. These tend to sell to people with higher and more stable incomes and assets than is the case with single widths—"house trailers."

Initially, manufactured houses were predominantly placed on leased land and financed by relatively short-term loans. Chattel loans still dominate, but over the years, buyers are increasingly putting their houses on their owned lots and financing the house and land with traditional long-term mortgages that have considerably lower interest rates. But even multiwidth manufactured houses don't compare in size with the recent wave of site-built McMansions with their indoor pools and running tracks.

Cyclical

Nevertheless, factory-built housing is highly cyclical and tied to employment growth, even more so than are single-family home sales. This difference isn't surprising since manufactured housing is still sold to a lower-income buyer on average than is a site-built home and, hence, is more sensitive to employment conditions.

Furthermore, the industry in the late 1990s suffered from the effects of earlier excessive easy credit. In the mid-1990s, eager lenders were attracted by the six percentage point or so difference between interest rates on chattel loans and mortgages, apparently not fully aware that those spreads reflected the differences in creditworthiness of borrowers. Lenders also dropped the required down payments from 10 percent to 3 percent and stretched repayments to 30 years from the traditional 20 years. On top of that, some manufacturers' rebates virtually eliminated those small down payments. Minimum credit scores for borrowers were lowered considerably.

Manufactured housing became the first housing-related sector to have its loans securitized, including a surge in so-called triple-A manufactured housing asset-backed securities (ABSs). This further promoted ample money, very loose lending standards, and poor assessments of risks by both credit rating agencies and buyers of securities backed by factory-built home loans.

Obviously, many less-than-creditworthy people bought manufactured houses, many of whom couldn't afford chicken coops much less houses of any description. At the same time, lenders rushed to finance dealers and their inventory, encouraging entry into what's always been an easy-entry, easy-exit business by many thinly capitalized independent dealers.

The results were predictable. Manufactured home shipments soared to exceed one-third the level of single-family home sales in the mid-1990s. The market became saturated, but shipments continued to rise. Then lenders retrenched. Inventories leaped and turnover plunged as many new homes shipped simply went to new dealer lots and not to final buyers. The number of independent dealers' sales sites plummeted about one-third from their peak, and repossessions also jumped since manufacturers normally agree to repurchase stranded units, which compete with and often undercut the prices of newly made units. With all of this excess inventory and independent dealers disappearing in great numbers, shipments collapsed and continued to decline to 49,800 in 2009, the lowest since the data started in 1959 (see Figure 3.8). Obviously, the triple-A manufactured housing ABSs were wiped out.

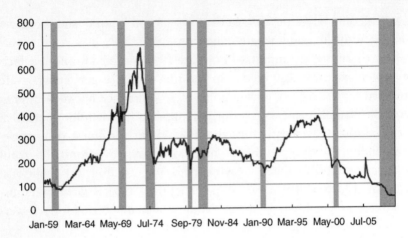

Figure 3.8 Manufactured Housing Shipments, 1959–Present (thousands of units)
Data source: U.S. Census Bureau.

Slow Learners

You might have thought that the harsh lessons taught by the manufactured housing industry in the late 1990s would have prevented a repeat in the 2000s by conventional housing, but they didn't. Those woes, however, made an indelible impression on me from my ringside seat as a Palm Harbor Homes director. So when I saw the same loose lending to subprime borrowers and same exuberant response in site-built housing a few years later, I jumped immediately to the last act of the tragedy. This was, as I explained in Chapter 1, a clear-cut example of history being relevant because lenders, builders, and homebuyers reacted to similar circumstances in similar—almost identical—ways. The factory-built housing analogy also stayed with me because that industry suffered two more whammies in the ensuing decade.

As mortgage underwriting standards for conventional housing virtually disappeared, homebuyers of very questionable credit quality could qualify. So people who could barely afford any house bought four-bedroom site-built houses instead of factory-built ones that have a lower image and higher financing costs on chattel loans. Then came whammy number 3. The collapse in conventional house prices (shown in Figure 1.2 in Chapter 1) might work to the advantage of factory-built units.

Homebuyers have turned tail on highly leveraged McMansions and now cotton to smaller, more cost-efficient abodes as they separate the places they live in from their investments. The median square footage of a single-family house dropped from 2,300 in early 2007 to 2,150 in late 2009. But the drying up of credit also has hurt the producers of manufactured houses—ditto for their customers, also stung by wage cuts, high unemployment, and uncertain job prospects. Still, even though manufactured home shipments have sunk to the lowest levels on record, as I'll explore in Chapter 11, this industry may have a very bright future.

Other Voices

You've read a lot of quotes from the 2002–2007 years of our forecasts of the mounting housing bubble and its eventual demise, and a few from those who disagreed with us every inch of the way. The home builders, of course, were extremely optimistic—at least until the roof caved in—and none more so than Robert Toll, CEO of Toll Brothers, who was always good for a quip. But notice how sobriety crept in as the years rolled by. In August 2005, he said, "We've got the supply and the market has got the demand; so it's a match made in heaven. . . . Why can't real estate just have a boom like every other industry? Why do we have to have a bubble and then a pop?" Two months later, he said housing market fundamentals looked strong through 2010. "That's pretty good moving and grooving," he said.

By early 2006, though, Toll's mood had shifted ever so slightly. He told *Barron's* in a February 2006 interview, "We don't see any doomsday scenario. Some of our markets are doing well, but none are as outstanding as during the summer of 2005. There's definitely an overhang of supply in certain markets." By April 2006, he was looking for a soft landing in housing, and in June, Toll said, "The housing market is experiencing an oversupply, to put it mildly."

Later that summer, Toll said, "It is difficult to characterize the position of home builders as other than a hard landing." He added that "it is the first downturn in the 40 years since we entered the business that was not precipitated by high interest rates, a weak economy, job losses, or other macroeconomic factors. Instead, it seems to be the result of an oversupply of inventory and a decline of confidence. Speculative buyers who spurred demand in 2004 and 2005 are now sellers; builders who built speculative homes must now move their specs; and nervous buyers are canceling contracts for homes already under construction."

The Shadow Knows

A year later, in September 2006, Toll said the U.S. housing market got ahead of itself due to greed on the part of buyers and sellers, and that it faced the highest level of speculative inventory ever. "Every day there's an article about how lousy housing is now and how dumb you have to be to buy a house now." In November 2006, he said, "Nobody wants to buy something that will cost less two weeks or two months from now." A month later, he said the housing market was experiencing something "harder than a soft landing."

Two months after that, in February 2007, Toll said, "It's amazing how many people get sick when prices fall" (so they can renege on house purchase contracts). A month later, saying that the spring selling season had been "pretty much a bust," Toll asked, "When will the market rebound? Who knows? The Shadow knows. I have no idea. I would've thought that it would've rebounded by now and I would've been dead wrong, and I was."

Toll wasn't alone among the rough-and-ready CEOs of home builders, virtually all of whom were very depressed in early 2007 as they surveyed the prospects for the year. Stuart Miller, CEO of Lennar, said, "The typical stronger spring selling season has not yet materialized." Jeffrey Mezger, KB Home's CEO, noted, "We're not ready to say that the markets have stabilized" and that prices had completed their decline. And Robert Toll's February 2007 remark that only "the Shadow knows" when the market will rebound was beaten by D.R. Horton CEO Donald J. Tomnitz, who famously said, "I don't want to be too sophisticated here, but '07 is going to suck, all 12 months of the calendar year." As close second runners-up, there's Ryland Group Chairman and CEO R. Chad Dreier's remark to an investor conference in June 2007, that "we do think if you're dumb enough to buy a home builder (share), you ought to buy us."

Reluctant Regulators

Regulators weren't exactly on top of this housing bubble, which expanded with little interference from them. As noted earlier, all the participants, aided and abetted by many in Congress, were enjoying the party and vigorously resisting interference by regulators with ongoing loose lending practices. Also, they had a tough job since regulation of housing and its financing is widely dispersed among sometimes conflicting bodies at the state and federal level. At the same time, subprime mortgages moved from traditional lenders to firms outside federal jurisdiction to often-limited state regulation. In 2005, 52 percent of subprime mortgages were originated by companies that lay beyond federal regulation, principally mortgage brokers and individual mortgage lenders.

The Office of the Comptroller of the Currency (OCC) regulates nationally chartered banks; the Office of Thrift Supervision (OTS) is in charge of S&Ls; the Fed regulates bank-holding companies and, with the FDIC and state regulators, state-charted banks. Furthermore, regulators have traditionally concentrated on the solvency of their charges, not the suitability of the loans they make. And securitization removed the traditional link between the lender and the borrower as lenders lost almost all contact with those taking out the mortgages and bore little residual default risk.

States stepped into the breach and a number, including Ohio, Pennsylvania, North Carolina, and Georgia, had various rules to prevent mortgage lenders from putting borrowers into loans they could not afford to repay. But banks regulated by the OTS and OCC didn't have to comply with state regulations.

Regardless, federal regulators were slow to realize the mushrooming subprime problem. FDIC Chairman Sheila Bair was probably more aware of the growing problems than any. Her ringing of a few alarm bells apparently led to attempts to run her out of Washington as a party pooper—until the housing bubble burst and she became Queen of the May. But even she said in retrospect that "early on, regulators didn't see extensive consumer complaints and credit distress" and that rising house prices covered up some of the problems.

Finally, in early 2007, the four federal regulators issued their "Interagency Guidelines for Non-traditional Mortgage Product Risks." Wonderful timing! In the years 2002–2007, while the regulators were unable to overcome lender resistance to at least keep lending standards from deteriorating, subprime loans lacking full documentation went from 30 percent to 50 percent of the total. Loan-to-value leaped from 85 percent to 94 percent. And, of course, more stringent regulation after housing started to collapse only encouraged lenders to tighten standards further and add to foreclosures.

The Rating Agencies

Why were the ultimate buyers of all the subprime mortgages and other trash willing to do so? In part because in the securitization and derivative creation process, the mortgage payments are divided into tranches with the top one getting paid first and almost certain to be paid unless the vast majority of the underlying mortgages default with zero recoveries, as discussed earlier. Also, investors believe the securitization process gave them disaster-proofing diversification.

In the main, however, investors trusted rating agencies that continued to give high credit ratings to what rapidly became toxic waste. Many investors, including pension fund trustees, ultimately were embarrassed to learn that their portfolios contain nearly worthless junk. Investors in collateralized debt obligations (CDOs), for example, received little information on what collateral was backing their investments. And CDOs were often invested in other CDOs, further obscuring the collateral.

Our good friend, housing expert Tom Lawler, notes seven reasons why rating agencies were slow to downgrade subprime mortgage-backed bonds or even put them on their negative watch lists—despite the message from investors as the spreads on these bonds versus Treasurys leaped to deep junk levels as their prices collapsed; despite the sharp jump in delinquencies and foreclosures (see Figure 3.9); despite the disappearance of many subprime lenders; despite the growing number of analysts who joined Tom and me in predicting big losses for these obligations; and despite the dim view investors took toward rating agencies themselves as their stock prices collapsed.

Figure 3.9 Residential Mortgages Past Due, 1972–2009
Data source: Mortgage Bankers Association.

Here's Tom's list:

1. Rating agencies have conflicts of interest. They're paid by the issuers of the bonds they rate and want to keep them happy and the product flowing. No bonds issued, no rating fees.
2. They may have figured that a rash of downgrades would trigger a rush for the exit and spawn panic in the mortgage market as pension funds and others that couldn't own non-investment-grade bonds dump the downgraded obligations.
3. Premature and unjustified downgrades could be embarrassing, so they'd wait to see the whites of the eyes of actual foreclosures, hoping that delinquencies wouldn't take that dire next step. Nevertheless, foreclosures leaped.
4. Many of the troubled subprime-related obligations were a year or less old. It would be embarrassing to rate something as junk that was rated investment-grade only a few months earlier.
5. Massive rating downgrades would screw up the time-tested statistic used by risk managers to gauge the probabilities of defaults as bonds age.
6. Rating agencies relied on models to predict delinquencies and defaults. Since house price declines, at least in nominal terms, did not occur in earlier post–World War II years, their models based on that history could not deal with the unfolding price drops.

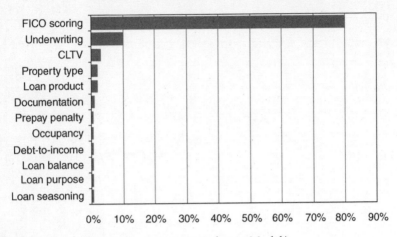

Figure 3.10 Typical Rating Agency Foreclosure Model★
★Explanatory power of mortgage loan characteristics based on Fitch's statistical model.
Data sources: Lawler Economic and Housing Consulting.

7. Their statistical models also found, historically, 80 percent of foreclosure risk is based on FICO credit scores (see Figure 3.10). So their projections neglected other factors that had become much more important, like underwriting standards, current loans as percentages of total values (CLTV), the suitability of the loan product, and the extent of income and other documentation.

The rating agencies have so much egg on their faces that when state regulators decided to pick a firm to help determine the risks in residential mortgage portfolios held in insurance company portfolios, they turned elsewhere. In late 2009, the National Association of Insurance Commissioners selected Pacific Investment Management (Pimco) to estimate losses in about 18,000 bonds in order to gauge the capital insurers' need to back them. Many of those issues were originally rated triple-A, but more recently were downgraded to junk, or below triple-B, the minimum for investment-grade status.

The End

I've discussed at length the housing bubble and why we saw it well ahead of time, what we wrote as it expanded, the resistance of the chorus of optimists along the way, and the slowness of regulators and rating agencies to understand the size and scope of the problem. Now let's explore the bubble's spectacular bursting, starting in early 2007.

In 2003, the big British bank HSBC bought U.S. personal finance company Household International for $14.8 billion and it became the center of its American subprime lending binge. HSBC had big expansion plans for that unit, and also bought billions of dollars of low-grade loans from other lenders. Its second-mortgage holdings leaped from $6.3 billion in September 2005 to $10.2 billion in March 2006. But delinquencies on those loans mushroomed, and in February 2007, HSBC set aside $1.76 billion to cover soured mortgages and other bad debt.

Then HSBC and other lenders that warehouse mortgages for lenders before they are securitized started to push those that had gone bad back to the original lenders. Their agreements allowed them to do that for mortgages that defaulted within the first few months or if fraud was involved in making the loans. In addition, mortgage lenders retained a portion of the loans they sold off, and that equity was the first to go when any loans in the package defaulted.

Expansion plans moved to the far back burner due to the bank's subprime mortgage disaster. Top management fired those in charge and brought in the workout crew. HSBC's CEO said it would take two or three years to clean up the mess. As an instant indicator of the bank's widespread retrenchment, HSBC said it would no longer provide high-interest-rate early loans to U.S. taxpayers expecting refunds from the IRS. It also announced that subprime mortgage lending had "virtually" ended.

Dramatic Effects

That announcement by HSBC in February 2007 made it clear that subprime residential mortgages were in deep trouble. The price index for BBB-minus mortgage securities backed by subprime mortgages, which had been moving down, virtually collapsed (see Figure 3.11). Also involved in triggering the subprime revelation was the nation's second largest mortgage lender, New Century, which took so little time in examining a borrower's credentials that it bragged about its ability to make a mortgage proposal in 12 seconds. Even as delinquencies grew

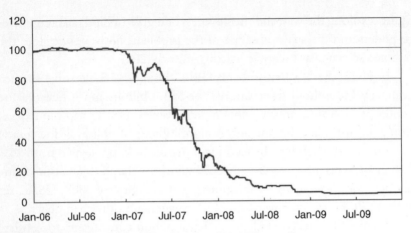

Figure 3.11 ABX Index BBB–Tranches (06-1 Vintage★)
★based on mortgages originated in first half 2006.
Data source: Markit.

in 2006, New Century denied problems, saying its careful underwriting was actually improving its results. But on February 7, 2007, New Century reported a loss for the previous quarter along with rising delinquencies and announced that earlier profits were cut by bad mortgages it had previously sold to banks but had to take back. Its stock fell 36 percent the next day.

In our April 2007 *Insight*, we wrote, "Those who hoped the plague would be confined to subprime mortgages are being disappointed," but amazingly few understood that at the time. In that report, we noted that the latest *Wall Street Journal* poll of 60 economists (not including me) "found that 80 percent believe the worst of the housing bust is behind us, only 22 percent say the subprime woes have led them to reduce their economic growth forecasts, and on average they see a mere 0.77 percent decline in house prices this year." Fed Governor Susan Bies, in a speech at the time, said that the troubled subprime market was just a "sliver" of the broader mortgage market, to which we replied, "Well, we don't know about her but we've suffered some pretty painful and expensive slivers, especially in our hands and other nerve-laden areas."

Our May 2007 *Insight* went on to say:

Stockholders and most economists continue to believe subprime mortgage woes won't sink the rest of housing and the economy as the

Dow Industrials hits record levels. They earlier believed housing is safe until interest rates skyrocket, but then came deflation in subprime, the soft extrusion of the housing bubble. Now they ignore leaping subprime problems as teaser rates reset and the spreading difficulties as Alt-A mortgages are infected, lenders retrench and are pressured by regulators, the likely downgrades by rating agencies, the capitulation of housing speculators and procrastinating homeowners as the spring selling season bombs, and the immense housing inventory overhangs. Hopes that capital spending will replace housing as a growth engine have also faded, and foreign economic growth won't be a replacement either. Rapid U.S. job growth won't offset faltering housing. Residential activity falls before business cycles peak and then declining construction employment and spending spread to the rest of the economy and overall jobs. A 25 percent fall in house prices will mushroom these negative effects.

The Basic Problem

The dire consequences of the housing collapse were fundamentally due to excess leverage. If all homebuyers had been required to make 20 percent down payments and to have good credit scores, adequate incomes to make monthly mortgage payments, and significant financial reserves, the 30 percent drop in house prices so far and the financial crisis it spawned would have caused much less damage. But then, without all the financial leverage, liars loans, and so forth, the exuberant demand for houses that created the leap in home building and the skyrocketing of prices would never have occurred.

The vast difference that leverage makes can be seen by contrasting the collapse in the U.S. housing bubble with that in Hong Kong, which was touched off by the 1997–1998 Asian financial crisis. Between mid-1997 and 2003, house prices there fell by two-thirds, but mortgage delinquencies over 90 days never exceeded 1.4 percent—far below the recent U.S. number of 5.2 percent that is still rising. In contrast to loans of 100 percent or more of property value in the United States, mortgage loans in Hong Kong are limited to substantially less than a property's value.

Furthermore, in Hong Kong, the mortgage lender can go after the homeowner's other assets in the event of foreclosure, but many U.S. states permit nonrecourse mortgages that encourage underwater borrowers to walk away from their houses. Hong Kong required documentation for borrower income and assets, but in the United States, no-doc loans were common in the housing salad days. Furthermore, Hong Kong monetary authorities have no reluctance to react early to a housing heat-up by cutting the limits on loan-to-value ratios and raising taxes on home sales. But note that the Hong Kong government does have a degree of control over real estate that's lacking in the United States: Land is scarce, and the government owns the available supply. So through land sales, it can influence the demand-supply balance and prices.

In contrast, recently, many American homeowners who are under-water with their mortgages exceeding their houses' values are defaulting even if they can afford the monthly payments, and then moving to cheaper rentals. For them and others, home ownership is no longer attractive (Figure 3.6). Estimates are that these strategic defaults exceeded one million in 2009, four times the 2007 level. One-quarter of mort-gagors are underwater and that number may reach 40 percent as house prices fall further, as I explain in Chapter 10. Many of these strategic defaulters use the difference between their earlier mortgage payments and lower rental costs for discretionary expenditures.

A Final Irony

A final irony to the housing collapse came with an agonizing deci-sion by the Mortgage Bankers Association (MBA), those folks who so unabashedly were involved in creating and distributing toxic subprime residential mortgages. With the housing collapse, MBA membership dropped from 3,000 to 2,400 and its staff fell from 150 to 107. So it was using only 40 percent of its Washington headquarters building in early 2010, with 10 percent rented to tenants and 50 percent vacant. When it bought the building in 2007 just as housing was collapsing, MBA CEO Jonathan Kempner said, "We have come to the inescapable conclusion that owning our own building was the smartest long-term investment for the association." In July 2008, Kempner resigned and in October 2009, MBA said it had put the building up for sale since contin-ued ownership was "economically imprudent." In February 2010, MBA sold its 10-story headquarters for $41.3 million, compared to its purchase price of $79 million in 2007 and the $75 million it borrowed from banks to finance the building. So, like so many of the previous homeowners the MBA encouraged to buy houses, the association has joined the ranks of the renters.

A Rare Investment Opportunity

By the mid-2000s, I was so convinced that the housing bubble would collapse that I searched for ways to make serious money if my forecast proved correct. Short-selling home-builder stocks, credit rating agencies, mortgage insurers, Fannie and Freddie, bank and nonbank mortgage lenders, building suppliers, home improvement retailers, residential-focused real estate investment trusts (REITs), and exchange-traded funds (ETFs) related to these equities were all possibilities. But, as noted in Chapter 1, you can lose a lot of money if you're short securities that rise in price. Even though you're right in the long run, you may never get there because security prices go against you in the interim and squeeze you out financially, psychologically, or both.

The Dow Jones Home Construction Index peaked in mid-2005, about the time I saw the housing industry topping out, but even if I'd been lucky enough to short those stocks at the peak, there were so many hair-raising rallies on the way down.

I was still searching for the answer when, in July 2006, I got a call out of the blue from Brad Rosenberg, the head trader at Paulson & Co. I wasn't familiar with the firm or its head, hedge fund manager John Paulson. A friend had sent him a copy of our April 2006 *Insight* and he'd read our "Not Home Alone" report that spelled out our forecast for a collapse in U.S. house prices, despite the fact that it hadn't occurred yet in other countries with exuberant housing activity such as in the United Kingdom and Australia.

I was invited in for a discussion of our views, and after an hour or so, we set up a consulting relationship. Paulson & Co. had just launched its Credit Opportunities Fund, designed to profit if subprime mortgages got into trouble. Indeed, if house prices only flattened, much less fell 25 percent as I was forecasting, the fund would do well. House prices

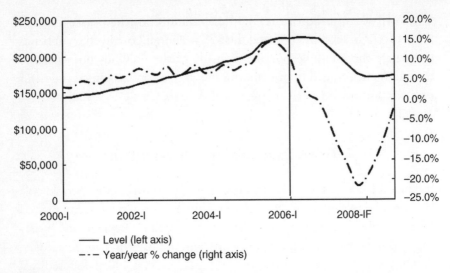

Figure 3.12   Existing Median Nationwide Single-Family Home Sale Prices
Data sources: National Association of Realtors; A. Gary Shilling & Co.; data after second quarter 2006
is AGS & Co. forecast.

and mortgage defaults are closely linked, much more so than other factors like unemployment, interest rates, and economic growth. John was very impressed with my graph of house prices, which showed my forecast for substantial declines. Ever since then, John has reminded me many times of how important that forecast was to his success with subprime mortgage-related securities. In fact, he suggested that I include it in this book, so here it is (Figure 3.12).

Impressed by Three Things

At that July 2006 meeting, John asked me to be one of the initial members of the advisory board he was establishing, and I readily agreed. The advisory board meets monthly, and through those meetings and other contacts with Paulson and his associates, I was impressed by three things. First, they were very disciplined in their research of various subprime-related securities and in the execution of their strategies. Second, the necessary understanding of the details of the securities they used to execute their strategies was beyond the capabilities of me and my staff. I couldn't begin to duplicate what they were doing. Third, the vehicles they used limited losses but allowed tremendous gains, many times the original investment. This achieved the objective of selling short but eliminated the problem of unlimited potential losses while prospective gains stop at 100 percent if the security falls to zero.

They were using credit default swaps (CDSs), which are essentially insurance policies on bonds and other fixed-income securities or derivatives of those securities. You don't have to own the securities to buy insurance on them, and this creates the opportunities for big gains. If the value of the securities falls, the CDS rises. If the bond or other underlying instrument rises in value, the CDS falls but never below zero. Conversely, the sellers of CDSs can only gain the amount the buyers can lose, but can suffer huge losses unless hedged if the value of the underlying securities plummets.

Because of gigantic losses by sellers of CDSs, some government lenders recently have suggested that CDSs should only be available for those who own the underlying securities because they believe their use by others helped create the financial crisis. The sale of CDSs by AIG to hedge funds and others nearly bankrupted the company as the underlying securities collapsed. That forced the Fed ultimately to inject $123 billion, much of which was lost.

This strikes me as similar to the attempts to blame the weakness in early 2010 in the euro currency on hedge fund sellers and divert it from the fundamental problems in the eurozone structure and Greece and its other weak members. Attempting to pin the 2007–2009 stock market collapse on short sellers is another example of the blame game, and the SEC reacted in early 2010 by restricting short selling, as discussed earlier. I believe that inherently weak markets will decline even without short selling of one form or another. Disallowing proper price signals from being transmitted simply prolongs the agony. Allowing banks to avoid marking toxic assets down to market prices is another example of avoiding market-determined prices. It probably doesn't change the final outcome, but delays it. If short sellers and other bear raiders are wrong in their assessments, markets will probably trap them into huge losses.

Note also that in the nineteenth century, it was common in England for people to take out life insurance policies on others they'd never met, often celebrities. More recently in the United States, some corporations buy life insurance policies on low-level employees that principally benefit the company if they die—"janitor insurance." Furthermore, investors buy existing life policies from older people who prefer to cash out.

Lots of Leverage

Back in 2006, Paulson & Co. was buying CDSs on BBB tranches of CDOs that were ultimately backed by pools of subprime residential mortgages (refer back to Figure 3.7). Notice that this tranche compounded the low quality of subprime residential mortgages because it was a low-end slice of a CDO that in total was composed of low-end pieces of RMBS securitizations. Furthermore, the confidence in subprime mortgages at that time was so great that CDSs were selling at only 1 percent of the value of the BBB tranches of CDOs. So an investment of $10 million would insure $1 billion.

Paulson reasoned that if the strategy didn't work, then his outside investors would be willing to spend a maximum of 25 percent over three years, or 8 percent a year, including Paulson's 1 percent annual management fee. Since the payments on the CDS purchase are made over time, most of the investors' money would earn the Treasury bill rate, then 5 percent, until the payments came due. So the gross maximum annual cost of the CDS, before this 5 percent offset, would be 12 percent. That allowed leverage of 12 to 1. If $1 billion in CDSs were purchased and the underlying BBB tranche became worthless due to subprime defaults, the gain would be $10 billion. Wow!

Now, I've lost 25 percent on investments. Been there, done that. So the downside of Paulson's strategy didn't bother me, and I saw plenty of upside. I did worry, however, about getting paid by those who sold the CDSs if they leaped. I asked about this and learned that Paulson settled its positions, plus or minus, on a daily basis with its trading partners. Interestingly, I must not have been the only person with this concern. I recall that Deutsche Bank, which was advocating the same strategy to investors, as I discuss later, had a page in its presentation book that explicitly said that the bank's balance sheet would support the CDS positions if those who ultimately had sold them didn't.

Pay Dirt

So I'd found the vehicle to make money if my forecast of a collapse in housing led by subprime mortgages was valid. I called John Paulson and asked if I could invest an amount that was below his minimum but a meaningful sum for me. He agreed and I invested in the Paulson Credit Opportunities Fund in October 2006. Not much happened for the next few months, but the timing for the fund, which had started at midyear, and for me was auspicious. In February 2007, with the HSBC $1.8 billion reserve for bad subprime loans and the announcement of a fourth quarter 2006 loss by New Century, subprime securities tanked (see Figure 3.11) and the values of CDSs written on them soared. Paulson closed out those positions as the value of the subprime-backed tranches approached zero and moved on to other successful investments. Paulson & Co. is reported to have made $20 billion for the firm and its clients in 2007 and 2008, $1.25 billion in one day in 2007. John Paulson personally earned $6 billion over those two years. My much smaller investment was up over $11\frac{1}{2}$ times as of May 2010.

Timing

Timing in this or any investment is obviously critical. A number of other investors were involved in the subprime CDS trade. Some got in too early and gave up while some were frustrated over initial losses but hung in for eventual big gains. One of the latter was Greg Lippmann of Deutsche Bank. On January 11, 2006, about six months before the initial call from Paulson & Co., I got an unexpected call from Peter Hooper, chief economist at Deutsche Bank Securities, whom I'd met on an economic outlook panel. A mortgage-backed trader at his firm had sent him one of our *Insight* articles predicting big trouble for housing.

That trader was Greg Lippmann, global head of ABS trading, who shared my views and called me the same day. Greg explained how I could make money with my negative subprime forecast, and tossed out terms like CDOs, tranches, and CDS that I barely knew. He said he'd e-mail me information. I decided, however, that the whole idea was too complicated and esoteric for me to consider seriously, and threw my notes of our phone conversation on my "file and forget" pile.

Then, in April 2007, after I'd become involved with Paulson and knew what CDSs were, I happened to be cleaning out that pile and discovered those notes. "Eureka!" I shouted to myself. "Greg in early 2006 explained exactly what I'm now doing through the Paulson Credit Opportunities Fund." So I called Greg and promptly visited him in New York City. Greg was surprised how much I'd learned about CDOs, subprime mortgages, CDSs, and so forth in the intervening year. We established a consulting relationship that worked to both our advantages.

I'm lucky, however, that I didn't follow Lippmann's advice at the beginning of 2006. Deutsche Bank executives allowed him to put on the subprime CDS trade in the fall of 2005 to a limited extent, but it went nowhere and in the summer of 2006, his superiors at Deutsche Bank grew impatient. They didn't close out his positions, but required periodic reviews. Meanwhile, Lippmann began to convince hedge fund clients of the merits of his idea. Nevertheless, most of them lost money by the end of 2006.

In early 2007, however, Lippmann's profits leaped as the subprime ABX Index collapsed. He resisted management pressure to cut his positions substantially that fall, and for the year, his group made close to $2 billion for Deutsche Bank. This helped offset losses elsewhere in the bank, many of them ironically on CDOs that were created to accommodate the subprime CDSs of Paulson and others who were negative on the mortgage market.

Spreading Effects

The collapse in the subprime mortgage market starting in early 2007 was the trigger that pummeled the rest of the housing sector, spawned the near-meltdown on Wall Street, and then spread to the rest of the economy and abroad. In Chapter 5, I survey this slow-motion train wreck and the amazing denial of most other forecasters while it was occurring. But first, I turn in Chapter 4 to one more great call, the demise of the financial bubble and the global recession.

Chapter 4

The Financial Bubble
(Great Call 7)

My seventh great call was that the speculative financial bubble that started to develop in the late 1990s would burst with severe consequences. In our December 2004 *Insight*, we wrote:

> Continuing speculation has left a big gap between the financial sphere and the economic world of goods and services. If history is any guide, this Great Disconnect will be eliminated sooner or later, and the reunion may be a violent and unpleasant affair. This suggests that the final bear market bottom, the terminal correction of the 1982–2000 bull run and its equity bubble in the late 1990s, may lie yet ahead. That would mean that the 2003 rally was not the beginning of a new bull market, but only a rally in an ongoing bear market.

This forecast proved to be entirely correct when the S&P 500 Index in early 2009 broke through the October 2002 low of 776 to reach 677 on March 9 (see Figure 1.6).

The long and substantial rally in stocks from August 1982 to March 2000 was driven by the unwinding of inflation in all of its aspects (refer to Figure 1.5 in Chapter 1). The falling interest rates that accompanied disinflation spurred the rise in price/earnings (P/E) ratios. At the same time, the ending of inflation eliminated the transfer of profitability from corporations to government via taxes on underdepreciation and inventory profits, as noted earlier. Corporate restructuring, which began in earnest in the early 1980s, and a much more hard-nosed attitude toward labor costs also boosted profits (Figure 2.4).

The length and intensity of the 17-year, eight-month bull market put fear to flight, leaving nothing but intense greed and unbridled speculation. Many became convinced that the five consecutive years of 20 percent-plus gains in the S&P 500 Index were the new and lasting order of things in the great New Economy. So they abandoned saving any of their earned income in the belief that stock appreciation would put their kids through college, finance early retirement, and cover a few round-the-world trips in between. In effect, the financial world parted company from economic reality, a phenomenon that had not been experienced since the late 1920s.

As in the Roaring Twenties, the speculative climate of the late 1990s did spill over into the real economy. Consumers spent freely because they no longer saw any reason to save. Dot-coms spent the money investors threw at them on advertising and capital outlays and went well beyond what Keynes had in mind when he said, "If human nature felt no temptation to take a chance...there might not be much investment merely as a result of cold calculation." Still, the real economy did not and probably could not reflect the full frenzy of financial speculation.

Plenty of Help

To be sure, investors had plenty of help in their flight from economic reality. Wall Street analysts were paid lavishly to tout investment banking clients' stocks that they knew were dogs. Wall Street wizards dreamed up the off-balance-sheet schemes that ultimately sank the Enrons of the world, with the cooperation of those firms' outside auditors. Accounting firms charged their clients huge fees for aggressive tax shelters that were very welcome by those who had sold those investments to insatiable investors for gigantic profits. Pension fund consultants convinced many fund trustees that stocks were the sole route to salvation by using data that only contained the post-1982 bull market years.

So powerful was the 1982–2000 bull market and so strong the aiding and abetting by the financial services industry that even the 2000–2002 bear market did not rejoin the financial and economic worlds. Many investors still believed they were entitled to 20 percent or greater annual returns, but were no longer sure that stocks would do the job. So they switched to other investments, which often leveraged their holdings manyfold.

Monetary Assistance

Furthermore, government policies not only failed to encourage a reuniting of the financial and economic spheres, but actively promoted the continuing separation of economic reality from financial fantasy. As discussed earlier, then-Fed Chairman Greenspan's "irrational exuberance" speech in December 1996 showed that he was aware of unfolding speculation at that time. Still, the central bank failed to act, apparently afraid of precipitating a bear market and recession. So the dot-com years followed and took speculation to its ultimate heights and subsequent collapse (previously seen in Figure 1.1 in Chapter 1).

The gigantic destruction of consumer net financial worth (see Figure 4.1) and the drop in capital spending that followed the collapse in capacity utilization (see Figure 4.2) threatened a major recession. This enhanced the already considerable fears over deflation and weak consumer spending at the central bank, especially after 9/11. So the Fed slashed interest rates (as we saw in Figure 1.3) and limited the recession as low interest rates and easy credit encouraged housing and consumer spending. So, too, did the tax rebates and two rounds of tax cuts during 2001–2003 as well as the jump in federal spending on homeland security and the Afghanistan and Iraqi wars, as noted in Chapter 3.

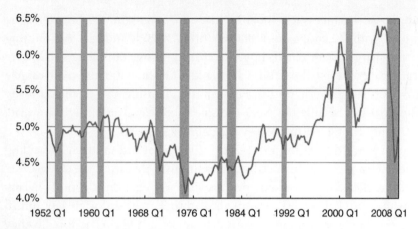

Figure 4.1   Household Net Worth as a Percentage of Disposable Personal Income
Data source: Federal Reserve.

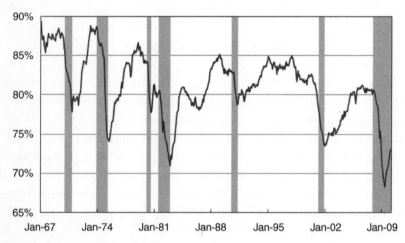

Figure 4.2   Capacity Utilization
Data source: Federal Reserve.

Cheap mortgage money (seen earlier in Figure 3.2) spawned speculation in housing, which many saw as the replacement for stocks in their
uninterrupted quest for riches. House prices and the consumer price
index (CPI) normally move together, but real estate speculation caused
a wide divergence (as we saw in Figure 3.4). The extent of homeowner
financial leverage was also made obvious by comparing the all-time high

in the value of household real estate in relation to disposable personal income in the early 2000s with the falling percentage owned after all mortgage encumbrance is removed (as seen in Figure 3.5). Homeowners more than borrowed the immense appreciation in their abodes' values.

Leveraging Fannie and Freddie

And they weren't alone in speculating in real estate. Fannie Mae and Freddie Mac moved from buying residential mortgages and then reselling them in packages to investors to retaining huge quantities of mortgages. This greatly increased the financial leverage of those elephantine government-sponsored enterprises and made them, in effect, the world's biggest hedge funds. Also, the federal government, largely through Fannie and Freddie, promoted down payments on home purchases of 3 percent or less for low-income, minority, and young families, as noted in Chapter 3.

Also propelling the great disconnect were the repeated bailouts of potential financial disasters, always under the "too big to fail" doctrine, which sometimes hides political sensitivity to financial setbacks even if they resulted from people's own follies. The Fed cut interest rates after the bankruptcy of Orange County in 1994. It also did so following the collapse of Long-Term Capital Management in 1998 and organized a Wall Street bailout of that firm. Government-sanctioned Fannie and Freddie bought adjustable-rate mortgages (ARMs), whereby homeowners who could barely afford the initial low mortgage payments were set up for certain trouble when their rates adjusted upward. And, of course, the big declines in the federal funds rate in the early 2000s and again more recently postponed but did not eliminate the woes of many low-income homeowners who couldn't retain their houses without considerable price appreciation.

These actions follow in a long tradition of government help in times of crisis. The panic of 1792 resulted from speculators trying to corner the market for federal government bonds, which leaped in price and then collapsed. So Treasury Secretary Alexander Hamilton borrowed from banks to buy government bonds and revive the market. The financial system stabilized and no banks failed.

In 1933, the Home Owners' Loan Corporation was created to buy defaulted mortgages from banks and refinance them at lower rates for fixed 15-year terms. The 1930s Depression spawned all manner of government interventions and changed the economic and financial landscapes with innovations ranging from the 1933 bank holiday to audit banks and close the insolvent ones to the Glass-Steagall Act, the SEC, the FDIC, farm subsidies, the WPA, PWA, TVA, and so forth. With the 1986–1995 savings and loan crisis sinking about half the country's 3,234 savings institutions, deposit insurance funds ran out so Congress created the Resolution Trust Corporation (RTC) and taxpayers got the $150 billion bill.

Borrow Short, Invest Long

The Fed's reduction in the short-term fed funds rate it controls in the early 2000s also created a big and inviting spread between short and long rates, a steep yield curve. This sired vast speculation as hedge funds, banks, brokers, and others borrowed cheap short-term money and bought Treasury bonds, junk bonds, convertible obligations, emerging country stocks and bonds, commodities, and currencies. And homebuyers engaged in their own carry trade as house price inflation vastly exceeded mortgage rates, especially on ARMs.

Office buildings, malls, hotels, and other commercial real estate moved into bubble territory in the early 2000s. Lower interest rates encouraged investors to reduce their expected operating return, or capitalization rates, and bid up prices accordingly. And that came in the face of weak rents and high vacancy rates.

As we said in our June 2004 *Insight* report,

> It's the height of ironies. In the late 1990s, the Fed refrained from credit restraint for fear of precipitating a recession and bear market, but in so doing allowed speculation to mount to the point that the three-year big bear raid resulted. Then, in its attempt to keep stock losses from wrecking the economy and to stave off deflation, the Fed pushed short rates so low that another huge wave of speculation resulted.

In effect, the Fed, with plenty of help from the administration and Congress, promoted continued speculation and the disconnect between the financial world (and let's include real estate in it) and the real economy. That's probably partly why, despite the nosedive in stocks in the three-year bear market, especially the ridiculously overpriced tech stocks, investors never capitulated.

Thus, gigantic levels of speculation remained despite the 2000–2002 stock collapse, and as we wrote in our November 2006 *Insight*,

> they won't be eliminated and the yawning Grand Disconnect between the real world of goods and services and the financial world of asset speculation won't disappear unless forced by significant events. Speculations never end voluntarily or in orderly fashions. Meanwhile, the game continues for five reasons.

Five Reasons

Reason A, the world has been awash in liquidity, which amply feeds speculation. Reason B, speculation feeds on itself, as was seen with the dot-com bubble and, more recently, in gold and emerging market stocks. There's nothing like making money to insure speculators that their bets are correct and should be redoubled. Reason C, institutional and other investors yearn for huge returns. Their clients demand them. Many pension funds still have 9 percent or so expected returns. And money managers who don't produce consistent high gains lose money to those who do. So there's great willingness to take sizable risks.

Reason D, perceived risks, at least until recently, have been low. With roaring profits, junk bond default rates remain low. The low anticipated volatility in stocks and bonds has desensitized many investors to the increased risks they are taking. So, too, is the conviction that the Fed will continue to bail out speculators. Finally is Reason E. Loose mortgage lending has been encouraged by the development of mortgage-backed securities that allow lenders to package mortgage loans and sell the securities to yield-hungry investors. So why not make riskier loans when they can be sold easily and the risks transferred with the sale? It's like a bookmaker who expands his business without adding risk by laying off his customers' bets to others.

Signs of Disconnect

There was ample evidence that the great disconnect was alive and well in the mid-2000s. Sure, like other services, the financial sector grows faster than the overall economy. As developed economies expand, financial services tend to become more widespread, more complex, and a bigger share of economic activity. Still, the upward departures from post–World War II trends in the financial sectors were substantial and measured the disconnect from the real economy. These bulges are especially significant because after huge speculation, as in the late 1990s, the corrections should have taken these series below their long-term trends for at least a few years. But that did not happen.

Stock market capitalization as a percentage of GDP historically ran about 50 percent, but spurted to 180 percent in the Internet bubble and never returned to trend in the 2000–2002 bear market (see Figure 4.3). As individual wealth builds over time, so do Americans' holdings of mutual funds. Again, however, the bulge in the late 1990s was never corrected.

Much of the speculation in financial markets and real estate was financed by borrowing, of course, and consumer debt and debt service in relation to take-home pay jumped in the early 2000s (Figure 4.4). It was especially revealing that debt service was well above its mid-1980s

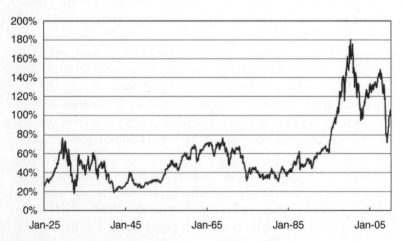

Figure 4.3 Market Capitalization as a Percentage of GDP
Data sources: Haver Analytics, Historical Statistics of the United States.

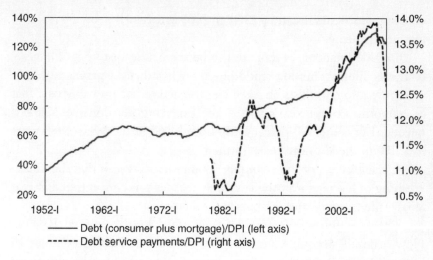

Figure 4.4 Debt and Debt Service Payments as a Percentage of Disposable Personal Income (DPI)
Data source: Federal Reserve.

peak because interest rates declined substantially in the interim. The effects of lower interest rates on monthly payments were much more than offset by much higher debt levels.

The continuing rapid growth in derivatives such as futures, options, and currency and interest rate swaps was also a sign of the great disconnect between the financial and economic worlds. The notional value of global over-the-counter derivatives jumped from $100 trillion in 2000 to almost $700 trillion in mid-2008. True, derivatives aren't money in the sense that you could use one to buy a gallon of milk in a supermarket. Nevertheless, they served to largely finance the housing bubble.

Review of Leverage

In the 1960–1980 years, it took a $1.68 increase in total net debt to finance an additional dollar of nominal GDP. Total net debt includes that of households, unincorporated business, the corporate sector, the financial sector, state and local governments, and the federal government. From 1980 to 2000, that number averaged $3.10. Then in the 2000–2009 years, it leaped to $5.10 on average and peaked at $7.70 in 2008 before collapsing to a still substantial $2.48 in 2009 as federal borrowing replaced private financing.

Outside financing is supposed to be the grease that keeps the gears of the economy running smoothly. It's what turns a primitive barter economy into a sophisticated, efficient structure. It's probably true that as economic complexity grows, more financing per dollar of GDP is needed. But is the 300 percent leap from $1.68 in the 1960–1980 years to $5.10 in the last nine years justified?

A brief review of the economy's components reveals that the mushrooming of leverage over the last three decades was concentrated in two areas—the financial and the consumer sectors.

The U.S. financial sector, as categorized by the Federal Reserve Flow of Funds accounts, includes the monetary authority, commercial banks, savings institutions, credit unions, property-casualty insurance companies, life insurance companies, private pension funds, state and local government employee retirement funds, federal government retirement funds, money market mutual funds, mutual funds, closed-end and exchange-traded funds, government-sponsored enterprises (GSEs), agency- and GSE-backed mortgage pools, issuers of asset-backed securities finance companies, real estate investment trusts, security brokers and dealers, and funding corporations.

Many of these diverse outfits function in different ways, employ widely different degrees of risk, and serve different markets. But they all are financial intermediaries, raising money in the form of deposits, insurance premiums, pension fund contributions, commercial paper, notes, bonds, equity issues, and so forth, and investing it in commercial loans, bonds, mortgages, stocks, commercial paper, consumer loans, and so on.

Note, however, that the Fed Flow of Funds data do not include derivatives. But even without that exploding component, financial sector financing has been growing rapidly. So rapidly that the ratio of new net debt and equity issues to gross value-added of financial corporate business (essentially the value-added of that sector) jumped from about 50 percent in the early 1970s to 187 percent in the fourth quarter of 2007 before collapsing. Meanwhile, the ratio to gross domestic product (GDP) climbed from around 4 percent to 14 percent before hitting the skids.

Big Debt and Equity

Also, with net borrowing, year after year, growing faster than GDP or gross value-added of financial corporate business, the cumulative debt and equity issues of the financial sector have risen tremendously in relation to either measure, from 400 percent in the early 1970s to 1,600 percent in the case of gross value-added of financial corporate business and from 20 percent to 130 percent for GDP. In contrast, from 1952 to the early 1970s, the cumulative net outside financing of the financial sector grew from 300 percent of GFCP to 400 percent, and from 9 percent of GDP to 20 percent.

Notice that we're using the cumulative net issuance of stocks and bonds, not their current values, which have increased much more over time, mainly because of the rises in the prices of outstanding stocks. Conversely, we don't record the recent write-downs of debt instruments. We're interested in the money financial institutions obtain from outside investors, not the value outside investors place on those securities.

These dramatic upward shifts in trends speak volumes about the extent to which the finance sector has become much more leveraged. Some components such as insurance and pension funds have not increased their leverage much, if any, in recent years. So this mushrooming cumulative debt and equity issuance ratio implies that financial businesses such as GSEs and security brokers and dealers that are chronically highly leveraged have gained in relative size and/or increased their leverage massively. The latter is certainly the case in the securities industry where the ratio of assets to shareholder equity has leaped in recent years, but more recently is being reversed with a vengeance.

Derivatives

As noted earlier, the Fed Flow of Funds data do not include derivatives, which have exploded in recent years. The numbers I cited are global and cover only over-the-counter derivatives, privately arranged deals between buyers and sellers, and do not include futures, options, and other derivatives that are traded on exchanges. At the same time, they include many hedges and other offsets that reduce net financial exposures.

Often, when derivatives are no longer needed, they aren't canceled but rather a new mirror-image derivative is created as an offset. So the total face value, or notional amount, rises, but not the net exposure.

In any event, the Bank for International Settlements (BIS) estimated that net over-the-counter derivatives exposure added, as of the first half of 2007, $2.7 trillion, or 17 percent, to the debt of the financial sector. And note that this is a huge addition to the debts of the limited number of banks, hedge funds, Wall Street houses, and other financial institutions that dominate in the derivatives business. The leap in debt and derivatives exposure in recent years suggests that it is massively excessive in the current world of financial woes and distrust, and will suffer massive reductions.

The household sector was also a big leverager for about three decades. Mortgage borrowing financed much more than house purchases. There has been such a thing as a 15-year car loan, formally known as a home equity loan. That's why I include mortgage borrowing in household financing, and it dominated household borrowing in the past decade.

Total household financing grew in step with both disposable personal income and GDP in the 1960s. But borrowing leaped, starting in the early 1980s, so the accumulated debt jumped in relation to GDP and disposable personal income (see Figure 4.4).

Surplus to Deficits

The household sector used to be a net saver, even after accounting for spending on residential construction, due to the high saving rate (seen in Figure 2.5 in Chapter 2). But that ended as the saving rate collapsed and mortgage borrowing leaped. When after-tax, or disposable, personal income is subtracted from personal outlays plus residential investment, the result in the 1970s and 1980s was a negative number, or a surplus (see Figure 4.5). More recently, that difference reached a deficit of over $600 billion at annual rates. Interestingly, individuals on balance borrowed considerably more than needed to cover that deficit, a $1,300 billion rate back in the boom times as they sucked money out of their houses to fund not only consumer spending but also investments.

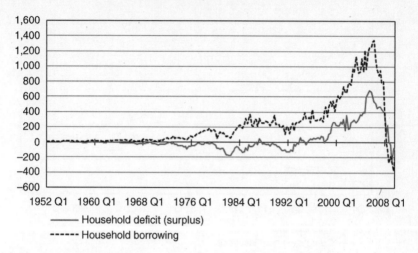

Figure 4.5 Household Borrowing and Expenditures★ ($ Billion)
★Personal outlays and household investment less disposable personal income.
Data sources: Bureau of Economic Analysis and the Federal Reserve.

With the collapse in housing activity, however, both mortgage borrowing and mortgage equity withdrawal also plummeted. So, too, did the borrowing in addition to the household deficit, the difference between the two lines in Figure 4.5. So Americans are increasingly forced not only to cut their borrowing, but to borrow only what they are required to. The growing negative effects on consumer discretionary spending and household investing are obvious.

Nonfinancial Corporations

Much has been made in recent years of the financial health of the nonfinancial corporate sector. Indeed, recently, cash flow exceeded capital spending, the reverse of the usual situation. Moreover, the ratios of nonfinancial corporate borrowing and equity issuance to corporate gross product (basically corporate sales) or to GDP have been volatile but essentially trending down since the early 1970s. Stock buybacks and mergers that extinguish equity have pushed down the total debt and equity issuance ratio. Still, financing has grown rapidly over the past 55 years so cumulative nonfinancial corporate debt issuance has risen more than 25 percentage points in relation to GDP (see Figure 4.6).

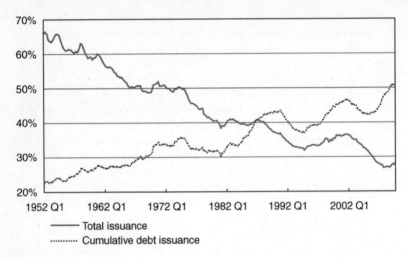

Figure 4.6 Nonfinancial Corporate Sector Cumulative Debt and Equity Issuance as a Percentage of GDP
Data source: Federal Reserve.

So, the nonfinancial corporate sector has almost doubled its cumulative debt-to GDP-ratio in the post–World War II era, but more than offset that growth with limited net equity issues. This, of course, has been a boon to shareholders and probably has been responsible for much of the rise in stock prices. But it's left nonfinancial firms with a lot more debt in relation to their equity issuance, that is, more leverage.

Federal Government

The federal government basically borrows what it needs to finance its deficits—or, as occurred briefly in the late 1990s and some earlier years, uses surpluses to retire securities (as was seen in Figure 3.1). It has no reason to hold more than working balances since excess borrowing only incurs interest costs, and the government's credit remains so superior that historically it hasn't worried much about market acceptance of borrowing at any time. Not surprisingly, the ratios of federal borrowing to receipts or to GDP have essentially the same shape as the deficit.

Despite the persistence of federal deficits in the post–World War II era, their ratios to receipts or GDP have been smaller on average than the growth rates in those measures. So, on balance, federal debt has fallen in relation to receipts and to GDP until the recent explosion, although it didn't get as low as it was in the 1970s before the Reagan Cold War military buildup. The much maligned federal government was much less profligate than the nonfinancial corporate, the household, and especially the financial business sectors, but now is running huge deficits (Figure 3.1) as government stimulus is attempting to replace private sector retrenchment.

State and Local Governments

Like the federal government, state and local governments basically borrow just enough to cover their needs. Unlike the federal government, however, almost all states require balanced budgets, at least excluding capital expenditures. But there are numerous ways around those requirements, as any imaginative politician can attest. Tax anticipation notes and other debt can be issued and treated as receipts. In the summer of 2009, California ran out of money and issued IOUs to pay its bills amidst its nonstop budget crisis. In New Jersey, the governor alone certifies that his proposed budget will be balanced and no one can second-guess him. In fact, for a number of years, I chaired the New Jersey State Revenue Forecasting Advisory Commission established by the legislature to keep an eye on the revenue forecasts of the governor.

In any event, the ratios of state and local borrowing to receipts and to GDP had plenty of volatility, but were trendless since the early 1950s until the recent recession-induced massive shortfall in corporate and individual income, sales, and property tax receipts. Consequently, the ratios of debt to receipts and to GDP have also showed volatility without strong trends until the past few years.

Pressures on state and local government revenues from weak tax collections are likely to persist for years, as I discuss in Chapter 7. Attempts to raise taxes and cut spending have been wholly inadequate, and huge deficits persist. Taxpayers want basic municipal services but at economically efficient costs. As their own incomes and assets remain under fire, they may demand cuts in state and local employee compensation since wages exceed those in the private sector by 34 percent on average and benefits are 70 percent more expensive. Since employee compensation is about half of state and local government costs, two-tier pay systems are being introduced, with new employees paid much lower wages and offered defined contribution instead of defined-benefit pension plans. Meanwhile, the pay of some existing employees is being frozen and pensions and retiree health benefits reformed.

Too Much Debt

Our analysis, summarized in Figure 4.7, shows that financial corporate debt and equity issuance has exploded in relation to GDP since the early 1970s while the household sector commenced its big leveraging in the early 1980s. The nonfinancial corporate sector and the federal government sectors, until recently, actually reduced their ratios while the state and local government sector has been flat.

Except for the household sector, the data are only beginning to reflect the ongoing massive financial deleveraging, and the household sector only shows any of this because the mortgage-related housing sector was the first to collapse. But the huge size of debts, the fears that

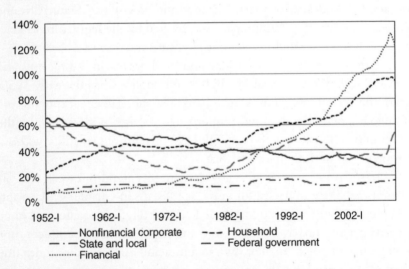

Figure 4.7 Ratios of Cumulative Sector Debts to GDP
Data source: Federal Reserve.

dominate financial markets, and government regulation almost guarantee further huge write-offs, charge-offs, debt cancellations, massive reductions of leverage, and subdued borrowing levels in the private sectors of the economy for years to come.

There are basically three ways of reducing financial leverage: selling assets for at least their cost, writing them down, or increasing capital. All three have proved difficult and are likely to remain so in the years ahead. The overleveraged household sector can't increase capital at present in view of weak real incomes and chronic high unemployment. Its assets are largely falling in value or already underwater, and write-downs of home equity don't reduce leverage much. In the long run, a saving spree will do the job, as I cover in Chapter 6. The private financial sector's capital-raising ability is limited by ongoing woes and many of its assets, especially related to commercial real estate, can only be sold at pennies on the dollar. So painful and capital-destroying write-downs will be significant in deleveraging despite congressionally approved limits in 2009 on mark-to-market accounting.

Everyone's Happy, But . . .

As we stated in our August 2004 *Insight*, in those bubble days,

> almost no one wants the financial and real estate spheres to reunite with the economic world, especially since the fusion could be bloody. Speculators in financial markets and real estate don't want the party to end. Those that lend to them don't want to see their attractive profits replaced by default write-offs. The financial services industry—which includes not only brokers, banks, hedge funds, money managers, and venture capitalists but also financial TV channels, myriad consultants, and purveyors of financial data and research—doesn't want its customer bases to shrink dramatically. And Washington, especially the Fed, doesn't want to preside over a painful reconvergence.
>
> Still, history suggests that the real and the financial world will rejoin at some point and that the reunion may be painful. Many of those speculators, including Fannie and Freddie, claim their positions are well hedged. Maybe so, but derivatives can transfer risks from one part to another but can't eliminate risks. Someone ends up holding the bag.

The critical question is, on balance, have risks been transferred from weak to strong financial hands or from strong to weak? No one knows the answer, but our guess is, it's the latter. Supporting our belief is the fact that in recent years, whenever trends in a wide variety of futures markets reversed, they did so violently. This suggests strongly that many weak-handed hedge funds and other speculators are all on the *same* side of the *same* trade at the *same* time. When their positions start to go against them, they are so leveraged that they have to get out immediately.

As I explore later, this was certainly true in 2008 when almost every investment class tanked. It's also true, however, that a number of banks and other financial houses ended up stuck with toxic derivatives, so toxic that they no longer are independent entities. Merrill Lynch, Bear Stearns, Lehman, Wachovia, and AIG are all in that category. Maybe they just regarded themselves as middlemen, created collateralized debt obligations (CDOs) and other lethal instruments strictly to facilitate trade, and intended to unload them before they could cause them trouble. But when financial markets started to dry up in the second half of 2007, potential buyers disappeared.

In our April 2005 *Insight*, I wrote:

> Our forecasts for the United States, China and, indeed, the world may sound dire, but realize that risk-taking and speculation have crept to very high levels without adequate concern. Many dismiss the thought of excessive risk-taking and speculation, reasoning that we're in a low-volatility world with the Fed firmly in command. That makes much higher levels of financial leverage entirely appropriate, they reason. They haven't yet rationalized these excesses under the rubric, "the New Economy," as the dot-com zealots did for their darlings in the late 1990s, but I wouldn't be surprised if they do.

The Bear Bust

The correctness of my great call on the financial bubble was revealed in late June 2007 when two big Bear Stearns hedge funds collapsed because of holdings of troubled subprime mortgage-related securities. Even though the subprime mortgage market was collapsing, starting

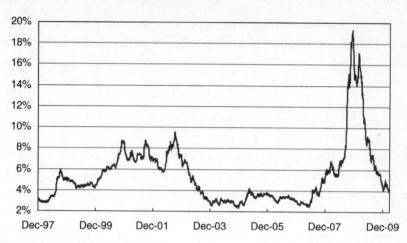

Figure 4.8 Junk Bond Spread
Data source: Bianco Research.

in February, few saw any further implications, as discussed in Chapter 3. Junk bonds were trading at tiny premium yields over Treasuries (see Figure 4.8), reflecting fearless investors and a default rate of just 0.8 percent in 2006 as ample liquidity made refinancing of even basket cases easy. In fact, junk bond owners willingly agreed to refinance those debts at lower rates, fearing that borrowers would refinance elsewhere and leave them with cash that could only be invested at still-lower rates. Between January 1 and April 19, 2007, $115 billion in debt was repriced.

Lender zeal also spawned *covenant lite* loans, which contain few requirements for the minimum profits, cash flow, and other factors needed to safeguard lenders. Still, lenders hungered for leveraged loans with new issues leaping from $300 billion in 2005 to $500 billion in 2006 and much more in 2007. Junk bond interest could often be paid in the form of more debt rather than cash (payment in kind), which puts more money in the hands of private equity firms that regularly use junk bonds to finance takeovers. In 2006, 21 percent of new junk bonds carried a very low "C" rating, but in the first half of 2007, the number was 33 percent.

Many leveraged loans were used to keep troubled companies afloat—*rescue financing*, it was called. This is one reason that bankruptcies remained so low until 2008, which in turn encouraged less fear of default and even more aggressive lending. In truth, however, these loans were just postponing the inevitable defaults, which were to then wipe out even more loans.

Fearless Zeal

Fearless zeal for yield also had pushed the spreads between emerging country debt and Treasurys to ridiculous lows (see Figure 4.9). And developing country stocks have way outpaced those in the United States (see Figure 4.10). Investment-grade bond issues were increasingly used not for productive investments or to improve balance sheets to the benefit of bondholders. Instead, they benefited stockholders as the proceeds were used for equity buybacks. Stock repurchases didn't generate cash flow that could pay interest and repay debt but they did raise the risks of default. The supply of investment-grade bonds was up 20 percent in the first half of 2007 from 2006, but the spread versus Treasurys was at a nine-year low.

Blind investor faith was clearly evident in enthusiastic buyers of collateralized debt obligations, those opaque derivatives that were ultimately supported by subprime mortgages, corporate debt, leveraged loans, and so forth, but which also owned other CDOs, as discussed earlier.

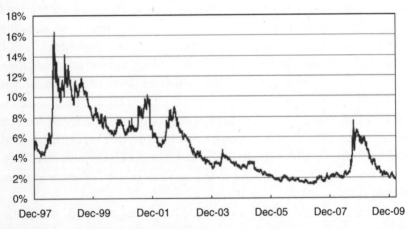

Figure 4.9 Emerging Market Bond Spread over Treasurys
Data sources: Bianco Research and the Federal Reserve.

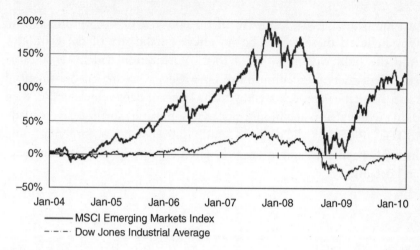

Figure 4.10 Emerging Market Stocks and Dow Jones Industrial Average since January 2, 2004
Data sources: Yahoo! Finance and Morgan Stanley Capital International.

Still, the top of the tree in unbridled investor faith was the special-purpose acquisition companies (SPACs), known as blank-check companies, which are empty shells that promise to use the proceeds of initial public offerings to buy other companies. Through May 2007, 30 SPACs had raised $3.5 billion, more than the $3.4 billion raised by 40 SPACs in all of 2006, and their average size jumped from $84.5 million to $115.9 million.

The Soft Underbelly

Not surprisingly, the first speculation to burst was the most vulnerable—the subprime mortgages of individuals with the lowest creditworthiness. The issuance of these mortgages had leaped in earlier years as loose lending made them available to an ever-widening circle of unqualified homebuyers.

Initially, the bulls dismissed this cesspool of putrid debt because—although it had skyrocketed—it was "only" 18 percent of total mortgages outstanding in 2006. Leaping delinquencies and foreclosures (shown previously in Figure 3.9) were of no concern to the optimists since they believed there would be no effect on the rest of the economy. And the bulls weren't worried that securitization had made it difficult for lenders to accommodate borrowers who are on the financial ropes since they are separated by many layers of debt vehicles. Also, they didn't worry that when modifications in subprime mortgages were made to keep borrowers afloat by stretching out repayments, forgiving some monthly payments, and so on, they often only postponed delinquencies and defaults.

The Reset Wringer

The housing optimists also ignored the tremendous number of subprime ARMs that would reset to much higher interest rates as the year progressed unless short-term interest rates nosedived. Until 2006, those with the usual 2/28 ARM—a fixed rate for two years and then floating for 28 years—had appreciation in their houses on average (seen earlier in Figure 1.2), so they could refinance or sell them to avoid reset shock. But with falling house prices, those up for mortgage rate reset had losses, and since they already spent an average 40 percent of after-tax income on housing, they couldn't afford the resets, which could increase monthly mortgage payments by 50 percent.

Indeed, there's clear evidence that many homeowners expected to lose their houses by 2006. Normally, homeowners pay their mortgages first to keep their abodes and then other debts if their funds are adequate. But with falling prices and looming ARM resets, many had little or negative equity in their houses and little to lose, so they paid credit card debt first. In early 2003, 32 percent of subprime borrowers were 30 days or more late on their payments; the number increased to 36 percent at the end of 2006. At the same time, 30-day or greater delinquencies on credit cards fell from 32 percent to 24 percent. Soon-to-be-evicted homeowners also reasoned that it normally takes six months to a year or more to foreclose on a house, so they could skip mortgage payments and live there rent-free in the meanwhile, as noted earlier.

Move-Up Market

Most importantly, the bulls even in early 2007 ignored the tremendous importance of the move-up market, mentioned in Chapter 3. In 2006, 36 percent of securitized mortgages were subprime or the somewhat better but none-too-good Alt-A loans. And 4.2 percent of Alt-A securitized loans were 90 days or more delinquent after 14 months, up from 1.6 percent in 2005 and 0.9 percent in 2004. But subprime and Alt-A loans were drying up as lenders tightened underwriting standards, aided and abetted by late-to-the-party regulators and bond rating agencies. Consequently, many owners of starter homes had few new homeowners to sell their house to so they could move up to bigger abodes. Those further up the ladder were getting similarly stuck, all the way to McMansion owners.

Bad Bear Bets

The subprime slime slid to Wall Street in a few months when it was revealed in June 2007 that two of Bear Stearns' hedge funds bet the wrong way on subprime mortgages. Its High Grade Structured Credit Strategies Fund was formed in 2004 and had gone 40 months without a loss. It used its $925 million in capital to bet $9.7 billion on the bull side and $4 billion on the bear side of the subprime mortgage market. The High Grade Structured Credit Strategies Enhanced Leverage Fund launched in August 2006 had $638 million in investor capital on March 31, 2007, and borrowed at least $6 billion to make $11.5 billion in bullish bets and $4.5 billion in bearish wagers. Either of those names is a mouthful, perhaps reflecting their complexity. Maybe they should simply rename them the Bet the Ranch on Subprime Junk Funds to reflect honestly their big net bullish positions in the $1.8 trillion market of securities backed by subprime mortgages.

From January through April 2007, the Enhanced Leverage Fund lost 23 percent, after increasing its positions as losses mounted, and investors and Wall Street lenders to the fund got nervous. After Bear Stearns refused to pay off those loans, Merrill Lynch tried to sell $850 million in collateral and soon found that the best fetched 85 to 95 cents on the dollar, but the lower rated mortgage-backed CDOs and other securities were worth only as little as 30 cents in the marketplace. The lenders demanded that Bear Stearns bail out the two funds, but it initially refused and made unreasonable demands, including a 12-month moratorium on margin calls and the release of the collateral back to the funds.

Such an attitude by Bear Stearns has precedent. Its CEO, James Cayne, refused to join the other major Wall Street houses in 1998 in bailing out Long-Term Capital Management. In 2007, many of those same 15 firms were Bear's lenders and the shoe was on the other foot. In any event, the lenders held firm and Bear, realizing that collateral dumping would collapse the value of similar assets it owned in other accounts, relented. Although the firm only had $40 million invested in the two funds, it agreed to lend $3.2 billion to the High Grade Fund, about double its $1.6 billion in borrowing. The more leveraged Enhanced Leverage Fund's problems were not immediately resolved and it owed $1.2 billion to its lenders. Bear's stock, already falling sharply, soon collapsed. And finally, the business itself disintegrated as a run on the bank forced the firm to sell out to JPMorgan Chase for a trivial sum on March 16, 2008 with a $30 billion loan from the Fed. The government intended the low sale price it sanctioned—$2 per share but later raised to $10—to convince Wall Street that taxpayers wouldn't bail out firms that made unsound bets.

The Scales Drop

When Bear was first pushed to the wall on Friday, June 22, 2007, the scales fell from investors' eyes and they saw ugly sights in many speculative arenas. The whole tenor of Wall Street attitudes shifted from bullishness as bad news was brushed aside to bearishness with good news questioned.

Sure, some university endowments initially bottom-fished for cheap subprime mortgage-backed securities, but Bear Stearns refused their fire sale bids. And persistent bulls pointed to earlier financial problems that had passed by without widespread and permanent damage: The $3.7 billion bailout of Long-Term Capital Management in 1998; the May 2005 debt downgrade to junk status of $450 billion of GM and

Ford debt; the $6.4 billion failure due to bad bets on copper prices of hedge fund Amaranth in September 2006. Nevertheless, the collapse in the late 1980s of the leveraged buyout (LBO) market financed by junk bonds and of its leader, Drexel Burnham Lambert, paved the way for the 1990 recession. And even greater distress was in the wings in mid-2007.

Wall Street firms like Goldman Sachs switched emphasis from arranging buyout money to devising exit strategies for private equity firms. The attitude of investors toward junk bonds changed dramatically. They pulled over $1 billion from junk bond mutual funds in a two-week period in late June. The takeover game disappeared after the Bear bust, and with it support for stocks. Hedge funds, which had been aggressive buyers of the leveraged loans and other debt needed to finance buyouts, became conspicuously absent. The whole view changed from a half-full to a half or more empty glass. Reflecting new concerns over global growth, the currencies of commodity exporters like Australia slipped and the prices of commodities such as copper fell. Meanwhile, the yen rallied as the carry trade was unwound.

The rating agencies, as usual, reacted to market reality, and didn't anticipate it. Earlier in 2007, they had an attack of common sense and realized that subprime mortgages with big delinquencies would later turn into big foreclosures. So they put the securities backed by those loans onto their credit watch lists. Subsequently, they slashed the rating on bonds backed by pools of subprime mortgages.

How Do You Price CDOs?

The biggest jolt from the Bear bust was the realization that CDOs and other derivatives are illiquid, trade infrequently, and therefore are not easily subject to market-determined prices. Also, because fund management and performance fees are determined by the value of the assets, there could be a bias toward valuations that are above market prices. This was why Bear Stearns agreed to bail out the High Grade Structured Credit Strategies Fund when Merrill Lynch and others found its securities were worth far less on the market than the prices at which Bear carried them. And it created immense potential write-downs for all who owned CDOs and similar illiquid derivatives.

CDOs have been around for two decades, but their issuances leaped in the early 2000s, from $84 billion in 2002 to $500 billion in 2006. As noted earlier, they are bundles of debt, ranging from subprime mortgages to corporate bonds to credit card debts and even other CDOs that are then sliced and sold to investors in various tranches. The tranches were often rated higher than the underlying loans because CDOs supposedly reduce risk through diversification. But the Bear bust revealed that assumption as false. CDOs also used borrowed money to enhance returns. Because of their structure, these CDOs were far removed from the underlying loans. A subprime mortgage loan was pooled with others to form a residential mortgage-backed security (RMBS), as we saw earlier in Figure 3.7. Then it and other RMBSs were used as collateral for a CDO. So without market prices for their thinly traded derivatives, it was hard to know what the underlying loans and, hence, the CDOs were worth.

Pricing Models

Earlier, I discussed the models used by rating agencies to forecast subprime mortgage foreclosures. They were based on times of rapid house price appreciation, and almost irrelevant to conditions of declining home values.

Similarly, rating agencies and Wall Street houses used models to price CDOs, based on such factors as interest rates, the illiquidity of similar investments, volatility, and the prices of similar instruments. This made CDO prices highly subjective and self-reinforcing since other CDOs were priced with similar formulas. This mark-to-model instead of mark-to-market approach was also fraught with peril when illiquid and highly leveraged securities were involved. Recall that illiquidity and leverage sank Askin Capital Management in 1994 when its mortgage-backed security-laden hedge fund suffered huge losses. That lethal combination also led to the demise of Long-Term Capital Management in 1998 despite the fact that its models were developed by Nobel Prize–winning economists.

Valuation models tended to smooth returns and make asset prices appear less volatile—and cause agonizing reappraisals. Bear's Enhanced

Leverage Fund initially reported a 6.75 percent loss for April 2007, but later revised it down to an 18 percent drop. And models provide huge opportunities for self-delusion. Most valuation models for CDOs backed by subprime mortgages used house prices provided by the Office of Federal Housing Enterprise Oversight. But these prices were believed by most housing experts to significantly overstate market prices. So even without optimistic assumptions, the history used in CDO pricing models gave them an upward bias.

Bear's Research

Furthermore, Bear Stearns' Synthetic Securitized Product group went much further in calculating the fair value of various subprime mortgage-backed securities even when the market said otherwise. It concluded that the fair value of the ABX-HE BBB-06-02 index shown in Figure 3.11 was 90.14 on February 11, 2007, compared with the then-market price of 82.68, or 9 percent higher.

The Bear researchers, in reaching their numbers, used the very optimistic assumptions of flat house prices in 2007 and 3.5 percent annual rises in later years. They acknowledged that their models greatly under-forecast delinquencies and defaults on the loans backing the bonds in question, but still used those models to predict bond prices with only limited and optimistic adjustments. If Ralph Cioffi relied on Bear's researchers' models in running those two big Bear Stearns hedge funds that collapsed, their overly optimistic valuations may have been a big part of his problem.

The Cockroach Theory

Our great friend, daily newsletter author Dennis Gartman, espouses the cockroach theory. When you see one cockroach, you know many more are lurking. We prefer to quote the King in *Hamlet*: "When sorrows come, they come not single spies,/But in battalions!"

Either way, it was clear to me in late June 2007 that the Bear bust was not likely to be a one-off problem. As we wrote in our July 2007 *Insight*,

Many other outfits have huge subprime mortgage-backed securities positions through their involvement in originating and owning these now toxic waste instruments. The Bear troubles revealed a frighteningly close correlation between low-rated CDO tranches and higher-rated ones. And if we're right in our forecast of a 25 percent peak to trough decline in median single-family house prices nationwide, not only will the BBB tranches be history, but also the A and AA pieces. Bad performance is flowing and will turn into a flood.

Some still hope that the Bear Bust will be contained, but we doubt it. The seas of liquidity that were flooding into CDOs and other derivatives, junk bonds, CLOs, and other vehicles are ebbing fast. That will sink the housing market and eliminate the house appreciation that consumers have relied on in lieu of income growth to fund their robust spending. So the consumer-led economy will slip into recession, probably by year's end, and spread worldwide as the many export-led economies around the globe lose their American consumer buyers.

In the remainder of 2007 and in 2008, events did unfold pretty much in line with this forecast with the recession officially starting in December 2007. Incredibly, most forecasters and stockholders continued to deny that a major global financial crisis was under way and a worldwide recession was close behind. I outline these developments and the continual denials in Chapter 5.

Chapter 5

The Results of Denial

I t's incredible that after the subprime residential mortgage market started to collapse in earnest in February 2007, even as the woes spread rapidly to the rest of housing, and even as the crisis spread to Wall Street with the Bear Stearns bust in June of that year and threatened to sink the domestic and global economies, most forecasters remained in denial. In August 2008, eight months after the recession had actually started, the *Wall Street Journal*'s poll of 53 economists, excluding me, found that only about half believed the U.S. economy was in recession and that most expected real GDP to rise from the fourth quarter of 2007 to the fourth quarter of 2008 (it actually dropped 1.9 percent).

Meanwhile, investors, policy makers, regulators, and Wall Street leaders did not appear to understand the depth and breadth of the financial crisis. Every step of the way, they felt sure that the latest problem would be the last problem, that the latest bailout would solve all difficulties and no more would be required. They weren't really aware that it was a financial crisis driven by deleveraging. And the stock market, although a good measure of sentiment, was only a sideshow.

SEC Shortcomings

Perhaps the least credible of all the Washington players was the SEC. The agency's own Inspector General recently reported that the SEC staff in 2006 "identified precisely the types of risks that evolved into the subprime crisis in the United States less than one year later," but "did not exert influence over Bear Stearns to use this experience to add a meltdown of the subprime market to its risk scenarios, according to the *Wall Street Journal*." The report went on to state that the SEC "made no efforts" to require Bear Stearns to reduce its debt or raise money after spotting "numerous shortcomings" in the firm's risk management of mortgages and "missed opportunities" to force Bear Stearns management to address the difficulties. The SEC also allowed internal rather than external Bear auditors to perform "critical" work in assessing the firm's risk management, and found too close a relationship between Bear Stearns traders and risk managers who lacked the necessary skills to understand the risks.

The SEC also botched its later attempts to prop up financial stocks by prohibiting new short positions on 799 financial equities, a list that grew to about 1,000, and many more than its earlier list of 19 financial stocks. The SEC placed a number of nonfinancial outfits like IBM, pharmacy chain CVS, GM, and Ford on the list, as well as hedge funds Fortress and GLG, but missed GE with its huge financial arm as well as Credit Suisse. An embarrassed SEC then turned the listing job over to stock exchange operators NYSE Euronext and NASDAQ OMX Group.

Initially, the securities regulator also required hedge fund and money managers to disclose their short positions promptly, without realizing that that would publicize trading strategies and could disrupt markets as others emulated winning trades. So it backtracked and required prompt reporting of short positions to the SEC with public release two weeks later. The SEC also had to reverse its short sale directives to permit short selling for market making and hedging activities, both normal procedures.

Borodino

In a way, the haplessness of policy makers was to be expected since they were dealing with the massive and painful deleveraging of the household and financial sectors—the fundamental problems—with deteriorating confidence of consumers and investors spawning chaotic and unpredictable zigs and zags along the way. As in military battles, chance events and fluid conditions can change the course of history.

In 331 B.C. at the Battle of Gaugamela, Alexander the Great was outnumbered 250,000 to 40,000 by the Persians. When he threw a javelin at Darius III, the Persian king, he struck his chariot driver instead. Darius's army thought their king had been hit and fled, leaving Alexander the victor and conqueror of Persia. In *War and Peace*, Tolstoy describes the Battle of Borodino in which the battlefield was shifting so rapidly that by the time Napoleon's orders reached the front, they were irrelevant. Even with radio communications, similar conditions existed in the D-day landing at Normandy, according to the movie *The Longest Day*.

Investors, Too

And don't forget that investors and Wall Street leaders showed no better understanding of the causes and depths of the financial woes as they unfolded than did policy makers. Every nasty revelation, they concluded, would be the last and every Washington bailout would end all difficulties forever and ever.

In February 2007, huge British bank HSBC took a $1.8 billion write-down to cover soured subprime mortgages, as noted in Chapter 3. For many, that was the first indication that the subprime slime, as I dubbed it, was a problem and only then did subprime mortgage-related securities begin their collapse (as shown in Figure 3.11 in Chapter 3). And that was just the beginning of HSBC's subprime woes. Through the third quarter of 2009, the bank had taken $67 billion in impairment charges on its U.S. operations and was losing 52 percent on the sales of foreclosed properties, including write-downs on the unpaid loans. HSBC announced earlier in 2009 it would no longer make new U.S. consumer loans, except on credit cards.

Still, most observers saw no serious threats to the economy or even the overall housing industry in early 2007. After all, they argued, subprime mortgages may be growing but were still only 18 percent of the total market in 2006. And housing in aggregate may be volatile but it

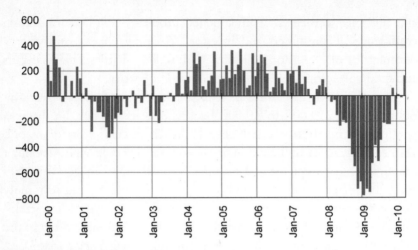

Figure 5.1 Payroll Employment (Thousands)
Data source: Bureau of Labor Statistics.

was still just 4.6 percent of the total economy on average. Furthermore, back in early 2007, the optimists—the overwhelming majority of fore-casters, security analysts, and investors—believed housing collapses were always precipitated by Fed tightening, and at that point, the Fed had completed its hikes in the federal funds rate from 1 percent to 5.25 percent, which brought it from extreme low levels back to a normal, but not constrictive, range (as seen in Figure 1.3 in Chapter 1). Besides, they also argued, mortgage rates hadn't risen much and any adverse effects were easily offset by looser lending standards.

The bulls also believed that housing was safe as long as employment gains persisted, and jobs were still being created in early 2007 (see Figure 5.1). They also looked for capital spending on equipment and structures as well as export growth to easily offset any weakness in housing. So investors shunted aside subprime mortgages problems, and after a brief nosedive in early 2007, stocks rose robustly—until June.

Bear Is the Bear

In that month, Bear Stearns revealed that its two big hedge funds with very long names were essentially bust because of bad bets on subprime mortgages, as discussed in Chapter 4.

The investor reaction was swift and severe. Stocks tanked (as seen in Figure 1.6 in Chapter 1), as did the junk bond market. That cut off leveraged buyouts (LBOs) by private equity firms that were financed by junk debt. The asset-backed commercial paper market virtually disappeared overnight and its interest rates leaped as investors suddenly distrusted the value of the subprime mortgage-related and other assets those borrowings were used to purchase. Derivatives based on subprime-related securities dropped like rocks (Figure 3.11). Pension funds, municipalities, and other investors from Australia to Europe to the United States were shocked—shocked!—to learn that the markets and the rating agencies were both downgrading their mortgage-backed securities, sometimes from high-grade to junk. Meanwhile, investors in leveraged loans and junk bonds sat on their hands with dismay.

On August 9, 2007, the Fed and other central banks responded to the crisis by pumping funds into banks and encouraging them to borrow from those lenders of last resort. The Fed cut the discount rate on August 17. And, the zeal for financial safety remained so great that on August 20, the three-month Treasury bill rate dropped to 2.51 percent interday, well below the earlier 5 percent level.

In reaction, the Fed cut both the discount and federal funds rates by 50 basis points on September 18, and investors breathed big sighs of relief and yelled, "Hooray! Hooray! The Fed has saved the day!" Stocks recovered and other depressed securities rallied, as exemplified by the AAA ABX index. Also, the spread between junk bonds and Treasurys, which had opened remarkably during the period of panic, closed considerably. The London Interbank Offered Rate (LIBOR), the rate at which U.S. banks lend to each other, leaped in August when banks didn't trust each other, much less customers, with loans. After the Fed rate cuts in September, however, LIBOR dropped but remained well above the federal funds rate that it normally hugs.

Lehman Brothers was able to sell $3 billion in investment-grade bonds. Rates on asset-backed commercial paper fell from lofty levels, and futures markets anticipated further cuts in the fed funds rate of more than 100 basis points by June 2008. Indeed, the euphoria and conviction that ease had solved all the problems of the world were so great that fears of financial collapse were replaced by worries about economic overheating and inflation as commodity prices continued to leap.

Table 5.1 Fed Ease and Business Cycle Peaks

Business Cycle Peak Dates	Effective Funds Peak	Months before/ after Business Cycle Peak
Q3 1957 (August)	October 1957	+2
Q2 1960 (April)	November 1959	−5
Q4 1969 (December)	August 1969	−4
Q4 1973 (November)	July 1974	+8
Q1 1980 (January)	April 1980	+3
Q3 1981 (July)	June 1981	−1
Q3 1990 (July)	March 1989	−16
Q1 2001 (March)	November 2000	−4
Q4 2007 (December)	July 2007	−5

Data sources: National Bureau for Economic Research and Federal Reserve.

Once again, Wall Street and investors exhibited tremendous denial of the deteriorating financial and economic climates. They preferred to view Fed ease as a boost to stocks, which reached their all-time high in October 2007, and the savior of the economy instead of proof that the economy was about to crater, as is almost always the case. Notice that the Fed normally cuts interest rates at the peak of the business cycle, give or take several months (Table 5.1). So the beginning of a Fed easing campaign signals that a recession is close at hand or already under way.

A Short Respite

So, in the course of the first nine months of 2007, investors first believed the subprime slime would be confined with no consequences for the rest of the economy. Then, as prime mortgages and the rest of housing plummeted, they maintained that the remainder of the economy and financial markets were still safe. Even the credit crisis that summer was assumed to be more than offset by Fed ease.

In fact, by September, some were suggesting that financial institutions had over-reserved for the unknown but clearly sinking values of collateralized debt obligations (CDOs) and other questionable securities, and would book profits when they were sold later at higher prices. The kitchen sink theory prevailed—the belief that institutions from mortgage lenders to Wall Street houses had thrown out everything bad, and then some. In reality, the cockroach theory prevailed—when you see one write-off, there are many more to come.

Another Downer

In late 2007, stocks again slid as financial institutions, led by Merrill Lynch and Citigroup, were forced to take huge write-downs on sub-prime mortgage-related securities. Banks are moneymaking machines, both figuratively and literally. The basic business of commercial banking is spread lending, borrowing at lower rates from depositors and lending at higher rates. As long as their loans are sound and they maintain depositor confidence, commercial banks can make attractive returns on their capital and pay healthy dividends to their shareholders.

But most publicly owned bank managements want rapid growth as well, and that means taking more risks and moving into other areas of finance such as asset management, corporate finance, proprietary trading, hedge funds, foreign lending, merchant banking, commodity trading, security brokerage, and so on. Many banks also exhibit herdlike instincts as they all rush into a new area of great profit promise and then all rush out when earnings prove disappointing.

This was true of consortium banks decades ago as a number of banks combined to set up a separate bank, usually operating overseas. Too many owners proved detrimental in most of those cases. Later, in the 1980s, many U.S. banks stampeded into Latin American loans only to be chased out in the 1990s when the finances of Mexico, Brazil, Argentina, and other countries there fell apart.

Land Development Loans

More recently, many big banks plunged into subprime mortgage securitization and investments only to get stuck when they were forced to determine realistic market values, as discussed earlier. A number, including smaller banks, mushroomed their lending for construction and land development. The increase from 5.0 percent of total loans and leases in 2002 to 8.1 percent five years later may not seem like a big deal, but bear in mind that these loans can be lethal in times of falling house prices.

The value of residential land is simply the difference between what a buyer will pay for the combined land and the house sitting on it and the cost of reproducing the house. Since construction costs aren't very volatile over time, the cyclical swings in house prices really amount to even bigger swings in land prices. If a house costs $500,000 to build and a buyer is willing to pay $1 million for the house and land, he's valuing the land at $500,000. A 20 percent drop in the value of the package would depress the land value by $200,000, or 40 percent, assuming building costs don't change.

This explains why many builders dumped land inventories or walked away from land options when house prices collapsed. This also explains why bank loans on land are vulnerable when prices drop.

No Trust

By late 2007, write-downs and the realization that more were coming on securities of unknown and perhaps unknowable value became so great that no financial institution trusted any other, especially highly leveraged and subprime-drenched Bear Stearns. Bear's asset-to-capital ratio was about 32 when its two hedge funds collapsed in June 2007, and its senior management in its infinite wisdom kept the ratio close to that level right to the end. But much of the borrowing to support those assets was overnight money, and lenders refused to renew their loans. So Bear suffered a liquidity crisis, a run on the bank. That forced the Fed to step in to prevent the collapse in the financial sector, to the tune of $29 billion in Fed money to guarantee Bear's securities in its shotgun marriage with JPMorgan Chase bank in March 2008, discussed in Chapter 4.

Then the frightened Fed extended access to its discount window beyond commercial banks to investment banks, in effect guaranteeing that another run on the banks couldn't occur. "That's it!" yelled Wall Street. "The Fed has saved us and it's clear sailing ahead." Stocks, as usual, jumped as euphoria returned to investors.

But while the Fed can insure liquidity by accepting any and all securities as collateral for loans, that doesn't guarantee solvency—a positive net worth when a firm's assets and liabilities are marked to market. All the Fed actions as of mid-2008 to pump money into the system—including expanding open-market operations, lowering the rate on discount-window loans to banks, creating the Term Auction Facility and the Term Securities Lending Facilities, opening the discount window to securities dealers, lending money to prevent the Bear Stearns bankruptcy, and extending swap lines to European and Swiss central banks—didn't do that. And solvency insures happiness, as Charles Dickens explained in *David Copperfield*: "Annual income 20 pounds, annual expenditure 19 pounds 19 shillings and six pence, result happiness. Annual income 20 pounds, annual expenditure 20 pounds and six pence, result misery."

The Myth of May

By May 2008, that reality became painfully obvious, especially for Fannie Mae and Freddie Mac. Collapsing house prices racked up huge losses for the pair. Furthermore, it became more and more obvious that their regulatory capital vastly overstated reality, not only compared to market capitalization (see Figure 5.2) but also when compared with standard accounting measures. After accounting for all the accounting legerdemain, Fannie and Freddie probably had negative asset values of $50 billion or more each.

Their stocks tanked and the interest rate spreads between their securities jumped as investors, especially foreigners who owned lots of them, dumped them in favor of Treasurys. So on July 13, a federal bailout plan was announced—only the first of many, as it later turned out. The Treasury would lend the pair as much as needed, up from an earlier limit of $2.75 billion each, and could also buy their equity. In addition, the Fed could lend to both "should such lending prove necessary."

Statements by Fed Chairman Bernanke and others suggested that the common and preferred shareholders of Fannie and Freddie and perhaps subordinated debt holders would be wiped out, and their stock prices dropped further. Nevertheless, investors overall were pleased with yet

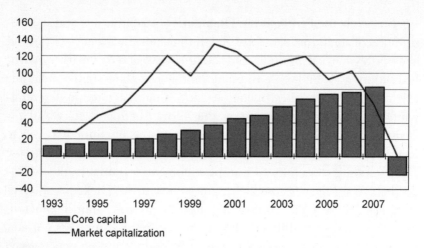

Figure 5.2   Fannie Mae and Freddie Mac Core Capital and Market Capitalization
($ Billion)
All points are for the end of the period.
Data source: Federal Housing Finance Administration.

another government bailout. Fannie and Freddie spreads versus Treasurys initially narrowed and the stock market rallied.

Underestimates

While the financial structure was unraveling, Wall Street leaders and government officials continually underestimated the problems. Despite nonstop write-downs and capital raising, Merrill Lynch CEO John Thain, who arrived in November 2007, consistently said the firm didn't need to raise more, as documented in Chapter 1. Apparently he finally decided otherwise when he arranged a hasty shotgun marriage with Bank of America on September 15, 2008. And Treasury Secretary Henry Paulson, the architect and czar of the Bush administration's bailout plan, also consistently underestimated financial woes, at least publicly, until late in the game. To his credit, however, the Treasury Secretary in late 2007 had his staff plan for potential disaster scenarios, including one involving the purchase of distressed assets from financial institutions. It was known as "break the glass," an apparent reference to breaking the glass in a fire alarm box to report a fire.

Down, But No Panic

Stockholders also had a relatively relaxed attitude toward the growing financial storm. Sure, the S&P 500 was down 20 percent from its October 2007 peak through early August 2008, but that barely met the popular definition of a bear market and wasn't huge compared to many past declines associated with recessions.

The bear market gathered steam after the weekend of September 13–14, 2008, when Lehman filed for bankruptcy, Fannie and Freddie went into conservatorship, AIG was bailed out by the Fed, and the run on money market funds became scary. In my view, policy makers, regulators, financial firm managements, and investors have failed to recognize that the household and financial sectors had mounted massive buildups in leverage in the preceding three decades (as seen in Figure 4.7 in Chapter 4).

The household sector did so by slashing down payments on houses and increased borrowing on credit cards, auto loans, student loans, and home equity loans. Borrowing in the private financial sector mushroomed with the creation of huge off-balance-sheet vehicles and skyrocketing derivatives. Major U.S. investment banks' combined assets jumped from under $2 trillion in 2003 to over $4 trillion in late 2007, and their leverage ratios rose by 50 percent in that time. Painful deleveraging was beginning in 2008, and it's far from being completed.

Not Prepared

If financial institution managements had understood the extent of their overleveraging, then write-downs, restructuring, and mergers would have come much earlier and perhaps much less painfully. If homeowners had comprehended their plight, the decline in house prices might have been swifter, but the excess inventories would be eliminated by 2015. If investors believed what I think is the eventual extent of deleveraging, stocks would probably have declined more sharply but reached a very solid bottom.

And if Washington had agreed with me, a master bailout plan would be in place and implemented rather than the ad hoc responses that occurred. Sure, the Bush administration and many in Congress believed in deregulation and free markets, and were reluctant to intervene. But painful deleveraging resulted in the worst financial crisis since the 1930s. In a sense, it may involve even greater risks than back then. In the Roaring Twenties, no one expected a government bailout if they took on excessive financial leverage and failed. Furthermore, financial institutions then were often owned by their senior managements, so firm risks and losses were personal risks and losses as well. Their actions were tempered by lots of fear.

Because of government regulation of securities markets in reaction to the Depression, a much more active Fed, the FDIC, and the bailouts of Lockheed in 1971, Chrysler in 1979, the savings and loans in the early 1990s, the airlines after 9/11, and so forth, players today have come to expect government help in times of financial crisis and, therefore, take great risks. Also, senior officials are managers, not the owners, of firms and get big payoffs even for failure.

The situation today is known as *moral hazard*, meaning that insurance against risks encourages more risk taking. I've described it more graphically by saying that raising the safety net encourages the circus daredevil to climb to yet a higher perch from which to take that half-mile dive into a wet sponge. Also, many financial houses didn't worry much about increased risks since they securitized questionable securities and sold them to investors. Only when the music stopped and they were stuck with not-yet-sold garbage did they begin to realize the extent of their exposure. That's far different from Jimmy Stewart's Bailey Building & Loan in *It's a Wonderful Life*, which made mortgage loans only to creditworthy borrowers since it would hold them to maturity.

What a Summer!

Despite the Fannie Mae and Freddie Mac rescue plan in July 2008, investors still did not believe the government was backing them 100 percent since the prospects of further huge losses as house prices fell threatened their solvency. Their stocks continued to fall and foreign investors continued to avoid their securities. The Bank of China dumped $4.6 billion of the $17.3 billion it held on June 30, which in turn was

$6 billion lower than at the end of 2007. In the week ending September 3, foreign central banks sold $9.8 billion in Fannie, Freddie, and other U.S. government agency securities. Even after the subsequent Fannie and Freddie rescue plan, Treasury Undersecretary David McCormick made a very unusual call to large Japanese investors to explain the plan and keep them from defecting from their holdings of about $100 billion in Fannie and Freddie securities.

Earlier, Fannie said it was cutting back its purchase of mortgages to preserve capital, a dire threat to the mortgage market where U.S. agencies were now the only game in town. After their September 7, 2008, seizure by the government, James B. Lockhart (the director of their regulator, the Federal Housing Finance Agency) told Congress that in August, the pair couldn't raise capital in any "meaningful size," even at their increasing borrowing costs. While rating agencies were slashing their ratings and foreign borrowers stopped buying their debt, their only alternative to financing from the Treasury was dumping of their mortgage assets in the already collapsing market.

The second Fannie and Freddie rescue plan involved the Treasury acquiring $1 billion in preferred stock in each company, warrants giving the government 79.9 percent ownership in each company with 10 percent dividends. The government also pledged up to $200 billion each to help them deal with their mushrooming mortgage delinquencies. When the two firms were put under conservatorship, the Federal Housing Finance Agency (FHFA) was given management control. Holders of stock and $36 billion in preferred stock were decimated but senior debt holders were backed by the government. That's not surprising since their $1.6 trillion in debt was so widely held, especially by foreigners. With the second Treasury bailout, the spreads between Fannie and Freddie senior debt and Treasury interest rates narrowed.

The next act in the Fannie and Freddie play took place in December 2009 when these two government-sponsored enterprises (GSEs) were granted unlimited draws on the Treasury for the next three years, up from the previous limits of $200 billion each. That set the Treasury up to inject money each quarter into Fannie and Freddie if revenues aren't big enough to cover anticipated losses. And rising delinquencies indicate continuing infusions. At the end of January 2010, 4.0 percent of single-family mortgages at Freddie were at least 90 days past due or in foreclosure, compared with 2.0 percent a year earlier. At Fannie, 5.3 percent were 90 days overdue in November 2009, up from 2.1 percent a year earlier.

Lehman Lurches

The threat of insolvency, not illiquidity, sank Fannie and Freddie. The same was true of Lehman, which had no liquidity problems since it had access to the Fed's discount window along with other investment banks after Bear Stearns' run-on-the-bank demise in March 2008, as noted earlier. Investors, however, did not comprehend the depth of Lehman's problems as they figured the government moves in response to Bear's collapse solved Wall Street's problem.

In April 2008, Lehman issued $4 billion in convertible preferred shares, more than planned because of robust demand. And the firm ran a 32-to-1 leverage ratio earlier that year compared to 24-to-1 at Goldman Sachs. In 2003, Lehman's holdings of Treasurys and mortgage- and other asset-backed securities were about equal; by 2006, Treasury holdings were about the same but asset-backed positions had tripled. Nevertheless, storm clouds were gathering as asset managers worried about counterparty risk. Still, Lehman only slowly prepared a plan to cut its leverage by selling its attractive asset management business. Its attempt to spin off $25 to $30 billion in commercial real estate assets into a separate company where they wouldn't be marked to market was not well received. Commercial real estate dominated Lehman's mortgage-related asset holdings and was 1.7 times its common equity. Some believed that the market value of those assets, 85 percent of original numbers according to Lehman, was 35 percent overstated.

In any event, time overran Lehman and the government refused to provide financial backing to potential buyers as it had with Bear Stearns' takeover by JPMorgan Chase. So potential buyers Barclay's, Bank of America, and the Korean Development Bank departed. Flack received in the wake of the Bear bailout and the abandonment of moral hazard concerns pressured Washington to reverse gears and let Lehman go. Also, Treasury Secretary Paulson reasoned that unlike the sudden collapse of Bear, markets had plenty of time to prepare for Lehman's demise. And he observed that unlike Bear, Lehman had access to the Fed's discount window.

Bankruptcy

So Lehman filed for bankruptcy on September 15, 2008, and with $639 billion in assets, it was the nation's biggest bankruptcy by a factor of six. That wiped out not only stockholders but also bondholders, who had been protected in the Bear Stearns bailout. Barclay's bought Lehman's North American business for $1.75 billion, including most of its employees, franchise technology, and clients, but not its toxic waste assets and liabilities. In contrast, in early 2007, Lehman had a stock market capitalization of $45 billion. Lehman's asset management business was sold ultimately to employees. Meanwhile, Japanese broker Nomura bought Lehman's Asia Pacific business for $225 million and its European and Middle East operations for two, count 'em, two dollars!

As would be expected, Lehman was less than candid in describing its financial woes as it careened toward disaster. It quietly borrowed $30 billion from the Fed and $12 billion from the European Central Bank (ECB) to avoid broadcasting its distress. On September 10, one day after the firm figured it needed at least $3 billion in new capital, an outside analyst on a conference call asked if Lehman needed to raise $4 billion. CFO Ian Lowitt responded, "We don't feel that we need to raise that extra amount." The usual federal probe followed, investigating whether Lehman overvalued its assets, misled investors about its financial health in conjunction with its June 2008 $6 billion stock offering and in its September 10 conference call, and improperly moved $8 billion from its London offices to New York just before filing for bankruptcy. The following April, former Lehman CEO Richard Fuld Jr., who was paid about $400 million from 2000 until Lehman folded, told ex-employees, "I spent too much time out of the office with clients and trusted other people to manage the risk."

In early 2010, a bankruptcy examiner's report said Lehman's financial statements were "materially misleading" and that its senior executives engaged in "actionable balance sheet manipulation." The CEO and three CFOs breached their "fiduciary duty" to disclose important facts about the firm's financial condition, especially Repo 105 accounting. In this maneuver, Lehman treated assets as having been sold to shrink its balance sheet when, in fact, they were only collateral for short-term loans. No U.S. law firm would bless the deals, so Lehman moved the securities to its European operations and used an English law firm for a legal opinion on the transactions. The bankruptcy examiner said Lehman CEO Fuld was "at least grossly negligent for failing to insure" that Lehman filed correct financial statements about its accounting for the transactions.

The SEC in early 2010 admitted that it wasn't aware of the Repo 105 accounting even though it had people in Lehman's offices at the time. Lehman's outside auditor and top brass also ignored warnings in a May 2008 letter from Matthew Lee, a Lehman senior vice president. He wrote that Lehman wasn't pricing tens of billions of dollars of illiquid assets in a "fully realistic or reasonable way." Also, in a June interview with Lehman's outside auditor he questioned the Repo 105 accounting.

Winners in the Lehman collapse are few but they include the 28 law firms, financial advisers, and consultants who are unraveling the mess. Between September 15, 2008, and the end of July 2009, they were paid $568.7 million in fees and expense reimbursements. Estimates put the final costs between $800 million and $1.4 billion.

Fallout

The speed of Lehman's collapse and piecemeal sale was as rapid as the fallout. Hedge funds that used Lehman as a prime broker worried about retrieving their assets and pulled money out of Morgan Stanley and Goldman Sachs, the two remaining big investment banks, just to be safe.

Freddie was concerned about repayment of a $1.7 billion loan to Lehman that was overdue, as was the interest. Probably in response to this Lehman fallout, Fannie began to require some banks to speed up the transfer of mortgage payments to investors in mortgage-backed securities that were guaranteed by Fannie. This, of course, reduced their cash and enhanced the risks of further bank problems.

The Norwegian government pension fund, which had over $800 billion in Lehman's stock and bonds, lost a bundle. And with the collapse in Lehman bond values, investors worried that others would follow. Also,

Figure 5.3 Moody's Seasoned Baa Corporate Bond Index, annual percent yield
Data source: Federal Reserve.

hedge funds and others that had done profitable credit default swaps
(CDSs) with Lehman fretted over collecting their money. Furthermore,
worried that other securities firms were vulnerable, these counterparties
rushed to buy CDSs on them, skyrocketing the costs. So there was a rush
to buy credit default swaps in that massive $62 trillion market, spiking
costs as well as corporate bond yields (see Figure 5.3). Swedish banks were
troubled because their collateral on loans to Lehman included high-risk
loans on real estate projects under construction. But the really big losers
from Lehman's demise were the money market funds and AIG.

Money Market Massacre

Bruce Bent says he invented money market funds in 1970 and preached
ironclad safety for these funds' investments. On his firm's web site, he
says that many have "lost sight of the purpose of a money market fund"
in their "foolhardy quest for a few extra basis points" while his company,
Reserve Management, believes cash funds are "definitely not money to
take risks with." I certainly agree that money market funds should be as
safe as Treasurys, and years ago opened and still maintain government
securities-only money market funds for myself and my family.

Sadly, in his quest for more money to manage, Bent broke his own standards. In 2006, his $63 billion Reserve Primary Fund prospectus was changed to include riskier commercial paper. Then on September 16, 2008, the fund announced that its net asset value had fallen below $1 per share, it had "broken the buck," because of $785 million in Lehman commercial paper and other securities that had to be written down to zero. This reduced the per-share value to 97 cents, the first breaking of the buck since the Orange County, California, bankruptcy in 1994. Since then, fund managers have injected capital into any troubled funds to make investors whole.

The S&P dropped Reserve's rating from AAA to its lowest level and already-nervous investors fled. That day, and the day before in the wake of the Lehman bankruptcy, large investors withdrew $40 billion from the fund and another run on the bank ensued. On September 17, $79 billion fled money market funds that total $3.4 trillion. To stop the run, two days later the government said it would insure money market funds for the first time, but only investments made through September 29. It was financed by the Treasury but supported by fees from the funds. Also, the Fed essentially lent the money market funds $230 billion through banks to offset illiquid asset-backed securities.

Meanwhile, investors had trouble getting their money out of Reserve Primary Fund because many of its remaining assets were in commercial paper selling at huge discounts. There was no cap on this Treasury coverage, which ran for three months. Simultaneously, the Fed moved to aid the money market funds and the corporations whose commercial paper they held by lending money to banks that bought those assets from desperate money market fund sellers and guaranteeing against any defaults by the industrial company issuers. The Fed financed $150 billion in two weeks but frozen credit markets forced it to move further to lend directly to nonfinancial businesses, $350 billion by January 2009.

This was only a piece of what later became known as *quantitative easing*. Traditional Federal Reserve stimulus by reducing interest rates (as seen in Figure 1.3 in Chapter 1) hadn't worked. The central bank was pushing on a string, locked in a Keynesian liquidity trap when oceans of bank liquidity didn't spur loans and business activity. So, direct injections of money were needed to at least stabilize financial markets. Later, the FDIC and others in Washington increased coverage on FDIC-insured deposits to $250,000. These moves allayed depositors' fears but increased moral hazard by encouraging them to leave money in shaky financial institutions.

As for Bruce Bent, he and his co-CEO son, Bruce Bent II, are charged with fraud by the SEC for "engaging in a systematic campaign to deceive the investing public into believing that the Primary Fund—their flagship money market fund—was safe and secure despite its substantial Lehman holdings."

Bye-Bye, Merrill Lynch

While Lehman was filing for bankruptcy, Merrill Lynch's John Thain arranged a hasty shotgun marriage with Bank of America, as noted earlier. He must have finally, *finally* concluded that the firm didn't have enough capital to withstand the deepening financial crisis. At the $44 billion sale price, Merrill was valued at two-thirds of its market capitalization of a year earlier and half its peak value in early 2007. Its stock, along with most financial shares, had fallen about 90 percent since then. Still, the merger price, $29 per share, was well above the $17.05 price right before the merger.

Thain worked hard to raise capital and get rid of bad assets. In July 2008, he sold $30.6 billion to private equity firm Lone Star at 22 cents on the dollar, and even then, financed 75 percent of the deal to get it done. He also sold Merrill's 20 percent holding in financial information giant Bloomberg, another example of selling the best and keeping the rest when that's all the market will buy, except at huge discounts.

Aside from his $9.7 million exit package, Thain was probably willing to put the deal together in 48 hours because he was a newcomer, having been at Merrill less than one year. I was Merrill's first chief economist from 1967 to 1971, as mentioned in Chapter 1. The company's culture may have changed considerably since then, but if it's anything like what I knew, it was so centered on loyalty that it would have been extremely difficult for a Merrill Lynch veteran to sell the firm.

Merrill Lynch was founded by Charlie Merrill in 1914, and two years later he was joined by Winthrop H. Smith, straight out of Amherst College, which Merrill had attended, as had I. Smith eventually ran

Merrill Lynch, Pierce, Fenner and Smith. His son was Winthrop H. Smith Jr., a former vice chairman of Merrill Lynch. On December 5, 2008, he addressed the special stockholders' meeting to approve the sale of the firm to Bank of America. Here are a few excerpts from his speech:

> Merrill Lynch to so many of us was Mother Merrill, and it is so sad that the CEO who preceded John Thain and the Board of Directors had no understanding of what that meant.... We had a swagger, and we were damn proud to be part of 'The Thundering Herd.'... But most of all, we were proud of our principles that we inherited from Charlie Merrill.... We were about character, spirit, leadership, ethics, and pride.
>
> Today did not have to come.... Today is not the result of the subprime mess or synthetic CDOs. They are the symptoms. This is the story of failed leadership and the failure of a Board of Directors to understand what was happening to this great company, and its failure to take action soon enough. I stand here today and say shame to both the current as well as the former Directors who allowed this former CEO to wreak havoc on this great company. Shame on them for allowing this former CEO to consciously and openly disparage Mother Merrill, throw our founding principles down a flight of stairs, and tear out the soul of the firm.
>
> Shame, shame, shame for allowing one man to consciously unwind a culture and rip out the soul of this great firm. Shame on them for allowing [Stan O'Neal] to retire with a $160 million retirement package and shame on them for not resigning themselves.
>
> Where is the accountability? No wonder that the Main Street that learned to trust Merrill Lynch in the 1940s has lost faith in Wall Street in 2008. Merrill Lynch is not alone in this. But in the past, Merrill Lynch rose above the crowd and distanced itself from the greed that brought others down. Our principled leaders steered us through many challenges, and we emerged stronger because of them.

In contrast to Thain, the many years that Richard Fuld Jr. served as Lehman's CEO is cited as a big reason why he hesitated so long in deleveraging the firm and selling the saleable pieces that bankruptcy became the only option. His Lehman shares were worth $993.5 million in February 2007 when the stock peaked at $86.18 per share. In late

2008, it traded at 33 cents, and his wife auctioned off a valuable modern art collection.

AIG

American International Group (AIG), one of the world's largest insurance companies, was also sunk by the tidal waves engulfing the financial sector after Lehman failed. Apparently, its insurance units are sound, and tight regulation by various governmental bodies keeps them that way. But a noninsurance unit based in London, AIG Financial Products, was heavily involved in writing credit default swaps (CDSs) to protect clients from losses on $294 billion in corporate debt, $141 billion in European residential mortgages, and $78 billion in collateralized debt obligations (CDOs), pools of securities that often contained subprime mortgage-backed securities.

This business was unusual and risky for an insurer, but AIG was known for aggressive business behavior. Accounting irregularities several years earlier led to a $1.64 billion settlement with authorities and the departures in 2005 of Hank Greenberg, the company's long-time CEO who built the business and set the tone. Greenberg and three AIG executives later settled for $115 million a 2002 lawsuit brought by shareholders on behalf of the company for diverting AIG money to another firm.

AIG relied on models developed by a Wharton and later Yale economist to price the CDSs it sold. In December 2007, AIG's CEO told investors worried about CDS exposure that those models were "very reliable" and gave the firm "a very high level of comfort." In a June 2006 SEC filing, AIG wrote that the CDSs it was selling could never have enough defaults to make any payout more than "remote, even in severe recessionary market scenarios." The firm's CDS exposure leaped to $80 billion in early 2006 when AIG stopped selling that credit protection because of declining underwriting standards on subprime mortgages.

Models Failed

Nevertheless, those models failed to take into account the write-downs of the underlying securities and the collateral the firm had to deliver to CDS buyers as the value of those contracts rose and AIG's corporate debt rating fell. That collateral ultimately jumped to $50 billion. It was revealed later that AIG was aware of these risks, and a federal criminal probe was launched to determine whether senior executives misled investors and the firm's outside auditor. The probe was dropped later.

In any event, Lehman's collapse caused CDS costs to mushroom, and AIG's involvement turned from very lucrative to huge losses. AIG Financial Products' losses reached $25 billion at the end of the second quarter of 2008 and dominated the $18 billion loss for the parent company in that and two previous quarters.

These problems plus rating downgrades and a tanking stock made the cost of replenishing capital much more expensive and difficult at any price. With rating downgrades, its bonds fell to junk levels. AIG had assets in excess of liabilities by $78 billion, but most of them were tied up in insurance subsidiaries and unavailable to cover CDS losses. Furthermore, many of its noninsurance assets were illiquid. And AIG, as an insurer, lacked access to the Fed's discount window. So AIG faced both a liquidity and a solvency crisis.

Only $80 Billion Needed

The firm needed $80 billion to avoid bankruptcy, so it accepted an $85 billion loan from the Fed as the only other alternative on September 16, 2008. In what became a standard bailout formula, the government in effect got a 79.9 percent equity stake in the company in warrants and the CEO was tossed out. The initial $85 billion government loan later rose to a bailout package of $123 billion, as noted earlier. With the high cost of government borrowing, AIG was under the gun to delever and sell assets to reduce interest costs and subsequently sold its crown jewel insurance units. In early 2010, the United Kingdom's Prudential PLC tried but failed to buy Asia-oriented American International Insurance, while Met Life purchased Alico, an AIG insurer oriented toward Japan but with business in more than 50 other countries.

Failure to incorporate the proper variables was lethal to AIG as well as to rating agency models, as discussed in Chapter 3. But even if properly specified, models of serious economic value are inherently flawed, as was the case with Long-Term Capital Management. If a model worked well enough to generate sizable and consistent profits, its developers would greatly expand its use and others would pile in as the good news leaked out, regardless of rigorous attempts to keep the models secret. That would alter the data universe on which the model was based and ruin its effectiveness.

That's what caused the stock market crash of 1987. Models assured institutional investors they could effectively utilize portfolio insurance. The theory was that they could continue to hold full portfolios of stock regardless of how overpriced they might be, because if equities started to fall, they could systematically sell them to lock in profits. The problem was that many, many investors were using the same models that selling compounded rapidly and the stock market fell 22 percent in one day, October 12, 1987.

Freeze Up

The credit markets were in disarray starting in August 2007, but with the bailout of Fannie and Freddie, Lehman's demise, Merrill Lynch's shotgun wedding with Bank of America, AIG's bailout, and the run on money market funds all coming in the first half of September 2008, short-term lending markets virtually froze up. Central banks vigorously pumped money into banks.

At mid-month, the Fed added $50 billion in repurchase agreements, the European Central Bank pumped in an extra $43 billion, the Bank of England added $9 billion, and the Bank of Japan, $14 billion. Then a few days later, the Fed added $180 billion to currency swap lines with foreign central banks, for a total of $247 billion, to give them plenty of bucks to meet vigorous demand abroad for greenbacks. Later, it increased those swap lines to $620 billion and then removed limits with major foreign central banks. It also added a record total of $105 billion in temporary reserves to the U.S. money markets while the ECB put in an additional $25 billion, the Bank of England another $45 billion, and the Bank of Japan a further $24 billion.

Later in that month, the Fed further increased currency swaps to $290 billion while the Reserve Bank of Australia put out $10 billion in repos and the Bank of Japan injected $30 billion. Furthermore, the Fed said it would accept riskier securities, even equities, as collateral for loans.

Won't Drink

Despite the flood of money provided by the central banks, the financial institutional horses didn't want to drink the central banks' water. Banks didn't trust each other with loans, much less customers, as witnessed by the high LIBOR rates, as they and investors rushed to the safety of Treasurys. By mid-September 2008, the overnight LIBOR rate leaped to 6.4 percent while Treasury bill yields several times that month actually fell below zero as panicked investors paid for the privilege of owning government securities. Some money market funds that invest only in government debt stopped taking new money since they couldn't find enough Treasurys to buy, and the low yields on what was available would dilute existing shareholders. In Russia, Switzerland, and elsewhere, stock trading was suspended temporarily to try to break the free fall. The commercial paper market broke down as buyers abandoned even one-day maturities.

In the week ending September 17, the commercial paper market shrank by $52.1 billion, and by $61 billion in the following week, while yields skyrocketed. Yields on one-day maturity asset-backed commercial paper leaped to the 5 to 8 percent range on September 17, from 2.15 to 3.5 percent two days earlier. The crisis in money market funds drastically curtailed the normally heavy purchases of commercial paper. In fact, they were being sold instead to cash out fleeing money market investors.

All the turmoil pushed the prices of exchange-traded funds (ETFs) significantly apart from underlying values that they normally track closely. The SEC limits on short selling also disrupted some ETFs that engage in that practice. Meanwhile, companies that had credit lines with banks were tapping them and hoarding the cash as precautions against tightening credit and more bank failures. GM announced that it would draw down the remaining $3.5 billion of a $4.5 billion credit line. The Federal Reserve's quarterly survey conducted in July found that 60 percent of U.S. banks had tightened their standards on loans to midsize and large companies in the previous three months.

Crisis Rates

Yields on bonds issued by financial companies on September 17, probably the worst day of the month-long crisis, hit a record high of 6 percentage points over Treasurys. The spreads between Treasurys and investment-grade corporate bonds jumped to more than 4 percentage points and hit 6.4 percentage points on October 1, while junk bonds saw 9-point spreads that ultimately rose to 19 points. And as municipal debt investors jumped ship in favor of taxable but safe Treasurys, yields on many tax-free municipal money market funds jumped to over 5 percent, far above Treasury yields. Normally, of course, municipal bonds yield less than taxable securities because of their tax-free nature.

Some frightened investors ran to gold as well as Treasurys. Indeed, the U.S. Mint ran out of American Buffalo one-ounce gold coins and temporarily halted sales until more could be made. It earlier suspended sales of the one-ounce American Eagle coin because of short supplies.

Reaction

With all this financial chaos, including a possible massive run on money market funds by individual investors, Washington was forced into further action. On September 18, word leaked out of a massive bailout plan and it was announced the next day. The guts of the plan was the Treasury's $700 billion Troubled Asset Relief Program that was supposed to buy troubled mortgages and mortgage-related securities from financial institutions, but was used to inject money directly into banks. The bailout bill also allowed the Fed to pay interest on bank reserves. Then the FDIC guaranteed new debt of almost all U.S. banks. Also on September 18, the SEC announced its temporary ban on short sales of financial stocks, as discussed earlier. Investors yelled, "Hurrah!" and stocks, as usual, leaped.

All these piecemeal and forced bailouts by Washington made clear the misunderstanding of the size of the financial crisis, the absence of a plan for dealing with it, and the lack of coordination among regulators, the Fed, the administration, and Congress. The same was true of the stress tests of the 19 largest financial institutions that were completed in May 2009. The October 2008 bank rescue by the Fed and Treasury forced all major financial institutions to take Troubled Asset Relief Program (TARP) money to avoid distinguishing the bad from the good. Of course, investors soon realized that neither Citigroup nor Bank of America was adequately capitalized to absorb prospective losses. And the stress tests, which didn't impose very stressful scenarios, made that publicly clear.

Faced with collapsing stocks and uncertainty over funding, Morgan Stanley and Goldman Sachs, the last two major investment banks, on September 21 decided to convert to traditional bank holding companies. They also probably figured that now that investment banks have the same access to the Fed's discount window as commercial banks, they would be regulated like commercial banks. So why not gain the advantage of funding through deposits? Indeed, since the opening of the discount window after Bear Stearns' collapse, Fed officials were stationed in the major investment banks.

Effortless Transfers

With almost effortless Internet transfer of funds magnified by investors' financial fears, bank deposits became very fickle. Depositor bank runs sank mortgage lender IndyMac as depositors withdrew $1.3 billion in late June and early July 2008. Similarly, depositors pulled $16.7 billion from Washington Mutual in a 10-day period in September, leaving the savings and loan in "an unsafe and unsound condition to transact business," according to the Office of Thrift Supervision that took it over, as I discuss later.

Then the U.K. nationalized mortgage lender Bradford & Bingley (B&B) sold its deposits and branches to Spanish bank Santander after a run on B&B. The government was left with $92 billion in mortgages and other loans. The firm had expanded in recent years in loans to rental apartment owners, an earlier booming area in the United Kingdom. But then B&B's lenders withdrew as property owners fell behind on mortgage payments in a softening market. Also, 20 percent of B&B's loans have little borrower documentation.

Note that all these bank runs occurred despite deposit insurance in the United States and the United Kingdom. Apparently, depositors didn't want to risk delays in getting their money back. Run now and let the regulators pick up the pieces later, seemed to be the sentiment.

Lower Leverage

Furthermore, the leverage of investment banks was two or three times the 10 to 12 ratios of commercial banks, so Morgan Stanley and Goldman needed to slash their leverage and profits as they converted to commercial bank status over the following two years and were faced with reserve requirements. And profits would be further depressed by the elimination of off-balance-sheet vehicles, huge fees from subprime securitization, and other lucrative activities that drove Wall Street earnings to unbelievable heights in recent years.

Boutique investment banks, private equity firms, and similar institutions will no doubt continue to exist and in some cases thrive. But the bloom of the big investment banks, if not off the rose itself, is gone and the best and the brightest from business schools will need to find another activity in which to get rich quick.

The swing of the cycle was amazing to watch. When I was at Merrill Lynch from 1967 to 1971, the firm considered itself a retail brokerage house and everything else—government and corporate bonds, commodities, investment banking, even OTC stock trading—was there to aid the broker selling listed stocks to individual investors. Merrill didn't even have an asset management business, which it considered a conflict of interest.

Bank Reign

In any event, today the commercial banks with their deposit bases and government protection are taking over in the financial arena. Note that only two days after Goldman decided to become a bank holding company—and a week after the Washington bailout announcement—cagey ol' Warren Buffett made his $5 billion investment in that firm with $5 billion more in warrants. And more recently, Mitsubishi UFJ acquired 21 percent of Morgan Stanley for $9 billion. Then, Buffett used the same formula to invest in GE—$3 billion in a perpetual preferred stock yielding 10 percent and warrants to buy $3 billion in common stock at a discount, which gave him an instant $300 million profit.

The 1933 Glass–Steagall Act separated commercial banking, investment banking, and insurance since Congress wanted to keep depositor money safe from risky investment banking activities. That Act was gradually chipped away in the 1980s and 1990s and finally and formally eliminated in 1999. Are we going back to the wild and woolly pre-Glass-Steagall days as the distinction between commercial and investment banks disappears? Probably not, at least for some years, since the increased regulation that is bound to result from the ongoing financial crises will be considerable and rigorous. The Volcker Rule, proposed by former Fed Chairman Paul Volcker in 2010, would separate commercial banking from proprietary trading and other risk activities, but the financial regulation bill that contains it has not yet been enacted by Congress as of this writing.

Washington Mutual

Washington Mutual (WaMu) was sunk by a bank run despite federal deposit insurance, as mentioned earlier. That distressed savings and loan had $300 billion in assets and 2,200 branches. But $50 billion of its assets were in largely subprime, no-doc ARMs. It tried to find a private buyer, including private equity firm TPG, which led a $7 billion infusion at WaMu in April 2008 and therefore had a stake to protect. The biggest bank failure in U.S. history by far on September 25 threatened the FDIC's $45 billion in assets, already strained by a $9 billion hit earlier that year when IndyMac failed. So the FDIC arranged a quick sale of WaMu's assets to JPMorgan Chase for $1.9 billion, leaving the holding company in FDIC hands and stockholders, bondholders, and TPG sucking wind.

Despite FDIC backing, WaMu's problem was liquidity as well as solvency. JPMorgan Chase, which in March 2008 offered $7 billion to $9 billion for the firm, said it would write off $31 billion of bad loans. WaMu concentrated on toxic adjustable-rate mortgages (ARMs), subprime loans, and home equity loans.

Wachovia was next in the seemingly never-ending string of financial firm failures and shotgun weddings. In October 2008, that acquisition-minded bank, which bought Golden West in May 2006, right at the peak of the housing bubble, was itself acquired by Wells Fargo. That upended an earlier deal to join Citigroup with government assistance. With the Golden West purchase, Wachovia had been saddled with $121 billion in option adjustable-rate mortgages centered in the stricken California housing market. Those mortgages allow homeowners to pay interest only or less, resulting in negative amortization, and have proved lethal as home prices plummet.

Phase 3

By late 2008, our earlier forecast that the recession would unfold in four phases was coming true. Phase 1, the collapse in housing led by the sub-prime slime, started early in 2007 and continued to unfold while phase 2, financial woes, commenced in mid-2007 when it became apparent that many financial institutions were very highly leveraged and invested in subprime and other overvalued assets. These two phases are essentially financial, while the goods and services side of the economy held up until late 2008.

Then came phase 3, the massive retrenchment by U.S. consumers, which started in earnest with the financial collapse in the fall of 2008. Denial about the housing collapse and financial near-meltdown came to an abrupt end. Consumers only spent about 20 percent of the $100 billion in tax rebates in mid-2008, and retail sales started to nosedive in September of that year. American consumers spent as long as there was funding available, but that ended, as I discuss in more detail in Chapter 6. Real incomes were falling in 2008, and the house appreciation that consumers had relied on to fund spending advances in lieu of income growth was disappearing fast (as seen in Figure 3.4 in Chapter 3) as house prices plummeted (shown in Figure 1.2 in Chapter 1).

Also pressuring consumers were falling stock prices (Figure 1.6) and tightening loan standards. They'd maxed out their credit cards and were up to their eyeballs in upside-down auto loans, student loans, and home equity borrowing. Consumers were pulling money out of their 401(k) accounts even though their savings were slim—and getting slimmer as stocks fell—despite the 10 percent tax penalty they faced for early withdrawal. Contribution rates to 401(k)s were also down as fewer and fewer had anything left to put into them after meeting living expenses. And the turmoil in financial markets, uncertainty over the safety of bank and money market deposits, and squabbling in Washington over bailouts were also depressing consumers.

Discretionary Drops

Discretionary spending of any kind was slashed. Auto sales collapsed from a 13.7 million annual rate in August 2008 to 12.5 million a month later and headed for a 9.1 million annual rate in February 2009. Consumers turned to drinking tap water instead of bottled, brown-bagging lunches, and buying generics and house brands instead of national brands at the supermarket. Charities including food banks suffered cutbacks. Hospitals, museums, and other nonprofits, especially those that depend on contributions from Wall Street, were hurt and worried. Upscale retailers like Neiman-Marcus suffered while consumers flocked to low-cost Wal-Mart.

In earlier years, homeowners paid their mortgage bills first, since they wanted to keep their homes, and made monthly payments on credit cards, auto, and student loans as funds permitted, as noted in Chapter 3. But after house prices fell precipitously (see Figure 1.2 in Chapter 1), many underwater homeowners figured they were going to lose their houses anyway, so they favored credit cards, which they treated as ATM sources of cash.

A study by TransUnion found that in the first quarter of 2008, for the first time, the percentage of consumers current on credit cards and delinquent on mortgages was 4.3 percent, greater than those in the reverse situation, 4.1 percent. And since then, the trend continued, with 6.6 percent in the third quarter of 2009 current on credit cards and delinquent on mortgages while 3.6 percent were current on mortgages but behind on their credit cards. The trend was more pronounced in the big housing boom/bust states, California and Florida, as you'd expect.

Nevertheless, by late 2008, lots of folks didn't even have the income to keep current on credit card debt repayments, so delinquencies leaped.

If, at the end of the month, it's a choice between making a credit card payment and putting bread on the table, financial responsibility may go by the boards.

There were lots of credit card and other nonmortgage consumer debts outstanding, many in the hands of financial institutions. Considering securitized debt alone, at the end of 2007, home equity, auto, credit card, and student loans totaled $1.4 trillion, or 1.7 times the $780 billion in securitized subprime mortgage loans. So, as consumer loan defaults grew, financial firms experienced another round of bad debt write-downs.

Since consumer spending accounts for 70 percent of GDP, the severe consumer retrenchment took down the goods and services economy with it. The result was the worst recession in the post–World War II era.

The nosediving economy finally got the attention of the majority of economists, who belatedly in October 2008 forecast a recession—after it was already 10 months old, as mentioned in Chapter 1. It's true that most of those forecasters are paid to be optimistic, come hell, high water, or recession! Still, it's hard to believe that so many economists didn't understand that the financial sector and the goods and services economy are completely intertwined. As Fed Chairman Bernanke said at the time, "There have been very few cases where you've had this kind of financial disruption without a significant effect on the economy."

Phase 4

The weak U.S. economy was accompanied by the unfolding of phase 4, the globalization of the recession. Consumer spending in Europe and Japan was weak; housing bubbles in countries like Ireland, Spain, and the United Kingdom were collapsing; and the U.S.-led financial crisis had spread abroad.

In the United Kingdom, mortgage lender HBOS was acquired by smaller-by-half Lloyds TSB Bank in a government-arranged deal after markets on which HBOS depended to borrow money froze up. The French government bought 30,000 unfinished houses, made more government-owned land available for private homebuilding, and tripled the number of homebuyers eligible for government-guaranteed mortgages to 60 percent.

In Iceland, the government nationalized the country's major banks, including Landsbanki Islands, which took Internet deposits from 400,000 U.K. and Dutch savers through Icesave and offered very high interest rates. German banks were also attracted and lent $21 billion to Icelandic borrowers, five times as much as the British. What amounted to a national Ponzi scheme converted Icelandic fishermen to investment bankers overnight, but Landsbanki failed when depositors wanted their money back. The Prime Minister said Iceland was at risk of a "national bankruptcy" as the financial iceberg slid into Reykjavik.

The U.K. and Dutch governments paid off those depositors, but demanded offsetting payments of $5.3 billion from Iceland. In March 2010, 93 percent of Icelanders voted in a national referendum not to repay the money even though settlement of the issue was necessary to get desperately needed funds from an IMF-led bailout. Iceland's krona is an international pariah, and its GDP in 2009 dropped a record 6.5 percent while unemployment leaped from near zero to 6.5 percent. Ex-fishermen are relearning their former trade. In April 2010, bond rating agencies threatened to move Iceland government issues to junk status.

Going back to late 2008, Chinese stocks plummeted from their October 2007 peak (see Figure 5.4) as the speculative bubble deflated and growth prospects dimmed. The central bank cut interest rates for

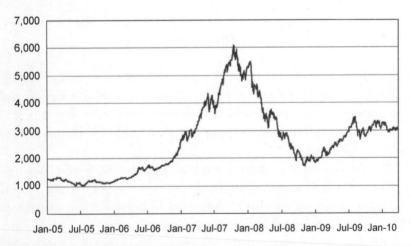

Figure 5.4 Shanghai Composite Index
Data source: Yahoo! Finance.

the first time in six years, and China's $200 billion sovereign wealth fund bought the shares of the nation's three largest banks on the open market. About two-thirds of Chinese stocks were already state-controlled.

Russia and Others in Trouble

Russia suspended equity trading several times in September 2008 due to its ongoing stock market collapse as global financial crises and slumping petroleum prices shook its economy. The government assembled a $120 billion rescue package to sustain a faltering bank system that desperately needed liquidity and the consolidation of Russia's 1,200 banks. The government also spent heavily to support the ruble. In effect, the money generated by high oil prices was used to recapitalize the banks. Russian real estate fell as loan costs leaped.

At the end of September 2008, Ireland reacted to the global financial crisis by guaranteeing up to $563 billion in bank debt, including securities and short-term borrowing, and deposits without limit. The French-Belgian bank Dexia specializes in lending to local governments, and lost heavily in its U.S. operations, so Belgium, France, and Luxembourg injected $9.2 billion to keep it afloat. The United Kingdom raised deposit insurance from $62,000 to $89,000.

On September 28, 2008, Fortis, the Dutch-Belgian bank, failed in its attempt to get French bank BNP Paribas and Dutch financial firm ING to bail it out. So Fortis and the Netherlands, Belgium, and Luxembourg governments pumped in $16 billion. Fortis got in over its head in the earlier $101 billion takeover, along with Royal Bank of Scotland, of ABN Amro Bank. Several days earlier, Fortis's interim CEO Herman Verwilst said he was "flabbergasted" over the stock decline. It fell 20 percent that day and was down 71 percent this year. Within hours, he was sacked.

Meanwhile, Germany's Hypo Real Estate Group, based in Munich but a big real estate lender in the United States, had lost bundles in American subprime-related securities. And its Irish Depfa unit was having trouble in rolling over its commercial paper. Subsequently, Hypo got a $51 billion bailout from the German government and a consortium of private banks.

The Indian central bank had to promise to pump money into ICICI Bank to stop a run touched off by worries over its foreign holdings, including Lehman assets. Hong Kong banks didn't want to lend to each other, so the Hong Kong Monetary Authority allowed them to use U.S. dollar assets as collateral at its discount window. And in South Korea, the government offered loans and debt guarantees to help small and midsize firms with short-term funding problems.

Bad, Bad Americans!

Furthermore, foreign governments didn't hesitate to point out American financial stumbles even as they addressed their own. The German Finance Minister said, "The United States will lose its status as the superpower of the global financial system." German Chancellor Merkel and French President Sarkozy called for a more international approach to financial regulation, clear pressure on the United States for reform. These statements were made, of course, before the 2010 eurozone crisis. Beijing's direct purchase of Chinese bank stocks, a retreat from free market capitalization, was provided cover by U.S. financial market intervention.

It's also true that the rest of the world depends critically on exports to the United States to generate economic growth. U.S. imports began to fall in 2007 and plunged as consumers retrenched, weakening foreign production. Then, as foreign economies dropped, so did U.S. exports, further depressing the U.S. economy.

The massive government bailouts here and abroad in reaction to the 2007–2008 financial crisis may have been necessary to prevent disintegration of financial structures and a severe depression. And given the reliance on government aid since the 1930s in times of national distress, they were probably politically necessary. But like any national trauma, the financial crisis greatly increased government involvement in the economy, as evidenced by a review of all the government actions in 2008–2009.

March 14, 2008	Fed spends $30 billion to subsidize JPMorgan Chase's purchase of Bear Stearns.
September 7, 2008	United States places Fannie and Freddie in conservatorship.
September 15, 2008	Fed and Treasury acquiesce in Lehman bankruptcy.
September 16, 2008	Fed approves $85 billion loan to AIG, takes 80 percent stake.

September 19, 2008	Treasury guarantees money market fund deposits; Fed offers to buy assets from the funds.
October 3, 2008	Congress approves $700 billion TARP.
October 14, 2008	Treasury uses $125 billion of TARP money to buy preferred shares in nine big banks; FDIC guarantees new bank debt via new Temporary Liquidity Guarantee Program.
November 23, 2008	Treasury, FDIC, and Fed rescue Citigroup by taking preferred shares; Treasury injects added $20 billion in TARP funds.
November 25, 2008	Fed creates Term Asset-Backed Securities Loan Facility (TALF) to revive securitization market; Fed begins purchasing mortgage-backed securities backed by Fannie and Freddie to bolster mortgage market.
December 19, 2008	Treasury approves loans of $13.4 billion for GM and $4.0 billion for Chrysler from TARP.
January 16, 2009	Treasury, Fed, and FDIC rescue Bank of America by taking preferred shares; Treasury invests another $20 billion TARP funds.
March 18, 2009	Fed begins purchasing Treasury securities, as much as $300 billion in coming six months.
April 30, 2009	Chrysler files for bankruptcy reorganization, sells to Fiat.
May 7, 2009	Fed announces stress test results of 19 largest U.S. bank holding companies.
June 1, 2009	U.S. takes 60 percent stake in GM, which files for bankruptcy.
June 17, 2009	JPMorgan Chase, Morgan Stanley, Goldman Sachs, and seven other banks repay their federal aid.
September 18, 2009	Treasury ends money market guarantee.
October 22, 2009	TARP paymaster decides compensation packages for top 25 executives at seven large TARP recipients.
December 9, 2009	Bank of America repays government aid.
December 14, 2009	Citigroup and Wells Fargo agree to pay back government aid.
December 24, 2009	Treasury decides to cover unlimited losses at Fannie and Freddie through 2012.

And that list doesn't include the $787 billion the Obama fiscal stimulus package enacted in early 2009 and the $1.25 trillion purchase of mortgage-related securities by the Fed. Also recall that the three great traumas of the twentieth century—the two world wars and the Great Depression—resulted in much more powerful central governments.

To a great extent, central bank money substituted for private funds, but with little net effect in stimulating business growth. Similarly, tax cuts and other fiscal stimuli replaced consumer retrenchment, but didn't do much to spur economic growth. Unwinding the unprecedented government involvement will be difficult. The Fed moved well beyond traditional monetary policy and subjected itself to serious political scrutiny in policy and regulatory realms. Fiscal intervention builds dependence on the federal government and powerful constituencies. Fannie and Freddie in housing come to mind, as does the Tennessee Valley Authority (TVA) much earlier. That started as a New Deal program to construct dams to tame the wild Tennessee River but morphed into a big coal-fired electric power producer.

Moral Hazards

The big bailouts have no doubt increased moral hazard by informing all parties that government will step in to solve big problems regardless of the folly of their creators. It's also now clear that to be too big to fail, financial institutions and homeowners don't need to be as big or as numerous as was earlier thought. Those bailed out probably figure that Washington has again proven that it couldn't allow serious financial crises, and that it has again raised the safety net. So after a period of R&R, they may well return with even bigger, more leveraged speculations. The decade of slow economic growth and deflation that I'm forecasting may keep speculation at bay for a number of years, but the urge to gamble remains embedded in the human soul.

Furthermore, bailout costs have added considerably to government deficits and debts worldwide, and to the cost of servicing those debts. Some academicians believe that when gross government debt exceeds 90 percent of GDP, economic growth is reduced by about one percentage point. I wonder, however, whether causality doesn't run the other way, since in non-wartime environments, big debts are the result of huge deficits caused by sluggish tax revenues and high unemployment benefits and other outlays in times of slow economic growth.

In any event, I examine in Chapter 6 the effects of increased government regulation and involvement in the economy as well as six other factors that will retard economic growth in the next decade.

Chapter 6

Slow Growth Ahead

F rom 1982 to 2000, the U.S. stock market was on a tear. The S&P 500 Index rose at a compound rate of 16.6 percent. Inflation withered so interest rates dropped (as seen in Figure 1.5 in Chapter 1), propelling the S&P 500 price/earnings (P/E) ratio from 8.9 in the third quarter of 1982 to 29.4 in the first quarter of 2000 at the end of the dot-com bubble. In those years, American business responded to excruciating foreign competition by restructuring with a vengeance. That boosted productivity and profits, which also benefited as declining inflation reduced taxable inventory profits and underdepreciation. And consumers went on a mad borrowing-and-spending binge.

Saving Less

The saving rate of American consumers fell from 12 percent in the early 1980s to 1 percent before the recent rebound (as shown in Figure 2.5 in Chapter 2). This meant that, on average, consumer spending rose about

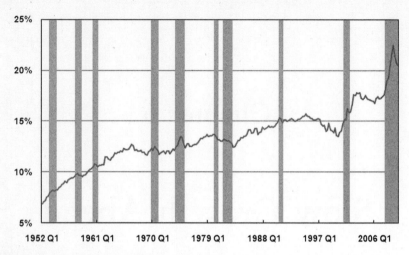

Figure 6.1   Household Debt to Assets
Data source: Federal Reserve.

a half percentage point more than disposable, or after-tax, income per year for a quarter century. The trend continued for so long that many accepted it as a fact of nature, subconsciously believing it would last forever and not realizing that it was unsustainable.

The fact that Americans were saving less and less of their after-tax income was only half the profligate consumer story. *Saving* is defined as the difference between disposable income and spending on durable goods like autos and appliances, nondurables like food and clothing, and services such as health care and recreation. If someone borrows to buy a car, his saving rate declines because his outlays go up but his disposable income doesn't. So the downward march in the personal saving rate was the flip side of the upward march in total consumer debt (mortgage, credit card, and auto debt) in relation to disposable income (as shown in Figure 4.4 in Chapter 4) and relative to assets (see Figure 6.1). Just like the falling saving rate, the rising debt and debt service rates couldn't continue forever.

First, Stocks

Not surprisingly, the advent of the declining saving rate coincided with the beginning of the great bull market in stocks in August 1982 (as seen in Figure 1.6 in Chapter 1). Rising stocks made people more optimistic, more willing to spend, and more inclined to save less and borrow more. Previously, starting in the mid-1960s, the severe inflation that resulted from excess government spending on Vietnam and Great Society programs had devastated stocks, which fell in inflation-adjusted terms by two-thirds from 1968 to 1982. Inflation depressed stocks by driving up interest rates (Figure 1.5) as well as very efficiently transferring corporate profitability to labor and government, leaving much less for shareholders (as shown in Figure 2.4 in Chapter 2).

With the unwinding of inflation and falling interest rates (Figure 1.5) as well as reviving profits, stocks began an unprecedented 17-year, eight-month bull market in August 1982 that lasted until March 2000. All of these factors boosted consumer confidence.

The rally was so robust that by the late 1990s, many felt that stocks would appreciate at least 20 percent per year forever, as they did for five consecutive years, 1995–1999. So, they reasoned, saving anything from current income was unnecessary since never-ending equity appreciation would fund all their future saving needs. Individual stockholders didn't liquidate their stocks appreciably during the big 1982–2000 bull market, but they looked at their equity portfolio as a continually filling piggy bank that allowed them to fund oversize spending by saving less and borrowing more on credit cards, auto loans, student loans, and from their home equity.

Sure, the saving rate, by definition, does not include capital appreciation, and some observers in the late 1990s argued that this absence made it a flawed measure. But the subsequent collapse in the dot-com and other tech stocks (as seen in Figure 1.1 in Chapter 1) that had sucked in so many naïve investors reestablished the validity and usefulness of the saving rate.

Next, Housing

Then the housing bubble almost seamlessly took over when stock appreciation turned to depreciation. House prices departed from their normal close link to the consumer price index (CPI) in the mid-1990s and subsequently racked up huge appreciation for homeowners. From a fundamental standpoint, the economic growth spurt ended in 2000, as shown by basic measures of the economy's health. The stock market, that most fundamental measure of business fitness and sentiment, essentially reached its peak with the dot-com blow-off in 2000 (Figure 1.6). The same is true of employment, goods production, and household net worth in relation to disposable (after-tax) income (as seen in Figure 4.1 in Chapter 4). Nevertheless, the gigantic policy ease in Washington in response to the stock market collapse in 2000 and the terrorist attacks of 9/11 gave the illusion that all was well and that the growth trend had resumed.

The Fed worried about a severe recession, financial crisis, deflation, and later a dire aftermath of 9/11. So the central bank eased massively, pushing its federal funds rate ultimately to 1 percent (as seen in Figure 1.3 in Chapter 1), a record low rate that rivaled the Bank of Japan's zero percent overnight rate (see Figure 6.2). At the same time, federal tax rebates and cuts (see Figure 6.3) and spending on homeland security and military efforts in Afghanistan and Iraq pumped lots more money into the economy. As a result of all these stimuli, the 2001 recession was brief and shallow. Speculation survived and simply shifted from stocks to commodities, foreign currencies, emerging market equities and debt, hedge funds, private equity, Bernie Madoff—and to a rapidly expanding housing bubble.

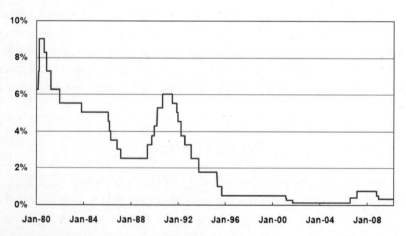

Figure 6.2 Japanese Discount Target Rate
Data source: Bank of Japan.

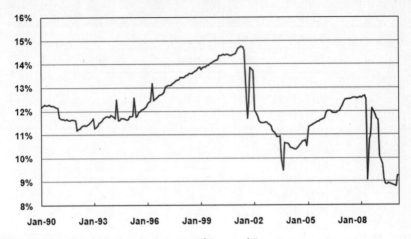

Figure 6.3 Personal Taxes—Percent of Personal Income
Data source: Bureau of Economic Analysis.

Easy Money

All this house appreciation made it easy for homeowners to save less and spend more, and they needed to do so in order to maintain their consumption growth because real wages and salaries were flat in the 2000s. American business had more than met foreign and domestic competition in recent years by holding down labor costs and employment. Combined with robust sales and strong productivity growth (see Table 6.1), the result has been the explosive growth in corporate earnings, which pushed profits' share of GDP to a record high level (Figure 2.4).

According to the Federal Reserve, Americans extracted $719 billion in cash from their houses in 2005 after a $633 billion withdrawal in 2004 and $439 billion in 2003. Back in the mid-1990s, it was less than $200 billion per year. This was easily accomplished with the help of accommodative lenders through refinancings and home equity loans. Other homeowners looked on their houses as golden geese that never stop laying, so they simply saved less and borrowed more on credit cards and other means to bridge the gap between their robust spending growth and meager income gains.

Make no mistake: House appreciation was extremely important to consumer spending by allowing Americans to save less and spend more. And the widespread nature and relatively even distribution of home

Table 6.1 Productivity in the U.S. Nonfarm
Business Sector

	NBER	**BLS**
1901–1910	2.34%	n/a
1911–1920	2.64%	n/a
1921–1930	2.07%	n/a
1931–1940	2.39%	n/a
1941–1950	2.46%	n/a
1951–1960	2.28%	2.14%
1961–1970	2.49%	2.71%
1971–1980	n/a	1.45%
1981–1990	n/a	1.61%
1991–2000	n/a	2.18%
2001–2009	n/a	2.36%

Data sources: National Bureau of Economic Research
(NBER) and Bureau of Labor Statistics (BLS).

ownership meant that the median homeowner was financially better
off during the housing bubble than in the dot-com stock bubble even
when stock prices were well below the 2000 peak.

In 2007, 69 percent of U.S. households owned their own abodes
while only 50 percent held equities or mutual funds. More importantly,
as of 2007, the latest data, the top 10 percent in terms of income owned
houses with $500,000 median value, five times the $100,000 median
price of those owned by the lowest 20 percent by income (Table 6.2).
In contrast, the top 10 percent held stocks worth $219,600, 34 times the
median $6,500 owned by the lowest 20 percent (Table 6.3).

Table 6.2 Median Value of Primary Residence

	1998	**2001**	**2004**	**2007**
All families; percent of income	115.8	131.0	175.7	200.0
Less than 20	63.8	69.2	76.9	100.0
20–39.9	86.9	85.2	109.8	120.0
40–59.9	98.5	101.2	148.3	150.0
60–79.9	127.4	138.5	192.2	215.0
80–89.9	158.7	186.4	247.1	300.0
90–100	260.7	319.5	494.2	500.0

By income class; data are in thousands of dollars.
Data sources: Federal Reserve, Survey of Consumer Finance.

Table 6.3 Median Value of Direct and Indirect* Stock Holdings

	1998	2001	2004	2007
All families; percent of income	31.8	40.4	35.7	35.0
Less than 20	6.4	8.8	8.2	6.5
20–39.9	12.7	8.8	10.9	8.4
40–59.9	15.3	17.5	16.5	17.7
60–79.9	24.4	33.9	29.0	34.2
80–89.9	57.3	75.6	62.1	62.0
90–100	173.8	291.3	225.1	219.6

By income class; data are in thousands of dollars.
* Indirect holds are mutual funds, retirement accounts, and other marginal assets.
Data sources: Federal Reserve, Survey of Consumer Finance.

So it's not surprising that researchers have found that a 10 percent gain in house prices leads to a 0.62 percent rise in consumer spending, about twice the rise that results from a 10 percent jump in stock prices. Also not surprising, amidst this consumer borrowing and spending orgy, consumer spending's share of GDP leaped from 62 percent to 71 percent (see Figure 6.4).

Instant Gratification

Unsustainable as this spending binge was, I'm convinced it would have continued as long as American consumers could fund it. A couple doesn't

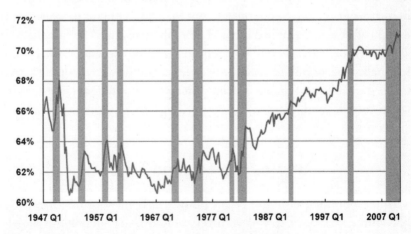

Figure 6.4 Personal Consumption Expenditures/GDP
Data source: Bureau of Economic Analysis.

wake up one morning and say to each other, "Dear, we're borrow-ing too much, saving too little, and spending too much. We've *got* to cut back." No, no. Americans have been trained—and I use that word deliberately—by retailers, the media, and even the government to keep spending regardless of their financial health. Achieve instant gratification by next-day delivery, and postpone the bill until later, maybe never, if it can be paid by extracting house appreciation.

But the forces that drove the 25-year consumer spending bubble couldn't continue forever and have been reversed. These include the decline in the consumer saving rate and the jump in household debt, the vast leveraging of the financial sector, increasingly free trade, the roaring stock market, soaring house prices, and loose financial regulation.

Individual investors no longer trust their stock portfolios to finance future financial needs, despite the strong rebound that started in March 2009 (Figure 1.6). While speaking on a *Forbes* magazine–sponsored Caribbean cruise in December 2007, soon after stocks had peaked, I asked for a show of hands among the audience of about 300 as to who thought their stock holdings would cover their financial requirements from then on out. Almost everyone raised his hand. I asked the same question on an identical Forbes Caribbean cruise in December 2009. Even though the S&P 500 was then up 60 percent from its low, the audience had dwindled by half and only two hands went up.

Furthermore, in 2009, investors yanked $9 billion from U.S. stock funds and put $375 billion into bond funds and continued those trends in the first half of 2010. In contrast, they added $152 billion to stock funds in 2003 after stocks reached their March low that year. The fact that the S&P 500 Index actually fell 3 percent in the 2000s decade has obviously demoralized shareholders and slashed their confidence in equities. And it will probably stay subdued if my forecast of limited stock returns in future years is valid.

House Appreciation Gone

With the plummet in house prices (shown in Figure 1.2 in Chapter 1), that source of money to finance oversize consumer spending is largely exhausted. Those with mortgages had equity of almost 50 percent of the house's value on average in the early 1980s. As of the fourth quarter of 2009, it was down to only 16.4 percent (as seen in Figure 3.5 in Chapter 3), due to home equity withdrawals and, especially in recent years, house price declines. Also at that time, 23 percent of those homeowners were underwater, with their houses worth less than their mortgages. Furthermore, mortgage lending standards shifted from trivial to tight (see Figure 6.5), making it difficult for those without considerable home equity and sterling credit to withdraw equity through cash-out refinancing, home equity loans, or otherwise.

So with investor uncertainty over their stock portfolios, home equity nearly exhausted, and high credit card delinquencies and charge-offs, American consumers have no choice but to curtail spending to save more and repay debt. The borrowing-and-spending binge of the past quarter century is being replaced by a saving spree. Note that as of the fourth quarter of 2009, household net worth as a ratio to after-tax income was lower than in the 1950s and 1960s (Figure 4.1) when the saving rate was much higher (see Figure 2.5).

Consumer retrenchment has continued despite repeated attempts by Washington to massively stimulate spending. As noted in Chapter 5, 80 percent of the 2008 tax rebates were saved. In both April and May 2009, personal taxes were cut by $49.8 billion at annual rates by the tax credit of $400 for working individuals and $800 for married couples filing jointly.

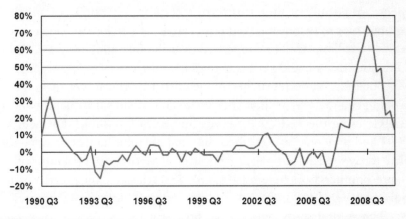

Figure 6.5 Net Percentage of Banks Tightening Standards for Residential Mortgage Loans
Data source: Federal Reserve.

In addition, in May those on Social Security and similar programs each got a $250 payment, or $157.6 billion in total.

As a result, after-tax income rose $140 billion at an annual rate in April and a further $178.1 billion in May. But savings jumped $146.2 billion in April, so consumers saved 104 percent of their after-tax income increase. In May, savings again leaped by $160.3 billion, or 90 percent of the after-tax income increase.

So consumers are saving virtually every dollar of those fiscal stimuli, and all it amounts to is two bookkeeping entries—an increase in the federal deficit matched by an increase in household saving. And bear in mind that higher-income folks, who normally do almost all of the saving, got no tax cuts and little of the Social Security payments. So, middle- and lower-income people have suddenly become big savers. The net effect was to push up the average saving rate (Figure 2.5).

My Rich Parents

With home equity exhausted and stocks distrusted, is there another big source of money to bridge the gap between consumer incomes and out-lays? One possible source of big, although not immediate, money to sustain consumer spending is inheritance. In 1993, two academicians estimated that the postwar babies, who have saved little for their retire-ment, would inherit more than $10 trillion in 1990 dollars from their parents. Not to be outdone, other researchers in 1999 concluded that at least $41 trillion would be inherited over the following 60 years. Wow! Quit your day job and get ready for a life of leisure!

But those same researchers concluded that the subset of boomers would get a mere $7 trillion after estate taxes. And subsequent work by AARP, using the Federal Reserve's Survey of Consumer Finances for 2004 and previous years, slashed the total for inheritances of all people alive today to $12 trillion in 2005 dollars. Most of it, $9.2 trillion, will go to pre-boomers born before 1946, only $2.1 trillion to the postwar babies born between 1946 and 1964, and $0.7 trillion to the post-boomers.

The AARP study goes on to show that the percentage of people receiving inheritances since 1989 has been quite consistent, so there's no reason to expect big jumps in their numbers any time soon. In fact, it's surprising that more boomers and post-boomers, as they age and their parents die, aren't getting inheritances. In 2004, 98 percent of post-boomers, 83 percent of boomers, but only 22 percent of pre-boomers had living parents. The reality, however, is that their parents are living longer, incurring more medical expenses, and giving more to charity before they die. So there's less to pass on, which probably accounts for the stability over time of these numbers receiving inheritances.

Furthermore, the value of all previous inheritances as reported in the 2004 survey was $49,902 on average, with $70,317 for pre-boomers, $48,768 for boomers, and $24,348 for post-boomers. Clearly, these are not numbers that provide for comfortable retirements and, therefore, allow people to continue to spend like drunken sailors.

The Rich Get Richer

The AARP also found that families with high net worth received bigger inheritances than those with less. Well, what would you expect? Rich kids often have wealthy parents. In any event, those in the top quintile had net worth of $449,739 in 2004 and got 36.5 percent of all inheritance dollars. The top two quintiles with net worth over $159,941 got 60 percent of the total. So most of the money is not going to those with few assets but to those who are already well off.

Finally, few people, 14 percent, expect inheritances in the future and only 14.9 percent of postwar babies do. So, far from supplying big money to promote consumer spending, the meager sizes of inheritances, the skewing toward those already well off, and the low expectations for future inheritances point to consumer retrenchment and a saving spree, especially among the heretofore spendthrift postwar babies.

Anything Else?

What other assets could consumers borrow against or liquidate to support spending growth in the future? After all, they do have a lot of net worth, $54 trillion for households and nonprofit organizations as of 2009. Nevertheless, there aren't any other big assets left to tap. Another big stock bonanza is unlikely for decades and the real estate bubble has collapsed. Consumer durable goods, especially autos, are already heavily financed, with the vast majority of the vehicles on the road purchased with borrowing.

Deposits in financial institutions totaled $7.8 trillion in 2009, but the growth over time as well as the majority, $6.1 trillion, were in time and savings deposits, largely held for retirement by financially conservative people. Is it likely that the speculator who owned five houses has sizable time deposits to fall back on?

Households and nonprofits held $4.2 trillion in bonds and other credit market instruments, but most owned by individuals were in conservative hands and unlikely to be liquidated or borrowed against to finance consumer spending. In fact, as noted earlier, individual investors have been shoveling money into bond mutual funds. Life insurance reserves can be borrowed but their total size, $1.2 trillion, pales in comparison to the $1.8 trillion that homeowners extracted from their houses in the 2003–2005 years. There was $6.5 trillion of equity in noncorporate business in 2009, but the vast majority of that was needed by typically cash-poor small businesses to keep their doors open.

Pension Funds

Pension funds might be a source of cash for consumers who want to live it up now and take the Scarlett O'Hara "I'll think about that tomorrow" attitude toward retirement. They totaled $11.8 trillion in 2009, but that number includes public funds and private defined-benefit plans that are seldom available to pre-retirees unless they leave their jobs.

The private defined contribution plans, typically 401(k)s, have been growing rapidly since employers favor them. In 1985, they were only half the size of defined-benefit pension plans, but in 2008 they totaled $2.5 trillion in assets while defined-benefit plans had $2.0 trillion. But sadly, many employees, especially those at lower income levels, don't share their bosses' zeal. Indeed, few eligible workers make the extra contributions to their 401(k)s that Congress allowed in 2001 for people 50 and older, even though 80 percent of 401(k) plans allow it.

Many don't participate in their company 401(k) plans and thereby take advantage of company contributions, even though their 401(k)s are the primary retirement plans for most employees. Furthermore, almost half of those who leave their jobs and have small or medium-size defined contribution plans don't roll them into IRAs, but instead cash out.

Furthermore, the amount that employees could net from withdrawals from defined contribution plans would be far less than the $2.5 trillion total, and probably less than the $1.8 trillion they pulled out of their houses in 2003–2005. That $2.5 trillion total includes company contributions that are not yet vested and therefore can't be withdrawn by employees. Also, withdrawals by those under age $59\frac{1}{2}$ are subject to a 10 percent penalty, with income taxes due on the remainder.

American consumers justified and collateralized their long-term decline in saving and rise in borrowing that accompanied their spending binge, first by soaring stock portfolios and then by leaping house prices. Those sources are ancient history and no others, including inheritance or pension fund withdrawals, are likely to fuel oversize consumer spending. Consumer retrenchment and a saving spree are the result.

The Postwar Babies

A saving spree in the next decade will also be encouraged by postwar-baby saving. Those 79 million born between 1946 and 1964 haven't saved much, like most other Americans, and they accounted for about half the total U.S. consumer spending in the 1990s. But they need to save as they look retirement in the teeth. Households with members age 50-plus had only $89,300 on average in retirement accounts on September 30, 2008, according to an AARP study, not enough to replace even one year of $95,000 in annual income for the typical household headed by someone age 50–59. A poll taken by the Employee Benefit Research Institute in January 2008 found that, excluding home values and defined-benefit plans, less than 23 percent of employees age 55 or older have savings and investments over $250,000, and 60 percent had less than $100,000 (see Figure 6.6).

Postwar babies need to save not only to finance retirement, but to repay debt. The Fed's 2007 Survey of Consumer Finance found that 55 percent of households with members age 55–64 had mortgages on

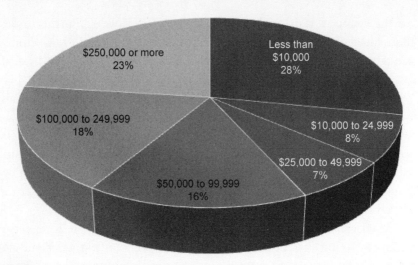

Figure 6.6 Savings and Investments for Americans Age 55 and Older (January 2008)
Data source: Employee Benefit Research Institute.

their abodes and 45 percent carried credit card balances. Even for those in the 65 to 74 age range, 43 percent still had mortgages on their primary residences and 37 percent owed on credit cards. With the stagnation in stock prices over the past decade and the collapse in house prices, early retirement is a forgotten dream for many baby boomers, and working beyond normal retirement age, if they can find work, is a looming reality.

It's ironic that when the household saving rate was 12 percent in the early 1980s (Figure 2.5), the demographic forces were the worst for saving. The postwar babies were in their twenties and thirties, the weakest saving ages when people spend heavily on cars, appliances, baby equipment, and other outlays associated with establishing households and raising families (see Figure 6.7). In contrast, the big savers at that time, those in their fifties and sixties, were the sparse Depression babies. These postwar babies are now in their career peak earning years, need to save for retirement, and can save because their kids are leaving home—well, some are today, although boomerang kids return home—and ending tuition payments. And if their kids are anything like our four offspring, they no longer have as many smashed-up cars to replace!

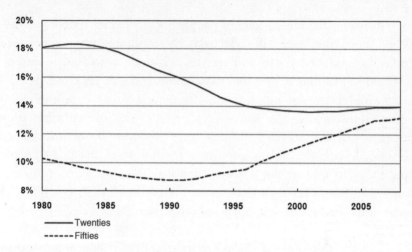

Figure 6.7 Percent of Population in Their Twenties and Fifties
Data source: U.S. Census Bureau.

Today, the postwar babies are in the big saving ages—and have additional incentives to save due to their earlier spendthrift ways coupled with the recent volatility in stocks and collapse in house prices. Many postwar babies who planned to retire early may have no choice but to work well beyond normal retirement age, as noted earlier. Meanwhile, the big-spending younger folks are relatively few (Figure 6.7). Less spending and more saving will also be encouraged by the chronic deflation I discuss in Chapter 8, as consumers postpone purchases in anticipation of lower prices.

Delayed Consumption?

Ironically, stock appreciation, saving out of current income, or anything else that racks up assets today will not solve the postwar baby problem a decade hence, even though that idea sounds plausible enough. After all, we all know that by saving and investing successfully, we can accumulate the money needed for retirement. But what works for the individual won't work for the whole nation. Economists call this the fallacy of composition. When one person or a small group retires and stops producing goods and services, but keeps consuming, its effect on total supply and demand is insignificant.

Not so for the huge group of people born between 1946 and 1964. When they retire, they will collectively be consuming large amounts of currently produced goods and services which they will no longer be involved in making. Where will those goods and services come from?

Saving today—in other words, forgoing current consumption—doesn't directly solve the problem since you can't move currently produced goods and services through time. Services, by definition, are consumed as produced. It's impossible to shift an airline flight people take today to one in the postwar babies' retirement years. You can't really shift goods through time, either. A car that's built but not sold today could be mothballed, but who would want to drive a 2010 model in 2020?

Consequently, even if the postwar babies saved like people do in Singapore, where the national saving rate exceeds 50 percent, and shoved it all into, say, stocks, pushing the Dow Jones Industrial Average to 10 zillion by 2020, they still could end up chewing gum for breakfast. Why? When they stop working, the supply of goods and services would fall. In retirement, they might spend less on themselves and on supporting their kids, and they might have lots of greenbacks as they liquidated their stocks—assuming their collective liquidation didn't kill the stock market. Nevertheless, there would not be enough goods and services to go around. The value of their assets would then be inflated away as excess dollars chased a reduced supply of products. The same would be true if their checks came from the government.

Still, heavy saving now will help if it is invested in plant and equipment, technology, and labor training and education that will increase productivity. If so, when the postwar babies retire, those still working will be so productive that the retirees' needs can be met without both workers and retirees getting significantly less.

Luckily, productivity growth because of today's convergence of new technologies will probably remain robust (Table 6.1) and there will be plenty of capacity in the U.S. economy for years to come. Beyond that, increasing production and exports from China and other new market economies as well as other supply-increasing forces promise plenty of global capacity. Nevertheless, the postwar babies will probably be required to retire later and have more constrained retirement and health care benefits than are called for in current formulas.

Chronic Unemployment

Chronic high unemployment is another important reason for a multi-year consumer saving spree. As I discuss later, unemployment rates may average not much below current levels over the next decade (as shown in Figure 2.1 in Chapter 2), despite substantial government-sponsored job creation. This will encourage saving to prepare for potential joblessness and uncertain financial futures, especially as American businesses continue to cut costs by curtailing employment and promoting productivity (Table 6.1) in response to fierce domestic and foreign competition.

In addition, domestic and global competition will probably keep the time between jobs long. Until recently, in the post–World War II years, the average number of weeks unemployed was about 15, but now it is almost 30. The number of people per job opening averaged about two from 2000 until the recent climb to six. At the bottom of the early 1980s recession, 26 percent of the jobless were considered long-term unemployed; now that number is 40 percent. And when people lose jobs today, many who are lucky enough to find new positions are paid less. Declining union jobs (see Figure 6.8) are a key reason that average real income has gone nowhere for a decade. So are two-tier wage systems. The 2007 auto industry labor agreements allow automakers to replace

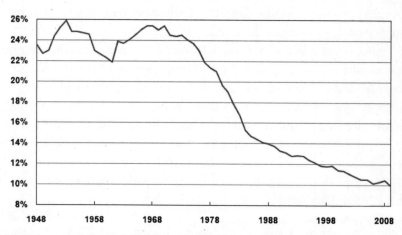

Figure 6.8 Union Membership as a Percentage of Labor Force
Data sources: Historical Statistics of the United States and Bureau of Labor Statistics.

workers who leave or retire with new employees paid $14 per hour, about half what older employees are paid. Ford started doing so in early 2010. And the new people get 401(k) retirement accounts instead of the defined-benefit pension plans enjoyed by existing workers.

Unemployment woes are also augmented by underwater homeowners who can't easily sell their abodes in high jobless areas and move to where jobs are more plentiful. The tendency of both spouses to work is also limiting job mobility and, ironically, adding to unemployment woes. When only the husband worked outside the home, if he lost his job he could seek employment in another city and the wife and family would follow. Today, if one spouse becomes unemployed, and the other is the sole breadwinner, the jobless spouse is reluctant to look for employment elsewhere because the other spouse may not be able to get relocated easily. It's not surprising that in 1987, 71 percent of Americans said they were satisfied with their jobs, but that number fell to 59 percent in 1995, 51 percent in 2000, and 45 percent in 2009.

Saving will also be encouraged in future years since high joblessness will discourage the reinstatement of many employee perks that have been eliminated in recent years. These include stock options, paid family leave, education reimbursement, and adoption assistance. College students who are being forced to drop out of school or switch to cheaper educational institutions because their parents are unemployed and lack adequate savings will remember this experience vividly. A September 2009 survey found 61 percent of higher education institutions had 10 percent or more financial aid applications than in the previous year.

Also, many parents are financially unable to help their offspring buy houses when cautious lenders say no. Home ownership for people ages 25 to 29 fell from 42 percent in 2006 to 38 percent in 2009, and 22 percent of those ages 18 to 34 say they've been turned down for a mortgage. Some 21 percent have moved back home or doubled up with a friend or relative. Many young people are also seeing their parents postpone retirement because of financial strains. All these forces will no doubt encourage today's youths to save robustly for their future welfare and for that of their children.

The chronically high unemployment is spawned in part by the slow economic growth I foresee, which in turn is the result of sluggish consumer spending growth attributed to the rising saving rate. So, to an extent, high unemployment and the consumer saving spree result from a simultaneous solution to the macroeconomic equation. But in my judgment, the absence of stocks and house appreciation to support excessive consumer spending and the need for the postwar babies to save will promote a chronically rising saving rate even without the spur of high unemployment.

Saving Is In

Saving may become the in thing in future years as people make a virtue out of necessity. Some say consumers are returning to the 1930s mantra, "Use it up, wear it out, make do, or do without." Conspicuous consumption and impulse buying seem to be giving way to more thoughtful purchases. Many of the aspiring affluent may drop out of the luxury goods market—but not give up on small luxuries that convey some degree of status, as I explore in Chapter 12.

Due to consumer caution as well as high unemployment and reduced commuting, the miles driven in passenger and commercial vehicles fell from 3.037 trillion in 2007 to 2.930 trillion in the 12 months ending October 2009. Consumers are favoring cheaper fast food, like $1 cheeseburgers, and the industry is complying. PepsiCo assumes the "age of thrift" will continue and is offering more promotions. The domestic nonalcoholic beverage industry suffered its second annual decline in a row in 2009. Bottled water sales fell in 2008 and 2009 after a decade of growth as consumers turned to tap water. Unilever has reversed its strategy of raising prices actively while letting volume fall as consumers balk. Procter & Gamble is using promotions aggressively to try to stem the consumer trend to lower-priced items and house brands. A December 2009 survey found that two-thirds had traded down in the previous 12 months and three-fourths of them said the cheaper producers were as good as or better than the more expensive brands.

To attract diners who want to save money, restaurants have resorted to lower-cost items on their menus or have substituted cheaper ingredients in recipes. Target is offering a 5 percent discount on every purchase to users of its credit card.

Already, coupon clipping has become not only a way to save money but also a serious business for many who amass huge quantities of goods that are bought cheaply on coupons. In some cases, coupons reduce supermarket items on sale to zero, but conscientious shoppers limit these purchases to avoid cleaning out the shelves. In 2009, the number of coupons redeemed jumped 27 percent from 2008 to 3.3 billion.

Layaway financing was popular in the Great Depression as consumers made periodic payments and then picked up their Christmas gifts or other purchases after they were completely paid for. Credit cards, with their enjoy-it-now-pay-later appeal, almost ran layaways out of business. But now they're reviving as credit card issuers tighten limits and consumers worry about crushing debt loads and job losses. And, of course, layaways are available to all, even those with bad credit. The popularity of debit cards in recent years may prove to have been a harbinger of a trend away from instant gratification through credit card financing.

Furthermore, lenders will probably remain cautious long after the current credit crisis is over, and it may take until the next generation of bankers before they again are willing to make risky loans. As noted earlier, lenders, especially banks, have shown tremendous herdlike instincts in the past, all rushing into questionable areas and then stampeding out after they suffer big losses, only to swear they'll never, ever take big risks again.

With today's lingering financial crisis, the worst since the Great Depression, loans of all sorts but certainly home mortgage, home equity, auto, credit card, student, and other consumer loans will probably be made parsimoniously for many years, and only to the very best credit risks.

In the 1930s, movies served a dual function of cheap entertainment and escapes from the daily drag of the Depression. They again appear to be doing so, to the extent that ticket prices are jumping, especially for 3-D films that accounted for most of 2009's 10 percent rise in box office sales. Movie attendance in the United States and Canada rose 5.5 percent in 2009, and ticket sales in early 2010 were up 10 percent from a year earlier.

For the next decade, I'm forecasting an average one percentage point increase in the saving rate annually, raising it to more than 10 percent in 10 years. At that point, it still may not exceed the 12 percent saving rate of the early 1980s (Figure 2.5), even though the demographics for saving have gone from the worst to the best in the interim. And even a decade of vigorous saving will probably not return household net worth even close to its former peaks (Figure 4.1) or eliminate completely the three decades of ever-increasing household financial leverage (Figure 4.7).

A Big Switch

For the past quarter-century, consumer spending has risen on average about a half-percent faster than after-tax income per year as the saving rate dropped from 12 percent to 1 percent, as noted earlier. As that spending has been magnified as it works its way through the economy, the total effect has been about 1.5 times as much. Since consumer spending has averaged about two-thirds of GDP over that period, the excess consumer outlays have added around 0.5 percentage points to real GDP growth out of its 3.3 percent average.

This extra economic growth and the rising debt associated with the consumer spending and borrowing binge (as seen in Figure 4.4 in Chapter 4) helped support consumer-related businesses, credit card issuers, and stock prices. And higher stock prices made people less inclined to save, in a self-feeding cycle. The extra consumer spending also spiked the trade and current account deficits (see Figure 6.9), which were financed by growing foreign ownership of U.S. assets.

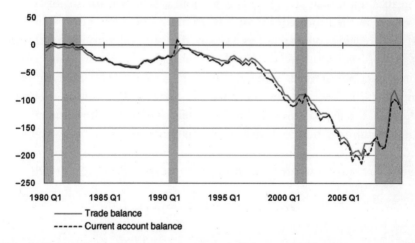

Figure 6.9 U.S. Current Account and Trade Balances ($ Billion)
Data source: Bureau of Economic Analysis.

The chronic one-percentage point annual rise in the consumer saving rate for the next decade or so that I forecast, however, will knock approximately one percentage point off real GDP growth after its effects work their way through the economy. That's a big contrast with 0.5 annual percentage point declines in the saving rate over the previous quarter century (Figure 2.5) that added around 0.5 percentage points to growth. That total swing of 1.5 percentage points will reduce real GDP growth from 3.7 percent per year in the 1982–2000 salad days to 2.2 percent.

Two Paradoxes

The newfound consumer zeal to save is involved in two interesting and interrelated paradoxes that are now at work in the U.S. economy. The first is well known, the *paradox of thrift*, so named by Lord Keynes in the 1930s Depression. It deals with the behavior of consumers, individually and collectively. People need to save for contingencies, their kids' educations, health care emergencies, and retirement. And until recently, they didn't, as witnessed by the quarter-century decline in the household saving rate. To make matters worse, they borrowed excessively, pushing total consumer and residential mortgage debt from 60 percent of after-tax income to 135 percent, as discussed earlier.

But additional saving curtails spending. So when the majority does what is in their individual best interest and favors saving over spending, the aggregate economy suffers a lack of demand. Economists call this the *fallacy of composition*. What's good for one isn't good for all. The tax cuts and extra Social Security payments in 2009 were 100 percent saved, as noted earlier. So the net effect was no additional consumer spending. Instead, the federal government increased its deficit to fund the tax cuts and consumers increased their saving an equal amount. It may be better to have higher household saving at the expense of a bigger federal deficit, but there was no immediate effect on consumer spending or GDP.

Business Cost-Cutting

The second paradox is one I'm not aware anyone else has explored. Throughout the 2000s and more intently in recent years, American business has been cutting labor costs, not so much through layoffs as by not hiring additional employees. Productivity growth has been strong as workers produced more per hour. Much of that productivity growth fell to the bottom line and corporate profits rose robustly.

This also is a paradox, another fallacy of composition. Every business, acting in its own best interest to meet domestic and foreign competition, needs to cut costs to promote productivity and profits, especially in today's slow-growth world. But when most businesses do so, there probably won't be enough labor income paid out to purchase the combined output of the business sector. In my two deflation books—*Deflation: Why It's Coming, Whether It's Good or Bad, and How It Will Affect Your Investments, Business and Personal Affairs* (Lakeview Publishing, 1998) and *Deflation: How to Survive and Thrive in the Coming Wave of Deflation* (McGraw-Hill, 1999)—I noted that that great economist Henry Ford paid his auto workers an unprecedented $5 per day so they could afford to buy the Model T's they built.

This paradox has been hidden until recently. Consumers lacked adequate purchasing power from their paychecks, so they saved less and borrowed more to bridge the gap between their income and their spending growth. But now that consumers have reversed from a 25-year borrowing-and-spending binge to a saving spree, the mask is off. Their incomes and spending are inadequate to buy all of the domestically produced goods and services plus net imports.

These two paradoxes are likely to reinforce each other in coming years. Weak labor income and even weaker consumer spending as household saving rises will limit growth in production. Reinforcing the resulting softness in labor income are continuing business efforts to cut costs even further to promote productivity growth. And the greater the risks of layoffs, short hours, and pay cuts, the more employees want to increase their saving to prepare for harder times ahead.

Financial Deleveraging

Beyond the U.S. consumer saving spree, there are seven other forces that will slow global growth in the years ahead (see Table 6.4). None of them can be quantified easily, but all are important retarders.

Table 6.4   Nine Causes of Slow Global Growth in Future Years

1. U.S. consumers will shift from a 25-year borrowing-and-spending binge to a saving spree. This will spread abroad as American consumers curtail the imports of the goods and services many foreign nations depend on for economic growth.
2. Financial deleveraging will reverse the trend that financed much global growth in recent years.
3. Increased government regulation and involvement in major economies will stifle innovation and reduce efficiency.
4. Low commodity prices will limit spending by commodity-producing lands.
5. Developed countries are moving toward fiscal restraint.
6. Rising protectionism will slow, even eliminate global growth.
7. The housing market will be weak due to excess inventories and loss of investment appeal.
8. Deflation will curtail spending as buyers anticipate lower prices.
9. State and local governments will contract.

Financial deleveraging is my second reason for reduced long-term economic growth (see Table 6.4). As I discussed earlier in Chapter 3, the recession really started in early 2007 in the financial arena with the collapse of subprime residential mortgages. Then it spread to Wall Street in mid-2007 with the complete mistrust among financial institutions and their assets, too many of which were linked to troubled mortgages. That panicked Washington into opening the money floodgates. The Fed started its interest rate–cutting campaign that ultimately drove its federal funds rate target to the zero to 0.25 percent range in August 2007 (Figure 1.3).

But the central bank soon found that banks were too scared to lend and creditworthy borrowers didn't want to borrow when Bear Stearns and Lehman collapsed and other large banks and Wall Street houses were on the brink. So the Fed embarked on quantitative easing that exploded its balance sheet (see Figure 6.10). Meanwhile, Congress and the administration joined in with the $700 billion TARP, the $787 billion fiscal bailout, and many other programs, as witnessed by the rapidly increasing federal deficit (seen in Figure 3.1 in Chapter 3).

BIS Warning

Central banks and governments are replacing financing by private institutions and bailing them out as they pressure them to delever. The Bank

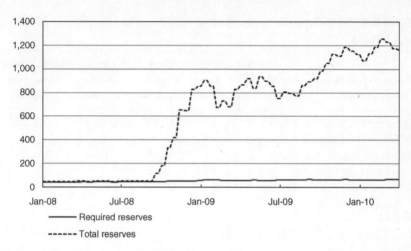

Figure 6.10 Required and Total Reserves of Depository Institutions ($ Billion)
Data source: Federal Reserve.

for International Settlements (BIS) in 2009 said only limited progress has been made in clearing up the global financial system, and any economic recovery will be short-lived and followed by a long period of stagnation unless bank balance sheets are corrected.

Among large banks, troubled Citigroup cut only 4.2 percent of its assets between December 31, 2008 and a year later, but CEO Vikram Pandit told the Congressional Oversight Panel, "We're selling 40 percent of the company." Citi has already sold 51 percent of its Smith Barney brokerage operation to Morgan Stanley, but as consumers retrench and pay off debts, it's having trouble unloading consumer lender Citi Financial, a $40 billion portfolio of credit card receivables and a ski lodge.

During the real estate boom, big banks securitized subprime mortgages and other questionable assets and then sold them to investors, who suffered when housing collapsed. Now, in order to sell mortgage-related securities, banks are being forced to issue covered bonds, a vehicle common in Europe, in which the loans remain on the balance sheets of the banks and tie up their capital as well as make them responsible if things go bad. This obviously makes them think twice and limits their leverage.

Furthermore, a number of medium-size and smaller banks are in dire straits. Many own troubled loans that finance commercial real estate projects that they'll probably eventually write off as delinquencies mount. Commercial real estate loans in relation to capital are heavy in banks with

Table 6.5 Bank Exposure to Commercial Real Estate (as of September 30, 2009; in $ Billion)

Commercial Banks (by Asset Size)	Total Assets	Total CRE Whole Loan Exposure	Total CMBS Exposure	Tier 1 Risk-Based Capital	CRE Whole Loans/Tier 1 Capital
Greater than $10 billion (85 banks)	$9,460	$843	$47,304	$749.3	112.5%
$1 billion to $10 billion (440 banks)	$1,159	$365	$1,943	$104.9	346.5%
$100 million to $1 billion (3,798 banks)	$1,104	$354	$0.708	$102.5	344.9%
Less than $100 million (2,588 banks)	$143	$27	$0.058	$16.3	165.2%

Data sources: Federal Deposit Insurance Corp. and SNL Financial.

$1 billion to $10 billion in assets and in those with $100 million to $1 billion (see Table 6.5). The big banks are now, in effect, guaranteed by the federal government. From the way major bank CEOs are grilled by congressional committees and ordered about, one wonders whether they have received General Schedule (GS) ratings that indicate their status as federal government employees. But medium and smaller banks are not too big to fail—that is, they are too small to rescue and lack easy access to private capital.

Like households, the financial sector spiked its borrowing and equity issues for three decades (Figure 4.7). Now its embarrassed leaders, pressured by regulators and everyone else here and abroad, will no doubt pursue the deleveraging process for years to come. Securitization, off-balance-sheet financing, derivatives, and other shadow bank-system vehicles that both stimulated and distorted economic activity are disappearing.

Chastened lenders will probably be overly cautious for years as they eschew all those fancy financing vehicles and move back toward banking 101, spread lending in which banks take deposits and then lend them at market-determined spreads. It's human nature to move from one extreme to the other, and overly conservative lending will probably prevent many reasonable risk takers from being financed for years to come. And, of course, the financial sector will be much less profitable as the lucrative fees and spreads from securitization, high leverage, and so forth are absent.

I saw a prime example of the profitability that can result from leverage several years ago while visiting a consulting prospect, the proprietary trading arm of Citigroup. That operation occupied three complete huge floors of what earlier was the Travelers building in lower Manhattan. Looking out over the sea of traders and computers, I wondered, how can all these highly paid people and expensive equipment and services make enough, trading Citigroup's money, to cover their costs and return a profit? Are they all trading geniuses who see opportunities that others miss? And since, in trading, for every winner there is a loser, if they're consistently profitable, who are the losers?

Leverage!

Sure, some of their gains came from spreads on trades they made for customers. But a lot came from what are essentially spread positions with lots of leverage. Borrowing through asset-backed commercial paper and then buying subprime-related securities might net two percentage points, but if the trade is leveraged 20-to-1, the return is 40 percentage points, a huge profit. But a mere 5 percent decline in the mortgage securities value wipes out the capital, and that indeed is what subsequently happened. I wonder how many traders are left on those three big floors.

Deleveraging of the financial sector will obviously have negative ramifications for the real economy it finances. We've already seen plenty of effects among small businesses, homeowners, and consumers. The credit crisis won't last forever, but it did reveal the extent to which consumers and businesses depend on borrowed money and lack equity and reserves to finance even normal operations. We're seeing that many larger businesses depend on commercial paper to finance inventories and buy supplies. Small businesses rely on bank loans and owners' personal credit cards to meet payrolls.

Many companies that import materials rely on bank letters of credit for financing and only pay after they've processed the materials and sold the finished goods. Then banks, worried about getting paid, curtailed letters of credit, which left goods stranded on the docks. Consumers depended on home equity withdrawals to fund day-to-day spending and used their credit cards like ATMs. More reliance on equity and less on borrowing is quite probable in future years and will no doubt curtail economic growth.

Cautious institutional and individual investors will probably limit the funds flowing into venture capital firms in the years ahead at the same time that slower economic growth will impede the businesses that many of them finance. And muted equity markets are likely to limit investors' appetite for initial public offerings, the normal exit strategy for venture capitalists. As banks avoid leveraged loans and investors are wary about junk bonds, private equity leveraged buyouts are likely to be muted for years.

Overseas, Western banks largely financed the rapid economic growth in the former Iron Curtain countries in Europe after the Soviet Union collapsed in 1991. Many companies in those lands funded their domestic businesses by borrowing Swiss francs and other hard currencies at lower rates than in their own inflation-prone countries. Individuals entered the same carry trade to fund their home mortgages.

With the financial crisis, however, lenders retreated as they delevered, local currencies were weak or likely to be devalued if pegged to strong currencies, and growth in those lands will be in jeopardy for years. The Latvian and Lithuanian economies nosedived, and their currencies, pegged to the euro in anticipation of entering the eurozone, risked devaluations.

The United Kingdom seems especially zealous to reduce financial leverage. In late 2009, Adair Turner, chairman of the Financial Services Authority, said he believed that the financial system got too big and got involved in more "clever" finance and trading than was needed to keep the economy humming efficiently. Lord Turner also believed there was too much debt in the system and that financial firms needed to delever. This is beginning to happen. In the year through March, the median investment-grade European company had a 5 percent decline in net debt while earnings before interest, taxes, depreciation, and amortization rose 1 percent.

More Government Regulation

U.S. consumer retrenchment and global financial deleveraging will keep worldwide economic growth subdued for many years. So, too, will my third reason, vastly increased regulation here and abroad, the normal reaction to financial and economic crises. *When a lot of people lose a lot of money, there is a cosmic need for scapegoats and increased regulation.* In September 2008, just before the vote on the big $700 billion financial bailout bill, Speaker Nancy Pelosi said on the House floor, "For too long this government, eight years, has followed a right-wing ideology of anything goes, no supervision, no discipline, no regulation. It has created not jobs, not capital; it has created chaos." Sure, many embarrassed financial wizards have sworn off their wayward ways and will be cautious for years, probably the balance of their careers. But that won't stop witch hunts.

Regulation and more government involvement in the economy are the normal reactions to big problems. Historically, it was during wars that governments assumed bigger, often dominant roles but afterward withdrew to let the economy pretty much run itself. The Civil War brought immense economic involvement by the governments on both sides, but for the rest of the nineteenth century, wildcat banking, private expansion of the Western frontier, and buccaneer capitalism had fairly free reign.

Until near its end, the twentieth century was one of increasing government involvement, not surprising since it was dominated by two world wars, the Cold War, and the Great Depression, as mentioned earlier. The Depression ushered in a whole new role for government, the welfare state as some would call it. Economic collapse that didn't seem to be curing itself quickly sired the New Deal programs, Social Security, and the widespread conviction that not only was the federal government responsible for ensuring full employment and decent livings for everyone, but also was able to deliver on that responsibility.

In the 1930s, the economic collapse was widely blamed on the laissez-faire financial sector. So the reaction was the Securities and Exchange Act; the Glass-Steagall Act that separated banks, brokers, and insurers; and the FDIC and the SEC. The Fed had been created earlier in 1913 in reaction to the Panic of 1907.

A consistent characteristic of regulation, however, is that it comes after the fact, in reaction to abuses and problems. By the time regulation of Wall Street was enacted in the 1930s, investors were so disillusioned with stocks that they had no interest in them—or in giving anyone the opportunity for new equity-related abuses—for almost two decades. In fact, it can be argued that well-intentioned regulators often do harm by inhibiting constructive changes. Glass-Steagall, which was gradually eroded but officially on the books until 1999, was considered a case in point by many—at least until the recent financial crisis.

The tide turns like all trends, the government involvement in the U.S. economy that started in 1933 got so overdone that by the 1970s, voters reacted, as discussed in Chapter 2. As a result, deregulation and a shrinking role for government were prevalent in the 1980s and 1990s in financial services, retail trade, telecommunications, transportation, and many other areas. But the dot-com stock bubble of the late 1990s and the 9/11 terrorist attacks in 2001 reversed the tide. The 9/11 attacks led to the nationalization of airport security, strip searches of passengers, the monstrous Department of Homeland Security, and so-called planters outside Washington buildings that look like the tank traps they are.

In any event, the voter revolt was first manifested with the passage of Proposition 13 in California in 1978, which limited property taxes, and it culminated with the 1980 election of Ronald Reagan, who said that "government is not the solution to our problems; government is the problem." In the late 1970s, that rebellion against government convinced me that the then frighteningly high inflation would fade, since in our view excess government spending is the root of inflation, as discussed in Chapter 9. So I wrote my first book in the early 1980s, *Is Inflation Ending? Are You Ready?* that correctly forecast the ensuing chronic fall in inflation rates and the salutary effects on both stock (Figure 1.6) and bond prices (Figure 1.5), even before the end of the Cold War was in sight.

When the dot-com bubble broke, the blame game moved into high gear. Wall Street firms and their analysts, like Jack Grubman, who promoted stocks they really believed to be garbage, were readily available. Then came the billion-dollar fines on Wall Street firms and the ridiculous directive to brokers to buy and promote the research of outside "independent" analysts, as noted earlier. The corporate accounting scandals early in the 2000s that sank Enron and WorldCom led to the Sarbanes-Oxley law, which added immensely to corporate accounting costs. Later, "late trading" abuses among mutual funds led to more fines and more regulation, but again, well after the fact.

Outside of Wall Street, problems like the Vioxx scandal have led to congressional calls for more drug regulation and safety. Energy deregulation in California starting in 1998 has been largely dismantled after power shortages led to frighteningly large swings in prices. And the Department of Education essentially nationalized the student loan markets after private lenders withdrew earlier in 2008.

Tainted food and lead paint on toys from China led to huge product recalls recently. In 2007, 45 million toys and other children's products were recalled for hazards ranging from lead paint to small but powerful magnets that might be swallowed. Recalls jumped 22 percent in the nine months ending June 30 from the year-earlier period. In reaction to faulty testing in China and other exporters, retailers stepped up standards and used their own testing services. Toymaker Mattel said its testing program adds 1.5 percent to the cost of goods sold.

An Invitation for More

With the bursting of the subprime mortgages bubble and the financial crisis it spawned, government involvement in financial markets mushroomed. Interestingly, in keeping with the Bush administration philosophy, then-Treasury Secretary Paulson made it clear that he fundamentally opposed bailouts and government intervention. Early on, he said, "I don't see a good result to come out of somehow injecting more public money into trying to prevent a correction in the housing market that is inevitable or in looking to somehow or another keep people in homes if they can't afford to stay in their homes." But after the crisis at Fannie and Freddie unfolded, he stated, "I would rather not be in the position of asking for extraordinary authority to support the GSEs, but. I am playing the hand I have been dealt."

Still, he played that hand to the utmost. When the housing bill that also provides for the rescue of Fannie and Freddie was being debated in Congress, he argued for unlimited bailout money for the pair. "If you want to make sure it's used, make it small enough and it will be a self-fulfilling prophecy." But leaving the amount open-ended "would be more confidence-inspiring and it would put the government in a stronger position and minimize the cost to the taxpayer." In other words, he went on, "If you've got a squirt gun in your pocket, you may have to take it out. If you've got a bazooka, and people know you've got it . . . you're not likely to take it out."

In 2008 at a mortgage security bailout congressional hearing, Paulson said, "I have never been a proponent of intervention, and I just think we have an unprecedented situation here and it calls for unprecedented action. There's no way to stabilize the markets other than through government intervention." His original proposal would give him czar-like control of the $700 billion bailout fund.

So Paulson the free-market devotee became Paulson the activist. In March 2008, he proposed a sensible overhaul of the current hodgepodge of financial market regulations, which would give the Fed oversight of risk throughout the financial system. Still, I have to ask, is overlapping and sometimes contradictory regulation by the Fed, the SEC, the Office of the Comptroller of the Currency, the Office of Federal Housing Enterprise Oversight, the National Credit Union Administration, the FDIC, and the Commodity Futures Trading Commission worse than that of one overall regulation czar that may be very efficient and precise, but could inflict terrible damage if it makes a mistake?

In March 2010, Senate Banking Committee Chairman Christopher Dodd introduced a bill that would permit the Fed to examine any bank holding company with over $50 billion in assets as well as large nonbank financial institutions. Furthermore, an autonomous Fed division would regulate consumer lenders. The government also would be able to take over and liquidate failing financial outfits, regulate financial derivatives, give shareholders more power over public company operations, and give the government increased ability to limit the risks taken by banks. The United Kingdom, as usual moving faster than the United States, has already increased the number of examiners per major bank to a maximum of 15 from the earlier limit of six.

Meanwhile, the Justice Department is looking into whether hedge funds colluded in selling short the Eurocurrency during the Greek crisis. And its Antitrust Division and Democrats in Congress seem interested in challenging the Supreme Court, which has been limiting the application of the 120-year-old Sherman Antitrust Act.

Expanded Fed

Even without the Treasury Secretary's grand plan, the role of the Fed expanded greatly, starting in the summer of 2008 when financial markets came close to freezing up. After the central bank realized that its cuts in the discount and fed funds rates (Figure 1.3) were doing little to ease the crisis, it embarked on a series of measures to make funds available to banks that couldn't borrow from other banks since they were too wary to lend. Later, that list was expanded to include opening the discount window to investment banks to insure that the run on the bank that sank Bear Stearns wouldn't recur.

Of course, with the Fed lending to investment banks for the first time since the 1930s, it was only a matter of time until it regulated them. Indeed, Chairman Bernanke said in July 2008 that lending to investment banks "could tend to make market disruptions less effective in the future. Going forward, the regulation and supervision of these institutions must take account of these realities." As noted earlier, already, Fed officials were stationed inside the four major firms and working alongside officials from the SEC to oversee those investment banks' operations. If investment banks borrow Fed money just as commercial banks do, why shouldn't they be regulated like their commercial cousins?

The Fed has also been active in urging derivatives issuers to improve and speed up their clearance operations. Furthermore, although the Fed traditionally leaves responsibility for the dollar's value against foreign currencies to the Treasury, Chairman Bernanke in June 2008 when the buck was quite weak made an extraordinary comment. He said that the buck's steep fall had contributed to an "unwelcome rise in import prices and consumer price inflation." Sure, inflation is the Fed concern, and so must its causes be as well. Still, the Fed Chairman expanded the central bank's sphere of influence into the currency market.

No Chance to Regulate

The Fed didn't have a chance to regulate the major investment banks because after Lehman went bankrupt, Merrill Lynch agreed to merge with Bank of America in September 2008, and the two remaining large investment banks, Morgan Stanley and Goldman Sachs, became bank holding companies. So they're now formally regulated by the Fed, anyway. Obviously, as bank holding companies, their leverage ratios were cut drastically over the two years of transition, and their investments and trading activity much more closely scrutinized, all to the detriment of earning power.

The Fed's involvement in financial institutions was also enhanced by its initial $85 billion loan to bail out AIG on top of its guarantee of $29 billion in Bear Stearns securities to facilitate its takeover in March by JPMorgan Chase. The government's direct involvement with financial institutions also includes the warrants the government now holds in Fannie and Freddie and AIG, and the other financial institutions into which it pumped money.

Some in Congress are questioning the newly developed power of the Fed and its chairman. "Why does one person have the right to grant $85 billion in a bailout without the scrutiny and transparency the American people deserve?" asked House Speaker Pelosi. House Financial Services Committee Chairman Barney Frank reported that Bernanke said, "I have $800 billion" (in Treasurys) when he was asked where he'd get the $85 billion for the AIG bailout. Mr. Frank, who speaks in paragraphs longer than German PhD dissertations but is always good for a one-liner, said later, "No one in a democracy, unelected, should have $800 billion to spend as he sees fit. That's not the way to run a democracy."

Crisis Inquiry Commission

In reaction to the financial crisis, the Congressional Financial Crisis Inquiry Commission was established, started hearings in January 2010, and must deliver a final report by December. Its chairman, Rep. Phil Angelides, was California's treasurer for eight years and is well known for tenaciously attacking executive pay, promoting human rights, and pushing corporations toward greater social responsibility. He apparently wants his commission to compile the complete chronology of the financial crisis, as did the 9/11 Commission. He's also studied the Pecora Commission that pilloried Wall Street in the wake of the 1929 Crash. He said at the first hearing that the commission would become "a proxy for the American people—their eyes, their ears, and possibly also their voice . . . if we ignore history, we're doomed to bail it out again."

At that hearing, the CEOs of Goldman Sachs, JPMorgan Chase, Morgan Stanley, and Bank of America were grilled. In reference to Goldman Sachs's business of selling mortgage-backed securities in the expectation they would decline, Angelides said, "It sounds to me a little bit like selling a car with faulty brakes and then buying an insurance policy on the buyer of those cars." It didn't help that Goldman Sachs decided to pay billions of dollars in executive bonuses for record 2009 earnings and that its CEO, Lloyd Blankfein, had earlier said he was just a banker doing "God's work."

In an April 2010 hearing, the Commission's vice chairman, former Republican Congressman Bill Thomas, tore into Charles Prince, former Citigroup CEO, when he tried to explain his infamous mid-2007 statement, "As long as the music is playing, you've got to get up and dance. We're still dancing." Prince was referring to Citi's risky loans for private equity buyouts, but Thomas said, "You weren't going to be the lemming that stopped and said: 'I don't want to keep walking.'"

The commission is also interested in government efforts to investigate and prosecute financial lawbreaking during the crisis. Attorney General Eric Holder earlier said that the Justice Department is "using every tool at our disposal—including new resources, advanced technology and communications capabilities, and the very best talent we have—to prevent, prosecute, and punish these crimes."

The Volcker Rule

In January 2010, President Obama proposed that banks that take FDIC-insured deposits be prohibited from proprietary trading—the Volcker Rule, named for its proponent, former Fed Chairman Paul Volcker. Just like the President's reference in December 2009 to "fat cat" bankers, this announcement shook Wall Street, especially since it's unclear how proprietary trading and transactions to serve clients can be separated and how legitimate hedging can be allowed. The President also proposed that banks be prohibited from investing in hedge funds. He also called for expanding the 1994 law that prohibits one bank from acquiring another if the combined entity would control more than 10 percent of national insured deposits by expanding the limit to cover nondeposit short-term bank borrowing from financial markets. This all seems aimed at reinstituting the 1930s Glass–Steagall Act and confining banks to spread lending, as mentioned earlier.

The financial reform bill, still not passed in Congress as of early July 2010, contains a number of these proposals. It also would allow regulators to seize and break up troubled financial institutions that threaten the system, require routine derivatives to be traded on exchanges and routed through a clearinghouse, create the Consumer Financial Protection Bureau within the Federal Reserve, require mortgage lenders to verify borrower income and credit history, require banks to keep 5 percent of credit risks on their balance sheets, tighten regulation of credit rating firms, and give shareholders nonbonding votes on executive compensation.

Central Bank Independence

Congressional attempts to cut the Fed's independence are to be expected after the central bank moved far beyond traditional monetary policy with quantitative easing, the initial direct loan to AIG of $85 billion, supporting the Treasury by buying its debt, and so forth. If housing collapses again in the future, will the Fed be expected to support it? Chairman Bernanke admits that the Fed did not curb the excessive risks of the banks it regulates, but will that force the central bank to be excessively vigilant in the future? The New York Fed decided to make those who bought credit default swaps (CDSs) from AIG whole, in effect paying them with government money pumped into that troubled insurer. And it told AIG not to disclose key elements of the agreement. What precedent does this set?

The independence of central banks globally is under fire, and not long after some of them achieved separation from government control. The Bank of England became independent in 1997 and the Bank of Japan a year later. Both of these, along with the European Central Bank (ECB) and the Fed, responded to the financial crisis with massive intervention well beyond traditional monetary policy, and all are in boats with their governments that are hard to abandon. On his first day in office, the new

British Chancellor of the Exchequer, George Osborne, asked Bank of England governor Mervyn King to endorse his budget plan. That violates the principle that central bankers don't comment on fiscal policy, but he got the endorsement. In November 2009, Japanese Banking Minister Shizuka Kamei said, "The Bank of Japan is asleep at the wheel as usual." That same month, the head of the new Budget Bureau said, "We need comprehensive measures to address the current economic situation. I hope the Bank of Japan will take steps in a way that will answer our hopes." He was later named Finance Minister and then said, "With help from monetary policy steps, I'd like to avoid the economy from falling into a double-dip recession."

In January 2010, French President Sarkozy once again said the euro, which the ECB influences through its interest rates, is too strong. Also that month, the South Korean government sent an official to a central bank policy meeting, exercising its right for the first time in a decade. Argentine President Christine Kirchner forced out the president of the central bank over her demand to transfer $6.57 billion in foreign reserves to pay off government bonds held by foreigners. In China, there's no question about central bank independence. That organization is a government department in charge of China's monetary policy.

A congressional panel in 2009 blasted Chairman Bernanke over his role in Bank of America's purchase of failing Merrill Lynch, but the chairman struck back by increasing his visibility with the American public, including a town hall–style meeting in Kansas City.

The eurozone has a common currency and central bank, but no parallel organization to manage a uniform fiscal policy that is run by the 16 individual members. So the ECB and its strong president, Jean-Claude Trichet, in effect represent overall economic policy for the group. But with the eurozone financial crisis in 2009–2010, the government of Germany and the other stronger eurozone economies are heavily involved. Also, German Chancellor Angela Merkel insisted that the International Monetary Fund (IMF) be involved in any bailout. Trichet resisted IMF involvement since it implied that the eurozone and the ECB couldn't handle their own problems, but he lost. He also bowed to political pressure to buy government bonds to help soften the eurozone debt crisis. Both he and the ECB have suffered at least a temporary loss of prestige and power, even if the eurozone survives intact.

Fiscal Control in Europe

With the €110 billion bailout of Greece and €750 billion standby credit for other EU members, EU officials have been pushing for authority to review national budgets that were previously left to individual countries. Furthermore, Eurostat, the bloc's statistics agency, has new authority to do limited audits on countries books to forestall the number massaging done earlier in Greece, Portugal, and elsewhere to reduce reported government deficits.

The EU's executive arm, the European Commission, wants to review budgets before they are sent to parliaments. "Coordination of fiscal policy has to be conducted on advance, in order to insure that national budgets are consistent with the European dimension, that they don't put at risk the stability of the other member states," said the EU's economics affairs commissioner in a statement.

Furthermore, the European Central Bank has moved considerably beyond its monetary policy role with its president, Jean–Claude Trichet, calling for "the equivalent of fiscal federation" in the EU. He proposes an independent agency that would review national budgets and hand out sanctions against countries that were out of line. Fiscal federation is anathema to many Europeans. The Germans believe it would result in a loss of sovereignty and transfer funds from German taxpayers to wayward Club Med lands. But the French and others favor more centralized fiscal control in the eurozone on top of the common currency.

The eurozone crisis has also resulted in direct intervention with financial institutions. In Greece, the big leap in debt since the advent of the eurozone was at the government level, but in Spain it was in the private sector. Much of the jump in Spanish private debt financed the housing boom. From 1995 to their peak in the second quarter of 2008, Spanish house prices leaped 213 percent, but have only retreated 11 percent since then. In contrast, U.S. house prices jumped 143 percent from 1995 to their first quarter 2006 peak and have fallen 29 percent since then. Spanish house prices probably have much further to decline, and this is bad news for Spain's 45 *cajas*, regional savings banks often run by local politicians and heavy into residential lending.

The *cajas* constitute about half of the banking sector. Estimates are they have €175 billion in real estate-developer loans equal to 273 percent of tangible equity, and might need €43 billion in new equity. Right before the June 30 deadline for tapping the government Fund for Orderly Bank Restructuring and pushed by the government and the Bank of Spain, 39 of the 45 *cajas* agreed to merge, 26 of them with €768 billion in assets doing so with state aid totaling €11 billion. Subsequently, the government moved to encourage stock ownership in the *cajas* and reduce political control.

Ireland has also stepped in to bail out troubled banks—and to regulate them more intensely. In March 2010, it set up a "bad bank" program under which the National Asset Management Agency would spend €8.5 billion to acquire over 1,200 loans with a face value of €16 billion, about twice their current value, from lenders. NAMA expects to acquire €81 billion in face value loans by February 2011.

The government also issued tough bank capital requirements that could put more banks under government ownership. Then in June, the Irish Financial Services Regulatory Authority intensified bank supervision to eliminate the loose lending practices that led to the earlier collapse of the Irish housing boom and the financial sector. New regulations include tighter bank liquidity buffers, limits on exposure to any other company, and new controls on pay and financial institutional management. It also is setting up a system to deal with failing banks.

Bank Exposure

One reason that central banks and governments in individual countries are concerned about their banks' health is because of their exposure abroad. Banks are so intertwined today by cross-border and global finance that problems in any one country, even tiny Greece, could easily multiply into a worldwide financial crisis. French banks have $75 billion in public and private sector Greek debt, and German banks hold $45 billion. In total, at the end of 2009, French banks had $493 billion in exposure to Greece, Ireland, Portugal, and Spain. Germany had $465 billion to those same countries. Of the $958 billion total, $174 billion was sovereign debt and $784 billion was private. Banks in the 16-member eurozone had $1.58 trillion, or 62 percent, of all international active bank exposure to that quartet.

Recently, the ECB warned that eurozone banks face $240 billion writedowns in 2010 and 2011. PricewaterhouseCoopers says German banks had $260 billion in nonperforming loans on their books at the end of 2009. These troubled loans could be lethal to some thinly-capitalized banks. European banks tend to have high leverage ratios—assets to equity—ranging from 21 to 49. In comparison, U.S. banks, many of which sank or had to be bailed out of the subprime mortgage-induced financial crisis, have subsequently reduced their leverage ratios from the 20 to 30 range to 12 to 17.

U.S. banks are far from immune from the European debt crisis. For the five largest, exposure to Europe equals percent of Tier 1 capital. Exposure to Spain, Greece, and Italy equal 25 percent of Tier 1 capital, and the five's exposure to Germany and France equals 61 percent. In total, U.S. banks have $1.5 trillion in exposure to major European countries plus the United Kingdom, or 48 percent of their global total.

Stress Tests

EU officials hope that the stress tests that are being applied to banks will reassure investors and other banks of their soundness. In 2009, the United States gave 19 major banks stress tests that found 10 needed a total of $75 billion more capital. Those tests did not use a particularly stressful scenario, but publishing the results of each bank did help reassure investors that the financial system would not collapse.

European banking supervisors also performed stress tests last year, but did not reveal the test assumptions or the results for individual banks for fear that bad news could sink weak banks and require expensive bailouts. This year they have agreed to do so, and the results are expected by the end of July. Originally, the list included about 25 large European institutions, close to the 22 tested in 2009, but has been expanded to 91 banks. The additions will include the large but questionable German Landesbanken.

Financial Standards

The results of the stress tests will also be used to help determine international standards for adequate bank capital. G-20 leaders have agreed to develop standards by the end of 2010, but major leaders have different ideas on this and related issues. Germany and France want an annual levy on banks' balance sheets to cover the costs of future bailouts. Canada, whose banks haven't required bailouts, thinks such a tax is unnecessary. The United Kingdom plans to tax its banks even if there is no international agreement to do so. Germany is also considering a tax on financial transactions to help pay for the €750 billion eurozone sovereign debt rescue and wants other eurozone lands to join her. Meanwhile, European finance ministers have approved measures to rein in hedge funds, and the United States is likely to follow suit.

Meanwhile, the new U.K. government is revising financial regulations by eliminating the watchdog Financial Services Authority, blamed for being asleep during the financial crisis and consolidating power within the Bank of England. The reorganization, to be implemented by the end of 2012, makes the Bank of England, in addition to running monetary policy, responsible for preventing systemic financial risks and for ongoing supervision of the financial sector, including foreign firms operating in the City of London. Two other FSA functions—consumer protection and law enforcement—will be assumed by new independent agencies. These changes will probably mean much more stringent bank regulation. Bank of England Governor Mervyn King has talked openly about breaking up big banks.

World Trade Organization head Pascal Lamy also believes that current international financial regulation will not prevent another financial crisis. In a recent speech, he said that the G-20 had "not yet, visibly, filled the regulatory gap in international finance that was the main cause, if not 'the' cause of the financial explosion." The European Commission has proposed a number of restrictions on banks and insurance companies. They include limits on the number of boards a person can sit on, prohibitions on one person being CEO and board chairman, restrictions on pay packages for departing executives and elevating risk management committees to board level. It also proposed legislation to tighten the oversight of credit rating companies.

Obama's Budget

The first Obama federal budget in February 2009 also pointed clearly to more government regulation and involvement in the economy, in health, education, and the environment. Beyond the financial sector, the bailout of U.S. auto producers led to considerable government control of that industry, almost day-to-day management by Washington.

Of all the signs of opulence carried over from the bubble years, corporate jets and big executive bonuses seem to bother Congress and the President the most. This reaction to big bonuses paid by firms that are taking huge write-offs, losing big money, and requiring massive government bailouts was predictable. The administration appointed pay czar Kenneth Feinberg to review and even force renegotiation of pay controls at those firms—with no appeal. In March 2010, he forced AIG to cut $45 million from 2009 retention bonuses, some paid to people who had left the firm. And he put $500,000 salary caps on 82 percent of the 119 top executives at the five companies he oversaw in early 2010 because they still had government bailout money—AIG, GM, Chrysler Financial, Chrysler, and GMAC. In addition, the Fed now reviews compensation of officers of the banks it regulates, and also wants to be sure that traders who take bigger risks aren't paid more.

Overseas, the United Kingdom applied a 50 percent tax on 2009 bank bonuses over $40,000 to discourage risk taking and encourage banks to retain more capital. France followed suit with a tax of 50 percent on bank employee bonuses over $40,000 for 2009, to soothe the public concern over high pay levels and help fund bank bailouts while pressuring financial institutions to beef up reserves. In early July 2010, the European Parliament passed a law limiting EU-country cash bonuses to 30 percent of a banker's total, and 40 percent to 60 percent will have to be deferred three years or more and clawed back for base investment performance. Over half must be paid in bank stock.

Even China is requiring its financial companies to limit top management bonuses to three times salaries and retain 40 percent of bonuses against future risks for three years. Bear in mind that all major Chinese banks and insurers are majority-owned by the government and top officers are appointed by the Communist Party. The government wants to control financial risks and "ensure a fair distribution of income in society." In late 2009, Hong Kong required senior bank executives to defer at least 60 percent of their bonuses for three years, with a clawback provision in the event of future losses.

The SEC, accused of being asleep at the switch while the excesses that led to the financial crisis ran rampant, subsequently flexed its muscles and extended its reach. It belatedly studied the now thoroughly discredited credit rating firms and concluded, lo and behold, that they put profits ahead of quality controls as they struggled to keep up with the explosive growth in mortgage-related debt vehicles during the boom years. The report found that the analysts involved in the ratings were well aware of the fees involved. One rating firm "regularly reduced loss expectations on subprime second lien mortgages" from what the firm's models showed but didn't publicly disclose that practice.

The SEC began oversight of rating firms in 2007, and it then proposed new rules requiring them to disclose historical ratings performance to help investors gauge their accuracy. The SEC also wanted the firms to avoid conflicts of interest such as letting a bond issuer determine which analyst will rate its issues and then wining and dining him. The agency also proposed a new rating scale to separate corporate bonds for inherently more risky securitizations, far too many of which were highly rated in yesteryear. More recently, in early 2010, the SEC voted to encourage public companies to inform shareholders about the effects of climate change on their businesses. Down under, Australia is bringing its securities regulation in line with the United States by giving its Securities and Investments Commission the power to levy higher fines and prison terms for insider trading, market rigging, lying, and market manipulation.

On another front, the SEC reacted to the collapse in bank and broker stocks by curbing the improper short selling of 17 financial stocks plus Fannie and Freddie. Attempts to limit short selling, going back to the aftermath of the South Sea bubble in 1733, have never been successful, but the SEC's increased involvement in this area will probably persist.

In late 2007 and early 2008, FDIC Chairman Sheila Bair was calling for modification of underwater mortgages to eliminate negative equity and give homeowners the incentive to stay in their abodes. She finally got her chance with the collapse of IndyMac. The FDIC, on taking control of that failed bank, suspended foreclosures in progress for IndyMac's $15 billion mortgage portfolio and instituted a mortgage modification program.

She justified these moves by saying they will limit FDIC losses. More likely, however, they were to benefit distressed homeowners. The FDIC's stated mission is to insure bank deposits, but Bair extended it into mortgage modifications. In addition, the FDIC is imposing higher fees on banks it insures whose pay policies encourage risky behavior that could threaten the banks' solvency. At the same time, the head of the Federal Housing Financing Agency that regulates the 12 Federal Home Loan Banks told them in May 2010 to reduce risks and stick to their core mission of making secure loans to banks.

Many Examples

Other examples of growing government regulation and involvement in the economy are rampant. The Environmental Protection Agency in January 2010 proposed tightening smog-reduction measures, which it estimates will cost between $19 billion and $90 billion annually, by forcing refineries, gas stations, power plants, and other businesses to reduce emissions of chemicals they contribute to smog. The medical bill enacted by Congress in March 2010 under gigantic administration pressure is really a health insurance, not a health care, law. It increases hugely the federal government involvement in the economy by forcing health insurers to take all applicants and forcing businesses and individuals to carry medical insurance or pay the equivalent in fines. The Department of Energy plans to give or lend over $40 billion to businesses developing clean technology like electric cars, better batteries, wind turbines, and solar panels. That increases the likelihood that the government, not the market, will decide which are the most promising. He who pays the piper calls the tune.

The administration also increased scrutiny of foreign bribery of U.S. companies. The proposed regulation of industrial carbon dioxide emissions has been sidelined by evidence of unscientific behavior by its advocates, but would have huge effects on a wide range of businesses. With increased involvement in energy, transportation, health, and finance, the government is affecting a third of the economy.

Fat Cats

The President has made clear his zeal to blame Wall Street more rigorously for the financial institutions' problems, and to make them pay for bailouts. In December 2009, he said in a CBS *60 Minutes* interview, "I did not run for office to be helping a bunch of fat cat bankers on Wall

Street" and "you guys are drawing down $10, $20 million bonuses after America went through the worst economic year that it's gone through in decades, and you guys caused the problem. And we've got 10 percent unemployment." In January 2010, he proposed a $90 billion tax over 10 years on financial firms that received government help.

He then talked about "obscene bonuses" and said this tax would "repay taxpayers in full for saving [banks'] skins in a time of need" and added, "We want our money back! And we're going to get your money back—every dime, each and every dime."

Larry Summers, the chairman of the President's National Economic Council, said on CNN's *State of the Union*, "Here is what I think they don't get. . . . It was their irresponsible risk taking in many cases that brought the economy to collapse." Interestingly, the Treasury estimated in April 2010 that the financial bailout will cost $89 billion. That's close to the proposed $90 billion tax and far less than the Congressional Budget Office's estimate a year earlier of $250 billion due to recovery of financial institutions and repayment of bailout money. The $89 billion number, however, excludes the open-ended cost of rescuing distressed homeowners through Fannie and Freddie. That $89 billion is about 0.6 percent of GDP compared to the 3.2 percent of GDP bailout of the savings and loan crisis 20 years ago. Of course, that figure doesn't include the effects of the financial crisis and recession, which reduced federal tax revenues considerably, probably by around $200 billion in 2009.

Higher Taxes

The administration is also interested in higher taxes to reduce the huge federal deficit (Figure 3.1) and has appointed a commission to recommend possible actions. The nonpartisan Tax Policy Center estimates that in a worst-case scenario it would take half a trillion dollars per year in revenue increases and/or spending cuts to reduce the deficit from 10 percent of GDP in 2009 to 3 percent. Since about half of households pay no income tax, higher income taxes to reduce the deficit to 3 percent of GDP would fall on upper-income families, and would push the top two brackets from 33 and 35 percent to 72.4 and 76.8 percent, the Tax Policy Center estimates. Since those taxpayers account for a big chunk of consumer spending, tax hikes of that magnitude would drive the currently weak economy into a major depression.

In recessionary 2008, the top 20 percent of households by income accounted for 38.4 percent of consumer income, almost identical to their 38.2 percent average over the previous 10 years. This implied that like lower income folks, they cut their spending when their incomes suffered in tougher times. It suggests they'd do the same in reaction to a tax hike-induced reduction in after-tax income.

Massive tax increases on high earners are unlikely, however. True, the President has advocated letting the Bush-era tax cuts expire at the end of 2010 for high-income taxpayers, pushing the top two brackets to 36 percent and 39.6 percent. Still, continuing high unemployment and a lethargic economy may encourage Congress to keep current tax rates in place.

If, contrary to my forecast, the economy skyrockets, the awesome revenue-generating capability of the federal tax system will reduce the deficit quickly. But if it remains tepid, with chronic high unemployment, as I project, major tax increases will only make it weaker. On the other side of the coin, I doubt that any serious economist other than an Obama loyalist believes the President's contention in his January 2010 State of the Union address that "because of the steps we took, there are about two million Americans working right now who would otherwise be unemployed." The administration's own report said 599,108 people were being paid economic stimulus funds in the fourth quarter of 2009, but even that number is questionable.

Other countries are also looking for ways to close their government budget gaps with higher taxes on someone. Some 42 percent of India investment funds are domiciled in Mauritius, and India plans to change the tax treaty with that country to impose a 10 to 15 percent capital gains tax. The United Kingdom, in addition to taxing bankers' big bonuses, has increased the top individual income tax rate from 40 to 50 percent.

Fannie and Freddie

The American Dream of home ownership is very powerful politically. So the collapse in house prices (Figure 1.2) almost guaranteed increased and chronic government support for homeowners. If house prices fall another 10 percent, as we forecast, about 40 percent of those with mortgages will be underwater, compared with 23 percent in early 2010, and the gap between their mortgage debt and house values will total about $800 billion. The government-sponsored enterprises (GSEs) Fannie Mae and Freddie Mac as well as the Federal Housing Administration, which is part of the Department of Housing and Urban Development, are the entities through which the government is supporting housing. Indeed, these three now fund or guarantee 99 percent of new mortgages, up from 55 percent in the housing boom days when private lenders with low underwriting standards were robust.

Back in mid-2008, many FDIC-insured institutions were heavily leveraged but still had an average capital-to-asset ratio of 7.9 percent. In contrast, Freddie and Fannie have less than 2 percent, so for each buck of capital, they owned or guaranteed $50 in mortgages. Lobbyists from the two convinced Congress that they didn't need more capital since defaults would be tiny as house prices rose forever. But when the housing sector nosedived, Fannie and Freddie's houses of cards fell apart. So in September 2008, both were seized by the government in a legal structure called *conservatorship*, as noted earlier. They are regulated, indeed controlled, by the Federal Housing Finance Agency. Initially, each had up to $200 billion backing from the Treasury, but it later was made open-ended through 2012.

Off-Balance-Sheet Vehicles

Washington regarded Freddie and Fannie as part of the government. Assistant Treasury Secretary Michael Barr said that because they are "owned by the taxpayers in the biggest housing crisis in 80 years, it is logical that they be used to stabilize the housing market." But since the two technically remain private corporations, their finances remain off the federal budget and their huge prospective losses from sour mortgages don't need to be counted in the federal deficit. It's ironic that the government is using Fannie and Freddie as the biggest off-balance-sheet financing vehicles in the economy at the same time it's blasting banks for using off-balance-sheet entities in earlier years.

Also, by using these GSEs to support housing, with an open credit line to the Treasury, the administration doesn't have to approach Congress for funding bit by bit. The Treasury simply injects enough money, quarter by quarter, to cover their losses. Through the end of 2009, that was $126 billion for the pair, and the Congressional Budget Office estimates the losses through 2020 at almost $400 billion.

This policy of supporting housing through Fannie and Freddie by recognizing their bad mortgages only slowly is attractive to politicians who love anything they can get credit for now, with the bill postponed until after the next election or, better still, until after they retire. It's a very different approach from the lessons of the Resolution Trust Corporation bailout of the failed S&Ls in the early 1990s, as outlined by then-director L. William Seidman. Assets in government hands lose value since there's no private owner to enhance their worth, so sell them quickly. Holding large inventories of distressed assets overhangs the market and depresses prices, another reason to sell them to private buyers soon. To rejuvenate markets, initial sales at low prices are needed to attract buyers and lead to higher prices.

Nevertheless, Treasury Secretary Timothy Geithner in March 2010 said, "There is a quite strong economic case, quite strong public policy case for preserving, designing some form of guarantee by the government to help facilitate a stable housing finance market," even after Fannie and Freddie are restructured or unwound. Furthermore, the administration doesn't seem to realize that the earlier attempts to make housing afford-able only fueled the bubble and were self-defeating. Cheap and readily available mortgage money spurred housing demand, pushed up prices, and, therefore, required even more subsidies for those who basically should have been renters, not homeowners, as explained earlier.

Fraught with Problems

Increased regulation may be the natural reaction to recent financial and economic woes, but it is fraught with problems. It's a reaction to past crises and, therefore, comes too late to prevent them. And it often amounts to fighting the last war since the next set of problems will be outside the purview of these new regulations. That's almost guaranteed to be the case since fixed rules only invite all those well-paid bright guys and gals on Wall Street and elsewhere to figure ways around them. A million-dollar-a-year Wall Street lawyer will beat a regulator with a $100,000 annual salary on most days. Also, government regulations are seldom removed even after they become irrelevant. Traffic lights and stop signs are installed after accidents occur. Did you ever see one removed, even if traffic dwindled to nothing?

Furthermore, government regulators have never, as far as I know, stopped big bubbles or caught big crooks. Consider the dot-com and then the housing blow-offs, both of which occurred while the SEC, the Fed, other regulators, Congress, and so on, sat on their hands. Think about Penn Square Bank, Beneficial Life, Enron, WorldCom, and Bernie Madoff, all of whom went on their merry ways until their self-induced collapses, completely free of regulatory interference. The SEC's own inspector general acknowledged that it repeatedly failed to investigate Madoff's Ponzi scheme or respond to the damning analysis presented to it by Harry Markopoulos. The SEC neglected investigation of the Ponzi scheme in favor of a minor part of Madoff's operation because, in the words of a senior examiner, "that's where my area, my team's area of expertise led." Furthermore, in April 2010, he reported that starting in 1997, that agency suspected that R. Allen Stanford was running a Ponzi scheme. Still, it waited until early 2009, after the SEC was embarrassed for missing Madoff's multibillion-dollar Ponzi scheme, to take action on Stanford's $7 billion swindle. In 1997, 1998, 2002, and 2004, SEC examiners were suspicious that Stanford could legitimately deliver the returns he promised investors, but deferred prosecution in part because of a culture that favored easily settled cases over more difficult ones. And in the same month, the inspector general revealed that 30 employees, including 17 senior officials, had viewed porn during the past five years on their office computers or on laptops while traveling.

This reminded me of an exchange I had in 1994 with Mary Schapiro, now SEC Chairman but then chairman of the Commodity Futures Trading Commission. We were both on an investment conference panel that discussed financial derivatives. I pointed out to her that security regulators spent a lot of time harassing small firms over minor technical infractions, but had missed all the major perpetrators. She naturally brushed over my comment, but I challenged her to name the big fish the regulators had caught on their own; she could only list minnows that were so small I'd never heard of any of them. That was true of regulators in 1994. The Madoff and Stanford affairs show it's still true today.

Most importantly, government regulation and involvement in the economy is almost certain to prove inefficient. Risk taking has been excessive, but government bureaucrats are likely to eliminate much of it, to the detriment of entrepreneurial activity, financial innovation, and economic growth, while government-imposed procedures spawn waste and inefficiency. I think of government efficiency in the same league as congressional ethics, airline food, postal service, military intelligence, the usual suspects, wild game management, beloved mothers-in-law, vegetarian vampires, jumbo shrimp, tax simplification, nutritional fast food, working vacations, and other oxymora.

Air Force Fuel

The lack of efficiency in government was proven by the ease with which the federal government found ways to cut its own costs. To emphasize his commitment to spending cuts, the President in mid-2009 ordered his cabinet secretaries to find $100 million in budget reductions. That's only 0.006 percent of the federal deficit. Still, the list they came up with shows the inherent wastefulness of government, which lacks any bottom-line discipline.

The Air Force found it could use commercial jet fuel with a few additives rather than special blends to save $52 million. The Office of Thrift Supervision in the Treasury identified unused phone lines costing $329,000. The Defense Department can save $573,000 by copying on both sides of the paper, while Homeland Security can cut $318,000 by e-mailing documents rather than printing them out. By reading newspapers free online rather than hard copies, various agencies can save $47,160. Here's our favorite: The Coast Guard's fleet of small boats have maintenance schedules geared to water skiing and bass fishing. Since our worthy Coast Guardsmen supposedly don't use those craft for such strenuous activities, they can save $2 million a year in maintenance.

In the late 1980s, our third son, Steve, worked a summer in the metal-working factory owned by a neighbor, Bill Kaupp. Steve is very mechanically apt and thoroughly enjoyed the experience. I, too, enjoyed a visit and tour by the owner in which he showed me support housings they made for gyroscopes. One rack had those ready to be shipped to commercial customers and another contained seemingly identical binnacles to be sent to the military. He told me his military and aerospace contracts paid about 10 times as much as his civilian customers. "Why?" I asked. "Because they demand much closer tolerances for the machining of the enclosures," he explained. "Does that make any difference for the functioning of the gyroscopes?" I queried. "Not as far as I know, but they want it and are willing to pay for the extra work."

My Regulation Plan

If it were up to me, and it obviously isn't, I'd design a system that would regulate financial firms lightly so they could innovate and experiment, but within a framework that would prevent them from threatening systemic failure to the point that government has no choice but to bail them out. That, of course, is the present problem so I'm advocating a quite different structure than at present.

This might involve limiting the size, scope, and complexity of individual firms so investors and regulators could understand what's going on. That would prevent AIG, basically an insurance company, from being sunk by unrelated CDS activity. Also, the management of a Merrill Lynch wouldn't have to take an embarrassing and destabilizing string of write-downs because it didn't understand the securities the firm held and their risks. Admittedly, this concept is easier to envision than it might be to implement.

A central clearinghouse for derivatives would also be useful, with the clearinghouse, not other traders, as the counterparty. That's now the arrangement with the Chicago Mercantile Exchange (CME) and other U.S.-organized futures exchanges, and would eliminate the scary question of who-owes-what-to-whom-and-how-good-is-his-credit that arose in and contributed to the collapses of Bear Stearns and Lehman. Senior regulators need to be paid enough to attract people as smart as those they regulate, and to retain them. Now, bright young people join the Justice Department, SEC, and other governmental entities only long enough to learn the ropes before being hired at much higher pay by the regulated to beat the regulators.

I suggest a clear plan to unwind a failing financial institution without systemic risks and major market traumas. This is similar to the thinking of former Secretary Paulson, who said in 2008, "We need to create a resolution process that ensures the financial system can withstand the failure of a large, complex financial firm." Bonuses should be paid out slowly over the years and clawed back, with even personal capital contributions from bank senior officers and traders if their profits turned to losses or their firms went bust.

I'm also in favor of the popular idea of requiring financial institutions to have much more capital. Debt-to-equity ratios of 50-to-1 for Fannie and Freddie were reckless. So were 30-to-1 ratios for Bear Stearns and Lehman. The more capital, the better able an institution is to weather shocks and the less likely it is to need a bailout or a liquidation. There is a trade-off, however, since more capital means lower profits and probably higher costs for the bank's customers.

Ironically, while many of us have been concerned about banks being too big to fail, the financial crisis has resulted in mergers and a further concentration among big banks. At the end of 2009, the world's 10 largest banks accounted for 70 percent of global banking assets, up from 59 percent three years earlier. In the United States, banks with over $10 billion in assets had $11.87 trillion in assets, or 80 percent of total bank assets, on September 30, 2009, compared with $5.74 trillion, or 67 percent of the total, 10 years earlier.

This financial regulatory plan is taken, almost word for word, from our October 2008 *Insight* report. Many of its features are contained in the regulatory bill being considered in Washington. We'll only know if they work when the next major financial crisis arrives, and that may be years, even decades, away.

Uncertainty

There's a final way government intervention and increased involvement in financial markets and the economy slow economic growth: With shifting financial regulation and political blow-ups like the flap over AIG and Wall Street bonuses as well as the degree of federalism in the euro-zone, confusion and uncertainty have leaped in the private sector, to the detriment of financing, spending, and investment. The uncertainty and potential costs of carbon emission taxes, increased health care for employees, renewed antitrust activity, and control over executive pay have a similar impact.

Some academics believe that the Great Depression was prolonged because the New Deal measures were so disruptive that banks and other financial firms as well as individual investors, consumers, and businessmen were too scared to do anything. Today's parallels are unnerving.

In January 2010, President Obama declared he would not let firms that had "soaring profits and obscene bonuses" curtail his financial reforms. "If these folks want a fight, it's a fight I'm ready to have." This sounds like President Roosevelt in his 1936 reelection campaign when he talked about the problems of "business and financial monopoly, speculation, reckless banking." He noted that Wall Street and business hated him and said, "I welcome their hatred." Then, warming to the topic, he continued, "I should like to have it said of my first administration that in it the forces of selfishness and the lust for power met their match. I should like to have it said of my second administration that in it these forces met their master."

The New Deal problems constituted huge increases in government regulation and involvement in the economy. Included were the 1933 "bank holiday" to halt bank runs, the National Recovery Administration with minimum wages and limits on hours, the replacement of a flat tax on corporate income with a graduated rate, a 1936 undistributed profits tax, the 1935 Wagner Act that instituted the closed labor shop, vigorous antitrust policies, and the 1935 Public Utilities Holding Company Act that made it tough for private utilities to raise equity capital. Today's regulatory initiatives may be similar in immense magnitude and impact on the economy and financial markets.

Commodity Crisis

The earlier collapse of the commodity bubble (see Figure 6.11) will also subdue global economic growth in future years, my fourth reason. Sure, commodity consumers benefit from lower prices by the same

Figure 6.11 Commodity Research Bureau (CRB) Commodity Index
Data source: Jefferies & Co.

amount by which producers lose. But while the share of total spending on commodity imports by consumers, especially in developed lands, is tiny, commodities account for the bulk of exports for producers, many of them developing countries such as Middle East oil producers. Forget those office towers in Persian Gulf sheikdoms that were planned to reach even farther into the sky.

Producers and exporters of industrial materials such as Australia, South Africa, and Canada will experience slower economic growth due to subdued global demand and weak prices; ditto for many Latin American commodity exporters. Demand from China for imports of industrial materials to fuel stockpiling and economic stimulus-inspired usage should be noticeably curtailed, as I discuss in Chapter 11.

Furthermore, security losses in 2008 devastated sovereign wealth funds, many of them in oil-rich countries as well as Asian exporters. In 2008, they were estimated to hold $3 trillion in assets, on their way to $10 trillion. A year later, the estimate was $1.8 trillion and optimistically forecast to rise to only $5 to $6 trillion by 2012. Lower oil prices have a lot to do with the downward revisions.

Fiscal Policy Reversal

The mid-2010 shift toward fiscal restraint in advanced lands is my fifth reason for slow economic growth in the years ahead. Only a few months ago, developed countries were all pumping fiscal stimuli into their economies to revive them from the worst recession since the 1930s. All their stimuli and the related government borrowing have basically been offsetting the deleveraging and retrenchment of their private sectors, as is clearly the case in the United States. But before those economies proved able to live without government life support, country leaders, with the partial exception of President Obama, decided to start withdrawing that immense government aid. What happened to cause this dramatic reversal? Did they decide that the stimuli weren't working? The bang per buck has been poor, but as an old history professor of ours used to say, "There are no 'ifs' in history." You'll never know what would have happened without the immense and global government aid. Maybe the world economy would have entered a depression. Besides, lack of success has not deterred politicians facing unemployed voters in the past from redoubling their efforts to stimulate.

More likely, this new zeal to limit government deficits, which started in Europe, was exactly what we foresaw way back in our December 1998 *Insight*, written just as the euro was about to be launched at the beginning of 1999. We stated that with a common currency and a one-size-fits-all monetary policy, individual countries would be forced to rely on fiscal policy to deal with local economic conditions and:

> the limit on fiscal stimulus will be default risks. Government bond investors and rating agencies will become the policemen and will blow the whistle.... It's even possible that economic differentials among countries may be so great that the common currency doesn't hold together, especially in the next European recession when unemployment leaps....

Well, the "next European recession" has arrived, starting in 2008, and "the economy differentials among countries" may prove to "be so great that the common currency doesn't hold together."

With the rating downgrades of Greek sovereign debt to junk quality and the rating cuts for Portugal and Spain, other developed country governments such as Britain worry that they may be next. Indeed, rating agencies have raised red flags for the United Kingdom and United States of eventual trouble if debt and deficit explosions are not contained.

Nevertheless, attempts to reduce fiscal stimuli to cut deficits may not work. The European Commission forecasts Spanish GDP to fall

0.4 percent this year. In cutting Spain's credit rating, S&P forecast only 0.7 percent average annual growth until 2016. Growth that slow will retard tax revenues and increase spending on unemployment and other benefits to the extent that deficit reduction will be very hard to achieve.

This problem exists in other European countries. Furthermore, unless GDP in a country grows faster than its deficit-to-GDP ratio, it's mathematically impossible for the government debt-to-GDP ratio to decline. With GDP growth in the years ahead likely to be below 3 percent in every European land, it will take draconian deficit cuts, that would almost certainly further depress GDP growth, to reduce the deficit-to-GDP ratios from their present levels to below those low economic growth rates.

G-20 Decision

This whole issue of fiscal restraint came to resolution, sort of, at the G-20 meeting in Toronto in late June 2010. Going into that meeting, the Obama Administration advocated a go-slow approach to fiscal stimuli removal for fear of precipitating a relapse. If global economies again falter, it's hard to envision another round of massive tax cuts and spending increases with government deficits and debts already sky-high, or another big expansion of money with central bank interest rates already close to zero.

Before the G-20 meeting, Obama wrote to his counterparts in other countries that "we should be prepared to respond as quickly and forcefully as needed to avert a slowdown in economic activity." The Administration worried about a "Hoover moment," a reference to the 1930s when the still-weak economy relapsed. This term is politically deliciously laughable. In 1936, long after Hoover left office in March 1933, FDR worried that deflation was about to turn to inflation (believe it or not) and convinced the Fed to tighten credit. The 1937 recession followed, only second in depth to the 1929-1933 collapse. At the time it was called the "Roosevelt Depression," but morphed into a "Hoover moment" in the current Democratic White House.

No doubt the basic reason for the difference between the United States and the other developed countries on the question of when to withdraw fiscal stimulus is that America has the globe's reserve currency, the dollar, and Treasurys, which the world lusts after while the rest fret about sovereign downgrades. The possibility of the euro as a reserve currency is destroyed, at least for now. Sterling as a reserve currency is ancient history and the Japanese don't want the yen to become one. So the buck reigns supreme, with no feasible alternative. The Swiss franc is a safe haven but too small a market to be an alternative. The recent rush to gold may reflect a disdain for all fiat currencies, but it, too, is a small market.

America's unique ownership of the greenback and Treasurys gives her the luxury of being fiscally profligate—at least until an alternative arises. That could be China in a decade or two, but only after the yuan becomes freely convertible, and establishes a history of freedom from the government control that Beijing cherishes.

Even in America

Still, Washington is concerned over huge and rising deficits (see Figure 3.1). The Administration has proposed a three-year freeze on non-security discretionary spending, which accounted for only 12.4 percent of the budget pie in 2009. The President suggested reviving "pay as you go" rules that would require spending increases to be offset by spending cuts elsewhere or tax increases. And he established the bipartisan White House Commission on Fiscal Responsibility and Reform to study and propose long-run reductions in the deficit. Early indications are that even Democrats on the panel favor more spending cuts than tax hikes to curb the deficit. U.S. debt is forecast to leap from 53 percent of GDP last year to 90 percent in 2020. So even the Administration is trying to balance fear of economic relapse with the yawning federal deficit.

The Fed has a similar dilemma. It has for months discussed publicly its exit strategy from earlier monetary and quantitative easing and the resulting excess bank reserves of over $1 trillion (see Figure 6.10). Also, Chairman Bernanke has urged Congress to establish a credible deficit reduction plan. But he also said the economy is too weak to start the cutting now. And Fed officials are discussing internally the actions they could take if the economy falters. They're also beginning to once again worry about deflation as inflation excluding food and energy slides below their 1.5 percent to 2 percent informal target.

Despite the sluggish economy, voters are up in arms over the mush-rooming federal deficit. A mid-2010 *Wall Street Journal* poll asked them about the attributes of a congressional candidate that would excite them, and cutting federal spending was in first place, the choice of 34 percent. And Congress is listening to the voters.

Academic Entries

There's also the nagging question of whether fiscal stimulus does much good for the economy. The Keynesian theory, the product of the 1930s, is that government spending creates demand and puts money in the pockets of consumers and businesses, which is then spent and re-spent. The ulti-mate multiplier, then, is bigger than 1.0 even though some of the money spending power leaks out to taxes and saving. But the Austrian School of economists like Friedrich Hayek and Ludwig von Mises believed the economy is much more complicated. Keeping school teachers employed and spending their salaries doesn't help laid-off construction workers in the aftermath of the housing collapse.

The Austrian view suggests that the government spending multiplier may be only 1.0, and that there are not any follow-on effects. More recent academic studies indicate that the multiplier is less than 1.0, perhaps much less. Note, however, that deficit spending occurs in the midst of economic declines. It probably is statistically difficult to separate the effects of economic weakness, which depresses spending and can increase saving in recessions, from the influence of increased government outlays. Also, the inherent inefficiencies of government reduce the effects of deficit spending and lower the multiplier. Spent any time in a post office or other government facility lately?

Regardless, the standard explanation for a low multiplier is that peo-ple take actions in the face of government spending increases or tax cuts, and the resulting deficit increases that offset at least part of their stimulating effects. German Chancellor Merkel says that Germans' con-cerns over the government debt increases spawned by deficit spending, including worries that their beloved welfare state could be jeopardized or their taxes raised to finance its continuance, would result in offsetting saving increases. If Germany instead cuts the deficit, "then the citizen is more willing to spend money because he knows that he can count on the pension, health and elderly-care systems," she says. Polls of German voters back up her statements.

It doesn't appear that most Americans are infected by the German conviction that they will have to pay for deficit spending, that there's no such thing as free lunch. But, as discussed earlier, they saved most of their 2008–2009 tax rebates and cuts. Another reason that the multiplier on government stimulus may be low, at least over time, is the spending that it encourages now is spending that would have occurred anyway but at a later date. Auto rebate programs, whether sponsored by auto producers or government tax credits, often simply borrow demand from the future. People buy cars now they could have purchased in future months. The homebuyer tax credits are another case in point. Demand spurted up to the first expiration of the credit last November 2009 and the second in April 2010. The data since then suggest that the earlier leap in activity is being offset by subsequent weakness.

Perhaps some of this logic permeated the Toronto G-20 conference and offset the normal Keynesian instincts of politicians who love to spend on constituents' pet projects, i.e., earmarks. If Keynes was right, it's silly to prematurely reduce fiscal stimulus but if the government stimulus multiplier is low, it may not be so silly in the face of sovereign rating downgrades. And, of course, with the initial difference between the U.S. position to wait and the rest of the G-20 to cut stimulus now, the outcome had to be a compromise.

The agreement was to halve government deficits by 2013 and "stabilize" debts by 2016. In exchange, the Obama Administration got language making growth the top priority. Despite the vagueness of the Toronto G-20 agreement, individual country plans to cut their deficits are much more precise, especially the weak ones like Greece, Portugal, Spain and Ireland, where market pressures and bailout agreements are severe. Others like the United Kingdom, Italy, and Japan fear market pressures will grow later and worry about possible rating downgrades.

My judgment is that withdrawal of fiscal stimuli in the near future will enhance the chances of a global second dip in the Great Recession, which already appears to be at 50 percent or higher. The bulk of the restraints, such as public sector pay freezes, constraints on unemployment benefits and tax increases, will fall on consumers who are already subdued spenders in developed countries. And then there is the high likelihood that fiscal restraint won't reduce government deficits in weak countries sufficiently to satisfy markets, as discussed earlier. Even though some like Greece are small economies, the intertwining of finance would then spread the woes throughout the eurozone and, indeed, the world.

Greek Austerity

With the €110 billion bailout of Greece came a stringent austerity program led by that world-class enforcer, the IMF. Greece is required to transform itself into an international competitor by cutting wages and pensions and raising the retirement age from 58 to 65, introducing a two-tier private wage system to encourage hiring of younger workers and opening construction, trucking, legal, drug, notary, engineering, architecture, auditing, and other industries to competition. They are now protected by tariffs and other barriers. Bonuses of government employees are to be cut and the top tier value-added tax will be raised to 23 percent from 21 percent while sin taxes are raised.

All told, the austerity measures are expected to save the Greek government €40 billion through 2013 and reduce the deficit from 13.6 percent of GDP in 2009 to 8.1 percent this year and to the EU ceiling of 3 percent by the end of 2014. The government says that in the first six months of 2010, it reduced the deficit to 4.9 percent of GDP, even below the 5.8 percent target. But should you trust those guys? In early 2009, the Greek government said the 2009 deficit would be 3.7 percent of GDP. Then the number jumped to 12.5 percent in October 2009 due to accounting errors and pension fund adjustments, and to 12.7 percent later and finally up to 13.6 percent. Naturally, the current regime blames the problem on its predecessors, whom the voters dismissed last October.

Furthermore, are those declines in the deficit-to-GDP ratio like when the IMF forecasts an economic contraction of 4 percent this year and 2.6 percent in 2011 before a modest revival of 1.1 percent in 2012 and 2.2 percent in 2013? With GDP falling, the deficit has to drop considerably just to keep the ratio from rising.

Other PIIGS

Portugal is less in the spotlight than Greece, but also under pressure to rein in their government deficit. That country's once strong textile industry has been decimated in recent years by lower cost production in China and Eastern Europe. Textile exports have steadily declined and production is down 25 percent since 2004 while the sector's employment is off by 20 percent. GDP growth since 2011 has averaged 0.5 percent annually, half the eurozone average.

Nevertheless, the public sector continued to expand robustly, pushing the government deficit-to-GDP ratio to 9.4 percent in 2009. So, with the sovereign debt downgrade and under international pressure, the Portuguese government approved a value-added tax increase of one percentage point. Companies with profits over €2 million are hit with an additional 2.5 percent tax on their earnings.

Most of the deficit-reduction measures are tax increases but top government officials will have salary cuts of 5 percent. All these measures last only to the end of 2011. By then, the government projects the deficit-to-GDP ratio to fall to 4.6 percent after dropping to 7.3 percent this year.

Sovereign debt rating downgrades and eurozone pressure is also forcing Spain to slash her government deficit. The IMF said bluntly that Spain needs a "radical overhaul" of its labor laws including reductions in mandated severance payments, which discourage full-time employment since some workers get 45 days severance for each year worked when they're laid off. The IMF also wants "wage flexibility" to allow lower wages for first-time workers and a boost in the retirement age from 65 to 67. Labor market rigidity and the collapse in the housing boom are largely responsible for Spain's 20 percent unemployment rate.

So far, the government has announced €15 billion in budget cuts in May on top of the €50 billion austerity package in January. The goal is to reduce the deficit-to-GDP ratio from 11.2 percent in 2009 to 9.3 percent this year and 6.5 percent in 2011 and then to 3 percent in 2013. Cuts include 5 percent declines in public sector wages this year and then freezes in 2011, freezes on public pensions next year and elimination of the €2,500 baby check for every newborn. The government also plans to cut public investment by €6 billion this year and next. And the severance pay for new hires will be reduced to 33 days for each year of employment and the government will pay for eight of those days.

Italy is really only partly one of the PIIGS since it's composed of the productive North as well as the Club Med South. Consequently, her 5.3 percent government debt-to-GDP ratio in 2009 makes Italy a picture of health. But her government net debt level, $2.2 trillion in 2009, is only exceeded by Japan with $5.5 trillion in 2008 and the United States with $8.3 trillion in 2009. And Italian debt is expected to grow, especially compared to GDP, which continues to rise slowly. At 101 percent of GDP, Italy's net government debt is the highest in the EU.

Italy suffers from flat tax revenues due to low growth as manufacturing in Northern Italy shifts to China and Eastern Europe—the same problem faced by Portugal. In the last decade, GDP growth in both countries averaged 0.5 percent per year. At the same time, the Italian government remains pressed to keep providing aid to the poorer South that depends heavily on government employment.

Nevertheless, Italy has embarked on a two-year austerity program to cut the budget by €25 billion by 2012. Wages are frozen in the public sector and funding for regional and local governments is being reduced. There's also a 10 percent cut in government ministry spending in both 2011 and 2012.

Ireland's economy suffered terribly from the recession, from which it is only beginning to recover, the collapse of its banking sector, and her huge dependence on exports. Unemployment exceeded 13 percent last year, a shock to the Celtic Tiger that enjoyed rapid growth after joining the eurozone with average annual economic growth of 5.3 percent in the 2000-2005 years.

The reaction of the government, however, was swift to try to slash the deficit of 14.3 percent of GDP in 2009, even higher than Greece's. Ireland's 2010 budget calls for €4 billion in spending cuts, or 17 percent of its 2009 deficit of €24 billion. Salaries of public employees have been cut by 5 percent to 15 percent to save €1 billion annually, €760 million in welfare cuts were enacted and child benefit payments have been reduced.

Northern Europe

Other Northern European lands are under less pressure for fiscal austerity but are faced with rising budget deficits and aging populations. The Netherlands deficit in 2009 was 5.3 percent of GDP and government spending on a budget basis rose from 45 percent of GDP 10 years ago to

51 percent this year in that wealthy welfare state and tax rates on higher incomes are rising.

France's deficit-to-GDP ratio at 7.5 percent in 2009 and its net government debt-to-GDP ratio, 51 percent, weren't low for a major eurozone country. The mushrooming social security deficit remains a major budgetary problem. The government plans to reduce the deficit to 3 percent of GDP by 2013 and reduce public debt by €100 billion. It has already announced €45 billion in spending cuts over three years and €5 billion increases in already high taxes in addition to the increase in the retirement age from 60 to 62 that I discussed earlier.

In Germany, the regional election defeat in May 2010 told the government in no uncertain terms that voters want the government deficit cut. So Chancellor Merkel dropped the proposed €16 billion tax cuts. She also stoutly resisted calls by the United States, France, and others to de-emphasize German exports and spend more to induce domestic consumption. "German export successes reflect the high competitiveness and innovative strength of our companies," she said. "Artificially reducing Germany's competitiveness would be of no use to anyone."

Quite the opposite, the German government announced €80 billion in budget cuts over the next four years, mainly through lower spending but with some tax hikes. The goal is to save €11.2 billion in 2011, €19.1 billion in 2012, €23.7 billion in 2013, and €27.6 billion in 2014. Most of the spending cuts will fall on social welfare and unemployment benefits and possibly military spending. The government wants to reduce the deficit, which hit 3.3 percent in 2009 and is forecast to run 5 percent this year, to 3 percent in 2013. A constitutional amendment passed last year requires a deficit no more than 0.35 percent of GDP starting in 2016. Boy, those Germans are tough!

The United Kingdom

The new U.K. coalition government is deeply concerned over possible downgrades from triple-A for sovereign debt after seeing the contagion from the Greek debt crisis spread among bond investors and rating agencies. With an 11.5 percent deficit-to-GDP ratio in 2009, it has genuine cause to be worried.

The newly-established Office of Budget Responsibility slashed the previous government's forecast of economic growth to 1.2 percent this year, 2.6 percent in 2011, 2.8 percent in 2012 and 2013, and 2.6 percent in 2014. Nevertheless, the government believes that spending cuts and tax increases equal to 8 percent of GDP over the next five years are necessary to avoid long-run trouble even at the expense of considerable short-run pain and risk to the fledgling economic recovery. The proposed budget restraint of £40 billion comes on top of the £73 billion in cuts enacted by the previous government, which included a five percentage point hike in the top tax rate. The government is obviously bracing for fights with labor unions and government employees in a country where about half the jobs depend directly or indirectly on the government. Still, the aim is to eliminate the structural deficit, the red ink even under normal economic conditions, by 2015.

Some 77 percent of the reductions are scheduled to come through spending cuts and the rest from tax increases. Cuts include a two-year public sector pay freeze and $11 billion reduction in welfare spending. Tax increases include an increase in the value-added tax from 17.5 percent to 20 percent, a capital gains tax hike from 18 percent to 28 percent and a tax on bank balance sheets.

Japan, Too

I continue to have trouble understanding the Japanese way of thinking. They're smart people and we're sure their thinking is logical, but quite different from ours. Here is a country mired in a deflationary depression for 20 years, highly dependent on exports at a time when the U.S. consumer, the key to export demand, is retrenching, a country where consumer spending has been dead flat for 15 years and accounts for a low 60 percent of GDP.

Yet the new Japanese Prime Minister Naoto Kan recently proposed a doubling of the sales tax from 5 percent to 10 percent over the next few years as the centerpiece of his economic program. He also plans to increase income taxes on high earners to raise revenue and also to narrow income inequality. At the same time, this anti-Keynesian plans to expand nominal GDP by 3 percent annually, a rate not seen since the early 1990s, by not only raising taxes but also by curbing government spending in order to reduce the high net debt-to-GDP ratio, now 112 percent on a net debt basis. The government plans to cap next year's new debt at this year's level and balance the budget, equal to 9.1 percent of GDP in 2009, in 10 years.

The increase in the sales tax from 3 percent to 5 percent in 1997 turned a budding recovery into instant recession in Japan. Nevertheless, the Prime Minister says Japan must enact fiscal austerity to avoid a Greek-like debt crisis. Also, he's no doubt fully aware that Japan's aging population will put increasing strains on government deficits and debts.

Mr. Kan also hopes to promote growth by encouraging investment in promising areas like the environment and health care, and attracting more foreign investment and tourists. The government also plans to cut the effective corporate tax from 40 percent to 25 percent, in line with other countries, to improve domestic firms' competitiveness and production in Japan as well as to attract foreign investment.

China, Too

Finally, Chinese monetary and fiscal policies are retrenching, but not for fear of rating downgrades. With $2.9 trillion in foreign currency reserves, most of last year's $585 billion in stimulus funded by state-controlled banks rather than government debt, and a still tightly-controlled currency, foreign investors' view of Chinese government debt is of little concern to Beijing. Nevertheless, China is tightening monetary and fiscal policy, as I discuss in Chapter 11.

The recent decision by China to again allow the yuan to appreciate may have been aimed in the short run at allaying foreign charges of currency manipulation and in the long run at fostering a more domestically-driven economy. Still, in the short term, it restrains economic growth by retarding all-important exports as well as inflation.

Chapter 7

No Help from Anywhere

I f you have been a believer in decoupling—the theory that even if the U.S. economy suffers a setback, the rest of the world, especially locales like China and India, would continue to flourish—recent events may have disabused you of that notion. Most countries depend on exports for growth, as noted earlier, and the U.S. consumer, the globe's biggest spender, has been the biggest buyer of those exports.

But a number of factors are making it obvious that overseas markets won't lead the way to strong economic growth.

Rising Protectionism

Without question, rising protectionism will slow or even eliminate global economic growth, my sixth reason for expecting slower economic gains in future years. Protectionism is aimed at sustaining, even increasing, domestic wages and prices. But as retaliation takes place, trade suffers.

Recessions spawn economic nationalism and protectionism, and the deeper the slump, the stronger are those tendencies. It's ever so easy to blame foreigners for domestic woes and take actions to protect the home turf while repelling the offshore invaders. The beneficial effects of free trade are considerable but diffuse while the loss of one's job to imports is very specific. And politicians find protectionism to be a convenient vote-getter since foreigners don't vote in domestic elections.

It's also easy to restrict imports under the guise of health and safety considerations. Years ago, the Japanese were considering an import embargo on U.S.-made skis because they hadn't been tested on Japanese snow. It says in Matthew's Gospel that God sends the rain on the just and the unjust, but I guess he has a different idea in the case of snow. More recently, in early 2010, Chinese provincial leaders declared that 48 of 85 samples of imported designer clothes failed Chinese standards, half of them because of improper laundry instruction labels. Meanwhile, China is promoting its own competing brands. And China has started to restrict imports of Argentine soybean oil because of higher than acceptable traces of solvents, even though China got 77 percent of its soybean oil imports in 2009 from Argentina.

Classically, protectionism takes the form of promoting domestic production by encouraging exports of goods and services while discouraging imports. Despite its lack of success, it's been tried often, going back to European mercantilism in the eighteenth century, Smoot-Hawley protectionism of the 1930s, and Japanese and Chinese mercantilism more recently.

As discussed earlier, the current recession started in the financial arena. First was the collapse in the residential mortgage market led by the subprime slime that commenced in early 2007, and then the follow-on Wall Street woes that started in the middle of that year when two big Bear Stearns hedge funds imploded. So it's not surprising that protectionism began in the financial arena and took the form of competing to safeguard a country's financial institutions. But at least that competition was positive for financial systems and economies, even if expensive for taxpayers.

As the financial crises spread and especially after the Reserve Primary Fund money market fund broke the buck in mid-September 2008 due to holdings of bad Lehman assets, bank depositors got nervous. Ireland was already in recession by then and, to preempt bank runs, the Irish government at the end of September guaranteed up to €563 billion in bank debt, including securities and short-term borrowing as well as deposits without limit in its six major financial institutions.

That put the heat on other eurozone countries that feared that with the Internet and a few keystrokes, depositors in their banks would transfer their funds to the unlimited safety of Irish banks. A number of them, especially Germany, objected to what they saw as unfair competition and a violation of European rules that ban state monopolies.

Follow the Leader

But Greece followed quickly Ireland's guarantee of bank deposits. Germany joined the crowd a day after criticizing Ireland, and in a few weeks, the practice spread elsewhere in Europe and even to the United States. Recall that the $700 billion bank bailout bill enacted in early October 2008 increased the FDIC insurance on deposits from $100,000 to $250,000 while the Fed guaranteed money market deposits to prevent further runs.

Then the U.K. government, embarrassed for not having prevented the Northern Rock bank run, the first in Britain in a century, worried about the status of its financial institutions. It also fretted about the health of London's financial hub, which depends heavily on international business, and about the total financial sector, which provides 21 percent of British jobs compared with 6 percent in the United States. Over the years 2005–2007, U.K. financial services grew at a 9.4 percent annual rate compared with 2.5 percent for the total British economy.

So Prime Minister Gordon Brown in early October 2008 upped the level of financial institutional protection. The government decided to guarantee unlimited bank deposits and $434 billion in bank debt and spend $63 billion to buy bank stock. Other countries followed instantly. France is guaranteeing $435 billion in senior bank debt and setting up a state company with $54 billion to recapitalize or bail out the banks. Germany guaranteed up to $544 billion of bank debts to other banks and bought $109 billion in bank shares. Spain guaranteed $136 billion in new bank issues, and set up a fund to buy $41 billion to $65 billion in "high quality" bank assets. Italy, with its usual genius for imprecision, planned to recapitalize banks and guarantee bond issues, but on a case-by-case basis.

Elsewhere, peer pressure forced Sweden to guarantee $200 billion in bank debt, to set up a facility to inject capital into troubled banks, and to double deposit guarantees to $67,000 even though Swedish banks were sound, having avoided the U.S. subprime problem. They learned their lesson in the early 1990s when real estate prices plunged and five of the seven largest Swedish banks needed capital injections. The government guaranteed the entire banking system, insuring creditors and depositors—but not shareholders—against loss, and spent 4 percent of GDP in the bailout.

Australia guaranteed all bank deposits and banks' wholesale term funding, such as loans to other banks, and bought residential mortgage-backed securities. New Zealand introduced retail deposit guarantees. The Swiss central bank took $60 billion in toxic waste from UBS and invested $5.3 billion for a 9 percent stake in that bank. UBS suffered $48 billion in write-downs and raised only $27 billion privately as offsets while customers withdrew $74 billion of their money in the third quarter of 2008. The Swiss Banking Federation didn't think Switzerland needed a comprehensive bailout plan similar to other countries, but felt UBS was being punished because that country had no plan.

North America Joins In

Canada considered guarantees on interbank lending to keep its banks competitive with those in other countries. And note that the international pressure to recapitalize the banks forced then–Treasury Secretary Paulson to use $250 billion of the $700 billion bailout money to buy U.S. bank shares.

It's also true that banks goaded governments to be sure that no other country gives its banks a better deal than their own. German bankers complained that U.K. banks had access to liquidity more cheaply and easily, while British bankers claimed that the U.S. bailout was more generous than the United Kingdom's. They say the government charge for guaranteeing their debt was too high, and that unlike Treasury share purchases in U.S. banks, British government purchases of preferred stock had to be bought back before they could pay dividends to other shareholders, probably not until 2012.

So the competition to protect each country's financial system became fierce. And an easy way for governments to check who was ahead or behind them was to look at the prices of credit default swaps (CDSs) on each country's debts. Those CDSs gauged investors' evaluations of how the bailout plans affect the government's finances. The costs of these insurance policies leaped in late 2008 for many countries, with Italy the least trusted of major developed lands, the United Kingdom under question, and Germany and the United States the best of the bunch. Note, however, that Iceland was off the chart.

Every Country for Itself

This every-country-for-itself attitude was also seen in the lack of international cooperation in the bailout of financial institutions in developed lands. Sure, eurozone countries agreed to ease mark-to-market accounting rules to reduce bank write-downs—that helps banks but makes them opaque for investors. And in October 2008, the world's major central banks made a coordinated half-percentage-point cut in their interest rates. But beyond that, not much else happened. No country wanted its banks to be at a disadvantage when capital can move so easily from one land to another, or to pay for another nation's financial troubles. The International Monetary Fund (IMF) managing directors, representing major countries, agreed to prevent additional major financial institutions from failing, but didn't specify any programs. The European Union as a governing organization proved to be nearly impotent in the financial crisis. Its rules to promote fair competition and fiscal discipline were ignored in the race to protect individual countries' banks.

French President Sarkozy proposed a pan-European fund to rescue banks, but Germany vetoed it. European leaders asked for global standards for financial regulation and a supervisory body for the world's 30 largest banks. British Prime Minister Brown asked for a "new Bretton Woods" conference to reshape global finance. Washington called these ideas nonstarters and Tokyo agreed.

Protectionism Spreads

Countries were competing to see which could provide the best protection for its financial institutions. Then protection spread to its more classical import-export arena with the advent in late 2008 of massive U.S. consumer retrenchment and the globalization of the downturn that depressed goods and services purchases and trade. And there's nothing like high and rising unemployment to spur attempts to limit imports and promote exports. Recall the high-unemployment, slow recovery of the early 1990s when Pat Buchanan and Ross Perot on the right and Dick Gephardt on the left beat opposite sides of the same protectionist drum.

Sadly, the United States appears to be among the leaders for protection of goods and services against foreign competition. Vice President Biden said it was legitimate to have some portions of "Buy American" in the 2009 stimulus package, and it did under the argument that taxpayers' money should support U.S. products. Obama advocates a super-competitive economy, which requires highly productive workers. Yet the fiscal stimulus law restricted H-1B visas, granted to foreigners with advanced education and skills, for employees of firms that receive Troubled Asset Relief Program (TARP—bank bailout) money. Then, a $1.5 billion Chinese-American wind farm project in Texas was threatened after congressional Democrats complained that federal subsidies would end up financing components manufactured in China and not create U.S. jobs.

Dumping, selling goods abroad at less than production costs because of subsidies, is always grounds for retaliation. China, with its huge growth in exports, is in many countries' crosshairs and in early 2010 was ranked the leading target for protectionist measures. In 2006, the European Union slapped a 16.5 percent tariff on Chinese shoes that it said were dumped in Europe and were killing the Italian shoe industry. In a Chinese-American deal to allow China to enter the World Trade Organization (WTO) in 2001, the United States doesn't have to prove dumping but only that imports from China have surged and American producers have suffered production losses. Almost a decade ago, we worked for a consulting client on such a case before the U.S. International Trade Commission involving wire coat hangers. Our client was both a domestic producer and importer of hangers, and resisting other U.S. manufacturers who were unhappy about leaping imports from China. The Commission ruled in favor of the other side, but President George W. Bush, who had the final say, vetoed their finding.

In 2008 and 2009, the U.S. Commerce Department found that illegal dumping or subsidies existed in imports from China, including automobile tires, steel pipe of various types, thermal paper, manganese dioxide, sodium nitrite, PET film, wire hangers, graphite electrodes, citric acid, lawn groomers, kitchen appliance shelves, magnets, steel wire, and steel mesh. It listed Germany for thermal paper and sodium nitrite; Australia for electronic manganese dioxide; India for matches; Turkey and South Korea for pipe and tube; Argentina for piston inserts; Taiwan, Indonesia, and Vietnam for polyethylene bags; Canada for citric acid; South Africa and Vietnam for intersprings; Brazil, Thailand, and the United Arab Emirates for PET film; France for sodium metal; Taiwan for magnets; and Mexico for pipe and tube.

U.S. dairy farmers want protection from cheap products such as cheese and powdered milk from New Zealand. The administration's protectionist bent appears to have the backing of many Americans. A survey in late 2009 found a disturbing degree of isolationist feeling. Some 49 percent believe the United States should "mind its own business internationally," up from 30 percent in 2002 soon after the shock of 9/11 and the highest reading since the Gallup Survey first asked the question in 1964. Isolationism and protectionism go hand in hand. And in a 180-degree reversal, the United States and the European Union in late 2009 complained to the WTO about Chinese export tariffs on strategic raw materials.

China's Policies

China discriminates against foreign companies bidding on government projects in favor of domestic firms in buying technology products and requires vendors to be accredited for their products if they contain "indigenous innovation." China is also developing a system to screen foreign companies' acquisitions of local firms in order to keep control of key government-linked outfits. Patent rules imposed in February 2010 threaten to raise the costs in China of foreign innovators in drugs and other industries, and force licensing of production to local firms at government-set prices. Google quit its search business in China rather than implement government censorship rules. American and European firms operating in China increasingly feel discriminated against in favor of domestic companies as China grooms state-owned firms to dominate their industries as "national champions." The government plans to increase to 50 percent in 2015 from 44 percent in 2009 the passenger vehicles produced by domestic companies.

In an early 2010 survey of its members, the American Chamber of Commerce in China found they "are troubled by a mounting number of policy challenges ranging from the inconsistent enforcement of laws to China's discriminatory domestic innovation policies and regulations that limit market access into sectors that have been increasingly open." Authorities there tend to "disfavor foreign rights holders" in disputes over intellectual property, and insist on access to the technology of foreign firms located in China. China appears to be flexing its economic muscles in the form of nationalism and disdain for foreigners operating in that country.

In early 2010, China's opaque legal system convicted four employees of iron ore–producing giant Rio Tinto of taking bribes from Chinese steel company customers to insure adequate supplies. Apparently, these payoffs are standard in China, but it wanted lower ore prices and was unhappy that Rio Tinto rejected a bid by Aluminum Corporation of China to raise its ownership of that Australian company. China accused the four of stealing state secrets, which include almost anything of economic value to a company that hasn't been publicly disclosed.

Fearing protectionism from the West, Asian lands are promoting intra-regional trade, with Japan pushing for an "East Asian Community." Trade within Asia is leaping, but our estimates are that, directly or indirectly, over half of the value-added of those exports ends up in the United States. At the same time, protectionism is growing among Asian and other developing lands. Brazil, Thailand, and Russia are concerned about China's trade tactics, and India filed more trade complaints against China than any other country in 2009. China's exports to India, Brazil, Indonesia, and Mexico are growing at 30 to 50 percent annual rates. China generates about 20 times as much electric power as India, and the resulting sizable and experienced power equipment manufacturing sector supplies the equipment for around 25 percent of India's new generating facilities. But India, which wants to increase power production in the five years ending March 2012, is favoring its own equipment manufacturers and asked state-controlled power producers to use Indian equipment on all their large projects. Also, only 1 percent of a project's workers in India can be foreign nationals.

Developed Countries Fight

In Europe, the European Union took the unprecedented step of approving prohibitively high tariffs on imported steel pipe from China *even before any of it enters Europe*. Wow! Talk about being preemptive! And trade disputes between Western countries flare up. In March 2010, French President Sarkozy blasted the American government for favoring Boeing for a new fleet of aerial-refueling tankers for the U.S. Air Force over a consortium of Northrop Grumman and European Aeronautic Defense and Space. Canada has asked the WTO to determine the legality of the United States' mandatory country-of-origin labeling that Canada believes prevents its own cattle and hog exporters from competing in U.S. markets.

The European Union is considering hedge fund rules to protect investors, reduce financial system risks, and increase transparency—but they also would just happen to raise the requirements for non-EU fund managers to prohibitive levels in terms of leverage, discipline, and location of depositories. The United Kingdom has long been very open to foreign purchases of British companies, so almost all of the investment banking, utility, steel, and chemical industries are foreign-controlled. But in March 2010, the U.K. Business Secretary, reacting to the takeover of Cadbury by U.S.-based Kraft Foods, considered changing the 2006 Companies Act to prevent short-term investors from acquiring U.K. companies. Furthermore, English workers at a French-owned oil refinery struck in 2009 because Total awarded a construction contract to an Italian firm that planned to use its own staff from abroad rather than local workers. Once again, high unemployment promotes protectionism.

Protectionism can always be justified as reasonable retaliation, the "you started it" philosophy. In early 2010, China restricted imports of U.S. poultry and auto parts in response to the earlier American imposition of high tariffs on tires from China. It also challenged EU and U.S. exports of chemical products and optical fibers as well as nylon exports from the United States, EU, Russia, and Taiwan when the United States launched an investigation into Chinese aluminum exports. The North American Free Trade Agreement (NAFTA) allows free access to American roads for Mexican trucks, but in 2009, Congress, with Teamsters Union backing, canceled a 2007 pilot program to allow Mexican trucks beyond the commercial border zone. So Mexico retaliated with $2.4 billion in tariffs on imports of U.S. goods.

Competitive Devaluations

Good old-fashioned competitive devaluations to spur exports and retard imports, a mainstay of the 1930s, may make a comeback. The idea is that a cheaper currency promotes imports while retarding exports, at least until trading partners make their currencies even cheaper. As noted earlier, it's the economic health of trading partners that primarily determines export levels, not exchange rates, but that doesn't stop government leaders from manipulating their currencies.

China stopped allowing its yuan to appreciate until late June 2010 (see Figure 7.1), in part because its labor costs are being undercut by countries like Vietnam and Bangladesh. In March 2010, Chinese Premier Wen Jiabao reacted to growing pressure on China to push up the yuan value by saying,

> I do not think the renminbi [yuan] is undervalued. We are opposed to countries pointing fingers at each other or taking strong measures to force other countries to appreciate their currencies. I can understand that some countries want to increase their share of exports. What I don't understand is the practice of depreciating one's own currency and attempting to press other countries to appreciate their own currencies solely for the purpose of increasing one's own exports. This kind of practice I think is a kind of trade protectionism.

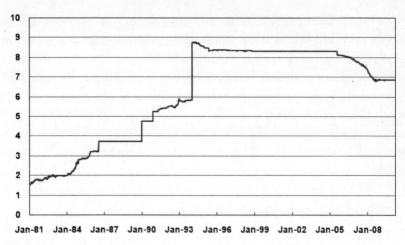

Figure 7.1 Chinese Yuan per U.S. Dollar, 1981–2009
Data source: St. Louis Federal Reserve.

With the understanding that protectionism helped make the Great Depression "great," country leaders still publicly espouse free trade and reject protectionism. Shortly after the U.S. fiscal stimulus law was signed by the President in 2009, he said in Canada that it wasn't protectionist and added, "Now is a time where we've got to be very careful about any signals of protectionism, because as the economy of the world contracts, I think there's going to be a strong impulse, on the part of constituencies in all countries, to see if they can engage in beggar-thy-neighbor policies." At the Davos meeting in January 2010, business and political leaders warned that a rising wave of protectionism could make the global recession worse. Chinese Premier Wen Jiabao said, "Protectionism serves no purpose as it will only worsen and prolong the crisis."

But also at Davos, Wen slammed the United States when he said the financial crisis was "attributable to inappropriate macroeconomic policies of some economies and their unsustainable model of development characterized by prolonged low savings and high consumption; excessive expansion of financial institutions in blind pursuit of profit," and a failure of government supervision of the financial sector. Russia's Putin called for a multiple regional reserve currency in addition to the dollar. "Excessive dependence on a single reserve currency is dangerous for the global economy," he said.

World leaders express confidence that global organizations like the WTO, IMF, and World Bank will forestall protectionism and economic nationalism, and they engage in endless meetings to promote free trade as well as global standards and cooperation for handling the deepening financial crisis. But almost nothing happens. U.S. free trade deals with South Korea, Colombia, and Panama await congressional approval. An early 2010 free trade pact between the EU and Central American countries must be approved by all EU member governments, a lengthy process at best.

Stealth Protectionism

Meanwhile, protectionism expands overtly as well as by stealth. U.S. steelmakers continue to file antidumping suits against foreign producers, a strategy they have employed successfully for decades, and India recently proposed increased steel tariffs. In the first half of 2008, WTO antidumping investigations were up 30 percent from a year earlier. Bank bailouts have been aimed at protecting local institutions, as discussed earlier, and the Japanese government bought stocks of Japan-based corporations to help company balance sheets, which also gave them a competitive advantage over the subsidiaries of foreign outfits.

Like America, France aided its own auto producers, not transplants, and has created a sovereign wealth fund to keep "national champions" out of foreign ownership. In late 2008 and early 2009, Russia imposed special road tolls on trucks from the European Union, Switzerland, and Turkmenistan. The European Union again is giving export refunds to dairy farmers, to the detriment of New Zealand. Indonesia used special import licenses to limit the inflow of clothing, shoes, and electronics and also is curtailing toy imports by allowing them to enter through only a few of its ports.

Limits on immigration are another form of stealth protectionism. Countries such as Malaysia, Singapore, and South Korea have relied on low-wage foreign workers from Bangladesh, Laos, Nepal, Cambodia, and Burma to help them compete with China and India. But backlashes from natives who fear competition from low-wage foreigners as well as health and safety concerns are resulting in closer screening of immigrants by government officials. Many immigrants, as a result, are leaving. Singapore has long grown with the major assistance of immigrants, but is concerned about low-skilled newcomers holding down productivity and living standards growth, and plans to concentrate on high-skilled immigrants.

Even Academicians

Even some academicians are now questioning the value of free trade. Alan Blinder, a Princeton economics professor and former vice chairman of the Fed, opposes tariffs and trade barriers, but he believes that a new industrial revolution is unfolding, this time in communications and technology, that allow services to be delivered worldwide electronically. As a result, he calculates that 30 million to 40 million American jobs are vulnerable to replacement by people overseas. Those at risk aren't necessarily less-educated, low-skilled people, but rather people in service jobs that don't require face-to-face contact. His ranking of highly off-shoreable jobs includes computer programmers and data entry keyers (no surprise, given Indians' growing involvement in this field), but also economists. Ugh! (Table 7.1).

Table 7.1 Highly Offshoreable Jobs

Occupation	Number of U.S. Workers
Computer programmers	389,090
Data entry keyers	296,700
Actuaries	15,770
Film and video editors	15,200
Mathematicians	2,930
Medical transcriptionists	90,380
Interpreters and translators	21,930
Economists	12,470
Graphic designers	178,530
Bookkeeping, accounting, and auditing clerks	1,815,340
Microbiologists	15,250
Financial analysts	180,910

Source: Working paper by Alan S. Blinder.

Working, But Unsustainable

Since the early 1980s, world trade has functioned in a smooth but unsustainable fashion. The rest of the world produced and America consumed. In many foreign lands, households were weak consumers and big savers, so production exceeded domestic consumption. Their production surpluses were exported, directly or indirectly, to the United States where consumers were saving less and less (as seen in Figure 2.5 in Chapter 2) and spending more and more. Over the past three decades, a 1 percent rise in consumer spending spiked imports by 2.4 percent on average. With their growing trade surpluses, foreign nations had growing piles of dollars that they recycled into Treasurys and other U.S. investments, helping to hold down interest rates and making it cheaper for spendthrift American consumers to borrow easily and cheaply to fund their leaping debts (as seen in Figure 4.4 in Chapter 4).

Interestingly, other major countries have much more muted relationships. A 1 percent rise in consumer spending in Canada boosted imports by only 1.4 percent, by 1.3 percent in France, by 1.0 percent in Italy, by 1.1 percent in Japan, and by 0.8 percent in the United Kingdom. The gap between the U.S. import response to economic growth and the responses abroad isn't surprising. The United States has the economy most open to imports, and American consumers were, until recently, a vacuum cleaner for the rest of the world's exports.

This difference in imports' response to economic growth in various countries explains the continual rise in the U.S. trade deficit. Even if economies around the world grew at the same rate, U.S. imports grew the fastest. This difference has been augmented in recent decades since the American economy has outpaced other developed countries.

This world trade system got a big boost after the Asian financial crisis in the late 1990s. Earlier, those lands had been living beyond their means and financing it with debts denominated in foreign currencies. When foreign investors got scared and refused to renew their loans, Asian currencies collapsed and deep recessions followed. In response, those lands emphasized exports, in part by keeping their currencies cheap against the dollar, and built huge foreign currency reserves from their mounting trade surpluses.

This system was unsustainable, but not, as many believed, because foreigners would eventually become overloaded with greenbacks and dump them. I've argued for years that yes, accidents can and do happen. But no major export-dependent country would risk the financial collapse and global depression that would probably result from dollar-dumping. That would be the end of their exports and economic growth.

Furthermore, the economic power in this system rested with the United States. Years ago, my firm was doing extensive consulting work with Emerson Electric and a number of its subsidiaries including USEM, which made large horsepower electric motors. I was on the phone with the head of USEM to set up a meeting. When it came down to the location, I said I'd be delighted to host him in our Manhattan offices, having no desire to travel two hours to his Connecticut headquarters. He said he preferred Connecticut, and after a few rounds of sparring, he said, "Gary, are you selling or are you buying?" My instant reply: "What time do you want me in your office?" When capacity is in excess, the buyer, not the seller, has the economic advantage.

The earlier world trade lineup proved unsustainable because of the collapse in the U.S. housing bubble and the follow-on stock market nose-dive and widespread financial crisis. That eliminated U.S. consumers' ability to continue to borrow to finance oversize spending and imports.

Now, with American consumers embarking on a saving spree, the United States will no longer be the buyer of first and last resort for the globe's excess goods and services, as shown by declining trade and current account deficits (see Figure 6.9). Furthermore, with slower global growth for years ahead, virtually every country will be promoting exports to spur domestic activity. When every country wants to export and none want to import, the pressure for protectionism leaps.

Excess House Inventories

My seventh reason for slow U.S. growth in coming years is the combination of the huge overhang of excess house inventories, the shock of price declines, underwater mortgages, and the resulting weakness of the sector for years to come. Inventories of single- and multifamily housing units are well off their peak, but still huge, and excess inventories are the mortal

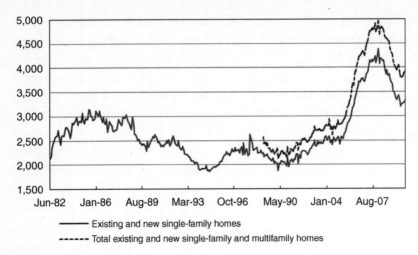

Existing and new single-family homes

Total existing and new single-family and multifamily homes

Figure 7.2   Home Inventories, 1982–2008 (Thousands of Units)
Data sources: National Association of Realtors, Census Bureau, A. Gary Shilling & Co.

enemy of prices. Unwanted houses are cleared out by chopping prices to attract bargain hunters. Figure 7.2 shows the reported inventories of new and existing single-family homes since 1982. The dashed line adds in inventories of existing multifamily units since they were first reported in 1999. The long-term average of the total is about 2.5 million, suggesting that number is about the normal working level of inventories. So anything above that, 1.3 million of the 3.7 million total in early 2010, is excess inventories. That's a lot considering that about 1.5 million houses are (Figure 3.3).

Excess inventories persist despite the collapse in new construction because household formation has also nosedived since the 2004–2005 peak (see Figure 7.3). A *household* is defined as one or more people occupying a separate dwelling unit. So households aren't formed in a vacuum, waiting to move into unoccupied units. No, no. Household formation is governed by all the forces behind people's willingness and ability to move into a separate abode. During the housing bubble, the prospects of quick profit induced many to leave their families early and ditch roommates to buy the biggest, most expensive houses that loose lenders would let them finance. But afterward, with declining house prices, stringent lending standards, and rising unemployment, they stayed put and household formation dropped sharply.

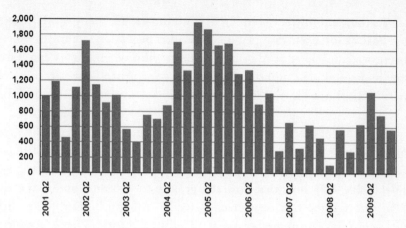

Figure 7.3 U.S. Household Formations, 2001–2010 (Thousands)
Data source: U.S. Census Bureau.

Disappearing Households

In fact, many households disappeared as foreclosures extinguished home-ownership. Some of the dispossessed move into rental units, so they're still occupying abodes, just different ones. But those who double up with family and friends are putting additional units on the market and adding to inventory. Notice (in Figure 3.6 in Chapter 3) that the housing boom–driven jump in home ownership is being reversed. And that's true for all individual age brackets and every ethnic group. Also, the size of new houses is falling as buyers conclude that, with declining prices nation-wide for the first time since the 1930s, an abode and a great investment are no longer contained in the same package—their owner-occupied houses.

Home mortgage delinquencies continue to skyrocket (Figure 3.9), but Washington mandated a moratorium on foreclosures as lenders and servicers were encouraged to modify mortgages to keep stressed home-owners in their houses. These attempts are faring poorly since many who couldn't afford chicken coops even when jobs were plentiful were allowed to finance and buy four-bedroom houses. An economic priv-ilege becomes an economic right when society believes it can afford it for everyone. We've learned, painfully, in the past few years that America can't afford home ownership for all, including those who don't have the incomes and assets to pay for it.

As these modification attempts continue to fail, many more houses will be foreclosed and dumped on the market by lenders, adding to excess inventories and downward price pressures. Ditto when the tax credit for new and some existing homeowners ended in April 2010. So most of these houses now in modification are hidden inventories, soon to be revealed.

So, too, are empty units owned by speculators who eventually give up on renting them or waiting for higher prices and, instead, list them for sale. And there's already plenty of hidden inventory. Our calculations (Table 7.2) show that from the peak in the housing boom in early 2006 through the first quarter of 2010, 5.4 million housing units, net of demolitions and removals, were added to the total. The 2.7 million growth in households and the 1.2 million rise in published inventories as well as other uses left 644,000 unaccounted for—over half a one million increase in hidden inventories during that period!

More House Price Weakness

Median single-family house prices nationwide have already fallen 29 percent from their peak in early 2006. I see excess inventories pushing them

Table 7.2   Hidden House Inventory—So Far

	1Q 2006	1Q 2010	Change
Housing units	125,503	130,873	5,370
Vacant units for rent or sale	5,268	6,424	1,156
Households	109,234	111,983	2,749
Rented or sold	1,071	841	−230
Occasional use	1,839	2,211	372
Usual residence elsewhere (URE)	1,328	1,292	−36
Seasonal	3,912	4,627	715

Data in thousands of units.

Hidden inventory = Additional units−(New households + Change in units for rent/sale + Change in units rented or sold + Change in units for occasional use + Change in URE units + Change in seasonal units).

Hidden inventory = 5, 370, 000 −[2, 749, 000 + 1, 156, 000 + (230, 000) + 372, 000 + (36, 000)+ 715, 000].

Hidden inventory = 644, 000.

Data source: Census Bureau.

down another 10 percent to 20 percent from here. As house prices remain weak due to excess inventories, those surplus homes will only slowly be absorbed in coming years and keep new house construction at low levels. This is a small component of GDP, but a volatile one. Its likely failure to return to even its long-term average of 6.1 percent of real GDP from 2.8 percent in the first quarter of 2010 for a number of years will rob economic growth of an important component.

Those who believe that population growth will promote a major revival in housing apparently don't realize that household formation, not population growth, is what's important. Just as faith in ever-rising prices propelled home ownership in the post–World War II era, the shock that house prices nationwide can and do fall substantially may well keep household formation (Figure 7.3) subdued for many years and home ownership (Figure 3.6) falling.

Furthermore, demographics are not favorable for housing in the next decade or so. The postwar babies are all housed, and those in the prime first-time homebuyer age are fewer in number (see Figure 7.4). Indeed, as the baby boomers retire and seek smaller living spaces, many of the McMansions built in the past decade may be divided into retiree apartments, reducing the demand for housing units. Furthermore, population growth may slow as high unemployment continues to retard the inflow of immigrants, an important component of past gains, and restrain births.

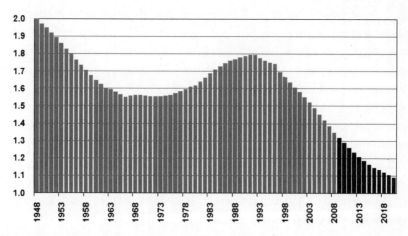

Figure 7.4 Ratio of U.S. Population Age 20–49 to Age 50+
Data source: U.S. Census Bureau (estimates after 2008).

Deflation Slows Growth

Chronic deflation, the result of global supply exceeding global demand is the eighth reason I'm forecasting slow economic growth in the next decade or so. As discussed in my two *Deflation* books a decade ago, and in many subsequent *Insight* reports, chronic deflation spawns self-fulfilling deflationary expectations. Today, who would have the guts to tell a friend he paid the full sticker price for a vehicle? Years of rebates have trained car buyers to expect continuing and even bigger rebates. So they wait to buy. That leads to excess inventories that require even larger price concessions. Buyer suspicions are confirmed so they wait longer, promoting more inventory buildup, more price cuts, and so on in a self-feeding cycle. A key effect, of course, is to retard spending and slow economic growth as well as promote more deflation.

The auto industry isn't alone in facing deflationary expectations. In early 2010, Dell's Optiplex 760 machines were listed at $966, on sale for $699, but offered to the Indiana Office of Technology, which manages 25,000 Dell desktops for state employees, at a further discounted price of $590 to encourage more purchases. At the same time, Constellation Brands offered promotions on expensive liquor brands to try to stem the switch by drinkers to cheaper brands. Coupons and rebate offers appear on store shelves and in newspapers. Supermarkets have developed a pattern of combining discounts on national brands with more prominent displays of house labels, and those that don't go along lose shoppers. About a third of shoppers buy only goods on sale, compared with one in six two years earlier. Kroger has been successful in attracting business with low prices and intends to continue that strategy in the long run as the cost of food eaten at home continues to fall.

The reality of deflation at the supermarket level is backing up to food producers who are finding they can no longer count on 2 or 3 percent annual retail food price increases to cover any rises in commodity, labor, packaging, and transportation costs. Similarly, in the United Kingdom, grocers worry that consumers have gotten hooked on big discounts and find reverting to full prices abhorrent. Back in the States, hotels and cruise lines with more than ample excess capacity find they must continue to offer big discounts to attract conscious consumers.

Worried Central Banks

Central banks and governments take deflation very seriously for two reasons. First, in deflation, conventional monetary policy is impotent; and second, deflation can spawn self-feeding deflationary expectations.

Japan has been mired in deflation for almost two decades despite consistent positive money supply growth (see Figure 7.5), as I discuss in more detail in Chapter 11. But even zero interest rates are positive in real terms in deflation (see Figure 7.6), so money isn't free. And it's been an almost continuous deflationary depression (see Figure 7.7) with cautious consumers waiting for ever-lower prices before buying. It's hard to believe, but conditions are so severe that in early 2010, the Japanese government pressed the Bank of Japan to set a target for inflation and then implement measures to achieve it. In March 2010, the Finance Minister said, "Two or three years is too long. If possible, I hope that the consumer price index turns positive by the end of the year," although he added that his goal reflected his "wishful thinking." How could any self-respecting central banker ever deliberately attempt to create inflation?

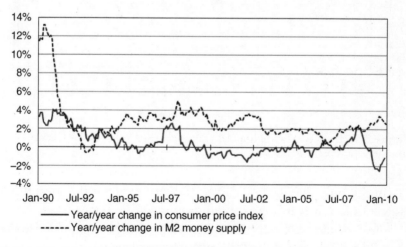

Figure 7.5 Japanese Money Supply and Prices, Year over Year Percent Change
Data sources: Bank of Japan and the Statistics Bureau of Japan.

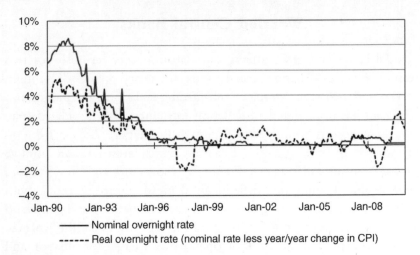

Figure 7.6 Real and Nominal Japanese Overnight Rates
Data source: Bank of Japan.

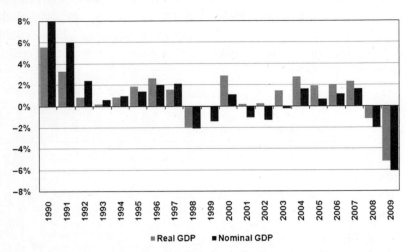

Figure 7.7 Japan Real and Nominal GDP, Year over Year Percent Change
Data source: Japanese Cabinet Office.

In the early 2000s, the Fed was so worried about deflation that it assigned a dozen of its top economists to study the Japanese experience in order to avoid a U.S. repetition. The U.S. central bank concluded that it would need to act early and massively to keep deflationary expectations from developing. The price index for personal consumption expenditures excluding food and energy, the Fed's favorite inflation measure, was

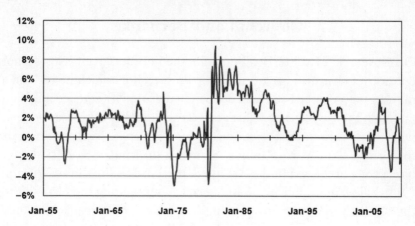

Figure 7.8 Real Effective Federal Funds Rate*
* Effective Fed funds rate less year/year percentage change in consumer price index.
Data sources: Federal Reserve and Bureau of Labor Statistics.

running below 1 percent at the time, although later revised upward. That has a lot to do with the Fed cutting its federal funds rate to 1 percent in June 2003 and keeping it there until June 2004.

Central bankers are well aware that economy-stimulating negative real interest rates (see Figure 7.8) are impossible to achieve in deflation since, as I understand it, nominal rates stop declining when they get to zero. Because of this concern, in February 2010, Oliver Blanchard, the chief economist at the International Monetary Fund (IMF), wrote that in "normal times in order to increase the room for monetary policy to react to such shocks," such as major banking crises, terrorist attacks, or pandemics, central banks may want to target inflation at 4 percent, twice the 2 percent or less that many now believe is appropriate. That would put short-term interest rates at around 6 to 7 percent, leaving plenty of space between there and zero to cut rates, if necessary.

But he's neglecting the loss of credibility to central banks if their increase in inflation targets to 4 percent suggests further acceptable increases in times of financial distress. More important, higher inflation targets risk the spawning of self-feeding inflationary expectations, as I explore shortly. Also, this argument suggests that when central bank rates get to zero, the monetary authorities are out of ammunition. That's simply not true.

Churchill and Bernanke

On November 21, 2002, Ben Bernanke, then a Federal Reserve governor but not yet chairman, gave a well-known speech in which he laid out a number of things the Fed could do to fight deflation if a zero federal funds rate didn't prove effective. That's the classic liquidity trap, as at present, where even zero interest rates don't induce lenders to lend or borrowers to borrow. On a visit to him in his office on January 8, 2003, I gave him a copy of the actions he had listed, preceded by lines from Winston Churchill's famous June 4, 1940, speech about fighting the Germans to the last ditch and never surrendering (see Table 7.3). Bernanke modestly said he was happy to be compared with Churchill.

Table 7.3   Churchill and Bernanke

Winston Spencer Churchill, June 4, 1940	Ben S. Bernanke, November 21, 2002
We shall not flag or fail. We shall go on to the end. We shall fight in France, we shall fight in the seas and oceans, we shall fight with growing confidence and growing strength in the air, we shall defend our island, whatever the cost may be, we shall fight on the beaches, we shall fight on the landing grounds, we shall fight in the fields and in the streets, we shall fight in the hills; we shall never surrender.	A central bank whose accustomed policy rate has been forced down to zero has most definitely not run out of ammunition [to fight deflation]. The Fed could find other ways of injecting money into the system . . . by lowering rates further out along the Treasury term spectrum . . . use its existing authority to operate in the markets for agency debt . . . make . . . loans directly to the private sector . . . offer fixed-term loans to banks at low or zero interest, with a wide range of private assets (including, among others, corporate bonds, commercial paper, bank loans, and mortgages) deemed eligible as collateral . . . go to the Congress to ask for the requisite power to buy private assets . . . buy foreign government debt.

To appreciate fully the self-feeding aspects of deflation, it may be helpful to recall the exact opposite: self-feeding inflation. During the high inflation of the 1970s, people became convinced that it would last indefinitely, and indeed that prices would accelerate. So they borrowed heavily to beat rising interest rates and used the money to invest in leaping tangibles. This strained credit supplies and pushed up interest rates, while rampant demand for real estate, coins, antiques, and artworks propelled prices. Suspicions were confirmed, spawning more of the same.

Just as in 1919, as I discuss in Chapter 1, consumers and businesses in the early 1970s bought more goods than they needed to in anticipation of rising prices. That put pressure on supplies, pushed up prices, and encouraged even bigger hedge-buying. Productive work and investments in the 1970s gave way to speculation, so there was little productivity growth to offset rising costs. This, too, added fat to the fires of inflation. Businesses didn't care much what they paid for labor and materials because cost increases could be passed through with ease, and with markups to boot. This practice fed on itself since costs accelerated as they moved through the production system and encouraged even bigger markups. Meanwhile, the resulting leaping inflation induced widespread cost-of-living adjustments and even higher labor costs.

During the early 1970s, I told clients how I'd succumbed to inflationary expectations even though I was predicting their demise. After the October 1973 energy price leap, I knew that drastically higher fertilizer prices would follow since natural gas is used in making its nitrogen component. But my local garden center owner hadn't caught on. So as he was closing at Thanksgiving for the winter, I bought his remaining supply of lawn fertilizer, and he even gave me a discount to avoid holding the inventory over the winter.

There it was, stacked up in my garage from the floor almost to the ceiling. I used part of it on my lawn the next summer, but still had room for another stack so I returned the following fall. His prices had risen, but not much so I repeated the exercise. I'm sure I would have kept repeating it until prices broke and I would have been stuck with a 10-year supply of fertilizer, but, fortunately, I ran out of garage space first.

Deflationary Expectations

Deflation, like inflation, is self-feeding. A key, but by no means the only, self-perpetuating mechanism is the anticipation of lower prices. But how much deflation does it take for consumers and businesses to wait for lower prices before buying? This is the same question we used to ask, in reverse, about inflation. In either case, there is no simple answer, as the central banks that fret over deflation no doubt agree. It depends on at least four factors:

1. *The breadth of deflation.* Declining prices have to spread across a wide spectrum of goods and services to be convincing. The declines in energy prices in 2009 were too narrow to be convincing (see Figure 7.9).

2. *The chronic nature of deflation.* The consumer price index (CPI) and producer price index (PPI) dropped year over year in 2009, but only for a few months due to declining energy prices. Furthermore, against the background of nonstop inflation since World War II, that experience was not long-standing enough to convince people that it would persist.

3. *Decelerating prices*, at least in the short run. Few Americans expect deflation, and most regard a return to significant inflation as inevitable, as I examine in Chapter 8. This probably means that

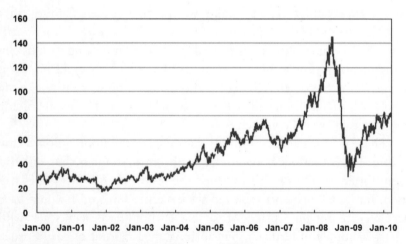

Figure 7.9 Crude Oil Prices (Dollars per Barrel)
Data source: Energy Information Administration.

it will take a pattern of smaller and smaller rates of inflation turning into bigger and bigger rates of deflation to be convincing. In other words, inflation rates have fallen from double digits to essentially zero in the past 25 years. If deflation sets in, but at a steady rate of, say, 1 percent per year, it will probably take a number of years before people believe in its permanence. More immediately convincing would be 1 percent deflation followed by a 2 percent decline in general prices the next year and 3 percent the following year.

4. *The amount of deflation.* Of course, the deeper the deflation, the more convincing it becomes. Deep deflation would be a big persuader as it promotes big drops in interest rates and tangible asset and commodity prices, and unbelievable consumer bargains, but also job losses in firms that don't cut their costs and prices. Those living on fixed incomes would feel like kings as their purchasing power grows while highly leveraged individuals and corporations fail.

Deflation, like inflation, must be significant enough to spur action. Even if you are convinced that a decline in shoe prices is in the offing, it may not be big enough to make you wait to buy. Waiting could entail another trip to the shoe store to check prices, and besides, if you buy a pair now, you get the use of them in the meantime.

In addition, the cost and discretionary nature of a good or service influences the sensitivity to deflation. An expected 5 percent decline in car prices may make you wait. If you're spending $30,000, that's a cool $1,500 in your pocket, and you can probably nurse your old bus along for another year anyway. Recall how rebate programs have pushed vehicle sales up and down like ping-pong balls. But an expected 10 percent drop in toothpaste prices may not make you get out the pliers so you can, by vigorous squeezing, make the old tube last until the lower price is in effect—or to brush your teeth with Ajax while waiting for that price drop.

The Trigger Point for Deflationary Expectations

Taking these four factors into account, what would it take to trigger deflationary expectations? Probably not as big a decline in prices as the 3 percent inflation rate level that seemed to touch off inflationary expectations in the 1970s. Even before that decade, folks had gained familiarity with rising prices throughout the postwar era and were sensitive to the inflationary beast. Been there, done that. Deflation, however, is a different animal, not seen since the 1930s, and few of us today have had firsthand experience with it. Widespread and chronic falling prices would be such a shock to most that it would probably take less deflation today than it took inflation earlier to get people's attention.

My judgment is that declines in the prices of most goods and a fair number of services, averaging 1 to 2 percent and lasting for several years, would do the job. Then, anticipation of lower prices by buyers and all of the other self-feeding aspects of deflation would kick in. Of course, few readers believe chronic deflation is in the wings, so I'm taking the next chapter to make the case that we may see ongoing annual declines in general price indexes of 2 to 3 percent. If I'm right, the world will be quite different than with the 2 to 3 percent annual inflation rates that most investors currently expect.

State and Local Duress

Another drag on U.S. economic growth in future years will be restrained state and local spending. The recession has made life tough for state and local governments. Revenues have plummeted but costs stubbornly refuse to follow. Taxpayers, under financial distress from falling house prices, uncertain stock prices, and high unemployment, deplore tax increases. But they don't want cuts in essential services. Something's got to give.

As unemployment leaped and personal income was compressed, state personal tax collections—a third of tax revenues in 28 states—fell. Corporate income taxes were also stressed. And as consumers hiked their saving rates for the first time in a quarter-century, state sales taxes also declined. That's bad news for state governments that get 55 percent of their revenues, before federal transfers, from these three sources. Local governments receive a third of their revenues from property taxes, which were still rising in 2009, but destined to fall as they catch up with declining house prices and commercial property values.

The federal government transferred $246 billion to state govern-
ments from the 2009 fiscal stimulus package of $787 billion to pre-
vent more schoolteacher layoffs ($54 billion), help fund Medicaid cost
increases ($90 billion), and to plug other holes in state budgets. This
filled 40 to 50 percent of state budget gaps, but $180 billion in com-
bined deficits is expected in the fiscal year starting July 1, 2010. This
is despite all states but Vermont being required to balance their budgets
to one degree or another, legitimately or creatively. Some $76 billion
was received in the first three months of 2010, but the money from
Washington will run out by 2012.

The state of New Jersey's budget is balanced when the governor certifies that it is. Period. There's no midyear course correction, regardless
of any obvious and substantial shortfall of revenues or overrun of outlays. I know, since in earlier years I was chairman of the New Jersey
State Revenue Forecasting Advisory Commission, appointed by the
state legislature to keep an eye on the reality of the governor's budget
projections.

Budget Legerdemain

This budget legerdemain no doubt is related to the rapid growth in
state spending in recent years, averaging about 7 percent annually, and
the 93 percent leap in debt from $1.2 trillion in 2000 to $2.4 trillion in
2009. State and local governments now use debt to fund investments that
used to be done on a current budget basis, and some issue debt to cover
up routine budget shortfalls. In the current financial crisis, Washington
is helping them by subsidizing 35 percent of the interest costs on taxable
Build America Bonds (BABs), which can be used to fund most of the
activities financed by regular tax-exempt municipal bonds. In the fourth
quarter of 2009, BABs accounted for $29 billion, or 32 percent, of all
municipal issuance.

It obviously takes a lot of gnashing of teeth in the outer darkness
for state and local governments to flatten, much less cut, their spending
after a decade of rapid growth. Jumping municipal employment is the
main reason for mushrooming spending in earlier years, and cutting what
are often unionized state and local workforces is very difficult. Since the

recession started in December 2007 through March 2010, private payroll employment has dropped 6.8 percent, but state and local jobs increased 1.8 percent. According to the Bureau of Labor Statistics, in the long run, including business expansions and recessions, layoffs and discharges in the public sector occur at only one-third the rate of the private sector. Public employees seldom lose their jobs due to cost cutting or poor performance.

Still, the breathtaking revenue shortfalls are forcing some labor cost cuts at the state and local levels. Los Angeles, faced with a $212 million budget shortfall in fiscal 2010 and $500 million the next year, cut 4,000 jobs to save $260 million. More than 20 states are considering mandatory days off without pay for government employees, and they have been instituted in California, Maine, Maryland, and Michigan.

Medicaid costs, which are mandated by Washington but paid in part by the states, mushroomed along with unemployment, even though some states have capped enrollment and cut out non–federally mandated services. They constituted 20.7 percent of state outlays in fiscal 2008. Rainy-day state funds, estimated at $36.5 billion in fiscal year 2009, were exhausted quickly.

Adding to the future financial woes of many state and local governments will be the cost of unwinding interest rate swaps. In earlier years, they issued low-cost variable-rate debt and then signed swap contracts with Wall Street banks to protect against rising interest rates. But interest rates fell instead as the Fed drove its federal funds rate to zero, and the municipalities face big losses. Those include Los Angeles, Chicago, Philadelphia, Denver, Kansas City, and Oakland, plus in the states of Massachusetts, New Jersey, New York, and Oregon, as well as a number of French cities. I simply don't understand why state and local officials think they can bet against Wall Street bankers and win.

Unfunded Pension Costs

Reported state and local bond debt and debt growth vastly understate financial obligations because of underfunded pension and retiree health care obligations. The Pew Center found that as of June 30, 2008, state reports show they are obligated for $3.35 trillion for pension benefits owed to current and retired employees. Nevertheless, they have only contributed $2.35 trillion, so those retirement plans are underfunded to the tune of $1 trillion. Moreover, the Pew Center study found that states on average have set aside only 7.1 percent of retiree health care and other nonpension benefits, and 20 states have reserved nothing.

Also, the Pew Center believes its estimate of the shortfall is conservative because it didn't account for the massive investment losses in the second half of 2008 and early 2009, in conventional investments such as stocks and corporate bonds as well as alternative investments such as foreign currencies, commodities, emerging market stocks and bonds, private equity, and hedge funds. Municipal pension funds have only partially recouped their losses since then.

The California Public Employees Retirement System (CalPERS)—the largest in the country—saw its assets drop from $260 billion on October 31, 2007, to $193 billion a year later, a loss of $67 billion, due to huge declines in real estate, stocks, and other investments. That pushed the ratio of the fund's assets to liabilities from 102 percent in June 2007 to a likely 68 percent in June of 2010, well below the 80 percent or more ratio for a healthy pension fund. As a result, CalPERS will probably require state employer members to increase their contributions from 13 percent of payroll up to 15 to 17 percent in July 2010. Furthermore, CalPERS earns fees by guaranteeing the bonds of municipalities, but will make less after its credit rating was cut in late 2009 to three notches from triple-A.

Another study noted that state and local pension plans use a much higher interest rate to discount the future cost of their liabilities than is likely in the ongoing low-inflation, low-interest-rate climate. Therefore, that study estimates underfunding at $3.2 trillion. Because of generous state and local governments, annual pension costs for state and participating local governments more than doubled from fiscal 2000 to $64 billion in fiscal 2008.

Raise Taxes, Cut Services

In reaction to their financial woes, many state and local governments have attempted to raise taxes and fees. The usual suspects include higher sin taxes on tobacco and alcoholic beverages as well as taxes on companies based out of state but doing some business in the state. Washington, D.C., the federal government, and 14 states all raised cigarette taxes last year. Virginia, North Carolina, Washington, Vermont, and Mississippi are considering selling the rights to distribute liquor to private interests for windfall profits and to eliminate the costs of running state stores. Colorado and Pennsylvania may loosen restrictions on private outfit alcohol sales to increase revenues and, of course, drinking.

In Texas, the government in March 2010 won a state Supreme Court case allowing it to tax strip joints. The clubs said pole dancing is free speech and can't be taxed, but the state argued successfully that the tax would deter male club attendees who would drink booze, watch the strippers, and then possibly move on to commit rapes.

States are aggressively chasing tax evaders. Nebraska plans to post online the names of 500 taxpayers who owe more than $20,000. Some like Ohio and Oklahoma are asking other states for data on tax dodgers. Missouri may garnish bank accounts to collect tax judgments. California, Connecticut, Illinois, Maryland, Virginia, and Vermont may join New York, North Carolina, Rhode Island, and Colorado in trying to collect sales taxes on online sales, despite a limiting decision by the Supreme Court in 1992. Of course, courts have no concern over government funding, but in financially stressed Illinois, the state Supreme Court ruled in March 2010 that a Roman Catholic medical center isn't a charitable operation and, therefore, has to pay property taxes. And if you're not run out of Dodge, you can play at the Kansas state-owned Boot Hill casino there which pays the government 27 percent of its revenue in what until 1948 was a dry state.

Until Republican Chris Christie was elected governor of New Jersey in November 2009, there was talk of extending the state sales tax to clothing. Other jurisdictions may enlarge sales taxes on services to hotel room and restaurant bills to professional services such as medical, legal, and—heaven forbid!—economic consulting fees. As of 2007, the latest data, only seven states had sales taxes on services, which continue to grow much faster then goods consumption. But tax increases are not only resisted by taxpayers but often self-defeating as taxpayers vote with their feet. Louisiana was forced to back down on a tax on Internet companies.

Minnesota's governor in early 2010 proposed a 20 percent cut in the corporate income tax and a 20 percent tax cut for small business to entice businesses to move into the state. In depressed Michigan, a Democratic state representative asked for a 44 percent drop in business taxes.

Service Cuts

State and local governments are also making some service cuts. Of course, there have been the usual threatened reductions in taxpayer-favored services, intended to scare them into accepting higher levies. California Governor Schwarzenegger said he'd close state parks, cut money to fight wildfires, and close state prisons, turning the inmates loose on the public. But he's not alone. Over half the states cut penal costs in fiscal 2010 and 17 closed prisons or reduced inmate populations.

In New York City, where politically inspired financial legerdemain is a fine art, past mayors have threatened to take cops off the beat to save money, but seldom to reduce the ranks of those sitting at desks drinking coffee. Nevertheless, this threat is much less effective as crime rates fall along with the numbers of those who typically perpetrate them, young males in their teens and twenties. Mayor Bloomberg proposed closing up to 20 fire companies and reducing the police force by 1,300 through attrition. That would cut New York's finest to 80 percent of their 2001 staffing levels. Some cities say they're no longer responding to whole categories of calls such as check fraud, shoplifting, traffic accidents involving minor injuries, and burglaries. So you're on your own with only your insurance company to help.

New York City's public hospital system faces a $1 billion deficit in fiscal 2010 and $1.5 billion in fiscal 2011 due to increasing numbers of uninsured patients, state cuts in Medicaid payments, and employee pension costs, which leaped from $50 million in 2004 to an estimated $333 million next year. So the system intends to eliminate 10 percent of its 38,000 employees over the next two years. Personnel costs are 70 percent of the budget. Meanwhile, St. Vincent's Catholic Medical Center in Manhattan filed for bankruptcy in April 2010 for the second time in five years.

Education expenses, nearly sacred in many cities and suburbs, are under fire as 25 to 30 states cut funding for K–12 education in fiscal 2010 and at least 15 are likely to cut outlays in fiscal 2011. Laws limiting class sizes are being eased or axed in Florida, Georgia, Oklahoma, and Nevada. California did so in 2009, resulting in 75 percent of the state's public elementary schools increasing class sizes in the 2009–2010 school year. A number of school districts have moved to four-day weeks. The missing hours are made up by longer school days, but costs are reduced for custodians, cafeteria staff, bus drivers, and utilities. The Kansas City School Board in early 2010 decided to close 26 of 61 schools due to half-filled buildings, poor student achievement despite excessive earlier spending, student flight to the suburbs and to charter schools, and a $50 million annual deficit.

What to Do?

These attempts to raise taxes and cut spending have proved wholly inadequate to solving state and local government funding problems. And those woes appear chronic, especially if my forecast of slow economic growth and even deflation is valid. Rises in taxable personal and corporate incomes will be muted. Retail sales and taxes on them will be sluggish as consumers persist for the next decade in their saving spree, replacing the borrowing-and-spending binge of the past decade, as noted earlier.

> House prices are likely to fall further in the next year or so, under the weight of gigantic excess inventories. Meanwhile, commercial real estate's high vacancies and severe financial problems will take years to resolve, keeping prices depressed for some time. So, all things considered, local government property taxes are likely to be curtailed for many years.

With Americans experiencing limited income growth and zealous to save more and pay off their debts, their interest in spending is less than enthusiastic, especially spending on taxes. Proposition 13 in California—which was enacted in 1978 and limits real estate taxes to

1 percent of assessed valuation and annual increases in valuation to 2 percent unless the property is sold—has served as a model for other states. In 2008, Indiana cut property taxes an average 30 percent, starting in 2010, and capped them at 1 percent of assessed valuation on residential homes, 2 percent on rental properties and farms, and 3 percent for businesses.

Default

For some municipalities, the way out of this dilemma may be to default on their bonds and other obligations. In the 1930s, there were many municipal defaults. A study by George Hempel in 1964 found that at their peak in 1935, 3,252 municipal bonds were in default (see Table 7.4). If short-term defaults are excluded, 15.4 percent of the average net municipal debt went into default in the 1930s, although all but 1 percent was eventually paid off. But in 1934, Arkansas defaulted on its general obligation bonds and their holders lost money.

Recently there have been few municipal failures, with some notable exceptions. In 1994, wealthy Orange County, California, defaulted on $1.7 billion when its treasurer, Robert Citron, the lemon of Orange County, made some very bad bets on the direction of interest rates with the aid of clever Merrill Lynch bankers. In January, Las Vegas Monorail, a nonprofit with over $600 million in municipal bonds outstanding, filed for Chapter 11 bankruptcy. The 3.9-mile monorail along

Table 7.4 Municipal Defaults in the 1930s

Type	Peak Number in Default	Date
States	1–3*	May 1, 1933
Counties	359	July 1, 1934
Cities and towns	851	January 1, 1935
School districts	882	August 1, 1935
Other districts	299	September 1, 1935
Special purpose/special districts	1,173	May 1, 1938

*The study questioned whether two or three states actually entered default.
Data source: McDonnell Investments.

the Las Vegas Strip has suffered with that city's discretionary spending–driven economy. Ridership fell 21 percent in 2008 and default became unavoidable.

More recently, Jefferson County, Alabama, the home of 660,000 people and the city of Birmingham, got into financial trouble as a result of $3.2 billion in bonds to finance federally mandated sewer improvements. That left the county with $7,000 in debt for each resident, among the highest in the country. Much of the sewer work went to inexperienced firms, many of which subsequently have been convicted of bribery while the then-president of the Jefferson County Commission, and later Birmingham's mayor, was convicted of taking kickbacks and sentenced to 15 years in prison.

The county is still deciding whether to try to renegotiate its debts or to file for bankruptcy since the state has refused to bail it out. Bankruptcy would severely damage its reputation and limit future borrowing. Also, despite their current stench, the sewer bonds earlier were considered safe and worry-free investments, much more so than others such as municipal bonds backed by land speculations in Florida. Either bankruptcy or settling with bondholders for cents on the dollar could shake up the whole municipal market as others with similar woes line up to follow suit.

It's Not the 1930s

Several factors suggest that a rerun of the municipal defaults of the 1930s is unlikely. Lax as debt ratings have been in recent years, they're tougher for municipal obligations than in the 1930s when almost all were rated triple-A or double-A. About 90 percent of the 310 cities with more than 30,000 residents were rated triple-A in 1929 and 98 percent were rated double-A or better. So, of defaulting issues, 48 percent were rated triple-A in 1929, which accounted for 80 percent of the dollar value of all defaults, and 78 percent were rated double-A or higher and covered 94 percent of defaults in dollar terms. In reaction, rating agencies subsequently tightened their standards. In 2009, 9 percent of new long-term municipal issues were rated triple-A and 46 percent were double-A rated.

Furthermore, unlike the 1930s, today bailouts are the order of the day, and state and local governments are queuing up for their fair share of government handouts. As noted earlier, $246 billion from last year's fiscal stimulus bill went to state and local governments, including the Build America Bond subsidies.

Nevertheless, a number of municipalities are considering Chapter 9 of the bankruptcy code, which allows them to work out a debt repayment plan while being protected from creditors. Chapter 9 was enacted in 1934 and only 600 cases have used it, in part because it requires state approval. The largest was the 1994 default of Orange County, mentioned earlier. Vallejo, California, a city of 116,000 near San Francisco, filed for Chapter 9 in 2008 after real estate values nosedived and it was stuck with generous labor contracts that built in big increases in pay and benefits for police, firemen, and retirees and consumed 90 percent of the city's budget. Now Harrisburg, Pennsylvania, and San Diego are considering Chapter 9, as well as Jefferson County, Alabama, while Pittsburgh has avoided it by operating under state supervision since 1994.

In the past, municipal general obligation bonds, which are backed by the taxing authority of the issuing state or local government, were considered safer than revenue bonds supported by revenues from toll roads, water authorities, or school districts. But in today's environment, I put more faith in a steady, dedicated stream of bridge tolls than in the taxing ability and credibility of some municipalities. Debt problems and pension underfunding make California, Illinois, New Jersey, and Rhode Island especially suspect.

Labor Costs

Sooner or later, taxpayers will probably force state and local governments to curb labor costs, which account for half their spending, or $1.1 trillion in wage and benefit outlays in 2008. Years ago, the social contract held that those employees received lower wages than private sector workers, so early retirement provisions and lush pensions allowed them to catch up in their later years. But since the early 1980s, the private sector has been globalized with very little growth in real incomes. Meanwhile, state and local government employees have continued to receive pay raises in excess of inflation and now have wages that are 34 percent higher than for private sector employees.

California Assembly Speaker Willie Brown, a well-known liberal and great friend of organized labor, wrote in early 2010 in the *San Francisco Chronicle*:

> *The deal used to be that civil servants were paid less than private sector work-ers in exchange for an understanding that they had job security for life. But we politicians—pushed by our friends in labor—gradually expanded pay and benefits . . . while keeping the job protections and layering on incredibly generous retirement packages. . . . [A]t some point, someone is going to have to get honest about the fact.*

Partly responsible for these trends is unionization. Employment in heavily unionized manufacturing has been falling for decades due to productivity growth and as production is moved abroad. And growing sectors such as technology, professions, and many service industries tend to be nonunionized. In 1973, 24.5 percent of private-sector workers were unionized, but in 2009 it was only 7.2 percent, down from 7.6 percent in 2008 (see Figure 7.10). In 2009, 10.1 percent of private-sector union jobs were lost, compared to the 4.4 percent decline in private payrolls as unionized manufacturing and construction employment plummeted. In contrast, government unionized jobs have grown from 24.1 percent in 1973 to 37.4 percent of government jobs in 2009, up from 36.8 percent in 2008.

In the early 1970s, over 80 percent of union members worked in private-sector jobs and less than 20 percent were employed by govern-ment. In 2009, 51.4 percent, over half, of the national 15.4 million unionized jobs were in government at some level, or 7.9 million. The private sector is less and less unionized over time while the govern-ment sector has had about a third of its workforce unionized for the last three decades (Figure 7.10). This has given state and local government unions considerable power to negotiate substantial increases in wages and benefits. Sections of the country with the highest unionization of the workforce have the highest pay of state and local employees and tend to have the highest compensation advantage over the private sector.

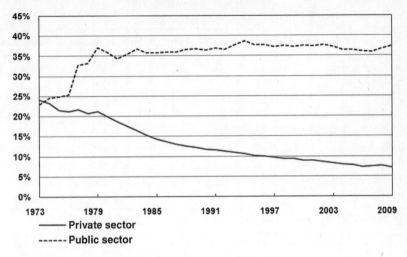

Figure 7.10 Union Membership—Percent of Workforce
Data source: Bureau of Labor Statistics.

Union Power

The power of unions and other forces have probably resulted in higher pay levels than needed to attract qualified employees. The U.S. Bureau of Labor Statistics found that the average quit rate among state and local employees was only a third that in the private sector. In California, 85 percent of the state's 235,000 employees are unionized, not including higher education staffs. Pension costs for state employees mushroomed 2,000 percent over the past decade. More than 15,000 retirees get over $100,000 per year in pensions.

As noted earlier, state and local employees receive 34 percent higher wages than in the private sector on average, but it's in benefits where they really shine, with a 70 percent advantage (see Table 7.5). Health insurance, retirement benefits, life insurance, and paid sick leave are not only much more available to public than private employees, but much richer. As shown in Table 7.5, in 2009, the costs of health insurance were 2.18 times as much for state and local employees as for private sector workers. No wonder that the tax in the 2010 health care bill on extremely generous, so-called Cadillac health insurance plans was vehemently opposed by public sector employees as well as the labor unions whose members now receive them.

Table 7.5 Average Compensation, 2009

	A. State and Local	B. Private Sector	Ratio A/B
Total compensation	$39.66	$27.42	1.45
Wages and salaries	$26.01	$19.39	1.34
Benefits	$13.65	$ 8.02	1.70
Paid leave	$ 3.27	$ 1.85	1.77
Supplemental pay	$ 0.34	$ 0.83	0.41
Health insurance	$ 4.34	$ 1.99	2.18
Defined-benefit pension	$ 2.85	$ 0.41	6.95
Defined-contribution	$ 0.31	$ 0.53	0.58
Other benefits	$ 2.53	$ 2.40	1.05

Data are given in dollars per hour worked.
Data source: Bureau of Labor Statistics.

As the table shows, in 2009, $2.85 per hour worked by state and local employees went for defined-benefit pension plans, despite their being extremely underfunded, compared to only $0.41 for private employees. Conversely, public employees get $0.31 per hour on average in payments to defined-contribution plans compared to $0.53 for private sector workers.

This reflects the dramatic shift away from defined-benefit plans by private employers in recent decades as they shifted to 401(k)s and other defined-contribution plans in which employees, not employers, are responsible for investment success. In 2009, defined-benefit plans were available to only 21 percent of private sector employees. Meanwhile, most state and local governments continued to offer defined-benefit plans, which were available to 84 percent of their employees. And public sector defined-benefit plans paid about twice as much as those in the private sector.

Early Retirement

Public sector defined-benefit plans and other retirement costs also are high because those employees can usually retire at age 55, after 30 years of employment, with pensions equal to 60 percent or more of final salary and indexed for inflation. Those in public safety in California can retire at age 50 after 30 years of service with benefits equal to 90 percent of their final year's pay.

Since many jurisdictions base pensions on salaries in the last one to three years on the job, some—like New York City—routinely give those close to retirement lots of overtime so they end up retiring at close to their base pay levels—*spiking*, it's called. New York Attorney General Andrew Cuomo in early 2010 cited the case of a cop with a base salary of $74,000 who got $125,000 in overtime in his last year of employment, pushing up his total retirement costs by $1.2 million. In contrast, private defined-benefit pensions are typically based on the last five years or career average pay.

Furthermore, in California, New Jersey, Utah, and other states, government employees can double-dip by retiring early and then resuming their previous jobs or taking other government positions. So they get salaries and pensions at the same time. In New Jersey, someone can hold simultaneous government jobs—say, small-town mayor and state senator, both part-time positions, while teaching full-time in a public school—all the while contributing to the state pension fund from three different jobs and ensuring a comfortable retirement.

Further, many state and local pension plan costs are increased by those who retire early due to disabilities but go on to take other jobs. I'm told that in my town, the garbage collectors don't even need to retire to take another job. Apparently, they race through their rounds in the morning so they finish by noon what's supposed to take eight hours, and then move on to other employment in the afternoon.

Taxpayer Revolt?

People working in the private sector apparently were willing to accept the fact of higher pay, more job security, and better retirement benefits for state and local government employees in past years. High employment and robust economic growth at least held out the hope that the lots of private sector workers would improve tomorrow. But with slow economic growth, limited income expansion, and high unemployment likely in future years, voter attitudes have changed.

Americans still want basic municipal services like police and fire protection, good schools for their kids, clean streets, and garbage collection. But they are coming to believe that they're paying too much for those services; that 34 percent higher wages for state and local employees compared to private sector workers isn't justified as pay cuts multiply in the private sector and those laid off earn much less if and when they can find another job; that 70 percent higher benefit costs is over the top, especially as private sector employees are paying more of their health care premiums and seeing their defined-benefit pension plans replaced by much more uncertain 401(k)s.

If a full-blown taxpayer revolt unfolds, there are plenty of things that can be done to reduce state and local government labor costs in an orderly way. Following in the footsteps of bankrupt GM, two-tier wage structures can be established with existing employees continuing at current salary levels, but new hires paid the much lower wages adequate to attract qualified people. And the new people can be enrolled in defined-contribution pension plans that require employee contributions, rather than defined-benefit plans, while their retirement ages can be increased.

Meanwhile, while waiting for existing employees to retire, their pay levels can be frozen. Also, pension formulas can be reformed to avoid the system being gamed by heavy overtime in final years on the job, and double-dipping can be eliminated. Retirees can be required to pay meaningful shares of the health care costs to limit government outlays and curtail what I call *recreational medicine*—taking a day off work at full pay to visit a physician, at employer expense, because of a minor ailment.

Action So Far

Recently, 10 states have required employees to increase their contributions to their benefit plans. Indiana's health savings accounts for state employees have been remarkably effective—since people are, in effect, spending their own money—and have cut costs by 11 percent. Others, including New York, Nevada, Nebraska, Rhode Island, and New Jersey, are reducing new-employee compensation by raising their retirement ages, moving toward defined-contribution plans, eliminating spiking, and reducing pension benefit payouts while increasing employee contributions.

At the same time, a number of states are underpaying their annual pension fund bills, only delaying the inevitable. With an $11 billion budget deficit, New Jersey Governor Christie is skipping entirely the state's $3 billion payment, following in the footsteps of his predecessor, Jon

Corzine, who essentially missed a $2.5 billion payment and permitted local governments to pay only 50 percent of their pension fund obligations. Virginia is paying $1.5 billion of $2.2 billion due. Illinois has not paid in full in past years, and Governor Pat Quinn has proposed paying $300 million less than the $4.5 billion due in fiscal 2011. In 2009, more than 50 percent of pension funds did not receive full payment.

Outsourcing to the private sector can also cut state and local government costs quickly. I've heard that garbage collection costs by private haulers in some towns can be only a third the expense of using public employees. With money-laden carrots, the Obama administration is encouraging states to relax rules that bar teacher pay-for-performance and charter schools. The powerful, 3.6 million-strong teachers unions have always demanded that teacher seniority determine pay, promotion, and job tenure, but are now beginning to accept looser seniority and tougher evaluations.

The ramifications of meaningful restraints on state and local government spending would be profound since that sector has been a source of stability in employment and the economy for decades. In the fourth quarter of 2009, state and local government spending accounted for 12.4 percent of GDP, at the top of the range that it's held since the early 1970s (see Figure 7.11). That share leaped in the early post–World War II

Figure 7.11 State and Local Government Consumption and Investment Expenditures as a Percentage of GDP
Data source: Bureau of Economic Analysis.

decades largely to educate the postwar babies. After they left high school and college, labor and other costs elsewhere in state and local budgets leaped. But in the next decade, municipal governments' share of GDP may decline significantly.

Please note that the nine economic growth-slowing forces I've discussed in this and the previous chapter make 2.0 percent annual advances in real GDP in coming years reasonable, maybe even optimistic. The switch from a quarter-century-long consumer borrowing-and-spending binge to a saving spree will cut 1.5 percentage points off the 3.7 percent rate of the lush 1982–2000 years. That alone brings growth down to 2.2 percent, and the eight other forces—global financial deleveraging, increased government economic involvement and regulation, weak commodity prices, fiscal restraint in developed countries, rising protectionism, depressed housing activity, deflation and state and local government spending—can easily reduce growth by 0.2 percentage points more.

Offsets?

There could, of course, be economic sectors of strength that would push economic growth higher than the 2.0 percent annual average I foresee. Robust spending on capital equipment and industrial structures is a possibility, but huge excess industrial capacity here and abroad is likely to persist in the years of slow growth ahead and depress new investment, as I discuss in Chapter 11. Also, developing countries in Asia, to say nothing of Europe, will probably be flooding the world with capital goods.

The exception in the capital equipment arena I foresee is productivity-enhancing equipment, and not necessarily new-tech gear. In an era when raising prices will be next to impossible for most companies and volume growth is limited, the route to profits growth will often be through cutting costs and enhancing productivity, as I explore in Chapter 12.

Also, it will take years before excess office buildings, malls, warehouses, and hotels are absorbed amid consumer retrenchment and slow economic growth, and before oceans of bad real estate debts are written off. The exceptions, as I discuss in Chapter 12, may well be rental apartments and medical facilities.

Many hope that net exports will be a source of strength. But the consumer saving spree that will dampen U.S. economic growth will have even more profound effects on the foreign economies that have depended for growth on American consumers to buy the excess goods and services for which they have no other markets. As I mentioned earlier, a 1 percent decline in American consumer spending reduces our imports—their exports—by 2.9 percent. The merchandise (goods) trade balances in Table 7.6 are for the most recently reported 12 months for each country, not for the same 12 months in all cases. Also, like all foreign trade data, these are full of discrepancies. With these caveats, however, the $550 billion U.S. deficit is matched by a net $500 billion surplus abroad.

In 2008, U.S. consumers accounted for 16.6 percent of global GDP compared to 14.9 percent in 1980. A clear result of the upward trend in consumers' share of GDP and declining saving rate (Figure 2.5) for a

Table 7.6 Merchandise Trade Balances

Country	Trade Balance	Country	Trade Balance	Country	Trade Balance
United States	−550.1	Czech Republic	9.0	Australia	−8.0
Japan	79.3	Denmark	14.9	Hong Kong	−39.9
China	144.9	Hungary	6.8	India	−105.8
United Kingdom	−132.5	Norway	55.0	Indonesia	21.3
Canada	−2.4	Poland	−5.0	Malaysia	37.0
Euro area	41.4	Russia	149.4	Singapore	29.9
Austria	−5.2	Sweden	10.0	South Korea	40.0
Belgium	20.0	Switzerland	20.1	Taiwan	15.5
France	−60.1	Turkey	−50.9	Thailand	13.1
Germany	210.4	Egypt	−24.2	Argentina	14.6
Greece	−44.1	Israel	−5.4	Brazil	19.3
Italy	−13.1	Saudi Arabia	104.4	Chile	15.4
Netherlands	53.2	South Africa	−1.4	Colombia	1.1
Spain	−70.7			Mexico	−2.3
				Venezuela	30.0

Data are in US$ billion.
Data source: *Economist*, July 8, 2010.

quarter-century has been the downtrend in the foreign trade and current account balances (as seen in Figure 6.9 in Chapter 6). I can't overemphasize the importance of the profligate U.S. consumer in fueling economic growth in the rest of the world.

Our analysis of Asian exports illustrates this reality. The intra-Asian trade, mentioned earlier, was much bigger than the direct exports to the United States, but when we accounted for the value-added of the components produced in, say, Taiwan that were sent for subassembly to Thailand, then to Malaysia for final assembly, with the finished product destined for the United States, over half of Asian exports ended up in America. Countries that remain dependent on exports, most of which go directly or indirectly to U.S. consumers, include China, which I give special attention to in Chapter 11.

With subdued U.S. consumer spending in the years ahead and the resulting weakness in American imports, economic growth abroad will be even weaker than in the United States. It's the classic case of America sneezing and the rest of the world catching a cold—or, in the present climate, America catching the cold and the rest of the world contracting pneumonia. Exports in Asia other than from Japan now account for about 50 percent of those countries' GDP versus only 12 percent in the United States.

Currencies versus Economies

Many believe that a weak dollar in future years will spur U.S. exports. We look for a robust buck, as I explain in Chapter 12, but in any event, our research shows that the links between currency values and export and import prices and between the buck and real imports and exports are very weak.

Note that the dollar is about three times as volatile as U.S. import or four times as volatile as export prices. Why? Partly because most dollar transactions have nothing to do with American trade. Greenbacks are heavily used in others' trade and as mediums of exchange in weak currency countries. Also, international capital flows involving the buck dwarf trade uses of the dollar. And some international trade involves long-term contracts that lock in prices for years.

More important, importers and exporters adjust their prices to off-set currency fluctuations. If the dollar falls 10 percent against the euro, importers of German cars don't want to raise their U.S. prices 10 percent to maintain their unit revenues in euros for fear of losing American market share. So they shave their prices and profits instead and also attempt to offset the euro's strength with cost cuts and productivity gains. Similarly, U.S. exporters could maintain their sales prices in dollars and see their prices in euros fall 10 percent. They prefer, however, to raise their dollar prices to improve their profits, especially since raising prices is otherwise so difficult in a world of surpluses.

As a result, the link between U.S. imports and the dollar is weak. Ditto for eurozone imports and the euro. If currency movements don't influence trade much, what does? It's economic growth, as implied by my earlier discussion on the global effects of U.S. consumer retrenchment. When an economy is growing, consumers and business buy more of everything, especially imports, and the reverse when economic activity is weak. This is also true for Japan, the United Kingdom, Germany, and the eurozone as a whole. Our statistical work backs this up by revealing that for each 1 percent rise in real GDP since 1974, U.S. real imports grew 2.9 percent but increased only 0.2 percent for each 1 percent rise in the dollar. Thus, currency fluctuations don't have much effect on import and export prices or on real imports and exports. Imports leap when the U.S. economy grows and exports climb when our trading partners' economies are robust.

Government Gooses?

Federal government is the only remaining sector of the economy that might support more robust growth in future years. The federal government will likely continue to be a big spender—with trillion-dollar deficits to prove it—but as a counterbalance to the slow growth in the private and municipal sectors and to chronic unemployment pressures, as I discuss in the next chapter.

Chapter 8

Chronic Worldwide Deflation

My great call on disinflation, made in the early 1980s, was followed by my prediction in the late 1990s of chronic deflation—to start with the next major global recession. Well, the great recession arrived at the end of 2007, so in several years we'll know whether my prognostication of chronic worldwide deflation will be my eighth great call. It would certainly qualify as one, according to my three criteria. It would be hugely important to economies and financial markets worldwide. It's certainly nonconsensus, since very few others believe deflation is possible in democracies with paper money, despite the clear evidence in Japan, the world's second largest economy (as seen in Figure 7.5 in Chapter 7). And I think I'll be right on the cause of deflation—an excess of supply over demand, with monetary policy playing only a minor and largely impotent role. The arrival of chronic deflation would also substantiate the two books I wrote on the subject, although it would be a Pyrrhic victory since that was so many years ago that they're both long out of print. The books are *Deflation: Why It's Coming, Whether It's Good or Bad, and How It Will Affect Your Investments, Business and Personal Affairs* (Lakeview Publishing, 1998), and *Deflation: How to Survive and Thrive in the Coming Wave of Deflation* (McGraw-Hill, 1999).

Few agree with my forecast of chronic deflation. As shown by the spread between the yields on 10-year Treasurys and Treasury inflation-protected securities (TIPS), investors expect inflation to run at 1.7 percent 10 years hence. They've never seen anything but inflation in their business careers or lifetimes, so they think that's the way God made the world. Few can remember much about the 1930s, the last time deflation reigned. They don't realize that inflation is a wartime phenomenon. In peacetime, deflation rules, as shown in Table 8.1. Notice that in the 92 war years since 1749, including shooting wars, the Cold War, the War on Poverty, and the recent War on Terror, wholesale prices rose

Table 8.1 Historic Inflation and Deflation

Period	Military Engagement	Number of Years	Annualized Wholesale Price Change
1749–1755	Peacetime	6	−0.50%
1756–1763	French-Indian War	8	2.27%
1764–1774	Peacetime	11	−0.35%
1775–1783	American Revolution	9	−12.31%
1784–1811	Peacetime	28	−1.91%
1812–1815	War of 1812	4	7.78%
1816–1845	Peacetime	30	−2.36%
1846–1848	Mexican-American War	3	−0.40%
1849–1860	Peacetime	12	1.05%
1861–1865	Civil War	5	14.75%
1866–1916	Peacetime	51	−0.74%
1917–1918	World War I	2	23.92%
1919–1940	Peacetime	22	−2.31%
1941–1945	World War II	5	6.12%
1946–1992	Cold War	47	4.20%
1992–2000	Peacetime	8	1.43%
2001–2009	War on Terror	9	2.53%

5.77 percent per year, on average. In the 168 years of peace, they fell an average 1.16 percent annually.

Starting in 1941, the nation suffered a uniquely long era of mostly war years, which actually started with rearmament in the late 1930s. This was followed by World War II, which promptly gave way to the Cold War that was augmented by the War on Poverty, and now the War on Terror. Fueled by excess government spending on Vietnam and Great Society programs, inflation rates began to rise in the late 1960s. By 1980, with double-digit rates prevailing, most forecasters believed high inflation would last forever. The Philadelphia Federal Reserve Bank's inflation expectations survey that year found professional forecasters looking for consumer price index (CPI) inflation of nearly 9 percent annually for the next 10 years. We were almost alone at the time in predicting a declining inflation trend and eventual drop to 3 percent rates or less. In fact, CPI inflation peaked in 1980, averaged 4.7 percent over the next decade, and dropped below 3 percent a few years later (as shown in Figure 1.5 in Chapter 1).

Inflation Biases

Furthermore, we all tend to have inflation biases. We worry more about rising prices that may strain household budgets than about falling prices, which can help them. Maybe that's why we tend to think that whenever we pay higher prices, it's because of the inflation devil himself, but that lower prices are a result of our smart shopping and bargaining skills. Airline ticket costs may be falling due to competition from discount airlines, but many people think they're responsible for their cheaper tickets as they visit airfare web sites and pick the lowest fares. Meanwhile, higher prices are seen as being the work of greedy corporations and other unassailable forces. Who doesn't feel helpless, both physically and financially, in the face of rising medical costs?

Also, we don't calculate the quality-adjusted price declines that result from technological improvements in many big-ticket purchases. This is especially true since many of those items are bought so infrequently that we have no idea what we paid for the last one. But we sure remember the cost of gasoline on the last fill-up a week ago.

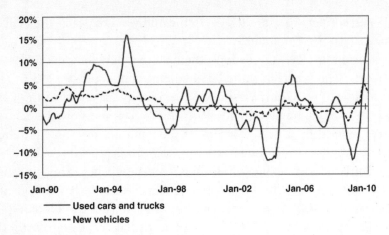

Figure 8.1 New and Used Automobile Prices, Year/Year Percent Change
Data source: Bureau of Labor Statistics.

Nevertheless, concentration on small purchases neglects the big price declines in recent years in expensive, infrequently purchased items that are often discretionary and can be postponed. New and used vehicles are in this category (see Figure 8.1). Computers are in the same boat, and adjusted for skyrocketing in computing power, their cost to consumers has virtually collapsed in the past 25 years while they have become more and more important expenditures.

Quality improvements are also important on lower-tech products. Even if a washing machine costs the same as a decade ago, the modern front-loading models are more convenient and use less energy and water. These quality enhancements are often forgotten even if people remember what they paid 10 years ago.

Despite the widespread belief that inflation is much higher than reported, the evidence is that the CPI is overstated. Back in the mid-1990s, the Senate Finance Committee established the Advisory Commission to Study the Consumer Price Index, which delivered its final report in December 1997. It found that the CPI was biased upward in four areas.

Four CPI Upward Biases

First, since the index has fixed weights, it doesn't account for the tendency to buy more of what's cheap and less of what's expensive. When apple prices fall and orange prices rise, consumers buy more apples and fewer oranges.

Second, the panel of retail stores sampled monthly by the Bureau of Labor Statistics (BLS) in its survey of selling prices changes only slowly over time. Therefore, rapidly expanding discounters like Wal-Mart are underreported while faltering, full-list-price mom-and-pop outlets are overweighted.

Third, the Commission found that the quality improvements are understated, which means that prices are recorded as higher than they would be with proper adjustment. And the fourth CPI upward bias quantified by the Commission results from the fixed-weight base period, currently 2007–2008 for the CPI. At that time, iPhones and lots of other new-tech gear didn't exist, but they now account for meaningful portions of consumer spending. Since their prices have fallen dramatically, the CPI is overstated since it doesn't include them.

In total, the Commission estimated that the annual rise in the CPI was overstated by 1.1 percent. The BLS made some corrections in 1999 that reduced the CPI by 0.2 percent per year, so it is still showing much more inflation than an unbiased measure would report. Consequently, when the official CPI less food and energy was 0.9 percent year-over-year in May 2010, the prices it is supposed to measure were really close to unchanged on balance.

Current Evidence of Deflation

Although few accept it, there is ample evidence of deflation currently. As usual, consumer electronics prices are falling, but with unusual speed. Apple introduced its iPhone in June 2009 for $599, but only three months later slashed the cost to $399. The prices of TV sets continue their downward march. And mobile phone software now allows shoppers to ferret out the best prices on electronics gear, cameras, and DVDs on their way to the mall. Some include GPS so shoppers can learn how close physically they are to the bargains. That's a deflationary application!

Procter & Gamble in early 2010 put more Duracell batteries in each pack but left prices unchanged—in effect, price cuts for a firm that hates to do so. With excess supply and muted consumer demand, many producers are absorbing any increase in the prices of raw materials, which are only tiny portions of many finished items, anyway. It won't make much difference to the prices of vehicles and other metal-intensive products, but with consumers keeping their goods longer, there was a shortage of scrap metal in early 2010 that was spiking prices—but from very low levels.

In April 2010, Wal-Mart launched a new wave of price cuts on thousands of items that will force competitors to follow. Prescription drug sales rose 5.1 percent in 2009 but that was at the low end of the range as users switched to generics. The number of generic prescriptions rose 5.9 percent while branded prescriptions dropped 7.6 percent.

In 2008, the value of all U.S. farmland and buildings fell 3.2 percent to $2,100 per acre, the first drop since 1987. At the other end of the spectrum, hesitancy among investors and lower returns have spurred venture capital firms to cut their fees. Their average annual return for the 10 years ending June 2009 was 14 percent compared to 34 percent for the 10 years ending June 2008. Private equity firms also cut their management fees, by 50 percent in some cases. New accounting rules that require corporations to reveal explicitly what they pay on merger and acquisition fees may put downward pressure on investment banking charges.

The rapid development of natural gas trapped in shale has dropped the price dramatically in recent years. That, plus the weak economy, pushed down electricity prices 40 percent in the first half of 2009 in the largest wholesale market, PJM Interconnection, which serves 13 states from Delaware to Michigan. California, often the nation's leader in everything from hula hoops to foreign cars, again in early 2010 planned to allow businesses to buy electricity directly from independent marketers, bypassing utilities, to take advantage of low prices. Wholesale electricity prices fell 29 percent from 2008 to 2009. Buying directly from wholesalers was suspended in 2001 after Enron effectively cornered the market, which forced the state to bail out utilities.

In Europe, many economies are in or close to deflation, and collapsing housing bubbles in Ireland and Spain imply prolonged years of falling price indexes. In February 2010, consumer prices fell 2.6 percent from a year earlier in Ireland with a 2009 year-end unemployment rate of 13.3 percent. In Spain, the jobless rate was almost 20 percent. Ireland, Portugal, and Spain all had 2009 declines in consumer prices from 2008, and inflation eurozone-wide is only about 1 percent.

The Root Cause of Inflation

In free markets, inflation results when ex ante demand exceeds supply, and deflation when ex ante supply exceeds demand, while prices are allowed to move up or down to bring supply and demand together. Historically, inflation is associated with wartime because it's then that the federal government creates excess demand for goods and services on top of an already fully employed economy. Recently, of course, Washington has been a big spender and is likely to remain so in the slow-growing economy I foresee, as mentioned earlier. But these huge outlays are, at best, offsetting severe weakness in the private sector.

The federal government is the only sector that can overspend enough to create inflation because it's the only one with the credibility in financial markets to float the immense borrowing to finance it. Other sectors, especially real estate, occasionally attempt huge and chronic outside financing but soon run out of lender credibility, as was seen in 2007–2008 with the collapse of subprime mortgages, Bear Stearns, and Lehman. Once inflation is well established, as in the 1970s, however, federal deficits don't appear that huge (see Figure 3.1 in Chapter 3), because federal receipts benefit as taxpayers are pushed into higher brackets and corporations are taxed on underdepreciation and inventory profits, as noted in Chapter 1.

Also, as discussed in Chapter 2, I don't believe that inflation is a monetary phenomenon. Any discussion of the money supply, of course, assumes that it can be precisely defined. But that isn't true, not in today's world of sophisticated financial instruments. Sure, the money supply includes currency in circulation, checking accounts, savings and time accounts, and money market accounts, all of which can be used or readily converted into forms that can be used to buy things—although the freezing up of money market funds in 2009 after Reserve Primary Fund broke the buck because of its holding of bad Lehman paper is a notable exception.

Money Definition

But should the money supply include reserves in cash-value life insurance policies that can be easily borrowed? And what about financial derivatives? They can't be used to buy milk in a supermarket, but many, through triple-A tranches of derivatives backed by subprime residential mortgages, were as good as cash back in the salad days of the housing bubble. Then there are credit, debit, and charge cards. Debit and credit cards do have specific limits, and should those amounts be included in the money supply? But charge cards have no limits. When you walk into a store with an American Express charge card, theoretically you have unlimited funds in your hand.

This lack of a definition of money is a serious problem for the monetarists who, like Milton Friedman, believe that inflation is always and everywhere a result of excess money. If you can't define the money supply, how can you measure its effects on prices? Furthermore, although money may be linked to inflation or deflation in some cases, it may not be the prime mover even then. Those who believe it is have to consider the monetary authorities to have been reckless and irresponsible for allowing the money supply to explode in the early 1940s and induce subsequent major inflation (see Figure 8.2), as discussed in Chapter 2.

Obviously, during World War II, monetary policy was merely the handmaiden of fiscal policy. With so much of production going to the military, there was limited output of civilian goods and services, far less than purchasing power in the fully employed economy. The

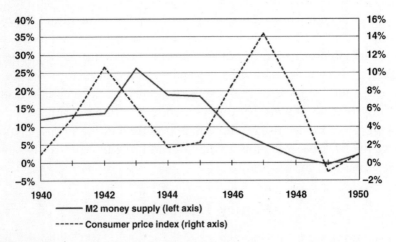

Figure 8.2 M2 Money Supply and Consumer Prices, 1940–1950
Data source: Historical Statistics of the United States.

government didn't want to risk reducing patriotism by raising taxes to soak up the surplus income and finance the war effort. So it resorted to other means—selling war bonds and mushrooming the money supply. The inflationary response to this fiscal policy–induced explosion in the money supply came later after wartime price and wage controls were removed (see Figure 8.2).

In any event, when the nation is not at war—a shooting war, a cold war, or the War on Terror—deflation is the norm as government spending in relation to gross domestic product (GDP) drops back. During those times, the productive capability of the nation, and now the world with globalization, is so great that supply chronically exceeds demand. That's what I believe lies ahead, assuming that the War on Terror will be wound down and not escalate into Cold War dimensions. That implies that deflation will reign until the next major war or some similar event. And unfortunately, unless human nature suddenly changes, there's another war out there in future years, waiting for us in the underbrush.

Seven Varieties of Inflation/Deflation

When we talk about inflation or deflation, we usually mean what is measured by the CPI, producer price index (PPI), GDP deflator, or other measures of aggregate price movements. I've identified, however, seven varieties of inflation/deflation that need to be kept in mind:

1. Commodity
2. Wage-price
3. Financial asset
4. Tangible asset
5. Currency
6. Inflation by fiat
7. Goods and services

1. Commodity Inflation/Deflation

In the late 1960s, the mushrooming costs of the Vietnam War and the Great Society programs in an already-robust economy created a

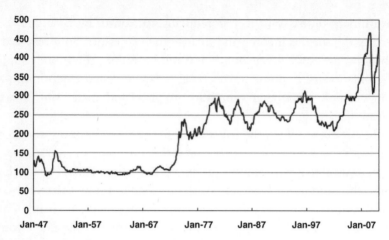

Figure 8.3 Knight Ridder Commodities Research Bureau Index
Data source: Haver Analytics.

tremendous gap between supply and demand in many areas. The history of low inflation rates for goods and services (we'll call it *CPI inflation* for short) in the late 1950s and early 1960s apparently created a momentum of low-price advances that held CPI inflation in check until about 1973 (Figure 1.5). But by the early 1970s, commodity prices started to leap (see Figure 8.3) and spawned a self-feeding upsurge. Worried that they'd run out of critical materials in a robust economy, producers started to double- and triple-order supplies to insure adequate inventories. That hyped demand, which squeezed supply, and prices spiked further. In turn, even more frenzied buying as many expected shortages to last forever, as discussed in Chapter 2.

The spot commodity index shown in Figure 8.3 rose 81 percent from November 1971 to October 1973. I use October 1973 because that marked the start of the Saudi oil embargo. Most observers still believe it touched off the inflation spiral, but the bulk of commodity inflation occurred beforehand. From October 1973 to the next peak in August 1974, the index rose "only" 25 percent.

At the time, even before the oil embargo, we were lucky enough to realize that what was occurring was not perennial shortages but massive inventory-building, as discussed in Chapter 2. Then, arriving inventories swamped sales, especially in late 1974 and early 1975, so production nosedived.

Another Commodity Bubble

Another commodity bubble started in the mid-2000s (shown in Figure 8.3). Robust demand for materials in the 1990s and early 2000s pushed up operating rates for base metal and other commodity producers. Still, they were reluctant to increase capacity, worried that future demand would not justify high initial costs of new mines, oil fields, and so forth. So commodity prices took off.

What greatly augmented the commodity bubble, however, was the overlay of speculators and investors. Many pension and endowment funds as well as individual investors became convinced that commodities were a legitimate investment class, like stocks and bonds. So they piled in and doubled their bets as prices soared. Crude oil was their darling and its price rose to $145 per barrel in July 2008 as many became convinced that the world would soon run out of oil and other key commodities (see Figure 7.9).

Those people are fans of M. King Hubbert (1903–1989), a geophysicist who joined Shell Oil in 1947. Hubbert believed that oil field production followed the classical bell curve, or normal distribution, and that oil gets increasingly expensive to extract and is of lower quality after a field's production peaks. Based on his theory, he predicted that production in the lower 48 states would peak in the early 1970s.

Few believed him at the time of his predictions, but, indeed, it did. His followers subsequently extended his concepts globally and believe that worldwide production will top out in 2010 or in 2012 at the latest. They are convinced that no big economically feasible oil fields remain to be found, so new finds will continue to fall short of demand increases. They discount the fact that reserves are often underestimated since oil fields produce more than original conservative estimates. Nor do they expect natural gas, liquefied natural gas, the oil sands in Canada, heavy oil in Venezuela and elsewhere, oil shale, coal, hydroelectric power, nuclear energy, wind, geothermic, solar, tidal, ethanol and biomass energy, fuel cells, and so forth to substitute significantly for petroleum.

Too Pessimistic

I have believed for some time that the Hubbert devotees are far too pessimistic. High prices are the best fertilizer for increasing supply in most anything. Continual technological improvements make the discovery of big new fields and increased production from existing ones likely. New technology for developing natural gas trapped in shale has mushroomed supply and collapsed prices. Nonpetroleum energy is sure to be exploited. France generates 80 percent of its electricity from nuclear facilities compared with 10 percent in the United States. The huge oil sands, which account for much of Canada's reserves and may contain more energy than Saudi Arabia's petroleum reserves, are being increasingly exploited.

I'm thoroughly convinced that human ingenuity will also beat threats of shortages anytime. Significantly higher automotive fuel mileage is no doubt in the cards, one way or another. Business users of energy invest in conservation technology when higher prices make the investments economical. Higher energy prices will spread the use of time-of-day prices among household users. There's also a trade-off between energy costs and conservation measures in house and office construction, with green now in.

Furthermore, oil demand grows more slowly than real economic growth due to greater efficiency in energy use over time. It's also due to the increasing share of GDP, especially in developed countries, accounted for by services with declining shares going to goods, especially goods that require lots of energy to produce.

In addition, recent oil field discoveries and the prospect of more finds are discrediting the peak theory. Many are the result of new technology that allows oil production under 6,000 feet of water. Petrobras discovered a huge field off the coast of Brazil in deep water and layers of salt. In 2009, BP announced a major new oil field in the Gulf of Mexico, although the oil spill may slow deep water drilling in that area. Tullow Oil made a major discovery in Uganda in an area where it already found a big reservoir. Anadarko also announced a major discovery in deep water off the coast of Sierra Leone, and the firm's 2007 discovery off Ghana may extend 700 miles west to Ivory Coast. Russia is inviting foreign energy producers to join with domestic firms to develop a vast Arctic gas field.

In any event, the global recession instantly converted commodity inflation to commodity deflation (Figure 8.3). Crude oil and many other commodity prices collapsed, and institutional and individual investors withdrew as they learned the hard way that commodities are speculations, not an asset class (see Figure 7.9).

Commodity prices have rebounded more recently, along with the hope that a return to rapid growth is not far off. Many investors are also impressed with the recent stockpiling of commodities by the Chinese, assuming that much more is in store. I believe, however, that slow global growth lies ahead, especially as U.S. consumers continue to retrench and slash the imports on which most foreign countries continue to depend for growth, directly or indirectly. I look for further weakness of commodities as supply continues to swamp demand in a world of muted economic growth. A return to the price norms of the 1980s and 1990s (see Figure 8.3) is certainly possible.

2. Wage-Price Inflation/Deflation

Wage-price inflation causes wages to push up prices, which then push up wages in a self-reinforcing cycle that can get deeply and stubbornly embedded in the economy. This, too, was suffered in the 1970s and accompanied slow growth. Hence the name *stagflation*. As with commodity inflation, it was spawned by excess aggregate demand resulting from huge spending and the Vietnam War and Great Society programs on top of a robust economy.

Back then, labor unions had considerable bargaining strength and membership (as seen in Figure 6.8 in Chapter 6). Furthermore, American business was relatively paternalist, with many business leaders convinced that they had a moral duty to keep their employees at least abreast of inflation. Most didn't realize that, as a result, inflation was very effectively transferring their profits to labor—and also to government, which taxed underdepreciation and inventory profits. The result was a collapse in corporate profits' share of national income and a comparable rise in the share going to employee compensation from the mid-1960s until the early 1980s (as shown in Figure 2.4 in Chapter 2).

I told many corporate CEOs at the time that they should look at their earnings in inflation-adjusted terms. They were getting slaughtered. Most replied that Wall Street analysts used nominal, not real, numbers, so they should, too. But stockholders were savvy. Corrected for CPI inflation, the S&P 500 Index fell 64 percent from its peak in November 1968 to July 1982.

The Peak

The wage-price spiral peaked in the early 1980s as CPI inflation began a downtrend that is still continuing (Figure 1.5). Voters rebelled against Washington, elected Ronald Reagan, and initiated an era of government retrenchment. The percentage of Americans who depend in a significant way on income from government rose from 28.7 percent in 1950 to 61.2 percent in 1980, but then fell to 53.7 percent in 2000, as discussed earlier. Furthermore, the Fed, under then-Chairman Paul Volcker, blasted up interest rates, and negative real borrowing costs turned to very high positive levels (see Figure 8.4).

As inflation receded, American business found itself naked as a jaybird with depressed profits and intense foreign competition. In response, corporate leaders turned to restructuring with a will. That included the end of paternalism toward employees as executives realized they were in a globalized atmosphere of excess supply of almost everything. With operations and jobs moving to cheaper locations offshore and with the economy increasingly high-tech and service-oriented, union membership and power plummeted (Figure 6.8).

In today's unfolding deflation, the wage-price spiral has been reversed. Contrary to most forecasters' expectations, but forecast in my

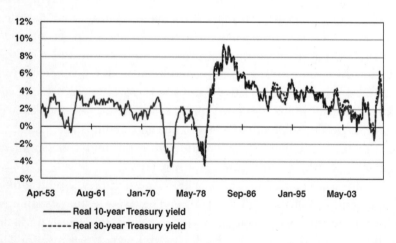

Figure 8.4 Real 10- and 30-Year Treasury Yields
Real yield = Nominal yield less year/year change in CPI.
Data sources: Federal Reserve and Bureau of Labor Statistics.

two *Deflation* books, wages are actually being cut and involuntary furloughs instituted for the first time since the 1930s. In inflation, oversize wages can be cut to size by simply avoiding pay hikes while inflation erodes real compensation to the proper level. But with deflation, actual cuts in nominal pay are necessary. Note that as wage cuts and furloughs become increasingly prevalent, the layoff and unemployment numbers (Figure 5.1 in Chapter 5, and Figure 2.1 in Chapter 2, respectively) will increasingly understate the reality of the declines in labor compensation.

Experts point out that layoffs reduce morale as those remaining ask, who's next? Those who can do so leave for other jobs in anticipation of the ax. Research shows that for every layoff, five additional employees leave voluntarily within a year. So recruiting and training replacements often outweighs the savings from layoffs. Lincoln Electric, the Cleveland-based maker of welding equipment, has had a no-layoff policy since the 1920s. To avoid layoffs in times of weak orders, Lincoln Electric cuts wages, reduces working hours, and transfers people to different jobs. In other words, everyone suffers the pain. Furthermore, the company, which distributes 30 percent of its annual profits in employee bonuses, enforces rigorous productivity and performance standards, and those who fall short get small bonuses or pink slips. Wages are based on piecework so the quality of employees' work can be monitored.

3. Financial Asset Inflation/Deflation

Perhaps the best recent example of financial asset inflation was the dot-com blow-off in the late 1990s. It culminated the long secular bull market that started in 1982 and was driven by the convergence of a number of stimulative factors. As discussed earlier, CPI inflation peaked in 1980 and declined throughout the 1980s and 1990s. That pushed down interest rates (Figure 1.5) and pushed up price/earning (P/E) ratios. American business restructured and productivity leaped starting in the 1990s (Table 6.1).

Another important driver of the economy, profits, and ultimately stocks was the U.S. consumer borrowing-and-spending binge that started in the early 1980s and ultimately drove their saving rate from 12 percent to 1 percent (Figure 2.5 in Chapter 2), their borrowing rate from 65 percent to 135 percent of after-tax (disposable) income (Figure 4.4 in Chapter 4), and consumption spending from 62 percent of GDP to 71 percent (Figure 6.4 in Chapter 6). The saving rate decline alone added about half a percentage point to annual real GDP growth, which averaged 3.7 percent per year in the period 1982–2000, as it worked its way through the spending system, as discussed earlier.

The secular bull market (Figure 1.6 in Chapter 1) saw a P/E leap that jumped the S&P 500 at a 16.6 percent annual rate from the second quarter of 1982 through the first quarter of 2000, much faster than the 8 percent growth in corporate profits and 6.4 percent rise in GDP. Ultimately, however, the good times led to rampant speculation, especially in dot-com and other new-tech stocks, and then to the 2000–2002 collapse (Figure 1.1 in Chapter 1).

The robust economy upswing that drove the 1982–2000 secular bull market really ended in 2000. Nevertheless, the gigantic policy ease in Washington in response to the stock market collapse and 9/11, as discussed earlier in Chapter 4, gave the illusion that all was well and that the growth trend had resumed.

Speculation Survives

As a result, the speculative investment climate spawned by the dot-com nonsense survived. It simply shifted from stocks to commodities, foreign currencies, emerging market equities and debt, hedge funds, private equity—and especially to housing, which also benefited from low mortgage rates, loose lending practices, securitization of mortgages, government programs to encourage home ownership, and, most important, the conviction that house prices would never fall, as discussed in Chapter 3.

The second leg down in the secular bear market I believe we're now in was, of course, triggered by the collapse of subprime mortgages and the financial crisis it spawned. And if I'm right that real GDP will grow about 2 percent per year for the next decade compared with 3.7 percent per year in 1982–2000, that secular bear will continue to prowl. Stocks aren't likely to decline nonstop, as I discuss in Chapter 10. But reflecting shorter, weaker economic expansions and longer, deeper recessions, bull markets are likely to be less robust than during the previous secular bull market, and bear markets will be frequent and more severe.

Since the early 1980s, then, we had a long bull market that gave way to financial inflation with the dot-com blow-off. That was followed by two bouts of financial deflation (Figure 1.6) as stocks declined by over 40 percent for only the third and fourth times since 1900.

A financial inflation/deflation cycle has also occurred among financial institutions that greatly leveraged their balance sheets over the past three decades (Figure 4.7 in Chapter 4). When the virtual explosion in risks involved in derivatives, mortgage securitizations, off-balance-sheet vehicles, and so forth is included, financial inflation was even greater. Now, deflation is the order of the day as financial institutions are being forced to raise capital, reduce risk, and cut leverage.

4. Tangible Asset Inflation/Deflation

Booms and busts in tangible assets are a fourth form of inflation/deflation. The big inflation in commercial real estate in the early 1980s was spurred by very beneficial tax law changes earlier in the decade and by financial deregulation that allowed naïve savings and loans to make commercial real estate loans for the first time. But deflation set in later in the decade due to overbuilding and the 1986 tax law constrictions. Bad loans mounted, and the S&L industry went bust and had to be bailed out by taxpayers through the Resolution Trust Corporation.

Today, commercial real estate is again back in deflation. Ironically, except for hotels, it's not so much a problem of overbuilding of shopping malls, office buildings, and warehouses in the past decade, as I explore further in Chapter 11. In fact, the modest expansion compared to the residential building bubble in recent years encouraged many investors to bid up prices and to leverage commercial properties heavily.

This left scheduled refinancing in trouble during the ongoing credit crunch. At the same time, the recession has pushed retail and office vacancies up (see Figure 8.5), hotel occupancies and revenues down.

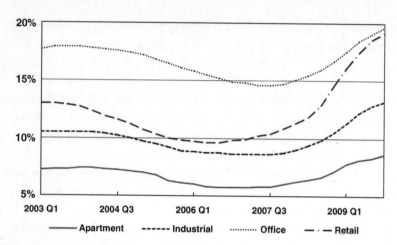

Figure 8.5 Commercial Property Vacancy Rates
Data source: Mortgage Bankers Association.

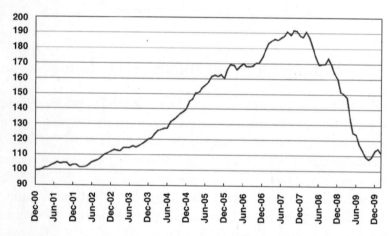

Figure 8.6 Moody's/Real Commercial Property Price Index
Data source: MIT Center for Real Estate.

Property prices are plummeting (see Figure 8.6) and delinquencies surging.

Commercial real estate inflation and deflation has occurred repeatedly since World War II. Intense house price inflation has not been seen for about a century (see Figure 3.4 in Chapter 3), at least not on a nationwide basis. The gut-wrenching house price deflation still in progress is the first since the early 1900s.

Housing Boom Drivers

As we've been discussing in *Insights* since 2002, the housing boom was driven by ample loans and low interest rates (Figure 3.2 in Chapter 3), loose and almost nonexistent lending standards, securitization of mortgages which passed seemingly creditworthy but in reality toxic assets on to often unsuspecting buyers, and most of all, by the conviction that house prices never decline, as noted earlier.

House price deflation actually started in early 2006 as the pool of unqualified buyers ran down and the bubble began to collapse from its own weight (Figure 1.2 in Chapter 1). It gathered steam when subprime mortgage trouble leaped in early 2007. Then it jumped to prime mortgages as the recession and stock bear market slashed the incomes and assets of those who really could afford to own houses as opposed to most subprime borrowers who couldn't. Housing deflation would, of course, be much worse if the industry weren't on government life support. As mentioned earlier, almost all new mortgages now are being guaranteed by Fannie and Freddie.

5. Currency Inflation/Deflation

We all normally talk about currency devaluation or appreciation. This is, however, another type of inflation/deflation and, like all the others, it has widespread ramifications. Relative currency values are influenced by differing monetary and fiscal policies, CPI inflation/deflation rates, interest rates, economic growth rates, import and export markets, safe haven attractiveness, capital and financial investment opportunities, the carry trade, attractiveness as trading currencies, military strength or weakness, and government interventions and jawboning, among other factors. In recent years, Japan, South Korea, and China have all acted to keep their currencies from rising to support their exports and limit imports. South Korea bought US$12.2 billion in July and August 2009 to keep its won down. Still, the Bank of Japan governor in late 2009 reversed gears and said that a stronger domestic currency may benefit the economy in the long run.

For most people in the large American domestic economy, currency fluctuations are probably remote. The vast majority of Americans get paid, spend, and invest in dollars. Even major currency fluctuations have little effect on living standards or spending habits. Imports and exports are relatively small pieces of GDP, imports being 15 percent and exports 12 percent. This is quite different from Hong Kong, where foreign trade exceeds domestic economic activity, or the Netherlands, essentially the outlet of the Rhine, where Dutchmen routinely also speak English, French, and German because of their global trade orientation.

Even in the United States

Even still, in the United States, the dollar's value relative to other currencies has significant effects. A weak buck attracts foreign tourists while a strong one discourages them. A cheap greenback may attract foreign investors but a declining dollar may portend more of the same and encourage them to take their money elsewhere. Many worry that China, with $2.4 trillion in foreign currency reserves, mostly in dollars, has been supporting the idea of a global currency as an alternative to the dollar, although it hasn't said it will abandon the buck. And I continue to doubt it will. Such action would no doubt precipitate a dollar collapse and global depression that would slaughter the exports on which China continues to depend for growth, to say nothing of collapsing the value of its dollar holdings. Indeed, China continues to expand its holding of U.S. Treasurys.

Currency values also affect the prices of imports and exports, and therefore the prices Americans pay and receive in foreign trade. Nevertheless, these effects are limited, as discussed earlier.

In recent years, currencies have been used extensively in the carry trade in which the currency of a low-interest-rate country, Japan in recent years, is borrowed and invested in a country with higher interest rates, such as Australia. The investors benefit from the interest rate spread and can make big money because of the huge leverage involved. But if the higher-yielding currency falls relative to the lower-yielding, they will lose money when they unwind the trade and repay their loan. In 2009, interest rates in the United States have dropped below even the

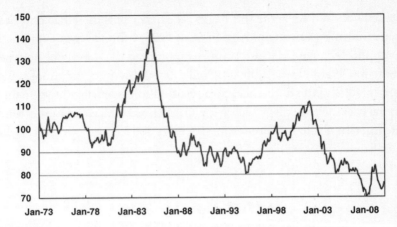

Figure 8.7 Trade-Weighted Dollar Index (versus Major Currencies)
Data source: Federal Reserve.

super-low Japanese rates for the first time in 16 years. So the buck began to serve as a funding currency. In recent years, fluctuations in the yen against the dollar have reflected global economic and financial sentiment, even on a daily basis. When investors are nervous, they buy the yen as a safe haven and as they unwind carry trades, but do the reverse when they feel confident.

The dollar has been weak in recent years (see Figure 8.7), but I'm bullish on the buck, as I cover in Chapter 12. Other currencies, however, have seen major, even terminal deflation. After World War I, Germany deliberately printed oceans of marks to pay war reparations, largely to France. It worked for a time because the money supply rose faster than the related decline in the mark against other currencies. But it also wrecked the economy through hyperinflation, which paved the way for the Nazi takeover.

Excessive use of the printing press also collapsed the foreign exchange as well as domestic value of the Chinese currency in the waning days of the Nationalist government in 1949 as the Communists moved toward victory. Similarly, by flooding the economy with paper money, the Zimbabwean government today has rendered its foreign exchange value worthless as domestic inflation rates run at levels of millions of percent.

In my wallet, I have a one hundred trillion Zimbabwe dollar bill that's probably worth only a few cents. Until December 2003, when

Turkey knocked six zeroes off its lira, the paper bills there had almost as many numbers. On a trip there in May 1998, I found I was continually being shortchanged because I sometimes missed the difference between a 500,000 lira bill and a 5,000,000 bill—but the waiters and shopkeepers certainly knew the difference! So I resorted to memorizing the pictures on the backs of the bills, which were all different. Well, with the currency reform, that challenge for visitors is over. A dollar is now worth 1.47 lira rather than 1,470,000 lira.

6. Inflation by Fiat

Way back in 1977, we developed the sixth variety, or *inflation by fiat* concept, which gained media attention in that era of the high wage-price spiral. This sixth form of inflation encompassed all those ways by which, with the stroke of a pen, Congress, the administration, and regulators raise prices. The rise in the minimum wage in 2009 is a case in point. So, too, was the President's decision to slap high tariffs on imports of Chinese tires. Agricultural price supports keep prices about at equilibrium. As a result, the producer price of sugar in the United States is 31 cents per pound compared to the 17-cent world price. Federal contractors are required to pay union wages, which almost always exceed nonunion pay, another example of inflation by fiat.

Environmental protection regulations may improve the climate, but they increase costs that tend to be passed on in higher prices. The cap-and-trade proposal to reduce carbon emissions is estimated to cost each American household $1,600 per year, according to the Congressional Budget Office. Pay hikes for government workers must be paid in higher taxes sooner or later, and can spill over into private wage increases. Increases in Social Security taxes raise employer costs and may be passed on in higher selling prices. Furthermore, government regulation and involvement in the economy tends to distort markets, increase costs, and reduce efficiency, as discussed in Chapter 6. And it's not clear that they have significant positive effects.

Then there are those lawyers, accountants, lobbyists, even economists in the private sector hired to figure out, influence, and adapt to government regulation. In 2007, they were only 0.2 percent of the population, according to our calculations, but numbered about 600,000, and many of those people are very well paid. Back in the late 1970s, we calculated that inflation by fiat added 2 percent to the CPI. And that was a conservative estimate since we only included measures that were clearly quantifiable.

There was some deflation by fiat in the 1980s and 1990s. One of the biggest changes was requiring welfare recipients to work or be in job-training programs. That reduced the welfare rolls from 4.7 percent of the population in 1980 to 2.1 percent in 2000, while the overall number that depended on government for meaningful income dropped from 61.2 percent to 53.7 percent, as noted earlier. But now, as an angry nation and left-leaning Congress and administration react to the financial collapse, Wall Street misdeeds, and the worst recession since the Great Depression, substantial increases in government regulation and involvement in the economy are assured—and with that, more inflation by fiat.

7. Standard Inflation/Deflation

The seventh and final variety of inflation/deflation is the standard inflation/deflation type caused by a substantial gap between aggregated supply and demand—CPI inflation, as I've been referring to it. Excess demand resulting from heavy spending and the Vietnam War and Great Society programs spawned that sort of inflation in the 1970s, as noted earlier. Commodity inflation preceded it and the wage-price spiral was part of the whole inflationary climate back then.

I've identified seven types of inflation/deflation that may occur individually but often happen simultaneously or in sequence as they interact with and promote each other. The huge spending on the Vietnam War and Great Society programs, starting in the mid-1960s, spawned first commodity inflation in the early 1970s, then a wage-price spiral and general CPI-style inflation. Currency deflation and general inflation both resulted from excessive money creation in Germany in the 1920s, China in the late 1940s, and Zimbabwe today.

Financial asset deflation in stocks in the years 2000–2002 and again in 2008–2009 as well as the tangible asset deflation in houses have sired a consumer saving spree along with other forces that should generate CPI-style general deflation. Commodity deflation has also curtailed spending by producers and therefore slower global growth and CPI deflation. Protectionism resulting from the deflationary, high-unemployment global economy may spur competitive devaluations—currency deflation that leads to retaliation and slows worldwide growth. That would enhance other forms of deflation.

Five of the seven forms of deflation are in place, and are largely understood by investors. Increasingly, observers realize that cuts in wages and hours worked are being used to reduce labor costs in addition to layoffs (wage-price deflation). The collapse in 2008 in commodities, and more recent weakness, is obvious to all (commodity deflation). Commercial real estate deflation is increasingly seen as another serious threat to the financial system and adds to housing price weakness (tangible asset deflation). The 2000–2002 and 2007–2009 stock collapses as well as the more recent slide are vivid to most investors (financial asset deflation). The dollar's strength in late 2008 and early 2009 as well as in early 2010 is well known.

The least accepted variety of deflation remains general price declines, or CPI deflation, as we've dubbed it. If we're right and the CPI and PPI fall chronically by 2 to 3 percent per year, that will be a big shock to almost everyone else who expects the opposite. Unlike CPI inflation, which is generally considered undesirable, deflation comes in two flavors: the good deflation of excess supply and the bad deflation of deficient demand.

Good Deflation

Good deflation is driven by new, productivity-soaked technologies that expand supply faster than demand can catch up. Actually, new technologies aren't really new by the time they generate good deflation. Think about computers. When first developed after World War II, they were physically huge and limited in potential size and computing power because, on a random basis, one of their thousands of vacuum tubes would burn out every minute or so and shut down the whole machine. Even after vacuum tubes were replaced by transistors, and later the development of PCs, computers had limited impact on the economy. Even though growing very rapidly in number and computing power, they

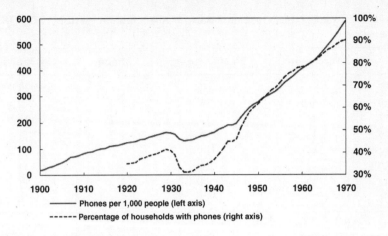

Figure 8.8 Telephone Usage
Data source: Historical Statistics of the United States.

started from a tiny base. Ditto for other post–World War II new technologies such as the Internet, telecommunications, and biotech. Only in
recent years are they collectively becoming large enough to have importance. And deflation-spawning productivity simply gushes from these
new technologies, both in their production and their use. Think about
the explosion in computer consumption in recent decades while prices,
adjusted for mushrooming computer power, simultaneously collapsed.
Note that in the 1930s, productivity grew a robust 2.39 percent annually
as the new techs of the 1920s, which I explore later, mushroomed, despite
the dire economy. For example, after a setback in the Great Depression,
telephone usage leaped as it proved too useful to avoid even in tough
times (see Figure 8.8).

   With rapid productivity growth, fewer and fewer hours-worked are
needed to produce goods and services. Estimates are that between 2000
and 2006, 65 percent of the jobs lost in manufacturing were due to
productivity growth, with only 35 percent due to outsourcing overseas.
Not only new technology but also a seasoned labor force should continue
to hype productivity in future years. Productivity growth in the 1990s
and in the past decade exceeded 2 percent per year (Table 6.1). This is
up from the 1970s and 1980s, when inflation diverted attention from
productive work and investment to speculation in tangible assets, when
the postwar babies were entering the workforce as raw recruits, and

Table 8.2 Value-Added in Commodity U.S. Output by Sectors, 1859–1899 (Percent)

	Agriculture	Manufacturing	Mining	Construction
1859	56	32	1	11
1869	53	33	2	12
1874	46	39	2	12
1879	49	37	3	11
1884	41	44	3	12
1889	37	48	4	11
1894	32	53	4	11
1899	33	53	5	9

Data source: Robert E. Gallman, *Trends in the American Economy in the Nineteenth Century* (UMI, 1960).

when the work ethic almost disappeared in the aftermath of Vietnam and Watergate. Today, the postwar babies are seasoned employees, work discipline has improved, and inflation has disappeared.

The same was true of the American Industrial Revolution. It commenced in New England in the late 1700s along with its genesis in England, but only came into full flower and became big enough to drive the economy after the Civil War. Agricultural value-added was almost twice that of manufacturing at the beginning of that conflict (see Table 8.2), but the explosion of factory output equalized the shares of the two by the mid-1880s. At the end of the century, factories outproduced farms by almost two to one. Between 1860 and 1914, employment in manufacturing and construction tripled, and the physical output of manufacturing rose six times.

Industrial growth was spurred, of course, by the needs of the Civil War, but after the war, the boom continued, fueled by rapidly changing industrial technology and rapidly expanding railroads, which provided an ever-increasing market potential. The number of patents granted in the nation grew from 25,200 in the 1850s to 234,956 between 1890 and 1900.

Typical of what was happening to manufacturing in the United States between 1860 and 1890 is the pressed-glass industry. During that time, glass manufacturers began to experiment with gas furnaces and continuous glass-melting tanks. Coal was firmly established as the best glass-making fuel, but natural gas proved to be perfect for glass-melting: It burns at intense heat, leaves no residue, has no bad effects on the glass, and made continuous melting tanks possible in 1879.

In addition to these general improvements, pressed-glass manufacturing benefited from new discoveries in glass chemistry. The use of lime instead of flint in the glass mixture reduced metal costs and gave rise to mechanical innovations that enhanced its properties. The straight wooden press lever, spiral springs, the adjustable mold guide, and the water-cooled plunger—all of which, I'm sure, are familiar to you—were among the new devices that became commonplace during this period. And, of course, the automatic bottle machine that spews out bottles and glasses faster than you can see relegated glass blowers to tourist exhibits and craft shops.

Here Comes the Choo-Choo

Railroads were first developed in England in the mid-1700s, but only after the Civil War did this new technology become big enough to drive the U.S. economy as they pushed across the continent, uniting first North and South, then East and West. In 1860, the United States had 30,626 miles of track, mostly in the East, Midwest, and South. But Americans knew there was a vast land of resources stretching toward the Pacific Ocean, and in a valiant competitive effort, railroad companies rushed to reach the West—with, to be sure, considerable government subsidies in the form of free land along the rights of way and lots of skullduggery. The dramatic increase in miles of track occurred in three building spurts: In 1866–1873, 30,000 miles were built; 1879–1883, 40,000 miles more; and 1886–1892, 50,000 additional miles were constructed. By 1900, the United States had 198,964 miles of track.

Trains crisscrossing the nation carried people westward and brought agricultural products and minerals east, thus opening up vast acreage for farmers, ranchers, and miners. Before the Civil War, cattle and hogs were primarily raised in the Ohio Valley, making Cincinnati the leading center of pork packing, with the meat products moving to market via the Ohio and Mississippi rivers. With the railroads and the invention of the refrigerated freight car, livestock production shifted westward, and Chicago became a leading shipping point for livestock and meat products. All of those cowboys in the Old West weren't raising cattle for chuckwagon dinners, but for Eastern markets that were only easily accessible by rail.

Agriculture in Bloom

Accessibility of Eastern markets also caused a great expansion of wheat growing, which, combined with cattle-raising, fed the exploding labor force concentrated in industrialized cities. Food surpluses created a marketable export that became more important than cotton. After 1873, the American balance of trade turned favorable, because of wheat and wheat flour, meat products, and live cattle exports. Although agricultural products were becoming a smaller percentage of U.S. output, agricultural productivity increased 40 percent from 1869 to 1899 as farm technology blossomed.

In the mid-1800s, John Deere of Illinois developed and sold a plow whose moldboard, share, and landslide were made of cast steel strong enough to break the tough sod of the prairies. In the late 1860s, John Oliver, also of Illinois, developed a plow of chilled iron (a soft-center steel), which was more durable and cheaper. Obed Hussey of Ohio and Cyrus H. McCormick of Virginia both came up with the same idea that would truly revolutionize the wheat-growing industry: the mechanical horse-drawn reaper. Hussey is credited with being first (1833), but McCormick was close behind (1834), and was a better marketer. When he began manufacturing in Chicago in 1847, he knew how to advertise and offer credit as well as instructions in maintenance and repairs. The number of reapers in use in the United States grew from 70,000 in 1858 to 250,000 in 1865. Improvement followed fast. Better reapers raked the cut grain and gathered it for a man on the reaper to bind. Harvester and thresher were combined (hence the term *combine*) in the 1890s.

An example of the productivity leap attributed to farm equipment is the drop in man-hours needed to prepare and harvest one acre of grain. In 1829–1830, the time required in Illinois was 61 hours, 5 minutes. By 1893, a Red River Valley spring-wheat farm took only 8 hours, 46 minutes to do the same thing. Largely because of mechanization, output per farm worker in wheat, corn, and oats increased between three and four times between 1840 and 1910, or at compound annual rates of 1.5 to 2.0 percent.

More Productivity Equals Lower Prices

Overall, U.S. productivity after the Civil War grew at a sustained rate unequaled at any other period of history. Real GNP per capita grew at an average annual rate of 2.1 percent from 1869 to 1898, and the population rose at about the same rate, encouraged by waves of immigrants. Consequently, real GNP grew 4.3 percent per year in the greatest period of sustained growth in American history. That compares with 3.7 percent in the 1982–2000 unsustainable salad years.

Notice, in comparison, the much slower growth in the United Kingdom and France during the latter part of the nineteenth and early twentieth centuries (see Table 8.3). Without meaningful immigration, population growth was much slower than in the United States, and the industrial revolution bloom was off the rose, especially in the pioneer industrialist nation, the United Kingdom. Canada, naturally, resembled

Table 8.3   Growth by Country, 1869–1913

Country	Period	GNP (Percent)	GNP (Percent) per Capita	Population (Percent)
United States	1869–1878 to 1904–1913	56.0	27.5	22.3
United Kingdom	1860–1869 to 1905–1914	25.0	12.5	11.1
France	1841–1850 to 1901–1910	18.6	16.3	1.9
Germany	1860–1869 to 1905–1914	35.6	21.6	11.5
Canada	1870–1879 to 1905–1914	47.1	24.7	17.8
Japan	1878–1887 to 1903–1912	49.2	33.7	11.6

Source: S. S. Kuznets, *Economic Development and Social Change* (October 1956).

the United States. After Bismarck assembled the various German states into one nation and industrialization commenced, growth was strong, but the immigrant population growth of the United States was missing. The same was true of Japan, after Commodore Perry's show of American naval and industrial firepower in 1854 convinced the leaders there that feudalism had to go in favor of industrialization.

The availability of so much output produced at such lower costs depressed prices considerably—even though the reduced prices vastly expanded sales, and ordinary Americans could afford to eat better and buy manufactured goods for the first time ever. Innovations in glass manufacture, detailed earlier, compressed the retail prices of pressed-glassware by as much as 89 percent between 1864 and 1888, from $3.50 for a dozen glasses to $0.40. Prices of food staples plunged dramatically. The overall wholesale price index dropped 49.7 percent between 1870 and 1896, or at a 2.6 percent annual rate. The wholesale price of a bushel of wheat fell from $1.58 in 1871 to 56 cents in 1894. Nails dropped from $4.52 for 50 pounds in 1871 to $2.00 in 1889.

Prices that farmers received for their products also fell. Between 1879 and 1889, wheat fell 37 percent and corn 25 percent. Farmers thought they were really getting shortchanged by these declines, but nonfarm prices fell as rapidly as farm prices in many cases, and in some cases, more rapidly. Fortunately for farmers, rates for railroad transportation were declining during the period despite concerns over freight rate gouging. Between 1866 and 1897, the charge for carrying wheat from Chicago to New York fell from 65 cents per 100 pounds to 20 cents, a 70 percent decline. Between 1870 and 1899, the charge for dressed beef transport declined from 90 to 40 cents, or 55 percent. Farm machine prices also dropped 60 percent between 1870 and 1900.

Figure 8.9 shows the rapid growth of real GDP as well as the drop in wholesale and consumer prices in the 1870–1896 good deflation years. The new technology of the late 1800s, then, dramatically increased the supplies of agricultural and manufactured goods, and that stimulated big leaps in demand. Still, supply outran demand on balance, because prices fell. At the same time, not only was productivity jumping in these new-tech industries, but also their output enhanced the productivity of their customers. Mechanical farm equipment speeded planting and harvesting. Steel girders made it possible to build taller buildings than with wood.

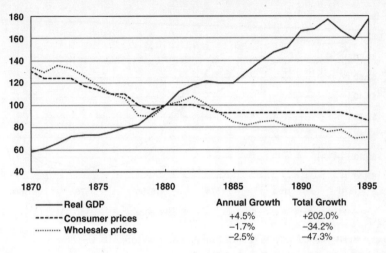

	Annual Growth	Total Growth
Real GDP	+4.5%	+202.0%
Consumer prices	−1.7%	−34.2%
Wholesale prices	−2.5%	−47.3%

Figure 8.9 Real GDP, Consumer Prices, and Wholesale Prices, 1870–1896 (1880 =100)
Data source: Historical Statistics of the United States.

Steel ships with steam boilers were much more efficient than wooden vessels under sail. This, too, increased new-tech output greatly. And even though prices were plunging in these new-tech industries, output volume was growing faster, so their revenues exploded.

Lower Prices Lead to Lower Nominal But Higher Real Wages

Nominal or money wages after 1870 began to fall, along with prices for many occupations, such as carpenters, painters, and blacksmiths (see Figure 8.10). Overall, nonfarm employees saw their monetary pay decline from $489 per year in 1870 to $420 in 1894, a fall of 14 percent. But prices were falling faster than wages, so real pay grew 29 percent, or at a 1.1 percent annual rate during those years. If we extend the period to 1900 and pick up the Spanish-American War effects, monetary wages were still down slightly, 1.2 percent over 30 years, while real incomes grew 1.4 percent annually. In an analysis conducted under the National Bureau of Economic Research, C. D. Lang concluded that real wages in manufacturing went up 50 percent from 1860 to 1890.

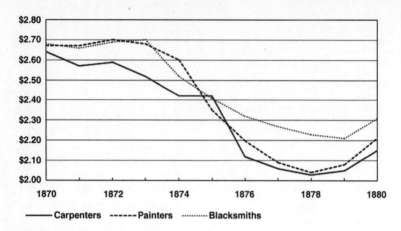

Figure 8.10 U.S. Daily Wages of Skilled Occupations, 1870–1880
Data source: Historical Statistics of the United States.

Good Deflation in the 1920s

So even though deflation was the order of the day after the Civil War, excess supply was the cause, not declining demand. In fact, as noted, demand and overall growth were nothing short of flamboyant. Although we'll probably never again see anything like the growth explosion of the Industrial Revolution and the opening of the West, good deflation has not been confined to that era. The Roaring Twenties were also a time of deflation driven by supply growing faster than demand, even though rapid productivity advances knocked prices down and made goods affordable for many more buyers.

Again, there were two major new technologies that drove productivity and growth and, again, both had been invented much earlier but only got big enough to have economic importance in the 1920s. Edison electrified parts of lower Manhattan in 1882, but it wasn't until the 1920s that electrification of factories and homes sparked. This in turn spawned further new technologies that required electric current, such as appliances and radio. Automobiles existed in the late 1800s as custom-built toys of the rich, but only with Henry Ford's mass production did they mobilize America in the 1920s and pave the way for highways and bridges, hotels, and motels.

Table 8.4 U.S. Consumer Goods Output, 1921–1929 ($ Million)

	1921	1929	Percent Change
Electrical refrigerators, washing machines, and stoves	$63	$177	179%
Radios	$12	$37	200%
Automobiles	$1,116	$2,567	130%
Automobile accessories	$170	$408	140%
Household furniture	$467	$600	29%
Heating and cooking apparatus	$187	$347	86%
House furnishings	$375	$643	72%
China and household utensils	$167	$274	64%

Data source: Historical Statistics of the United States.

In the eight years following the sharp 1920–1921 recession, discussed in Chapter 1, industrial production almost doubled as wholesale prices fell on balance. The value of output of various durable consumer goods during the same period jumped anywhere from 29 percent to 200 percent (see Table 8.4). New technologies, especially electricity, were responsible for much of the boom. Electrification of factory power equipment grew from 33 percent in 1914 to 74 percent in 1929.

Not to be left behind, the American housewife found her efficiency improved through electricity as it powered such appliances as electric irons, washing machines, vacuum cleaners, and refrigerators. The manufacture of electric machinery and appliances became one of the decade's leading industries.

Construction also took during the 1920s. Normal construction had slowed during World War I, so builders were ready to go once money was available, and modern improvements made even recently constructed buildings old-fashioned. Building construction in 120 cities (one-third of which was in New York City) climbed from $373 million in 1918 to $3.4 billion in 1925.

Ford's Assembly Line

Of course, the granddaddy of all boom industries during the 1920s was the automobile. Henry Ford's application of interchangeable parts and his introduction of the moving assembly line increased the production of cars by the whole industry from 65,000 in 1908 to 1 million in 1915. Between 1913 and 1914, the labor time required to put together a Model T chassis dropped from 2 hours and 38 minutes (down from an original 12 hours and 28 minutes) to 1 hour and 33 minutes. Consequently, the price of the Model T runabout dropped from $500 on August 1, 1913, to $260 on December 2, 1924.

As noted earlier, Henry Ford paid his workers an unprecedented $5 per day, reasoning that if they couldn't afford to buy the cars they were assembling, he wouldn't sell many. I've known this for years, but never figured how $5 per day would buy anyone a car. Now I know. At $5 per day, 300 days a year (they worked Saturdays then), the assembler made $1,500 and paid few taxes. A Model T at $260 was definitely affordable.

Other prices fell as well in the 1920s, even after the 1920–1921 collapse, including items like home furnishings and apparel. Food prices rose a bit after the 1920–1921 plunge, in which they fell much more than industrial prices, but the weakness in the latter after that collapse made the Roaring Twenties a time of overall deflation, the good deflation of excess supply.

In addition to today's wave of new tech, big-output growth in future years will result from the globalization of production. With U.S. consumer retrenchment and a shrinking pool of global imports, export-dependent lands such as Germany as well as developing nations will be competing even more fiercely for the remaining markets. China talks of developing a consumer-led economy, but that's probably at least a decade away and after government retirement and health care programs are developed to replace the current need of households to save, as I discuss in Chapter 11. Meanwhile, the rising share of Chinese GDP accounted for by exports and declining share by consumption will likely persist.

Bad Deflation

In contrast to good deflation that occurs when overall supply grows rapidly and exceeds demand, bad deflation reigns when demand drops below supply. That, of course, is the story of the 1930s when incomes and demand collapsed following the 1929 Crash that revealed how over-leveraged the financial system was. Bankruptcies spread rapidly and were followed by massive layoffs and pay cuts for those still working. The association of pay cuts with the Depression and resulting pressure to maintain nominal wages is probably the main reason why wage reductions since the 1930s have been few—until recently, as explained earlier.

Wholesale prices and employment nosedived in tandem as unemployment leaped. The American Federation of Labor estimated that in October 1930, there were approximately 4.6 million unemployed workers. In October 1931, the number rose to 7.8 million; to 11.6 million in October 1932; and early in 1933, to more than 13 million—almost 25 percent of the civilian labor force.

Wages fell faster than prices, even more so when periods of unemployment and short hours are included. The declines had to be spread over a lot of unemployed people as well, especially at a time when government relief programs were tiny. My good friend John Farmer, a columnist for Newhouse newspapers, told me that in the Depression, his family lived in Jersey City, New Jersey, and his father drove a bus from New York to Atlantic City. His mother's sister's husband was out of work quite a bit, so his father supported his own family and, from time to time, helped his in-laws as well. Then World War II started at the end of the decade and his brother-in-law got a job in a shipyard. Obviously, many people could only afford the bare necessities of life in the bleak days of the Depression. Of course, the United States was not alone in those dreadful years of the early 1930s: The Depression was global (see Table 8.5).

Worse than Its Predecessors

To get a perspective on just how severe this shortfall in demand really was, compare changes in real consumption and real gross national product with changes occurring between 1839 and 1843, a similar depression, called the "Hungry '40s" (see Table 8.6). Even in that terrible deflationary depression, real consumption and real GNP increased. Notice that the declines in the money supply, prices, and number of banks were similar in the two periods. It's hard to pin the depth of the 1930s Depression solely on the decline in the money supply and on the Fed.

Table 8.5　Percentage Change in Industrial Production and GDP, 1929–1932

Country	Industrial Production	GDP
Austria	−34.3%	−22.5%
Belgium	−27.1%	−7.1%
Denmark	−5.6%	4.0%
Finland	−20.0%	−5.9%
France	−25.6%	−11.0%
Germany	−40.8%	−15.7%
Italy	−22.7%	−6.1%
Netherlands	−9.8%	−8.2%
Norway	−7.9%	−0.9%
Spain	−11.6%	−8.0%
United Kingdom	−11.8%	−5.8%
United States	−44.7%	−28.0%
Czechoslovakia	−26.5%	−18.2%
Hungary	−19.2%	−11.5%
Poland	−37.0%	n/a
Romania	−11.8%	n/a

Data source: United Nations.

It's also hard to pin it on American business or even the Hoover administration. Because the federal government ran a budget surplus in 1929, there was leeway to offset the weakening economy with fiscal stimulus. In November 1929, President Hoover called for tax cuts and expanded public works programs. He also gathered the captains of industry and made them promise to help sustain purchasing power by maintaining wage levels and increasing capital spending. After that

Table 8.6　Comparison of 1839–1843 with 1929–1933 in the United States

Change in:	1839–1843	1929–1933
Money stock	−34%	−27%
Prices	−42%	−32%
Number of banks	−23%	−42%
Real gross investment	−23%	−91%
Real consumption	+21%	−19%
Real gross national product	+15%	−30%

Data source: 13-D Research.

meeting, Henry Ford raised the wages of his autoworkers from his cel-
ebrated $5 per day to $7 per day. Nevertheless, neither Ford nor other
manufacturers could withstand the onslaught of the Depression. The
average hourly wage of those production workers lucky enough to keep
their jobs in manufacturing fell 21 percent from 1929 to 1932, and
because hours were cut as well, average weekly earnings fell 32 percent.
Many weren't so lucky. By 1932, 38 percent of those production jobs in
manufacturing that existed in 1929 had been eliminated.

Japan's Bad Deflation

Japan also has suffered bad deflation over the past two decades after the
collapses of its 1980s housing and stock market bubbles (Figures 2.3 and
2.2 in Chapter 2, respectively). But in Japan, the lack of demand wasn't
caused by a dearth of employment and income as in the United States
in the early 1930s, but because the government delayed cleaning up its
financial institutions while consumers refused to spend their incomes.
And note that no amount of monetary ease and deficit spending could
prevent deflation.

I've been forecasting chronic good deflation of excess supply because
of today's convergence of many significant technologies such as semiconductors, computers, the Internet, telecom, and biotech that should hype
productivity and output. Ditto for the globalization of production. Still,
in my two *Deflation* books and subsequent reports, I say clearly that
the bad deflation of deficient demand could occur—due to severe and
widespread financial crises or due to global protectionism. Both have
unfolded, as explained earlier.

Furthermore, with slower global economic growth in the years ahead
due to the U.S. consumer saving spree, worldwide financial delever-
agings, increased government regulation, state and local government
contraction, massive excess house inventories here and abroad, low commodity prices, and protectionism, slow growth and excess global capacity
will probably be chronic problems. So deflation in the years ahead is
likely to be a combination of good and bad. The chronic 1 to 2 percent deflation from excess supply that I forecast earlier still seems likely,
but now I am adding 1 percent due to weak demand, for a total of

2 to 3 percent annual declines in aggregate price indexes for years to come.

I'm well aware that most forecasters and investors believe that the recent explosion in the Fed's balance sheet and $1 trillion–plus federal deficits guarantee not meaningful deflation but serious inflation. I explain why I disagree in the next chapter.

Chapter 9

Monetary and Fiscal Excesses

Most forecasters vigorously disagree with my forecast of chronic deflation. They believe that inflation is part of the modern economy. With the exception of Japan, it has been among developed countries since the 1930s, and that decade of the Great Depression is irrelevant in today's world of active, even hyperactive, monetary and fiscal policies, most contend. In fact, the huge excess reserves piled up at the Fed (shown in Figure 6.10 in Chapter 6) and the likely continuation of $1 trillion federal deficits (see Figure 3.1) positively, absolutely, without question, guarantees rapid inflation—maybe not immediately, but chronically in future years, they maintain. These excesses certainly will precipitate inflation, but only if they generate aggregate demand in excess of overall supply. That I doubt very much.

After the Fed started cutting its discount rate in August 2007 and then the federal funds rate in September (shown in Figure 1.3 in Chapter 1), it soon realized that the financial crisis was so severe that banks didn't want to lend and creditworthy borrowers didn't want to borrow. The central bank was stuck in a liquidity trap where no amount of reserves offered or low interest rates spurred demand. So it embarked on a long list of quantitative easing measures to pump money into the financial system that later extended to the initial $85 billion bailout loan to AIG and the massive purchase of Treasury bonds, mortgage-backed securities, and Fannie Mae and Freddie Mac debt, as discussed earlier. The result was the explosion of Fed assets.

No Immediate Threat

As of mid-2010, excess bank reserves at the Fed (Figure 6.10) remained only a distant potential threat as the money supply was barely growing. Normally, when the Fed creates bank reserves by buying Treasurys, they promptly are lent and re-lent by the banks to create money. Notice that in early 2007, before the financial crisis erupted, bank reserves were about $100 billion and the M2 money supply $7 trillion (see Figure 9.1), so

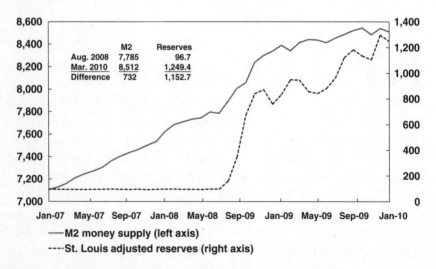

Figure 9.1   M2 Money Supply and Total Bank Reserves ($ Billion)
Data source: St. Louis Federal Reserve.

the banks multiplied each dollar of reserves into \$70 of M2. But from August 2008, when quantitative easing got under way hugely, through March 2010, reserves rose \$1,152.7 billion, but M2 was up only \$732 billion. The effect of the increased reserves wasn't 70 to 1 but less than 1 to 1!

For these idle reserves to spawn inflation, three steps are necessary, none of which I expect to occur. First, economic growth has to be much stronger than I foresee, robust enough to make banks feel it's safe to lend, and to make creditworthy borrowers interested in taking on debt. At present, corporations are loaded with cash—6 percent of assets as of the fourth quarter of 2009 compared to a norm of about 4 percent—and are repaying loans. In fact, many are contemplating dividend increases or acquisitions as uses of excess funds. Consumers, meanwhile, are reducing debt (as seen in Figure 4.4 in Chapter 4).

I emphasize *creditworthy* borrowers because many financial institutions, big and small nonfinancial businesses, homeowners, and consumers who borrowed easily in the loose lending standards and lax climate of yesteryear were not creditworthy under prudent credit specifications. They're even less so in today's atmosphere of serious financial regulation, deleveraging financial institutions, tight lending standards, and high unemployment. Those borrowers are in dire financial straits and are a huge burden for Washington to bail out. But they're not part of the lending and borrowing business going forward.

Personal Credit Cards

Notice that many smaller businesses are now forced into the use of personal credit cards and asset-based loans, the last resort before the loan sharks. The latter are loans against specific assets that the lenders can seize easily in case of default. Their interest rates are lower than on credit cards, but significantly higher than on loans based on the firms' overall creditworthiness.

There is, of course, a slim, remote, inconsequential, highly improbable chance that I'm dead wrong in my forecast and, instead, the economy takes off like a scalded dog. Then creditworthy borrowers and lenders would be eager to do business. The excess bank reserves would turn into loans and M2 money, further spurring the economy toward full employment and the excess demand that creates inflation.

But this brings me to the second step in the process: the length of time it would take to fully utilize excess labor and capacity, and on a global basis. The unemployment rate remains high in the United States (see Figure 2.1 in Chapter 2) and even higher in many European countries. Global capacity to produce vehicles is about 90 million per year, but just 60 million are likely to be made and sold in 2010. Developing countries have plenty of excess capacity since the retrenchment of U.S. consumers has robbed them of all-important exports. China's huge 2009 fiscal stimulus program has created substantial industrial capacity that historically has been used to produce exports, but is or soon will be underutilized. Back in the States, capacity utilization is still at very low levels (as shown in Figure 4.2 in Chapter 4). In my judgment, it would take three or four years before all the excess labor and business capacity were absorbed.

So it's on to step three in the process by which excess bank reserves inspire serious inflation. The Fed and other central banks must sit on their hands while demand surges, eats up excess capacity, and threatens inflation. That violently goes against the grain of central bankers. I wonder if, before they take their oaths of office, they don't go to medical facilities for inoculations of the anti-inflation gene. They may fear deflation as they did in the early 2000s, but they hate inflation with a passion.

The 1937 Experience

Now, it is true that the Fed remains very cautious over the prospects for a rapid economic revival. Chairman Bernanke, a student of the Great Depression, is well aware of the Fed's mistakes back then. The central bank not only tightened monetary policy soon after the 1929 Crash, but again in 1936 by raising reserve requirements three times. At the same time, FDR wanted to balance the budget. In the mid-1930s, banks were scared to lend, much like today, and held huge reserves at the Fed. The credit authorities and FDR worried that those reserves would be lent to businesses and individuals, kindling exuberant demand and inflation. Banks responded by reducing loans.

The downward pressure on the economy was augmented by federal spending cuts. World War I veterans pressured Congress for a big bonus, which was paid and spent in 1936 but not extended to 1937. At the same time, Social Security taxes were collected for the first time—the Supreme Court ratified the Social Security Act on my birth date, May 25, 1937, so happy birthday, Gary! Capital gains taxes were also increased. The effect was the severe 1937 recession, the "Roosevelt Depression," as it was then called, as I discussed in Chapter 6. The unemployment rate, which had reached 25 percent in 1933 but then declined to 15 percent in 1937, climbed back to 19 percent a year later.

The Fed has been widely criticized for not only knocking its federal funds rate down to 1 percent in 2003 and thereby keeping speculation alive, but also for increasing it in steady, predictable 0.25 percentage point increments every six weeks for 17 times, starting in June 2004, as discussed earlier (Figure 1.3). Many feel this took the shock and awe out of Fed policy. The current Fed under Chairman Bernanke is obviously very aware of this criticism, so its public statements in early 2010 to the effect that it intended to make no changes in basic monetary policy for some time suggested that the central bank was indeed very concerned over the basic health of financial markets and the economy.

Subdued Inflation

The Fed's Federal Open Market Committee in June 2010 again kept its federal funds rate in the 0–0.25 percent range, and repeated its expectation that rates will remain near zero for "an extended period." In a somewhat more subdued outlook on the economy than in recent months, the Fed said that while the recovery was "proceeding," consumer spending is "increasing but remains constrained."

And the Fed statement said that "financial conditions have become less supportive of economic growth on balance, largely reflecting developments abroad," namely Europe. A Fed research paper suggests that the central bank will wait until 2012 to start raising interest rates.

Nevertheless, Bernanke and other high Fed officials have worked diligently to assure financial markets that they would withdraw financial stimulus when it was no longer needed. On February 18, 2010, the

Fed raised the discount rate from 0.5 percent to 0.75 percent. This was symbolic since, with all the excess reserves, borrowing from the discount facility had dwindled to below $15 billion right before the announcement from more than $100 billion. But that move showed that the Fed still is a force to be reckoned with, contrary to some suggestions that it had become a toothless tiger. Also, much of the Fed's liquidity injection instituted in reaction to the financial crisis has been unwound, and the Fed on March 16, 2010, said it would close the last of those programs on June 30.

The Fed purchases of $300 billion in Treasurys, $1.25 trillion of GSE mortgage-backed securities, and $175 billion in Fannie and Freddie debt ended on schedule in March 2010. Furthermore, a month earlier, the president of the Federal Reserve Bank of St. Louis said the Fed should gradually begin to sell its mortgage portfolio, possibly later in the year and after the economy is clearly in a sustainable recovery, despite concerns that such sales would boost mortgage rates. And in June, the president of the Atlanta Fed said that "the time is approaching when it will be appropriate to consider recalibrating interest rate policy," although he stressed that the time has not yet come.

Reverse Repos

The central bank has also made several test runs of reverse repo operations, designed to withdraw bank reserves on a short-term basis. In January 2010, Fed Vice Chairman Donald Kohn warned the financial community to be prepared because, he said, "Many banks, thrifts, and credit unions may be exposed to an eventual increase in short-term interest rates," which, of course, the Fed controls. He also said long-term interest rates could rise due to heavy government borrowing to fund deficits and fewer foreign purchases of Treasurys from trade surplus countries if those surpluses continue to shrink and give them fewer dollars to recycle into U.S. assets (see Figure 6.9 in Chapter 6).

Also in late 2009, the Fed got congressional approval to pay interest on reserves and now does at a 0.25 percent annual rate. The central bank has said that one way to deal with excess reserves if they threaten to spur too rapid growth is to encourage banks to place them in term deposits of up to one year maturity. To make them attractive, they probably would need to pay more than 0.25 percent, and Fed officials, including Bernanke, have stated that higher rates for term deposits would necessarily push up the all-important federal funds rate.

Interestingly, that would eat into the Fed's immense profits, the difference—after operating costs—between what it earns on its portfolio of Treasurys, mortgage-related securities, 10 percent preferred stock of AIG, and returns on other bailout financing, and what it pays for funds. That cost was essentially zero on the bank's reserve that it creates until the recent 0.25 percent interest on reserves. Now, I'm genuinely sure that Fed officials are strictly policy-oriented with no thought of making, much less maximizing, their profits, which they pay to the federal government, anyway. But the bigger their assets, the larger their profits, and in 2009, with a $2.2 billion balance sheet, the Fed's net income was $52.1 billion and they sent $46.1 billion to the Treasury, even with historically low-interest returns on their assets.

Offsets to Central Banks

These who worry about excess bank reserves spurring inflation also aren't considering the huge destruction of liquidity taking place in the private sector. Homeowners' equity has largely evaporated (see Figure 3.5 in Chapter 3) and consumers are slashing their borrowing power as their credit card debts are written off and residential mortgage delinquencies (shown in Figure 3.9 in Chapter 3) turn to foreclosures. The financial sector is also starting to delever (see Figure 4.7 in Chapter 4) and the decline has a long way to go to return to trend.

Over-the-counter derivatives are only one segment of the previously exploding, now collapsing shadow banking system. Their notional value leaped from $100 trillion in 2000 to almost $547 trillion in December 2008, according to the Bank for International Settlements. Netting out all of the offsets and double-counting reduced this to $32.2 trillion, up from $11.1 trillion in June 2007. With deleveraging, that measure fell to $25.4 trillion in June 2009—a $6.8 trillion drop in only six months! Recall that the M2 money supply rose a mere $732 billion between August 2008 and March 2010 while bank reserves jumped a trifling $1.2 trillion (see Figure 9.1). These derivatives, even in netted form, continue to dwarf the M2 money supply of about $8.5 trillion. As I noted earlier, derivatives can't buy a gallon of milk in a supermarket, but they financed much of the U.S. housing bubble and lots of other economic activity.

Big Federal Deficits

The slow economic growth in future years that I'm projecting will curtail the growth in federal individual and corporate tax and other government revenues. At the same time, federal outlays will continue to rise rapidly due to ongoing fiscal stimulus of one stripe or another. Consequently, the deficit projection of the Congressional Budget Office (seen in Figure 3.1 in Chapter 3), which assumes 4.3 percent annual growth in real GDP in the next decade compared to my 2.0 percent projection, will be low. The slow growth I foresee also will force Washington to create large numbers of jobs on an ongoing basis. Thus, I look for federal deficits to continue in the $1 trillion or greater range for years, even before the leap in outlays when the postwar babies start drawing on Medicare and Social Security in huge numbers (see Figure 9.2). Meanwhile, the unemployment picture is already dim.

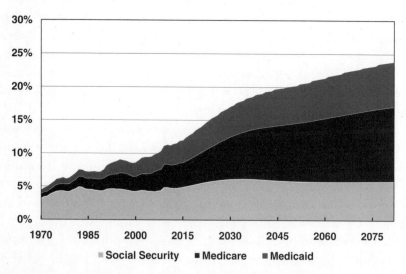

Figure 9.2 Social Security, Medicare, and Medicaid as a Percentage of GDP
Data sources: Congressional Budget Office and the Social Security Administration.

The unemployment rate of around 10 percent in mid-2010 (see Figure 2.1 in Chapter 2) considerably underestimated the excess supply of American labor. Notice that the gap has widened between the headline number and the broader measure that also includes those who have given up looking for work, those working part-time but desirous of full-time positions, those forced to leave work to care for sick relatives, and so forth. The total, including all of those marginally attached to the labor market, was 16.5 percent of the labor force in June 2010. The same story is told by the decline since 2000 in the ratio of employment to working age population and the labor force participation rate (those employed or looking for work as a percentage of working-age population).

Furthermore, the average time between jobs in mid-2010 was a record high 35 weeks—over half a year—compared with 16 weeks at the beginning of the recession. More than 45 percent of the jobless have been unemployed for 27 weeks or more. And even though the number claiming continuing unemployment benefits fell in 2009, it's because the jobless reached their time limit on that program, normally 26 weeks. After that, they were eligible for another 13 to 20 weeks of extended unemployment benefits. Those who don't qualify for extended benefits could get up to 53 weeks of benefits under Emergency Unemployment Compensation. The total number in these three programs leaped from 4 million in mid-2008 to 9.2 million in June 2010.

Labor Cost Control

Throughout the past decade, American business has been controlling labor costs by not hiring people as opposed to laying them off, as discussed earlier. Notice that layoffs and discharges were fairly steady before the recession and rose little when it hit, compared to the collapse in job openings (see Figure 9.3). Also, at the business peak in 2007, job openings were 11.7 percent below the 2000 peak even though real GDP had grown 18.5 percent in the meantime. Not surprisingly, the number of unemployed per job opening jumped from 1.5 in 2007 right before the recession started to 5.0 in June 2010. Additionally, 8.4 million jobs were lost in the downturn, or 6.4 percent of payroll employment, more than twice the average percentage drop in previous post–World War II recessions.

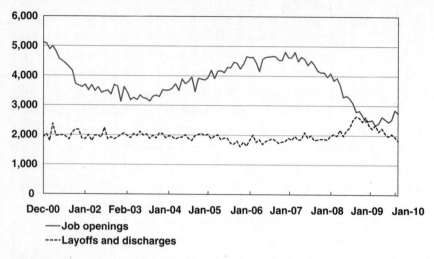

Figure 9.3 Job Openings and Layoffs and Discharges, 2000–2010 (Thousands)
Data source: Bureau of Labor Statistics.

Not only jobs but compensation is weak, as shown by average weekly wages, which actually fell in 2009. Labor's bargaining power also continues to fall as the percentage of workers in unions slides. Last year, union membership in the private sector dropped 10 percent to 7.2 percent of the total from 7.6 percent in 2008, as noted earlier. This was the biggest fall in 25 years as industries with heavy unionization, namely construction and manufacturing, slid. A small gain in public union jobs kept the total flat at 12.3 percent in 2009, but down from 25 percent in the early 1980s. The trend in private union membership also continues to be down as job creation focuses on traditionally nonunionized businesses and geographic locations.

Chronic High Unemployment

High unemployment will probably be chronic. Figure 9.4 is a scatter diagram of the year-over-year percentage change in real GDP against the year-over-year change in the unemployment rate over the post–World War II years, as well as a fitted curve. The 2 percent average real GDP growth we foresee over the next decade is far below the 3.3 percent needed to keep the unemployment rate stable. Faster growth pushes the

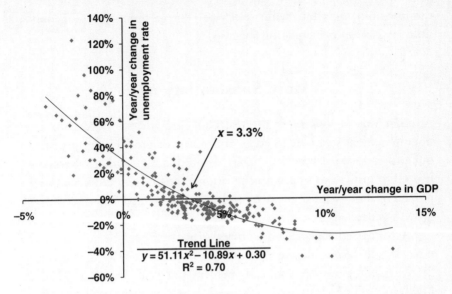

Figure 9.4 Year/Year Change in Unemployment Rate as a Function of the Year/Year Change in Real GDP

unemployment rate down, but growth slower than 3.3 percent means a rising unemployment rate year after year. In fact, the fitted curve indicates that 2 percent real GDP growth is linked to a 10.7 percent annual growth in the unemployment rate. If the rate were 10 percent this year, it would be 11.07 percent next year. By 2018, the unemployment rate would be 23 percent with a 2 percent annual real GDP growth in the interim.

When we fitted the curve shown in Figure 9.4, we didn't realize it but it is a somewhat more sophisticated version of Okun's Law, first proposed by economist Arthur Okun in 1962. Our analysis found that a first- and second-order equation fit the scatter diagram well, while Okun and subsequent updates use linear equations. In any event, one of those updates was run by the Federal Reserve Bank of Kansas City using data from the second quarter of 1948 through the second quarter of 2007 (our database was the first quarter of 1948 through the fourth quarter of 2009). The Kansas City equation says that to keep the unemployment rate steady, real GDP must grow 3.3 percent at annual rates, precisely the same as our numbers. It also implies that at 2 percent real GDP growth, the unemployment rate will rise 0.9 percentage points per year, only a little lower than our equation suggests.

More Substantiations

Another way of looking at the real GDP growth rate needed to keep unemployment steady is to add our forecast of productivity growth to our projection of labor force gains. If productivity growth were zero, real GDP growth in step with the labor force's rise would keep unemployment about stable, but with productivity rising, additional economic growth is needed.

As discussed earlier, productivity growth should be robust in the next decade despite slow economic advances. In the 1990s, it averaged 2.18 percent per year, and 2.36 percent per year during 2001–2009 (Table 6.1). The combined average, 2.3 percent per year, may be on the low side since it undershoots recent performance.

The labor force's growth since 1990 averaged 1.1 percent per year as the labor force ran a fairly steady percentage of the population (see Figure 9.5). In 2006, the Bureau of Labor Statistics forecast that in the next 10 years through 2016, the labor force would grow slightly more

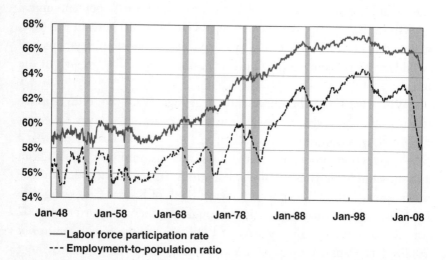

Figure 9.5 Employment to Population Ratio and Labor Force Participation Rate
Data source: Bureau of Labor Statistics.

slowly, at 0.8 percent per year. Labor force growth has declined in recent years, however, in part because of big layoffs in construction, hospitality, and other industries that attract legal and illegal immigrants. The Pew Hispanic Center estimates that net immigration from Mexico plunged to 175,000 in the 12 months ending in March 2009 from the 653,000 peak in 2005.

So you can argue that job scarcity in the years ahead will limit immigration, discourage natives from entering the workforce, and otherwise reduce the growth in the labor force. But this amounts to a chicken-and-egg question. If, as we suspect, the federal government creates jobs to combat high and rising unemployment, the labor force will probably rise at roughly its historic rate, or around 1 percent annually.

The 1 percent annual growth plus 2.3 percent annual productivity growth implies that a real GDP rise of 3.3 percent per year is needed to keep unemployment steady. Again, that's precisely the same as derived from Okun's Law and from our own analysis. It's reassuring when three different approaches yield the same number.

Slow Productivity to the Rescue?

Some, however, suggest that slower economic growth will bring slower growth in productivity. That would reduce the upward pressure on unemployment since more people would be employed than with faster productivity growth. But there's no evidence that productivity growth necessarily slows with a chronically weak economy. In the depressed 1930s, productivity grew 2.39 percent annually, among the highest decades since 1900 (Table 6.1). In that decade, much of the new technology of the 1920s—electrification of homes and factories and mass-produced automobiles—was being implemented, despite the Great Depression and its slow growth aftermath, as mentioned earlier.

Similarly, as noted earlier, the new-tech burst of the past decade or so in computers, the Internet, biotech, telecom, and semiconductors will no doubt promote rapid productivity growth in coming years. In addition, the residuals for the equation shown in Figure 9.4 show no different pattern in the 1970s and 1980s when productivity growth was lower than in the past decade when it's been high.

Finally, the mind-set of American business will probably promote robust productivity growth in future years. As in the past decade, the emphasis will be on producing more with fewer people. American businesses will likely continue to be more interested in not hiring people than in firing them (Figure 9.3).

Big Federal Spending

If we're right, then, on our forecast of slow economic growth in the next decade, unemployment will be high and chronically rising—absent huge federal intervention. And that intervention is assured since no government—left, right, or center—can withstand high and rising joblessness for long.

Some of this federal intervention will probably take the form of more federal employees and direct purchases of goods and services. But most of it will be transferred to individuals as federal unemployment benefits, extra Social Security checks, and so on, and to state and local governments to fund everything from leaf-raking and other make-work projects to more productive activities like repairing roads and bridges. Massive job creation is the obvious response to keep unemployment to politically acceptable levels. Many government-sponsored jobs will no doubt be in medical services. That sector was going to expand anyway without the new health care law as the postwar babies age. Health care is already huge, employing 13.7 million, or 10.5 percent, of payroll employees, and covers a full range of skills from attendants in nursing homes to medical researchers to health insurance and hospital administrators to developers of medical equipment to brain surgeons.

In any event, slow economic growth will keep upward pressure on the labor supply as Americans look for work and downward force on jobs and compensation in future years. Circumstances may change, of course, but it appeared that a quarter of the 8.4 million jobs lost during this GR recession will never return.

One can argue, of course, that massive creation of jobs by the federal government will enhance economic growth as the resulting wages are spent and respent. But I believe that much of that money will be saved, continuing the new trends (see Figures 2.5 and 4.4). Households have a long way to go to get debts in relation to after-tax income back to the 65 percent level of the early 1980s. In the first quarter of 2010, it was 122 percent, down from 131 percent in the first quarter of 2008, mostly because of write-offs of mortgage, credit card, and other consumer debt. Also, as discussed earlier, our assumption that the household saving rate will rise to 10 percent may well be on the low side. Note as well that in the 1930s, all the government make-work programs such as WPA, PWA, CCC, TVA, and so on did little to revive the economy. It finally took rearmament and World War II to restore spending and economic growth.

Many Feet in the Trough

Current as well as future increased federal immersion in the economy builds constituencies that fight fiercely to preserve their government goodies. Significant government involvement in the economy, which started with the New Deal in the early 1930s, has already done so. Newt Gingrich's antigovernment strategy in the mid-1990s was rejected as people worried about federal government closures delaying their Social Security checks. President George W. Bush's 2005 Social Security reforms landed with a resounding thud due to Democratic opposition and public fear that benefits might not be guaranteed as they are now and that their growth might be curtailed.

In the aftermath of September 11, defense spending has once again accelerated while a new, sprawling federal bureaucracy—the Department of Homeland Security—was created. Furthermore, Bush signed into law the costly Medicare prescription drug benefit program. The declining ratio of federal spending to GDP that occurred due to the end of the Cold War was reversed to the upside in 2000, largely due to the increase in military and homeland security outlays.

So many Americans rely on federal, state, and local governments for meaningful portions of their incomes that significant cuts in total government spending are extremely difficult, even if there were no pressure for more spending to create unemployment-combating jobs. We first analyzed this issue in 1979 and found that about half of Americans are government beneficiaries. We updated our study in 2006 and found that in 2004, then the latest data, 56.5 percent were in that category. In 2007, the number reached 58.2 percent.

The Hard Numbers

We counted all the Americans who depend on government, directly or indirectly, for a major part of their income—major in the sense that they would be very upset if it disappeared or shrank substantially and would oppose politicians who had any such plans. This means, for example, that we included government employees and Social Security recipients as government beneficiaries, but not children who receive government lunch subsidies. Many schoolchildren receive federal milk money, but most of their parents are unaware of it, although the dairy industry that receives the subsidies knows where their bread is buttered. On the other side of the trillion-dollar Treasury bill, some wealthy folks on Social Security aren't influenced by the relatively small size of their benefits, but they are proportionally few.

At the same time, we were very careful to avoid double-counting, even being conservative in some of our estimates of government beneficiaries to offset any inherent double-counting in other areas. For example, virtually all those on Medicare are also receiving Social Security, so we counted them only once—as Social Security recipients.

Overview

Comprehensive data starts in 1950, but if it were available back to the early 1930s, it would no doubt show that then only a trivial portion of the population depended on government for a meaningful share of its income. The years 1950–1980, however, witnessed a rapid rise in many groups of government dependents.

Federal civilian employees and military personnel rose with overall population, but the shares of state and local employees more than doubled. At those levels, legions were employed to administer the many social services and other programs that streamed out of Washington. Also, at the local government level, schoolteachers were hired to instruct the mushrooming postwar baby population.

In the pensions and transfers area, Social Security retirees went from 1.7 percent of the population in 1950 to 10.3 percent in 1980, while survivors receiving Social Security jumped from 0.6 percent to 3.3 percent, disability recipients mushroomed from 0.0 percent to 2.1 percent, and welfare recipients climbed from 1.4 percent to 4.7 percent. Food stamp recipients who are not on welfare leaped from 0.0 percent to 4.6 percent in 1980.

The Private Sector's Share

Government not only employs people and gives them money but also buys goods and services that benefit employees in the private sector. Services that governments buy rose from 3.0 percent of the population in 1950 to 4.0 percent in 1980 as government's share of GDP rose, mostly in the early 1950s, with the onset of the Cold War and the leap in defense outlays.

The big action, however, was the decline in the beneficiaries of agriculture subsidies, not because the amount paid out fell but because of the decline in the number of farmers as agricultural productivity surged. In 1950, farmers heavily dependent on government largesse, about a third of the total employed in agriculture, were 1.6 percent of the American population, but 0.4 percent in 1980 and 0.3 percent in 2007.

Rising government regulation over the years pushed up the number of private sector employees such as lawyers and accountants who benefited from dealing with regulation and those in industries such as steel and sugar that enjoyed higher prices and production due to government-imposed protectionism, as noted earlier. This is a small sector, but it quadrupled from 0.1 percent of the population in 1950 to 0.4 percent in 1980.

With the net increase from 17.0 percent to 44.3 percent of the population in folks dependent on governments at all levels between 1950 and 1980, those with jobs not directly financed by government fell from 34.2 percent to 17.8 percent.

Dependents

A key factor in changing the government beneficiaries picture in the 1960s and 1970s was the shrinking percentage of the population who are dependent on others for their financial support—children under 18, married women not in the labor force, and college students. That number fell from 49 percent in 1950 to 38 percent in 1980 and on to 32 percent in 2007. This, in turn, was the result of the rapid rise of women in the labor force as their participation rate jumped from 33 percent in 1948 to 60 percent in the late 1990s, where it leveled off. Also, the average household size dropped from 3.37 people in 1950 to 2.7 in 1980 and 2.61 in 2007 as delayed marriages, working women, single-parent families, divorces, and declining fertility rates reduced the number of people per household. In addition, many of the postwar babies, born between 1946 and 1964, moved beyond their eighteenth birthday by the late 1960s and were no longer dependents.

To avoid double-counting, we subtracted from this dependent pool those already counted as government beneficiaries—children on welfare; married women over 65 and not in the labor force and, therefore, probably on Social Security; and students receiving government loans and grants. The remaining dependents are then apportioned between government employees, including private employees working on government contracts, and the remaining private employees. Implicitly, we're assuming that government employees have, on average, the same number of children and other dependents as private sector workers. Between 1950 and 1980, dependents in total fell from 48.9 percent of the population to 37.9 percent.

The big jump in government employees from 5.0 percent in 1950 to 8.1 percent of the population in 1980 pushed up their dependents as a share of the population. It rose from 5.4 percent in 1950 to 9.6 percent in 1980, so total government employees and dependents' portion of population climbed from 10.4 percent to 17.7 percent. Conversely, as the percentage of private employees who don't benefit from government in major ways fell, from 34.2 percent to 17.8 percent, it dragged down their dependent percentages from 37.1 percent to 21.0 percent of the total population.

On balance, the total portion of the population that weren't major beneficiaries of government support fell from 71.3 percent in 1950 to 38.8 percent in 1980. This means that government beneficiaries, including dependents, jumped from 28.7 percent to 61.2 percent.

Long-Term Decline?

The 1980s were a watershed in the American economy in many ways. After the trauma of Vietnam, frustrations over Great Society programs that didn't work, and Watergate, voters no longer saw government as the solver of the nation's problems. This was especially true of the federal government, but it also extended to the state and local levels—recall Proposition 13 in California in 1978 that drastically limited property taxes and, therefore, government spending. The trend was capped by the 1980 election of President Reagan, who declared that government wasn't the solution to the nation's difficulties, government *was* the problem.

In fact, the Reagan administration was largely unsuccessful in curbing government spending, especially in view of the Cold War defense spending jump it initiated. Still, in my judgment, this shift in voter sentiment led to the peaking and decline in inflation, starting in the early 1980s, as discussed earlier. That, in turn, left American business—which keeps its books in current dollars and didn't understand the ravaging effects of inflation on profits—exposed. In real danger of being wiped out by foreign competition at the dawn of serious globalization, American business rose to the occasion and the massive wave of restructuring commenced. This spawned major private job creation, which helped shift the shares in favor of the private, not the government sector. The number of private employees increased from 17.8 percent of the total population in 1980 to 24.6 percent in 2000, and with their dependents from 38.8 percent back to 46.3 percent.

Welfare Reform

This helped offset the rising headcounts in government employees and stabilize the percentage at around 8 percent. The decline in federal civilian employees' share and in military personnel, with the end of the Cold War, basically offset the rise in local employees' portion.

Elsewhere, the shares of state and local retirees grew while veterans on pensions declined as World War II vets died. The Social Security segments were relatively stable as retirees, survivors, and disabled grew pretty much in step with total population.

Welfare reform in the 1990s, however, had a major impact. The number of recipients fell from 4.7 percent of the population in 1980 to 2.1 percent in 2000, and further to 1.6 percent in 2004 and 1.4 percent in 2007. Many dropped out of the system when they were required to work or get trained in order to collect benefits. Also, in the late 1990s, the states gained big incentives to curtail welfare payments when they became responsible for benefits beyond the block grants provided by the federal government.

Private employees dependent on government fell from 4.8 percent of the total population in 1980 to 4.3 percent in 2000, and their total share, including dependents, fell from 10.4 percent to 8.2 percent in 2000 as the pool of dependents continued to atrophy.

A Funny Thing

The 1980–2000 era, then, looked like a major reversal in the previous 50-year trend toward an ever-larger number of Americans, indeed a majority, depending on government for a meaningful share of their incomes. But then a funny thing happened on the way to a more private sector–dependent economy. Government beneficiaries jumped from 53.7 percent in 2000 to 56.5 percent in 2004 and 58.2 percent in 2007.

Some of this was due to globalization that shifted private sector jobs abroad. At the same time, new tech–inspired productivity growth has been strong, eliminating many jobs on the domestic front. On balance, employment gains since the 2001 recession through 2007 were sluggish by past business cycle recovery standards, as discussed earlier.

In addition, in the years 2000–2007, there was a big jump in food stamps. The share of government budgets for employee compensation and the government employee headcount portion of the population have been about flat in the past several decades. But the share of government spending for goods and services has been falling while the portion spent on transfers has been rising. Indeed, the percentage of personal income from all transfers—Social Security, welfare, government and private pension funds, and so on—is on an upward trend.

Ominous

This trend is ominous because it's only a taste of what lies ahead when the postwar babies retire and move heavily into Social Security, Medicare, and Medicaid (Figure 9.2). And don't forget the private sector employees who retired before 65 and will be eligible for full Social Security and Medicare benefits later. Many in heavily unionized industries such as autos and utilities can retire with full benefits after 25 to 30 years of service. Airline pilots are required to retire at age 60.

Nevertheless, recent bear market losses on 401(k)s, house appreciation, and stocks are forcing many to work beyond planned retirement dates. Also, looming strains on Social Security and Medicare Trust Funds will probably lead to further increases in eligibility ages.

The first wave of boomers will turn 65 in 2011 (the last reach retirement age in 2029), but so far, Washington appears mostly unwilling to address the issue. The Census Bureau estimates that 57.8 million boomers will be alive in 2030—one year after all are 65 years or older. That is equal to 16 percent of the total population, most of whom will be eligible for Social Security. In 2008, 16.6 percent of Americans already collected Social Security retirement benefits. The government projects that total mandatory outlays will more than double between 2005 and 2016. It expects the annual growth in Medicare costs to reach 9.8 percent in 2018, up from 7.4 percent in 2008. Medicaid is forecast to rise 7.9 percent per year in the next decade while Social Security outlays rise 6.8 percent annually in 2018 versus 4.8 percent in 2008.

Many in and out of Washington don't seem aware that with the postwar babies now in their peak earning years, the Social Security Trust Fund enjoyed a big net inflow of $180 billion at the end of 2008 and an estimated $137 billion in 2009, which has reduced the non–Social Security deficit. This surplus, of course, will fade and turn to a whopping deficit unless major changes are made.

And changes will be made, probably through a combination of higher payroll taxes for Social Security and Medicare, later retirement dates, as noted earlier, and slower growth in benefits. Already, some states are attacking their share of Medicaid costs, spurred by their requirement to balance their annual budgets in the face of collapsing revenues, as I discussed earlier.

My Fearless Forecast

Two major forces, then, will push up in the next decade the percentage of Americans who depend significantly on government for financial support. The first is retiring postwar babies as they receive Social Security benefits and Medicare support. The second is the jobs created by the federal government to offset the high and chronically rising unemployment that otherwise would result from slow economic growth.

Beyond these two forces, the underlying pressures that favor a rising share of the population that depends significantly on government will continue to operate, barring a rejection of government involvement in the economy such as occurred in the early 1980s. And that seems unlikely in an era of slow economic growth and chronically looming high unemployment—unless the Tea Party movement gains serious traction.

Private sector job growth will continue to be restrained by globalization and outsourcing abroad as well as the rapid productivity growth discussed earlier. In contrast, U.S. governmental bodies have no foreign competition and no incentives to promote productivity or efficiency. In fact, the official economic statistics value government services at cost, implying that there are no productivity gains in government.

Social Security

The government estimates that Social Security pension and disability recipients will rise from 51.7 million in 2009 to 67.4 million in 2018—unless some of the restraining measures cited earlier are enacted. That will push the percentage of the population involved from 16.5 percent in 2007 to 19.6 percent in 2018, a 3.5 percentage point increase. Recall that we assume that everyone on Medicare is also receiving Social Security benefits, so to avoid double-counting we don't list Medicare recipients separately.

In contrast, the Census Bureau projects the growth in Medicaid beneficiaries to be only slightly faster than the overall population growth. These numbers may be on the low side in the slow economic growth decade I foresee, but to be conservative, we did not adjust them upward. In any event, to avoid double-counting, we don't list Medicaid recipients separately since almost all of them are already included among those receiving welfare, food stamps, and Social Security.

Make-Work Projects

The increase in Social Security benefit payments and the ongoing drift toward a greater share of the population being dependent on the government for meaningful financial support is peanuts compared to the number of people for whom Washington is likely to create jobs in the next decade to prevent skyrocketing unemployment. Our forecast of 2 percent annual real GDP growth over the next decade and the 10.7 percent annual rise in the unemployment rate it implies (Figure 9.4) would push the unemployment rate from our 9.3 percent average monthly forecast for 2010 to 23.2 percent in 2018, as noted earlier.

Let's assume that the federal government creates enough jobs or otherwise takes enough people off the unemployment rolls to reduce the unemployment rate to 8.5 percent in each year from 2010 to 2018. That chronic 8.5 percent is still a high level and could cause a lot of political flack and social unrest. Nevertheless, it would require a tremendous increase in new government-created jobs, rising from 2.8 million in 2010 to 24.8 million in 2018. That would increase the number of Americans dependent on government for major financial support by 0.9 percent of the population in 2010, up to 7.4 percent in 2018.

This increase, together with the rise in Social Security beneficiaries and the underlying upward shift, puts the number of Americans who depend significantly on government for financial support at 67.3 percent in 2018—over two-thirds! Let's hope that by then, more rapid economic growth has resumed and reduced the pressure for government job creation, and that serious restraint on Social Security and Medicare benefits will be enacted. Otherwise, the percentage who depend on government will rise even further as more postwar babies retire and sign up for Social Security.

Surprisingly Low

What's amazing, and perhaps speaks well of Americans' conservative fiscal instincts, is that the river of government goodies isn't already a flood with over 50 percent of the population on the receiving end. Why haven't voters voted themselves more handouts? And what will it be like if the ratio climbs over 60 percent? Will the threat of runaway deficits and worries over an increasingly government-controlled economy provide adequate restraints? Maybe.

As the population ages, the political climate is likely to become more conservative. Still, retirees can become organized around programs they favor and have high voter turnouts. And they will be on the receiving end of the big growth in government benefits in future decades. Furthermore, the threat of high and chronically rising unemployment will keep up the pressure for government spending and job creation.

Deficits Equal Inflation?

With the prospect of huge federal deficits for the next several years, why won't significant inflation follow? After all, excessive government spending is the root of inflation. Still, it's excessive only if the economy is already fully employed, as in wartime. And that's not the case now, nor is it likely in the slow economic growth years ahead. The continuing $1 trillion deficits result from a sluggish economy, which retards revenues and hypes government spending.

Looking at it from the financial side, the federal government debt expansion is replacing the contraction in the private sector (see Figure 9.6)—the socialization of debt, if you will. If, contrary to my forecast, the economy leaps, federal revenues will, as usual, grow much faster as corporate profits skyrocket in relation to sales and expanding personal incomes push taxpayers into higher tax brackets.

Inflation would also reduce the federal deficit. The White House budget office estimates that a one percentage point annual increase in the inflation rate over 10 years would cut the deficit a cumulative $462 billion, even if it also resulted in one percentage point higher interest costs on federal debt. This means the low interest rates I expect with deflation, and which I discuss in Chapter 11, won't nearly offset the effects on the deficit of falling overall prices. This is inflation in reverse, with weak nominal incomes moving individual taxpayers into lower tax brackets and subduing nominal corporate profits. With deflation, gains in real personal incomes and profits may not show up in taxable increases in the nominal figures. If wages are flat but the CPI falls 3 percent in that year, real wages are up 3 percent. Nevertheless, that 3 percent rise isn't taxable. Unless and until the federal government changes its spending and tax policies, deflation will increase deficits, perhaps substantially.

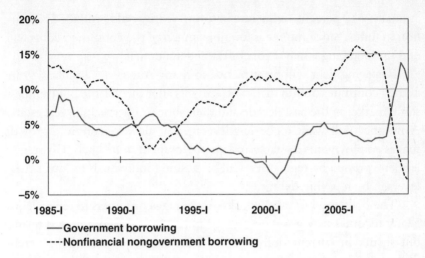

Figure 9.6 Government and Nongovernment Net Borrowing as a Percentage of GDP

Data source: Federal Reserve.

U.S. Savers to the Rescue

How will the chronic high federal government deficits be financed? In the past, federal deficits were financed substantially by foreigners as they recycled back to the United States the dollars gained from their trade and current account surpluses. The earlier growing U.S. current account deficit (Figure 6.9) measured the increasing gap between domestic saving and investment, or, in effect, the need for foreigners to not only finance government deficits but also make up for declining U.S. consumer saving (Figure 2.5).

But now, the current account and trade deficits are shrinking as American consumers retrench and slash imports. Further declines will accrue in future years if exports grow faster than imports, so foreigners will have smaller American current account deficits to finance. At the same time, much more of federal deficits will probably be financed by rising U.S. consumer saving.

Although the stock bulls may salivate over the prospect that increased saving will mean more equity purchases, we believe that most of the money will go to debt repayment (Figure 4.4)—the flip side of a saving spree (Figure 2.5). Since after-tax income is now about $11 trillion annually, a 10 percent saving rate in future years would produce $1.1 trillion in funds. Since money is fungible, much of the consumed debts will end up financing a major part of the federal deficit.

Repaying debt will be attractive to many Americans in future years as they continue to shun many investments after the volatile but trendless stock market in the past decade and their shocking setbacks in real estate. A number will want to be less leveraged as slower economic growth makes employment less stable and unemployment more likely. Chastened lenders, pressed by regulators, will be pushing individuals to lower their leverage by repaying debt.

The deflation I foresee will also encourage consumers to repay debts. Many incomes may grow on average in real or inflation-adjusted terms, but shrink in current dollars. Still, debts are denominated in current dollars and therefore will grow in relation to those current dollar incomes and the ability to service them. This will be the reverse of inflation, which reduces the value of debts in real terms and makes it easier to service them as incomes rise with inflation.

Memories of rude phone calls from collectors of overdue credit card, auto, and student loans will also haunt U.S. consumers for years and encourage debt repayment. With ever-rising college tuition and fees, declining public funding for state schools, and squeezed family resources, total student loans leaped 25 percent in the 2008–2009 academic year to $75.1 billion. Two-thirds of college students borrow for their education, and have an average debt load of $23,186 by graduation time. Back in 1997, 58 percent borrowed and owed $13,172 when they left college. Many graduates will need decades to pay off their student loans. Outstanding federal and private student loan debt totals about $730 billion, and only 40 percent of it is actively being repaid.

United States like Japan

Interestingly, the United States is moving toward the financial conditions of Japan. For the past 15 years, the Japanese government has been running huge deficits (see Figure 9.7) and mounting debts as it attempts to stimulate its way out of its deflationary depression (as seen in Figure 7.7 in

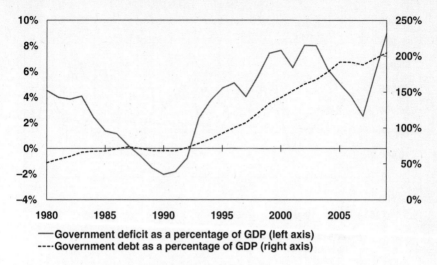

Figure 9.7 Japanese Government Debt and Deficit as a Percentage of GDP
Data source: International Monetary Fund.

Chapter 7). But consumers simply saved much of the resulting increases in incomes as they persisted in anticipating even bleaker times ahead. So households earlier, and Japanese business more recently, saved so much that they easily funded government deficits and have money left to export.

That's the equivalent of Japan's big current account and trade surpluses—until the recent weakness in exports (see Figure 9.8). Note that foreigners own only 5.8 percent of Japanese government bonds at the end of September 2009 and domestic investors owned the rest. In contrast, half of U.S. Treasuries are owned abroad.

The U.S. federal deficit may also be in part financed by higher taxes on corporations and upper-income individuals in future years. Profits' share of GDP was at an extreme several years ago, especially relative to labor's share (Figure 2.4 in Chapter 2), and likely to be cut one way or another. Also, the Obama administration seems determined to raise taxes on higher-income taxpayers. Furthermore, the share of total income going to the top 20 percent has been leaping for decades and seems likely to be reduced by taxes or other means in future years (see Figure 9.9).

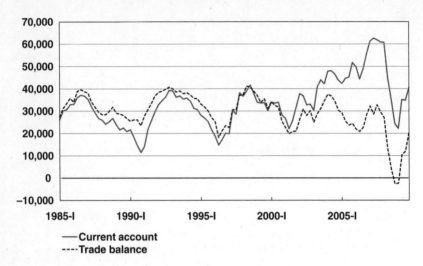

Figure 9.8 Japanese Current Account and Trade Balance (in 100 Million Yen)
Data source: Japanese Ministry of Finance.

I appreciate your reading this book thus far to learn about my track record, philosophy of forecasting and analyzing the economy and financial markets, and outlook for slow growth and deflation in the next decade. Now let's move on to my investment strategies, starting with my prognostication for stocks in the long run in Chapter 10.

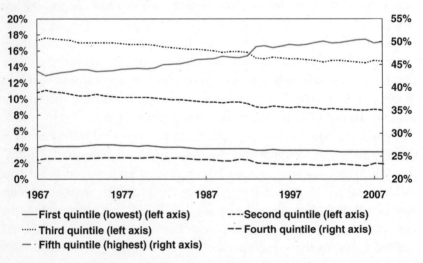

Figure 9.9 Shares of Aggregate Income by Quintile
Data source: U.S. Census Bureau.

Chapter 10

The Outlook for Stocks

Before discussing my specific investment themes for an era of slow economic growth and deflation, I'll address the outlook for stocks in general over the next decade or so.

I've never understood the U.S. individual investors' fascination with stocks, almost to the exclusion of all other investment vehicles. Stock backers point to long-run annual gains of about 10 percent, but neglect to note that about half of that came from dividends, which were much bigger parts of the total return in earlier years, and may be again in the future.

Perennial stock bull Jeremy Siegel of the Wharton School says that since 1802, stocks have returned 7 percent per year on average after adjusting for inflation. But a lot of his early data are suspect. In the early 1800s, few stocks existed and his index from 1802 to 1820 is based on seven stocks, all banks. Through 1845, one financial stock was added, an insurance company. From 1834, 24 railroads were added to the index. Also, Siegel's list excludes stocks where prices were hard to find or returns appeared "non-typical," "erratic," or "inflexible," according to the 1935 book, *Fluctuations in American Business*, by the originators of the index, Walter Buckingham Smith and Arthur Harrison Cole. In fact, there were over 1,000 stocks listed on 10 exchanges between 1790 and 1860, including Charleston, South Carolina, New Orleans, and Norfolk, Virginia. So Professor Siegel's stock returns are based on an index that excludes 97 percent of stocks in the earlier years and includes only the best of the survivors. He also appears to have used very aggressive estimates for dividends in the early years.

Since the weak, failing, and bankrupt companies were excluded from the index, the calculated stock performance had an upward bias. This *survivor bias* still exists today as Standard & Poor's and other stock index generators drop weak and fading companies and replace them with robust and growing firms. So the performance of the Dow or S&P 500 over time is much stronger than the performance of the companies that were in those indexes, say, 30 years ago. In the first quarter of 2009 and the three previous quarters, the S&P 500 Index replaced 42 stocks, 17 of which were from the troubled financial sector, and 18 of which reported operating losses in 2008 (see Table 10.1). The deleted included eight of the 15 largest detractors from 2008 earnings.

Table 10.1   S&P 500 Changes by Sector

	Added	Deleted	Net Change
S&P 500	42	42	0
Utilities	4	0	4
Information technology	6	3	3
Health care	5	2	3
Industrials	6	4	2
Energy	5	3	2
Materials	3	2	1
Consumer staples	4	4	0
Telecom services	0	0	0
Consumer discretionary	4	7	(3)
Financials	5	17	(12)

Data from April 1, 2008 through March 31, 2009.
Data sources: Standard & Poor's and Goldman Sachs Global ECS Research.

Another reason that many investors cotton to stocks may be the gambling instinct, the zeal to tell friends at cocktail parties about the small equities they discovered that doubled overnight. It's the thrill of the quick gains, of showing others how clever they are. Try explaining the sparkle of Treasurys, which most believe are only suitable for widows and orphans, and your friends will hightail it to the bar for another drink. Of course, those who love to reveal their winning stocks seldom discuss their losers or their overall portfolio performance.

The Long-Run Rationale for Stocks

Despite all these caveats, stocks do rise over time, essentially because of economic growth. Notice in Figure 10.1 that in the post–World War II era, GNP and profits reported by the Commerce Department rose at almost the same rate. From 1947 through 2009, nominal GDP grew an average 6.78 percent per year and profits only slightly slower, 6.70 percent. The S&P 500 reported earnings grew slower, 5.74 percent per year, but much of the difference was because of the collapse in 2008 due to

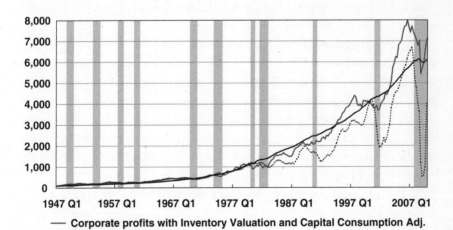

Figure 10.1 Corporate Profits, GDP, and S&P Reported Earnings, 1947–2009 (1Q 1947 = 100)

Data source: Bureau of Economic Analysis.

the recession, financial crisis, and immense write-offs, despite the 2009 revival.

In fact, the S&P 500 reported earnings were $14.88 per share in 2008 versus $66.18 in 2007, a decline of 78 percent. That one-year disaster axed the average annual climb to 3.71 percent in 1947–2008 from 6.39 percent in 1947–2007. Amazing what a difference one year out of 61 years can make, but then the year-to-year decline in S&P 500 reported earnings *was* 78 percent.

Puzzling

From 1947 to 2007, the average annual S&P reported earnings gain of 6.39 percent was much closer to the profits rise of 7.22 percent, but still below it and below the growth in GDP. This is puzzling because of the upward survival bias in the S&P 500 Index, discussed earlier. Also, you'd expect earnings by any measure to grow faster than the economy due to operating leverage, as sales rise and spread fixed costs over more units of output—to say nothing of financial leverage. Furthermore, the corporate sector's share of GDP has grown from 53 percent after World War II to 60 percent right before the current recession and the effective corporate tax rate fell from about 9 to 4 percent.

S&P 500 operating earnings were first reported in 1988, and are definitionally closer to the Commerce Department definition of profits since they both omit write-downs, goodwill adjustments, and other noneconomic accounting adjustments—"earnings without the bad stuff," as one former chief accountant for the SEC so aptly put it. From 1988 through 2009, corporate profits grew faster than GDP, but S&P 500 operating earnings and reported earnings lagged. Indeed, over those 20 years, corporate profits' annual growth averaged 5.48 percent compared with 5.02 percent for GDP as profits' share of GDP rose (see Figure 2.4 in Chapter 2).

But S&P 500 reported earnings only grew 3.72 percent annually over those 20 years and S&P 500 operating earnings still lagged corporate profits growth with a 4.19 percent annual advance. The year 2008 killed not only reported but operating earnings, which in the first quarter were negative for the group as a whole for the first time ever. Even when we go back to 2007, S&P operating earnings grew 6.69 percent in the 1988–2007 era, behind the 7.00 percent annual rise in corporate profits, and the 5.54 percent gain per year in S&P reported earnings lagged even more.

Of course, there are many factors that account for these differences. Beyond the corporate sector, GDP includes the output of government and nonincorporated business. The mix of S&P 500 earnings differs from corporate profits since it includes foreign earnings of U.S. multinationals. Also, the mix differs in periods like the late 1990s when technology dominated the S&P 500 and later when financial earnings were preeminent before they collapsed. Furthermore, the S&P 500 includes the vast majority of stock market capitalization, but not all.

The Importance of Price/Earnings Ratios

My purpose here is not to explain all of these differences but simply to note that, at best, at very best, earnings expand in step with the aggregate economy. So stockholders' portfolios overall are simply riding up with GDP in the long run—except for critical intermediate trends in the price-earnings ratio and profits/GDP ratio.

Price-earnings ratios (P/Es), even on the aggregate S&P 500 Index, show considerable short-term volatility but still experienced three distinct trends since World War II. The ratio started at a low level after the war, 5.9 in the second quarter of 1949. Stocks had been thoroughly discredited by the Great Depression and its aftermath, and after the war, many thought the economy would sink back into depression.

But then the GIs returned from overseas as the victors in a global war that left the United States as the sole superpower. Veterans were greeted as heroes by an upbeat country and many used the GI Bill of Rights to attend college—often the first in their families to do so. It was a totally different atmosphere than what greeted the returning Vietnam veterans, who had faithfully served their country but were treated as pariahs since they were associated with a losing cause.

After World War II, home building took off, not only to house the returning vets but also to make up for the lack of residential construction in the Depression era 1930s and during the war. Just as pessimism in the

1930s and the absence from the home scene had depressed births, the postwar optimism and economic revival spawned the baby boom that reigned from 1946 to 1964.

Low Inflation

After the initial burst of inflation when wartime price and wage controls were removed, and again during the Korean War, inflation rates remained low (shown in Figure 1.5 in Chapter 1). Interest rates rose somewhat, especially after the Treasury and the Fed agreed to unpeg them in 1951, but remained relatively low. Corporate profits' share of GDP was volatile but on a relatively high level as business activity leaped (Figure 2.4). Even the advent of the Cold War against a militant Soviet Union in the late 1940s didn't deter the postwar expansion.

As the economic boom replaced fears of a relapse into depression, stocks revived for the first time since 1929. And the attitude toward equities changed remarkably. In the 1920s, bonds were the investment of choice for the few pension funds and endowments that existed as well as for most individual investors. Only 3 percent of Americans owned stocks in 1929 despite the fact that many followed the stock market. Stocks were considered highly speculative and manipulated, and the 1929 Crash, subsequent depression, and revelations of wrongdoing only reinforced those convictions for the next 15 years.

Interest Rates and Dividend Yields

Right after World War II, stock dividend yields were nearly three times the 20-year Treasury yield due to low stock prices and the necessity to pay big dividends to attract investors who did not expect much if any price appreciation. Many bought stocks because their dividend yields were much higher than bond yields (see Figure 10.2).

But as stock prices gradually rose along with the postwar boom and as dividend yields fell, the concept of total return gradually took hold. The idea was that stocks' attractiveness was determined by the sum of appreciation and dividend yield, not just by dividends alone. And the price of a stock was considered to be the present value of the future

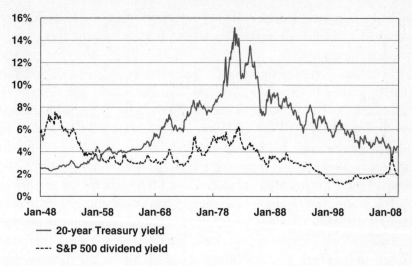

Figure 10.2 Twenty-Year Treasury and S&P 500 Dividend Yields, 1948–2009
Data sources: Haver Analytics and Federal Reserve.

stream of dividends or earnings and a P/E–determined later value of the equity, all discounted by the relevant interest rates.

The idea of applying an assumed P/E to a forecast of terminal earnings always struck me as circular. After all, earnings growth and P/Es are highly correlated, and an overly optimistic earnings forecast, for example, would probably result in an overly optimistic P/E assumption on future earnings. Nevertheless, this concept gained widespread appeal as the years passed.

Then, in the 1950s, the institutionalization of stocks commenced. Pension and endowment funds and other financial institutions not only proliferated with postwar wealth, but also bought stocks in size for the first time as they diversified out of bonds. That led to a bonanza on Wall Street. Stock commissions were based on the costs of selling 100-share lots to individuals. But they became immensely profitable when institutions started buying 10,000-share blocks because the clearing costs weren't much higher than on 100-share trades. But that's another story.

I remember hearing about the meeting of an equity portfolio manager with the trustees of a pension fund that previously owned only bonds and never replaced them until they matured. "I notice in your report that you sold one of your stocks," remarked one of the older trustees. "Yes," replied the equity manager. "It hit our price target so we decided to move on." "Then you made a mistake in buying it in the first place?" queried the trustee.

The net effect of all the favorable factors in the early post–World War II years pushed P/Es on the S&P 500 from the second quarter of 1949 low of 5.90 to the 18 range in the late 1950s, a level that, with cyclical fluctuations, held until the late 1960s. As a result, stocks jumped at an 11.3 percent annual rate from the second quarter of 1949 to the fourth quarter of 1968, far outdistancing the 6.7 percent annual rise in GDP, 6.6 percent climb in corporate profits, and 4.6 percent annual advance in S&P 500 reported earnings. Interestingly, reported earnings grew slower than GDP despite the faster growth in gross corporate product than GDP and the declining effective corporate tax rate. Our great long-term friend and client Fred Fern, CEO of Churchill Capital Management, aptly refers to that period as a secular bull market (see Figure 10.3), and I thank him for developing the concept I'm discussing here.

The Bear's Back

In the mid-1960s, government spending on the Vietnam War leaped, as did Great Society outlays. Coming on top of an already strong economy,

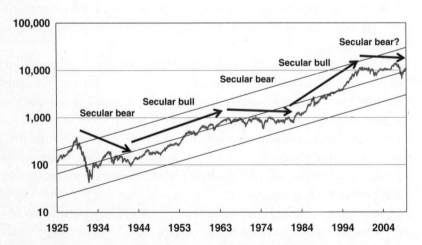

Figure 10.3   Secular Bull and Bear Markets (Dow Jones Industrial Average)
Data source: Churchill Capital Management.

these huge spending increases pushed aggregate demand well in excess of aggregate supply, with the inevitable result—serious inflation (shown in Figure 1.5 in Chapter 1). The ensuing rise in interest rates depressed P/Es, which tend to be inversely correlated.

Furthermore, inflation depressed the corporate earnings to which the P/E is applied in determining stock prices. Inflation transferred earnings to the government, which taxed the resulting inventory profits and the taxable profit-creating effects of historic cost depreciation, which under-shot replacement costs, as noted earlier. Profits were also transferred to employees since most businesses felt duty-bound to keep their workers abreast of inflation and didn't realize its devastating effects on corporate earnings (see Figure 2.4 in Chapter 2).

Also in the late 1960s and 1970s, the unpopularity of the Vietnam War and the draft led to a general breakdown of support for authority in this country, which further eroded productivity (Table 6.1 in Chapter 6), output, and profits. Furthermore, the numerous postwar babies, then in their twenties (Figure 6.7), were raw recruits in the work force, untrained, undisciplined, and highly unproductive.

In addition, the high inflation of those years pushed up the price of tangible assets such as gold, antiques, artwork, and real estate as hedges against generally rising prices and as alternatives to weak stock and bond prices. So a great deal of effort and money was diverted from productive work and investment to speculation in tangible assets.

Weak Stocks

The unsurprising result of all these negative forces was a decline in S&P 500 P/Es from the 18 range of the late 1960s to 8.9 in the third quarter of 1982. Stocks in nominal terms were flat for years. Note that the Dow Jones Index seesawed back and forth around the 1,000 level (Figure 10.3). But in inflation-adjusted terms, the S&P 500 Index fell 64 percent from November 1968 to July 1982.

That index in nominal terms vastly underperformed the annual growth in GDP (9.5 percent), corporate profits (5.7 percent), and S&P 500 earnings (6.4 percent) as it declined 0.41 percent at annual rates from the fourth quarter of 1968 to the third quarter of 1982. And note that reported earnings were helped by the rising share of gross corporate product in GDP and falling effective corporate tax rates in those years. Nominal economic profits were rising during that inflation era, but it was a lousy time to own stocks as P/Es collapsed.

Another Secular Bull

Inflation rates peaked in 1980 (Figure 1.5), in our judgment because the voters became disillusioned with Washington's ability to lead the country and control inflation, as explained earlier. That shift in sentiment was probably also key to the Fed, under Chairman Paul Volcker, dramatically hiking interest rates to recession-inducing levels, first in 1979 (see Figure 1.3 in Chapter 1).

It took time for the reversal of inflation to soak in. Most thought double-digit price increases were here to stay, even in 1983 when my first book, *Is Inflation Ending? Are You Ready?* was published. In it, I argued that yes, inflation is ending because of the shifting mood of the country, but no, you aren't ready, because even then, investors were still zealous over the tangible-asset beneficiaries of inflation while largely uninvested in stocks and bonds, which would benefit from declining inflation rates, as mentioned in Chapter 2. Events unfolded as my book forecast, but few believed me so the book's sales were poor, as noted in Chapter 2.

As inflation unwound in the 1980s and 1990s, interest rates fell (Figure 1.5). That pushed up P/Es, which jumped from 8.9 in the third quarter of 1982 to the dot-com extreme of 20.5 in the first quarter of 2000.

Naked as a Jaybird

As inflation faded in the 1980s, it left American business naked as the proverbial jaybird as inflation-induced profits disappeared. Also, mounting foreign competition threatened to wipe out much of U.S. manufacturing as imports leaped. So producers responded with a massive restructuring drive that depressed labor's share of the economy and boosted corporate profits' share (Figure 2.4). Heavy investment in high tech was an important but not the only driver of the related productivity leap. The postwar babies by the 1980s were experienced workers and the social ferment of the late 1960s and 1970s had largely abated.

Another important driver of the economy, profits, and ultimately stocks was the U.S. consumers' borrowing-and-spending binge that started in the early 1980s and ultimately drove their saving rate from 12 percent to 1 percent (see Figure 2.5 in Chapter 2) and their borrowing rate from 65 percent to 135 percent of after-tax (disposable) income (shown in Figure 4.4 in Chapter 4), as covered in Chapter 6. The saving rate decline alone added about half a percentage point to annual real GDP growth, which averaged 3.7 percent per year in the years 1982–2000, as it worked its way through the spending system.

Other Help for Profits

Declining interest rates also benefited corporate earnings during the long 1982–2000 bull market by reducing the interest costs on corporate debt. And the widespread use of stocks to buy other companies substituted for debt and thereby eliminated some interest costs altogether, while labor compensation in the form of stock options, especially in the bull's latter years, further reduced corporate costs. The surge in stocks in corporate defined-benefit pension funds slashed company contributions and, in many cases, returned money from overfunded pension funds to corporate earnings. Also, corporate tax rates fell sharply, in large part due to leaping exports combined with the lower tax rate that U.S.-based corporations paid on export profits. As it became clear post-Enron, aggressive accounting also hyped reported earnings for many companies.

The gigantic enthusiasm for dot-com and other new-tech companies in the late 1990s provided more than ample funds that went into a capital equipment and software boom.

During the secular bull market from the third quarter of 1982 through the first quarter of 2000, GDP rose at a 6.4 percent annual rate, corporate profits grew 8.1 percent annually, and reported S&P 500 earnings climbed 7.9 percent per year. With the jump in P/Es, stocks climbed even faster. The average 16.6 percent per year rise in the S&P 500 convinced many Americans that they could save less and borrow more since ever-rising stock portfolios and perennial good times would take care of all future saving needs. Ultimately, of course, the good times led to rampant speculation, especially in dot-com and other new-tech stocks, and then to the 2000–2002 collapse (see Figure 1.1 in Chapter 1).

A Secular Down Cycle

The robust economy upswing that drove the 1982–2000 secular bull market really ended in 2000, as shown by basic measures of the economy's health. Stocks, which gauge economic health as well as fundamental sentiment, have really been trending down since 2000 (seen earlier in Figure 1.6 and now in Figure 10.3). The same is true of employment, goods production, and household net worth in relation to disposable (after-tax) income (see Figure 4.1 in Chapter 4). Nevertheless, the gigantic policy ease in Washington in response to the stock market collapse (Figure 1.1) and 9/11 gave the illusion that all was well and that the growth trend had resumed. The Fed rapidly cut its target rate from 6.5 percent to 1 percent and held it there for 12 months to provide more-than-ample monetary stimulus (Figure 1.3). Meanwhile, federal tax rebates and repeated tax cuts generated oceans of fiscal stimulus, as did spending on homeland security, Afghanistan, and then Iraq.

As a result, the speculative investment climate spawned by the dot-com nonsense survived, as discussed earlier. It simply shifted from stocks to commodities, foreign currencies, emerging market equities and debt, hedge funds, private equity—and especially, as discussed in Chapter 3, to housing (Figure 3.4), which also benefited from low mortgage rates, loose lending practices, securitization, government programs to encourage home ownership, and especially the conviction that house prices would never fall.

Investors still believed they deserved double-digit returns each and every year, and if stocks no longer did the job, other investment vehicles would. This prolongs what we earlier dubbed the great disconnect between the real world of goods and services and the speculative world of financial assets, as I explained in Chapter 4.

Unsustainable

Even before these final speculative binges, the forces driving the economy in its long expansion were unsustainable, as mentioned earlier. These forces included the decline in the consumer saving rate and jump in consumer debt, the vast leveraging of the financial sector, increasingly freer trade and globalization, and loose financial regulation, all of which have been reversed.

When stocks collapsed in 2000–2002, house appreciation (Figure 1.2 in Chapter 1) seamlessly took over to continue the declines in the household saving rate to 1 percent. Americans saw their houses as continually filling piggybanks because, they believed, home price appreciation would continue indefinitely. They tapped that equity freely with home equity loans and cash-out refinancing.

The flip side of saving less is borrowing more, as shown by the leap in household debt (Figure 4.4). Not surprisingly, amidst this consumer borrowing-and-spending binge, consumer spending's share of GDP leaped from 62 percent in the early 1980s to 71 percent (see Figure 6.4).

No More Borrowing Sources

Now, however, consumers have run out of borrowing power after house prices collapsed, and they don't trust their stock portfolios to cover future saving needs. Furthermore, as discussed earlier, there are no other major consumer assets that could be borrowed against. So consumers are being forced to embark on the saving spree we have been predicting for some years. As explained earlier, the retrenching of U.S. consumers along with the other forces depressing economic growth are likely to reduce real GDP annual gains to about 2 percent over the next decade. I'm also forecasting chronic deflation of 2 to 3 percent, as discussed in Chapter 8, so nominal GDP might not gain at all.

Just as it took the sobering 1930s to put the Great Gatsby opulence of the 1920s in perspective, today—with two breathtaking stock declines, the housing collapse, and severe financial crises—we are beginning to appreciate the exuberance of the 1980s and 1990s. Furthermore, the years ahead will probably be unsettling since economic expansions are likely to be shorter and less robust while recessions are deeper and more frequent.

Corporate profits will probably grow even slower than GDP. In a democracy, neither labor nor management gets the upper hand indefinitely, and the leap in profits' share of GDP from the early 1980s until recently was unsustainable (Figure 2.4). Indeed, the Obama administration and the Democrats controlling Congress are determined to reduce profits' share and push labor's share higher as they redistribute income, as noted earlier.

Individual investors, with huge losses in home equity and stock values that haven't gained in a decade, may retreat for years from equities they own directly, through mutual funds and in their 401(k)s and IRAs. That's what they did in the secular bear market of the 1970s when the money in mutual funds fell 42 percent between May 1972 and March 1980. As mentioned earlier, in 2009, investors put $375 billion into taxable bond mutual funds but pulled $9 billion from stock funds. As also noted earlier, their increased saving will probably be used for debt repayment, not equity investment. And in the equities they still own directly or indirectly, they'll probably favor safe dividends over uncertain appreciation, as I discuss in Chapter 12.

Grade School Math

Individuals and institutional investors are also likely to be discouraged by the length of time it takes to recoup stock losses. Grade school math tells us that after stocks fall 50 percent, they have to double to get even, and that can take a long time. After losing 89 percent of their value in the 1929 Crash, stocks didn't fully recover until 1954. After the 2000 peak, it took 7.2 years for stocks to bottom and return to that level. After the 1973 top, it took 7.5 years. From the recent 677 S&P 500 low on March 9, 2009, the index climbed 58 percent as of early July 2010, but it still would need to rise 46 percent to reach the peak of 1,565 on October 9, 2007.

Institutional investors are also likely to be cautious for years after the shock they suffered in 2008 when virtually all of their investment classes fell. That included U.S. stocks, foreign stocks in developed countries, emerging market stocks and bonds, junk and even investment-grade bonds, commercial and residential real estate, commodities, and foreign currencies against the dollar. In fact, Treasurys, gold, and the yen were about the only things that rose in price in 2008, as I discuss in Chapter 12.

Price/earnings ratios are probably in a declining trend that could last a decade, at least declining from the 20.5 top reached in the first quarter of 2000. With the S&P 500 Index at 1,072 as of early July 2010, the P/E on the previous two months' S&P 500 reported earnings was 16.9.

You might think this level would be justified in future years by the low interest rates I'm forecasting. I'm looking for 3 percent yields on 20- to 30-year Treasury bonds, as I cover in Chapter 12. If we add, say, one percentage point to account for the greater risk of stocks versus bonds, that would give an earnings yield, or corporate earnings/stock price ratio, of 4 percent. Inverting that ratio results in a 25 P/E. It is true that earnings and Treasury yields tend to move together, at least since the 1960s (see Figure 10.4), but notice that since the early 1980s, earnings yields were consistently below Treasury yields. Does anyone believe that stocks have been safer than Treasuries?

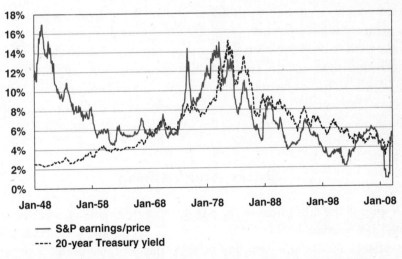

Figure 10.4 S&P 500 Earnings/Price Ratio and 20-Year Treasury Yields
Data sources: Haver Analytics and Federal Reserve.

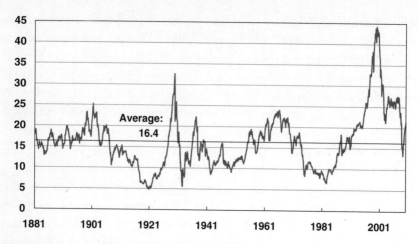

Figure 10.5 Cyclically Adjusted Stock Price-to-Earnings Ratio (S&P 500 Price to Average Earnings from Previous 10 Months)
Data source: Robert Shiller.

My friend Robert Shiller of Yale has compiled data back to 1881, and uses the average of corporate profits over the past 10 years to avoid short-term volatility. On that basis, P/Es average about 16 over time (see Figure 10.5). When that ratio is about 20, as in early 2010, stocks are headed for poor returns, an annual decline of 2 percent for the next decade, according to Professor Shiller. With dividends added in, returns are slightly positive. Only after a substantial fall are stocks cheap enough to spark above-average growth, as shown in Figure 10.3. He also notes that it just isn't the current P/E above 20 that's the problem. Since 2001, the P/E has only spent seven months, in late 2008 and early 2009, below the average level of 16.4, so there's lots of catching up on the downside ahead to revert to the long-run average.

Stocks Aren't Cheap

Despite all the disruptions of the past decade—the dot-com stock blow-off, the housing bubble and collapse, the global financial crisis, the possible demise of the euro, and brewing major problems in China and Japan—stocks still aren't cheap. As I noted earlier, the extreme leverage in the U.S. consumer sector and in the financial area globally will probably take a decade or more to unwind, and that's the good news. If it happened in only a year or so, the worldwide economy would be in a collapse much worse than the 1930s Great Depression. Yet in early 2010, stock and commodity markets around the world reflected an investor conviction that 2008 was just a bad dream from which they'll awaken and then return to the sunny, speculative days of yesteryear. Some of that euphoria, however, evaporated with the eurozone financial crisis, agonizing reappraisals of the U.S. economic outlook, and sell-off of stocks.

With my forecast of a 2 percent annual rise in real GDP and 2 to 3 percent deflation in the next decade, nominal GDP growth will be about zero. And so will stock appreciation, excluding the effects of a secular decline in P/Es.

So the total return on stocks in the years ahead will be significantly influenced by dividend yields, as I explore in Chapter 12. If dividend yields climb from the present 2 percent on the S&P 500 Index to the 3 percent level that in earlier times was the floor (see Figure 2.6 in Chapter 2), then the total nominal average return on the stock market at best will be about 3 percent—zero nominal appreciation plus the dividend yield. In real terms, with 2 to 3 percent deflation, the total return would be 5 to 6 percent, in line with historical standards.

But the likely secular decline in P/Es would push that return down. A decline from the 20.6 number for March 2010, using Bob Shiller's measure, to 14 would be a modest fall over 10 years by historic standards. Still, it would cut total returns by more than 3 percent annually. In my judgment, total real returns on the U.S. stock market, at best, will average 2 to 3 percent over the next decade, with essentially all of it coming from dividend yields.

Returns that low will be a shock to many investors. Many pension funds are still planning for 8 percent or so in nominal returns with about 5 percent in real terms, with their assumptions of 3 percent inflation. A late 2009 survey of financial planners found the average expecting a 6 percent long-term return on stocks after inflation, investment expenses, and taxes, and some were looking for 9 percent net returns. Another poll revealed an average expectation of 7.4 percent return after those three expenses.

Buy and Hold?

In the slow economic growth world I foresee, with more frequent, deeper recessions and weaker recoveries, the same pattern is likely in stocks—more frequent, deeper bear markets and less robust bull markets than in the exuberant 1982–2000 secular bull market years. Consequently, the buy-and-hold strategy, which was validated by the earlier long, steadily rising market, is no longer appropriate. CNBC's Jim Cramer, who always can be counted on to emphatically flog the latest fad, on March 26, 2009, said that buying and holding is "the lazy man's strategy" and that you're not "a trader or a traitor" to buy and sell in time periods shorter than infinity.

The proponents of the buy-and-hold strategy also note that trying to time the ups and downs of the stock market is difficult. It can kill your performance. Well-known Wall Street observer Charlie Ellis pointed out, for example, that from 1926 through 1996, almost all of the total gain on stocks occurred in only 60 months, or a mere 7 percent of the total. Conclusion: If you weren't aboard during that 7 percent of the time, you blew it, and because you don't know in advance when those luscious months will occur, you'd better be fully invested all the time. Forget trying to time the market.

I looked at this issue some years ago, and wrote an article for the March/April 1992 *Financial Analysts Journal* entitled, "Market Timing: Better than a Buy and Hold Strategy." We've updated that study and you already have a pretty good idea of my conclusion from that article's title, but let me tell you exactly how I reached it.

From December 31, 1946, through February 2010, the Dow rose at an 8.7 percent compound annual rate, including the reinvestment of dividends but with no deductions for taxes. In other words, $1 invested soon after World War II was worth $213.30 at the end of February 2010.

Why Mess with Mother Nature?

Performance this good might suggest that the best investment policy is simply to increase your assets by purchasing high-quality stocks and then either sit back and relax or leave for a long trip to Hongo Bongo,

Table 10.2   Stock Market Total Returns, S&P 500 Index, December 1946 through February 2010

	50 Strongest Months	50 Weakest Months	All Other Months	Appreciation (Times)	Average Annual Return
1	long	long	long	213.3	8.7%
2	0	long	long	6.6	3.0%
3	long	0	long	10,190.7	15.5%
4	0	0	long	315.2	9.4%
5	0	short	long	10,897.1	15.6%
6	short	short	long	255.9	9.1%
7	long	short	long	352,309.7	22.1%

where communications with the outside world are nonexistent. It seems to imply that investors should keep their cotton-pickin' hands off their portfolios, that trying to time the market by moving into and out of stocks merely risks ruining a good thing.

Another, and perhaps most important, reason for the buy-and-hold strategy, as Charlie Ellis noted, is that stocks haven't appreciated in a smooth fashion, but in spurts, and the investor who is in and out of the market risks being out at times of great appreciation. We found that if the investor missed the 50 strongest months in those 63 years, his total annual return would have shrunk from the 8.7 percent annual growth shown in the first line of Table 10.2 to a shocking pittance of 3.0 percent annual gain and only 6.6 times appreciation (line 2).

Bye–Bye to Bad Times

Before you conclude that, like honesty, being fully invested is the best policy, let's consider several alternatives. Suppose, just suppose, that an investor had the clairvoyance to be fully invested in the S&P 500 except for the 50 weakest months in that era. I'm using the 50 weakest simply for symmetry with the 50 strongest. Line 3 of Table 10.2 indicates that this vastly improves investment results. This $1 invested in December 1946 would have grown at a 15.5 percent annual rate to $10,191—32.5 *times* the compound return of the fully-invested-at-all-times approach.

Why this vast improvement in return? It has a lot to do with the simple yet crucial fact that, after a given percentage loss in a stock's price, a bigger percentage gain is necessary to return to the original price. If, for example, a stock drops 50 percent in price, it must then double to get back to its starting point. Despite its simplicity, and I call it grade school math, this reality is not well understood. By avoiding the 50 weakest months, the investor would have had much more money to invest the rest of the time.

The benefit of being out of stocks during the periods of big market decline is even more powerfully shown in line 4. There I assume that the portfolio was out of stocks in both the 50 strongest and 50 weakest months of the postwar era. As shown, the average return of 9.4 percent was better than the 8.7 percent return in a portfolio that was fully invested all the time.

This is extraordinary—better performance even though the 50 months of greatest market advance are excluded. The 50 strongest months witnessed less gain than the declines experienced during the 50 weakest months. Being out of the market in the weakest months is very beneficial, even if the investor also misses the strongest months. This fact is extremely comforting to anyone trying to time the market since he can hardly expect to be in cash in the biggest down months of bear markets without also being absent during some of the frequent final blow-off months of the bull markets that precede them.

The Final 500

A shining example of the benefit of sitting out a bear market, even if the exit is early, can be found in 1987. In the spring of that year, some astute investors recognized the frothy, speculative nature of the U.S. stock market and liquidated their portfolios, only to see the Dow Jones Average spurt another 500 points, or 22.5 percent.

Nevertheless, at year's end, they were well ahead of those who had held stocks throughout the year and seen much more than that final 500 points removed by the Crash and its aftermath. And those bears weren't scared by devastating losses and therefore were in much better psychological shape to assess analytically the 1988 investment outlook.

Investors could choose not only to own no stocks in the months of greatest stock market decline, but to sell them short. Line 5 (Table 10.2) shows the results when the portfolio was out of the market during the 50 strongest months of the 1947–2010 era and short the DJIA during the 50 weakest. Even if the 50 most robust months are missed entirely, the investor had far better performance by being short the 50 weakest months than if he were fully invested at all times. Line 5 indicates that $1 turned into $10,897—a 15.6 percent compound annual gain compared with the 8.7 percent annual gain from the buy-and-hold strategy with $1 growing to $213.3 (line 1).

The difference between an 8.7 percent compound annual gain and 15.6 percent may not seem great, but it makes for a difference in portfolio value of 51 times in the course of 63-plus years ($10,897 compared to $213.3). Compounding is potent! This difference is huge, but it makes sense. If the investor sells short and the stock falls 50 percent, he has gained one-half on the value of the stock. If he had been long instead, he would have lost 50 percent. Consequently, the bear, with 150 percent of his starting portfolio, is three times better off than the bull, whose portfolio has dropped to 50 percent of its original value. Repeating and compounding this sort of gap over time results in a huge difference.

The Perennial Bear

Take it one step further and suppose the investor is a skeptic and shorted the S&P 500 not only in the 50 weakest months, but also in the 50 strongest months, and went long otherwise. Despite his error in taking exactly the wrong action in the strongest months, his short position in the 50 weakest proves to be so beneficial that he winds up with a 9.1 percent annual gain (line 6), more rewarding than the perpetual bull (line 1). This, to me, makes a very powerful statement. Being negative on stocks in the weakest times pays well even for the investor who is negative during the strongest months as well! He could make a lot of mistakes in being bearish and still have an excellent performance.

This reality has worked for us in portfolios we manage. We've missed being long in some strong stock rallies and sometimes have even been short, but our willingness to be short in bear markets has produced overall superior returns. There's less competition in selling stocks short since many investors consider it unpatriotic, as noted earlier. Nevertheless, timing is still critical since bear markets tend to be shorter and more intense than bull rallies.

The best results would obviously be achieved by the portfolio that was long in the 50 strongest months and short in the 50 weakest (line 7 in Table 10.2). As usual, we assume the portfolio was long in all other months, whether the S&P 500 rose or fell. Any investor clairvoyant enough or lucky enough to own that portfolio would have seen each dollar invested in the S&P 500 at the end of December 1946 turn into $352,310 by February 2010—a 22.1 percent annualized gain. Super! The combined, compounded effect of being long the bull months and short the big bear months is spectacular.

The moral of this exercise is clear: It's profitable to be in stocks during bull markets, but it's even more profitable to be short stocks, or at least out of the market, during bear markets—even if many of the major bull market months are missed completely.

I'm convinced that this analysis and my conclusion for market timing will be valid in the years ahead. It may be meaningful for you. If you forgo the last exuberant months of a bull market, you'll still be ahead—financially and psychologically—if you're also on the sidelines when the big bear emerges from hibernation.

Further proof: A Spanish research firm found that if you removed the 10 best days for the Dow Jones Industrial Average in the years 1900–2008, two-thirds of the cumulative gains were lost. But if you missed the 10 worst days, it found, the actual gain on the Dow tripled.

Closet Timers

Furthermore, many investors engage in market timing whether they admit it or not. Portfolio rebalancing involves reducing holdings in sectors that have risen and adding to those that have fallen to reestablish set sector percentages. This amounts to market timing since the underlying assumption is that those stocks that jumped will fall in the next period while the fallen will rise. I, however, have never understood this strategy of selling your winners and buying more of your losers. I'm stuck on the

Wall Street adage, cut your losses and let your profits run. Or as my great friend Dennis Gartman puts it, do more of what's working and less of what isn't.

I also eschew the buy-and-hold strategy because of what's known in classical statistics as the *gamblers ruin paradox*. The odds may be in your favor in the long run—in this case, your stocks may provide great returns over, say, 10 years. But if you hit a streak of bad luck, your capital may be exhausted before that long run arrives.

Or, more likely, a severe bear market will scare you out at the bottom. Many investors bail out then and don't reenter until the next bull market is well advanced. This explains why the returns of mutual fund investors lag well behind the performance of the funds in which they invest. A widespread retreat is what makes a good bottom. All those who can be shaken out are. They've reached the puke point at which they regurgitate their last equities and swear never to ingest any more, as noted in Chapter 3.

Active Managers

The current challenge to the buy-and-hold strategy has spilled over to the passive versus active management arena. The rational implementation of the buy-and-hold strategy is passive management, such as index funds. Investment fees tend to be lower than for active management, and statistics indicate that these higher fees prevent most active managers from beating their benchmarks in the long run.

Nevertheless, active managers are supposed to be superior in bear markets since they can shift to cash and defensive stocks. Still, 58 percent of active U.S. stock managers failed to beat their benchmarks in 2008, and all of those benchmarks fell. So they lost lots of money. And only a few of the 42 percent who bested their benchmarks had positive returns. Just one of 1,700 diversified U.S. stock funds showed a gain in 2008, and that was a mere 0.4 percent. The average of these funds dropped 39 percent, precisely in line with the S&P 500's decline. As I've said and written many times: On the way up, performance is relative, but on the way down, it's absolute. No investor can be happy with a portfolio manager who beats his benchmark but still loses the investor's money.

Furthermore, in recoveries from bear markets, many active managers behaved just like individual investors and remained on the sidelines too long. In the three upswings before the 2009–2010 rally, index funds beat managed funds on average. In the 12 months after the March 2002 stock bottom, only 30 percent of active managers exceeded their benchmarks.

Another problem for investors is the tendency of active managers who are hot this year to be cold next year. So investors tend to give them money in response to great performance last year just as their luck is running out. Past performance is no indication of future results. Regulators require investment advisors to state this to investors, and academic studies substantiate it.

The Best of the Best

The ultimate antitheses of the buy-and-hold devotees are the few astute investors who can sense that an asset is so cheap that the downside risk is minimal while the upside is substantial. This is what Baron Rothschild was talking about when he said the time to buy stocks is when blood is running down the streets of Paris. George Soros is credited with this knack. Warren Buffett's stellar track records, increased prestige, and deep pockets allowed him to basically lend much needed capital during times of great stress to Salomon Brothers years ago and more recently to GE at very high rates of interest and considerable equity gains when the firms revived. John Paulson, Greg Lippmann, and a handful of other hedge fund managers realized in 2006 that credit default swaps on securities backed by subprime residential mortgages were dirt cheap, and offered huge profit potential with limited loss exposure. But most of us can't tell when cheap is the cheapest it will get, and when enough blood is running down the Paris streets to signal a gigantic buying opportunity.

As you've read in this chapter, I expect subdued performance in U.S. stocks in aggregate in the next decade as they reflect the slow economic growth and deflation I'm forecasting. Within the overall equity market, I expect specific sectors to be especially weak. These and other investment sectors I suggest you sell or avoid are the subject of Chapter 11.

Chapter 11

Twelve Investments
to Sell or Avoid

I 'm convinced that for successful long-run investing you need a well-thought-out forecast of the economic, financial, and political framework within which investment opportunities will develop. Then, as the parade passes, you'll be prepared to know which uniform colors among the many worn by the marchers to look for. And when you spot the vanguard, you'll be reasonably certain that many wearing similar garb will pass the reviewing stand soon. In other words, my strategy is to use my forecasts to determine investments, but to let the markets tell me when the time for it all to come to fruition is indeed at hand.

I've used many pages in this book to examine economic and financial bubbles, especially the U.S. housing and global financial bubbles that have burst in recent years as well as the eurozone financial crisis. I went on to document the denial of many that these bubbles even existed, much less that their breaking would have profound and lasting effects. Then I proceeded to make the case for a decade or so of slow economic growth and chronic deflation and the implications for the U.S. stock market. Many, of course, reject my arguments. They believe that 2008 was a confined correction of excesses with no lasting effects other than to pave the way for a return to carefree consumer spending, rapid economic growth, and a robust stock market. They also believe the huge expansion in Federal Reserve credit and immense federal government spending will generate galloping inflation in a year or two.

If I have not persuaded you otherwise, you probably should stop reading this book right here. But if you do believe my analysis and forecasts have merit, you'll probably be interested in my investment strategies for an era of slower economic growth and deflation. In this chapter, I discuss 12 sectors to sell or avoid, and in Chapter 12, I cover the ones I recommend buying.

The 12 investments to sell or avoid are:

1. Big-ticket consumer purchases.
2. Credit card and other consumer lenders.
3. Conventional home builders and suppliers.
4. Antiques, art, and other tangibles.
5. Banks and similar financial institutions.
6. Junk securities.
7. Flailing companies.
8. Low- and old-tech capital equipment producers.
9. Commercial real estate.
10. Commodities.
11. Developing country stocks and bonds.
12. Japan—a slow train wreck.

Not a Stock Picker

Be aware, however, that I'm not a stock picker. My approach is top-down, as outlined early in this book. I start by examining the economic, financial, and political spheres and then the forecasts they seem to point to. From there, I distill the investment themes and strategies for implementing them. In managing our portfolios, we seldom use individual securities except for Treasurys since we're interested in broader industries and financial sectors. Instead, we rely on exchange-traded funds (ETFs), which are increasingly available as are some mutual funds on a wide variety of stock and bond sectors, commodities, and currencies.

In our more aggressive portfolios, we also use futures contracts, which often allow pure plays on investment themes. For example, if global industrial production is likely to be weak, copper prices will probably fall since the red metal is used in almost every manufactured good from machinery to computers to vehicles to plumbing fixtures. Shorting the stocks of copper producers would seem like a logical strategy, but falling demand for copper might precipitate a wave of mergers that would hype the stocks' prices. But selling short copper futures offers a pure play on copper prices.

1. Big-Ticket Consumer Purchases

Sell big-ticket consumer discretionary purchases such as autos, appliances, airlines, cruise lines, and leisure and hospitality providers—for two powerful reasons. First, as consumers persist in their saving spree they'll continue to curtail spending on expensive postponable items. Cash-for-clunkers in 2009 generated a stampede of new car buyers with junkers worth less than the $4,500 government rebate, but most Americans can run their vehicles a year or so longer than normal when they're seriously saving, even though the age of vehicles continues to rise.

Second, as widespread price declines persist, they will be anticipated. Prospective buyers will wait for lower prices. As a result, excess inventories and unused capacity will mount, forcing prices lower. That will confirm prospective buyers' suspicions so they'll wait for still-lower prices in a self-feeding downward spiral of deflationary expectations, as I discussed in Chapter 8.

Let's say that deflation has set in and airline ticket prices are falling. You want to visit your dear Aunt Suzy who lives across the continent. She's still in good health, so you say to yourself, I'll wait until next year. Airfares will be even cheaper then and besides, I'm trying to save and can do so by making the trip later when airfares are lower. Because you and lots of others reason this way and postpone trips, demand will be weak. So airlines will cut ticket prices to try to entice travelers and to meet their competitors' price reductions. When that year's wait is over, you'll notice the drop in fares and, because Aunt Suzy's still in good shape, you'll postpone your trip again and call her occasionally instead. And so it will go for airlines and industries that produce big-ticket consumer discretionary items as they're hit with the double whammy of consumer zeal to save and self-feeding deflationary expectations.

Deflationary expectations not only soften demand for large discretionary purchases but also maintain downward pressure on prices. So producers and distributors of these large-ticket items are hit with both weak volume and weak prices. The auto industry has been devastated by rebates that it just can't shake off due to customer expectations of continuing special incentives. The July 2009 "cash for clunkers" federal tax credit was seen by car buyers as just one more rebate, but one that was sponsored by Washington. In fact, Peter Fong, Chrysler's head of sales at the time, prepared a plan for an additional $4,500 discount. Apparently, that was too much of a response to car buyers' wishes because it was "giving away margin" in the words of Chrysler CEO Sergio Marchionne, and Fong was fired shortly after.

In addition, vehicle buyers are switching from profitable big SUVs to smaller vehicles. Germany's Daimler is teaming up with France's Renault and Japan's Nissan to produce small cars by sharing engines and small car platforms. They also plan to collaborate on research and development of fuel-efficient technologies for hybrids and battery-powered cars. Daimler has been losing money on its small Smart cars and A-class and B-class models. Volkswagen is buying a 20 percent stake in Suzuki to increase its position in small, cheap cars. Still, with lower profits on small cars and tremendous and growing excess capacity for global vehicle production, the outlook for most automakers is dim.

Eat at Home

Other areas that are already affected by increased consumer saving include apparel and restaurants as people downgrade to fast food or eat at home.

As noted earlier, supermarkets have witnessed a shift from high-priced national brands to house brands and other cheaper alternatives.

Even the rich, normally immune to recessions, have cut back and downgraded. Used business jet prices have fallen, even on newer models, as the rapid growth in jet ownership has reversed with deliveries of new jets off 66 percent in the first half of 2009 from a year earlier.

A Merrill Lynch study found that the number of people in the world with $1 million or more in investable assets fell from 10.1 million in 2007 to 8.6 million in 2008. Those assets dropped from $40.7 trillion to $32.8 trillion. Their equity holdings fell in step with the S&P 500, about 40 percent, and their real estate also dropped in value.

The pressure on wealthy consumers will likely persist for years. They own a vast majority of the stocks held by individuals, and I expect much slower growth in equities than the 16.6 percent compound annual growth rate in the 1982–2000 secular bull market, as discussed in Chapter 10. Their real estate, both residential and commercial, is also likely to rise slowly in value over the next decade.

Furthermore, the left-leaning Obama administration and Congress seem dedicated to redistributing income and taxing the rich to fund their health care and other initiatives, as discussed earlier. They are joining if not leading the public in blaming excessive risk taking in pursuit of high pay for the financial crises and severe recession. Washington has all but declared war on big bonuses and large compensation in general—easy targets amid rising unemployment, wage cuts, and involuntary furloughs. This fervor is probably now at its zenith, but it is likely to persist for years as the painful deleveraging of the household and financial sectors continues.

Income Shares

Ever since the data series began in 1967, the share of income of the top 20 percent has trended up while all other shares fell, as noted in Chapter 9 (Figure 9.9). These are shares, not income levels—which have grown on balance for all quintiles. Also, studies have found considerable rotation in and out of the various quintiles, with many of those in the top bracket in a given year absent from it in earlier and later years. Still, the stagnation in purchasing power for many middle-income people in the past decade on top of the collapse in their homes' values has created considerable anger, which Obama hopes to cash in on.

So have the ongoing efforts of American business to restrain hiring throughout this decade in order to enhance productivity and profits (Table 6.1), as discussed earlier. This is encouraged by the declining power of organized labor in the private sector, generally weak labor markets, and intense foreign competition. Job openings have nosedived in recent years (Figure 9.3 in Chapter 9).

2. Credit Card and Other Consumer Lenders

Credit card and other consumer lenders will probably continue to be squeezed for years. They had their heyday during the long consumer borrowing-and-spending spree (see Figure 4.4 in Chapter 4). Consumers were trained by the media, retailers, and even the government to believe they deserved instant material gratification. Buy now, put it on the plastic card, and pay later—much later—became the norm. And creditworthiness was no problem for credit card issuers and other consumer lenders. They sliced and diced consumers' financial statuses, used sophisticated models to determine payment risks, and charged fees and interest rates to fit any risk category.

But their models and analyses inherently assumed that the borrowing-and-spending binge, as well as the ability to repay, would last indefinitely. What a revolting development when consumers retrenched and cut back on their use of credit, debit, and charge cards! What a surprise it was when consumers suddenly went further and switched to a saving spree and began to pay down credit card and other revolving debt! What a shock when heavy layoffs (Figure 5.1 in Chapter 5), leaping unemployment (Figure 2.1 in Chapter 2), collapsing house prices (Figure 1.2 in Chapter 1), and inadequate consumer incomes spiked credit card delinquencies! What a disappointment when Congress in 2009 restricted credit card fees and interest charges! Credit card issuers dropped their direct mail offers to consumers from about 7 billion in 2007 to around 1.8 billion in 2009.

Developments in the past several years are virtually all negative for the credit card business now and will be for years to come. Horror stories abound of people with $20,000 annual incomes who managed to run up $50,000 in credit card debt and then became unemployed. A cottage industry to help these people deal with their financial woes exploded in size. Debit cards are replacing credit cards as consumers realize they can't trust themselves to restrain debt and need to accumulate the money in a bank account before spending it. Layaway plans are replacing the buy now, pay later approach, as discussed earlier. With the switch from a quarter-century-long consumer borrowing-and-spending binge to a long-run saving spree, the credit card business has moved from a growth industry to a laggard.

3. Conventional Home Builders and Suppliers

Home building was a growth industry in the salad days of low mortgage rates, lax underwriting standards, securitization of mortgages that passed seemingly creditworthy but in reality toxic assets on to unsuspecting buyers, laissez-faire regulation, and, most of all, conviction that house prices never fall (Figure 1.2). Now all these conditions have reversed with lending standards tighter, on balance; securitizations of mortgages essentially dead, with government agencies the only buyers; much more vigilant regulation; and homeowners aware that they can lose money, even all of the equity in their highly leveraged houses. As discussed earlier, home ownership rates (Figure 3.6 in Chapter 3) are falling as those who earlier bought houses to get in on the speculative bonanza are foreclosed out of their abodes, while prospective homeowners wait for still-lower prices.

Conventional home building is likely to be depressed for years. Excess inventories, the residue from the earlier home building boom, have only been partially absorbed (Figure 7.2 and Table 7.2 in Chapter 7) despite the collapse in housing starts (Figure 3.3 in Chapter 3). New inventory is added as many of the homeowners foreclosed out of their abodes go back to living with parents or with friends, and as owners of investment properties that are empty or rented at below carrying costs give up and dump their houses on the market. Excess inventories will probably take years to work off. Meanwhile, excess inventories are the mortal enemy of prices, which will continue to be under pressure, especially since the new homeowner tax credits have expired and as the moratorium on

foreclosures ends after attempts to modify mortgages to keep home owners in their houses largely fail. In March 2010, about 5.5 million houses
were estimated to be in serious delinquency or in early stages of foreclosure. About seven million may eventually be foreclosed. After excess
inventories are worked off, house prices should decline with general
deflation in the usual relationship, as noted earlier.

About 35 to 40 percent of all borrowers with 30-year fixed-rate
mortgages that conform to Fannie Mae and Freddie Mac standards have
mortgage rates over 6 percent and could cut them by one full percentage
point by refinancing. Still, falling house prices make that impossible for
many since they are underwater with their mortgages exceeding their
houses' values. Also inhibiting refinancing are stricter lending standards,
higher fees, unemployment and declining incomes, and problems dealing
with second mortgages. Those who do refinance are generally in solid
financial condition, not the seriously stressed homeowners. Nevertheless,
60 percent of mortgages modified in the fourth quarter of 2008 defaulted
again within 12 months.

In April 2009, the administration launched its Home Affordable
Modification Program (HAMP) to help struggling homeowners who
owed between 80 and 105 percent of the value of their abodes by reducing interest rates to as low as 2 percent, extending mortgages up to
40 years, and, as a final resort, cutting mortgage principal, as noted
in Chapter 3. The goal is to reduce monthly mortgage payments to
affordable levels, but the program has largely failed. Through February
2010, only 170,207 permanent modifications had been made despite the
financial incentives to borrowers and lenders, while HAMP was initially
trumpeted to aid 2 to 3 million. And 88,663 have dropped out of the program. Also, many of those with permanent modifications will probably
default again since, on average, their monthly debt payments, including
on credit card and other consumer debts, are a crushing 60 percent of
pretax income. In March 2010, the administration modified HAMP to,
among other liberalizations, make the program more attractive to holders
of second mortgages, but it will probably continue to be a failure.

Many underwater homeowners are uninterested in home mortgage
modifications because they foresee no chance of returning to positive
home equity. Indeed, many who can afford their monthly mortgage
payments are engaging in so-called strategic defaults by walking away

from their abodes to rent or buy houses with lower monthly payments. As discussed in Chapter 3, a quarter of homeowners with mortgages are underwater and that number is likely to reach 40 percent. And rentals are readily available and cheap. Vacancies in apartments are at record levels (as shown in Figure 8.5 in Chapter 8) as the unemployed double up or move in with family, and effective rental rates fell 3 percent in 2009. The supply of rental apartments has been hyped by busted condo buildings that are being converted to rentals.

Land owned or optioned by home builders may also be a continuing concern. The value of residential land is simply the difference between what a buyer will pay for the combined land and the house sitting on it and the cost of reproducing the house, as discussed earlier.

Smaller Houses

Furthermore, home buyers are reversing gears on the size of houses they desire. In the housing boom, they wanted the biggest houses they could finance to make huge profits on extremely leveraged finances. With a 5 percent down payment and appreciation of 10 percent a year, the homeowner made a cool 200 percent on his investment annually, neglecting interest costs, maintenance, and taxes, in addition to having a place to live, as noted earlier.

But after seeing that house prices can and do decline—and can easily wipe out homeowners' equity and then some—interest is moving to smaller houses, shelter instead of shelter plus an investment. The 30 percent decline in house prices nationwide to date puts those who bought at the peak with 5 percent down way underwater. So McMansions are fast becoming undesired, and knocking their prices down to market-clearing levels will probably depress housing activity in future years. Furthermore, the profitability of building smaller houses is lower, even if they are packed onto smaller lots.

Also, many of those large houses may be subdivided into multiple dwelling units, adding extra excess inventory. I've noted, only half in jest, that many a large McMansion may be turned into a retirement home for multiple postwar babies. The surplus of McMansions will also be augmented by the postwar babies as they downsize in their later years, dump their large abodes, and move into smaller single-family houses and apartments. And the younger generation probably will be uninterested in those larger houses except at very low prices because of their high taxes and utility and maintenance costs, preferring instead smaller single-family homes and apartments.

In my hometown of Fremont, Ohio, on the same block as the house my parents owned for 69 years, are a number of mansions built in the Roaring Twenties. When I was growing up after World War II, they had been split up into apartments, occupied by several of my grade school teachers and the principal.

4. Antiques, Art, and Other Tangibles

Antiques and art are often valued for enjoyment or investment because they were made with now-obsolete methods. American furniture made after the mid-1800s when it was first produced in factories is generally worth much less than that produced earlier by handcraftsmen. A modern reproduction of an eighteenth century highboy may be technically superior to the original, but is worth far less. Ditto for a digital copy of a beautiful sixteenth century Dutch still life painting.

Antiques, art, jewelry, and similar tangible assets tend to appreciate in value during periods of high inflation, and when upper-income people who typically buy them are flush with cash. I doubt they will do well, however, in the atmosphere of slow economic growth, deflation, and pressure on high incomes. The subdued auction sales by Sotheby's and Christie's in recent years and the highly unusual declines in diamond prices by Tiffany may be symptomatic of what lies ahead. The value of these tangible assets is more likely to be in the enjoyment they give their owners than as rapidly appreciating investments. My wife and I love eighteenth-century American and English furniture, but we see our pieces as gorgeous furniture, not appreciating assets.

Further, illiquidity has always made antiques and collectibles questionable investments. The lack of standardization and wide spreads between purchase and sales prices present considerable problems. On PBS's *Antiques Roadshow*, people in various cities bring in the antique treasures they've found in their attics to be evaluated by experts. The pros give lengthy and interesting discussions of the background of selected pieces, their designers, and where and when they were made. But the high point is always the same. The expert asks the owner how much she thinks her antique is worth and then shocks her with its huge value, as the camera zooms in for a close-up of the overjoyed collector. I hope this fine program will survive in deflation days.

5. Banks and Similar Financial Institutions

During the financial free-for-all days, large banks moved well beyond traditional spread lending—taking deposits and then lending them with interest rate spreads to cover their costs, loan risks, and reasonable profits. They hyped their leverage—and their risk—as they set up off-balance-sheet vehicles and engaged in proprietary trading and in the origination of and investment in derivatives. Regulators stood by under the theory that free markets would discipline excessive risk taking. Both the big banks and the regulators, however, knew or should have known that they were too big to fail and take the financial system down with them. So those financial institutions were really playing a game of heads we win, tails we get bailed out by the government.

And fail they did, and bailed out they have been. Many investors seem to believe that's the end of the unpleasantness and now it's back to business as usual. The recent big trading profits by some financial institutions certainly point in that direction. I doubt it, though. The financial sector expanded its leverage over about four decades (see Figure 4.7 in Chapter 4) and its deleveraging will probably consume most or all of the next decade. Big risk-taking CEOs like Ken Lewis at Bank of America have been forced out, sending a clear message to the senior officers who remain. The collapse of Bear Stearns, bankruptcy of Lehman, and forced merger of Merrill Lynch into Bank of America are also indelible reminders.

Stringent, probably excessive regulation in and beyond the new financial reform bill is replacing the laissez faire model. Led by Fed Governor Daniel Tarullo, the Fed's 2,858 bank supervisors have switched from saying yes to almost anything the banks want to do to saying no. Higher capital requirements and other limits on risk taking will curb bank profitability. So will the limits on executive pay aimed at reducing the incentive to take big risks. And note that restrictions on executive compensation spread well beyond the financial sector to companies such as Polo Ralph Lauren, Sysco, Eli Lilly, Ingersoll-Rand, and Freeport-McMoRan Copper & Gold.

Fannie Mae and Freddie Mac are stuck with around $300 billion in delinquent mortgages, so they are forcing the banks that underwrote defective ones to take them back. Many borrowers lied about their income, said the loans were for owner-occupied homes when they were for vacation houses, had fraudulent appraisals, didn't provide proper documentation, and so forth. In total, lenders bought back around $20 billion in loans in 2009, and half of them were written off because they were hopelessly delinquent while the rest often required steep write-downs. Freddie returned $4.1 billion in single-family mortgages to lenders in 2009, more than twice the $1.8 billion in 2008. These buybacks and hits to bank capital may well increase in 2010 and later as delinquencies and foreclosures persist.

Furthermore, one wonders whether Goldman Sachs will be forced to make up the $1 billion of losses, $4 billion with triple damages, on a collateralized debt obligation (CDO) that the SEC in April 2010 said the firm improperly marketed without adequate disclosure. Is this just the tip of the iceberg in the hunt for those responsible for huge losses on CDOs and other derivatives?

After the collapse of many big banks, their senior officers would probably behave very conservatively for a generation, but the administration, Congress, and regulators who blame them for the mess will make sure they do. And the government reaction to the financial collapse in the 1930s tells us that the longer the era of slow economic growth, high unemployment, and deflation, the more stringent the regulation and restraint on financial institution risk taking and profits will be.

Smaller Banks

Regional and community banks are also likely to be unattractive investments for a number of years. Ironically, in the go-go days, many of them were unwilling to virtually abandon their underwriting standards to compete with nonbank residential mortgage lenders. So they lent to the commercial real estate market instead, as noted earlier. That's proving to be a jump from the frying pan into the fire, given the bleak outlook for commercial real estate that I'll discuss later.

Due to bad commercial as well as residential real estate loans, smaller banks have dropped like flies, almost 200 from the beginning of 2008 through March 2010, and about 80 percent of them had commercial real estate woes. Individually, they aren't too big to fail, but collectively they are since they are the primary financers of smaller businesses. Those businesses don't have access to commercial paper and other credit market vehicles and must rely on their local banks for loans—or on the personal credit cards of their owners.

Commercial banks hold about $1.5 trillion in commercial and multifamily housing debt. They also have around $500 billion in land and construction loans that are especially toxic since raw land and unfinished buildings provide no revenue but incur outlays for taxes, completion of the structures, guarding against vandalism, and so on. In early 2009, Congress relaxed accounting standards that permitted banks to avoid marking commercial mortgages down to market, which would have eliminated much or all of their capital in many cases.

But between 2010 and 2014, about $800 billion of that mortgage debt held by banks comes due, and about two-thirds of the loans are underwater. Will bank examiners allow them to roll over underwater loans under the theory that a rolling loan gathers no loss? Will banks be permitted to extend those loans and pretend they are solid? Meanwhile, many banks simply delay and pray that somehow commercial real estate, despite tremendous excess capacity, will revive. Middle-size banks have about 350 percent of their capital in commercial real estate loans, much more than either bigger or smaller banks.

Nevertheless, small banks aren't immune. In February 2010, the Congressional Oversight Panel, as part of its review of the Troubled Asset Relief Program (TARP), reported that almost 3,000 small U.S. banks may be forced to drastically cut their lending because of commercial real estate loan losses. They all had commercial real estate loans amounting to at least 300 percent of their capital or construction and land development loans equal to over 100 percent of capital. The 300 percent level raises red flags for regulators.

Private-Label Mortgages

From June 2007 through 2008, banks with less than $10 billion in assets bought more than $4 billion in private-label mortgage bonds that are not issued or guaranteed by government agencies. Many of them were downgraded to junk status as homeowner defaults surged. Some of those banks believe the bonds will eventually pay off, but regulators forced them to reserve extra capital against likely losses.

The Obama administration has moved to give small banks access to the $30 billion in TARP money if they use the money for small business loans. But with government money comes more government involvement and regulation, which tends to stifle bank earnings. And any that participate in TARP must sell the government warrants that give it the right to buy the bank's common stock at a set price.

Banks are being forced to reduce highly profitable proprietary trading, securitizations, and so on, and get back into traditional spread lending. But that basic commercial banking function is likely to be less profitable in a world of slow growth and deflation than during rapid growth and inflation. Loans are made in current, not inflation-adjusted dollars. So when inflation is reducing their value and business is booming, borrowers can usually repay without difficulty. But with slow growth in business revenues, pressure on the profits of borrowers, and deflation pushing up real loan values, the risk of nonrepayment jumps. To offset this, the interest spreads of lenders need to be bigger.

But that will be difficult in deflation. The yield curve will probably flatten so the spread between bank borrowing of short-term deposits or other instruments and longer-term loans will narrow. Short-term rates will probably be higher than at present in the years ahead as the Fed moves up its federal funds target somewhat from the current range of zero to 0.25 percent (see Figure 1.3 in Chapter 1) as the financial crisis recedes. At the same time, as deflation is accepted as the norm, longer-term interest rates will probably decline. Short-term interest rates are unlikely to be high enough to make it very profitable for banks to attract and service deposits, but they may have no choice if plans in the United States, the United Kingdom, and elsewhere to tax banks' wholesale funding are enacted. They can, of course, increase fees on checking and other accounts, but they are limited by competition from money market funds and other alternatives.

Mark to Market

Concern over pricing of financial assets mushroomed in 2007–2008 when fixed-income markets became dominated by nonstop downward repricing of securities to levels that few were convinced were their bottoms. And their illiquidity exacerbated the trend in a continual negative spiral as lower prices and more write-downs frightened buyers, forcing prices even lower and drying up bids.

Earlier, oceans of excess liquidity sloshing around the globe, zeal for high investment returns, and low volatility in many securities markets drove investors to immense speculation in many areas. And that speculation was implemented through gigantic financial leverage not only in housing but also in emerging market equity and debt, commodities, commercial real estate, and so forth.

As the many speculative bubbles inflated, everyone was buying these securities, virtually no one was selling, and few worried about what they would bring in difficult markets. In fact, their illiquidity gave free reign to pricing techniques that flew higher and higher from reality. Many were priced by models that, in the case of subprime-related mortgage securities, were based on a history of ever-rising house prices (Figure 1.2). So delinquencies and defaults were tiny since rising house prices allowed even the least creditworthy borrower to refinance or sell his house to avoid foreclosure.

Furthermore, those models were developed by those who were paid management and performance fees that were directly tied to the value of the securities priced by the models. No inherent conflict of interest, of course! And the securities and models that priced them were so complex that few questioned whether the resulting prices were realistic. So the prices used for CDOs and many other derivatives were based on hope, an extreme speculative climate, and self-serving and unrealistic models that assumed almost no risk of financial difficulties.

In the midst of all the 2007–2008 turmoil, financial institutions, pressured by accountants and regulators, attempted to mark these many opaque securities to market rather than mark to model. AIG's auditors in early 2008 forced the firm to write down mortgage-related insurance contracts, credit default swaps (CDSs), by $4.88 billion for October and November 2007 activity, superseding the firm's mark-to-model approach. In late 2007, the firm told investors its losses would be a mere $1 billion. Then the auditors insisted that the CDSs be marked to market even though they seldom trade, and the firm took an additional $6.24 billion write-down for December 2007 contracts.

Mark to Market: Pros and Cons

Advocates of the mark-to-market approach, including me, believe that markets are the only valid and impartial pricers of almost anything. They note that the models used to price subprime-related securities ridiculously overpriced them. Other approaches, such as interpolation between actual sale prices of similar securities to establish prices, are suspect since many securities aren't similar enough to make comparisons valid. Basing values on costs is clearly misleading, especially in rapidly falling markets. The collapses of both Bear Stearns and Lehman were in part caused by counterparty fears that those firms were vastly overvaluing their assets—and they were right, as noted earlier.

But critics of marking to market say that there might not be any recent trades in the securities in question, and those that do occur in falling, highly illiquid markets may be unreasonably low, as in 2007–2008. They also point out that pricing in relation to indexes of securities like the subprime mortgage ABX (Figure 3.11 in Chapter 3) and the commercial real estate CMBX might be inaccurate in relation to overall market conditions. Bears on subprime housing were vigorously selling securities related to the ABX index, thereby depressing it, the critics maintain. And those who own subprime-related securities were also selling to offset losses on their holdings. So current prices might have understated a security's value in the long run when current stressful conditions subside.

In fact, however, statements like that last one are nothing more than forecasts. Maybe market prices are artificially depressed, but maybe not. In early 2008, some hedge funds thought that bonds selling at 80 cents on the dollar were cheap. But then they fell to 60 cents and later to 40 cents. As my friend Ed Moos puts it, they get cheap, cheaper, and cheapest—and then you sell!

Optimists also said the various CMBX indexes that reflect the value of bonds backed by mortgages on office buildings, hotels, warehouses, and the like, traded at levels that implied a collapse in commercial real estate that they didn't believe was likely. They noted that the CMBX indexes are supposed to reflect the performance of commercial mortgage-backed securities, but the market for those bonds evaporated, making it hard to determine their worth.

Also, they insisted during the 2007–2008 financial crisis, that hedge funds and other speculators were selling CMBX-related vehicles to bet against commercial real estate, thereby depressing those indexes artificially. Furthermore, since the CMBX indexes have become the benchmarks for commercial mortgage bond prices, the yields on those bonds were being forced up.

One Price for Everything?

Critics also say that marking to market values everything on the basis of the last sales even though the securities involved aren't necessarily for sale, and certainly not the whole issue. This approach treats everything as constantly for sale, whether it is or not, they maintain. But what, pray tell, is the difference between using market prices for illiquid securities and using them, as is normal, for highly liquid issues?

Many of the largest stocks by market capitalization, which is determined by multiplying the current stock price by the number of shares outstanding, are considered highly liquid, but only a tiny fraction of their shares trade on an average day. Exxon Mobil has a market cap of nearly $320 billion, but a mere 0.52 percent of its stock trades per day. Yet the whole company is valued on the basis of the current price, $67.77 per share on April 19, 2010.

Is this realistic? A buyer today couldn't buy even 5 percent of any of these stocks without profoundly changing the price, nor could a seller. Exxon Mobil trades 24.4 million shares a day on average, but a buyer or seller of even 1 million shares wouldn't dream of entering the open market with a trade of that size. He'd employ block traders who are paid handsomely to find the other side of the trade to avoid big disruptions to the market. Yet the whole company is valued on the basis of the last trade, be it only 100 shares.

Beyond that, a strategic buyer who sees a company fitting into its business, or a private equity firm that believes a corporation can be reorganized, may think that the enterprise value of a company is much more than the current market capitalization. Those beliefs are what keep merger and acquisition experts in business.

So there probably isn't a fundamental difference between what the market price of a subprime mortgage-backed CDO tells us about the intrinsic value of the securities and what the last trade price of Microsoft reveals about the total value of that company. To say that the CDO price is artificially depressed is really only a forecast that it may sell at a higher price later. A bigger subsequent price will generate a profit for the holder, but that remains to be seen and doesn't prove that the current price is understated. The only price for a security that isn't a forecast is the current market price. The job of vulture funds is to buy securities they believe are cheap, but they are not guaranteed success.

Liquidity Matters

Consequently, the only difference between marking to market an infrequently traded CDO tranche and the last sale price of a company with huge market capitalization is liquidity. Investors don't think much about the liquidity of GE's stock because there is so much of it. Most investors can buy and sell GE shares all day without disturbing the price because there are enough traders on the other side to balance their actions. But even for big stocks, that's not always true.

Just as illiquidity has plagued owners of many derivatives as the financial market goes through massive deleveraging, it was vividly in evidence in the 1987 crash. Institutional investors were sold on the portfolio insurance strategy, which said that they could sell stocks progressively as they declined to avoid major losses. That encouraged them to hold bigger, riskier positions than otherwise. Unfortunately, too many tried the same approach, so on October 19, almost all were sellers and few were buyers. The 22.6 percent decline in the Dow Jones Industrial Average that day vividly testified to the resulting lack of liquidity.

Winston Churchill said that "democracy is the worst form of government except for all the others." Similarly, the free market determination of security prices isn't perfect, but it's probably well ahead of any other possibility.

6. Junk Securities

During the dark days of the financial crisis, the yields on junk bonds leaped to 19.3 percentage points over Treasurys (Figure 4.8 in Chapter 4) as investors worried about complete financial collapse and widespread defaults among low-grade issues. Triple-C rated bonds, the lowest junk tier, sold at 42.6 cents on the dollar at the beginning of 2009, and yielded 44.3 percentage points over Treasurys in December 2008.

But the bailout of the big banks and easing of the financial crisis allayed investor fears, and junk spreads collapsed to levels lower than in many pre–financial crisis years. Institutional investors piled in, followed by individual investors, many of whom sought alternatives to low returns on bank deposits and money market funds and who also bought investment-grade corporate and municipal bonds. So the spreads on junk bonds dropped to 5.5 percentage points in March 2010, and on triple-C bonds they narrowed to about 9 percentage points. In 2009, junk bonds returned 57 percent and low-quality leveraged loans returned 52 percent, much more than the 24 percent gain on the S&P 500 Index, despite the fact that 11 percent of junk issuers defaulted that year. In 2009, 265 companies defaulted on bonds, double the 2008 tally and more than the previous high of 229 in 2001.

In any event, I believe this rally was way overdone. In addition, the slow-economic-growth, deflationary scenario I project for the next decade will be lethal for many junk bonds, both those issued as high-yield instruments by companies with shaky balance sheets and fallen angels that have been downgraded to junk status. Slow revenue and cash flow growth, to say nothing of deflation, will make it difficult if not impossible for a number of financially weak and weakening firms to service their bonds and other debts as the principals of those instruments rise in real terms.

Really Equity

Rating agencies forecast default rates on junk bonds in 2010 to fall to the 4- to 7-percent range. Also, the zeal for yield in 2009 allowed many below-investment-grade companies to issue $145 billion in bonds, mostly to refinance debt. Nevertheless, Moody's says that 995 of the 1,300 companies it rates as junk have $800 billion in debt maturing in the next five years, $700 billion of it between 2012 and 2014.

I've always felt that junk bonds are essentially stocks. Real, for-sure bonds are backed by so much corporate cash flow that the prospects of interest payments not being met are extremely low. Only in the face of fallen angels destined for bankruptcy do investors worry about getting their semiannual interest checks. By contrast, junk bond price levels and the likelihood of meeting interest payments depend primarily on companies' quarter-by-quarter earnings and cash flow. That's no different than what principally determines stock prices and dividends.

Sure, stock bulls point out the prospects for growing earnings and stock appreciation, which isn't the case with bonds unless interest rates decline. Still, in the slow growth, deflationary world I foresee, growth in earnings and stock prices will be limited, as explored in Chapter 10, hardly enough to give equities a clear advantage.

So let's look at junk bonds as low-quality equities with big dividend yields, and assume that their spread versus Treasurys (Figure 4.8) measures their market value, dividend yields, and ability to continue their high dividend payments. From this standpoint, these dividends don't seem big enough to offset the risks that they won't be paid in the climate I foresee. Slow economic growth robs many financially weak companies of volume expansion, and deflation kills their pricing power. But if junk bond yields rise substantially, they then could be attractive in a world in which investors are likely to be interested in meaningful dividends of various kinds. That assumes that investors view junk not as bonds with temptingly high interest yields, but as low-grade equities with large but risky dividends and little prospects for capital appreciation.

7. Flailing Companies

Companies with below-average revenue growth, high fixed costs, and big debts represent a lethal combination in an era of slow growth and deflation. Without robust revenue growth, the only route to profit gains or even stability is cost-cutting. High fixed costs due to strong labor unions are especially troubling. As I've discussed earlier, during inflation, employees who are paid more than their value-added can be reduced to the proper pay levels by simply not giving them raises. Then inflation reduces their real pay. But in deflation, their wages and benefits must be reduced directly or through involuntary furloughs if layoffs aren't feasible. This is extremely difficult if employees are organized in strong unions, as Chrysler and GM found out.

Similarly, heavy debts are a problem amid slow revenue growth and deflation. The principals remain fixed in nominal terms but grow in real terms. So revenue and cash flow growth may not be adequate to retire those debts. Furthermore, in the case of bond issues, interest payments are often fixed for the lives of their bonds as well and may be difficult to meet in a slow growth, deflationary climate.

8. Low- and Old-Tech Capital Equipment Producers

Investors should avoid many low- and old-tech capital equipment producers. Industrial capacity is so excessive here and abroad that a meaningful surge in capital spending in advanced countries is probably years away (see Figure 4.2). The principal exception is productivity-enhancing equipment, new or old tech, that will improve user productivity and profits in an era in which volume growth and price increases are nearly impossible for most businesses, as I cover in Chapter 12.

Note that the volatility of the producers of equipment is much greater than that of the users. Auto sales declined by over 40 percent in the current recession, but orders for machine tools, automatic transfer lines, and other equipment fell much more as auto assemblers and parts makers almost froze orders. Recall as well how the recession-sired excess capacity in airlines caused massive cancellations and postponements of orders for Boeing's Dreamliner.

Some believe that the recent large negative gap between capital spending and cash flow (see Figure 11.1) will cause the leaping corporate cash to burn holes in CEO pockets. For the 500 largest companies, cash rose from 8 percent of assets in 2008 to 9.8 percent in 2009. My analysis suggests otherwise. When operating rates are low, as at present

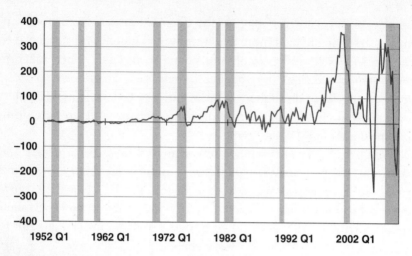

Figure 11.1 Nonfarm Nonfinancial Financing Gap
Data source: Federal Reserve Board.

(Figure 4.2), producers don't need more capacity and worry that revenues, prices, and profits won't be adequate to justify even existing capacity.

Our statistical models of capital spending show that in accounting for the year-over-year change in the equipment and software or in equipment and software plus nonresidential structures components of GDP, the *level* of operating rates is far and away the most important explanatory variable, much more than the year-over-year *change* in operating rates. This indicates that even if capacity utilization is growing rapidly, if it remains at low levels, the growth in capital spending will be subdued.

Much Less Important

Other variables, such as the year-over-year changes in cash flow, profits, and interest costs, were statistically significant in our models, but much less important in explaining the change in capital spending. And our models don't quantify and add in the extra corporate caution spawned by the recession and financial crises.

Besides the depressing effects of excess capacity, low-tech and old-tech companies suffer from other ongoing problems. Foreign competition continues to grow as their technology is transferred to China and other cheap production locales. Some suffer rising cost pressures due to lack of productivity gains. High-cost labor forces are sometimes a problem. And many sell into saturated, slow growth markets.

U.S. motor vehicles are a case in point. Its capacity utilization is even lower than for industry as a total. It recovered, in the aftermath of GM and Chrysler bankruptcies and the cash-for-clunkers rebates, to 52 percent at the end of 2009, but a far cry from the 90 percent or higher levels of earlier years. Global capacity to produce motor vehicles is now 86 million and headed toward 100 million by 2015, but now only about 55 million are being sold annually worldwide, a 65 percent utilization rate at present.

Reliable worldwide total capacity utilization data are not available, but they clearly are in excess and getting more so in what will soon be the world's second largest economy, China. As I discuss later, much of China's recent $585 billion stimulus program in 2009 went into bank loans to finance construction of steel, cement, and power plants and other industrial capacity. How will all that capacity be utilized?

In the past, it has ended up producing exports with U.S. consumers buying the lion's share, directly or indirectly. However, with American households retrenching, the viable alternative for mushrooming industrial capacity is domestic consumption in China. But China is not far enough along the road to industrialization to yet have a big middle class of discretionary spenders who can utilize all that industrial capacity.

Bottom-Line Growth Stocks

Along with other American businesses, many producers of old-tech capital equipment have been very good at cutting costs to preserve profits in recent years in the face of weak demand. But history suggests that cost-cutting cannot sustain profits growth for long without revenue growth. In the 1980s, when American businesses zealously restructured to counter withering foreign competition, we developed a concept I dubbed *bottom-line growth stocks*.

The idea was that some companies would prove so adept at continuous restructuring and cutting costs that even though they lacked strong top-line revenue growth, their profits, the bottom line, would rise at growth-stock speed. Our concept created a bit of a stir on Wall Street at the time. Unfortunately, it didn't work. Few firms proved able to continually cost-cut their way to significant profits growth without meaningful revenue advances.

The Real and Financial Economies

It goes without saying that excess capacity in the real, or goods and services, economy puts distinct downward pressure on prices. That compounds the negative effects of low capacity utilization on old-tech capital spending. It's also true that the financial and real economies interact, and deleveraging in the financial arena will create more excess capacity in the goods and services world. That's the lesson many learned the hard way in 2007 and 2008. They thought that the subprime mortgage woes that unfolded in early 2007 were isolated events even after they sank Bear Stearns in midyear. They didn't realize that the stock market nosedive starting in late 2007 and evaporation of lending would slaughter consumer spending in late 2008.

Excess debt and other financial imbalances, then, are important to both the financial and real economies. The extreme financial leverage that the U.S. household and financial sectors took four decades to build will probably take a decade or more to unwind (Figure 4.7).

9. Commercial Real Estate

Ironically, except for hotels, it's not so much a problem of overbuilding of shopping malls, office buildings, and warehouses in the past decade. In fact, the modest expansion compared to the residential building bubble encouraged many investors to bid up prices, depressing capitalization rates that link rental income to property values, and to leverage commercial properties heavily, as noted in Chapter 8.

This left scheduled refinancing in trouble. At the same time, the great recession pushed retail vacancies up (Figure 8.5) as retailers closed stores and reduced the space in those that remained. Rising sales per square foot justified store expansion in the 1990s and early 2000s, but that measure of productivity peaked at $454 per square foot in mall stores in 2007 and fell to $401 at the end of 2009. In the first quarter of 2010, lease rates in malls were down 3 percent from a year earlier, and vacancy rates rose to 8.9 percent. Landlords of retail space are renting to new tenants at 25 to 40 percent lower than rents paid by previous tenants.

Hotel occupancies and revenues continue to decline and office and apartment vacancies are still rising. Property prices are plummeting (Figure 8.6) while mortgage delinquencies are surging and reached 7.14 percent in March 2010 on securitized commercial mortgages. Fitch Rating expects the delinquency rate to leap to 11 percent by the end of 2010. Warehouses are empty as consumer retrenchment curtails goods imports from Asia and elsewhere. In the slow economic growth I see ahead, excess capacity and deflation in commercial real estate are likely to persist with the exception of rental apartments, as I explain in Chapter 12, and medical services–related real estate, which will continue to benefit from robust demand growth.

Businesses will cut costs not only by holding down employment and therefore the need for office space, but also by moving in the partitions to fit the remaining people into less space. Increasing use of telecommuting will also reduce need for office buildings. In March 2010, average net office rents were down 7.4 percent from a year earlier and the first-quarter vacancy rate was 17.2 percent. More teleconferencing will also cut hotel-utilizing business trips. At the same time, consumers will restrain discretionary travel and the hotel and motel use involved. Weak consumer spending will keep mall and warehouse space under pressure.

Furthermore, a great deal of real estate debt must be refinanced soon amid falling occupancy, rents, and sales prices as well as tight credit markets, as I covered earlier in conjunction with bank loans. Estimates are that $155 billion in securitizations are coming due by 2012 and two-thirds won't qualify for refinancing with prices down 35 to 45 percent from their 2007 peaks. Meanwhile, $525 billion of commercial mortgages held by banks and thrifts will come due by 2012. About 50 percent won't qualify for refinancing since they exceed 90 percent of the underlying property value. Lenders prefer loans of no more than 65 percent, down from 80 percent in the loose lending years. Still, banks persist in extending loans in the hope that all will be well somehow.

With commercial property prices likely to continue to fall with muted demand and deflation, rents, not appreciation, will be the source of investor returns after covering operating costs, taxes, declining values of the land and structures, and so on. But not only are current rents insufficient to provide economic returns on current depressed property values, even with today's low interest rates, they are also falling. This is quite different from the inflationary days of yore when owners could simply cover costs with rents and make their returns from appreciating building values. Also, taxes on those capital gains were only paid when building owners sold, but taxes on profits from rental income are due annually and at much higher rates.

Commercial Mortgage Rates

With our forecast of 3 percent yield on 30-year Treasury bonds, long-term commercial mortgage rates are likely to run about 4 percent. But if commercial real prices follow general inflation/deflation as they have in the past and fall 2 to 3 percent annually, real mortgage rates will run 6 to 7 percent. This will contrast sharply with earlier days when property appreciation exceeded financing rates. And in another reversal from the days of rising rents, tenants will demand shorter leases so they can renew at lower costs while landlords will desire longer leases to lock in present rental rates.

In this environment, even with rapidly falling costs for land and building materials, commercial construction will remain depressed until excess space is absorbed—and that may take many years. Property values need to fall faster than rents to eventually provide acceptable returns to investors. Current rents are estimated to be only 50 to 70 percent of the levels needed to encourage new construction, and lenders, quite logically, are unwilling to make new construction loans under these circumstances. (I thank my great friend and superb real estate investor, Art Hill of AHC Management LLC, for this insightful analysis and forecast.)

With high vacancies continuing to depress rents, property values will be marked down to well below new construction costs. Landlords will continue to offer generous concessions to attract tenants. A building, regardless of its age, is worth something as long as rent exceeds operating costs. When high vacancies and low rents reign, it's usually a matter of wiping out the equity of a series of owners and all of the lenders until that price is reached. As part of that process, Morgan Stanley in March 2010 told investors in its $8.8 billion real estate fund that two-thirds of their money may be lost because of fallen property prices.

Banks are extending many commercial real estate loans and pretending they aren't troubled—but many are. At the end of March 2010, restructurings of nonresidential loans, most of them on commercial real estate, totaled $24 billion, seven times the level two years earlier. Banks hold $176 billion in troubled commercial property loans. Regulators are allowing underwater loans to be carried as "performing" because writing them down would destroy tons of bank capital and push many institutions to the wall. But the truth is that commercial property prices are 42 percent below their October 2007 peak. Delinquencies in the first quarter of 2010 on commercial property loans were 9.1 percent, up from 1.5 percent three years earlier. About 45 percent of restructurings were 30 days or more delinquent compared to 28 percent in the first quarter of 2008.

Real estate investment trusts (REITs) used to be bought by investors seeking steady rental income for commercial properties, but in recent years they have behaved like the aggregate stock market—only more so. The Dow Jones Equity All REIT index lost three-fourths of its value from February 2007 to March 2009, but doubled from then to early 2010. And REITs then sold 20 percent above the market value of their real estate holdings. Publicly traded REITs bought just $4.6 billion in property in 2009, down 67 percent from 2008. They raised $24 billion in new stock in 2009, with the hope of buying distressed properties at fire sale prices. But since banks have not been forced to foreclose on troubled commercial mortgages, as discussed earlier, REITs are finding limited uses for their cash. It looks like investors jumped the gun in buying new REIT equity and bidding up their stock prices. Unless commercial real estate rebounds swiftly in 2011, which I doubt, disappointments may be legion.

10. Commodities

Global excess supply conditions will keep commodity prices under pressure, as will muted demand. American use of crude oil and petroleum products fell 4.2 percent in 2009 from a year earlier, the fourth consecu-tive annual decline. U.S. gasoline consumption in early 2010 was running 3 percent below the 2007 level, contrary to its usual steady growth trend. Consumer retrenchment and lower commercial demand were at work, but also less commuter travel due to high unemployment. Commuting accounts for the largest share of vehicle miles, 27 percent. These forces will likely persist in the slow growth, deflationary world I foresee. In addi-tion, the new fuel efficiency regulations call for cars and light trucks to be 34 percent more fuel-efficient for the 2016 model year than for 2009.

Commodity prices will also be subdued by the continuing realization by institutional and individual investors that commodities aren't an asset class, but speculations. Furthermore, the rush by pension and endowment funds as well as individual investors into commodities in recent years through ETFs and futures markets has been partly self-defeating. The result of their big buying has been to bid up the prices of more distant futures contracts in relation to nearby benchmark contract prices—a *contango*, as it's called. So when the benchmark contracts held expire and are rolled into the next ones, they are at higher prices. Consequently, even though the price of the underlying commodity is rising, the investor may make little or nothing. The benchmark corn contract tripled from $2.40 per bushel in January 1990 to $7.65 in mid-2008, but an ETF that held the benchmark contracts would have only broken even because of contango costs.

As I discussed earlier in Chapter 8, I disagree with those who believe the world is running out of crude oil or other basic commodities. Instead, I believe that human ingenuity beats shortages every time. The only shortage I'm aware of is castrati to sing in the beautiful Baroque operas by Handel and others that I thoroughly enjoy. Back on March 28, 1978, when the scare over crude oil shortages was extreme, I wrote a report while at White, Weld, pointing out two previous panics over the exhaus-tion of key commodities that proved false as alternative products were developed. Here are excerpts.

In Jamestown, Virginia, the original colonists who arrived in the early 1600s tried many occupations in their attempt to support themselves and produce goods that could be traded with England. One area that did thrive, at least briefly, was glass blowing, and numerous glass articles were exported to England. In the 1600s, hardwood charcoal was the most practical fuel for smelting iron, and the rapidly developing British iron and steel industry was consuming huge amounts of charcoal. In fact, the demand for charcoal by the iron and other industries was so great that by the end of the century, the British countryside was virtually denuded of hardwoods. Charcoal prices rose to the point that it was economical to fuel glass furnaces in Virginia with the abundant hardwood there and then ship glass articles 3,000 miles to England.

Charcoal also became so expensive that many British iron makers quit the business because of high production costs. Many observers expected the iron business—and industry—to grind to a halt because of the charcoal shortage.

Then in the early 1700s, it was discovered that coke made from abundant coal supplies could replace charcoal in iron smelting. After technical problems were worked out, charcoal prices collapsed and the British iron industry was saved, as were the remaining hardwood trees. Although employment statistics in Virginia at that time are sparse, it seems clear that a number of glass blowers joined the ranks of the unemployed.

Another energy shortage was threatened in the mid-1800s when it looked as though the world was going to run out of whales and, thus, the whale oil that was then widely used for lighting. In the 1850s, kerosene was introduced as a substitute, but with petroleum selling at $20 a barrel it was a prohibitively expensive one. In 1859, however, Edwin L. Drake, a retired railroad conductor, drilled his famous well and initiated the large-scale oil industry. In less than three years the price of oil dropped to 10 cents a barrel, so the world didn't have to go back to candles, and the whales were given a reprieve.

These examples are not just interesting bits of history. Then as now, the problem was not one of a worldwide energy shortage but rather a shortage of known supplies of a particular type of energy in a particular place. There may be an eventual shortage of currently known oil supplies, especially in the lower 48 States, but considering undiscovered oil reserves, nuclear potential, solar, and other sources, the world has abundant energy at what may prove to be surprisingly low costs.

I concluded back in 1978 that the so-called energy crisis was—and still is—a problem that can and will be solved not only by conservation but, more importantly, by the development of additional and new types of energy supplies. The process, however, could be greatly aided and disruptions minimized by government encouragement on the supply side—especially by allowing the price mechanism to do its proper job.

I believe that most commodity-producing companies and their suppliers of equipment and supplies will be unattractive investments in the coming years of weak demand, excess capacity, and soft prices. The same is true for economies such as Persian Gulf sheikdoms that depend heavily on commodity exports.

There is, however, one commodity sector I'm favorably disposed to—North American energy, as I explore in Chapter 12.

11. Developing Country Stocks and Bonds

As late as the end of 2007, most forecasters believed in decoupling. Even if the U.S. economy suffers a setback, they said, the rest of the world, especially developing countries like China and India, would continue to flourish. Indeed, the strength of those economies could even aid the United States as they bought more American exports.

I disagreed, and persisted in my long-held conviction that almost all developing countries depended on exports for growth, as shown by the persistent trade surpluses in those lands (Table 7.6) and the huge size of Asian exports relative to GDP. Further, our research revealed that the majority of exports by Asian countries, excluding Japan, went directly or indirectly to the United States.

Admittedly, this calculation involved a lot of judgment calls. On the surface, intra-Asian trade dwarfs the sum of all those countries' exports to the United States. But it's only the value-added in that intra-Asian trade that matters and the rest is double-counting. If, say, Taiwan produces a semiconductor that is shipped to Thailand to be used in a component that then moves to South Korea for subassembly and then to China for final assembly of a computer that is exported to the United States, adding up the exports of all four countries way overcounts the combined value-added. But separating out the portion of individual country exports that end up in the United States as opposed to remaining in Asia or moving elsewhere is tough.

Our November 2007 *Insight* report, "The Chinese Middle Class: 110 Million Is Not Enough," found that China was not yet developed sufficiently to have enough people with discretionary spending to support the economy domestically. It remained export-led, with U.S. consumers buying most of its exports, directly or indirectly. So, with our forecast of a major retrenchment by U.S. consumers, we predicted big trouble for China.

I wrote in our November 2007 report:

> So we conclude that the rapid growth of major developing lands, especially China, is still driven by direct and indirect exports to U.S. consumers. Local middle classes aren't big enough yet or likely to be for at least a decade to generate domestically led growth, much less promote U.S. expansion through massive imports from America. All the PCs owned by citizens of those countries and the 450 million cell phone users in China and 150 million in India are the result of exports earnings and direct foreign investment. And with U.S. consumers likely to end their 25 years of borrowing and spending and mount a saving spree as American housing collapses, exports to the United States, and hence growth in local spending in Asia, will be severely restricted.

Industrial Revolution's Significance

I still believe that China, India, the Asian Tigers, Latin American lands with the possible exception of Brazil, and other developing countries are not yet industrialized enough to have the vast middle classes needed to create economies that are led by domestic spending.

Probably the greatest effect of the Industrial Revolution was to create those middle classes. Earlier, European economies were two-class societies. Those on top owned almost everything and controlled most of the income. They spent lavishly on their palaces, entertainment, armies, and so forth, but still had large saving rates. Those on the bottom spent all their income to subsist, but they had very little. So, as in Asia today, national saving rates back then were large. Their counterpart was potential output far in excess of domestic demand, and those countries tried to export it in return for gold. This, of course, was the strategy of the mercantilists who held sway before the Industrial Revolution.

But with the Industrial Revolution came the middle class, all those people who wanted a better life, conspicuous consumption, and education for their children. And they had the money to pay for these desires. Hence the advent of domestic spending–led economies in developed countries—except in Japan, which clings to its feudalistic "export or die" mentality.

Today's array of developing countries are probably decades away from achieving big enough middle classes to eliminate their dependence on exports for growth. They still have the flip side of those big trade surpluses, huge private saving rates. Nevertheless, after the Asian collapse in 1997–1998, many of those countries sought, without notable success, to reduce the odds of being caught in another wave of falling dominoes by cutting their dependence on volatile global demand for their exports.

South Korea's Try

One of them tried exceptionally hard to force-feed domestic spending in what turned out to be an interesting experiment. South Korea offered tax breaks and other big incentives in 2000 to get consumers to use credit cards. And they did so with gay abandon, fueling robust consumer spending.

But then the government became worried about excessive lending and tightened regulations in 2002. The predictable results? A collapse in consumer spending that spawned a recession in the first half of 2003. Credit card delinquency rates leaped to the 28 to 59 percent range for the four major issuers under realistic accounting. This created a big problem for the government, which, after spending $129.5 billion to bail the banks out of the 1997–1998 crisis, was faced with rescuing credit card issuers and institutions that own their securities. So much for that noble experiment. Developing countries will have to grow their middle classes to much bigger sizes before their export dependence fades.

This exercise has been repeated more recently in India. The largest private sector bank, ICICI Bank, got heavily involved in credit card and consumer loans. But the default rate on its credit card loans jumped to 12 percent, and to 8 percent on consumer loans. So the bank is retreating. Consumer borrowers in India don't hesitate to default on loans because there are few repercussions and taking delinquents to court, for example, is difficult.

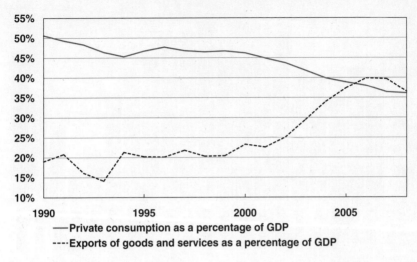

Figure 11.2 Chinese Exports and Consumption as a percent of GDP
Data source: Asian Development Bank.

Our analysis back in 2007 revealed that in China, it took about $5,000 per capita to have meaningful discretionary spending power. About 110 million Chinese had that much or more, but they constituted only 8 percent of the population and accounted for just 25 percent of GDP compared to 36.5 percent for exports (see Figure 11.2). If all goes well, China's middle class will approach 20 percent of the population in about 2020. In India, that class was a mere 5 percent of the population in 2007. In contrast, it took $26,000 per capita in the United States to have discretionary spending power and 80 percent of Americans had at least that much in that year. China's middle and upper classes have only 6 percent of Americans' purchasing power.

Asian Nosedives

Well, as they say, the rest is history. The Chinese and most other developing Asian countries nosedived as U.S. consumers retrenched (Figure 5.4 in Chapter 5). But recently, in the wake of China's huge $585 billion stimulus program in 2009; massive imports of industrial materials like iron ore and copper; jumps in construction of cement, steel, and power plants and other industrial capacity; and a pickup in economic growth (Figure 11.3), many forecasters again believe in decoupling.

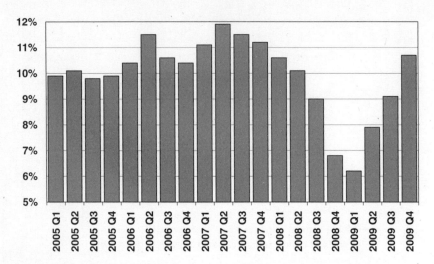

Figure 11.3   Chinese GDP, Year/Year Percent Change, 2005–2009
Data source: China National Bureau of Statistics.

Note that since the U.S. economy, with $14.3 trillion in 2009 GDP, was 2.9 times as large as China's $4.9 trillion, that $585 billion in Chinese stimulus was the equivalent of $1.7 trillion in America—2.1 times as large as the 2009 U.S. $787 billion fiscal stimulus package.

The current fascination with China, as in 2007, may in part be due to investors who are looking for high returns, but are wary of the U.S. economy and stock market, and even more so Europe's. A study of 82 companies that incorporated "China" in their names since late 2006 found that their returns from 20 trading days before the change to 20 days after were 31 percentage points higher than the total stock market. The longevity of the "China" effect is questionable. Many similarly small companies that included some form of "tech" or "electronics" in their names in the tech-crazy early 1960s lost 90 percent of their stock value. In the 1998 and 1999 Internet boom, putting "com" in a company's name got 53 percentage points better performance than other tech stocks—until they went bankrupt. In the years 2004–2007, adding "oil" or "petroleum" to a firm's name was good for an 8 percent hike in stock prices, but only briefly.

The veneration over rapid growth in Asian developing countries, especially China, also reminds us of the similar admiration, envy, and even dread over Japan back in its bubble days of the 1980s. After Japanese interests bought Pebble Beach, Iowa farmland, and Rockefeller Center, what was safe from their zillions? Any book on Japanese management style was an instant best-seller, and Japanese practices like *kanban*, or just-in-time inventory control, were adapted by many American firms. Like Japan earlier, China today is good at absorbing Western technology and using it to flood the world with exports. But that country is less skilled in seeing the big global picture and how its economy fits in.

Contrarian

Fortunately, back in the late 1980s, the contrarian in me said there was something wrong with these widespread forecasts of Japanese global dominance. After some research, I concluded in the late 1980s that the then-booming Japanese economy, real estate, and stock markets were unsustainable bubbles. In my 1988 book, *After the Crash*, I compared the 1980s in Japan with the 1920s in the United States, and forecast that the 1990s in Nippon would be a depression similar to the 1930s in America. That, too, is history.

Nevertheless, investors, despite the big setbacks of 66 percent in developing country stocks (Figure 4.10 in Chapter 4), charged back in 2009 and the MSCI Index rose 116 percent from the bottom in October 2008 through mid-March 2010. Grade school math, however, reveals that the index would still have to climb 36 percent to return to its October 2007 peak. Similarly, emerging market bond yields leaped relative to Treasurys but subsequently fell back to pre–financial crisis spreads. Indeed, in early 2010, investors switched from the higher-rated emerging countries' debt to the bottom-of-the-barrel bonds issued in Venezuela, Ukraine, Indonesia, Turkey, and El Salvador.

Brazil

Still, I remain skeptical. Sure, some countries such as Brazil and other South American countries with limited export exposure were not hurt too severely by the global recession. Brazil's economic output fell a mere 0.2 percent in 2009 as the government, with ample cash reserves, ordered the development bank to open its spigot as private credit shrank. Brazil is a major exporter of iron ore, steel, coffee, soybeans, sugar, and beef. In 2007, huge new oil fields were discovered offshore under miles of water and salt formations, as noted previously. Earlier, Brazil developed ethanol as a gasoline substitute. When I was there several years ago, gas stations sold both gasoline and ethanol, and drivers selected the cheaper because cars run on either.

But Brazil still has big problems that impede its full development. Government spending is a big share of the total economy and graft and consumption are legendary. The power of provincial governments often stymies federal government reforms. Infrastructure spending on roads, railroads, bridges, port facilities, airports, and pipelines has not kept up with economic growth. When I was there in 2008, many upper-income people in São Paulo commuted by helicopter because the roads were so congested.

Strict labor laws, dating from the 1940s, make it so expensive to start companies and hire employees that many entrepreneurs operate in the underground economy and pay workers off the books. Estimates are that the underground economy is 40 percent of the total, accounts for half of all urban jobs, and cuts overall annual economic growth by 1.5 percent. A massive 2007 infrastructure program remains stuck in bureaucracy with only 11 percent of the planned projects completed and over half yet to be launched. Crime is so high that it's unsafe to walk on Rio de Janeiro's beaches at night. And schools are underfunded and the quality of public education is low.

Among other developing countries, the Peronist government of Argentina has used central bank reserves to pay off foreign debts left over from its 2001 currency devaluation and economic crisis. Argentina has potentially a very productive agricultural sector that can be a major exporter, but the government is controlling beef prices and exports to the extent that ranchers have reduced their herds from 61 million in 2007 to 50 million head in 2009. Taxes on agricultural exports have farmers up in arms. Inflation is much higher, by all reports, than is shown by government statistics, which are produced by those loyal to the president, who replaced technocrats.

Vietnam's economy grew at a rapid 7.5 percent annual rate from 2000 to 2007, but spawned inflation, which peaked in August 2008 at a

28 percent annual rate. The previous surge in direct foreign investment has dried up, and with it rapid export growth. Consequently, Vietnam is one of the few Asian lands with big fiscal and current account deficits, despite its large, low-cost labor force. In order to counter the noncompetitive effects of inflation and to attract foreign manufacturing, the central bank devalued its currency, the dong, by 5 percent in November 2009 and another 3.4 percent in February 2010. But past devaluations and expectations of more to come appear to be spawning dollar hoarding along with weakness in business and consumer confidence.

Regardless of individual country-specific conditions, most developing economies depend on exports for growth, and the U.S. consumer has been the biggest buyer of those exports and far and away the globe's biggest spender. As the American consumer saving spree continues to shrink the U.S. trade and current account deficits (Figure 6.9 in Chapter 6), those developing economies will be subdued. I doubt that the recent rebounds in emerging market stocks and bonds correctly forecast robust, decoupled economic growth that is sustainable.

Tight Control

A tightly controlled economy can get results quickly, and that's what happened with China's $585 billion stimulus program. Unlike the $787 billion U.S. fiscal effort, there was no arguing in congressional committees, no need to wait for environmental approvals before infrastructure projects could be announced, no holdups because mortgage lenders didn't have the staffs to modify mortgages. Most of the money was channeled through the government-controlled banks, whose lending increased $1.4 trillion, or 32 percent, over the course of 2009 after being flat since early 2006, and the money supply leaped by 29 percent. Those loans financed public and industrial infrastructure and real estate, which accounted for eight percentage points of China's 8.7 percent economic growth in 2009 (Figure 11.3). Some also spurred real estate, and property prices in January 2010 were up 9.5 percent from a year earlier. Employment gained along with economic activity, and in the third quarter of 2009, there were 94 job openings for every 100 applicants, up from 85 in depressed 2008 and close to the pre-crisis average of 97.

Top-down economic control can get quick results, but it tends to result in stop-go economic performance. That's certainly true in China, as can be seen in the rollercoaster Shanghai stock index (Figure 5.4). The renewed boom has pushed new residential property prices up 20 percent nationwide at an annual rate. Industrial production jumped 20.7 percent in January–February 2010 from a year earlier, up from the 18 percent rise in the fourth quarter of 2009. Consumer prices rose 2.7 percent in February after falling for nine consecutive months in 2009, while producer prices in February 2010 were up 5.4 percent from a year earlier. In the same month, the director of the National Bureau of Statistics said that "asset price increases pose a challenge for macroeconomic policy." Yet with prices of high-end apartments in major cities rising much faster than house prices in general, developers accelerated their activity.

Overheating Fears

So the Chinese government in early 2010 was once again concerned with an overheating economy, much as it was in 2007. Inflation has gotten a number of Chinese dynasties tossed out over the millennia, and threatened the Mao Dynasty when it inspired the Tiananmen Square protests in 1989. Income inequality remains a problem in supposedly egalitarian China. The continual flow of Chinese from rural areas to more prosperous cities has increased average living standards, but the difference between the rich and the rest continues to widen. In 2009, per-capita annual income was around $2,500 in cities compared to $750 in the hinterland, and the gap has increased in the past decade. Adjusting for lower costs in rural areas, however, reduces the gap to about two to one. The housing boom has pushed up prices to the point that apartments in Beijing are affordable to only the top 20 percent because they're selling at around 18 times average incomes. With a condo costing $150,000 to $200,000, an urban couple earning $7,000 or $8,000 per year is definitely out of the market.

Consequently, the Chinese government is cutting back on stimulus. Total government spending is scheduled to grow 11 percent in 2010 compared to 21 percent in 2009. The government is budgeting only a 7.3 percent rise in public works investment in 2010 after a doubling in 2009.

Urban fixed-asset investment, China's gauge of capital spending, rose 26.6 percent in January–February 2010 from a year earlier, the lowest gain in a year and down from a 30.5 percent growth in all of 2009. Railway spending grew 21.8 percent in January–February versus 50 percent in December 2009, and agriculture capital outlays decelerated to 9 percent from 37 percent.

Finances are also a concern. As is widely known, the stated government deficits excluded many enhancing items. Early in 2010, China counted money that will be spent in 2010 but was budgeted in 2009 as being spent that year. That maneuver violated China's cash accounting procedures but kept the 2010 budget deficit at 2.8 percent of GDP rather than hiking it to 3.5 percent.

Many spending and financing activities are pushed down to local governments where they disappear into off-balance-sheet categories. Those vehicles, which avoid rules against local government debt, were used in 2009 to borrow heavily from state banks to finance infrastructure projects such as dams, railroads, and bridges. Estimates are that those off-balance-sheet entities borrowed $880 billion to $1.6 trillion. Banks have been ordered to stop lending to these vehicles, so future infrastructure spending is in jeopardy. Furthermore, the central government gets most of the tax revenues so local authorities may not be able to repay these debts.

Bond buyers have become concerned over local government issues, and the central government will probably end up on the hook to bail them out. Some 26 of 28 provinces have budgeted slower growth in 2010 than in 2009 and, on average, expect their investments to rise 11 percentage points slower in 2010 than in 2009. The China Banking Regulatory Commission is worried about bank lending and wrote in June 1010 that "Domestically, the soundness of the banking sector is being tested by the increasing pressure of a nonperfoming loan rebound, by the potential credit risks associated with lending to local-government financing platforms, and by the real estate sector and industries with excess capacity."

Central Bank Tightens

Meanwhile, the Chinese central bank nudged up three-month Treasury bill rates in January 2010 to 1.37 percent. That's only up from

0.96 percent in early 2009, but rates hadn't increased since August 2009. The central bank also increased reserve requirements from 15.5 percent to 16 percent in January 2010 and then to 16.5 percent in February. The People's Bank of China (PBOC) seems to prefer reserve requirements in executing monetary policy, but in Western central banks, changing reserve requirements is considered a sledgehammer tactic. Can you recall the last time the Fed did so? The Fed prefers open market operations and adjusting the federal funds rate—that is, when the financial system isn't, as at present, in a liquidity trap when interest rates don't matter, as discussed earlier.

Note, however, that in China, interest rates don't matter as much as in the United States, even in normal times. Prodigious Chinese savers can't invest abroad and so have few choices except to deposit their money in state banks, even at low interest rates. World Bank President Robert Zoellick in March complained that the banks use their cheap deposits to lend to other state-owned firms. That pushes their profits above market-determined levels and adds to China's super-high national saving rate as well as fueling cheap exports. Also, the yuan exchange rate was pegged until recently (see Figure 7.1 in Chapter 7) and foreign money doesn't flow in or out in response to interest rate exchanges. Indeed, with a pegged currency and huge trade surpluses, the PBOC has to soak up the resulting inflow of dollars and other currencies through bond offerings and add to foreign currency reserves to avoid hyping the money supply even further.

Furthermore, unlike Western central banks, the PBOC tells the big state-controlled banks how much they can lend. So, in a year like 2010 when they know the central bank is tightening, they rush out to lend early in the year before the ax falls. In January 2010, the banks had lent 20 percent of the $1.1 trillion target set by the PBOC for the whole year. That target is 18 percent higher than in 2009, but in that year when the central bank encouraged an open floodgate, bank loans rose 30 percent from 2008. In February, they made $103 billion in new loans, half the January total and way below the $157 billion February 2009 level. Under PBOC direction, large state-controlled banks suspended lending in January after the huge outflow of $146 billion in the first two weeks.

The decision in June 2010 to again allow the yuan to fluctuate is also causing problems. In anticipation, capital flooded into China in the first quarter, money that also has to be sopped up by the central bank since the currency, while no longer pegged, isn't floating freely but is in what the bank calls a "managed floating exchange rate." This change may allay the fears of foreign critics who believe a cheap yuan is responsible for China's trade surplus, but it's not likely to make much difference. In 2005–2008, the yuan gained 21 percent against the dollar, but the U.S. trade deficit with China grew by one-third to $268 billion. As discussed earlier, it's the economic health of trading partners, not exchange rates, that largely determine export levels, and U.S. consumer retrenchment is the key to curbing China's exports, not a stronger yuan.

Open, Closed, or In Between

In a completely controlled economy, as China's used to be, the leaders may make economically-inefficient decisions but their authority is not disputed. In an open economy, as in Singapore, the markets make the decisions, for better or for worse, and politicians aren't involved. But in a partly open–partly market-driven economy, as is currently the case in China, control is very difficult. Government leaders making major decisions have to guess at market responses and unintended consequences. With a "managed floating exchange rate," for example, they have to estimate how much hot money will enter China in anticipation of a stronger currency, and then figure out how to neutralize any undesired consequences.

Real Estate

Real estate investment continued on a tear in early 2010 with spending up 31 percent in January–February versus a year earlier, compared with 25 percent in the fourth quarter of 2009. But house sales started to cool, rising 37 percent in January–February 2010 from a year earlier compared with 50 percent in 2009. In May 2010, sales fell 3.4 percent from a year earlier, the first decline since 2008, and were off 16 percent from April. Excess inventories may develop rapidly as demand cools since new construction starts in May were double the year-earlier level while developer land purchases jumped 44 percent. In the first quarter, property loans rose

44 percent from a year earlier compared to a 22 percent gain for all loans. With Chinese exports curtailed by U.S. consumer retrenchment, capital spending threatened by government restraints and excess capacity, and consumer spending less than robust, housing was the big generator of 2009 growth and is China's best hope for sustained economic gains. Construction accounted for 60 percent of China's economic growth in 2009.

But leaping prices bother the government, which has moved progressively, and especially in April 2010, to prevent speculation, even though the restraints in 2008 led to a collapse. Second-home buyers must now put down 50 percent of the purchase prices compared to 30 percent for first-time home buyers. The government is also pressing banks to contain mortgage lending, and some have recently raised mortgage rates. Also, new taxes may be imposed on residential property.

Chinese Consumers

With politically sensitive high unemployment rates in developed countries, government leaders in Europe and the United States are threatening China with protectionist measures as its economy continues to be export-led. China's mounting foreign currency reserves, $2.4 trillion in 2009 and up from $166 billion in 2000, make their point. Chinese officials say they're aiming for a domestically driven economy and are aware of the challenge to create one. Premier Wen Jiabao told the National People's Congress in early 2010, "There is insufficient internal impetus driving economic growth" as he warned of ongoing weakness in the global economy that will hamper Chinese exports. As I noted earlier, the key domestic weakness is the low level of consumer spending (Figure 11.2). Chinese consumers buy only 36 percent of GDP compared to over half in other Asian lands such as India and the Philippines and 71 percent in the United States. And, as our analysis revealed, it will be some years before the Chinese middle and upper income classes are big enough to drive the domestic economy.

Still, the Chinese government doesn't seem to be in any rush to stimulate consumer spending despite the goal set in 2004 to raise its share of the economic pie. In its 2010 budget, Beijing restrained not only capital spending growth, but also outlays on subsidized housing, social security, and education, compared to 2009 advances. The government continues to favor big business, such as bailing out state-controlled airlines while smaller competitors fail. It resists international calls for a stronger yuan that could make imports cheaper for consumers, although it might also retard exports and jobs.

In 2009, China instituted massive $14.8 billion tax breaks and subsidies for car buyers, compared to the U.S. $3 billion "cash for clunkers" program and $1.7 billion tax deduction for car purchases. The response in China was tremendous, but just as consumers began to postpone purchases in anticipation of even bigger subsidies, the government cut them back. So car sales in China are expected to rise only 5 to 6 percent in 2010 compared to the 50 percent leap in 2009 as potential buyers have less incentive. Also, many who might have purchased vehicles in 2010 or later have already done so. In June 2010, dealers had to offer discounts to move the metal. So the government reinstated some rebates on small-engine cars.

Big Savers

A key reason why Chinese spending is subdued is because households are such big savers. Even with their limited income, they save almost 30 percent of it on average (see Figure 11.4). They save because in a Confucian culture, people feel responsible for providing for their families. They also save a lot to cover unemployment, old age and medical costs, job insecurity risks, and their children's education. When the Communist leaders moved the economy from a cradle-to-grave nanny state to a progressively free market orientation starting in 1978, no meaningful unemployment, government retirement, or health systems were instituted to replace dismantled government programs, free education, housing, and lifetime job guarantees. Sure, Chinese pay low taxes, but with low taxes come low services, so Chinese must save prodigiously to provide for their own welfare and retirement.

The Chinese government is planning to institute retirement and health care plans, but probably will do so gradually. The government in 2009 set a goal of providing basic medical care for all Chinese by 2020.

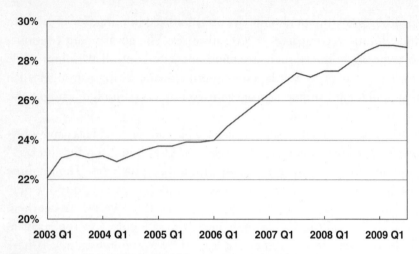

Figure 11.4 Chinese Household Saving Rate (Annual Average)
Data source: China National Bureau of Statistics.

But that's a decade away, and in China, basic medical care is very basic! The national pension fund hopes to double its assets to $300 billion by 2015, but that would be only 6 percent of 2009 GDP. More important, government retirement, health care, and other plans won't do as much to stimulate spending as many hope. That's because they'll require much higher taxes to offset their costs plus administrative expenses. More than one Chinese emperor was ousted and his dynasty terminated because of unpopular taxes on the peasant farmers.

Rising wages in China, however, may help consumer spending. Tightening labor markets have spawned wage increases of 20 to 30 percent, mostly for factory workers producing goods for foreign companies. Improving conditions in rival areas have reduced available labor as has China's one child per family policy. Manufacturers, however, plan to offset higher labor costs with higher productivity.

Excess Capacity

If Chinese consumer spending doesn't leap in the next several years, the nation will have a serious problem utilizing all the industrial capacity that's been built. The National Bureau of Statistics says that industrial capacity utilization in the fourth quarter of 2009 was 81.5 percent, even after that year's economic boom, and below the 84 percent in the first three quarters of recessionary 2008.

Capacity utilization numbers can be deceptive in the midst of a capital spending boom. It takes a lot of steel and cement to build more steel and cement plants, so while the process is going on, operating rates are much higher than after the bubble breaks and everyone wonders where all the excess capacity came from. This happened in the United States during the late 1990s tech bubble, the same phenomenon I foresee in China, but at a much higher level of technological sophistication than steel and cement plants. In the late 1990s, U.S. Internet usage was expected to grow by 100 percent every six months, so fiber optics producers strained to make enough cable to carry all that future traffic. But when the cable was installed and the reality of much slower Internet usage set in, only about 3 percent of capacity was being utilized.

Furthermore, I've never trusted Chinese government statistics, which seem more designed for propaganda purposes than to accurately depict the economy. Doesn't it seem odd that in China, where there are places you can't get into except by oxcart and then only in the dry season, the National Bureau of Statistics produces GDP numbers just 21 days after the close of the quarter in question? In the United States, with much better communications, data-gathering techniques, and analytical and statistician horsepower, it takes 29 days to come up with the first estimate of GDP. Then there's the consistency with which the economic growth forecasts of Chinese leaders prove to be accurate and the small size of any later revisions, compared to U.S. numbers.

Risks to Profits

Private analysts are probably more realistic than government statistics in estimating that China has enough unused steel-making capacity to equal the total output of Japan and South Korea, both big producers. Chinese businesses worry that excess capacity in industries such as steel, electrical power, chemicals, and cement will wound profits for years. Even the central bank deputy governor, Zhu Min, warned that the capital spending boom has resulted in massive surplus capacity in heavy industries such as steel, and that China's challenge is to strengthen consumer demand to absorb it.

But consumer spending is unlikely to absorb China's mushrooming industrial capacity as it continues to fall as a share of GDP and now accounts for only 36 percent compared to 71 percent in the United States. In past years, Chinese exports absorbed the rapid expansion in industrial capacity and were on a strong growth trend until U.S. consumers curtailed their purchases of Chinese products. Exports still account for 36.5 percent of GDP (Figure 11.2), but only 11 percent in the United States.

It is possible, of course, that Chinese leaders, constantly under pressure to create jobs, plan to have one crew build a steel plant, the next one dismantle it, the third crew rebuild it, and so forth. This, however, seems rather impractical and wasteful, and the plan could leak out, even in media-censored China, to embarrass the top brass.

Eight Percent Minimum

The Chinese economy is growing rapidly but it needs about 8 percent annual advances just to absorb all the people moving from rural areas to the cities, as noted earlier. In my view, that economy is still fundamentally driven by exports, which will continue to suffer as U.S. consumers retrench. China is probably a decade or more away from having a big enough middle class of free spenders who can drive the economy domestically. Meanwhile, its economy has been supported by massive government spending, which the government seems unwilling to continue due to financial strains and undesirable economic effects such as a housing boom and excessive industrial capacity.

That unutilized capacity portends weak profits and trouble for years for the loans that financed it. My judgment is that it will, as usual, be used for exports aimed at the United States and Europe. That will add to global excess supply and to downward pressure on prices. China and other export-dependent emerging economies will be fiercely competing in a world of slow growth and deflation for limited import demand by developed lands.

Meanwhile, Chinese economic policy persists in a stop-go pattern. The tightening phase in 2010 is reminiscent of 2007, which was augmented by the 2008 global recession. By late 2007, the Chinese government was trying to control the capital spending boom, which had outlays equal to 45 percent of GDP, far higher than India's 35 percent or the United States, where that component was 12 percent of GDP. Officials tightened up on the licensing of new electric generating plants, and imposed curbs on investment in autos, textiles, and other industries where excess capacity loomed.

The central bank was also concerned about 11 percent GDP growth in 2007 (Figure 11.3), far above the official 8 percent target, and about the flood of money coming in from exports and direct foreign investment. It raised its target interest rate five times by November 2007 to 7.29 percent for one-year loans, but that was still low relative to economic growth rates. The central bank also raised reserve requirements eight times that year to soak up excess liquidity. And it restarted, after a two-decade hiatus, a requirement for special deposits with the monetary authorities by financial institutions.

Unfortunate Timing

Absorption of export revenues and direct foreign investment money pushed foreign exchange reserves to total $1.43 trillion at the end of September 2007, up from $1.33 trillion at the end of June. The M2 money supply at the end of July was up 18.5 percent from a year earlier, and lending by all financial institutions at the end of July rose 16.5 percent from a year earlier and for the first seven months equaled 87 percent of 2006's total.

In our November 2007 report, we concluded that

> the risk is that the Chinese government and central bank finally curb the capital spending boom and excess liquidity just as exports weaken. Then, as excess capacity mounts, direct foreign investment inflows will disappear. And deflation will reign with a vengeance as producers slash prices to vie for the remaining domestic and export demand.

That's essentially what happened in 2008 as the effects of the Chinese fiscal and monetary restraint coincided with the worldwide economic slump. Economic growth dropped from 11 percent rates to 6 percent, which in China constituted a major recession. Of those who went back to their villages to celebrate the 2009 lunar new year, 20 million didn't return because their factory jobs had vanished along with Chinese exports. Don't be surprised if the same pattern develops in the next several years. Ironically, the Chinese economic restraint in 2010 is coinciding with the eurozone financial crisis, which threatens to spread to another global recession.

12. Japan—A Slow Train Wreck

My 1988 book, *After the Crash*, written when the Japanese bubble economy was still mushrooming, compared Japan's 1980s exuberance in real estate, stocks, and its economy with the Roaring Twenties in the United States. I went on to predict a deflationary depression in Japan in the 1990s, similar to that in America in the 1930s, as discussed in Chapter 2.

As Japan entered its long slump in the early 1990s, I suggested that, for two reasons, it could last even longer than its U.S. counterpart 50 years earlier. First, huge World War II spending is what really revived the United States, and nothing like that was on the horizon. Second, even though Japan could have learned how to use economy-reviving tools from the U.S. experience, its decision-making process is so torturously slow, by American standards, that it could take more than a decade to resolve its financial problems and clear the decks for renewed economic growth.

Where's the Action?

Well, as they say, the rest is history. The Nikkei stock index hit its peak of almost 39,000 on the last trading day of 1989, and then, in a sawtooth pattern, declined to less than half that, and is still in a downtrend (Figure 2.2 in Chapter 2). Japan has suffered repeated recessions since 1990, with weak growth in between (Figure 7.7 in Chapter 7).

Deflation has become a way of life in Japan, with prices falling more often than they've risen since 1990. Land prices sprinted 329 percent from 1980 to their peak in 1990, but fell back to 1980 levels (Figure 2.3). The unemployment rate has trended up from 2 percent in 1990 to 5 percent in early 2010.

As a result, it's not surprising that although Japan remains the second largest economy in the world, its status is slipping. Per-capita GDP leaped beyond that of the United States in the late 1980s but then stalled and now is a quarter lower than America's and only nineteenth highest in the world. In 1988, eight of the globe's 10 largest public companies by market capitalization were Japanese. Now, none make the list.

Monetary Response

The Bank of Japan (BOJ) helped collapse the 1980s housing and stock bubbles by raising interest rates starting on May 31, 1989, as mentioned in Chapter 2. Those rate increases were followed by the bursting of the stock and real estate bubbles soon thereafter.

After the bubbles broke, the central bank slashed its reference overnight rate to zero and has kept it close to that level ever since (Figure 7.6 in Chapter 7), and pumped money into the economy (Figure 7.5), but to no avail. Notice (Figure 7.6) that even if nominal rates are zero, in deflation, dispirited borrowers are discouraged by positive real rates. And zero is as low as central bank rates can go. Japan's financial system remains in the classic liquidity trap where no interest rate is low enough to encourage scared borrowers to borrow or reluctant lenders to lend. Substantial quantitative easing by the BOJ as it bought government bonds didn't help much, either. And so far, government pressure on the central bank to promote inflation hasn't worked. Indeed, the trend since the mid-1990s has been to repay loans.

Until 2001, Tokyo allowed banks to roll over bad business loans because calling them would force many companies into bankruptcy and spike unemployment, while writing off those loans would destroy bank capital. So the zombie banks that everyone knew were walking dead were allowed to continue to exist.

In 2001, however, Junichiro Koizumi was elected Prime Minister with promises to let fail those troubled companies that previously were propped up under the Japanese culture of long-term harmonious relations and job retention. Further, he said that bad bank loans to those firms and other questionable loans would be cleaned up one way or another. Despite his successful efforts, Japan's deflationary depression continued.

Fiscal Action

While monetary stimulus proved ineffective, the Japanese government worked diligently to try to revive the economy through fiscal means. Still, much of the government spending was squandered in paving rural riverbeds, building bridges to nowhere, and other projects motivated by Japan's archaic political representation system that favors rural areas. Little was spent on projects that would encourage economic activity, such as additional runways at Tokyo's big Narita airport or freeways in that traffic-clogged city. In fact, in early 2010, Japan opened the Ibaraki Airport, which cost $243 million and is expected to lose $22 million in its first year of operation. It's located a 90-minute bus ride from Tokyo and has only one flight a day, to Seoul.

On balance, fiscal stimulus was more than offset by economic weakness in many years in the 1990s, resulting in a multiplier of less than 100 percent, even a negative multiplier in 1997. Much of this questionable government infrastructure spending has been financed by Japan Post. It not only delivers the mail but also has huge nationwide banking and insurance operations with $3 trillion in assets, making it one of the world's biggest financial institutions. In effect, the government used Japan Post for its slush fund for the financing of politically popular public projects (how's that for alliteration?). In October 2007, the government began a 10-year process of privatizing Japan Post under a plan initiated by the Koizumi administration.

But the later Prime Minister, Yukio Hatoyama, was elected in part by promises to undo Koizumi's free market initiatives, and his successor, Naoto Kan, is continuing his policies. So the plans to privatize Japan Post have been rescinded and initiatives to sell equity in its banking and insurance arms have been frozen. Indeed, the postal services minister has proposed big increases in the limits on consumer deposits in postal savings accounts and insurance, which, of course, compete with private sector institutions. I'm old enough to remember America's postal savings accounts in World War II. I recall, however, that the U.S. Post Office went out of that business shortly afterward to concentrate on its inefficient, constitutionally guaranteed monopoly on mail delivery.

As a result, government deficits in Japan in the 1990s and most of the 2000s in relation to GDP were much bigger than in the United

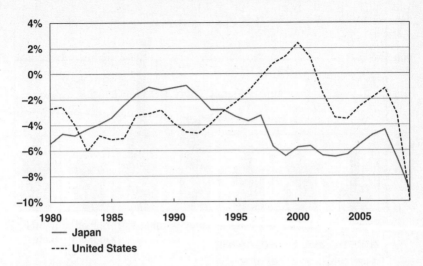

Figure 11.5 Japanese and U.S. Central Government Budget Balances as a Percentage of GDP, 2003–2009
Data sources: Office of Management and Budget and Japanese Ministry of Finance.

States (see Figure 11.5). And Japanese net government debt has leaped in relation to GDP, from 15.1 percent in 1990 to 105 percent in 2009. In most countries, gross government debt includes borrowings by one branch of the government from another, and should be netted out to determine what is coming from outside sources. These intergovernment transactions are especially large in Japan, so its gross debt-to-GDP ratio of over 200 percent dropped to about 100 percent on a net basis, about the same level as profligate Italy among G-7 countries (see Figure 11.6).

Japanese Consumer Savers

Financing Japanese government debt and deficits has not been a problem in Japan. The good news is that until recent years, big-saving Japanese consumers provided the funds so the government deficits were financed domestically. The bad news is that until recently, big-saving Japanese consumers provided the funds, which meant they weren't spending the money. In fact, there was so much saving left over that Japan had money to export. That's shown in its perennial trade and current account surpluses (see Figure 9.8 in Chapter 9).

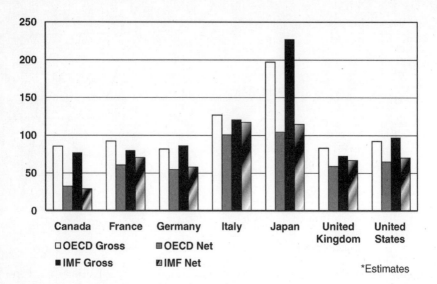

Figure 11.6 Debt as a Percentage of GDP, 2010
Data sources: Organisation for Economic Co-operation and Development (OECD) and the International Monetary Fund (IMF).

Of people I've rubbed noses with, Brazilians are the most optimistic, Americans slightly less positive in outlook, Europeans more fatalistic, and the Japanese the most negative. They seem to look for the worst to happen, all of the time. Only when Japanese businessmen are out drinking with their buddies do they seem happy.

Years ago, my wife and I were in Tokyo and attended a kabuki play. It was a marvelous production with the colorful costumes, emphatic speeches, and chanting choruses. The playgoers got headsets that provided a wonderful English translation. So we knew that when one of the principal actors made a dramatic outreach of his arm, he wasn't hailing a cab but rather signaling the impending doom of the cosmos.

Ninety-Seven Percent Dead

During the intermission, the translator discussed the history of classical Japanese drama. He cited a scholar who had studied the Kabuki plays, the Noh plays that preceded them, and the even-earlier Japanese legends. His study included only those written before World War II, which is important because that was an unmitigated disaster for Japan. Before it happened, unconditional surrender and foreign occupation of Japan were unthinkable.

That Japanese scholar found that in all of classic literature, the hero ends up dead 97 percent of the time. Wow! That instantly confirmed my suspicions about the Japanese character. Even the ancient Greek dramas didn't have that high a body count!

Not only has much of Japanese fiscal stimulus been spent on public works of little value, but until recently, the financially cautious employees ultimately paid to do the work saved much of it. Then they lent it back to the government, directly or indirectly, through banks and insurance companies to fund the deficits created by big public outlays. Sure, it's nice to fund huge government deficits internally and not rely on the kindness of strangers abroad. But if Japanese consumers had spent the money like spendthrift Americans of yesteryear, the Japanese economy would have been much stronger and there would not have been the need for nonstop big fiscal stimulus programs. In September 2009, foreigners held only 5.8 percent of Japanese government banks. In the United States, 30 percent of Treasuries are held by foreign governments, and foreign private holdings bring the number to about 50 percent.

Different Thinking

I must confess, every time I visit Japan, I come back convinced that I understand less about how the Japanese people think than I did on my previous trip. They dress about the same as Americans. They drive on the left, but the downtown buildings in their cities look about the same. They're smart people and I'm sure their thinking is logical, but it's quite different from ours. How do you otherwise explain that the most chauvinistic nation I'm aware of has English names on all the cars produced and sold in Japan?

In the 1930s U.S. deflationary depression, American consumers lacked incomes. So the results were completely logical: No money, no spending. In the 1990s–2000s Japanese deflationary depression, consumers in Japan had the money but didn't want to spend it. Where's the logic? Were they too scared about the future? Were they content with their lifestyles and not desirous of more goods and services? Maybe, but the increase in the national sales tax to 5 percent in 1997 turned the modest economic recovery then under way into instant recession (see Figure 7.7 in Chapter 7).

American consumers are moving toward the Japanese model as they embark on a long-run saving spree, as discussed in Chapter 9. They're using much of that money to buy Treasurys directly and to repay debts. And since money is fungible, it's recycled back to finance Treasury deficits. But unlike their Japanese counterparts, U.S. consumers need to save. They don't trust volatile stocks (Figure 1.6) to finance future financial needs. Through cash-out mortgage financing and home equity loans, combined with the nosedive in house prices (Figure 1.2), their home equity is depleted (Figure 3.5). U.S. households' net worth in relation to disposable (after-tax) income is lower than in the 1950s (Figure 4.1). The postwar babies haven't saved for retirement and desperately need to. And with chronically high unemployment (Figure 2.1), American households are only beginning to increase their saving rate from a record low level (Figure 2.5) and reduce their debt and debt service levels from record highs (Figure 4.4).

Unsustained Pattern

The kabuki dance between the Japanese government and consumer continues. In April 2010, the government announced plans to spend a $10.6 billion emergency reserve to kick-start the economy and the Bank of Japan is offering one-year loans to banks at 0.1 percent interest rates if they lend the money to companies. Still, bank loans in June 2010 fell from a year earlier for the seventh straight month. Meanwhile, consumers are embracing cheap fashions, but even the retailers of those goods were seeing a shift from earlier explosive growth to declining sales in early 2010. Consumer prices in April fell 1.5 percent from a year earlier after a 1.2 percent slide in March, so Japanese consumers continue to wait for even-lower prices before buying.

Regardless of the logic of the Japanese government fiscal stimulus being saved by consumers and then recycled back to the government to finance its deficits and then some, the mechanism is unsustainable.

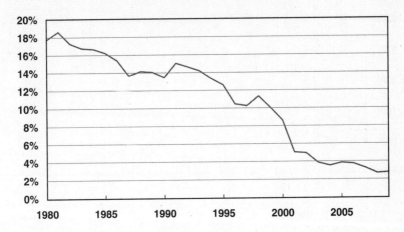

Figure 11.7 Japanese Saving Rate, 1980–2009
Data source: OECD.

Consumer spending has been essentially flat since the mid-1990s, while exports have provided what little growth there was in the economy. Furthermore, consumer borrowing has gone nowhere since 1990. But their saving rate has fallen sharply since the 1990s, especially since 1998, from very high levels to 2.8 percent in 2009 (see Figure 11.7). What's going on there?

Kentaro Kalayama, a visiting scholar at the Japanese Ministry of Finance, points to four factors that have pushed down the consumer saving rate. First, the economic stagnation in Japan has reduced consumer incomes and robbed consumers of the growth that earlier went into high saving. Second, increases in old-age pensions and public long-term care insurance reduced financial risks and the need to save, especially by older people. Third, attitudes in Japan have changed, with consumers putting more emphasis on enjoying life here and now and less on preparing for the future with saving and investment.

Finally, Japan's population is falling (see Figure 11.8), the most rapidly of any G-7 country. Fertility rates there are also the lowest of major developed countries at 1.21, well below the 2.1 needed to sustain population in the long run. Many younger Japanese women now have professional job opportunities available to them and are delaying or avoiding marriage and being confined at home as mothers. In addition, the number of older Japanese is growing much faster than their counterparts elsewhere, and

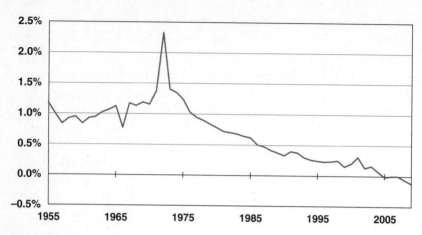

Figure 11.8 Japanese Population, Year/Year Percent Change, 1955–2009
Data source: Japanese Statistics Bureau.

the Japanese have the highest life expectancy of any developed country. Older people save less than younger folks as their incomes drop in retirement, and they systematically cash in their savings since they still consume.

Also, Japan is the least friendly to immigrants of any major country so it lacks the influx of people from abroad who are usually younger and save more. There's no such thing as an immigration visa, although foreigners have been allowed in during times of labor shortages for extended "training sessions." As I understand it, baseball is not a native Japanese sport and, like golf, was the result of emulation during the American occupation after World War II. Yet Japanese baseball teams are allowed no more than three foreigners.

Commodore Perry

In 1853, American Commodore Matthew C. Perry arrived in Japan to negotiate a trade treaty with that country, which then limited foreign trade to the Netherlands and in only one port. He also went because the United States was tiring of the way the Japanese welcomed our shipwrecked sailors—by killing them on the beaches. The representatives of the shogun, the feudal leader of Japan, tried to throw him out so Perry shot up a few portside buildings to demonstrate American naval power.

He then presented a letter of demands from President Millard Fillmore and left to return a year later with twice as many ships. They also had modern steam engines and other industrial equipment on their decks, and Perry invited the Japanese warlords on board to see what industrial might was all about. They promptly signed the American treaty, but also concluded that, militarily, their swords and spears were a bit behind the times. So they threw out the shogun, resurrected the figurehead emperor in the late 1800s Meiji Restoration, and embarked on the forced industrialization of Japan. It proceeded so quickly that they nearly beat the Russians in their 1906 war.

Today, Perry is respected in Japan for opening the country to the rest of the world. As I write, I am looking at a First Day of Issue envelope with a 10-yen stamp issued on May 17, 1960, and given to me years ago by a Japanese friend. The stamp has a sailing ship in a storm with a Japanese flag and the cover envelope says in English, "The Centennial Anniversary of the Japanese-American Treaty of Amity and Commerce."

The Ministry of Finance economist cited earlier believes the Japanese consumer saving rate will continue to fall as the population ages and consumers continue to put a higher value on spending now rather than saving for later. He concludes that "the saving rate will continue to decline or level off at least" and that "the slogan of 'saving is a virtue' could be a relic." Still, even with the enjoy-the-good-life-now motive, consumer spending in Japan has been flat since 1990. In contrast, that attitude pushed U.S. consumer spending from 62 percent of GDP in the early 1980s to 71 percent now (Figure 6.4). Does it boil down to how optimistic a culture is?

A Substitute for U.S. Consumers?

I expect the retrenchment of U.S. consumers to continue for a decade and to push the saving rate back into double digits (Figure 2.5). That will remove American consumers as the buyers of first and last resort for the world's excess good and services and the direct and indirect drivers of economic growth in many countries, including Japan and China. Notice in Figure 6.9 (Chapter 6) that the U.S. current account and trade deficits

Table 11.1 Ratio of Working-Age to Retirement-Age Populations

Year	Canada	France	Germany	Italy	Japan	United Kingdom	United States
1960	7.7	5.3	6.3	7.5	10.5	5.6	6.5
1990	5.9	4.7	4.5	4.7	5.8	4.3	5.3
2010	4.7	4.1	2.8	3.9	3.4	4.5	5.3
2030	3.5	3.3	3.0	3.4	3.0	3.9	4.9
2040	2.6	2.6	2.1	2.4	2.6	3.0	3.1

Data sources: Federal Reserve Bank of St. Louis and OECD.

grew earlier as U.S. consumers spent freely on everything in clothing imports, and for every 1 percent increase in their spending, U.S. imports rise 2.4 percent. Now they're retrenching and those U.S. deficits have been cut in half. As this trend continues and most countries want to export and there is no big net importer, protectionism is sure to result.

Will another country replace the United States as the economic engine that absorbs the globe's excess goods and services? Maybe, but none have yet volunteered for the job. It's unlikely to be Europe, with its traditional disdain for imports in favor of job-sustaining local production. Japan, however, could end up being the world's next big importer. All major countries have rapidly aging populations, but Japan's is the most extreme. One reason for this is the long life spans of the Japanese. In future years, Japan, like the United States, Canada, and European nations, will face a dwindling number of workers to support retirees (Table 11.1). In 1990, Japan had 5.8 people of working age for every one of retirement age, but that ratio is projected to fall to 3.0 by the year 2030. In contrast, the ratio in the United States should drop from 5.3 in 1990 to 4.9 in 2030. Compared with other developing countries, Japan will be devoting much more of its economic strength to taking care of nonworking citizens in future years.

But due to decades of saving more than was needed for domestic investment, Japan has been exporting capital. Those outflows have cumulated into $765 billion in U.S. Treasury obligations and a total of $2.8 trillion net foreign assets around the globe at the end of 2009. Japan in the decades ahead could simply sell those piles of foreign assets and use the money to buy the imports needed to supply its retirees. Otherwise, those still working will be strained to produce enough for themselves and retirees, and the result could be intergenerational warfare to split an inadequate economic pie.

No other major developed country that faces an aging population except Japan has that horde of foreign assets to cash in. Unfortunately, this will not happen as long as Japan has its "export or die" mentality.

What's Supporting Japan's Current Account?

With their falling saving rate, Japanese consumers are no longer financing the government deficits with enough money left over to sustain chronic current account surpluses (Figure 9.8 in Chapter 9). So what sector is filling the breach? By definition, the current account balance is the difference between gross national saving by consumers, business, and government, and total gross saving by the same three sectors. In this context, *gross* refers to measures before the subtraction of capital consumption or depreciation. If it's positive, as in Japan, saving exceeds investment needs and the rest is exported. If negative, as in the United States, saving is insufficient to finance domestic investment and funds need to be imported to fill the gap.

In Japan, household gross saving in excess of gross capital spending is slipping as the saving rate swoons (Figure 11.7). That trend is likely to continue, as discussed earlier. The government continues to run a deficit as its gross saving is about zero while gross investment is positive. So that leaves it up to the corporate sector where interesting things are happening. Notice in Figure 11.9 that gross corporate saving from retained earnings and depreciation continues the uptrend since the 1980s, but that gross capital spending has been flat since 1990. Thus, as of the mid-1990s, the business sector has been a saver on balance, and. most of that uptrend in gross saving has come from capital consumption in the nonfinancial corporate sector.

Opposite in the United States

In contrast, in the United States, the negative spread between gross national saving and investment is reflected in the zero difference between

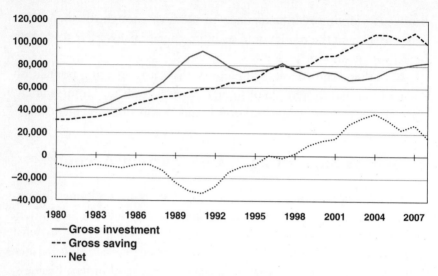

Figure 11.9 Japanese Business Gross Savings and Investment (in Billions of Yen)
Data source: ESRI.

household saving and investment as of 2008, with 2009 numbers yet to be reported. The U.S. government, of course, is running big deficits and, therefore, negative differences between gross saving and investment. And in the business sector, gross saving and investment have remained about equal over the years.

Back in Japan, the stagnation in corporate capital spending (see Figure 11.9) and its decline as a share of GDP come in the face of rising exports. Now, we know that in recent years, Japanese exports have more and more been capital goods that it sends to China and other Asian lands, which then make U.S.-bound consumer products. That explanation is a bit oversimplified, but gets to the essence of the process. So in recent years, Japanese business has been very efficient in producing capital goods exports without increasing its capital spending. Indeed, core machinery orders fell 9.1 percent in May 2010 from April.

But as U.S. consumers continue to retrench and retard imports, China will cut its growth in already excessive industrial capacity, and that will include capital equipment and other Japanese exports. Absent strong domestic demand, weak exports, in turn, will keep capital spending subdued and, in time, Japanese gross corporate saving in the form of capital

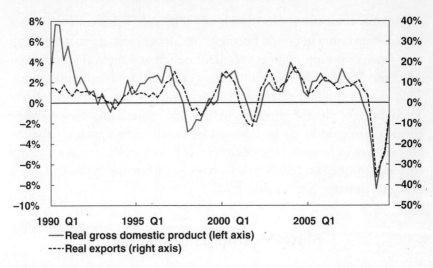

Figure 11.10 Japanese Real GDP and Exports—Year/Year Percent Change
Data source: Japanese Cabinet Office.

consumption and retained earnings will weaken. The net effect will be to depress Japan's current account, probably to negative territory—unless the economy comes to life with much more consumer income and saving and with the disappearance of government incentives to run big deficits by providing fiscal stimulus. Japan's current account fell 8.1 percent in May 2010 from a year earlier. Bear in mind that exports have been the only area of strength, except for government spending, in the Japanese economy for years. Notice the close link between exports and GDP growth since 1990, shown in Figure 11.10. That's why the government in early 2010 mounted a campaign to spur exports of infrastructure goods such as super-fast bullet trains and nuclear reactors.

Interest Rate Woes

A current account deficit in Japan would cause serious problems because it would then be importing, not exporting, money. And since this would probably occur in a moribund economy, few investment opportunities would attract foreign capital or encourage Japanese with foreign assets to sell them to return the money home. So interest rates would need to rise appreciably from current low levels of a little over 1 percent for 10-year Japanese government bonds. Furthermore, debt rating agencies are tiring over Japan's nonstop huge government deficit and mounting sovereign debt, and Standard & Poor's and Moody's have threatened downgrades. Such actions would further hike Japanese interest rates and bond yields. Then, Japan's immense government debt (see Figure 11.6), even if almost entirely domestically owned, would be much more expensive for the government to finance. Higher rates would also end the yen as a funding currency for the carry trade in which investors borrow in yen and invest in higher-interest-rate countries.

Slow-Motion Train Wreck

Japan looks like a slow-motion train wreck. Despite its 20-year deflationary depression, the yen has strengthened on balance over those two decades, much to the frustration of many currency traders. But Japan's aging and declining population and troubled export outlook may finally be catching up with it. I won't make a precise forecast, but in my judgment, the yen will weaken considerably against the dollar in the next five to 10 years.

There are, then, a number of investment areas to sell or avoid in the atmosphere of slow economic growth and deflation I foresee over the next decade. You might consider the 12 I've just discussed. But there will be winners, 10 by my analysis, as discussed in Chapter 12.

Chapter 12

Ten Investments to Buy

There are a number of winning investment sectors in an era of slower economic growth that investors should consider. In this chapter, I explore 10 of them:

1. Treasurys and other high-quality bonds.
2. Income-producing securities.
3. Food and other consumer staples.
4. Small luxuries.
5. The U.S. dollar.
6. Investment advisers and financial planners.
7. Factory-built housing and rental apartments.
8. Health care.
9. Productivity enhancers.
10. North American energy.

1. Treasurys and Other High-Quality Bonds

Full disclosure: I've been a bull on 30-year Treasurys since 1981 when I stated, "We're entering the bond rally of a lifetime." It's still under way, in my opinion. Their yields back then were 14.7 percent, but my forecast called for huge declines in inflation and, with it, a gigantic fall in bond yields to my eventual target of 3 percent. The 30-year Treasury yield actually fell to 2.6 percent at the end of 2008 amid serious fears of financial meltdown and a stampede to the world's ultimate safe haven, Treasurys. So in our January 2009 *Insight*, we declared "mission accomplished" and removed Treasury bonds from our recommended list. In 2008, the 30-year Treasury returned 42 percent—37.5 percent in appreciation and 4.5 percent in yield—while the S&P 500 fell 39 percent. And I assure you that stodgy old Treasury bonds are only suitable for widows and orphans!

But then Treasurys sold off in the early months of 2009, pushing the yield on the 30-year bond close to 5 percent. So we've subsequently reactivated the strategy with our forecast of a return in yields to 3.0 percent or lower. Treasurys will continue to be a safe haven in a troubled world and benefit from deflation.

A decline in yields from 4.0 percent in July 2010 to 3.0 percent may not sound like much, but the bond price would appreciate 20 percent. If it occurs over two years, then two years' worth of interest is collected, and the total return on the 30-year Treasury would be 28 percent. On a 30-year zero-coupon Treasury, which pays no interest but is issued at a discount, the total return would be 34 percent.

Notice that my zeal for Treasury bonds is driven by the prospect for appreciation, not yield. Going back to the early 1980s, I've never been interested in the level of bond yields but only in the appreciation as it goes down. I've liked Treasury bonds for the same reason investors like stocks—appreciation. Who would own the S&P 500 Index solely for its current miserly dividend yield of 2 percent?

Lock Up for Infinity?

A vivid example of this reality occurred in March 2006—before the 2007–2009 nosedive in stocks and leap in Treasury bond prices. I was invited by Professor Jeremy Siegel to Wharton for a public debate on stocks versus bonds. He, of course, favored stocks and I advocated Treasury bonds. At one point, he addressed the audience of about 500 and said, "I don't know why anyone in their right mind would tie up their money for 30 years for a 4.75 percent yield [the then-yield on the 30-year Treasury]." When it came my turn to reply, I asked the audience, "What's the maturity on stocks?" I got no answer, but pointed out that unless a company merges or goes bankrupt, the maturity on its stock is infinity—it has no maturity. My follow-up question was, "What is the yield on stocks?" to which someone correctly replied, "It's 2 percent on the S&P 500 Index."

So I continued, "I don't know why anyone would tie up money for infinity for a 2 percent yield." I was putting the query, apples to apples, in the same framework as Professor Siegel's rhetorical question. Of course, he isn't the only one who hates bonds in general and Treasurys in particular. And because of that, Treasurys, unlike stocks, are seldom the subject of irrational exuberance. Their leap in price in the dark days in late 2008 (see Figure 1.5 in Chapter 1) is a rare exception to a market that seldom gets giddy, despite the declining trend in yields and related decline in prices for almost three decades.

Stockholders inherently hate Treasurys. Shareholders say they don't understand them. But their quality has been unquestioned, at least until recently, as I discuss later. Treasurys and the forces that move yields are well-defined—Fed policy and inflation or deflation (Figure 1.5) are among the few important factors. Stock prices, by contrast, depend on the business cycle, conditions in that particular industry, Congressional legislation, the quality of company management, merger and acquisition possibilities, corporate accounting, company pricing power, new and old product potentials, and myriad other variables.

Stockholders also understand that Treasurys normally rally in weak economic conditions, which are negative for stock prices, so declining Treasury yields are a bad omen. It was only individual investors' extreme distaste for stocks in 2009 after their bloodbath collapse that precipitated the rush into bond mutual funds that year. They plowed $69 billion into long-term municipal bond funds alone in that year, up from only $8 billion in 2008 and $11 billion in 2007.

Those who worry more about inflation than deflation also hate bonds, which tend to fall in price as inflation rates rise. These worriers include individual and institutional investors. Wall Street denizens also hate Treasurys, as I learned firsthand while at Merrill Lynch and then White, Weld. Investment bankers didn't want me along on client visits when I was forecasting lower interest rates. They wanted projections of higher rates that would encourage corporate clients to issue bonds immediately, not wait for lower rates and cheaper financing.

Professional managers of bond funds are a sober bunch who perennially fret about inflation, higher yields, and subsequent losses on their portfolio. And if yields fall, they don't rejoice over bond appreciation but worry about reinvesting their interest coupons at lower yields. Even the 18 primary dealers who have the privilege of dealing directly with the Fed on Treasurys seem to always see the dark side. In a poll of all 18 in April 2010 when the yield on the 10-year Treasury note was 3.8 percent, most expected 4 percent or higher yields at the end of 2010. In August, it was down to 3.0 percent.

Kudlow's Call

CNBC's Larry Kudlow was extremely doubtful of my 3 percent forecast for the yield on 30-year Treasurys and even lower rates for 10-year Treasury notes. So in late 2007, he told me on camera that if the 10-year note yield fell below 3.5 percent, he'd take me to dinner in a fine New York City restaurant with our wives. On May 15, 2008, the Shillings were treated to a wonderful dinner by the Kudlows at upscale La Grenouille. As of late August 2010, yields on the 10-year bond were about 2.5 percent.

I've been pretty lonely as a Treasury bond bull for 29 years, but as noted in Chapter 1, I'm comfortable being in the minority and tend to make more money in that position than by running with the herd. Incidentally, I continue to favor the 30-year bond over the 10-year note, which became the benchmark after the Treasury in 2001 stopped issuing the "long bond," as the most recently issued 30-year bond is called. At that time, the Treasury was retiring debt because of the short-lived federal government surpluses (see Figure 3.1 in Chapter 3) caused by the post–Cold War decline in defense spending and big capital gains and other tax collections associated with the Internet stock bubble (shown in

Figure 1.1 in Chapter 1). But after the federal budget returned to deficits as usual, the Treasury resumed long bond issues in 2006. In addition, after stock losses in the 2000–2002 bear market, many pension funds wanted longer-maturity Treasurys to match against the pension benefit liability that stretched further into the future as people live longer.

I also prefer the long bond because maturity matters to appreciation when rates decline. Because of compound interest, a 30-year bond increases in value much more for each percentage point decline in interest rates than does a shorter maturity bond. Note that at recent interest rates, a one percentage point fall in rates increases the price of a 5-year Treasury note by about 5 percent, a 10-year note by around 8.5 percent, but a 30-year bond by around 20 percent. Unfortunately, this works both ways, so if interest rates go up, you'll lose much more on the bond than the notes if rates rise the same for both.

If you really believe, as I do, that interest rates are going down, you want to own the longest-maturity bond possible. This is true even if short-term rates were to fall twice as much as 30-year bond yields. Many investors don't understand this and want only to buy a longer-maturity bond if its yield is higher.

Others only buy fixed-income securities that mature when they need the money back. Or they will buy a ladder of bonds that mature in a series of future dates. This strikes me as odd, especially for Treasurys that trade hundreds of billions of dollars' worth each day and can be easily bought and sold without disturbing the market price. Of course, when you need the cash, interest rates may have risen and you'll sell at a loss, whereas if you hold a bond until it matures, you'll get the full par value unless it defaults in the meanwhile. But what about stocks? They have no maturity so you're never sure you'll get back what you pay for them.

Mom's Misunderstanding

I saw this common investor attitude firsthand in the mid-1980s when I took over the management of my parents' securities. I don't think it was that they trusted my investment prowess as much as the fact that their broker of some 30 years retired. Soon after we restructured the portfolio, I got a call from my mother.

"Gary," she said, "I see that you put Treasury bonds in our account that won't mature for 30 years."

"That's right, Mom," I replied. "We think interest rates are going down and so they'll appreciate nicely."

"But Gary," she rejoined, "Dad and I won't be around in 30 years."

"Maybe, Mom," I noted, "but we won't necessarily still have them in your portfolio in 30 years even if you are still alive." Well, Dad died in 1999 at age 91 and Mom lived to 100.

It may surprise you that there's about 20 percent left in this "bond rally of a lifetime." After all, the decline in Treasury bond yields from 14.7 percent to 4.0 percent has already been accomplished, so the expected further fall to 3 percent doesn't sound like much. But as you'll note from Table 12.1, the decline in yields from 15 percent to 14 percent results in 7.0 percent appreciation for a 30-year coupon bond, but a fall from 4 percent to 3 percent gives a 19.6 percent gain.

So there's still time, brother, to make substantial money in the long bond. You may recall that line from the 1959 movie, *On the Beach*. In the aftermath of nuclear war, Australia is the only place left where people have not yet died from irradiation. Consequently, the Christian

Table 12.1 Coupon Bonds—Return on 1 Percentage Point Decline in Interest Rates

Yield	30 Years	25 Years	20 Years	15 Years	10 Years	5 Years	2 Years
15%							
14%	7.0%	6.9%	6.7%	6.2%	5.3%	3.5%	1.65%
13%	7.5%	7.4%	7.1%	6.6%	5.5%	3.6%	1.68%
12%	8.1%	7.9%	7.5%	6.9%	5.7%	3.7%	1.70%
11%	8.7%	8.5%	8.1%	7.4%	6.0%	3.7%	1.73%
10%	9.5%	9.2%	8.6%	7.8%	6.2%	3.8%	1.75%
9%	10.3%	10.0%	9.2%	8.3%	6.5%	3.9%	1.78%
8%	11.3%	10.9%	9.9%	8.8%	6.8%	4.0%	1.80%
7%	12.5%	11.9%	10.7%	9.3%	7.1%	4.2%	1.83%
6%	13.8%	13.0%	11.6%	10.0%	7.5%	4.3%	1.85%
5%	15.4%	14.3%	12.6%	10.6%	7.8%	4.4%	1.88%
4%	17.4%	15.9%	13.7%	11.4%	8.2%	4.5%	1.90%
3%	19.6%	17.7%	15.0%	12.2%	8.6%	4.6%	1.92%
2%	22.0%	19.8%	16.4%	13.1%	9.0%	4.7%	1.95%

evangelists are advocating repentance and acceptance of Christ while they conduct parades, complete with signs that read, "There's Still Time, Brother!" But don't carry this little joke too far. We're not suggesting that once 3 percent long bond yields are reached, those securities become lethal. Far from it. With 2 to 3 percent deflation, the real yield would be 5 to 6 percent, at least twice the post–World War II average of 2.5 percent.

Zero-Coupon Bonds

Bond interest payments are important in boosting total return because of the compounding effect. As bond yields fall, though, the reinvestment interest rates decline as well. When yields were 10 percent, the interest received could be reinvested at 10 percent. At a 5 percent interest rate, the reinvestment earns only half as much.

The problem can be eliminated with zero-coupon bonds—also known as stripped bonds, or strips, because the coupons often are separated, or stripped, from the bond itself. They pay no interest, only one final payment at maturity. They are bought at a discount to that fixed final price and, in effect, the current interest rate is locked in. At 5 percent yields, for example, a zero coupon Treasury that matures in 30 years at $1,000 sells at $228.60 since $228.60 compounded at 5 percent for 30 years equals $1,000.

By eliminating this reinvestment risk, zero-coupon bonds deliver much more bang per buck as interest rates fall than do interest-paying bonds, as shown earlier. On a 30-year zero-coupon bond, a decline in rates from 15 percent to 14 percent boosts the price by 30 percent, and a drop from 4 percent to 3 percent leads to 34 percent appreciation (see Table 12.2).

By comparing Tables 12.1 and 12.2, you're seeing two big differences between coupon and zero-coupon bonds. First, the price increases per decline in yields are much greater, especially for long-maturity bonds. Consequently, a yield drop from 6 percent to 3 percent boosts the 30-year zero price by 137 percent compared with 63 percent for the coupon bond, excluding coupon payments. Second, the appreciation for each percentage point decline in yield increases very slowly for zeros compared with coupon bonds, due to the absence of the coupon reinvestment risk.

Table 12.2 Zero-Coupon Bonds—Return on 1 Percentage Point Decline in Interest Rates

Yield	30 Years	25 Years	20 Years	15 Years	10 Years	5 Years	2 Years
15%							
14%	30%	24%	19%	14%	9%	4.5%	1.8%
13%	30%	25%	19%	14%	9%	4.5%	1.8%
12%	31%	25%	19%	14%	9%	4.5%	1.8%
11%	31%	25%	20%	14%	9%	4.6%	1.8%
10%	31%	25%	20%	15%	9%	4.6%	1.8%
9%	32%	26%	20%	15%	10%	4.7%	1.8%
8%	32%	26%	20%	15%	10%	4.7%	1.9%
7%	32%	26%	20%	15%	10%	4.8%	1.9%
6%	33%	26%	21%	15%	10%	4.8%	1.9%
5%	33%	27%	21%	15%	10%	4.9%	1.9%
4%	33%	27%	21%	15%	10%	4.9%	1.9%
3%	34%	27%	21%	16%	10%	4.9%	1.9%
2%	34%	28%	22%	16%	10%	5.0%	2.0%

Not Tax-Friendly

Coupon and zero-coupon bonds, however, are not tax-friendly. The appreciation in zeros in lieu of interest payments is taxed annually, even if they aren't sold. So, too, is the appreciation caused by falling interest rates when zeros and coupon bonds are rolled over to maintain long maturities. They work best in tax-free accounts, and I used them for years in IRAs and pension portfolios we manage. Stocks that aren't sold avoid capital gains taxes, but their dividends suffer income levies. Small beers? Not so for long-term holders, since most of the gains racked up over a multiyear span come from the compounding effect on reinvestment dividends, and they get very big in relation to the original investment over time.

I hope this discussion of zero-coupon bonds has disabused you of another popular misconception—that bonds are only for very conservative portfolios. There's plenty of bang per buck in long-term Treasurys, even more in long-term zeros, and if you're still bored, try Treasury bond futures. We use them often in aggressive portfolios we manage, and they are not for the fainthearted. Nevertheless, due to heavy positions in 30-year Treasury and other futures, *Futures* magazine ranked me as the country's number one Commodity Trading Advisor.

Treasury Inflation-Protected Securities (TIPS) offer some protection against rising inflation, but if, unlike us, you look for higher inflation rates, why own any bonds? The difference between TIPS and coupon Treasury yields is investors' prediction of future inflation plus the inflation risk premium. So TIPS yields move with inflation-adjusted Treasury yields, but if we're entering a world of deflation as I expect, TIPS won't give you any of the wonderful appreciation we foresee for Treasury bonds. In July 2010, the spread between 10-year TIPS and Treasury coupon note yields implied that investors expected CPI inflation over the next 10 years to run 1.7 percent annually, down from 2.45 percent predicted in January.

Even if I'm dead wrong and inflation rises, TIPS don't work well in taxable accounts. The Treasury increases the principal in line with consumer price index (CPI) inflation every six months and pays the coupon interest rate on that adjusted value. But the investor pays ordinary income tax on the interest and the principal adjustment, so he loses in real terms. Furthermore, since that adjustment to principal isn't paid by the Treasury until maturity, if inflation spikes, tax payments could exceed interest receipts in the interim.

Three Sterling Qualities

I've also always liked Treasury coupon and zero-coupon bonds because of their three sterling qualities. First, they have gigantic liquidity with hundreds of billions of dollars' worth trading each day. So all but the few largest investors can buy or sell without disturbing the market. Second, in most cases, they can't be called before maturity. This is an annoying feature of corporate and municipal bonds. When interest rates are declining and you'd like longer maturities to get more appreciation per given fall in yields, issuers can call the bonds at fixed prices, limiting your appreciation. Even if they aren't called, callable bonds don't often rise over the call price because of that threat. But when rates rise and you prefer shorter maturities, you're stuck with the bonds until maturity. It's a game of heads the issuer wins, tails the investor loses.

Third, Treasurys, at least until recently, have been considered the best-quality issues in the world. This was clear in 2008 when 30-year Treasurys returned 42 percent, as noted earlier, but global corporate bonds fell 8 percent, emerging market bonds lost 10 percent, junk bonds dropped 27 percent, and even investment-grade municipal bonds fell 4 percent in price. In early 2010, however, bond-rating agency Moody's said that while the United States, the United Kingdom, France, and Germany faced no immediate risk of losing their triple-A rating, there is a slight risk that, if they don't get their huge deficits and mushrooming debts under control, they could be downgraded. Notice in Figure 11.6 that even after removing the double-counting that pushes gross Japanese government debt/GDP to over 200 percent and close to 100 percent in the United States, the net ratios are large in major countries and they continue to grow. Moody's worries that economic growth won't be sufficient to reduce these ratios, but tax increases and government spending cuts could strangle their economies. Also, the percentage of government revenue spent on debt service could put the U.S. government's rating in jeopardy.

In early 2010, bond guru Bill Gross warned that "if core sovereigns such as the United States, Germany, United Kingdom, and Japan 'absorb' more and more credit risk, then the credit spreads and yields of these sovereigns should look more and more like the markets they guarantee. Sovereign yields will narrow in spreads compared to other high-quality alternatives." Well, we'll see.

Treasury Secretary Timothy Geithner, naturally, sees no chance of a rating downgrade. "Absolutely not," he said in early 2010. "That will never happen in this country." Well, "never" is a long time, but I take comfort in the reality that Treasurys are still ahead of whatever is in second place. As noted in Chapter 11, U.S. consumers will be buying more Treasurys directly and indirectly in future years as their saving spree persists, and have been joining China in direct Treasury purchases in recent years.

Although foreign central governments own 30 percent of Treasurys, about 50 percent when other foreign holders are included, they're unlikely to dump them. Accidents can and do happen, but wholesale selling of Treasurys would no doubt precipitate a global depression that would slaughter the exports and growth of China, Japan, and other export-led, big Treasurys owners, as noted in Chapter 7. The dollar would collapse, making their remaining holdings worth much less. And if they wanted to exit U.S. debt, what other asset would be big enough and of high enough quality to be of interest?

Oh, What I Could Have Done!

Stocks, even with the survivor bias in their indexes discussed in Chapter 10, way, way underperformed Treasury bonds in the 1980s and 1990s in what was the longest and strongest stock bull market on record. The superiority of Treasurys has been even more pronounced since then. One reason that few realize this is because they don't know much about bonds, despite the simplicity of Treasury obligations, and so they ignore them. Furthermore, commissions on stocks are usually much bigger than on Treasurys, so brokers favor them. Another reason is that most of those promoting stocks compare them with short duration fixed-income securities that did not have long enough maturities to appreciate much as interest rates declined since the early 1980s.

Investment strategists cite numbers like a 6.7 percent annual return for Treasury bond mutual funds for the decade of the 1990s. For the past decade, they mention a 5.2 percent annual gain compared to 2.1 percent for U.S. stock funds, 4.7 percent for international equity funds, and 5.6 percent for corporate bond funds. But those government bond funds have average maturities and durations far shorter than on 30-year coupon and zero-coupon Treasurys that I favor. In fact, in official parlance, any Treasury with a maturity between one and 10 years is a note, while bonds have maturities over 10 years.

Figure 12.1, my all-time favorite graph, shows the results of investing $100 in a 25-year zero-coupon Treasury bond at its yield high (and price low) in October 1981, and rolling it into another 25-year Treasury annually to maintain that 25-year maturity. That avoids the declining interest rate sensitivity of a bond as its maturity shortens with the passing years, as I explained earlier. In March 2010, that $100 was worth $13,532 with a compound annual return of 18.8 percent. In contrast, $100 invested in the S&P 500 at its low in July 1982—when investors began to realize that devastating inflation was abating—was worth $2,255 in March 2010

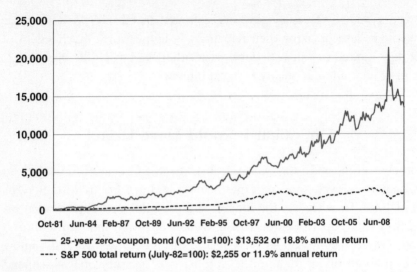

Figure 12.1 Comparative Stock and Bond Performances
Data sources: Bianco Research and Haver Analytics.

for an 11.9 percent annual return including dividend reinvestment. So Treasurys outperformed stocks by six times!

By now, you know I've had a long love affair with Treasury bonds. In the early 1980s, I put my money where my mouth was and personally took a highly leveraged position in 30-year Treasurys that soon achieved lifelong financial independence for the Shillings.

The Long Bond

I'm also sentimental about the long bond, because that almost became the name of a boat. We never owned a powerboat at our beach house on Fire Island, off the south coast of Long Island, because my wife and I wanted our four kids to learn to sail and figured that a power boat would be a big distraction. By the mid-1980s, however, the children had become good sailors, and I was becoming increasingly frustrated by what I call the tyranny of the ferry schedule. You need to take a ferry to get to Fire Island, and I do have a chronic tendency to run late—very late. So owning a power boat was an attractive idea.

At the time, we were doing consulting work for CML Group, based in the Boston area and named for Charles M. Leighton, the CEO and a former professor at Harvard Business School. The firm owned a number of upscale consumer product lines, including Boston Whaler boats. I asked Charlie Leighton if I could take out some of our consulting fees in trade, specifically in the form of a Whaler. He said fine, and to let him know when I'd have a half-day free so I could visit the Whaler facilities in Hingham, south of Boston.

We arranged a time when I was going to be in Boston anyway, and they sent a limo to pick me up. The head of the Whaler division, Joe Lawler, and the boat's original designer, who had sold the business years earlier but was still on the payroll, personally gave me a tour of the manufacturing operation. It was interesting to see how they sprayed the fiber glass on the molds, installed floats inside the seats, and did the finishing.

Then we went to the showroom. "What do you want to do with your boat?" Joe asked. I explained that I wanted to use the Whaler to get back and forth across the Great South Bay, to go fishing out in the ocean, to take the kids waterskiing, and so forth—in other words, I needed your all-purpose boat.

The Big Job

"Well," he said, "if you want to fish in the ocean, you'll need the big job over here. And you should have two engines in case one conks out 30 miles offshore with a storm brewing." We also decided that I'd need the console and windshield to hide behind in heavy weather, the built-in fish tanks, heavy-duty railings, miscellaneous storage lockers, and so on.

On the ride back to the airport in Boston, I began to wonder about the cost of the *Long Bond*, as my boat would be christened. I got to see when the numbers—at Whaler's lowest wholesale prices—arrived from Joe a few days later. Then came the sharp pencil work. I figured the depreciation on the boat, the cost of the money tied up, maintenance, summer docking fees, winter storage costs, fuel, insurance, license fees, and taxes. Then I estimated how often I'd use it on fishing trips, waterskiing, cruising, and, of course, ferry-avoiding trips across the bay.

The results were shocking. The ferry ride then cost $5, but each trip across the bay in the *Long Bond* would run $500. Now, it wasn't a matter of being able to afford the craft. This wasn't quite up to the vessel J. P. Morgan was referring to when he said that if you have to ask the price, you can't afford a yacht. I wasn't even scared off by the old definition of a boat—a hole in the water into which you pour money. I just simply couldn't justify paying 100 times the ferry's fare for the privilege of avoiding its tyranny. Needless to say, the *Long Bond* remains unbought—and unlaunched.

If Treasury bond yields settle in to 3 percent in the years ahead, their returns will be attractive in the deflationary climate I foresee, with 5 to 6 percent real yields, as noted earlier, very attractive for a safe investment. Similarly, high-quality corporate and municipal bonds are likely to be attractive on the basis of their real yields in deflation, even without any further price appreciation. And the returns on Treasury bonds may about equal those on stocks, as discussed in Chapter 10, even more so on a risk-adjusted basis.

2. Income-Producing Securities

This includes the high-quality corporate and municipal bonds just mentioned as well as stocks of utilities, consumer product companies, health care firms, and others that pay meaningful dividends that are likely to rise. Master limited partnerships are also possibilities, but only if their underlying businesses are secure enough to continue significant income flows to limited partners and stockholders. Banks used to pay significant dividends but slashed them when their earnings collapsed. Nevertheless, their deleveraging and reversion to safer but less growth-oriented businesses will probably pressure them to again pay attractive dividends.

After a long hiatus, companies that pay substantial, predictable, and meaningful dividends may be coming back into style for two distinct reasons. First, in a post-Enron/Arthur Andersen world and after gigantic write-downs have made reported earnings for many companies questionable, a company paying meaningful dividends is, in essence, assuring investors that it is generating the real earnings and real cash flow needed to finance those dividend checks. Furthermore, a significant dividend payer will almost certainly continue to be run in a prudent and stable manner. Dividend cuts forced by the down phases of volatile earnings patterns are not loved by investors, as was shown when many financial institutions slashed or eliminated their dividend in 2008. Second, dividends may provide the lion's share of earnings for many companies in future years, as I discussed in Chapter 10.

What's Real?

Many investors may revert to the reality that the only known return on equity investments is dividends. The rest are hopes and promises. Indeed, Charles H. Dow said, "To know values is to know the meaning of the market. And values, when applied to stocks, are determined in the end by the dividend yield." In earlier years, stocks were priced on the basis of their dividends. Since dividends are junior claims to interest payments, and stocks are more volatile than bonds, dividend yields exceeded bond yields in the early post–World War II years (see Figure 10.2 in Chapter 10).

Then the leap in stock prices in the 1950s and early 1960s pushed dividend yields below bond yields, so stock theorists shifted to earnings yields, the inverse of P/Es, to make stocks still look reasonably priced (Figure 10.4 in Chapter 10). Now, I've never understood the logic of discounting the future stream of earnings to ascertain the stock price, as noted in Chapter 10. Sure, future earnings may indicate the firm's ability to pay future dividends, but it may not. A company with rapidly growing net income may have to retain and reinvest every nickel to achieve that growth, leaving nothing for dividends. I guess the assumption is that everybody looks to earnings to price stocks, including the guy you eventually sell your share to. This sounds like a variation on the greater fool theory.

Lest you think I'm being antediluvian, consider the extremes that Wall Street analysts went to in the 1990s in order to make stocks that were ridiculously high, even on a P/E basis, look reasonable. In our January 2000 report, written just before the dot-com bubble broke, I noted the emphasis on "pro forma" and other forms of earnings overstatement, creative accounting, and cash "burn rates" for Internet companies. When even those accounting gimmicks failed to make soaring stocks look reasonable, the Wall Street wizards priced stocks, especially those with no present or likely future earnings, in multiples of sales.

Genuine Growth Stocks

To be sure, some corporations will not need to pay meaningful dividends in the years ahead because they will be regarded as real for-sure growth companies. Investors will be perfectly happy to let them retain and reinvest their earnings. But skeptical investors in future years will probably insist that those in the growth stock category have a history of steady growth in GAAP earnings and every prospect that this pattern will continue. Most others will be under pressure to pay dividends. Corporations that made dot-com promises in the late 1990s to provide fabulous earnings later—much later—if investors only give them lots of up-front money turned out to be rank speculations, definitely should have been beneath the investment horizon for most investors.

Dividends were hardly necessary during the long bull market from August 1982 to March 2000 (see Figure 1.6 in Chapter 1). That stock leap, which saw the S&P 500 Index rise at a compound annual rate of 15.3 percent for 17 years and eight months, was driven by the unwinding of inflation (Figure 1.5 in Chapter 1), which drove down interest rates and pushed up P/Es. According to stock valuation theorists, lower interest rates make future discounted earnings worth more today. Or, to put it another way, lower interest rates make bond returns less competitive with stocks. Interestingly, rising P/Es accounted for a 7.2 percent compound annual rise in the S&P 500 index in the 1982–2000 bull market. At the same time, disinflation largely eliminated the damage inflation did to corporate profits, as discussed in Chapter 10, and the consumer borrowing-and-spending binge hyped economic growth.

In that long bull market, then, stock appreciation was so exuberant that dividends didn't matter. In the face of such stock appreciation, what's a few percentage points in dividend yield? Dividends were only paid by backwash companies with no attractive investment prospect, the bulls roared. "Keep the money and turn it into stock appreciation," they bellowed.

So corporate managements deemphasized dividends as stocks soared. Dividend yields, which in the earlier postwar era had always found a floor at 3 percent, fell to close to 1 percent as payout ratios fell to new lows (Figure 2.6 in Chapter 2). The combination of leaping stocks and falling dividend payout ratios had this dramatic effect on dividend yields, reducing them by over two-thirds in the 1990s.

Corporate chieftains also responded to stockholder desires to receive capital appreciation, not dividends, in the long bull market due to the tax inefficiency of dividends. As is well known, they are often taxed twice, once as part of corporate income and again on investors who pay taxes. In contrast, capital appreciation is taxed only once, at the shareholder level, and then at lower capital gains rates.

Dividends Needed Now

In the years ahead, however, meaningful dividends will be needed to achieve acceptable returns on stocks in an era of slow growth and deflation, as explained in Chapter 10. I look for a return to the earlier floor of a 3 percent dividend yield on the S&P 500 from the recent 2 percent level even though that will be difficult. The way the math works out, the dividend yield multiplied by the P/E equals the payout ratio, the percentage of after-tax profits paid in dividends. A dividend yield of 3 percent multiplied by the current P/E of 22 implies a payout ratio of 66. A number of firms have plenty of free cash to hike their payouts substantially (see Figure 11.1). Still, even with the recent rapid buildups, in the post–World War II years, the average payout ratio rarely topped 65 percent, and then only briefly in recessions when profits fell much more than dividends (Figure 2.6).

In any event, my earlier forecast of 3 percent dividend yields plus around zero stock appreciation equals a total return on equities of 3 percent. That's 5 to 6 percent in real terms with 2 to 3 percent deflation, very acceptable by historical standards but, again, a far cry from levels to which investors in the late 1990s became accustomed.

Some argue that higher dividend yields aren't needed since Treasury bond yields are low, even more so if my forecast of lower yields is valid. But the link between the two is rather tenuous, as discussed in

Chapter 10 (Figure 10.2). Also, while dividend yields were well below Treasury yields in the 1982–2000 salad days for stocks, they will no doubt be much higher—I'm forecasting both will be around 3 percent—when stock appreciation is limited and dividends are key to positive nominal stock returns. Furthermore, future returns on money market funds and other short-term investments will enhance the appeal of stocks with meaningful dividends.

Others worry that higher taxes on dividends will kill their appeal relative to capital gains. But taxes on capital gains are also likely to rise if Obama has his way. Of course, little likely stock appreciation in future years means little likely capital gains tax, and makes dividends appealing even at higher tax rates. Also note that dividend yields in early post-World War II years, when tax rates were even above those proposed, were 3 percent or higher. To the extent that taxable stockholders dominate markets, maybe dividend yields also will be forced up to offset higher tax rates.

An alternative to paying dividends, of course, is buying back shares. The advantage is that stock buybacks are one-shot affairs with no obligations for the corporation to repeat buybacks in a regular pattern. From the shareholders' viewpoint, however, that is a disadvantage because they are unpredictable. Furthermore, announcements of repurchase programs are not the same as actual buybacks, which often lag well behind, and many times the announced totals are not repurchased. In addition, stock buybacks affect only those selling their shares, not the vast majority who don't sell. No money is transferred to them. So even though by reducing the shares outstanding they spread earnings and dividends over fewer shares, buybacks directly pay departing shareholders, unlike dividends, which reward those who still own the stock, at least own it up to the record date.

Buy High, Sell Low

Also disturbing is the fact that share buybacks have often been cases of buy high, sell low. In earlier years when stocks were flying, much corporate money was spent in repurchasing stocks, many of which are worth a lot less today. Ample corporate cash had generated a revival of stock buybacks. In the fourth quarter of 2009, buybacks by S&P 500 companies were $48 billion, up 98 percent from their low in the second quarter of 2009, but still down 72 percent from their high in the third quarter of 2007 when stocks peaked.

Beyond paying dividends and share buybacks, a third use of available corporate cash, of course, is acquisitions. Acquiring managements obviously believe they are thereby benefiting their companies and shareholders. Still, most mergers and many acquisitions fall short of expectations. Look no further than the disastrous AOL–Time Warner merger in which AOL, with no more substance than its virtual business, used dot-com stock to buy a solid enterprise.

Stock repurchases by Microsoft and other high-tech companies are often used to offset the shareholder-diluting effects of the stock options exercised by employees. This can help earnings and dividends in a minor way by avoiding dilution. Companies may be more inclined to raise dividends per share if the cost of doing so hasn't been dramatically increased by a huge jump in shares outstanding.

Still, although stock options may be important motivators for employees, they do transfer value from shareholders to those people. After all, options aren't exercised unless the stock is well above the issue price. So when a corporation buys in stock when options are exercised and sells the stock to employees at a lower price, the difference is transferred from shareholders' ownership of the company to those employees.

Attitude Change

Another reason that dividend-paying stocks are likely to be popular in coming years is a change in attitude by institutional investors, especially endowments and pension funds. In 2008, virtually all of the 40 investment classes I've identified fell (see Table 12.3). That included U.S. stocks, foreign stocks in developed countries, emerging market stocks and bonds, junk and even investment-grade bonds, commercial and residential real estate, commodities, and foreign currencies against the dollar. In fact, Treasurys, gold, and the dollar against foreign currencies except the yen were about the only things that rose in price in 2008—classic safe havens.

Table 12.3   Investment Performance, 2008

30-year Treasury bonds	+42%
Global corporate bonds	−8%
Emerging market bonds	−10%
Junk bonds	−27%
Municipal bonds	−4%
Gold	+6%
Commodities—Reuters/Jefferies CRB Index	−37%
Crude oil	−54%
Copper	−54%
Corn	−11%
Natural resource mutual funds	−49%
Hedge funds—Barclay Index	−22%
Private equity	−32%
Euro versus dollar	−5%
British pound versus dollar	−23%
Yen versus dollar	+19%
Canadian dollar versus dollar	−23%
Commercial real estate—MSCI US REIT Index	−42%
House prices—Case-Shiller 20-city index	−19%
Art—Sotheby's sales	−11%
Christies' sales	−20%
Real estate—direct ownership	−10%
Real estate—mutual funds	−40%
Stocks—Dow Jones World Index	−43%
United States	−39%
Canada	−35%
United Kingdom	−31%
Germany	−40%
France	−43%
Italy	−50%
Ireland	−66%
Japan	−42%
Australia	−41%
New Zealand	−33%
China	−65%
India	−52%
South Korea	−41%
Mexico	−24%
Brazil	−41%
Argentina	−50%

Furthermore, in 2008, all types of stocks were highly correlated—large and small cap value and growth; high tech; defensive stocks such as utilities, consumer staples, and medical care; financials; raw materials; and so forth. The same was true of foreign developed country and emerging market stocks. With globalization, the days are gone when a global sleuth can discover gems in the remote reaches of Asia or Latin America, as Sir John Templeton and his staff did decades ago. And the similarity of stock performance is even greater when the various classes are adjusted for risk. Emerging markets may climb more in bull markets but have greater falls when the bear arrives. There's no such thing as free lunch.

Despite the stark reality that almost all investments were highly correlated with all others, many remain unconvinced that diversification attempts are nearly useless. Consider Dave Kanas in the April 7, 2009 *Wall Street Journal*: "There's a great desire now to stay safe by holding only cash or only Treasurys. This kind of behavior is really just the same as chasing performance. Be disciplined. Stick to a diversified strategy and rebalance your holdings every year to reduce your exposure to the high-fliers."

These dramatic declines in 2008 came after a huge expansion in alternative investment products available not only to institutions but also to individual investors. In 2008, a quarter of the new mutual funds and exchange-traded funds (ETFs) were focused on real estate, commodities, and hedge fund–like investments. Morningstar that year added an "alternative" asset class to its mutual fund lineup, and the new group includes funds investing in currencies as well as long/short, market-neutral absolute return, and bear market strategies. Managed futures funds for small individual investors interested in futures investments driven by computer models were also popular.

Not the Plan

Investments weren't supposed to behave that way in 2008. For years, pension and endowment funds have been increasing their exposure to alternative investments such as commodities, foreign currencies, hedge funds, private equity, emerging market equity and debt, and real estate for two reasons. They believed they'd not only get higher returns than on conventional stocks and bonds, but also zero or, better still, negative correlations among these diverse investments. If U.S. stocks and bonds fell, their alternative investments would make money, they figured. Endowment portfolios averaged 10 percent in alternatives in 1995 but 30 percent in 2008. But way back in 1994, I said it ain't so.

In the late 1980s and early 1990s, we were doing very well in the aggressive portfolios we managed in a number of areas including currencies and, of course, 30-year Treasury bond futures. And many hedge funds and others that were similarly invested were also making big bucks. Unlike stocks, where everyone who's long makes money when they rise, futures is a zero-sum game. For every winner, there is a loser. I knew who the winners were but became curious over the identities of the losers.

I asked a number of managers who had been involved in these trades much longer than I, and the only logical investors they identified were genuine hedgers. Let's say that the manager of a big bond portfolio for an insurance company is worried, as most perennially are, that interest rates may rise. So he sells some 30-year Treasury futures contracts against part of his holdings. He's the seller, we bond bulls are the buyers. If interest rates go down, as they did in those years, we gain, he loses, but he's not entirely unhappy. After all, his hedge was an insurance policy. He broke even on the hedge because his losses on his shorts were offset by price appreciation on that part of his portfolio. And the bulk of his bond holdings was unhedged, so he made money overall, just not as much as if he'd had no hedge.

Game Change

In early 1994, the game changed radically. The rallies or declines in the sectors we were long or short futures became much shorter and the reversals much more violent. It became much more difficult to build positions, step by step, adding on top of already-established profits. It became much more likely that by the time a full position was built, a big reversal would wipe out the gains and maybe then some. I concluded that either the hedgers had atrophied or, more likely, the number of speculators such as we had leaped. As defined by government classification, *speculator* does not refer to wild gamblers and unsavory characters, but to any investor in futures or related products that is not a legitimate hedger. A euphemism for "speculator" is "passive investor." Speculators pursuing the same positions we were back then, but on a much larger scale, included well-known hedge fund managers Julian Robertson and George Soros.

Then another phenomenon confirmed my conclusion. I noted that when areas where I know a lot of speculators were involved unexpectedly reversed, the same happened in other areas, often totally unrelated, where they also had sizable stakes. A government report showing surprising strength in the economy would logically precipitate a decline in Treasury bond futures as investors worried about inflationary consequences. But it's hard to find a causal connection with a simultaneous decline in corn futures, except that many who were long Treasurys were also long corn.

I concluded that there was so much highly leveraged hot money floating around the world that regardless of whether it was managed by investment fundamentals (our approach), momentum strategies, technical principal, or any other investment style, it all ended up on *the same side of the same trades at the same time.* So when one investment position turned adverse, others, even fundamentally unrelated investments, retreated as investors withdrew to preserve their capital. One estimate is that speculators held 41 percent of all futures long positions in 2008, up from 7 percent in 1998.

Clear Proof

Clear proof of my 1994 observations occurred in 2008. Far from zero or negative, the correlations of all asset classes except Treasurys, the yen, and gold were essentially 1.0, as shown earlier in Table 12.3. They all went down. Heavy use of and overconfidence in mathematic models contributed to the bloodbath of 2008 through early 2009, as was the case with the 1987 crash and the 1998 collapse in Long-Term Capital Management. So did the illiquidity of many mortgages and other illiquid assets that forced banks and hedge funds to sell the only things they could find markets for: their liquid assets, especially stocks. Therefore, many endowments and pension funds lost 30 to 40 percent of their portfolios in

2008. The median public pension fund decline was 26.8 percent. This left many with an embarrassing lack of liquidity, especially with impending cash calls due to commitments to hedge and private equity funds.

Some were forced to float bonds or otherwise borrow for spending needs. Harvard raised $1.5 billion in taxable bonds and $600 million in tax-exempt bonds. Harvard lost 30 percent of its endowment in fiscal 2009 ending June 30 and was forced to lay off 275, or 1 percent, of its faculty and staff; in addition, it planned to cut work hours for 40 more. Dartmouth's endowment fell 23 percent in fiscal year 2009 and the university had to cut its operating revenues budget by $50 million since the endowment provides 35 percent of the total. In response, Dartmouth hiked its charges 4 percent to $52,275 in the 2010–2011 academic year for tuition, fees, and room and board. It also will end its no-loan financial program and require scholarship students to take out some loans, the first among Ivy League schools.

Amherst, my alma mater, raised $100 million in bonds due to its liquidity squeeze and big endowment loss. And Yale, where David Swensen pioneered the heavy use of alternative investments, cut its spending after losing 25 percent of its endowment value in the last six months of 2008. In early 2008, the California Public Employees Retirement System (CalPERS), which suffered a 23 percent drop in its assets in the fiscal year ending June 30, 2009, the worst in its 78-year history, was considering reducing its assumptions on future portfolio growth from a very optimistic 7.75 percent per year. In any event, since 75 percent of California state pensions come from CalPERS investments and only 25 percent from employee and government contributions, Governor Schwarzenegger proposed a 5 percent increase in state employee contributions. A Stanford study put the combined shortfall of CalPERS, California State Teachers' Retirement System, and University of California Retirement System at $500 billion, compared with the funds' own estimates of $55 billion.

The $96 billion Ontario Teachers' Pension Plan in Canada is well-known for using alternative investments to boost returns. But even during the 2009 rebound, returns on those investments fell short of their benchmarks and it was a "confounding" year, according to the Plan's CEO.

These disappointing investment returns came in the face of huge current and future benefit payouts for both private and public pension plans, as discussed in Chapter 7. Public pension plans are required by law to honor their benefit commitments to government retirees. Meanwhile, private plans, unlike public plans, have annual federally regulated funding targets, which went up to 96 percent in 2010 and 100 percent for 2011 compared with the earlier 90 percent. On average, the U.S. corporate pension funding level was 85 percent at the end of 2009 compared to 65 percent for public plans. Shortfalls in private plans must be made up in seven years, although those below a 60 percent funding level are frozen.

Not My Job

Most of the trustees of pension and endowment funds are not finance experts compensated for such unnerving setbacks as they suffered in 2008 and early 2009. They aren't paid at all but are volunteers in many cases. In the years ahead, they will no doubt insist on much more conservative investment policies, retreating from alternative investments and putting much less emphasis on stocks in general and more on fixed-income investments.

They'll likely emphasize more U.S. well-known companies in their stock portfolios and those that pay significant and rising dividends. Like bonds that pay regular interest, dividends are here-and-now money, which will probably be more preferred with less faith in returns from private equity that are out in the wild blue yonder.

Pension and endowment funds are important institutional investors, and their strategies will have meaningful influence on markets. So their retreat from alternative investments may further dampen emerging market stocks and bonds, real estate, and commodities, as well as enthusiasm for foreign currencies, hedge funds, and private equity.

Pensions and endowments are not alone in adopting more conservative investment strategies. Mutual funds and other financial service firms are finding ready markets for managed-payout funds that provide steady cash flow for retiring postwar babies without the high cost and restrictions of annuities. The 2008 through early 2009 stock market swoon embarrassed so-called lifestyle funds that had excessive stocks and fewer bonds relative to their benchmarks for investors as they age—*target-date funds*, they're called—so they have increased fixed-income allocations.

Pension and endowment funds will also continue to worry about the drawbacks of alternative investments. Most of them are illiquid, as the 2008 experience revealed. A number have considerable leverage that is hidden by the nature of their positions, but revealed when things go wrong. Precommitments to private equity and other partnerships and pools can be onerous if the cash flows that were supposed to fund them don't materialize. CalPERS, often the respected leader among pension funds, will probably cut back on outside private equity, real estate, and other alternative investments it manages when it cuts its asset appreciation assumptions. It was early in private equity investments, which leaped from $1 billion in 1990 to $25 billion recently.

Also, the models used in projecting many alternative investment returns can and do fail. That's true if only because so many managers invest using essentially the same models that their database, and hence their accuracy, is thrown off materially. I call this the Heisenberg uncertainty principle of investing. As an undergraduate physics major at Amherst, I learned about Professor Werner Heisenberg, a German physicist in the early twentieth century, who postulated that determining the exact position of anything is impossible. Even if you bounce the tiniest photon of light off an object to specify its location, you move it—and in an unpredictable way.

In finance, a model that seems to precisely predict, say, stock prices is similarly doomed to failure. If its developer uses it extensively, markets will be affected and the data on which it's based will no longer be valid. Even attempts to use it sparingly and keep it secret will probably be frustrated as the miracle model leaks out. The problem of overuse killed Long-Term Capital Management in 1998 since that firm became so huge that it essentially became the sole occupant of its universe. The same was true of portfolio insurance, which precipitated the 1987 stock market crash.

Many model-driven hedge funds floundered recently because they used essentially the same models so they ended up on *the same side of the same trade at the same time*. A new model-driven hedge fund, ROC Capital Management, presents itself as transparent and will give clients more information than most. Still, it will keep the details of its models confidential.

Theory Follows Fact

As usual, theory follows fact. The fact is that almost all asset classes fell in 2008, so new ideas are being generated to explain why asset class diversification didn't work. Professor John Geanakoplos at Yale has changed his long-held belief that interest rates—the price of money—are the most important indicator of supply and demand conditions in credit markets. Central banks missed the boat during the housing bubble by concentrating on interest rates, he says, not the mushrooming size of loans and securitizations and synthetic securitizations. The resulting immense financial leverage disconnected investor activity from efficient market theory, he believes. And when the subprime mortgage market started to crater—I date it in February 2007 with the $1.8 billion bad asset reserves taken by HSBC—lenders demanded more margin and the downward spiral set in as lower asset prices spawned demand for more margin, which forced borrowers to sell more and push prices down further, and so on. The good professor's theory sounds like my 1994 observation that too much highly leveraged money was on *the same side of the same trades at the same time.*

Historically, 90 percent of a portfolio's volatility depended on asset allocation, but after diversification failed utterly in 2008, some public pension funds are having agonizing appraisals. They are looking at investments not as stocks, bonds, commodities, and the like that earlier were assumed to behave independently, but as groups based on how they perform in different economic environments such as slow growth or high inflation. Private equity and real estate, for example, are in the same boat as stocks in their reaction to a major recession. Liquidity was not considered an investment objective for pension funds with long-time horizons until it disappeared in 2008. Joseph Dear, CalPERS's chief investment officer, said, "CalPERS's portfolio did not have meaningful exposure to assets that could have been a hedge in times of financial crisis and provide adequate liquidity to the fund."

Already, it is evident that significant changes in institutional investor attitudes have occurred. Pension and endowment funds lined up to withdraw money from a number of real estate funds that are open to redemption, and pressured those that are closed to be accommodative. They have also retreated from the many hedge funds that had substantial losses. Some hedge funds have moved toward conventional asset management and away from leveraged strategies in response.

Several public and private pension funds are cutting their exposure to derivatives due to hidden risks. These include state funds in Oklahoma, California, and Maryland. New Jersey and Illinois legislatures are considering restrictions. Counterparty risks and derivatives whose values cannot be checked by audits are worries.

Leading institutions pressured private equity and other alternative investors to ignore legally binding future capital calls as they try to conserve cash and reduce their involvement. Buyout firm TPG, with some clients strapped to fund $20 billion in commitments, allowed them to reduce their pledges by up to 10 percent. TPG didn't call more than 30 percent of investors' total commitments in 2009 and cut management fees. California State Teachers' Pension System, with $160 billion in assets, committed $250 million to Blackstone Group's newest private equity funds, a sharp drop from the $1.7 billion invested in the firm's prior fund.

Response of Corporations

The pressure, then, by stockholders is on corporations to increase their dividend and it will probably persist for years. The rebound of earnings in early 2010 and the growing size of corporate cash suggests they will respond. U.S. nonfinancial corporations hoarded $1 trillion in liquid assets in early 2010, with $580 billion in cash that could be used to pay dividends. And academic research reveals that companies with lots of cash become less profitable over time, with profit margins 1.5 percentage points lower than less cash-rich firms. Benjamin Graham said in 1949 that "The typical management will operate with more capital than necessary if the stockholders permit it—which they often do." Nevertheless, excess cash can invite corporate takeover bids.

In 2009, dividends in S&P 500 stocks fell $52 billion, or 21 percent, to $196 billion as profits swooned. Cuts and dividend eliminations were especially noticeable among hard-pressed financial institutions, but also among nonfinancials. Daimler eliminated its 2009 dividend, for the first time in 14 years, due to revenue declines of 20 percent and a loss of

$3.5 billion. In early 2010, dividend resumptions and increases were limited as corporate managements remained cautious. But better cash flow in media companies resulted in dividend increases. Starbucks, shifting away from a capital-intensive store-growth model after major setbacks in 2008–2009, announced its first-time dividend and plans to pay out 35 to 40 percent of net income in the future. In the first quarter of 2010, dividends rose but were still down 8 percent from a year earlier, and 21 percent from the first quarter of 2008.

In April 2010, 25 companies in the S&P 500 index raised their dividend and one initiated a dividend. That's similar to the 26 that raised them in April 2007 and contrasts with the 14 raises and 10 cuts in April 2009.

Dividends will be critical to total stock returns, and companies that make meaningful, reliable, and rising dividends should be in favor. Also, as discussed earlier, the shock to many pension and endowment funds of huge losses in 2008 and the resulting lack of liquidity is already turning them to investing in dividend-payers. Few sectors outside utilities and energy today pay meaningful dividends. Banks and other financial institutions used to, but they slashed payments when their earnings collapsed. However, their deleveraging and reversion to safe and sound spread lending is eliminating their earlier growth stock image and will pressure them to again pay significant dividends. Other industries will be encouraged to follow, especially those with limited growth potential and stable earnings.

3. Food and Other Consumer Staples

Items like laundry detergent, bread, and toothpaste are basic essentials of life that are purchased in good times and bad. In fact, as we've seen lately, consumers are buying more of their calories in supermarkets as they economize by eating at home rather than in restaurants. Note, however, that they are downgrading, as discussed earlier, from national brands to cheaper house brands, and will likely continue to do so in the slow growth economy, high-unemployment years ahead. Among retailers, the winners may continue to be discounters. Producers of national brands will need to continue to adapt to consumer downgrading by emphasizing cheaper "value" products.

Consumer staples producers and food processors have advantages in times of deflation. The costs of their raw materials will fall and they may not need to drop their prices commensurately, once they adjust to a thriftier consumer. So if they can keep cutting the labor and other costs, attractive profits growth is possible. Also, unlike big-ticket consumer purchases, they're unlikely to suffer from the deflationary expectations discussed earlier. Even if you know for sure the price of toothpaste will be lower next month, if you're out now, you won't brush your teeth with Ajax and delay purchasing another tube until prices drop, as I remarked earlier.

I'm forecasting slow economic growth and deflation in the next decade, not nonstop recession. Nevertheless, it may be useful to examine the performance of consumer staples and other defensive stock groups in previous bear markets associated with recessions.

We looked at the performance of a number of industry groups in bear markets, as defined by the recession-related periods of S&P 500 decline, starting with the 1957–1958 recession. Our list is representative, but it is not comprehensive, largely because of the changes in S&P 500 industry groupings over time as the composition of business shifts. For example, we don't list home builders since Standard & Poor's apparently did not consider them a significant group of public companies in earlier decades. Also, a major change in classifications in 2000 made it difficult to list consistent industries over the entire period. The category of Consumer Furnishing and Appliances was split into two, Home Furnishing and Household Appliances, so we used the old series through the 1990 bear market and Household Appliances since then.

These changes in industry classifications, of course, are on top of the usual changes within industry groups as firms merge, new ones enter, and old companies exit. And don't forget that recessions differ in terms of which economic sectors do best and worst.

No Absolute Winners

Keeping all these caveats in mind, we found that none of the industry groups we considered produced consistent absolute gains in past bear markets, and they all fell when the bear raided in 2007–2009. Chemicals and Paper & Forest Products in the basic materials category are obviously highly cyclical, and their stocks fell in all past bear markets as earnings dropped. Among consumer cyclicals, Automobiles and Building Materials always fell, but Publishing, Apparel, Footwear, Department Stores, and Furniture & Appliances had absolute gains in some bear markets. But note that when those industries did decline, they often fell more than the S&P 500. In the 1959–1960 bear market, Household Furniture & Appliances fell 27 percent, almost three times the 9 percent drop in the S&P 500.

In transportation, Airline stocks rose in the 1980–1982 stock slide as did Railroads in the 2000–2002 bear market, but otherwise fell. Energy was a loser except in the 1990 stock sell-off, and Capital Goods stocks always fell. Interestingly, Computer Hardware stocks, despite their high-tech growth image, declined in all bear markets except the one in 1959–1960.

Among financial classifications, Money Center Banks, Consumer Finance, Life/Health Insurance, and Property/Casualty Insurance sometimes rose in bear markets, but all fell in at least four of the past seven recession-related declines. Electric utilities rose more often than they fell, but Natural Gas Utilities always declined.

In consumer staples, Soft Drinks, Foods, and Household Products stocks rose in more bear markets than they fell, but the reverse was true for Broadcasting and Retail Food Chains. The category of Major Pharmaceuticals in the health care arena rose in four past bear markets but fell in three and was down again this time.

Relative Performance

Many institutional portfolio managers are charged solely with beating their benchmark, regardless of whether they rise or fall, so they win even if their portfolios are down but by less than their standards. For the rest of us, it's probably fair to say that on the way up, performance is relative, but on the way down, it's absolute. Losing less money than some stock average is still losing money, as I noted earlier. In any event, the better places for a portfolio of long stocks to be in past recessions were Electric Utilities, Soft Drinks, Foods, and Household Products—in other words, utilities and consumer staples, in line with popular sentiment. But none had positive returns in the 2007–2009 stock collapse. There was no place to hide.

4. Small Luxuries

As U.S. consumers retrench, the motto for many is, "Use it up, wear it out, make do, or do without." Conspicuous consumption has given way to thoughtful, value purchases, especially if they're green, as consumers make a virtue out of necessity. The aspirational shoppers, those stretching to buy high-priced prestige products, have become window shoppers in the atmosphere of tight credit, high unemployment, and depressed consumer net worth (shown in Figure 4.1 in Chapter 4). DeBeers, which produces and sells 40 percent of the world's rough-cut diamonds, slashed output 49 percent in 2009 in reaction to retrenching U.S. consumers, the biggest buyers of diamonds.

Nevertheless, consumers, especially when they're hard-pressed, tend to buy the very best of what they can afford, even if it's within a low-priced category. I developed this investment theme of small luxuries years ago when I noticed this tendency in apartheid South Africa. Urban blacks there often carried the elegant, slim, and expensive umbrella typical of investment bankers in London. They couldn't afford cars or even taxi fares, but they did achieve status and satisfaction with fine umbrellas. More recently, I learned of an unemployed man who enjoyed the status of morning coffee at 7-Eleven six days a week. By reusing his cup and the one he took home to his wife, he got a 32-cent discount per $1.37 serving and saved $655 a year on this small luxury.

Today, even the rich have become less so. In 2008, the number of millionaires in the United States fell by 15 percent, and losses on real estate and securities since 2007 have made many upper-income folks feel a lot poorer. Median chief executive pay at S&P 500 companies dropped 15 percent in 2008. That reversed the trend in the period from 1980 to 2005, during which the boss's pay jumped sixfold. A recent survey found that 48 percent of affluent Americans believe they may suffer future financial losses. Luxury goods sales fell 15 percent in 2009, according to Bain & Co. Sales of some very expensive car brands like Bentleys,

Maseratis, Maybachs, and Lamborghinis fell by as much as 50 percent. As noted earlier, the top 20 percent of households by income cut their spending in 2008 at about the same rate as everyone else, refuting the belief that the rich are immune from recessions.

I think manufacturers and retailers that can adapt to the demand for small luxuries will be winners in this environment. Some are adopting the small luxury mode by offering essentially the same products at lower prices by cutting their manufacturing costs. Neiman Marcus is reversing its norm of selling unrestrained luxury by pressing suppliers for lower-cost versions of designer styles. This includes leather totes for $695 compared with $1,400 for the snakeskin models. Nordstrom, serving a lower-level luxury market, has worked with vendors on exclusive but cheaper lines like Easy Money jeans priced under $100. These jeans "favor your financial assets while enhancing your personal ones." Coach now prices half its handbags between $200 and $300, compared with one-third in 2008, and is working with suppliers to improve its profit margins.

Secure Enough?

Saks is introducing brands with a wider scope of entry-level goods and plans to increase its sales of exclusive-to-Saks lines from 10 percent to 20 percent in the next few years. These lines are designer products at lower prices. Chloe, the French firm that sells handbags for $1,200 and up, introduced a canvas version at 50 percent off comparably-sized leather models. Jimmy Choo's high-end footwear line now includes rubber-soled flats for $365. Diogeo planned to introduce in the United States, in the summer of 2010, a "cheap chic" vodka from Sweden, called Rook, to compete with Constellation Brand's Svedka for $13 per 750 ml bottle. My good longtime friend the Right Reverend John S. Spong, retired Episcopal bishop of the Diocese of Newark (northern New Jersey), has a great way of describing self-confidence that many buyers of small luxuries lack. Jack cites the ads for House of Stuart, an off, off, off-brand of cheap scotch, which read, "Are you secure enough to serve it?"

Others are putting their prestigious names on different products. C.F. Martin reintroduced its stripped down 1930s guitar for under $1,000.

Average prices for its other models are in the $2,000 to $3,000 range and its top-of-the-line guitar costs $100,000. California winemakers are emphasizing cheaper wines as sales of those over $25 per bottle slump. Consumers are retrenching and dining out less at upscale restaurants where fine wines are sold. Tiffany sales of products over $50,000 are weak, but high-quality small items continue to sell well—always in its trademark blue box. Procter & Gamble (P&G) has not cut prices on its top-of-the-line products that sell at premiums to retain high-quality images. Consumers still splurge on such small luxuries as Gillette's five-blade Fusion razor and Olay's Pro-X moisturizer. But P&G introduced cheaper "value" versions of Tide and other products to compete with the growing consumer interest in house brands.

The firm in June 2010 introduced the Gillette Fusion ProSlide, a spring-loaded razor with a five-blade cartridge and battery-powered vibrator. A four-pack of manual cartridges will sell for $16.99, $17.99 for the battery-powered version, a 15 percent premium to regular Fusion blades that already sell for twice the average price of similar razors. Gillette says the blades are so thin you need a magnifying glass to see the edges, and it includes a "snowplow guard" to prevent hydroplaning. Fusion razors sell $1 billion a year, and to keep selling them in tough times, Gillette advertises that this small luxury provides a shave for only $1 per day.

Not to be outdone, Energizer Holdings also introduced the latest version of its Schick Hydro with a hydrating "reservoir" of aloe-infused lubrications so that "Hydro goes beyond just removing hair; it actually cares for your skin," Schick says. The five-blade Hydro will sell for 20 percent over Schick's premium Quattro blades. As for me, I'm a reverse snob so I buy whatever razor is the cheapest at Costco, which recently was a 52-pack of two-blade Gillette Custom Plus Pivot disposables, which have "extra lubricating power," for $22.99 or 44 cents each. And I get over a week's daily shaves from each one.

A Bathroom Luxury

Then there's toilet paper, which I never considered a luxury of any size, but apparently it is. Georgia-Pacific plans to introduce a new premium line after the success of a three-ply tissue called Quilted Northern Ultra Plush. That fancy paper was introduced in September 2008, just as consumers stopped buying just about everything else, but it proved a huge success. With $135 million in sales in its first year on the market, Ultra Plush was the most successful nonfood product launch of 2009, industrywide.

Some producers of luxury goods redesign them and market them under different names. Swatch Group sells low-cost Swatch watches in addition to expensive Berquet and Omega time pieces. Movado Group, in addition to its upscale models, makes less-expensive watches that are sold under Tommy Hilfiger, Hugo Boss, Lacoste, and Coach labels. And the firm in 2009 introduced its Bold line, which looks quite different from its Museum watches and sells for half as much or less. In contrast, some luxury purveyors market their wares without the label. Since the Democrats in Washington have declared war on Wall Street and executive compensation, many fancy hotel resorts have dropped the word *resort* from their names and marketing materials aimed at business conference planners.

Another route to small luxury success is to continually introduce new and improved models that make their predecessors obsolete. Apple is the master at this strategy, and the iPhone made the cell phone in my jacket pocket utterly antediluvian. Of course, the new iPad positively reeks of small luxuriousness since it's too big for your pocket and will be visible to all your envious friends.

Covetousness is nothing new, of course. Decades ago, before cell phones, car phones appeared and the transmission equipment took up half the trunk. The story going around then was that Joe, who envied his friend Herb's car phone, finally could afford one. On his first trip out, he used his car phone to call Herb on his car phone. Herb answers and Joe says, "Herb, I just wanted to call you on my brand new car phone," to which Herb replies, "Just a minute, Joe, I've got a call on my other car phone."

The risk, of course, is that in offering lower-priced models, upscale brands cheapen their image and lose their luxury appeal. Cadillac and Packard were both luxury cars in the 1920s. Packard introduced lower-priced models in the 1930s when the Depression killed sales of its top models, but that irreparably damaged its image.

Interestingly, luxury auto producers today are offering downscale models, but with limited success. Mercedes promoted its mid-size E class sedans on TV and radio ads, even citing how much lower their prices are than its bigger models, and plans to introduce a four-cylinder C class car. Mercedes also promotes large used cars for those who don't want to downsize. And if you can't even afford a small luxury Mercedes, you can always buy a few shares of Daimler stock to enjoy vicarious prestige.

5. The U.S. Dollar

Dumping on the dollar has been the favorite sport of investors and the financial media for years (see Figure 8.7 in Chapter 8). Then the financial meltdown in 2008 drove investors to the dollar as the global safe haven, but in early 2009 that status faded as fears of financial collapse melted. Buck busters cited the record low short-term interest rates, with the federal funds target rate at zero to 0.25 percent, even lower than in Japan. This made the greenback the preferred funding currency for the carry trade in which it was borrowed and then sold for higher-yielding currencies, such as the Australian dollar or the Norwegian krona. The falling dollar against those currencies also enhanced the profitability of those trades.

Buck dumpers also emphasized the tremendous number of dollars being pumped out by the Fed and the Treasury in their attempt to revitalize the economy, and the Fed's clearly stated commitment to keep short-term interest rates low for an extended period. Furthermore, the left-leaning Congress and administration didn't help the dollar with their twin goals of increasing government regulation and control of the economy and redistributing income from the higher-income people to lower-income households. These anticapitalistic policies tend to discourage foreign investors and encourage Americans to invest abroad.

My Two Hours with Milton Friedman

Some weak-dollar fans believe the answer to the chronic U.S. trade deficit (shown in Figure 6.9 in Chapter 6) is to get the dollar cheap enough that relatively high-cost American labor can compete against much cheaper

Asian workers. In reality, the dollar's weakness has not done much to slow the transfer of jobs abroad to foreign firms or U.S. multinationals that move capital overseas to fund facilities there that produce U.S.-bound exports. Years ago, however, Milton Friedman told me there was a different solution to the wage gap problem.

He was rigorously consistent in advocating free markets for almost every phase of human endeavor. People should be free to use drugs and tobacco, but taxed to provide for the health care they would need as a result, he maintained. School vouchers would bring competition into public education. I once heard him slam Social Security and other government welfare programs, saying that private charities would rise to the challenge and do a better job.

I experienced Friedman's free market convictions and doctrinaire approach in a one-on-one meeting in May 1987. I knew him only slightly, but heard he was interested in my 1986 book, *The World Has Definitely Changed*. My thesis was that the global economy had moved from a world of shortages to one of surpluses, and it supported my long-held view that inflation was on the way out.

I called him before a trip to San Francisco and he invited me to meet in his apartment there. A colleague dropped me off and agreed to pick me up two hours later. Friedman greeted me in his bathrobe and slippers with a three-day stubble. I immediately handed him a copy of my book and started to explain its thesis. "Excuse me," he interrupted, "there's no such thing as shortages or surpluses. Markets eliminate both."

Hard to Argue

And so the debate began. I argued, or at least tried to argue, that cost differences, especially labor cost gaps, made goods production expenses much cheaper outside the United States, particularly in Mexico, which was then the big supplier of low-cost imports. So the almost inexhaustible supply of cheap foreign labor was a key reason for global surpluses.

I say I "tried to argue" this point because Friedman constantly and aggressively interrupted, often in mid-sentence with "Excuse me" and then proceeded to tell me that any such cost differences were only temporary. He was well known to be a dirty debater, and his immense intellect made it easy for him to shift an argument he was losing to other grounds before you knew it.

The discussion was all very pleasant, but it was clear that he thought my ideas and analysis had no intellectual value whatsoever. As we entered the second hour, I was increasingly frustrated but had to stick it out until my ride arrived. I was reluctant to sink to his level of debate by interruption. After all, he was one of the world's great intellects and a Nobel Prize winner.

But, as my departure time approached, I screwed up my courage when he interrupted one too many times. "Excuse me, professor, I'd like to finish *my* sentence. In a theoretical world of completely free markets, costs between the United States and Mexico may equalize as Mexican wages rise from $1 per hour to $5 while American workers' pay drops from $20 to $5. But in the real world where production can be outsourced and where American labor has union and voter power, that simply won't happen. Jobs will move offshore or protectionism will unfold, or both." I'm sure, however, that I didn't change his mind.

The Reserve Currency

Despite all its drawbacks, however, the dollar remains the world's reserve currency and safe haven, regardless of suggestions by the Chinese and others that the dollar should eventually be replaced by a global currency. This status for the buck appears to be reemerging and will grow if I'm right that hopes for rapid economic growth in the years ahead will be dashed. Furthermore, until early 2010, almost everyone was on the dump-the-dollar side of the boat, a situation similar to that early in 2008 that preceded the dollar's jump which started in midyear (Figure 8.7). History suggests that when that happens, the winds often shift and all those folks will get tossed into the water as the boat sails in the reverse direction.

The recent strength in gold prices suggests that many investors distrust all currencies, not just the dollar. Nevertheless, the supply of gold is far too small, even at current prices, to again serve as money. Gold in private and government hands is worth about $5 trillion, compared to global M3 money supply of $60 trillion. Gold would have to sell at

$13,164 per ounce, versus $1,212 at present, to replace the M3 money supply dollar-for-dollar.

Before the current recession proved them wrong, the majority believed that most foreign economies were decoupled from the United States and would continue to grow even if America's economy faltered. Those convictions were dashed, but have returned, especially for China and other Asian countries. We continue to believe, however, that most foreign economies depend directly or indirectly on exports to the United States to fuel growth, as described earlier. With U.S. consumers retrenching, those countries are scrambling to compete for a shrinking pool of American imports, and want a stronger, not weaker, greenback to make their exports more attractive.

Fewer Exported Dollars

As I discussed earlier, U.S. consumer retrenchment is slashing our trade and current account deficits and, therefore, the dollars placed in foreign hands that are recycled into Treasurys and other dollar-denominated assets. But the related increased saving by American households is being channeled directly or indirectly into financing meaningful chunks of the huge federal deficits, much as has been the case in Japan since the early 1990s, as discussed earlier. This increased funding from domestic sources should aid the buck. Furthermore, U.S. consumer retrenchment will probably cut economic growth more abroad than in the United States as American imports continue to weaken. Each 1 percent decline in consumer spending cuts U.S. imports by 2.4 percent, according to historical norms. Therefore, many countries may promote the dollar against their own currencies to enhance their exports.

Railroads versus Horses

The euro is fundamentally vulnerable, in my view, because the euro-zone has a one-size-fits-all monetary policy but its economies vary in strength from Germany and the Low Countries at the top to Portugal, Italy, Spain, Greece, and Ireland at the bottom. Those lands can't use independent monetary policies to stimulate their economies since that's the providence of the European Central Bank (ECB). So they need to resort to fiscal stimuli and increasing government borrowing to finance the resulting deficits. A number, led by Greece, have suffered sovereign debt rating downgrades, which increase their borrowing costs, and more are likely. In April 2010, Fitch cut Greece's debt rating to the lowest investment-grade level. The noble experiment of a common currency in the eurozone without political unity and a common fiscal policy may not stand the test of tough times. It would be a miracle if this grand idea did work.

Americans are lucky because this country was largely developed after the advent of the railroad. That and Lincoln's decision to keep the nation together at all costs has given us a huge economy with a common language and culture and tremendous labor mobility—just the ticket in an era of globalization and its economies of scale.

In contrast, Europe was developed when travel was by foot or horseback. The result is a continent of diverse countries that is fun to visit since there's a different culture only 50 miles away. But it's hell in today's economic world due to language and cultural barriers and the lack of labor mobility. Unemployed Californians move to North Dakota where jobs are plentiful—if they can sell their houses—but Sicilians are unlikely to migrate to Germany in search of work. Besides, they don't speak German, and bratwurst with sauerkraut isn't their favorite dish. To a degree surprising to Americans, many Europeans are born, live, and die in the same city, even the same neighborhood.

The eurozone is the descendant of the decision between the German and French leaders after World War II that their normal means of interacting over the previous century—all-out warfare—was no longer feasible. They hoped that economic integration would drastically reduce the chances of war and that a common currency would promote a common economy and, ultimately, some sort of political unity. And the common currency and one central bank would prevent political leaders from inflating their way out of unemployment or fiscal crises. Neither could national central banks finance fiscal deficits and the volatility they sired. In early May 2010, former German Chancellor Helmut Kohl, then 80, confirmed my view when he said, "Today I am convinced more than ever that European unification is a question of war and peace for Europe and for us, and the euro is part of our guarantee of peace."

As we predicted in our December 1998 *Insight*, however, the structure of the eurozone was deeply flawed to start with. In the late 1990s, European leaders were so zealous to launch the eurozone at the beginning of 1999 that they winked at their own requirements. In 1997, the benchmark year, government deficits were supposed to be 3 percent or less of GDP and debts below 60 percent of GDP—and those limits were supposed to be stuck to in future years in order to force all eurozone countries into a common, disciplined fiscal mold. Belgium and other prospective members were far from the debt limits but were accepted if their ratios were falling. The 60 percent debt limit has never been met by the eurozone as a whole. Furthermore, many countries fudged their deficit numbers by one-off measures like selling off mobile phone spectrum licenses to goose revenues. So 11 of the 12 original members met the deficit limits, but three—Spain, France, and Portugal—later revised their deficits to more than 3 percent of GDP.

Greece never reached the target, but the cradle of democracy was allowed into the eurozone in 2001. Wayward members are supposed to be fined but never have been, and 9 of the original 12 members, including leaders Germany and France, exceeded the deficit level in at least one year. In 2005, the deficit standard was essentially thrown out by allowing breaches in recessions. Furthermore, it's been revealed recently that Greece and Portugal understated military outlays and subsidies to state enterprises in earlier years that, when properly recorded, pushed deficits up substantially, from 1.7 percent of GDP for Greece in 2003 to 5.7 percent after revisions.

Also, the eurozone charter since inception forbids countries from lending to each other, but the early 2010 bailout plan for Greece involved exactly that. Another limitation of the eurozone is that the European Central Bank has one goal—maintaining price stability that it interprets as inflation close to but below 2 percent per year. In contrast, the Fed has the twin goals of "stable prices" and "maximum employment."

PIIGS Pulled Along

Reasonable economic growth since the eurozone commenced in 1999 allowed weak economies, namely Greece but also the other PIIGS members—Portugal, Italy, Ireland, and Spain—to be pulled along by the stronger northern members, namely Germany, France, and the Low Countries. But growth also hid their vast economic differences. In the Club Med set, tax avoidance is a honed skill, labor rigidity is legendary, and public and private labor unions exert immense economic power. Greek income tax revenues were 4.7 percent of GDP in 2007, the latest available data, compared to 8 percent in the European Union on average. This is quite different than in the Teutonic north, although a number of German bigwigs have been embarrassed lately over tax-dodging accounts in Liechtenstein and elsewhere. Estimates are that 25 percent of the Greek economy operated off the books and doesn't pay taxes, compared to 22 percent in Italy, 19 percent in Spain, 19 percent in Portugal, 15 percent in Germany, and only 7 percent in the United States. This costs the Greek government about $21 billion a year in lost tax collections.

The European Commission estimates that bureaucracy in Greece—the cost of work devoted to dealing with government officials—equals 7 percent of GDP, twice the EU average. The cost is even higher since red tape discourages economic growth-spurring foreign investment and, therefore, GDP. Permanent government employees have lifetime jobs. Bribery, patronage and other forms of corruption also reduce GDP by 8 percent in Greece, according to a Brookings Institution study. That study also finds a close correlation between corruption and government deficits. It states that the Greek government deficits of 6.5 percent of GDP in the last five years would have been surpluses if that country were as clean as Sweden or the Netherlands, which did have surpluses over the last decade.

4-4-2 System

The World Bank ranks Greece the most corrupt among the 16 eurozone countries, and also the worst among the EU 27 along with Bulgaria and Romania, according to Transparency International. Estimates are that one-fourth of all taxes in Greece aren't paid, a third of that due to bribes. So tax collectors operate on the 4-4-2 system with 40 percent of taxes due going to the collector, 40 percent kept by the taxpayer, and 20 percent received by the government.

Greeks also retire much earlier than most, at 58, even though they live as long as the Germans. And Germany recently decided to raise the retirement age gradually from 65 to 67. Furthermore, in Greece, brass instrument players, masseurs in steam baths, pastry chefs, and hairdressers who use hair dyes can leave at age 50 because their working environments may cause breathing problems later. Spain's official retirement age is 65, but 60 for miners, firemen and policemen, and bullfighters can hang up their capes at 55—if the bulls don't get them first. As part of externally-imposed austerity, Greece agreed to raise retirement ages and cut pension benefits. As expected, public and private unions called a strike in response.

In France, where the 35-hour work week and five-week annual vacations are the law and where the government recalculated GDP to include the value of leisure, the official retirement age is 60, down from 65 in 1983. And the French actually retire earlier on average, at 58.7. But France's pension system is projected to run a €100 billion annual deficit by 2050, so President Nicolas Sarkozy has proposed a retirement age increase to 62. Naturally, French labor unions mounted not one but two nationwide protests, and the second in June involved twice the number of its May predecessor. Nevertheless, a survey found that two-thirds believe the pension system is in danger of collapse and about the same number think an increase in retirement age from 60 to 62 is warranted.

The global recession revealed the vast differences among the eurozone countries and the vulnerability of a common-currency union that lacks political and economic union. Without the euro, at least several of the PIIGS no doubt would have followed the usual path over the last decade—using easy-money policies to stimulate their economies and periodic devaluations to offset the resulting domestic inflation as well as their inherent economic inefficiency. Instead, the needed corrections have been postponed, perhaps to one big drop off the cliff—a big buildup to a big letdown rather than small, more orderly descending steps.

These vast differences can be seen in the 2009 government debt-to-GDP ratio, which ranges from −52 percent in Finland to 97 percent in Italy (see Figure 12.2), and in the unemployment rates in December 2009, from 4.0 percent in the Netherlands up to 19.5 percent in Spain. Holland, interestingly, keeps unemployment low through government "short-work" programs that subsidize pay for employees of companies that don't need them to work full-time.

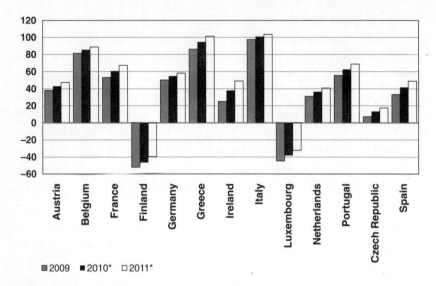

Figure 12.2 Net Debt as a Percentage of GDP: Eurozone, 2009–2011
*Estimates.
Data source: OECD.

These vast differences among eurozone countries resulted in bickering over how to bail out Greece, if necessary. German Chancellor Angela Merkel first called for expulsion of delinquent members of the eurozone, but few other leaders agreed. Then she insisted on IMF involvement in any bailout, but French President Nicolas Sarkozy objected, as did ECB President Trichet. Czech President Václav Klaus worried that bailouts will result in too much centralization of power. The sense of European unity seems to be receding as time passes and memories of World War II and German reunification fade.

The weak eurozone countries blame Germany for being too dependent on exports with insufficient stimulus for consumer spending. Germany's exports are 40 percent of GDP and 43 percent of them go to eurozone countries, with 12 percent sent to the PIIGS. And the hardworking Germans see no reason to bail out what they regard as lazy, unproductive, and overpaid southern neighbors. Since the monetary union started in 1994, unit labor costs have fallen 15 percent in Germany but have risen 3.5 percent in Greece, 10 percent in Spain, and 13 percent in Ireland. Furthermore, the Greeks are still smarting over the German invasion and occupation in World War II—remember the movie *The Guns of Navarone*? Their politicians apparently have forgotten the 115 million deutsche marks the German government gave them in 1960, a considerable sum back then. "How does Germany have the cheek to denounce us over our finances when it has still not paid compensation for Greece's war victims?" Margaritis Tzimas of the main opposition party told the Greek Parliament. Deputy Prime Minister Theodoros Pangalos said in a BBC interview, "They took away the Greek money and they never gave it back" in regard to German World War II actions.

No Good Solution

The ongoing eurozone crisis was triggered when the global recession revealed the extreme fundamental weakness of Greece and the other PIIGS and the rating downgrades of their debt as rating agencies cited their lack of competitiveness.

Although there are no secession provisions, if Greece defaults on its government debts, drops out of the eurozone, and goes back to using devalued drachmas as a currency, the eurozone might not survive. Argentina's default in 2001 and painful aftermath may be a parallel since one of the key differences between the two spendthrift countries is the hoped-for backing of Greece by the strong countries in the eurozone. Like Argentina, Greece would then need to rewrite all of its contracts in its new current terms. It would try to convert assets and liabilities into the new currency and devise a new monetary policy.

As with Argentina, lawsuits initiated by foreign holders of Greek debt would be plentiful. Trust in the new currency would be doubtful. Foreign banks would suffer tremendous losses. Everyone would pull euro deposits from Greek banks in fear they would be frozen, much as Argentina froze dollar deposits when it defaulted, and deposits elsewhere in the eurozone might flee for safer havens. And of course, if Greece defaulted and withdrew from the euro, Portugal, Spain, Italy, and Ireland might well follow.

The Alternative

These disastrous consequences of a Greek tragic exit from the eurozone are clearly why the strong members were willing to accept the alternative, bailing it out to the tune of €110 billion, even though the likelihood that Greece will shape up and fly right is slim. The bailout, of course, elevates the moral hazard of rewarding profligacy.

Investors, however, doubted that Greek leopards were going to change their spots by the end of 2011, the target date for Greece being able again to borrow in capital markets. Indeed, with the Greek government deficit optimistically projected to fall from 13.6 percent of GDP in 2009 to 8.1 percent in 2010 and to 4.9 percent in 2013, the resulting deficits for the next three years will require €50 billion in financing—plus another €70 billion to refinance maturing existing debt for a total of €120 billion. Furthermore, earlier promises to bail out Greece and even announcing the details of the plan did not halt the leap in interest rates on Greek bonds. And shortly before the bailout, Greece's debt rating was cut to junk status even though the European Central Bank reversed its earlier policy and continued to accept Greek government debt as collateral for loans to commercial banks.

Not Enough

When the €110 billion Greek rescue plan didn't allay investor fears, Europe accelerated to an additional €750 billion facility 10 days later. A €60 billion EU emergency fund would be available for any eurozone country in financial trouble, then €440 billion in funds guaranteed by other eurozone governments and €25 billion from the IMF. This really amounted to Germany, France, the Netherlands, and other strong countries using high credit. Maybe the IMF, with its history of tough love toward the countries it helps, will finally enforce meaningful fiscal discipline in Club Med countries. And from a long term as well as a short term standpoint, the sooner fiscal discipline is achieved in Europe, the better. Like all developed lands, European countries have aging populations and huge unfounded liabilities for health and retirement costs. Estimates are that those liabilities equal nine times the GDP of Greece, five times in Portugal, and 4.5 percent in the United Kingdom.

The recent weakness in the euro is obviously reflecting the turmoil in the eurozone and in Europe overall. And it reflects the fall from grace of that currency, which until recently was increasingly considered an alternative to the dollar in country foreign currency reserves. China is said to hold $630 billion of its $2.4 trillion in foreign currency reserves in euros. South Korea, with $270 billion in reserves, recently said that eurozone woes make the euro less attractive as a reserve currency. Iran's central bank has begun switching $55 billion of its foreign currency reserves into dollars and gold from euros. That reverses President Ahmadinejad's order last September to move hard currency reserves out of dollars and into euros. The bank holds $97 billion in reserves. Russia has $400 billion in foreign currency reserves and shifted away from the euro last year. Mutual fund investors in Europe and the United States are abandoning the common currency, and money flowed out of Europe at a $50 billion annual rate in January and February.

Furthermore, the euro has become a funding currency for the carry trade. With the ECB interest rate at 0.25 percent, investors borrow low-cost euros and sell them to buy the currencies of higher interest countries like Australia, where the central bank rate is 4.5 percent, or to invest in equity markets they favor. These actions, of course, further depress the euro against other currencies.

In one area, Europeans like a weakening euro since it makes their exports cheaper and more attractive elsewhere while discouraging higher-cost imports. But they also worry about the euro falling to the point that wholesale abandoning causes it to collapse completely. Our January 2010 *Insight* discussed the possibility of euro parity with the dollar. When that report was written in late December, the euro sold at $1.43, down from its $1.51 peak a month earlier and all-time high of $1.60 in April 2008. It's now $1.26 and a further substantial slide could trigger a mass exodus.

Intervention?

The response might be currency intervention by the ECB, aided by the Fed and other major central banks to try to stabilize the euro. Neither the Fed nor the ECB have intervened in currency markets since 2000 and both are aware of the general ineffectiveness of attempts to manipulate freely convertible currencies. The United States, Europe, Japan, the United Kingdom, and Canada bought $3 billion to $5 billion in euros in September 2000 to support the common currency, then recently introduced at the start of 1999. Still, it fell from $0.89 to $0.83 in October of that year.

Debt restructuring is highly likely among the PIIGS. It's already under way among Spanish banks ladened with troubled real estate loans, as discussed in Chapter 6. Because of the now-collapsing housing boom, Spain's big surge in debt was in the private sector, not at the government level as in Greece. Government debt restructuring in Greece is probably unavoidable. The amounts involved are huge. In 2009, Greece had $288 billion in net government debt outstanding, Portugal had $132 billion, and Spain had $510 billion.

Furthermore, eurozone debt has crossed borders freely. French banks held $75 billion in Greek government debt and German banks are stuck with $45 billion, as noted earlier. So if Greece restructures, financial institutions in many other countries would be hurt as would their governments if they needed to be bailed out. The European Central Bank holds huge amounts of Greek government bonds as collateral for loans to commercial banks and could face big losses that would erode its credibility and faith in the euro.

Lower Growth

The survival of the eurozone, at least in its current form, has to be a serious concern. And the implications are far-reaching. The World Bank estimates that debt defaults and a full-blown financial crisis in Europe would cut world economic growth this year to 2 percent and 0.7 percent in 2011 from the 3.3 percent rises it forecasts for both years.

It's amazing that amidst all this uncertainty, Estonia still wants to join the eurozone and has been endorsed by the European Commission to enter in 2011, but Poland and the Czech Republic decided to wait until the financial crisis subsides. The eventual configuration of the eurozone and the fate of the euro remain highly speculative. Nevertheless, we believe the ongoing woes are severe enough to drive the common currency back to parity with the dollar.

No Anglo-Saxon Model

Even during the 2000s when English-speaking countries were growing faster than the eurozone, Continental Europeans were unwilling to accept the Anglo-Saxon economic model and preferred more paternalistic strictures instead of lowering their social safety nets to achieve faster growth. They have long resisted restructuring since they believe that capitalism should be softened by strong labor protection and generous state benefits. The current recession and financial crisis, which started in America, further convinced them to stay with more regulated, less efficient, and less entrepreneurial economies with stagnant incomes. In the eurozone, 21 percent of the labor force under 25 were unemployed in the fourth quarter of 2009, compared to 9 percent of those over 25.

Unlimited Sick Leave

In Europe, many employees are entitled to extensive or even unlimited sick leave, and the Belgians really take advantage of it. Some government departments average 35 days of paid leave a year, seven times the U.S. average. Many call in sick in order to pack before vacations and to sleep off holiday hangovers when they return. Half of Belgians on sick leave say they suffer from depression. The average European was sick 11.3 days in 2005 versus 4.5 in the United States, and that cost the European economy 1.3 percent of GDP.

French President Sarkozy campaigned for the presidency in 2007 on a platform of spurring the French work ethic to energize the economy. But with this recession, he reverted to the usual model of state intervention. Promoting "national champions," companies that would dominate industries globally, was one of his programs. He granted tax cuts to companies that promised not to cut jobs. And he initiated a happiness component of GDP, which boosts the total by counting leisure as production. France Telecom, responding to a series of employee suicides, will partially base top managers' bonuses on social criteria including employee happiness as measured by factors such as work absenteeism. But if employees can take sick leave at will, how can a manager avoid absenteeism among his staff and the resulting hits to his bonus?

These structural forces plus their inherent lack of labor mobility, their language barriers, and their diverse cultures suggest that the euro will be weak relative to the dollar in the longer run, even if it survives the recent PIIGS crisis.

Further, history teaches that in the long run, the developed country with the fastest productivity growth has the strongest currency with reserve currency status. In that regard, the United States appears to have a clear advantage over Japan and Europe for many years from the combination of productivity-soaked new technology and business that is not only willing to continually cut costs and promote productivity but also is relatively free from government interference to do so—despite the ongoing wave of government regulation and expanding involvement in the economy.

Holland, Then Britain

In the eighteenth century, Britain's productivity was below Holland's, the top dog, because the Netherlands was the master of the new technology of the day, global trading. It controlled not only the mouth of the Rhine, the gateway to Europe, but also most of the trading routes to Southeast Asia. And the Dutch guilder was the world's top currency. But then the Dutch got fat and happy and spent lots of time having their portraits painted by Rembrandt, Vermeer, and the boys. Meanwhile, British productivity was leaping and the United Kingdom overtook the Netherlands in productivity level about 1785. Around the same time, the Industrial Revolution started in England and catapulted that country into a commanding lead in productivity—and in global power. In the nineteenth century, the United Kingdom's per-capita income was a third higher than that of France and twice the German level. Sterling became the world's reserve currency.

But, as in Holland earlier, the British got too comfortable with success and let their productivity growth rate slip below that of two upstarts—Germany and especially the United States, in the late 1800s. By then, the American Industrial Revolution was in full flower and railroads were spreading across the continent, as discussed in Chapter 8.

U.S. productivity growth averaged 2.1 percent per year from 1870 to 1890, far exceeding the United Kingdom's 1.3 percent rate. As that 0.8 percent gap compounded, American productivity levels spurted beyond those of Britain in the 1890s. Not surprisingly, by 1901, U.S. per-capita GDP exceeded that of the United Kingdom. Many believe that it was the disaster of World War I that knocked the United Kingdom off the throne, but it actually occurred 13 years before the war started, and the seeds were sown 45 years before that, when U.S. productivity growth leaped above that of Britain. Think about it! America, a mere colony in the eighteenth century, then a thorn in the side of mighty Britain in the late eighteenth and early nineteenth centuries, overtook the mother country at the beginning of the twentieth century and has been in the lead ever since.

It's not surprising, then, that the dollar replaced the pound sterling as the world's reserve currency. Nevertheless, currencies that other countries hold as part of their national treasuries die hard—they hate to desert old friends—so sterling did not begin to fall against the dollar until World War I, and remained in some countries' official reserves until well beyond World War II.

Other Currencies

British sterling was also under fire in early 2010 and may remain so for some time (see Figure 12.3). The U.K. economy remains in deep trouble, with even higher external debt than in the United States in relation to GDP (gross debt of 72 percent in 2009 compared to 54 percent in this country), which has caused bond rating agencies to threaten a downgrade of U.K. government debt, as noted earlier. Also, the troubled British financial sector accounts for 18 percent of total jobs compared with 6 percent in the United States, so as global finance delevers, the British economy is relatively worse off. As of early 2010, it looked like the recession in the United Kingdom was continuing, adding to the political uncertainty among the electorate.

The U.K. trade deficit remains large, 2.5 percent of GDP in the fourth quarter of 2009. And 30 percent of government debt of $1.6 trillion is in foreign hands, as are half of all U.K. bonds. This, too, looms over sterling.

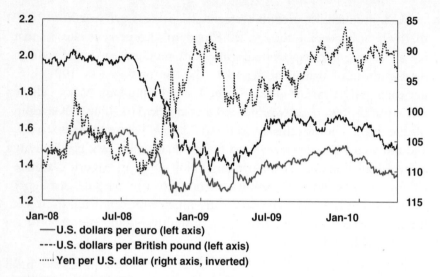

Figure 12.3 Euro, Pound, and Yen Exchange Rates
Data source: Federal Reserve.

Commodity-driven currencies, principally the Canadian, Australian, and New Zealand dollars, are also likely to weaken against the greenback as commodity prices fall. The Japanese economy remains weak and back in deflation, as I discussed in Chapter 11. But the yen's involvement in the carry trade makes it a tricky currency to forecast. Still, in the long run, I expect it to fall against the greenback, as I mentioned in Chapter 11.

Purchasing Power Parity

Some forecasters put faith in the purchasing power parity (PPP) concept, which maintains that currencies' equilibrium values are those needed to make the cost of a standard market basket of goods and services the same across national boundaries. On a PPP basis, the Organisation for Economic Co-operation and Development (OECD) says the euro is 21 percent overvalued against the dollar. Similarly, the IMF calculates that the Chinese yuan is 76 percent undervalued versus the buck.

The problem with PPP is that it applies only to internationally tradable goods and services, a tiny fraction of currency transactions. Estimates are that less than 10 percent of international dollar transactions have anything to do with U.S. imports or exports. The rest involve capital flows, currency trading, hedging, and trade among other countries that is done in dollars, currency speculation, and so on.

Nevertheless, a fun version of PPP is the Big Mac Index, which measures the change in exchange rates needed to make the cost of a Big Mac in other countries the same as in the United States (Table 12.4). Big Mac prices suggest that the Eurocurrency is about 28 percent overvalued against the greenback and the yuan is 49 percent undervalued—not wildly different than the more sophisticated PPP calculations cited earlier!

Table 12.4 Big Mac Index

Country	Big Mac Price ($)
Norway	6.87
Switzerland	6.16
Euro area	4.62
Canada	4.06
Australia	3.98
Hungary	3.75
Turkey	3.71
United States	3.58
Japan	3.54
United Kingdom	3.48
South Korea	3.00
United Arab Emirates	2.99
Poland	2.86
Saudi Arabia	2.67
Mexico	2.56
South Africa	2.44
Russia	2.39
Egypt	2.37
Taiwan	2.36
Indonesia	2.28
Thailand	2.16
Malaysia	1.12
China	1.83

Data sources: McDonald's and *Economist*.

The Chinese Yuan

In 1993, the Chinese devalued the yuan by 50 percent as it went from 5.81 per buck to 8.72 per dollar (see Figure 7.1 in Chapter 7). That put other Asian lands at an export disadvantage and, in addition to excessive reliance on borrowing abroad in hard currencies, may have been an important cause of the 1997–1998 financial and economic collapse in Asia. In any event, the yuan was pegged until 2005 when the Chinese government, under intense pressure from the United States and Europe to curb China's huge and growing trade deficit, allowed it to rise in a controlled manner to 6.8 per dollar in mid-2008, an increase of 21 percent. But with the global recession and weakness in the Chinese economy and in exports (Figures 11.3 and 11.2, respectively, in Chapter 11), the government again pegged the yuan to the greenback.

China in 2009–2010 faced renewed pressure from Europe and the United States to move its currency higher. As noted earlier, a strong currency probably won't curb Chinese exports appreciably since exports depend primarily on a country's trading partners' economic health. If their economies are strong, they're buying more of everything, including their imports—their trading partners' exports. But U.S. and European politicians can't do much directly to improve the strength of trading partners' economies and, hence, exports from the United States and Europe. And they don't want weaker U.S. and European economies and, hence, declines in imports. So about all they can do is yell and scream about China's robust exports and chronic trade surpluses. Also, with the yuan tied to the dollar and the dollar weak in 2009, Asian competitors of China such as South Korea, Indonesia, Thailand, and Malaysia felt that their trade positions versus China were being weakened.

Of course, with $2.4 trillion in foreign currency reserves, China can do pretty much what it wants in the international arena, but resisted calls for a stronger yuan for a number of reasons. Since the Chinese economy is still dependent on exports for growth, the government worried about anything that will restrict its international competitiveness. Government officials note that many Chinese exporters have profit margins of less than 2 percent, and a number of them that couldn't cut costs or improve productivity following the 2005 revaluation had to fold up. Chinese officials, reflecting the European domination of China a century ago, vehemently want to control their own destiny, free of U.S. and European pressure. East Asian countries are deepening a currency pool that can be drawn on to protect 13 regional currencies. China, along with Japan and South Korea, will provide 80 percent of the additional $40 billion, and no doubt it will be controlled by those countries. Importantly, these new funds will be accessible without IMF involvement. In the past, 80 percent of the pool was available only to countries involved in bailouts by the IMF, which China and other Asian lands regard as U.S.-controlled.

In any event, China gave in to the foreign pressure in late June 2010 and instituted a "managed floating exchange rate," as discussed in Chapter 11. The timing was right before the G-20 meeting in Toronto at which China otherwise would have come under considerable heat for keeping its currency pegged. The immediate results indicate that the government intends to not only maintain tight control of the currency but also allow it to move very slowly, up or down.

Strong Buck Effects

In any event, I look for dollar strengthening that will persist for years as the buck is again regarded as the safe haven amid slow economic growth and deflation that are tougher on foreign economies than on that of the United States. Furthermore, the greenback will no doubt remain the global reserve currency in the foreseeable future. The shift of reserves to others, principally the euro, will continue, but there's no alternative to the dollar in sight.

A strong dollar in the years ahead will favor U.S. investments. It will attract foreign money for anticipated currency gains as well as safe haven status. It will promote U.S. deflation, making high-quality U.S. bonds attractive to foreigners as well as Americans. A rising buck will also discourage U.S. investment abroad due to currency losses. It will, however, help foreign exporters by making their products cheaper for Americans, offsetting some of the effects of U.S. consumer retrenchment and the negative effects on U.S. imports.

6. Investment Advisers and Financial Planners

Investment advisers and financial planners should be in strong demand in the years ahead. Low investment returns will discourage do-it-yourself investing and encourage the use of professionals. The postwar babies will be desperate to build assets in their remaining years before retirement, and anxious to get all the professional help they can afford. Individual investors, still smarting over gigantic 2008 losses, will doubt their own investment abilities for many years. Those benefiting also include trust companies, banks oriented to high net worth investors, mutual fund managers, and life insurance companies.

Furthermore, some insurance companies have decided to concentrate on underwriting and selling policies while outsourcing the management of their portfolios. In 2009, over $1.1 trillion was transferred from insurers to managers following $980 billion in 2008. Swiss Reinsurance moved $23 billion to bond management specialist Black Rock. Allstate chose Goldman Sachs to manage one $5 billion equity portion of its $100 billion total portfolio.

The challenge, however, is for these asset managers to be profitable at fees that don't consume major shares of investment returns. If stocks return only several percent in nominal terms including dividends, fees of one percentage point or more on assets won't be feasible. At the retail level, the trick is for asset managers to make customers feel like individual clients but at low costs. Otherwise, the business will likely shift to low-cost index mutual funds and similar mass investment approaches.

Economies of scale in asset management are tremendous since total fees tend to rise much more than costs as assets under management grow. But stock prices and, therefore, portfolios are likely to grow more slowly in the world I see ahead than in the 1982–2000 boom years. Also, the big shift into 401(k) plans that helped many managers is largely over, now that they comprise 80 percent of total pension assets.

7. Factory-Built Housing and Rental Apartments

Factory-built housing and rental apartments will benefit from the separation of abodes from investments. As noted earlier, they used to be combined in owner-occupied houses back when owners believed house prices never fall. So they bought the biggest homes they could finance. The collapse in house prices has shown them otherwise. Further weakness in the prices of single-family houses and condos due to the depressing effects of excess inventories (Figure 7.2 and Table 7.2 in Chapter 7) will add fat to the fire. So, too, will further price weakness even after excess inventories are eliminated due to general deflation. As shown in Figure 3.4 (Chapter 3), corrected for the size of houses and inflation/deflation, single-family house prices have been flat for over a century.

Factory-built houses can be any size, but they tend to be smaller than site-built homes. They also cost about 50 percent less per square foot for comparable or better quality in fill-in locations in established neighborhoods because they are constructed in enclosed, weather-impervious locations. When finished on site, multiwide units can look almost identical to site-built houses.

But note that this price advantage does not hold for big subdivisions where site-built contractors essentially set up factories on location. Also, conventional home builders are themselves shifting with demand to smaller houses. Factory-built housing will also benefit from downsizing by the postwar babies in future years and their migration to Sunbelt locations where those structures tend to be made and sold, as well as from demand for second homes.

Factory-built housing was depressed in the late 1990s when its own bubble spawned by overlending collapsed, as discussed earlier (Figure 3.8 in Chapter 3). Then it suffered a second blow when loose lending on site-built houses attracted many with low-rate mortgage loans who otherwise would have bought factory-built units with higher-rate chattel loans. The third whack came with the collapse in conventional housing and the drying up of all forms of home loans. The industry is still struggling, but should have an exciting future.

Rent versus Buy

Even with the tax deductibility of mortgage interest, renting a single-family house or apartment is cheaper than home ownership, absent price appreciation. Repeated analyses by my firm over the years have shown this to be true, and even more so in a period of deflation when nominal house prices will probably fall on average. Over time, houses have sold for about 15 times rental costs. But that's in the post–World War II years when owners of rental properties expected inflation to enhance their 6.7 percent return—before the cost of income tax–deductible maintenance and property taxes. When I was young, when house price appreciation was not expected in the aftermath of the 1930s, the norm for rentals was 10 percent of the house's value. If I'm right about deflation, houses and apartments may sell for closer to 10 times rentals than the 15 times norm, much less than the 20 times in the housing boom days.

Of course, some people have intense pride in home ownership, especially those like me who are major do-it-yourselfers. My wife and I bought our 5,000-square-foot house in Short Hills, New Jersey, an upscale New York commuter suburb, in 1968. Years ago, a friend and I replumbed the place, which was built in 1907, with new copper pipes from the street in and installed three and a half new baths. I planted most of the shrubs on the three-quarter-acre lot myself and have 13 of my 80 beehives on the property. We've remodeled the house extensively over the years, including replacing steam heat with 23 heating zones and 15 thermostats, installed a heated driveway, and completely air-conditioned the place. Our four kids are grown and long gone and my wife would like to downsize from rattling around in this big house. But I know this house inside and out, and there aren't many things about it I can't repair myself. I've got no desire to move and start all over with a different house.

Rental apartments are now in ample supply (see Figure 8.5 in Chapter 8), and the surplus grows as troubled condos are converted to rentals. But the separation of abodes from investments should work to their advantage in future years. I'm not suggesting that Americans will give up on single-family owner-occupied housing. The idea of a single-family home of your own is just too deeply embedded in the American culture. But many who have no pride of home ownership and who would vastly prefer to yell for the "super" (New York-ese for the building superintendent) than to apply a wrench to a leaky pipe have bought houses and apartments in past decades only to participate in capital appreciation.

If I'm right, they'll be more inclined in future years to occupy rental apartments. This might be especially true of empty-nesters who don't like to mow their lawns and who decide to unload their money pits—especially because these homes are no longer appreciating rapidly. At the front end of the life cycle, young couples may decide that because houses are no longer a great investment, there's no reason to strain their financial, physical, and emotional resources to buy big, expensive houses as soon as possible. So they'll stay in rental apartments a bit longer and wait until their kids are of the age that a single-family house makes sense.

It will take a surprisingly small shift in housing patterns to make a big difference in the demand for and construction of rental apartments. Today, there are 130 million housing units in the United States, of which 36 million are rented. If only 1 percent of total households decided to move to rentals, the demand for apartments would increase by over one million, most of which would need to be newly built, after current vacancies are absorbed. This is a big number compared to new apartment starts of 333,000 on average over the past 10 years.

Rental apartments and smaller single-family abodes will also appeal to the growing number of postwar babies as they retire, downsize, and want less responsibility and more leisure time. Investors can participate in rental apartments, either through direct ownership or through real estate investment trust (REIT) stocks. There are also REITs that concentrate on rental sites for manufactured houses.

8. Health Care

Health care is a huge sector, accounting for 16 percent of GDP and growing rapidly. It will continue to grow, in view of the new law instituting universal health insurance and as the postwar babies age and need more medical services.

Furthermore, two major features of the current system almost guarantee explosive growth. First, most Americans don't pay directly for their health care, which is financed by employer-sponsored insurance or the government through Medicare and Medicaid. That plus the fact that it's "my life" that's involved means that, except for deductibles and co-pays, there's no restraint on usage. Many participate in what I call "recreational medicine"—take a day off from work at full pay to visit a physician, at employer expense, because of a minor ailment.

Second, in paying for service plans, medical providers have many incentives to perform extra procedures, including defensive medicine to avoid litigation over mistakes, because more office visits enhance their incomes. Several years ago, a dermatologist cut out a small precancerous growth on my lip. He said it would probably heal well, but wanted me to come back two weeks later to be sure. He had no concern for the value of the hour or so it would take me to drive to his office and sit in his waiting room for him to take a 30-second look, but he would collect an additional fee. Instead, I looked in the mirror two weeks later, decided the cut had healed and skipped the office visit.

The health care sector is also likely to expand in the slow economic growth years I see ahead because the federal government will be pressed to keep high and chronically rising unemployment at bay by massive job creation, as discussed in Chapter 9. Health care fits the bill. It employs skills ranging from nursing home attendants to medical researchers. Until the new health insurance law is fleshed out and implemented, there is considerable uncertainty over investment opportunities in future years. Will health insurers be harmed by a government-sponsored competitor? Will drug prices be more tightly controlled by federal regulators? How about drug store medical benefit administrators, and markups and profits on pharmacy benefit managers? Indeed, the new health care law does require the drug industry to reduce by half the price paid by Medicare beneficiaries (donut-hole coverage gap) starting in 2011. And how about the medical loss ratio caps that will limit health insurer costs and profits?

Cost Containment

Nevertheless, I look for long-run winners among those that promote cost containment, such as diagnostic testing labs and diagnostic equipment makers, outfits that provide home health care services and supplies, and outpatient services and clinics. Also included are manufacturers of noninvasive diagnostic and surgical equipment. Companies that provide health care information and services on and off the Internet and companies involved in physician and hospital management information systems as well as market research services should benefit from the new law.

Pressures on costs may not bother the price-insensitive wealthy. So companies managing upscale nursing homes, assisted-living homes, and rehab clinics may thrive. Ditto those aiding costly elective procedures, like laser eye-surgery. The rich and desperate will also pay for biotech hopes when the alternative is death.

In contrast, many medical products and services that seek to prolong lives, but at ever-increasing costs, may suffer. Ditto for Medicare- and Medicaid-reimbursed nursing homes and long-term-care homes, since government limits on pricing may offset the future huge demand for them. In the years ahead, health care may provide many opportunities to make money the old-fashioned way—skill, luck, clairvoyance, brains, hard work, and so much government subsidy you simply can't miss. But with government subsidy can come government control that can take a lot of the fun out of the game. Also, state control over health insurance premiums can be very challenging for insurers. In 2009, the Maine insurance regulator, Mila Kofman, ruled that Anthem Blue Cross and Blue Shield, a unit of WellPoint, should have no profit margin on its Maine business because of the depressed economy and the company's financial health. The firm sought premium increases averaging 18.5 percent that included its normal 3 percent "margin for profit and risk."

Even though drugs are often cheaper than surgery, big drug companies may be unattractive since their oversize costs will take years to work off and few blockbusters are in the pipeline. They've cut drug costs to Medicare under administration pressure. Generic drug providers are a better bet, but the field is crowded and prices are driven rapidly to commodity levels, as witnessed by recent industry consolidation.

Hospital chains may be unattractive unless attending physicians are employees, not outside contractors who have no interest in those institutions' financial health. Interestingly, an increasing number of physicians are giving up medical practices to work for larger, professionally managed health care organizations due to the increased costs of insurance paperwork and electronic recordkeeping as well as the desire for regular hours. In 2005, two-thirds of medical practices were physician-owned and had been for years, but that share fell below 50 percent by 2008 and continues to drop, according to the Medical Group Management Association.

Finally, medical office buildings and other health care facilities are likely to continue to be attractive investments. Demand for more services requires more space, and the consolidation of medical service providers into hospital-controlled facilities is hospitable for outside investors.

9. Productivity Enhancers

In a slow economic growth, deflationary environment, increased profits through price and volume increases will be difficult for many firms. So the current cost-cutting zeal will remain in place. Labor cost-cutting has been in vogue lately, but does have its limits. So anything—high tech, low tech, no tech—that helps customers reduce costs and promote productivity will be in demand.

Ironically, the very new technologies that will continue to increase oversupply and promote deflation—computers, semiconductors, the Internet, biotech, and telecom—will be in demand to help combat its effects. Furthermore, chronic deflation will be a shock to many companies accustomed to operating in inflation, but not to a number of new-tech firms. It isn't a question of whether computer chip prices will fall in any given year, but only by how much.

A basic characteristic of new technology is that it is continually surpassed by newer technology. In deflation, buyers of consumer and capital goods hold off purchases in anticipation of lower prices, and in so doing, force prices lower as excess capacity mounts and undesired inventories pile up. But in areas of rapidly advancing technology, buyers can't wait for lower prices on existing products because they will soon be obsolete. Bear in mind, however, that many big U.S.-based technology companies get major portions of their profits from overseas, and those earnings will be hurt by a chronically rising dollar. Also, their consumer-related business will be subdued by consumer retrenchment, especially if it involves major discretionary purchases, as discussed in Chapter 6.

Cost-cutting also can come from low-tech sources. Outsourcing of call centers as well as information technology (IT) is a case in point. Routine medical and legal work is now being done much more inexpensively in India than in the United States. Temporary help agencies may thrive as companies increasingly curb costs by using temps only at the time of day or season of the year they're needed, and avoid paying high benefit costs.

As noted earlier, the growing size of new technologies should keep productivity growing robustly in the next decade (Table 6.1). So, too, will the application of other cost-cutting measures. An important aspect of this whole exercise will be its net effects on employment growth. Will those employed in businesses that help customers cut costs and their incomes exceed the employment and income losses in industries that utilize them? Only time will tell.

10. North American Energy

Investments related to North American energy sources should do well in the next decade. The rationale is simple. The United States is increasingly dependent not only on imported energy, especially crude oil, but also petroleum products, which follows from local resistance to the construction of new refineries. Import growth, of course, results from rising demand for oil while domestic production falls.

Furthermore, energy imports, especially of crude oil, are coming from a number of countries with military and political instability, including Russia, Iran, Nigeria, and Venezuela. And whether the United States imports oil directly from, say, Iran or not is immaterial. Crude oil is fungible, and supply disruptions in any country are instantly transmitted worldwide.

Without these geopolitical concerns, there probably would be little pressure to undertake big developments of what is often higher-cost energy in North America. After all, low-cost North American energy has long been exploited because of political safety and proximity to markets of supply sources on this continent. But unless the world suddenly becomes a very safe and harmonious place, investors, energy companies, and Washington are all likely to increasingly favor North American energy.

I like petroleum, natural gas, coal, the Canadian oil sands, liquefied natural gas (LNG), nuclear power, and shale gas. Renewable energy sources such as ethanol, wind farms, solar, and geothermal all require heavy government subsidies that strike me as unreliable. The government giveth and the government taketh away. Solar panel maker First Solar took a big hit when Germany, where it had 65 percent of its sales in 2009, slashed subsidies.

Oilman T. Boone Pickens, who morphed into a clean energy advocate, in January 2010 shelved his plans for a huge wind farm in the panhandle of Texas, where they say there's nothing between there and the North Pole but a barbed wire fence. Cheap natural gas, the lack of electricity transmission, the credit crunch, and subdued demand for electricity were the culprits that even government subsidies for wind-generated power couldn't overcome. American electricity output in 2009 fell 3.7 percent, the biggest drop since 1938, after falling 1 percent in 2008.

Oil and Natural Gas

In the petroleum area, new drilling techniques are turning previously barren areas of the Gulf of Mexico into promising oil fields, even though interrupted by the BP oil spill. Before that, in March 2010, the Obama administration proposed permitting oil and natural gas exploration in the attractive eastern Gulf of Mexico as well as taking steps to determine the hydrocarbon potential off the coasts of Middle and South Atlantic states. At the same time, however, it also vetoed energy development off the coasts of California and North Atlantic states and in Alaska's Bristol Bay.

Natural gas is attractive long-term because of its clean-burning characteristics. The International Energy Agency sees gas use growing 50 percent faster than that of oil in the next 30 years, and overtaking coal as the number two energy source by 2020, accounting for one-fourth of total energy demand.

New technology has unleashed gas trapped in shale and flooded the market. As a result, U.S. demand for higher-cost imported LNG is weak. Natural gas from shale and other unconventional sources leaped from 10 percent of total U.S. production in 1990 to 40 percent in 2009. Proven reserves jumped from 177 trillion cubic feet in 2000 to 245 trillion cubic feet in 2009 and continue to rise. At current usage levels, they will supply the country for 90 years. In March 2010, Shell's CEO said that new sources of natural gas from unconventional formations such as shale gas and coal-fed methane gas had added a century's worth of usage to North American supplies.

Despite low natural gas prices, drilling activity for unconventional gas such as from shale is rising. And new technology has made drilling for gas faster and cheaper, although adequate supplies of water needed to fracture nonporous shale to release the gas may be a problem. Major energy companies ranging from ExxonMobil to Japan's Mitsui to Norway's Statoil to France's Total are buying into U.S. shale gas one way or the other. Consol Energy, the fourth largest U.S. coal producer, is acquiring Dominion Resources' natural gas business, probably in part because coal producers face limitations on surface mining and taxes on carbon dioxide, which has twice the emissions from burning coal as from gas per unit of energy output. In a departure from past strategy, gas producers are interested in 5- or 10-year contracts with electric utilities, suggesting that they now expect prices to stay low, given the abundance of U.S. natural gas.

T. Boone Pickens is zealous to reduce imported crude oil and is backing the use of natural gas to power heavy trucks and buses, although the additional cost per vehicle would be about $10,000. Countries such as Iran, Argentina, and Brazil have natural gas-fueled vehicles, and I saw that firsthand in Holland way back in 1959. I was hitchhiking in Europe and got a ride with a Dutchman to Amsterdam. At the outskirts of the city, he stopped his car and opened the trunk. It was pretty well filled with a tank of compressed natural gas, which he burned in the city to reduce pollution. So he flipped the switch to shift from gasoline to natural gas and we drove on.

Coal and Nuclear

Coal, especially thermal coal used for electricity generation, is plentiful in the United State, both from deep shaft mines in Appalachia and lower BTU content strip-mined coal in the West. At current production rates, the United States has 250 years' worth of reserves. America has the largest coal reserve but other countries also have sizable amounts, including Russia, China, India, and Australia (see Table 12.5). Coal accounts for

Table 12.5   Total Recoverable Coal (Billions of Short Tons) as of January 1, 2006

United States	262.7
Russia	173.1
China	126.2
India	62.3
Australia and New Zealand	85.1
Africa	54.7
Brazil	7.8
Canada	7.3
WORLD TOTAL	929.3

Data sources: Energy Information Administration, International Energy Outlook 2009.

about 30 percent of U.S. energy use, half of which is for electricity generation, and is virtually all produced domestically.

The problem with coal, of course, has been the sulfur, carbon dioxide, and other undesirable products of its combustion, but technological advances are solving these problems. Also, technology is being developed to gasify coal and to turn it into gasoline and diesel fuel. That, and more electricity-generating plants in the coal fields, will eliminate potential bottlenecks in transporting coal by rail.

Nuclear energy in the United States has had a bad name after the mishap at the Three Mile Island facility in 1979. Many have a frenzied reaction to the thought of a nuclear reactor exploding, and worry about a lethal meltdown such as occurred at Chernobyl in Russia in 1986. High cost has also been a factor.

Still, safety and cost-cutting technology continue to advance, and nuclear power doesn't produce pollution and create global warming threats. China and India are considering nuclear power as their needs expand. The United States lags far behind nuclear power generation in countries like France, where 80 percent of electricity is generated in nuclear plants. In the United States, it's only about 10 percent. The Obama administration has allowed the first new facility in 15 years to get under way, with $18.5 billion in federal loan guarantees, which the President proposes to increase to $54 billion. Two new standardized plant designs have been developed, which will improve cost efficiencies, and small, efficient facilities are being tested.

Despite the global revival in building nuclear power plants, uranium oxide prices in early 2010 were $42 per pound, down from $54 in the summer of 2009. They are expected to remain well below the $140 peak several years ago as worldwide supplies remain ample.

Babcock & Wilcox has developed a reactor that generates about one-tenth the power of big units, so utilities could add them one by one as electricity demand increases. Their cost per kilowatt of output is about the same but they can be built in factories and moved to the site by rail or barge, cutting construction time in half. And since this model is air-cooled, the installations don't need to be near big bodies of water as with the water-cooled big ones, and could be located in the arid West. General Atomics in early 2010 announced a 12-year program to develop a helium-cooled nuclear reactor that would be small enough to be moved by truck. It would provide a quarter of the output of conventional reactors and could utilize used fuel, which still contains 90 percent of its original energy.

Raising the temperature of water used to cool nuclear plants has become a political issue. New York environmental regulators in early 2010 denied a water-quality certification needed to extend by 20 years Entergy's license for its Indian Point facility. Environmentalists believe the 2.5 million gallons of water circulated through the nuclear plant each day is damaging the Hudson River's ecosystem and killing millions of fish.

I'm well aware of the need for lots of water to cool conventional reactors. For years, I've hunted ducks and geese at the marsh belonging to my good friend, Frank Harris. It's on the south shore of Lake Erie in Ohio and immediately adjacent to the Davis Besse nuclear power plant. Unfortunately, the birds often prefer the facility's cooling ponds to Frank's marsh, out of gun range and where we're not allowed to go, even to retrieve dead ducks. Frank jokes that the birds are easy to see at dawn when shooting begins because their eyes glow from the nuclear radiation.

Oil Sands

Canadian oil sands contain huge quantities of bitumen, which is turned into petroleum. Some experts believe that tar sands reserves could be larger than the crude oil reserves of Saudi Arabia. There's a big difference, however—production costs.

It takes pennies per barrel to get the oil out of the ground in Saudi Arabia, but about $50 or more per barrel to mine and process the tar sands into petroleum. But a lot of the processing cost is energy, now supplied mainly by natural gas, which has fallen substantially in price. The oil sands now produce about 1.5 million barrels of crude oil per day, over half of Canada's output. In any event, with oil prices remaining relatively high, oil sands output is expanding rapidly in this politically and militarily safe area.

The future for North American energy sources, then, seems bright, but in most cases requires high prices for a number of years in order to convince energy companies that the projects are worthwhile and for the construction, infrastructure, technological development, and so on to take place. The global recession and conservation measures depressed energy consumption, and slow economic growth and deflation in future years will limit energy demand expansion. Earlier forecasts of 2 percent annual rises in oil consumption worldwide are being cut to 0.5 to 1 percent, and some experts see a peaking in global demand by 2016. Still, crude oil prices seem to have stabilized in the $60 to $80 per barrel range, high enough to keep producer and investor interest in North American energy robust.

Twelve to Sell, Ten to Buy

So there you have it: my 12 investment areas to sell or avoid in an era of slow economic growth and deflation, and 10 areas to buy. Some of these are already unfolding. Others may do so only in future years, even if my basic forecast is correct. In either case, I hope my lists help you prepare for the investment climate over the next decade.

About the Author

Dr. A. Gary Shilling is president of A. Gary Shilling & Co., Inc., economic consultants, managing individual and institutional accounts. The firm also publishes *Insight*, a monthly report of economic forecasts and investment strategy. He has been a *Forbes* magazine columnist since 1983 and writes the "Financial Strategy" column.

He received his bachelor's degree in physics, magna cum laude, from Amherst College, where he was also elected to Phi Beta Kappa and Sigma Xi. Earlier, as a high school senior, he ranked twelfth in the nation in the Westinghouse Science Talent Search. Dr. Shilling earned his master's degree and doctorate in economics at Stanford University. While on the West Coast he served on the staffs of the Federal Reserve Bank of San Francisco and the Bank of America.

Before establishing his own firm in 1978, Dr. Shilling was senior vice president and chief economist of White, Weld & Co., Inc. Earlier he set up the economics department at Merrill Lynch, Pierce, Fenner & Smith at age 29 and served as the firm's chief economist. Prior to Merrill Lynch, he was with Standard Oil Co. (New Jersey) (now Exxon Mobil) where he was in charge of U.S. and Canadian economic analysis and forecasting.

A frequent contributor to the financial press, in addition to writing his regular *Forbes* column, he is a member of the *Nihon Keizai Shimbun* (*Japan Economic Journal*) board of economists and of the *Investment Advisors* magazine panel of investment strategists. He appears frequently on radio and television business shows. Recognized as an effective and dynamic speaker, he often addresses national and international business groups including the Young Presidents' Organization and the Bohemian Grove in a Lakeside Talk.

Dr. Shilling has published numerous articles on the business outlook and techniques of economic analysis and forecasting, and he serves as associate editor of *Business Economics*, the journal of the National Association of Business Economics. His fourth book, *Deflation: Why It's Coming, Whether It's Good or Bad, and How It Will Affect Your Investments, Business and Personal Affairs*, was published by Lakeview Publishing in June 1998, and Korean and Chinese editions were also published. Its sequel, *Deflation: How to Survive and Thrive in the Coming Wave of Deflation*, was published by McGraw-Hill in July 1999 and was translated into a Chinese edition. His latest book is *Letting Off Steam: A Collection of Commentaries on Matters Great and Small, Complex and Mundane, Serious and Frivolous*. He is also the creator of The Deflation Game, a board game that illustrates and reinforces his long-term forecast that deflation is a greater likelihood than a return to high inflation.

Dr. Shilling does not yet manage any mutual funds, but CNBC anchor Bill Griffeth was so impressed with his investment approach that he profiled him along with 19 well-known mutual fund managers in his book, *The Mutual Fund Masters* (Probus Publishing, 1995).

Dr. Shilling is well known for his forecasting record. In the spring of 1969 he was among the few who correctly saw that a recession would start late in the year. In 1973 he stood alone among nationally recognized experts in forecasting that the world was entering a massive inventory-building spree to be followed by the first major worldwide recession since the 1930s. In the late 1970s, when most thought that raging inflation would last forever, he alone said that the shifting political mood of the country would lead to an end of severe inflation, as well as to potentially serious financial and economic readjustment problems, and a shift in investment strategy from one favoring tangible assets to emphasis on stocks and bonds. Subsequently, he has become known as "Doctor Disinflation."

On January 2, 1986, the *Wall Street Journal* noted:

One year ago, 23 of the 24 economists in this newspaper's survey predicted that the yield on 30-year Treasury bonds, then 11.53%, would close 1985 in double digits. Instead, the bond closed Tuesday (December 31, 1985) at 9.27%.... The only forecaster who had expected a single-digit yield was A. Gary Shilling....

Six months later, the June 3, 1986, edition of the *Journal* stated:

Mr. Shilling's interest-rate forecasts of six months ago proved to be very close to the mark. He had expected a 6% rate on three-month Treasury bills and an 8% yield on 30-year Treasury bonds by the middle of this year. Those were by far the closest of the 25 analysts polled last December.

In January 1987, the *Journal* said,

According to the average estimate of 25 economists surveyed by the *Wall Street Journal* a year ago, the 30-year Treasury bond yield would rise to 9.76% by Dec. 31, 1986, from 9.27% at the end of 1985. That prediction turned out to be more than 2-1/4 percentage points too high. The best estimate came from Mr. Shilling, who said 8%.

The July 5, 1991, edition of the *Wall Street Journal* stated,

Mr. Shilling was one of the few analysts a year ago to forecast a recession. At that time, he said a recession "may already have started," a forecast that now looks prophetic.

The *Journal's* July 6, 1992, edition said:

Looking back at the July 1991 survey, nobody even came close in forecasting today's short-term rates. The average forecast a year ago for three-month T-bills at mid-1992 was 6.08%. That was too high by 2.45 percentage points. Mr. Shilling came closest at 4.50%.

The January 4, 1993, *Journal* edition, noting that Treasury bill rates were 3.15 percent at the end of 1992, assessed forecasts made one year earlier and declared, "Gary Shilling came very close, with his prediction of 3%. . . . [He was] among the few at the time who predicted that short-term rates would drop in 1992, as they did. The average at that time called for the T-bill yield to increase to 4.25% by the end of 1992."

The January 22, 1993, edition reviewed the track records of interest rate forecasters polled semiannually by the *Journal* since 1981 and said,

> The economist with by far . . . the best record in picking when to buy long-term bonds: A. Gary Shilling, who heads an economic consulting firm and manages money. During the 1980s, Mr. Shilling . . . saw sharply lower interest rates ahead . . . investors who bet on his rate forecasts by putting their money in long-term bonds did very well.

The July 7, 1997, edition stated that "Mr. Shilling . . . had the best overall forecast" of the economy, interest rates, exchange rates and inflation "among the . . . 57 economists polled in the latest survey."

The January 2, 2003, edition, in reviewing the forecasts of its poll made six months earlier, stated

> In June, only one forecaster . . . Gary Shilling, expected the Fed to cut short-term interest rates in the second half, as it did in November. . . . Only one forecaster, again Mr. Shilling, expected the Dow Jones Industrial Average to finish the year below 9,000. Twenty-seven of the 55 saw it finishing the year above 10,000.

(It finished at 8,342.)

Twice, a poll of financial institutions conducted by the *Institutional Investor* magazine ranked Dr. Shilling as Wall Street's top economist. *Futures* magazine rated him the country's number one commodity trading adviser. In 2003, *MoneySense* magazine named him the third best stock market forecaster in the world, right behind Warren Buffett.

Dr. Shilling's outlook for 2008 was extremely accurate, and all 13 of his investment strategies published in his January 2008 *Insight* worked. The random odds of batting 13 for 13 are one in 8,192.

Dr. Shilling is on the board of directors of the American Productivity and Quality Center; Palm Harbor Homes; and the Episcopal Preaching

Foundation, Inc., of which he is chairman. He is an advisory director of Austin Trust Company and a member of the New York Society of Security Analysts. In 1999, he was awarded an honorary doctor of law degree by Tiffin University, and in 2006, an honorary doctorate of humane letters by Church Divinity School of the Pacific. In 2008, Dr. Shilling was awarded an honorary doctor of humane letters by Berkeley Divinity School at Yale and in 2009 an honorary doctor of canon law from the University of the South (Sewanee).

He is a former member of the New York Stock Exchange, former director of the American Republic Life Insurance Co. of New York, the Henry H. Kessler Foundation, Inc., the Episcopal Church Foundation, Kent Place School, National Life of Vermont, and Aim Packaging, Inc. He is also a former trustee and treasurer of the General Theological Seminary (Episcopal), a former chairman and trustee of the New Jersey Shakespeare Festival, a former trustee of Bates College, a former director of the Heartland family of mutual funds, and former chairman of the New Jersey State Revenue Forecasting Advisory Commission. He was formerly a member of the National Commission on Jobs and Small Business. Dr. Shilling served as an informal economic adviser to President George H. W. Bush; and as executive in residence at the Amos Tuck School of Business Administration, Dartmouth College, and at Sewanee: The University of the South. He has testified before various congressional committees including the Joint Economic Committee and the House Banking Committee.

He is also an avid beekeeper.

Index

AARP, 168–169, 171
ABSs (asset-based securities), 77
ABX index, 85, 86, 378
Acquisitions, 210, 443
Active managers, 361–362
Adjustable-rate mortgages (ARMs), 4–5, 59, 116, 150, 151
Ads, Internet/new-tech company, 49–50
After the Crash (Shilling), 38, 397, 410
Agricultural productivity, 299–301, 302
AIG (American International Group), 91, 143–145, 192, 194, 377–378
AIG Financial Products, 143–144
Allstate, 480
Alt-A loans, 117
American International Group (AIG), 91, 143–145, 192, 194, 377–378
Analysts, 15, 49
Angelides, Phil, 192–193
Antiques, art, and other tangibles, 372–373
Antiques Roadshow (television program), 372–373
Apple, 277, 459
Argentina, 195, 398, 469
ARMs (adjustable-rate mortgages), 4–5, 59, 116, 150, 151
Asset-based securities (ABSs), 77
Asset classes, correlations among, 443–447, 451
Australia, 200, 228
Austrian School of economists, 216
Automobile industry. *See also specific companies*
    capacity utilization, 385
    China, 405

deflation and, 304, 305–306
as investment to sell/avoid, 365, 366
labor agreements, 175–176
luxury brands, 456–457, 459–460
prices, 276

Bagehot, Walter, 21
Bailouts:
    banks and similar financial institutions, 373
    cost estimate for, 203
    Fannie Mae, 131–132, 134–136, 189–190
    financial bubble and, 99–100, 113–114, 147–148
    Freddie Mac, 131–132, 134–136, 189–190
    preparation for, lack of, 133–134
Bair, Sheila, 81, 201
Bank for International Settlements (BIS), 106, 182–183
Bank of America:
    capitalization, 148
    CEO forced out, 373
    Lehman Brothers and, 136
    Merrill Lynch merger with, 24, 26, 132, 141
Bank of England, 144, 194–195, 199
Bank of Japan. *See also* Japan
    credit market freeze, 145–146
    currency inflation/deflation, 291
    independence of, 194, 195
    inflation, 245
    interest rates, 162, 416
    Japanese bubble, 38
    monetary response to economic slump, 411

Bankruptcy code, 261
Banks. *See also specific banks*
    bailout of, 373
    central, 194–195, 245–248
    commercial, 149–150, 375
    consortium, 129
    exposure abroad, 197–198
    investment, 149–150, 191–192
    as investment to sell/avoid, 373–380
    mergers among, 210
    mortgage buybacks, 374
    pay policies, 201–202
    regional/community, 374–375
    reserves, excess, 312–314, 316–317
Barclay's, 136, 137
Battles, military, 125
Bear market, 288–289, 346, 347–348. *See also*
    Bull market; Stock(s)
Bear Stearns, 112, 117–122, 124, 126, 130
Belgium, 465, 473
Benchmark contracts, 390
Beneficiaries, government, 325–334
    decrease in, 329–330
    dependents, 327–328
    future trends, 330–334
    increase in, 326–328
    percentage of population, 325–328
    private sector and, 327
    welfare reform, 330
Bent, Bruce, 139–140, 141
Bernanke, Ben. *See also* Federal Reserve (Fed)
    deflation, 248
    Fannie Mae and Freddie Mac, 131
    financial crisis, 153
    fiscal restraint, 215
    Great Depression, 314
    lending to investment banks, 191
    monetary policy, 315
    power of, 192
Bies, Susan, 86
Big Mac Index, 477
BIS (Bank for International Settlements), 106,
    182–183
Blanchard, Oliver, 247
Blank check companies, 20, 115
Blinder, Alan, 237
Bond(s). *See also* Treasurys
    coupon, 430–431
    covered, 183
    developing country, 392–410
    junk, 113, 381–382
    long, 428–429
    state/local government defaults on,
        259–261
    stripped, 431–432
    yields, 147

    zero-coupon, 431–432
Bonuses, 200, 203
Borrowing. *See* Debt
Borrowing-and-spending binge, 159–166,
    287–288, 349
BP, 284, 488
Bradford & Bingley, 148
Brazil, 397–398
Britain. *See* United Kingdom
Brown, Willie, 262
Bubbles. *See also* Dot-com bubble; Financial
        bubble; Housing bubble
    anatomy of, 22–27
    characteristics of, 1–3
    commodity, 211–212, 283
    electric lighting, 23
    history of, 18–22
    inventory, 4, 9–11, 33
    Japanese, 37–39, 396–397
    length of, 3
    overenthusiasm and, 23
    railroad, 20
    reassurances and, 24–26
    short sales and, 13–16
    South Sea, 19–20
    tulip bulb, 18–19
Budget(s):
    federal, 54, 199–200
    state/local, 252–254, 258–259
Buffett, Warren, 149–150, 362
Bull market. *See also* Bear market; Stock(s)
    dividends and, 440–441
    financial asset inflation/deflation and,
        288–289
    follies taught by, 44–45
    saving rate and, 160–161, 165
    secular, 346, 348–350
Business Cycle Dating Committee of the
        National Bureau of Economic Research, 6
Buy-and-hold strategy versus market timing,
    356–362

California Proposition 13, 188, 258–259
California Public Employees Retirement System
    (CalPERS), 255, 448, 450, 451
Calls, great:
    characteristics of, 3–4, 29
    disinflation, 33–37
    dot-com blow-off, 40–52
    financial bubble, 95–122
    housing bubble, 53–94
    inventory bubble (early 1970s) and recession
        (1973-1975), 33
    Japanese bubble, 37–39
    list of, 5
    missed calls, dealing with, 6

negativity involved in, 6–7
recession (1969-1970), 29–32
CalPERS (California Public Employees
    Retirement System), 255, 448, 450, 451
Canada, 199, 228, 233, 301–302, 491–492
Capacity utilization, 97, 98, 383–386,
    406–408
Capital equipment producers, low- and old-tech,
    383–386
CardioNet, 14–15
Carry trade, 56
CDOs. See Collateralized debt obligations
    (CDOs)
CDSs. See Credit default swaps (CDSs)
Central banks, 194–195, 245–248. See also specific
    banks
Charcoal, 390–391
China:
    bank bonuses, 200
    capacity utilization, 406–408
    central bank, 195, 401–403, 409
    currency, 234–235, 293, 402–403, 476, 477,
        478–479
    currency reserves, foreign, 292
    as developing country, 399–410
    domestic spending, 392–393, 395–396,
        404–405, 406, 408
    economic growth, 306
    economic policy, 408–410
    economy type, 403
    exports, 189, 393, 408
    fascination with, 396, 397
    fiscal policy, 223
    GDP, 396, 407, 409
    global recession and, 154–155
    overheating fears, 400–401
    protectionism, 226, 231–232, 234–235
    protectionist measures against, 230–231,
        232–233, 404
    real estate, 403–404
    saving, 405–406
    stimulus program, 395–396, 399–401, 405
Christie, Chris, 256, 266–267
Chrysler, 366, 383, 385
Churchill, Winston, 248, 380
Citigroup, 129, 148, 183, 185, 193
CMBX indexes, 378–379
Coal, 489–490
Cockroach theory, 121–122, 129
Coleridge, Samuel Taylor, 1
Collateralized debt obligations (CDOs):
    financial bubble, 114, 118, 119–121
    Goldman Sachs, 374
    housing bubble, 61, 82, 92, 94
    mark-to-market approach, 380
    pricing models, 120–121

Commercial banks, 149–150, 375
Commercial mortgages. See Mortgages,
    commercial
Commercial paper market, 146
Commercial real estate, 289–290, 378–379,
    386–389
Commodities, 9, 211–212, 281–285,
    389–392
Companies. See also specific companies
    blank check, 20, 115
    drug, 485
    flailing, 382–383
    insurance, 480
    limiting size, scope, and complexity of, 209
    nonfinancial, 107–108
    special-purpose acquisition, 20, 115
Composition, fallacy of, 173, 180, 181
Computers, 296–297
Consortium banks, 129
Constellation Brands, 244, 457
Consumer(s):
    borrowing-and-spending binge, 159–166,
        287–288, 349
    debt, 102–103
    lenders to, 368–369
    net worth, 97, 98
    purchases, big-ticket, 365–368
    retrenchment by, 151–153, 159–181,
        351, 463
    saving, 159–181, 175–177, 351
    spending and GDP, 165, 179
    staples for, 453–456
    wealthy, 367, 456–457
Consumer price index (CPI). See also Prices
    deflation, 296
    forecasts, 275
    historic, 16
    inflation, 282, 295
    money supply and, 280, 281
    Treasury yields and, 16
    upward biases, 276–277
Contango, 390
Contrarians, 12
Corn, 390, 447
Corporations. See Companies
Cost-cutting by business, as paradox, 180–181
Coupon bonds, 430–431
Coupon usage, 178
Covenant lite loans, 113
Covered bonds, 183
CPI. See Consumer price index (CPI)
Cramer, Jim, 356
Credit cards, 152–153, 171–172, 368–369
Credit default swaps (CDSs):
    AIG, 143–144
    housing bubble, 91, 92, 93–94

Credit default swaps (CDSs) (*Continued*)
Lehman Brothers bankruptcy, fallout from, 138–139
prices on each country's debts, 229
Credit market freeze, 145–146
Credit rating firms. *See* Rating agencies
Crude oil. *See* Oil
Currency. *See also* Dollar (U.S.)
competitive devaluations of, 234
East Asian pool, 479
euro, 463–464, 471, 476, 477
exports and, 270–271
inflation/deflation, 291–294
pound sterling, British, 475–476
reserve, 214–215, 462, 475, 479
swaps, 145–146
yen, 291, 292–293, 476
yuan, 234–235, 293, 402–403, 476, 477, 478–479
Current accounts:
Japan, 337, 338, 421, 423
United States, 179

Daimler, 366, 452–453, 460
Debt. *See also* Collateralized debt obligations (CDOs)
consumer, 102–103
corporate, 383
eurozone, 467–468
federal, 108–109
Greece, 464, 468–470
increase in rate, 160
Japan, 337, 412–413, 414
postwar babies, 171–172
repayment of, 335–336
Spain, 472
state and local government, 109–110
total net, 103–104
Debt-to-equity ratios, 210
Decoupling, 225, 392, 395
Defaults, state/local government, 259–261
Deficits:
deflation and, 334
financing of, 335–336, 337
forecasts, 318
Germany, 216–217
housing bubble and, 54
inflation and, 334
Japan, 337, 412–413, 414
tax increases to reduce, 203–204
Deficit-to-GDP ratio, 214, 218, 219–220, 221
Deflation. *See also* Disinflation; Inflation
automobile industry and, 304, 305–306
bad, 306–309
cause of, 279

central banks and, 245–248
commodity, 281–285
CPI, 296
currency, 291–294
current evidence of, 277–278
expectations of, 250–252
factors influencing, 250–251
federal deficit and, 334
financial asset, 287–289
good, 296–306
growth and, 244–252
interest rates and, 376
Ireland, 278
Japan, 245–246, 309
as peacetime phenomenon, 274–275, 281
productivity and, 297–301, 304–306
projections, 309–310
standard, 295
tangible asset, 289–291
types, 281–296
wage-price, 285–287
Deflation: How to Survive and Thrive in the Coming Wave of Deflation (Shilling), 47, 51, 181, 274
Deflation: Why It's Coming, Whether It's Good or Bad, and How It Will Affect Your Investments, Business and Personal Affairs (Shilling), 45–46, 51, 181, 274
Depression (1839-1843), 307, 308. *See also* Great Depression
Derivatives:
central clearinghouse for, 209
financial bubble and, 103, 104, 105–106
over-the-counter, 317–318
pension fund exposure to, 452
Deutsche Bank, 92, 93, 94
Developing country stocks/bonds, 392–410
Disinflation, 33–37. *See also* Deflation; Inflation
Diversification, 445–446, 451
Dividend(s):
bull market and, 440–441
changes in, 452–453
importance of, 438–439, 441–442
yields, 41, 42, 344–345, 439, 441–442
Dodd, Christopher, 190
Dollar (U.S.):
attitudes toward, 460–461
consumer retrenchment and, 463
currency inflation/deflation and, 292–293, 294
investments to buy, 460–479
other currencies compared to, 214–215
as reserve currency, 214–215, 462, 475, 479
Dot-com bubble:
accounting gimmicks, 439–440

advertising by Internet/new-tech companies, 49–50
bursting of, 48–49
conditions leading to, 40–41
declines after, 47–48
excesses of, 43–44
as financial asset inflation example, 287, 288
follies taught to investors during, 44–45
forecast of, 2, 45–47
as great call, 40–52
recovery from, 50–52
speculation, 41–43
Wall Street analysts during, 15, 49
Dow, Charles H., 439
Down payments, house, 58–59
Drugs, prescription, 278, 485

ECB. See European Central Bank (ECB)
Education expenses, 258, 267
Electricity, 23, 278, 304, 305, 488
Ellis, Charlie, 356, 357
Endowments:
attitude change by investors, 443–445, 451–452
diversification in, 445–446
investment strategies of, 449–450
returns of, 447–449
Energizer Holdings, 458
Energy, 391–392, 487–492
ETFs (exchange-traded funds), 146
Euro, 463–464, 471, 476, 477. See also Eurozone
European Central Bank (ECB):
bank exposure, 198
euro, 471–472
fiscal control, 196
goal of, 465
Greek financial crisis, 468, 470
independence of, 194, 195
interest rate, 471
responsibilities of, 463–464
European Commission, 196, 199
European Parliament, 200
European Union, 233, 236. See also specific countries
Eurozone. See also specific countries
crisis, 195–199, 469–474
differences in individual countries, 463–474
government debt-to-GDP ratio, 467–468
retirement age, 467
sick leave, 473
Exchange-traded funds (ETFs), 146
Experts, denial of housing bubble by, 69–71
Exports. See also Protectionism
China, 189, 393, 408
currency fluctuations and, 270–271

Japan, 420–421, 422–423
net, 269–270
protectionism and, 226, 230–236
Extraordinary Popular Delusions and the Madness of Crowds (Mackay), 18–19
Exxon Mobil, 379, 489

Factory-built housing, 75–79, 480–483
Fannie Mae. See also Freddie Mac
bailout of, 131–132, 134–136, 189–190
housing bubble, 62–63, 65
as housing support, 205–206
Lehman Brothers bankruptcy, fallout from, 138
mortgage buybacks, 374
as powerful constituency, 158
real estate speculation, 99
Farm equipment, 300–301, 302
Farrell, Bob, 1–2, 31
Fed. See Federal Reserve (Fed)
Federal Deposit Insurance Corporation (FDIC), 81–82, 140–141, 147, 150, 201–202
Federal Housing Finance Agency, 135, 202
Federal Reserve (Fed):
AIG and, 192, 194
bank/financial institution regulation, 373–374
credit tightening, 43
currency swaps, 145–146
deflation, 245–247
discount rate, 315–316
disinflation, 36
excess bank reserves at, 312–314, 316–317
Fannie Mae and Freddie Mac bailouts, 131
financial bubble, 97, 99, 100–101
fiscal restraint, 215
housing bubble, 81, 82
independence of, 194, 195
investment bank regulation, 191–192
liquidity, actions to ensure, 130–131
money market funds, 140
rate cuts in reaction to financial crisis, 127–128
recession (2001), 162
role, expanded, 190, 191–192
Federal Reserve Bank, 5, 54–56, 247, 315
Feinberg, Kenneth, 200
Financial asset inflation/deflation, 287–289
Financial bubble, 95–122. See also Great Recession
bailouts, 99–100, 113–114, 147–148
Bear Stearns, 112, 117–122, 126, 130
capacity utilization, 97, 98
cockroach theory, 121–122, 129
collateralized debt obligations, 114, 118, 119–121

Financial bubble (*Continued*)
   covenant lite loans, 113
   debt, consumer, 102–103
   debt, federal, 108–109
   debt, state and local, 109–110
   debt, total net, 103–104
   derivatives, 103, 104, 105–106
   disconnect, signs of, 102–103
   financial sector leverage, 104–105, 111
   financial services industry and, 96–97
   government policies and, 97, 99–101
   household sector leverage, 106–107, 111
   housing bubble and, 99, 100, 106–107,
    115–119, 125–126
   inflation unwinding and, 96
   junk bond spread, 113
   leverage, 103–104, 110–111
   market capitalization as percentage of GDP,
    102
   move-up market, 117
   nonfinancial corporations, 107–108
   rating agencies, 119, 120
   reasons for, 101
   rescue financing, 113–114
   special-purpose acquisition companies, 115
   speculation, 95–96, 112
   subprime mortgages, 115–119
Financial Crisis Inquiry Commission, 192–193
Financial instability hypothesis, 22
Financial institutions. *See also* Banks; Financial
   sector; *specific institutions*
   bailout of, 373
   bonuses, 200, 203
   debt-to-equity ratios, 210
   financial bubble and, 96–97
   government regulation of, 202–203
   as investment to sell/avoid, 373–380
   protectionism, 226–230
   stress tests, 147–148, 198
   subprime mortgage-related securities,
    write-downs on, 129
Financial planners, 480
Financial reform bill, proposed, 194
Financial sector. *See also* Financial institutions
   deleveraging of, 182–186
   leverage in, 104–105, 111
Financial Services Authority (United Kingdom),
   199
Financial standards, 198–199
Firms. *See* Companies
Fiscal restraint, 212–223
Fisher, Irving, 24
Fitch Rating, 387, 464
Follies taught by bull market, 44–45
Food and other consumer staples, 453–456

Ford, Henry, 305–306, 308–309
Forecasting principles, 7–13
Fortis,. 155
401(k) plans, 170–171
France:
   bank bonuses, 200
   bank exposure abroad, 197
   central bank independence, 195
   eurozone countries and, 465–466, 467
   financial standards, 199
   fiscal policy, 221
   global recession and, 153
   GNP growth, 301
   protectionism, 227, 229, 233, 236
Frank, Barney, 62–63, 192
Freddie Mac. *See also* Fannie Mae
   bailout of, 131–132, 134–136, 189–190
   housing bubble, 62–63, 65
   as housing support, 205–206
   Lehman Brothers bankruptcy, fallout from,
    138
   mortgage buybacks, 374
   as powerful constituency, 158
   real estate speculation, 99
Friedman, Milton, 36, 280, 461–462
Fuld, Richard, Jr., 137, 138, 142–143
Full disclosure, 49
Funds. *See also* Pension funds; *specific funds*
   hedge, 56, 446–447, 450, 451–452
   Internet transfer of, 148–149
   money market, 139–141, 279
Futures contracts, 365, 390, 446–447

G-20, 198–199, 214, 217
Gade, George A., 7–9
Gamblers ruin paradox, 361
Gas, natural, 488–489
Gasoline. *See* Oil
Gaugamela, Battle of, 125
GDP. *See* Gross domestic product (GDP)
Geanakoplos, John, 451
Geithner, Timothy, 206, 434
General Electric (GE), 149–150, 380
General Motors (GM), 146, 383, 385
Georgia-Pacific, 458–459
Germany:
   bank exposure abroad, 197, 198
   central bank independence, 195
   deficit spending, 216–217
   eurozone countries and, 465–466, 468–469
   financial institution protection, 227, 228, 229
   financial standards, 199
   fiscal policy, 196, 221
   global recession and, 155, 156
   GNP growth, 301, 302

hyperinflation, 293
Gillette Fusion razors, 458
Glass manufacturing, 298–299, 302
Glass-Steagall Act (1933), 150, 187, 188
Globalization of recession, 153–156
Globe Permits, 20
GM (General Motors), 146, 383, 385
GNP (gross national product), 301–302, 308
Gold, 147, 462–463
Golden West, 151
Goldman Sachs:
  Allstate and, 480
  Buffett's investment in, 149
  collateralized debt obligations, 374
  conversion to traditional bank holding
    company, 148, 149
  Fed regulation of, 191–192
  financial bubble, 119
  Financial Crisis Inquiry Commission hearing,
    193
  housing bubble, 70
  Lehman Brothers bankruptcy, fallout from,
    138
Government, federal. *See also specific agencies*
  budget, 54, 199–200
  debt, 108–109
  economy, involvement in, 34–35
  financial bubble and, 97, 99–101, 156–158
  job creation by, 324–325, 333
  as support to growth, 271
  wastefulness of, 208–209
Government, state/local. *See also specific locales*
  budgets, 252–254, 258–259
  contraction of, 252–268
  debt, 109–110
  defaults on bonds/other obligations, 259–261
  labor costs, 261–264
  pension costs, 254–255, 264–265, 266–267
  service cuts, 257–258
  spending as share of GDP, 267–268
  tax increases, 255–257
  taxpayer revolt, 258–259, 265–266
  unionization, 262–263
Government spending multiplier, 216–217
Graham, Benjamin, 452
Great Depression:
  deflation, bad, 306–309
  end of, 34
  government interventions, 100, 187, 188, 211
  productivity, 323
  reassurances before, 24
  short sales, 15
Great Recession, 123–158. *See also* Financial
  bubble; Housing bubble
  AIG, 143–145

bailouts, 131–136
banks, investment versus commercial,
  149–150
calling of, official, 6
credit market freeze, 145–146
crisis rates, 147
Fannie Mae and Freddie Mac bailouts,
  131–132, 134–136
Fed actions, 127–128, 130–131
funds, transfer of, 148–149
globalization of, 153–156
government actions, 156–158
investors, 126–128
land development loans, 129–130
Lehman Brothers, 136–138, 142–143
Lehman Brothers bankruptcy, fallout from,
  138–139
liquidity, 130–131
Merrill Lynch, 141–142
money market funds, 139–141
moral hazards, 134, 141, 158
reaction to, 147–148
respite, short, 128–129
retrenchment by consumers, 151–153,
  159–181, 351, 463
SEC shortcomings, 124
subprime mortgage-related securities,
  write-downs on, 129
underestimates of, 132
Wachovia, 151
Washington Mutual, 148, 150
Greece:
  bank deposit guarantee, 227
  debt rating, 464
  eurozone countries and, 465–467
  fiscal policy, 196, 218
  government funding crisis, 468–470
Greenspan, Alan, 43, 97
Gross, Bill, 434
Gross domestic product (GDP):
  China, 396, 407, 409
  consumer spending and, 165, 179
  corporate profits and, 341, 342
  deficit-to-GDP ratio, 214, 218, 219–220, 221
  market capitalization as percentage of, 102
  real, 302–303
  saving rate and, 180
  Social Security, Medicare, and Medicaid as
    percentage of, 318
  S&P operating earnings and, 342–343
  S&P reported earnings and, 341–343, 346
  state/local government spending as share of,
    267–268
  unemployment and, 320–323
Gross national product (GNP), 301–302, 308

Growth, slow global:
    causes, overview of, 181–182
    commodity crisis and, 211–212
    deflation and, 244–252
    financial deleveraging and, 182–186
    fiscal restraint and, 212–223
    government regulation and, 187–211
    housing market and, 239–243
    offsets to, 268–271
    protectionism and, 225–239
    saving and, 159–181
    state and local government contraction and,
        252–268

HAMP (Home Affordable Modification
    Program), 370
Hand-to-Mouth Buying and the Inventory Situation
    (Gade), 7–9
Health care, 483–486
Health insurance, 484, 485
Hedge funds, 56, 446–447, 450, 451–452. *See
    also specific funds*
Heisenberg uncertainty principle of investing,
    450
Henkel-Clauss, 11
Holder, Eric, 193
Holland, 154, 220–221, 292, 467, 474
Home Affordable Modification Program
    (HAMP), 370
Homes. *See* Housing
"Home Sick" (Shilling), 65
Hong Kong, 87–89, 156, 200, 292
Hoover, Herbert, 214, 308
Hotels, 386, 387, 459
Households, 240–241, 243
Household sector leverage, 106–107, 111
Housing:
    builders/suppliers, conventional, 79–80,
        369–372
    factory-built, 75–79, 480–483
    homebuyers, first-time, 58–59
    homeownership rate, 58, 59
    inflation/deflation, 291
    inventories, 239–240, 242–243
    market for, 239–243
    prices, during housing bubble, 56, 57, 63–64,
        73–74, 89–90
    prices, historical, 4
    prices, projected, 242–243
    size trends, 371–372
    value of primary residence, median, 164
Housing bubble, 53–94. *See also* Great Recession
    denial of, 69–71, 79–80
    down payments, tiny, 58–59
    end of, 84–85

    factory-built housing, 75–79
    financial bubble and, 99, 100, 106–107,
        115–119, 125–126
    forecast of, 3
    inventory problem, 71–72
    as investment opportunity, 89–94
    leverage, 56–59, 68, 87–88, 92
    mortgage lending standards, 60, 77, 78
    mortgages, interest-only, 59–60
    mortgages, subprime, 60–62, 65, 86–87
    peak of, 3, 4, 69–70
    problem, basic, 87–88
    rating agencies, 82–84
    regulation, lax, 62–63, 81–82
    saving rate and, 161, 163–165
    securitization, 60–61, 77
HSBC (bank), 85, 93, 125, 451
Hubbert, M. King, 283
Hypo Real Estate Group, 155

Iceland, 154, 229
ICICI Bank, 155–156, 394
IMF. *See* International Monetary Fund (IMF)
Immigration, 236–237, 418
Imports, 226, 230–236, 420–421, 422–423. *See
    also* Protectionism
Income-producing securities, 438–453
Income shares, 337, 338, 367
India, 155–156, 204, 232–233, 394, 395
Industrial Revolution, 298–301, 393–394
IndyMac, 150, 201
Inflation. *See also* Deflation; Disinflation
    bank reserves and, 313–314
    biases, 275–276
    by fiat, 294–295
    cause of, 279
    commodity, 281–285
    CPI, 282, 295
    currency, 291–294
    federal deficit and, 334
    financial asset, 287–289
    forecasts, 311
    interest rates and, 376
    money and, 280
    post-World War II, 344
    self-feeding, 249
    standard, 295
    stock prices, effect on, 30–31
    tangible asset, 289–291
    types, 281–296
    unwinding of, 16–17, 96
    wage-price, 285–287
    as wartime phenomenon, 274–275, 280–281
Inheritance, 168–169
Initial public offerings (IPOs), 49

Insurance, 480, 484, 485. *See also specific companies*
Interest spreads of lenders, 376
International Monetary Fund (IMF):
  bubbles, 22
  central bank independence, 195
  deflation, 247
  financial institution protection, 229
  Greek financial crisis, 468, 470
  Spanish fiscal policy, 219
  yuan, 476
Internet bubble. *See* Dot-com bubble
Internet/new-tech company ads, 49–50
Internet transfer of funds, 148–149
Inventory bubble, 4, 9–11, 33
Inventory-building, 7–9
Investment advisers, 480
Investment banks, 149–150, 191–192
Investments, correlations among, 443–447, 451
Investments to buy, 425–492
  dollar (U.S.), 460–479
  energy, North American, 487–492
  food and other consumer staples, 453–456
  health care, 483–486
  housing and rental apartments, factory-built, 480–483
  income-producing securities, 438–453
  investment advisers and financial planners, 480
  luxuries, small, 456–460
  productivity enhancers, 486–487
  Treasurys and other high-quality bonds, 426–438
Investments to sell/avoid, 364, 365–424
  antiques, art, and other tangibles, 372–373
  banks and similar financial institutions, 373–380
  capital equipment producers, low- and old-tech, 383–386
  commercial real estate, 386–389
  commodities, 389–392
  companies, flailing, 382–383
  consumer purchases, big-ticket, 365–368
  credit card and other consumer lenders, 368–369
  developing country stocks and bonds, 392–410
  home builders and suppliers, conventional, 369–372
  Japan, 410–424
  junk securities, 381–382
Investors:
  confidence of, 166
  financial bubble and, 96–97
  follies taught to, 44–45
  Great Recession, 126–128
  institutional, 352–353, 443–452

overenthusiasm of, 23
speculation by, 95–96
IPOs (initial public offerings), 49
Ireland:
  deflation, 278
  eurozone countries and, 465–466
  financial institution protection, 226–227
  fiscal policy, 197, 220
  global recession and, 155
Is Inflation Ending? Are You Ready? (Shilling and Sokoloff), 36–37, 188, 348
Italy, 219–220, 227–228, 465–466, 467

Japan. *See also* Bank of Japan
  bubble, 37–39, 396–397
  character of people, 414–415
  currency, 291, 292–293, 476
  current account, 337, 338, 421, 423
  debt, 337, 412–413, 414
  deficits, 337, 412–413, 414
  deflation, 245–246, 309
  demographics, 417–418, 420
  economic slump, 410–411
  fascination with, 396–397
  financial institution protection, 229
  fiscal policy, 222–223, 412–413, 416–417
  forecasts, 410
  GNP growth, 301, 302
  immigration policy, 418
  imports and exports, 420–421, 422–423
  interest rates, 416, 423–424
  as investment to sell/avoid, 410–424
  monetary response, 411
  protectionism, 226, 236
  real estate prices, 39
  saving, 413, 415–418, 419, 421
  stock prices, 38–39
  trade balance, 337, 338
  trade treaty with U.S., 418–419
  U.S. compared to, 336–338, 412–413, 419–420, 421–422
Japan Post, 412
Jefferson County, Alabama, 260
Jobs, 237, 319–320, 324–325, 333. *See also* Unemployment
JPMorgan Chase, 118, 130, 150
Junk securities, 113, 381–382

Kamei, Shizuka, 195
Kan, Naoto, 222–223
Kanas, Dave, 445
Kempner, Jonathan, 88
Kennedy, Brian, 14–15
Keynes, John Maynard, 96, 180, 217
Keynesian theory, 216, 217

King, Mervyn, 194–195, 199
Kohl, Helmut, 464
Kohn, Donald, 316
Kudlow, Larry, 428

Labor. *See* Unionization; Wages
Lamy, Pascal, 199
Land development loans, 129–130
Landsbanki Islands, 154
Las Vegas Monorail, 259–260
Law, John, 19
Lawler, Tom, 82–84
Layaway financing, 178, 369
Layoffs, 287, 319–320
Lehman Brothers, 136–139, 142–143
Lenders. *See also specific types*
    consumer, 368–369
    interest spreads of, 376
Lereah, David, 69–70
Leverage:
    financial bubble, 103–104, 110–111
    financial sector profitability from, 185
    housing bubble, 56–59, 68, 87–88, 92
    investment versus commercial banks, 149
Lighting, electric, 23
Lincoln Electric, 287
Lippmann, Greg, 93–94, 362
Liquidity, 130–131, 136, 380
Livestock production, 299–300
Loans. *See also* Mortgages; Mortgages,
    commercial; Mortgages, subprime
    Alt-A, 117
    covenant lite, 113
    future, 178
    land development, 129–130
Long bonds, 428–429
Long-Term Capital Management, 99, 118, 120,
    144–145, 450
Luxuries, small, 456–460

Mackay, Charles, 18–19, 20
Madoff, Bernie, 207, 208
Malabre, Alfred L., Jr., 31
Mandelcorn, H., 32
Manufactured housing, 75–79, 480–483
Market capitalization as percentage of GDP, 102
"Market Timing" (Shilling), 356
Market timing versus buy-and-hold strategy,
    356–362
Mark-to-market approach, 377–380
Mark-to-model approach, 377, 378
Medicaid, 254, 318, 331, 332
Medicare, 318
Mergers and acquisitions, 210, 443
Merkel, Angela, 195, 216–217, 221, 468

Merrill, Charlie, 141, 142
Merrill Lynch:
    financial bubble, 132, 141–142
    inflation and stocks, 30–31
    reassurances from, 24–26
    recession (1969-1970) forecast, 6–7, 29–30
    research analysts, 15
    as retail brokerage house, 149
    subprime mortgage-related security
        write-downs, 129
Mexico, 234
Middle classes, 393–394
Mieno, Masushi, 38
Models, failure of, 143–145
Money market funds, 139–141, 279
Money supply, 279–280, 281, 312–313
Moody's, 382, 424, 434
Moral hazards, 134, 141, 158
Morgan Stanley, 138, 148, 149, 183, 191–192
Mortgage Bankers Association, 70, 88–89
Mortgages. *See also* Mortgages, commercial;
        Mortgages, subprime
    adjustable-rate, 4–5, 59, 116, 150, 151
    buybacks of, 374
    delinquencies, 152–153
    interest-only, 59–60
    lending standards for, 60, 77, 78, 167
    modifications of, 201, 370
    postwar babies and, 171–172
    private-label, 376
    rates, 54–55
    refinancing of, 370
    underwater, 370–371, 375, 389
Mortgages, commercial:
    bank exposure to, 183–184
    rates, 388
    refinancing, 386, 387
    regional/community banks and, 374–375
    underwater, 375, 389
Mortgages, subprime:
    ABX index for, 85, 86, 378
    collapse of, 4–5
    financial bubble and, 115–119
    housing bubble and, 60–62, 65, 86–87
    Merrill Lynch write-downs on, 129
Move-up market, 117
Movie attendance, 178
Multiplier, government spending, 216–217

National Association of Realtors, 62, 69
National Bureau of Economic Research,
        Business Cycle Dating Committee, 6
Neiman Marcus, 152, 457
Netherlands, 154, 220–221, 292, 467, 474
Net worth, 97, 98, 169

New Century, 85–86, 93
New Jersey, 109, 253, 265
Newspaper ads by Internet/new-tech companies, 49–50
New York City, 257, 265
New York Times ads for Internet/new-tech companies, 50
Nifty Fifty, 21
Nikkei stock index, 38–39
Nonconsensus forecasts, 12–13, 16–17
Noyes, Alexander Dana, 21–22
Nuclear energy, 490–491

Obama, Barack:
 budget, 199–200
 financial firms, 202–203
 financial reforms, 211
 fiscal restraint, 214, 215
 protectionism, 230, 235
 taxes, 203, 204, 442
Obama administration, 337, 367, 488, 490
Office of the Comptroller of the Currency (OCC), 81, 82
Office of Thrift Supervision (OTS), 81, 82, 208
Office space, 387
Oil:
 consumption of, 389–390
 drilling and exploration, 408
 embargo, 282
 prices, 250, 283–284, 391
 sands, 491–492
Okun, Arthur, 321
Okun's Law, 321
O'Neal, Stan, 24, 142
On the Beach (movie), 430–431
Options, stock, 443
Orange County, California, bankruptcy, 99, 140, 259
OTS (Office of Thrift Supervision), 81, 82, 208
Over-the-counter derivatives, 317–318

Palm Harbor Homes, 75–76, 78
Paradoxes, 180–181, 361
Paulsen, Jim, 70–71
Paulson, Henry, 132, 136–137, 189–190, 210, 228
Paulson, John, 89–90, 93, 362
Paulson & Co., 89–91, 92–93
Paulson Credit Opportunities Fund, 89–90, 93, 94
Payout ratio, 42, 441
Pelosi, Nancy, 187, 192
Pension funds. See also Retirement
 attitude change by investors, 443–445, 451–452

diversification in, 445–446
 investment strategies of, 449–450
 returns of, 447–449
 state and local government, 254–255, 264–265, 266–267
 trends, 170–171
Perry, Matthew C., 418–419
P/Es (price/earnings ratios), 343, 344–347, 353–354, 355, 440
Pew Center, 254–255
Pickens, T. Boone, 488, 489
Polaroid, 21
Ponzi scheme investigations, 207
Portugal, 218–219, 278, 465, 466
Postwar babies, 168–169, 171–174
Pound sterling, British, 475–476
PPP (purchasing power parity), 476–477
Pressed-glass industry, 298–299, 302
Price/earnings ratios (P/Es), 343, 344–347, 353–354, 355, 440
Prices. See also Consumer price index (CPI)
 automobile industry, 276
 decelerating, 250–251
 historical, 8–9
 home, historical, 4
 home, in housing bubble, 56, 57, 63–64, 73–74, 89–90
 home, projected, 242–243
 oil, 250, 283–284, 391
 quality-adjusted, 275, 276, 277
 real estate, commercial, 290, 291
 stock, 30–31, 38–39
Prince, Charles, 193
Procter & Gamble, 177, 277, 458
Productivity:
 agricultural, 299–301, 302
 deflation and, 297–301, 304–306
 enhancers for, 486–487
 Great Depression, 323
 projections, 323–324
 United Kingdom, 474–475
 United States, 164, 475
Profits, corporate, 40–41, 341, 342, 352
Protectionism, 225–239
 devaluations, competitive, 234–235
 financial institutions, 226–230
 import-export arena, 226, 230–236
 stealth, 236–237
Purchasing power parity (PPP), 476–477
Putin, Vladimir, 235

Quality improvements, 275, 276, 277
Quantitative easing, 140
Quilted Northern Ultra Plush toilet paper, 458–459

Railroads, 20, 299–300, 302
Rating agencies. *See also specific agencies*
   financial bubble, 119, 120
   housing bubble, 82–84
   Japan, 424
   junk bond forecast, 381–382
   SEC and, 200–201
Razors, 458
Reagan, Ronald, 188, 329
Real estate. *See also* Housing; Housing bubble;
      Mortgages
   China, 403–404
   commercial, 289–290, 378–379, 386–389
   Japan, 39
   speculation in, 98–99
Real estate investment trusts (REITs), 389, 483
Recalls, product, 189
Recession (1920–1921), 7–9
Recession (1937), 214, 314–315
Recession (1969-1970), 7, 29–32
Recession (1973-1975), 7, 10–11, 13, 21, 33
Recession (2001), 162
Recession (2007-). *See* Great Recession
Regan, Donald T., 7, 31–32
Regional/community banks, 374–375
Regulation, government:
   banks and similar financial institutions,
      373–374
   financial regulatory plan, 209–210
   growth and, 187–211
   history of, 187–189
   housing bubble and, 62–63, 81–82
   inflation by fiat and, 294–295
   problems with, 206–208
   rebellion against, 188
Regulation FD (Full Disclosure), 49
REITs (real estate investment trusts), 389, 483
Rental units, 371, 481–483
Rescue financing. *See* Bailouts
Reserve Management, 139, 140, 141, 279
Reserve Primary Fund, 140, 141, 279
Residential mortgage-backed securities (RMBs),
      61, 120
Resolution Trust Corporation (RTC), 100, 206
Retail space, 386–387
Retirement, 171, 173–174, 467. *See also* Pension
      funds
Rio Tinto, 232
RMBs (residential mortgage-backed securities),
      61, 120
Roaring Twenties, 304–306, 410
Roosevelt, Franklin Delano, 214, 314
"Roosevelt Depression," 214, 314–315
RTC (Resolution Trust Corporation), 100, 206
Russia, 155, 236

Sarkozy, Nicolas, 195, 229, 233, 467,
      468, 473
Saving and saving rate:
   bull market and, 160–161, 165
   China, 405–406
   consumer, 159–181, 175–177, 351
   decrease in, 159–160
   financial bubble and, 114–115
   fiscal stimulus programs and, 167–168, 180
   forecast concerning, 178–179, 180
   GDP and, 180
   historical, 41, 42
   housing bubble and, 161, 163–165
   increase in, 159–181, 351
   Japan, 413, 415–418, 419, 421
   popularity of, 177–178
   postwar babies, 171–173
   retirement, 171
   stocks and, 160–161, 165
   unemployment and, 175–177
   young people, 176
Schapiro, Mary, 207–208
Schick Hydro razors, 458
Schwarzenegger, Arnold, 257, 448
SEC. *See* Securities and Exchange Commission
      (SEC)
Securities:
   asset-based, 77
   income-producing, 438–453
   junk, 113, 381–382
   residential mortgage-backed, 61–120
   subprime mortgage-related, 129
   Treasury Inflation-Protected, 433
Securities and Exchange Commission (SEC):
   Bear Stearns and, 124
   financial crisis, shortcomings during, 124
   full disclosure, 49
   Goldman Sachs CDOs, 374
   Ponzi scheme investigations, 207
   rating agencies, 200–201
   short sales, 124, 201
Securitization, and housing bubble, 60–61, 77
Service cuts, by state/local governments,
      257–258
Shakespeare, William, 11–12
Shiller, Robert, 354, 355
Short sales, 13–16, 124, 201, 359–360
Sick leave, 473
Siegel, Jeremy, 339–340, 426–427
Silius Italicus, 13
Singapore, 174, 236–237, 403
Smith, Winthrop H., Jr., 142
Social Security, 318, 331, 332, 333
Sokoloff, Kiril, 36–37
Solvency, 131, 136

Soros, George, 362, 447
South Korea, 156, 195, 394
South Sea bubble, 19–20
S&P 500 Index:
    earnings, operating, 342–343
    earnings, reported, 341–343, 346
    earnings/price ratio, 353
    financial bubble, 96
    inflation, corrected for, 285
    investor confidence and, 166
    price/earnings ratio, 354
    returns, total, 357
    survivor bias, 340
SPACs (special-purpose acquisition companies),
    20, 115
Spain:
    debt restructuring, 472
    deflation, 278
    eurozone countries and, 465, 466, 467
    financial forecasts, 213–214
    financial institution protection, 227
    fiscal policy, 196–197, 219
Special-purpose acquisition companies (SPACs),
    20, 115
Speculation:
    dot-com bubble, 41–43
    financial asset inflation/deflation
        and, 288
    financial bubble, 95–96, 112
    increase in, 446–447
    real estate, 98–99
Spending binge, 159–166, 287–288, 349
Spiking, 265
Spinning, 49
Stagflation, 33, 285
Stanford, R. Allen, 207, 208
Steel industry, 10, 26–27
Stimulus programs:
    China, 395–396, 399–401, 405
    failure of, 167–168, 180
    Japan, 411, 412–413, 416–417
    saving and, 167–168, 180
Stock(s):
    appeal of, 339–341
    bottom-line growth, 385–386
    buy-and-hold strategy versus market timing,
        356–362
    buybacks of, 442–443
    developing country, 392–410
    growth, 385–386, 440
    holdings, median value of, 165
    institutionalization of, 345–346
    investor confidence and, 166
    market capitalization as percentage of GDP,
        102

options, 443
price/earnings ratios, 343, 344–347,
    353–354, 355, 440
prices, 30–31, 38–39
rationale for, 341–342
returns, average annual, 339–340
returns, projected, 355
saving rate and, 160–161, 165
short selling of, 359–360
Treasurys versus, 426–427, 435–436
Stress tests, 147–148, 198
Stripped bonds, 431–432
Subprime mortgages. See
    Mortgages, subprime
Summers, Larry, 203
Supermarkets, 244, 367, 453
Survivor bias, 340
Sweden, 228

Tangible assets, 289–291, 372–373
TARP (Troubled Asset Relief Program),
    147–148, 375, 376
Taxes:
    federal deficit and, 203–204
    increases in, 203–204, 255–257
    as percent of personal income, 163
    revolt against, 258–259, 265–266
    state/local government, 255–257, 258–259,
        265–266
    United Kingdom, 204
Taxpayer Relief Act of 1997, 63
Technologies:
    new, 49–50, 296–297, 486, 487
    old, 383–386
Telephone usage, 297
Templeton, John, 22, 445
Thain, John, 24–26, 132, 141, 142
Thomas, Bill, 193
Thrift, paradox of, 180
Thurman, Randy, 14
TIPS (Treasury Inflation-Protected Securities),
    433
Toilet paper, 458–459
Toll, Robert, 79–80
Total (oil company), 233, 489
TPG (firm), 150, 452
Trade. See also Exports; Imports
    carry, 56
    intra-Asian, 392
    Japan, 337, 338, 418–419
    merchandise trade balances, 269
    United States, 179
    world, 238–239
Treasury Inflation-Protected Securities (TIPS),
    433

Treasurys:
  coupon bonds, 430–431
  foreign holders of, 434–435
  as investment to buy, 426–438
  long bonds, 428–429
  qualities, 433–434
  stocks versus, 426–427, 435–436
  Treasury Inflation-Protected Securities, 433
  yields, 16, 286, 353, 426, 430, 432
  zero-coupon bonds, 431–432
Trichet, Jean-Claude, 195, 196, 468
Troilus and Cressida (Shakespeare), 11–12
Troubled Asset Relief Program (TARP),
    147–148, 375, 376
Tulipomania, 18–19
Turkey, 293–294
Turner, Adair, 186
Twenties, Roaring, 304–306, 410

UBS (bank), 228
Unemployment, 34, 175–177, 307, 319,
    320–323. *See also* Jobs
Unionization, 175, 262–263, 320, 382–383
United Kingdom:
  bank bonuses, 200
  bank examiners, 190
  financial deleveraging, 186
  financial institution protection, 227, 228–229
  financial standards, 199
  fiscal restraint, 221–222
  global recession and, 153, 154, 155
  GNP growth, 301
  productivity, 474–475
  protectionism, 233
  tax increases, 204
United States. *See also* Dollar (U.S.); *specific topics*
  bank exposure abroad, 198
  financial institution protection, 227, 228, 229
  Japan compared to, 336–338, 412–413,
    419–420, 421–422
  productivity, 164, 475
  protectionism, 230–231, 233, 234, 235, 236
  trade and current account deficits, 179

Uptick rule, 15–16
U.S. Commerce Department, 231
U.S. International Trade Commission, 230–231
U.S. Justice Department, 190, 193
U.S. Quarterly Economic Outlook, 50

Van Hook, Bob, 11
Vietnam, 398–399
Volcker, Paul, 36, 150, 193
Volcker Rule, 150, 193

Wachovia, 151
Wage-price inflation/deflation, 285–287
Wages:
  average weekly, decrease in, 320
  corporate earnings and, 40–41
  good deflation and, 303–304
  Great Depression, 307, 308–309
  state/local government, 261–264
  two-tier systems, 175–176
Wall Street Journal ads for Internet/new-tech
    companies, 50
Wal-Mart, 152, 277, 278
Washington Mutual (WaMu), 148, 150
Watches, 459
Welfare reform, 295, 330
Wen Jiabao, 234, 235, 404
Wheat-growing industry, 300–301, 302
Wind-generated power, 488
World Bank, 22, 466, 472
World Has Definitely Changed, The (Shilling), 461
World Trade Organization (WTO), 199, 236
World War II, 34, 36, 280–281, 343–346

Yen, 291, 292–293, 476
Yield(s):
  bond, 147
  dividend, 41, 42, 344–345, 439, 441–442
  Treasury, 16, 286, 353, 426, 430, 432
Yuan, 234–235, 293, 402–403, 476, 477,
    478–479

Zero-coupon bonds, 431–432